ISBN 978-1-5280-6355-5
PIBN 10054873

For support please visit www.forgottenbooks.com

A COMPILATION

MESSAGES AND PAPERS

PRESIDENTS

WASHINGTON
GOVERNMENT PRINTING OFFICE
1897

A COMPILATION

OF THE

MESSAGES AND PAPERS

OF THE

PRESIDENTS

1789–1897

PUBLISHED BY AUTHORITY OF CONGRESS

BY

JAMES D. RICHARDSON

A REPRESENTATIVE FROM THE STATE OF TENNESSEE

VOLUME IV

WASHINGTON
GOVERNMENT PRINTING OFFICE
1897

Prefatory Note

In historic value this volume is equal to, if it does not surpass, any one of the series which has preceded it. It comprises the eight years of our history from March 4, 1841, to March 4, 1849, and includes the four years' term of Harrison and Tyler and also the term of James K. Polk. During the first half of this period the death of President Harrison occurred, when for the first time under the Constitution the Vice-President succeeded to the office of President. As a matter of public interest, several papers relating to the death of President Harrison are inserted. A number of highly interesting vetoes of President Tyler appear, among which are two vetoing bills chartering a United States bank and two vetoing tariff measures. During President Tyler's Administration the protective tariff act of 1842 was passed; the subtreasury law was repealed; the treaty with Great Britain of August 9, 1842, was negotiated, settling the northeastern-boundary controversy, and providing for the final suppression of the African slave trade and for the surrender of fugitive criminals; and acts establishing a uniform system of bankruptcy and providing for the distribution of the sales of the public lands were passed. The treaty of annexation between the United States and the Republic of Texas was negotiated, but was rejected by the Senate.

During the Administration of President Polk Texas was finally annexed to the United States; Texas, Iowa, and Wisconsin were admitted into the Union; the Oregon boundary was settled; the independent-treasury system was reenacted; the Naval Academy was established; acts were passed establishing the Smithsonian Institution and creating the Department of the Interior; the war with Mexico was successfully fought, and the territory known as New Mexico and Upper California was acquired. The acquisition of territory by Mr. Polk's Administration added to the United States California and New Mexico and portions of Colorado, Utah, and Nevada, a territory containing in all 1,193,061 square miles, or over 763,000,000 acres, and constituting a country more than half as large as all that held by the Republic before he became President. This addition to our domain was the next largest in area ever made. It was exceeded only by the purchase by President Jefferson of the Louisiana Territory, in which was laid so deep the foundation of the country's growth and grandeur. If our country had not already attained that rank by the acquisition of the Louisiana Territory, the further additions made by Mr. Polk's Administration advanced it at once to a continental power of assured strength and boundless promise.

JAMES D. RICHARDSON.

APRIL 27, 1897.

Contents of Volume IV

Illustrations

William Henry Harrison

March 4 to April 4, 1841

William Henry Harrison

WILLIAM HENRY HARRISON, third and youngest son of Benjamin Harrison, one of the signers of the Declaration of Independence, was born at Berkeley, Charles City County, Va., February 9, 1773. Was educated at Hampden Sidney College, Virginia, and began the study of medicine, but before he had finished it accounts of Indian outrages on the western frontier led him to enter the Army, and he was commissioned an ensign in the First Infantry on August 16, 1791; joined his regiment at Fort Washington, Ohio. Was appointed lieutenant June 2, 1792, and afterwards joined the Army under General Anthony Wayne, and was made aid-de-camp to the commanding officer. For his services in the expedition, in December, 1793, that erected Fort Recovery he was thanked by name in general orders. Participated in the engagements with the Indians that began on June 30, 1794, and was complimented by General Wayne for gallantry in the victory on the Miami on August 20. On May 15, 1797, was made captain and given the command of Fort Washington. While there he married Anna, daughter of John Cleves Symmes. Resigned his commission on June 1, 1798, peace having been made with the Indians, and was immediately appointed by President John Adams secretary of the Northwest Territory, but in October, 1799, resigned to take his seat as Territorial Delegate in Congress. During his term part of the Northwest Territory was formed into the Territory of Indiana, including the present States of Indiana, Illinois, Michigan, and Wisconsin, and he was appointed its governor and superintendent of Indian affairs, which he accepted, and resigned his seat in Congress. Was reappointed successively by Presidents Jefferson and Madison. He organized the legislature at Vincennes in 1805. Held frequent councils with the Indians, and succeeded in averting many outbreaks. On September 30, 1809, concluded a treaty with several tribes by which they sold to the United States about 3,000,000 acres of land on the Wabash and White rivers. This and former treaties were condemned by Tecumseh and other chiefs, and an outbreak became imminent, which was averted by the conciliatory course of the governor. In the spring of 1811 Indian depredations became frequent, and Governor Harrison recommended the establishment of a military post at Tippecanoe, and the Government consented.   On September 26 Harrison marched from Vincennes with about 900 men, including 350 regular infantry, completed Fort Harrison, near the site of Terre Haute, Ind., on October 28, and leaving a garrison there pressed on toward Tippecanoe.   On November 6, when near that town, was met by messengers demanding a parley, and a council was proposed for the next day.   At 4 o'clock the following morning a fierce attack was made by the savages; at daybreak the Indians were driven from the field.   For this victory he was highly complimented by President Madison in his message of December 18, 1811, and was also thanked by the legislatures of Kentucky and Indiana. On August 25, 1812, soon after war was declared against Great Britain, was commissioned major-general of the militia of Kentucky, though not a citizen of that State.   On August 22, 1812, was commissioned a brigadier-general in the Regular Army, and later was appointed to the chief command of the Northwestern army, with instructions to act in all cases according to his own discretion and judgment.   No latitude as great as this had been given to any commander since Washington.   On March 2, 1813, was commissioned a major-general.   Was in command of Fort Meigs when General Proctor, with a force of British troops and Indians, laid unsuccessful siege to it from April 28 to May 9, 1813. Transporting his army to Canada, he fought the battle of the Thames on October 5, defeating General Proctor's army of 800 regulars and 1,200 Indians, the latter led by the celebrated Tecumseh, who was killed. This battle, together with Perry's victory on Lake Erie, gave the United States possession of the chain of lakes above Erie and put an end to the war in uppermost Canada.   For this victory he was praised by President Madison in his annual message to Congress and by the legislatures of the different States.   Through a misunderstanding with General John Armstrong, Secretary of War, he resigned his commission in the Army May 31, 1814.   In 1814, and again in 1815, he was appointed on commissions that concluded Indian treaties, and in 1816 was chosen to Congress to fill a vacancy, serving till 1819.   On March 30, 1818, Congress unanimously voted him a gold medal for his victory of the Thames.   In 1819 he was chosen to the senate of Ohio, and in 1822 was an unsuccessful candidate for Congress.   In 1824 was a Presidential elector, voting for Henry Clay, and in the same year was sent to the United States Senate, and succeeded Andrew Jackson as chairman of the Committee on Military Affairs.   He resigned in 1828, having been appointed by President John Quincy Adams minister to the United States of Colombia.   He was recalled at the outset of Jackson's Administration, and retired to his farm at North Bend, near Cincinnati, Ohio. In 1835 was nominated for the Presidency by Whig State conventions in Pennsylvania, New York, Ohio, and other States, but at the election on November 8, 1836, was defeated by Martin Van Buren, receiving only 73 electoral votes to the latter's 170. December 4, 1839, he was nominated for the Presidency by the national Whig convention at Harrisburg, Pa., and was elected on November 10, 1840, receiving 234 electoral votes to Van Buren's 60. Was inaugurated March 4, 1841. Called Congress to meet in extra session on May 31. He died on Sunday morning, April 4, 1841. His body was interred in the Congressional Cemetery at Washington, but in June, 1841, it was removed to North Bend and placed in a tomb overlooking the Ohio River.

INAUGURAL ADDRESS.

Called from a retirement which I had supposed was to continue for the residue of my life to fill the chief executive office of this great and free nation, I appear before you, fellow-citizens, to take the oaths which the Constitution prescribes as a necessary qualification for the performance of its duties; and in obedience to a custom coeval with our Government and what I believe to be your expectations I proceed to present to you a summary of the principles which will govern me in the discharge of the duties which I shall be called upon to perform.

It was the remark of a Roman consul in an early period of that celebrated Republic that a most striking contrast was observable in the conduct of candidates for offices of power and trust before and after obtaining them, they seldom carrying out in the latter case the pledges and promises made in the former. However much the world may have improved in many respects in the lapse of upward of two thousand years since the remark was made by the virtuous and indignant Roman, I fear that a strict examination of the annals of some of the modern elective governments would develop similar instances of violated confidence.

Although the fiat of the people has gone forth proclaiming me the Chief Magistrate of this glorious Union, nothing upon their part remaining to be done, it may be thought that a motive may exist to keep up the delusion under which they may be supposed to have acted in relation to my principles and opinions; and perhaps there may be some in this assembly who have come here either prepared to condemn those I shall now deliver, or, approving them, to doubt the sincerity with which they are now uttered. But the lapse of a few months will confirm or dispel their fears. The outline of principles to govern and measures to be adopted by an Administration not yet begun will soon be exchanged for immutable history, and I shall stand either exonerated by my countrymen or classed with the mass of those who promised that they might deceive and flattered with the intention to betray. However strong may be my present purpose to realize the expectations of a magnanimous and confiding people, I too well understand the dangerous temptations to which I shall be exposed from the magnitude of the power which it has been the pleasure of the people to commit to my hands not to place my chief confidence upon the aid of that Almighty Power which has hitherto protected me and enabled me to bring to favorable issues other important but still greatly inferior trusts heretofore confided to me by my country.

The broad foundation upon which our Constitution rests being the people—a breath of theirs having made, as a breath can unmake, change, or modify it—it can be assigned to none of the great divisions of government but to that of democracy.   If such is its theory, those who are called upon to administer it must recognize as its leading principle the duty of shaping their measures so as to produce the greatest good to the greatest number.   But with these broad admissions, if we would compare the sovereignty acknowledged to exist in the mass of our people with the power claimed by other sovereignties, even by those which have been considered most purely democratic, we shall find a most essential difference.   All others lay claim to power limited only by their own will. The majority of our citizens, on the contrary, possess a sovereignty with an amount of power precisely equal to that which has been granted to them by the parties to the national compact, and nothing beyond.   We admit of no government by divine right, believing that so far as power is concerned the Beneficent Creator has made no distinction amongst men; that all are upon an equality, and that the only legitimate right to govern is an express grant of power from the governed.   The Constitution of the United States is the instrument containing this grant of power to the several departments composing the Government.   On an examination of that instrument it will be found to contain declarations of power granted and of power withheld.   The latter is also susceptible of division into power which the majority had the right to grant, but which they did not think proper to intrust to their agents, and that which they could not have granted, not being possessed by themselves.   In other words, there are certain rights possessed by each individual American citizen which in his compact with the others he has never surrendered. Some of them, indeed, he is unable to surrender, being, in the language of our system, unalienable.   The boasted privilege of a Roman citizen was to him a shield only against a petty provincial ruler, whilst the proud democrat of Athens would console himself under a sentence of death for a supposed violation of the national faith—which no one understood and which at times was the subject of the mockery of all—or the banishment from his home, his family, and his country with or without an alleged cause, that it was the act not of a single tyrant or hated aristocracy, but of his assembled countrymen.   Far different is the power of our sovereignty.   It can interfere with no one's faith, prescribe forms of worship for no one's observance, inflict no punishment but after well-ascertained guilt, the result of investigation under rules prescribed by the Constitution itself. These precious privileges, and those scarcely less important of giving expression to his thoughts and opinions, either by writing or speaking, unrestrained but by the liability for injury to others, and that of a full participation in all the advantages which flow from the Government, the acknowledged property of all, the American citizen derives from no charter granted by his fellow-man. He claims them because he is himself a man, fashioned by the same Almighty hand as the rest of his species and entitled to a full share of the blessings with which He has endowed them. Notwithstanding the limited sovereignty possessed by the people of the United States and the restricted grant of power to the Government which they have adopted, enough has been given to accomplish all the objects for which it was created. It has been found powerful in war, and hitherto justice has been administered, an intimate union effected, domestic tranquillity preserved, and personal liberty secured to the citizen. As was to be expected, however, from the defect of language and the necessarily sententious manner in which the Constitution is written, disputes have arisen as to the amount of power which it has actually granted or was intended to grant.

This is more particularly the case in relation to that part of the instrument which treats of the legislative branch, and not only as regards the exercise of powers claimed under a general clause giving that body the authority to pass all laws necessary to carry into effect the specified powers, but in relation to the latter also. It is, however, consolatory to reflect that *most* of the instances of alleged departure from the letter or spirit of the Constitution have ultimately received the sanction of a majority of the people. And the fact that many of our statesmen most distinguished for talent and patriotism have been at one time or other of their political career on both sides of each of the most warmly disputed questions forces upon us the inference that the errors, if errors there were, are attributable to the intrinsic difficulty in many instances of ascertaining the intentions of the framers of the Constitution rather than the influence of any sinister or unpatriotic motive. But the great danger to our institutions does not appear to me to be in a usurpation by the Government of power not granted by the people, but by the accumulation in one of the departments of that which was assigned to others. Limited as are the powers which have been granted, still enough have been granted to constitute a despotism if concentrated in one of the departments. This danger is greatly heightened, as it has been always observable that men are less jealous of encroachments of one department upon another than upon their own reserved rights. When the Constitution of the United States first came from the hands of the Convention which formed it, many of the sternest republicans of the day were alarmed at the extent of the power which had been granted to the Federal Government, and more particularly of that portion which had been assigned to the executive branch. There were in it features which appeared not to be in harmony with their ideas of a simple representative democracy or republic, and knowing the tendency of power to increase itself, particularly when exercised by a single individual, predictions were made that at no very remote period the Government would terminate in virtual monarchy. It would not become me to say that the fears of these patriots have been already realized; but as I sincerely believe that the tendency of measures and of men's opinions for some years past has been in that direction, it is, I conceive, strictly proper that I should take this occasion to repeat the assurances I have heretofore given of my determination to arrest the progress of that tendency if it really exists and restore the Government to its pristine health and vigor, as far as this can be effected by any legitimate exercise of the power placed in my hands.

I proceed to state in as summary a manner as I can my opinion of the sources of the evils which have been so extensively complained of and the correctives which may be applied. Some of the former are unquestionably to be found in the defects of the Constitution; others, in my judgment, are attributable to a misconstruction of some of its provisions. Of the former is the eligibility of the same individual to a second term of the Presidency. The sagacious mind of Mr. Jefferson early saw and lamented this error, and attempts have been made, hitherto without success, to apply the amendatory power of the States to its correction. As, however, one mode of correction is in the power of every President, and consequently in mine, it would be useless, and perhaps invidious, to enumerate the evils of which, in the opinion of many of our fellow-citizens, this error of the sages who framed the Constitution may have been the source and the bitter fruits which we are still to gather from it if it continues to disfigure our system. It may be observed, however, as a general remark, that republics can commit no greater error than to adopt or continue any feature in their systems of government which may be calculated to create or increase the love of power in the bosoms of those to whom necessity obliges them to commit the management of their affairs; and surely nothing is more likely to produce such a state of mind than the long continuance of an office of high trust. Nothing can be more corrupting, nothing more destructive of all those noble feelings which belong to the character of a devoted republican patriot. When this corrupting passion once takes possession of the human mind, like the love of gold it becomes insatiable. It is the never-dying worm in his bosom, grows with his growth and strengthens with the declining years of its victim. If this is true, it is the part of wisdom for a republic to limit the service of that officer at least to whom she has intrusted the management of her foreign relations, the execution of her laws, and the command of her armies and navies to a period so short as to prevent his forgetting that he is the accountable agent, not the principal; the servant, not the master. Until an amendment of the Constitution can be effected public opinion may secure the desired object. I give my aid to it by renewing the pledge heretofore given that under no circumstances will I consent to serve a second term.

But if there is danger to public liberty from the acknowledged defects of the Constitution in the want of limit to the continuance of the Executive power in the same hands, there is, I apprehend, not much less from a misconstruction of that instrument as it regards the powers actually given. I can not conceive that by a fair construction any or either of its provisions would be found to constitute the President a part of the legislative power. It can not be claimed from the power to recommend, since, although enjoined as a duty upon him, it is a privilege which he holds in common with every other citizen; and although there may be something more of confidence in the propriety of the measures recommended in the one case than in the other, in the obligations of ultimate decision there can be no difference. In the language of the Constitution, "all the legislative powers" which it grants "are vested in the Congress of the United States." It would be a solecism in language to say that any portion of these is not included in the whole.

It may be said, indeed, that the Constitution has given to the Executive the power to annul the acts of the legislative body by refusing to them his assent. So a similar power has necessarily resulted from that instrument to the judiciary, and yet the judiciary forms no part of the Legislature. There is, it is true, this difference between these grants of power: The Executive can put his negative upon the acts of the Legislature for other cause than that of want of conformity to the Constitution, whilst the judiciary can only declare void those which violate that instrument. But the decision of the judiciary is final in such a case, whereas in every instance where the veto of the Executive is applied it may be overcome by a vote of two-thirds of both Houses of Congress. The negative upon the acts of the legislative by the executive authority, and that in the hands of one individual, would seem to be an incongruity in our system. Like some others of a similar character, however, it appears to be highly expedient, and if used only with the forbearance and in the spirit which was intended by its authors it may be productive of great good and be found one of the best safeguards to the Union. At the period of the formation of the Constitution the principle does not appear to have enjoyed much favor in the State governments. It existed but in two, and in one of these there was a plural executive. If we would search for the motives which operated upon the purely patriotic and enlightened assembly which framed the Constitution for the adoption of a provision so apparently repugnant to the leading democratic principle that the majority should govern, we must reject the idea that they anticipated from it any benefit to the ordinary course of legislation. They knew too well the high degree of intelligence which existed among the people and the enlightened character of the State legislatures not to have the fullest confidence that the two bodies elected by them would be worthy representatives of such constituents, and, of course, that they would require no aid in conceiving and maturing the measures which the circumstances of the country might require. And it is preposterous to suppose that a thought could for a moment have been entertained that the President, placed at the capital, in the center of the country, could better understand the wants and wishes of the people than their own immediate representatives, who spend a part of every year among them, living with them, often laboring with them, and bound to them by the triple tie of interest, duty, and affection. To assist or control Congress, then, in its ordinary legislation could not, I conceive, have been the motive for conferring the veto power on the President. This argument acquires additional force from the fact of its never having been thus used by the first six Presidents—and two of them were members of the Convention, one presiding over its deliberations and the other bearing a larger share in consummating the labors of that august body than any other person. But if bills were never returned to Congress by either of the Presidents above referred to upon the ground of their being inexpedient or not as well adapted as they might be to the wants of the people, the veto was applied upon that of want of conformity to the Constitution or because errors had been committed from a too hasty enactment.

There is another ground for the adoption of the veto principle, which had probably more influence in recommending it to the Convention than any other. I refer to the security which it gives to the just and equitable action of the Legislature upon all parts of the Union. It could not but have occurred to the Convention that in a country so extensive, embracing so great a variety of soil and climate, and consequently of products, and which from the same causes must ever exhibit a great difference in the amount of the population of its various sections, calling for a great diversity in the employments of the people, that the legislation of the majority might not always justly regard the rights and interests of the minority, and that acts of this character might be passed under an express grant by the words of the Constitution, and therefore not within the competency of the judiciary to declare void; that however enlightened and patriotic they might suppose from past experience the members of Congress might be, and however largely partaking, in the general, of the liberal feelings of the people, it was impossible to expect that bodies so constituted should not sometimes be controlled by local interests and sectional feelings. It was proper, therefore, to provide some umpire from whose situation and mode of appointment more independence and freedom from such influences might be expected. Such a one was afforded by the executive department constituted by the Constitution. A person elected to that high office, having his constituents in every section, State, and subdivision of the Union, must consider himself bound by the most solemn sanctions to guard, protect, and defend the rights of all and of every portion, great or small, from the injustice and oppression of the rest.   I consider the veto power, therefore, given by the Constitution to the Executive of the United States solely as a conservative power, to be used only, first, to protect the Constitution from violation; secondly, the people from the effects of hasty legislation where their will has been probably disregarded or not well understood, and, thirdly, to prevent the effects of combinations violative of the rights of minorities.   In reference to the second of these objects I may observe that I consider it the right and privilege of the people to decide disputed points of the Constitution arising from the general grant of power to Congress to carry into effect the powers expressly given; and I believe with Mr. Madison that "repeated recognitions under varied circumstances in acts of the legislative, executive, and judicial branches of the Government, accompanied by indications in different modes of the concurrence of the general will of the nation," as affording to the President sufficient authority for his considering such disputed points as settled.

Upward of half a century has elapsed since the adoption of the present form of government.   It would be an object more highly desirable than the gratification of the curiosity of speculative statesmen if its precise situation could be ascertained, a fair exhibit made of the operations of each of its departments, of the powers which they respectively claim and exercise, of the collisions which have occurred between them or between the whole Government and those of the States or either of them.   We could then compare our actual condition after fifty years' trial of our system with what it was in the commencement of its operations and ascertain whether the predictions of the patriots who opposed its adoption or the confident hopes of its advocates have been best realized.   The great dread of the former seems to have been that the reserved powers of the States would be absorbed by those of the Federal Government and a consolidated power established, leaving to the States the shadow only of that independent action for which they had so zealously contended and on the preservation of which they relied as the last hope of liberty. Without denying that the result to which they looked with so much apprehension is in the way of being realized, it is obvious that they did not clearly see the mode of its accomplishment.   The General Government has seized upon none of the reserved rights of the States.   As far as any open warfare may have gone, the State authorities have amply maintained their rights.   To a casual observer our system presents no appearance of discord between the different members which compose it. Even the addition of many new ones has produced no jarring.   They move in their respective orbits in perfect harmony with the central head and with each other.   But there is still an undercurrent at work by which, if not seasonably checked, the worst apprehensions of our antifederal patriots will be realized, and not only will the State authorities

be overshadowed by the great increase of power in the executive department of the General Government, but the character of that Government, if not its designation, be essentially and radically changed.   This state of things has been in part effected by causes inherent in the Constitution and in part by the never-failing tendency of political power to increase itself.   By making the President the sole distributer of all the patronage of the Government the framers of the Constitution do not appear to have anticipated at how short a period it would become a formidable instrument to control the free operations of the State governments.   Of trifling importance at first, it had early in Mr. Jefferson's Administration become so powerful as to create great alarm in the mind of that patriot from the potent influence it might exert in controlling the freedom of the elective franchise.   If such could have then been the effects of its influence, how much greater must be the danger at this time, quadrupled in amount as it certainly is and more completely under the control of the Executive will than their construction of their powers allowed or the forbearing characters of all the early Presidents permitted them to make.   But it is not by the extent of its patronage alone that the executive department has become dangerous, but by the use which it appears may be made of the appointing power to bring under its control the whole revenues of the country.   The Constitution has declared it to be the duty of the President to see that the laws are executed, and it makes him the Commander in Chief of the Armies and Navy of the United States.   If the opinion of the most approved writers upon that species of mixed government which in modern Europe is termed *monarchy* in contradistinction to *despotism* is correct, there was wanting no other addition to the powers of our Chief Magistrate to stamp a monarchical character on our Government but the control of the public finances; and to me it appears strange indeed that anyone should doubt that the entire control which the President possesses over the officers who have the custody of the public money, by the power of removal with or without cause, does, for all mischievous purposes at least, virtually subject the treasure also to his disposal.   The first Roman Emperor, in his attempt to seize the sacred treasure, silenced the opposition of the officer to whose charge it had been committed by a significant allusion to his sword.   By a selection of political instruments for the care of the public money a reference to their commissions by a President would be quite as effectual an argument as that of Cæsar to the Roman knight.   I am not insensible of the great difficulty that exists in drawing a proper plan for the safe-keeping and disbursement of the public revenues, and I know the importance which has been attached by men of great abilities and patriotism to the divorce, as it is called, of the Treasury from the banking institutions.   It is not the divorce which is complained of, but the unhallowed union of the Treasury with the executive department, which has created such extensive alarm.   To this danger to our republican institutions and that created by the influence given to the Executive through the instrumentality of the Federal officers I propose to apply all the remedies which may be at my command. It was certainly a great error in the framers of the Constitution not to have made the officer at the head of the Treasury Department entirely independent of the Executive. He should at least have been removable only upon the demand of the popular branch of the Legislature. I have determined never to remove a Secretary of the Treasury without communicating all the circumstances attending such removal to both Houses of Congress.

The influence of the Executive in controlling the freedom of the elective franchise through the medium of the public officers can be effectually checked by renewing the prohibition published by Mr. Jefferson forbidding their interference in elections further than giving their own votes, and their own independence secured by an assurance of perfect immunity in exercising this sacred privilege of freemen under the dictates of their own unbiased judgments. Never with my consent shall an officer of the people, compensated for his services out of their pockets, become the pliant instrument of Executive will.

There is no part of the means placed in the hands of the Executive which might be used with greater effect for unhallowed purposes than the control of the public press. The maxim which our ancestors derived from the mother country that "the freedom of the press is the great bulwark of civil and religious liberty" is one of the most precious legacies which they have left us. We have learned, too, from our own as well as the experience of other countries, that golden shackles, by whomsoever or by whatever pretense imposed, are as fatal to it as the iron bonds of despotism. The presses in the necessary employment of the Government should never be used "to clear the guilty or to varnish crime." A decent and manly examination of the acts of the Government should be not only tolerated, but encouraged.

Upon another occasion I have given my opinion at some length upon the impropriety of Executive interference in the legislation of Congress— that the article in the Constitution making it the duty of the President to communicate information and authorizing him to recommend measures was not intended to make him the source in legislation, and, in particular, that he should never be looked to for schemes of finance. It would be very strange, indeed, that the Constitution should have strictly forbidden one branch of the Legislature from interfering in the origination of such bills and that it should be considered proper that an altogether different department of the Government should be permitted to do so. Some of our best political maxims and opinions have been drawn from our parent isle. There are others, however, which can not be introduced in our system without singular incongruity and the production of much mischief, and this I conceive to be one. No matter in which of the houses of Parliament a bill may originate nor by whom introduced—a minister or a member of the opposition—by the fiction of law, or rather of constitutional principle, the sovereign is supposed to have prepared it agreeably to his will and then submitted it to Parliament for their advice and consent.   Now the very reverse is the case here, not only with regard to the principle, but the forms prescribed by the Constitution.   The principle certainly assigns to the only body constituted by the Constitution (the legislative body) the power to make laws, and the forms even direct that the enactment should be ascribed to them.   The Senate, in relation to revenue bills, have the right to propose amendments, and so has the Executive by the power given him to return them to the House of Representatives with his objections.   It is in his power also to propose amendments in the existing revenue laws, suggested by his observations upon their defective or injurious operation.   But the delicate duty of devising schemes of revenue should be left where the Constitution has placed it—with the immediate representatives of the people.   For similar reasons the mode of keeping the public treasure should be prescribed by them, and the further removed it may be from the control of the Executive the more wholesome the arrangement and the more in accordance with republican principle.

Connected with this subject is the character of the currency.   The idea of making it exclusively metallic, however well intended, appears to me to be fraught with more fatal consequences than any other scheme having no relation to the personal rights of the citizens that has ever been devised.   If any single scheme could produce the effect of arresting at once that mutation of condition by which thousands of our most indigent fellow-citizens by their industry and enterprise are raised to the possession of wealth, that is the one.   If there is one measure better calculated than another to produce that state of things so much deprecated by all true republicans, by which the rich are daily adding to their hoards and the poor sinking deeper into penury, it is an exclusive metallic currency. Or if there is a process by which the character of the country for generosity and nobleness of feeling may be destroyed by the great increase and necessary toleration of usury, it is an exclusive metallic currency.

Amongst the other duties of a delicate character which the President is called upon to perform is the supervision of the government of the Territories of the United States.   Those of them which are destined to become members of our great political family are compensated by their rapid progress from infancy to manhood for the partial and temporary deprivation of their political rights.   It is in this District only where American citizens are to be found who under a settled policy are deprived of many important political privileges without any inspiring hope as to the future.   Their only consolation under circumstances of such deprivation is that of the devoted exterior guards of a camp—that their sufferings secure tranquillity and safety within.   Are there any of their countrymen who would subject them to greater sacrifices, to any other humiliations than those essentially necessary to the security of the object for which they were thus separated from their fellow-citizens? Are their rights alone not to be guaranteed by the application of those great principles upon which all our constitutions are founded? We are told by the greatest of British orators and statesmen that at the commencement of the War of the Revolution the most stupid men in England spoke of "their American subjects." Are there, indeed, citizens of any of our States who have dreamed *of their subjects* in the District of Columbia? Such dreams can never be realized by any agency of mine. The people of the District of Columbia are not the subjects of the people of the States, but free American citizens. Being in the latter condition when the Constitution was formed, no words used in that instrument could have been intended to deprive them of that character. If there is anything in the great principle of unalienable rights so emphatically insisted upon in our Declaration of Independence, they could neither make nor the United States accept a surrender of their liberties and become the *subjects*—in other words, the slaves—of their former fellow-citizens. If this be true—and it will scarcely be denied by anyone who has a correct idea of his own rights as an American citizen—the grant to Congress of exclusive jurisdiction in the District of Columbia can be interpreted, so far as respects the aggregate people of the United States, as meaning nothing more than to allow to Congress the controlling power necessary to afford a free and safe exercise of the functions assigned to the General Government by the Constitution. In all other respects the legislation of Congress should be adapted to their peculiar position and wants and be conformable with their deliberate opinions of their own interests.

I have spoken of the necessity of keeping the respective departments of the Government, as well as all the other authorities of our country, within their appropriate orbits. This is a matter of difficulty in some cases, as the powers which they respectively claim are often not defined by any distinct lines. Mischievous, however, in their tendencies as collisions of this kind may be, those which arise between the respective communities which for certain purposes compose one nation are much more so, for no such nation can long exist without the careful culture of those feelings of confidence and affection which are the effective bonds to union between free and confederated states. Strong as is the tie of interest, it has been often found ineffectual. Men blinded by their passions have been known to adopt measures for their country in direct opposition to all the suggestions of policy. The alternative, then, is to destroy or keep down a bad passion by creating and fostering a good one, and this seems to be the corner stone upon which our American political architects have reared the fabric of our Government. The cement which was to bind it and perpetuate its existence was the affectionate attachment between all its members. To insure the continuance of this feeling, produced at first by a community of dangers, of sufferings, and of interests, the advantages of each were made accessible to all. No participation in any good possessed by any member of our extensive Confederacy, except in domestic government, was withheld from the citizen of any other member. By a process attended with no difficulty, no delay, no expense but that of removal, the citizen of one might become the citizen of any other, and successively of the whole. The lines, too, separating powers to be exercised by the citizens of one State from those of another seem to be so distinctly drawn as to leave no room for misunderstanding. The citizens of each State unite in their persons all the privileges which that character confers and all that they may claim as citizens of the United States, but in no case can the same persons at the same time act as the citizen of two separate States, and *he is therefore positively precluded from any interference with the reserved powers of any State but that of which he is for the time being a citizen.* He may, indeed, offer to the citizens of other States his advice as to their management, and the form in which it is tendered is left to his own discretion and sense of propriety. It may be observed, however, that organized associations of citizens requiring compliance with their wishes too much resemble the *recommendations* of Athens to her allies, supported by an armed and powerful fleet. It was, indeed, to the ambition of the leading States of Greece to control the domestic concerns of the others that the destruction of that celebrated Confederacy, and subsequently of all its members, is mainly to be attributed, and it is owing to the absence of that spirit that the Helvetic Confederacy has for so many years been preserved. Never has there been seen in the institutions of the separate members of any confederacy more elements of discord. In the principles and forms of government and religion, as well as in the circumstances of the several Cantons, so marked a discrepancy was observable as to promise anything but harmony in their intercourse or permanency in their alliance, and yet for ages neither has been interrupted. Content with the positive benefits which their union produced, with the independence and safety from foreign aggression which it secured, these sagacious people respected the institutions of each other, however repugnant to their own principles and prejudices.

Our Confederacy, fellow-citizens, can only be preserved by the same forbearance. Our citizens must be content with the exercise of the powers with which the Constitution clothes them. The attempt of those of one State to control the domestic institutions of another can only result in feelings of distrust and jealousy, the certain harbingers of disunion, violence, and civil war, and the ultimate destruction of our free institutions. Our Confederacy is perfectly illustrated by the terms and principles governing a common copartnership. There is a fund of power to be exercised under the direction of the joint councils of the allied members, but that which has been reserved by the individual members is intangible by the common Government or the individual members composing it. To attempt it finds no support in the principles of our Constitution.

It should be our constant and earnest endeavor mutually to cultivate a spirit of concord and harmony among the various parts of our Confederacy. Experience has abundantly taught us that the agitation by citizens of one part of the Union of a subject not confided to the General Government, but exclusively under the guardianship of the local authorities, is productive of no other consequences than bitterness, alienation, discord, and injury to the very cause which is intended to be advanced. Of all the great interests which appertain to our country, that of union—cordial, confiding, fraternal union—is by far the most important, since it is the only true and sure guaranty of all others.

In consequence of the embarrassed state of business and the currency, some of the States may meet with difficulty in their financial concerns. However deeply we may regret anything imprudent or excessive in the engagements into which States have entered for purposes of their own, it does not become us to disparage the State governments, nor to discourage them from making proper efforts for their own relief. On the contrary, it is our duty to encourage them to the extent of our constitutional authority to apply their best means and cheerfully to make all necessary sacrifices and submit to all necessary burdens to fulfill their engagements and maintain their credit, for the character and credit of the several States form a part of the character and credit of the whole country. The resources of the country are abundant, the enterprise and activity of our people proverbial, and we may well hope that wise legislation and prudent administration by the respective governments, each acting within its own sphere, will restore former prosperity.

Unpleasant and even dangerous as collisions may sometimes be between the constituted authorities of the citizens of our country in relation to the lines which separate their respective jurisdictions, the results can be of no vital injury to our institutions if that ardent patriotism, that devoted attachment to liberty, that spirit of moderation and forbearance for which our countrymen were once distinguished, continue to be cherished. If this continues to be the ruling passion of our souls, the weaker feeling of the mistaken enthusiast will be corrected, the Utopian dreams of the scheming politician dissipated, and the complicated intrigues of the demagogue rendered harmless. The spirit of liberty is the sovereign balm for every injury which our institutions may receive. On the contrary, no care that can be used in the construction of our Government, no division of powers, no distribution of checks in its several departments, will prove effectual to keep us a free people if this spirit is suffered to decay; and decay it will without constant nurture. To the neglect of this duty the best historians agree in attributing the ruin of all the republics with whose existence and fall their writings have made us acquainted.

The same causes will ever produce the same effects, and as long as the love of power is a dominant passion of the human bosom, and as long as the understandings of men can be warped and their affections changed by operations upon their passions and prejudices, so long will the liberties of a people depend on their own constant attention to its preservation. The danger to all well-established free governments arises from the unwillingness of the people to believe in its existence or from the influence of designing men diverting their attention from the quarter whence it approaches to a source from which it can never come. This is the old trick of those who would usurp the government of their country. In the name of democracy they speak, warning the people against the influence of wealth and the danger of aristocracy. History, ancient and modern, is full of such examples. Cæsar became the master of the Roman people and the senate under the pretense of supporting the democratic claims of the former against the aristocracy of the latter; Cromwell, in the character of protector of the liberties of the people, became the dictator of England, and Bolivar possessed himself of unlimited power with the title of his country's liberator. There is, on the contrary, no instance on record of an extensive and well-established republic being changed into an aristocracy. The tendencies of all such governments in their decline is to monarchy, and the antagonist principle to liberty there is the spirit of faction—a spirit which assumes the character and in times of great excitement imposes itself upon the people as the genuine spirit of freedom, and, like the false Christs whose coming was foretold by the Savior, seeks to, and were it possible would, impose upon the true and most faithful disciples of liberty. It is in periods like this that it behooves the people to be most watchful of those to whom they have intrusted power. And although there is at times much difficulty in distinguishing the false from the true spirit, a calm and dispassionate investigation will detect the counterfeit, as well by the character of its operations as the results that are produced. The true spirit of liberty, although devoted, persevering, bold, and uncompromising in principle, that secured is mild and tolerant and scrupulous as to the means it employs, whilst the spirit of party, assuming to be that of liberty, is harsh, vindictive, and intolerant, and totally reckless as to the character of the allies which it brings to the aid of its cause. When the genuine spirit of liberty animates the body of a people to a thorough examination of their affairs, it leads to the excision of every excrescence which may have fastened itself upon any of the departments of the government, and restores the system to its pristine health and beauty. But the reign of an intolerant spirit of party amongst a free people seldom fails to result in a dangerous accession to the executive power introduced and established amidst unusual professions of devotion to democracy.

The foregoing remarks relate almost exclusively to matters connected with our domestic concerns. It may be proper, however, that I should give some indications to my fellow-citizens of my proposed course of conduct in the management of our foreign relations. I assure them, therefore, that it is my intention to use every means in my power to preserve the friendly intercourse which now so happily subsists with every foreign nation, and that although, of course, not well informed as to the state of pending negotiations with any of them, I see in the personal characters of the sovereigns, as well as in the mutual interests of our own and of the governments with which our relations are most intimate, a pleasing guaranty that the harmony so important to the interests of their subjects as well as of our citizens will not be interrupted by the advancement of any claim or pretension upon their part to which our honor would not permit us to yield. Long the defender of my country's rights in the field, I trust that my fellow-citizens will not see in my earnest desire to preserve peace with foreign powers any indication that their rights will ever be sacrificed or the honor of the nation tarnished by any admission on the part of their Chief Magistrate unworthy of their former glory. In our intercourse with our aboriginal neighbors the same liberality and justice which marked the course prescribed to me by two of my illustrious predecessors when acting under their direction in the discharge of the duties of superintendent and commissioner shall be strictly observed. I can conceive of no more sublime spectacle, none more likely to propitiate an impartial and common Creator, than a rigid adherence to the principles of justice on the part of a powerful nation in its transactions with a weaker and uncivilized people whom circumstances have placed at its disposal.

Before concluding, fellow-citizens, I must say something to you on the subject of the parties at this time existing in our country. To me it appears perfectly clear that the interest of that country requires that the violence of the spirit by which those parties are at this time governed must be greatly mitigated, if not entirely extinguished, or consequences will ensue which are appalling to be thought of.

If parties in a republic are necessary to secure a degree of vigilance sufficient to keep the public functionaries within the bounds of law and duty, at that point their usefulness ends. Beyond that they become destructive of public virtue, the parent of a spirit antagonist to that of liberty, and eventually its inevitable conqueror. We have examples of republics where the love of country and of liberty at one time were the dominant passions of the whole mass of citizens, and yet, with the continuance of the name and forms of free government, not a vestige of these qualities remaining in the bosoms of any one of its citizens. It was the beautiful remark of a distinguished English writer that "in the Roman senate Octavius had a party and Antony a party, but the Commonwealth had none." Yet the senate continued to meet in the temple of liberty to talk of the sacredness and beauty of the Commonwealth and gaze at the statues of the elder Brutus and of the Curtii and

Decii, and the people assembled in the forum, not, as in the days of Camillus and the Scipios, to cast their free votes for annual magistrates or pass upon the acts of the senate, but to receive from the hands of the leaders of the respective parties their share of the spoils and to shout for one or the other, as those collected in Gaul or Egypt and the lesser Asia would furnish the larger dividend. The spirit of liberty had fled, and, avoiding the abodes of civilized man, had sought protection in the wilds of Scythia or Scandinavia; and so under the operation of the same causes and influences it will fly from our Capitol and our forums. A calamity so awful, not only to our country, but to the world, must be deprecated by every patriot and every tendency to a state of things likely to produce it immediately checked. Such a tendency has existed—does exist. Always the friend of my countrymen, never their flatterer, it becomes my duty to say to them from this high place to which their partiality has exalted me that there exists in the land a spirit hostile to their best interests—hostile to liberty itself. It is a spirit contracted in its views, selfish in its objects. It looks to the aggrandizement of a few even to the destruction of the interests of the whole. The entire remedy is with the people. Something, however, may be effected by the means which they have placed in my hands. It is union that we want, not of a party for the sake of that party, but a union of the whole country for the sake of the whole country, for the defense of its interests and its honor against foreign aggression, for the defense of those principles for which our ancestors so gloriously contended. As far as it depends upon me it shall be accomplished. All the influence that I possess shall be exerted to prevent the formation at least of an Executive party in the halls of the legislative body. I wish for the support of no member of that body to any measure of mine that does not satisfy his judgment and his sense of duty to those from whom he holds his appointment, nor any confidence in advance from the people but that asked for by Mr. Jefferson, "to give firmness and effect to the legal administration of their affairs."

I deem the present occasion sufficiently important and solemn to justify me in expressing to my fellow-citizens a profound reverence for the Christian religion and a thorough conviction that sound morals, religious liberty, and a just sense of religious responsibility are essentially connected with all true and lasting happiness; and to that good Being who has blessed us by the gifts of civil and religious freedom, who watched over and prospered the labors of our fathers and has hitherto preserved to us institutions far exceeding in excellence those of any other people, let us unite in fervently commending every interest of our beloved country in all future time.

Fellow-citizens, being fully invested with that high office to which the partiality of my countrymen has called me, I now take an affectionate leave of you. You will bear with you to your homes the remembrance of

the pledge I have this day given to discharge all the high duties of my
exalted station according to the best of my ability, and I shall enter upon
their performance with entire confidence in the support of a just and
generous people.

MARCH 4, 1841.

SPECIAL MESSAGE.

To the Senate of the United States: MARCH 5, 1841.

I hereby withdraw all nominations made to the Senate on or before
the 3d instant and which were not definitely acted on at the close of its
session on that day.   W. H. HARRISON.

PROCLAMATION.

[From Statutes at Large (Little, Brown & Co.), Vol. XI, p. 786.]

BY THE PRESIDENT OF THE UNITED STATES OF AMERICA.

A PROCLAMATION.

Whereas sundry important and weighty matters, principally growing
out of the condition of the revenue and finances of the country, appear
to me to call for the consideration of Congress at an earlier day than its
next annual session, and thus form an extraordinary occasion, such as
renders necessary, in my judgment, the convention of the two Houses
as soon as may be practicable:

I do therefore by this my proclamation convene the two Houses of
Congress to meet in the Capitol, at the city of Washington, on the last
Monday, being the 31st day, of May next; and I require the respective
Senators and Representatives then and there to assemble, in order to
receive such information respecting the state of the Union as may be
given to them and to devise and adopt such measures as the good of
the country may seem to them, in the exercise of their wisdom and discretion, to require.

In testimony whereof I have caused the seal of the United States to
be hereunto affixed, and signed the same with my hand.

[SEAL.]   Done at the city of Washington, the 17th day of March,
A. D. 1841, and of the Independence of the United States the
sixty-fifth.

W. H. HARRISON.

By the President:

DANIEL WEBSTER,
Secretary of State.

· DEATH OF PRESIDENT HARRISON.

PUBLIC ANNOUNCEMENT.

[From the Daily National Intelligencer, April 5, 1841.]

WASHINGTON, *April 4, 1841.*

An all-wise Providence having suddenly removed from this life William Henry Harrison, late President of the United States, we have thought it our duty, in the recess of Congress and in the absence of the Vice-President from the seat of Government, to make this afflicting bereavement known to the country by this declaration under our hands.

He died at the President's house, in this city, this 4th day of April, A. D. 1841, at thirty minutes before 1 o'clock in the morning.

The people of the United States, overwhelmed, like ourselves, by an event so unexpected and so melancholy, will derive consolation from knowing that his death was calm and resigned, as his life has been patriotic, useful, and distinguished, and that the last utterance of his lips expressed a fervent desire for the perpetuity of the Constitution and the preservation of its true principles. In death, as in life, the happiness of his country was uppermost in his thoughts.

DANIEL WEBSTER,
Secretary of State.

THOMAS EWING,
Secretary of the Treasury.

JOHN BELL,
Secretary of War.

J. J. CRITTENDEN,
Attorney-General.

FRANCIS GRANGER,
Postmaster-General.

[The Secretary of the Navy was absent from the city.]

ANNOUNCEMENT TO THE VICE-PRESIDENT.

[From the Daily National Intelligencer, April 5, 1841.]

WASHINGTON, *April 4, 1841.*

JOHN TYLER,
Vice-President of the United States.

SIR: It has become our most painful duty to inform you that William Henry Harrison, late President of the United States, has departed this life.

This distressing event took place this day at the President's mansion, in this city, at thirty minutes before 1 in the morning.

We lose no time in dispatching the chief clerk in the State Department as a special messenger to bear you these melancholy tidings.

We have the honor to be, with the highest regard, your obedient servants,

DANIEL WEBSTER,
Secretary of State.

THOMAS EWING,
Secretary of the Treasury.

JOHN BELL,
Secretary of War.

JOHN J. CRITTENDEN,
Attorney-General.

FRANCIS GRANGER,
Postmaster-General.

ANNOUNCEMENT TO REPRESENTATIVES OF THE UNITED STATES ABROAD.

[From official records in the State Department.]

DEPARTMENT OF STATE,
Washington, April 4, 1841.

SIR: It has become my most painful duty to announce to you the decease of William Henry Harrison, late President of the United States.

This afflicting event took place this day at the Executive Mansion, in this city, at thirty minutes before 1 o'clock in the morning.

I am, sir, your obedient servant,

DANL. WEBSTER.

ANNOUNCEMENT TO REPRESENTATIVES OF FOREIGN GOVERNMENTS IN THE UNITED STATES.

[From official records in the State Department.]

DEPARTMENT OF STATE,
Washington, April 5, 1841.

SIR: It is my great misfortune to be obliged to inform you of an event not less afflicting to the people of the United States than distressing to my own feelings and the feelings of all those connected with the Government.

The President departed this life yesterday at thirty minutes before 1 o'clock in the morning.

You are respectfully invited to attend the funeral ceremonies, which will take place on Wednesday next, and with the particular arrangements for which you will be made acquainted in due time.

Not doubting your sympathy and condolence with the Government and people of the country on this bereavement, I have the honor to be, sir, with high consideration, your obedient servant,

DANL. WEBSTER.

ANNOUNCEMENT TO THE ARMY.

[From official records in the War Department.]

DEPARTMENT OF WAR,
Washington, April 5, 1841.

It is with feelings of the deepest sorrow that the Secretary of War announces to the Army the death of the President of the United States. William Henry Harrison is no more. His long and faithful services in many subordinate but important stations, his recent elevation to the highest in honor and power, and the brief term allotted to him in the enjoyment of it are circumstances of themselves which must awaken the liveliest sympathy in every bosom. But these are personal considerations; the dispensation is heaviest and most afflicting on public grounds. This great calamity has befallen the country at a period of general anxiety for its present, and some apprehension for its future, condition—at a time when it is most desirable that all its high offices should be filled and all its high trusts administered in harmony, wisdom, and vigor. The generosity of character of the deceased, the conspicuous honesty of his principles and purposes, together with the skill and firmness with which he maintained them in all situations, had won for him the affection and confidence of his countrymen; but at the moment when by their voice he was raised to a station in the discharge of the powers and duties of which the most beneficent results might justly have been anticipated from his great experience, his sound judgment, the high estimation in which he was held by the people, and his unquestioned devotion to the Constitution and to the Union, it has pleased an all-wise but mysterious Providence to remove him suddenly from that and every other earthly employment.

While the officers and soldiers of the Army share in the general grief which these considerations so naturally and irresistibly inspire, they will doubtless be penetrated with increased sensibility and feel a deeper concern in testifying in the manner appropriate to them the full measure of a nation's gratitude for the eminent services of the departed patriot and in rendering just and adequate honors to his memory because he was himself a soldier, and an approved one, receiving his earliest lessons in a camp, and, when in riper years called to the command of armies, illustrating the profession of arms by his personal qualities and contributing largely by his successes to the stock of his country's glory.

It is to be regretted that the suddenness of the emergency has made it necessary to announce this sad event in the absence of the Vice-President from the seat of Government; but the greatest confidence is felt that he will cordially approve the sentiments expressed, and that he will in due time give directions for such further marks of respect not prescribed by the existing regulations of the Army as may be demanded by the occasion.

JOHN BELL, *Secretary of War.*

GENERAL ORDERS, NO. 20.

HEADQUARTERS OF THE ARMY,
ADJUTANT-GENERAL'S OFFICE,
Washington, April 7, 1841.

The death of the President of the United States having been officially announced from the War Department, the Major-General Commanding in Chief communicates to the Army the melancholy intelligence with feelings of the most profound sorrow. The long, arduous, and faithful military services in which President Harrison has been engaged since the first settlement of the Western country, from the rank of a subaltern to that of a commander in chief, are too well known to require a recital of them here. It is sufficient to point to the fields of Tippecanoe, the banks of the Miami, and the Thames, in Upper Canada, to recall to many of the soldiers of the present Army the glorious results of some of his achievements against the foes of his country, both savage and civilized.

The Army has on former occasions been called upon to mourn the loss of distinguished patriots who have occupied the Presidential chair, but this is the first time since the adoption of the Constitution it has to lament the demise of a President while in the actual exercise of the high functions of the Chief Magistracy of the Union.

The members of the Army, in common with their fellow-citizens of all classes, deeply deplore this national bereavement; but although they have lost a friend ever ready to protect their interests, his bright example in the paths of honor and glory still remains for their emulation.

The funeral honors directed to be paid by the troops in paragraph 523 of the General Regulations will be duly observed, and the troops at the several stations will be paraded at 10 o'clock a. m., when this order will be read, after which all labors for the day will cease; the national flag will be displayed at half-staff; at dawn of day thirteen guns will be fired, besides the half-hour guns as directed by the Regulations, and at the close of the day a national salute. The standards, guidons, and colors of the several regiments will be put in mourning for the period of six months, and the officers will wear the usual badge of mourning on the left arm above the elbow and on the hilt of the sword for the same period.

By order of Alexander Macomb, Major-General Commanding in Chief:

R. JONES, *Adjutant-General.*

ANNOUNCEMENT TO THE NAVY.

[From official records in the Navy Department.]

GENERAL ORDER.

NAVY DEPARTMENT, *April 5, 1841.*

The Department announces to the officers of the Navy and Marine Corps the death of William Henry Harrison, late President of the United States, which occurred at the Executive Mansion, in the city of Washington, on the morning of the 4th instant, and directs that, uniting with their fellow-citizens in the manifestations of their respect for the exalted character and eminent public services of the illustrious deceased, and of their sense of the bereavement the country has sustained by this afflicting dispensation of Providence, they wear the usual badge of mourning for six months.

The Department further directs that funeral honors be paid him at each of the navy-yards and on board each of the public vessels in commission by firing twenty-six minute guns, commencing at 12 o'clock m., on the day after the receipt of this order, and by wearing their flags at half-mast for one week.

J. D. SIMMS,
Acting Secretary of the Navy.

OFFICIAL ARRANGEMENTS FOR THE FUNERAL.

[From official records in the State Department.]

WASHINGTON, *April 4, 1841.*

The circumstances in which we are placed by the death of the President render it indispensable for us, in the recess of Congress and in the absence of the Vice-President, to make arrangements for the funeral solemnities. Having consulted with the family and personal friends of the deceased, we have concluded that the funeral be solemnized on Wednesday, the 7th instant, at 12 o'clock. The religious services to be performed according to the usage of the Episcopal Church, in which church the deceased most usually worshiped. The body to be taken from the President's house to the Congress Burying Ground, accompanied by a military and a civic procession, and deposited in the receiving tomb.

The military arrangements to be under the direction of Major-General Macomb, the General Commanding in Chief the Army of the United States, and Major-General Walter Jones, of the militia of the District of Columbia.

Commodore Morris, the senior captain in the Navy now in the city, to have the direction of the naval arrangements.

The marshal of the District to have the direction of the civic procession, assisted by the mayors of Washington, Georgetown, and Alexandria, the clerk of the Supreme Court of the United States, and such other citizens as they may see fit to call to their aid.

John Quincy Adams, ex-President of the United States, members of Congress now in the city or its neighborhood, all the members of the diplomatic body resident in Washington, and all officers of Government and citizens generally are invited to attend.

And it is respectfully recommended to the officers of Government that they wear the usual badge of mourning.

> DANL. WEBSTER,
> *Secretary of State.*
>
> T. EWING,
> *Secretary of the Treasury.*
>
> JNO. BELL,
> *Secretary of War.*
>
> J. J. CRITTENDEN,
> *Attorney-General.*
>
> FR. GRANGER,
> *Postmaster-General.*

[The Secretary of the Navy was absent from the city.]

[From official records in the War Department.]

DISTRICT ORDERS.

WASHINGTON, *April 5, 1841.*

The foregoing notice from the heads of the Executive Departments of the Government informs you what a signal calamity has befallen us in the death of the President of the United States, and the prominent part assigned you in those funeral honors which may bespeak a nation's respect to the memory of a departed patriot and statesman, whose virtue and talents as a citizen and soldier had achieved illustrious services, and whose sudden death has disappointed the expectation of still more important benefits to his country.

With a view to carry into effect the views of these high officers of Government in a manner befitting the occasion and honorable to the militia corps of this District, I request the general and field officers, the general staff, and the commandants of companies to assemble at my house to-morrow, Tuesday, April 6, precisely at 10 o'clock, to report the strength and equipment of the several corps of the militia and to receive final instructions for parade and arrangement in the military part of the funeral procession.

The commandants of such militia corps from the neighboring States as desire to unite in the procession are respectfully invited to report to me as soon as practicable their intention, with a view to arrange them in due and uniform order as a part of the general military escort.

The detail of these arrangements, to which all the military accessories, both of the regulars and militia, are expected to conform, will be published in due time for the information of all.

For the present it is deemed sufficient to say that the whole military part of the procession, including the regular troops of every arm and denomination and all the militia corps, whether of this District or of the States, will be consolidated in one column of escort, whereof Major-General Macomb, Commander of the Army of the United States, will take the general command, and Brigadier-General Roger Jones, Adjutant-General of the Army of the United States, will act as adjutant-general and officer of the day.

WALTER JONES,
Maj. Gen., Comdg. the Militia of the District of Columbia.

ADJUTANT-GENERAL'S OFFICE,
Washington, April 6, 1841.

The Major-General Commanding the Army of the United States and the major-general commanding the militia of the District of Columbia, having been charged by the executive officers of the Government with the military arrangements for the funeral honors to be paid to the patriot and illustrious citizen, William Henry Harrison, late President of the United States, direct the following order of arrangement:

ORDER OF THE PROCESSION.

FUNERAL ESCORT.
(In column of march.)

Infantry.

Battalion of Baltimore volunteers.
Company of Annapolis volunteers.
Battalion of Washington volunteers.

Marines.

United States Marine Corps.
Corps of commissioned officers of the Baltimore volunteers, headed by a major-general.

Cavalry.

Squadron of Georgetown Light Dragoons.

Artillery.

Troop of United States light artillery.
Dismounted officers of volunteers, Marine Corps, Navy, and Army in the order named.
Mounted officers of volunteers, Marine Corps, Navy, and Army in the order named.
Major-General Walter Jones, commanding the militia.
Aids-de-camp.
Major-General Macomb, Commanding the Army.
Aids-de-camp.

CIVIC PROCESSION.

United States marshal for the District of Columbia and clerk of the Supreme Court.
The mayors of Washington, Georgetown, and Alexandria.
Clergy of the District of Columbia and elsewhere.
Physicians to the President.
Funeral car with the corpse.

Pallbearers.—R. Cutts, esq., for Maine; Hon. J. B. Moore, for New Hampshire; Hon.
C. Cushing, Massachusetts; M. St. C. Clarke, esq., Rhode Island; W. B. Lloyd,
esq., Connecticut; Hon. Hiland Hall, Vermont; General John Granger, New
York; Hon. G. C. Washington, New Jersey; M. Willing, esq., Pennsylvania;
Hon. A. Naudain, Delaware; David Hoffman, esq., Maryland; Major Camp, Vir-
ginia; Hon. E. D. White, North Carolina; John Carter, esq., South Carolina;
General D. L. Clinch, Georgia; Th. Crittenden, esq., Kentucky; Colonel Rogers,
Tennessee; Mr. Graham, Ohio; M. Durald, esq., Louisiana; General Robert
Hanna, Indiana; Anderson Miller, esq., Mississippi; D. G. Garnsey, esq., Illinois;
Dr. Perrine, Alabama; Major Russell, Missouri; A. W. Lyon, esq., Arkansas;
General Howard, Michigan; Hon. J. D. Doty, Wisconsin; Hon. C. Downing,
Florida; Hon. W. B. Carter, Iowa; R. Smith, esq., District of Columbia.
Family and relatives of the late President.
The President of the United States and heads of Departments.
Ex-President Adams.
The Chief Justice and associate justices of the Supreme Court and district judges
of the United States.
The President of the Senate *pro tempore* and Secretary.
Senators and officers of the Senate.
Foreign ministers and suites.
United States and Mexican commissioners for the adjustment of claims under the
convention with Mexico.
Members of the House of Representatives, and officers.
Governors of States and Territories and members of State legislatures.
Judges of the circuit and criminal courts of the District of Columbia, with the
members of the bar and officers of the courts.
The judges of the several States.
The Comptrollers of the Treasury, Auditors, Treasurer, Register, Solicitor, and
Commissioners of Land Office, Pensions, Indian Affairs, Patents, and Public
Buildings.
The clerks, etc., of the several Departments, preceded by their respective chief
clerks, and all other civil officers of the Government.
Officers of the Revolution.
Officers and soldiers of the late war who served under the command of the
late President.
Corporate authorities of Washington.
Corporate authorities of Georgetown.
Corporate authorities of Alexandria.
Such societies and fraternities as may wish to join the procession, to report to the
marshal of the District, who will assign them their respective positions.
Citizens and strangers.

The troops designated to form the escort will assemble in the avenue
north of the President's house, and form line precisely at 11 o'clock
a. m. on Wednesday, the 7th instant, with its right (Captain Ringgold's
troop of light artillery) resting opposite the western gate.

The procession will move precisely at 12 o'clock m., when minute guns
will be fired by detachments of artillery stationed near St. John's church
and the City Hall, and by the Columbian Artillery at the Capitol. At

the same hour the bells of the several churches in Washington, George-town, and Alexandria will be tolled.

At sunrise to-morrow, the 7th instant, a Federal salute will be fired from the military stations in the vicinity of Washington, minute guns between the hours of 12 and 3, and a national salute at the setting of the sun.

The usual badge of mourning will be worn on the left arm and on the hilt of the sword.

The Adjutant-General of the Army is charged with the military arrangements of the day, aided by the Assistant Adjutants-General on duty at the Headquarters of the Army.

The United States marshal of the District has the direction of the civic procession, assisted by the mayors of the cities of the District and the clerk of the Supreme Court of the United States.

By order: ROGER JONES,
                        Adjutant-General United States Army.

CERTIFICATE OF THE DEATH OF PRESIDENT HARRISON.

[From official records, written on parchment, in the State Department.]

WASHINGTON, *April 4, A. D. 1841.*

William Henry Harrison, President of the United States, departed this life at the President's house, in this city, this morning, being Sunday, the 4th day of April, A. D. 1841, at thirty minutes before 1 o'clock in the morning; we whose names are hereunto subscribed being in the house, and some of us in his immediate presence, at the time of his decease.

W. W. SEATON,
        Mayor of Washington.

THOMAS MILLER, M. D.,
        Attending Physician.

ASHTON ALEXANDER, M. D.,
        Consulting Physician.

WM. HAWLEY,
        Rector of St. John's Church.

A. HUNTER,
    Marshal of the District of Columbia.

WM. THOS. CARROLL,
        Clerk of Supreme Court U. S.

FLETCHER WEBSTER,
        Chief Clerk in the State Dept.

DANL. WEBSTER,
        Secretary of State.

THOMAS EWING,
        Secretary of the Treasury.

JNO. BELL,
        Secretary of War.

J. J. CRITTENDEN,
        Attorney-General.

FR. GRANGER,
        Postmaster-General.

JOHN CHAMBERS,
C. S. TODD,
DAVID O. COUPLAND,
        Of the President's Family.

Let this be duly recorded and placed among the rolls.

                                    DANL. WEBSTER,
                                        Secretary of State.

Recorded in Domestic Letter Book by—

                                    A. T. McCORMICK.

REPORT OF THE PHYSICIANS.

[From the Daily National Intelligencer, April 5, 1841.]

WASHINGTON, *April 4, 1841.*

Hon. D. WEBSTER,
    Secretary of State.

DEAR SIR: In compliance with the request made to us by yourself and the other gentlemen of the Cabinet, the attending and consulting physicians have drawn up the abstract of a report on the President's case, which I herewith transmit to you.

Very respectfully, your obedient servant,

THO. MILLER,
    Attending Physician.

On Saturday, March 27, 1841, President Harrison, after several days' previous indisposition, was seized with a chill and other symptoms of fever. The next day pneumonia, with congestion of the liver and derangement of the stomach and bowels, was ascertained to exist. The age and debility of the patient, with the immediate prostration, forbade a resort to general blood letting. Topical depletion, blistering, and appropriate internal remedies subdued in a great measure the disease of the lungs and liver, but the stomach and intestines did not regain a healthy condition. Finally, on the 3d of April, at 3 o'clock p. m., profuse diarrhea came on, under which he sank at thirty minutes to 1 o'clock on the morning of the 4th.

The last words uttered by the President, as heard by Dr. Worthington, were these: "Sir, I wish you to understand the true principles of the Government. I wish them carried out. I ask nothing more."

THO. MILLER, M. D.,
    Attending Physician.

FRED. MAY, M. D.,
N. W. WORTHINGTON, M. D.,
J. C. HALL, M. D.,
ASHTON ALEXANDER, M. D.,
    Consulting Physicians.

OATH OF OFFICE ADMINISTERED TO PRESIDENT JOHN TYLER IN THE PRESENCE OF THE CABINET.*

[From the Daily National Intelligencer, April 7, 1841.]

I do solemnly swear that I will faithfully execute the office of President of the United States, and will to the best of my ability preserve, protect, and defend the Constitution of the United States.

JOHN TYLER.

APRIL 6, 1841.

DISTRICT OF COLUMBIA,
    City and County of Washington, ss:

I, William Cranch, chief judge of the circuit court of the District of Columbia, certify that the above-named John Tyler personally appeared before me this day, and although he deems himself qualified to perform the duties and exercise the

* The Secretary of the Navy was absent from the city.

powers and office of President on the death of William Henry Harrison, late President of the United States, without any other oath than that which he has taken as Vice-President, yet as doubts may *arise*, and for greater caution, took and subscribed the foregoing oath before me.   W. CRANCH.

APRIL 6, 1841.

PROCLAMATION.
TO THE PEOPLE OF THE UNITED STATES.
A RECOMMENDATION.

WASHINGTON, *April 13, 1841.*

When a Christian people feel themselves to be overtaken by a great public calamity, it becomes them to humble themselves under the dispensation of Divine Providence, to recognize His righteous government over the children of men, to acknowledge His goodness in time past, as well as their own unworthiness, and to supplicate His merciful protection for the future.

The death of William Henry Harrison, late President of the United States, so soon after his elevation to that high office, is a bereavement peculiarly calculated to be regarded as a heavy affliction and to impress all minds with a sense of the uncertainty of human things and of the dependence of nations, as well as individuals, upon our Heavenly Parent.

I have thought, therefore, that I should be acting in conformity with the general expectation and feelings of the community in recommending, as I now do, to the people of the United States of every religious denomination that, according to their several modes and forms of worship, they observe a day of fasting and prayer by such religious services as may be suitable on the occasion; and I recommend Friday, the 14th day of May next, for that purpose, to the end that on that day we may all with one accord join in humble and reverential approach to Him in whose hands we are, invoking Him to inspire us with a proper spirit and temper of heart and mind under these frowns of His providence and still to bestow His gracious benedictions upon our Government and our country.   JOHN TYLER.

[For "A resolution manifesting the sensibility of Congress upon the event of the death of William Henry Harrison, late President of the United States," see p. 55.]

John Tyler

April 4, 1841, to March 4, 1845

John Tyler

JOHN TYLER, second son of Judge John Tyler, governor of Virginia from 1808 to 1811, and Mary Armistead, was born at Greenway, Charles City County, Va., March 29, 1790. He was graduated at William and Mary College in 1807. At college he showed a strong interest in ancient history; was also fond of poetry and music, and was a skillful performer on the violin. In 1809 he was admitted to the bar, and had already begun to obtain a good practice when he was elected to the legislature. Took his seat in that body in December, 1811. Was here a firm supporter of Mr. Madison's Administration; and the war with Great Britain, which soon followed, afforded him an opportunity to become conspicuous as a forcible and persuasive orator. March 29, 1813, he married Letitia, daughter of Robert Christian, and a few weeks afterwards was called into the field at the head of a company of militia to take part in the defense of Richmond, threatened by the British. This military service lasted but a month. He was reelected to the legislature annually until, in November, 1816, he was chosen to fill a vacancy in the United States House of Representatives. Was reelected to the Fifteenth and Sixteenth Congresses. In 1821, his health being seriously impaired, he declined a reelection and retired to private life. In 1823 he was again elected to the Virginia legislature. Here he was a friend to the candidacy of William H. Crawford for the Presidency. In 1824 he was a candidate to fill a vacancy in the United States Senate, but was defeated. He opposed in 1825 the attempt to remove William and Mary College to Richmond, and was afterwards made successively rector and chancellor of the college, which prospered signally under his management. In December, 1825, he was chosen by the legislature to the governorship of Virginia, and in the following year was reelected by a unanimous vote. In December, 1826, the friends of Clay and Adams combined with the Democrats opposed to John Randolph and elected Mr. Tyler to the United States Senate. In February, 1830, after taking part in the Virginia convention for revising the State constitution, he returned to his seat in the Senate, and found himself first drawn toward Jackson by the veto message (May 27) upon the Maysville turnpike bill; supported Jackson in the Presidential election of 1832, but broke with the Administration on the question of the removal of the deposits from the United

States Bank, and voted for Mr. Clay's resolution to censure the President. He was nominated by the State-rights Whigs for Vice-President in 1835, and at the election on November 8, 1836, received 47 electoral votes; but no candidate having a majority of electoral votes, the Senate elected Richard M. Johnson, of Kentucky. The legislature of Virginia having instructed the Senators from that State to vote for expunging the resolutions of censure upon President Jackson, Mr. Tyler refused to obey the instructions, resigned his seat, and returned home February 29, 1836. On January 10, 1838, he was chosen president of the Virginia Colonization Society. In the spring of 1838 he was returned to the Virginia legislature. In January, 1839, he was a candidate for reelection to the United States Senate; the result was a deadlock, and the question was indefinitely postponed before any choice had been made. December 4, 1839, the Whig national convention, at Harrisburg, Pa., nominated him for Vice-President on the ticket with William Henry Harrison, and at the election on November 10, 1840, he was elected, receiving 234 electoral votes to 48 for Richard M. Johnson, of Kentucky. By the death of President Harrison April 4, 1841, Mr. Tyler became President of the United States. He took the oath of office on April 6. Among the more important events of his Administration were the "Ashburton treaty" with Great Britain, the termination of the Indian war in Florida, the passage of the resolutions by Congress providing for the annexation of Texas, and the treaty with China. On May 27, 1844, he was nominated for President at a convention in Baltimore, but although at first he accepted the nomination, he subsequently withdrew his name. On June 26, 1844, Mr. Tyler married Miss Julia Gardiner, of New York, his first wife having died September 9, 1842. After leaving the White House he took up his residence on his estate, Sherwood Forest, near Greenway, Va., on the bank of the James River. Was president of the Peace Convention held at Washington February 4, 1861. Afterwards, as a delegate to the Virginia State convention, he advocated the passage of an ordinance of secession. In May, 1861, he was unanimously elected a member of the provisional congress of the Confederate States. In the following autumn he was elected to the permanent congress, but died at Richmond January 18, 1862, before taking his seat, and was buried in Hollywood Cemetery, in that city.

INAUGURAL ADDRESS.

To the People of the United States.　　　WASHINGTON, *April 9, 1841.*

FELLOW-CITIZENS: Before my arrival at the seat of Government the painful communication was made to you by the officers presiding over the several Departments of the deeply regretted death of William Henry Harrison, late President of the United States. Upon him you had conferred your suffrages for the first office in your gift, and had selected him as your chosen instrument to correct and reform all such errors and abuses as had manifested themselves from time to time in the practical operation of the Government. While standing at the threshold of this great work he has by the dispensation of an all-wise Providence been removed from amongst us, and by the provisions of the Constitution the efforts to be directed to the accomplishing of this vitally important task have devolved upon myself. This same occurrence has subjected the wisdom and sufficiency of our institutions to a new test. For the first time in our history the person elected to the Vice-Presidency of the United States, by the happening of a contingency provided for in the Constitution, has had devolved upon him the Presidential office. The spirit of faction, which is directly opposed to the spirit of a lofty patriotism, may find in this occasion for assaults upon my Administration; and in succeeding, under circumstances so sudden and unexpected and to responsibilities so greatly augmented, to the administration of public affairs I shall place in the intelligence and patriotism of the people my only sure reliance. My earnest prayer shall be constantly addressed to the all-wise and all-powerful Being who made me, and by whose dispensation I am called to the high office of President of this Confederacy, understandingly to carry out the principles of that Constitution which I have sworn "to protect, preserve, and defend."

The usual opportunity which is afforded to a Chief Magistrate upon his induction to office of presenting to his countrymen an exposition of the policy which would guide his Administration, in the form of an inaugural address, not having, under the peculiar circumstances which have brought me to the discharge of the high duties of President of the United States, been afforded to me, a brief exposition of the principles which will govern me in the general course of my administration of public affairs would seem to be due as well to myself as to you.

In regard to foreign nations, the groundwork of my policy will be justice on our part to all, submitting to injustice from none. While I shall sedulously cultivate the relations of peace and amity with one and all, it will be my most imperative duty to see that the honor of the country shall sustain no blemish. With a view to this, the condition of our military defenses will become a matter of anxious solicitude. The Army, which has in other days covered itself with renown, and the Navy, not inappropriately termed the right arm of the public defense, which has spread a light of glory over the American standard in all the waters of the earth, should be rendered replete with efficiency.

In view of the fact, well avouched by history, that the tendency of all human institutions is to concentrate power in the hands of a single man, and that their ultimate downfall has proceeded from this cause, I deem it of the most essential importance that a complete separation should take place between the sword and the purse. No matter where or how the public moneys shall be deposited, so long as the President can exert the power of appointing and removing at his pleasure the agents selected for their custody the Commander in Chief of the Army and Navy is in fact the treasurer. A permanent and radical change should therefore be decreed. The patronage incident to the Presidential office, already great, is constantly increasing. Such increase is destined to keep pace with the growth of our population, until, without a figure of speech, an army of officeholders may be spread over the land. The unrestrained power exerted by a selfishly ambitious man in order either to perpetuate his authority or to hand it over to some favorite as his successor may lead to the employment of all the means within his control to accomplish his object. The right to remove from office, while subjected to no just restraint, is inevitably destined to produce a spirit of crouching servility with the official corps; which, in order to uphold the hand which feeds them, would lead to direct and active interference in the elections, both State and Federal, thereby subjecting the course of State legislation to the dictation of the chief executive officer and making the will of that officer absolute and supreme. I will at a proper time invoke the action of Congress upon this subject, and shall readily acquiesce in the adoption of all proper measures which are calculated to arrest these evils, so full of danger in their tendency. I will remove no incumbent from office who has faithfully and honestly acquitted himself of the duties of his office, except in such cases where such officer has been guilty of an active partisanship or by secret means—the less manly, and therefore the more objectionable—has given his official influence to the purposes of party, thereby bringing the patronage of the Government in conflict with the freedom of elections. Numerous removals may become necessary under this rule. These will be made by me through no acerbity of feeling—I have had no cause to cherish or indulge unkind feelings toward any—but my conduct will be regulated by a profound sense of what is due to the country and its institutions; nor shall I neglect to apply the same unbending rule to those of my own appointment. Freedom of opinion will be tolerated, the full enjoyment of the right of suffrage will be maintained as the birthright of every American citizen; but I say emphatically to the official corps, "Thus far and no farther." I have dwelt the longer upon this subject because removals from office are likely often to arise, and I would have my countrymen to understand the principle of the Executive action.

In all public expenditures the most rigid economy should be resorted to, and, as one of its results, a public debt in time of peace be sedulously avoided. A wise and patriotic constituency will never object to the imposition of necessary burdens for useful ends, and true wisdom dictates the resort to such means in order to supply deficiencies in the revenue, rather than to those doubtful expedients which, ultimating in a public debt, serve to embarrass the resources of the country and to lessen its ability to meet any great emergency which may arise. All sinecures should be abolished. The appropriations should be direct and explicit, so as to leave as limited a share of discretion to the disbursing agents as may be found compatible with the public service. A strict responsibility on the part of all the agents of the Government should be maintained and peculation or defalcation visited with immediate expulsion from office and the most condign punishment.

The public interest also demands that if any war has existed between the Government and the currency it shall cease. Measures of a financial character now having the sanction of legal enactment shall be faithfully enforced until repealed by the legislative authority. But I owe it to myself to declare that I regard existing enactments as unwise and impolitic and in a high degree oppressive. I shall promptly give my sanction to any constitutional measure which, originating in Congress, shall have for its object the restoration of a sound circulating medium, so essentially necessary to give confidence in all the transactions of life, to secure to industry its just and adequate rewards, and to reestablish the public prosperity. In deciding upon the adaptation of any such measure to the end proposed, as well as its conformity to the Constitution, I shall resort to the fathers of the great republican school for advice and instruction, to be drawn from their sage views of our system of government and the light of their ever-glorious example.

The institutions under which we live, my countrymen, secure each person in the perfect enjoyment of all his rights. The spectacle is exhibited to the world of a government deriving its powers from the consent of the governed and having imparted to it only so much power as is necessary for its successful operation. Those who are charged with its administration should carefully abstain from all attempts to enlarge the range of powers thus granted to the several departments of the Government other than by an appeal to the people for additional grants, lest by so doing they disturb that balance which the patriots and statesmen who framed the Constitution designed to establish between the Federal Government and the States composing the Union. The observance of these rules is enjoined upon us by that feeling of reverence and affection which finds a place in the heart of every patriot for the preservation of union and the blessings of union—for the good of our children and our children's children through countless generations. An opposite course could not fail to generate factions intent upon the gratification of their selfish ends, to give birth to local and sectional jealousies, and to ultimate either in breaking asunder the bonds of union or in building up a central system which would inevitably end in a bloody scepter and an iron crown.

In conclusion I beg you to be assured that I shall exert myself to carry the foregoing principles into practice during my administration of the Government, and, confiding in the protecting care of an everwatchful and overruling Providence, it shall be my first and highest duty to preserve unimpaired the free institutions under which we live and transmit them to those who shall succeed me in their full force and vigor.

JOHN TYLER.

[For proclamation of President Tyler recommending, in consequence of the death of President Harrison, a day of fasting and prayer, see p. 32.]

SPECIAL SESSION MESSAGE.

WASHINGTON, *June 1, 1841.*

To the Senate and House of Representatives of the United States.

FELLOW-CITIZENS: You have been assembled in your respective halls of legislation under a proclamation bearing the signature of the illustrious citizen who was so lately called by the direct suffrages of the people to the discharge of the important functions of their chief executive office. Upon the expiration of a single month from the day of his installation he has paid the great debt of nature, leaving behind him a name associated with the recollection of numerous benefits conferred upon the country during a long life of patriotic devotion. With this public bereavement are connected other considerations which will not escape the attention of Congress. The preparations necessary for his removal to the seat of Government in view of a residence of four years must have devolved upon the late President heavy expenditures, which, if permitted to burthen the limited resources of his private fortune, may tend seriously to the embarrassment of his surviving family; and it is therefore respectfully submitted to Congress whether the ordinary principles of justice would not dictate the propriety of its legislative interposition. By the provisions of the fundamental law the powers and duties of the high station to which he was elected have devolved upon me, and in the dispositions of the representatives of the States and of the people will be found, to a great extent, a solution of the problem to which our institutions are for the first time subjected.

In entering upon the duties of this office I did not feel that it would be becoming in me to disturb what had been ordered by my lamented predecessor. Whatever, therefore, may have been my opinion originally as to the propriety of convening Congress at so early a day from that of its late adjournment, I found a new and controlling inducement not to interfere with the patriotic desires of the late President in the novelty of the situation in which I was so unexpectedly placed. My first wish under such circumstances would necessarily have been to have called to my aid in the administration of public affairs the combined wisdom of the two Houses of Congress, in order to take their counsel and advice as to the best mode of extricating the Government and the country from the embarrassments weighing heavily on both. I am, then, most happy in finding myself so soon after my accession to the Presidency surrounded by the immediate representatives of the States and people.

No important changes having taken place in our foreign relations since the last session of Congress, it is not deemed necessary on this occasion to go into a detailed statement in regard to them. I am happy to say that I see nothing to destroy the hope of being able to preserve peace.

The ratification of the treaty with Portugal has been duly exchanged between the two Governments. This Government has not been inattentive to the interests of those of our citizens who have claims on the Government of Spain founded on express treaty stipulations, and a hope is indulged that the representations which have been made to that Government on this subject may lead ere long to beneficial results.

A correspondence has taken place between the Secretary of State and the minister of Her Britannic Majesty accredited to this Government on the subject of Alexander McLeod's indictment and imprisonment, copies of which are herewith communicated to Congress.

In addition to what appears from these papers, it may be proper to state that Alexander McLeod has been heard by the supreme court of the State of New York on his motion to be discharged from imprisonment, and that the decision of that court has not as yet been pronounced.

The Secretary of State has addressed to me a paper upon two subjects interesting to the commerce of the country, which will receive my consideration, and which I have the honor to communicate to Congress.

So far as it depends on the course of this Government, our relations of good will and friendship will be sedulously cultivated with all nations. The true American policy will be found to consist in the exercise of a spirit of justice, to be manifested in the discharge of all our international obligations to the weakest of the family of nations as well as to the most powerful. Occasional conflicts of opinion may arise, but when the discussions incident to them are conducted in the language of truth and with a strict regard to justice the scourge of war will for the most part be avoided. The time ought to be regarded as having gone by when a resort to arms is to be esteemed as the only proper arbiter of national differences.

The census recently taken shows a regularly progressive increase in our population. Upon the breaking out of the War of the Revolution our numbers scarcely equaled 3,000,000 souls; they already exceed 17,000,000, and will continue to progress in a ratio which duplicates in a period of about twenty-three years. The old States contain a territory sufficient in itself to maintain a population of additional millions, and the most populous of the new States may even yet be regarded as but partially settled, while of the new lands on this side of the Rocky Mountains, to say nothing of the immense region which stretches from the base of those mountains to the mouth of the Columbia River, about 770,000,000 acres, ceded and unceded, still remain to be brought into market. We hold out to the people of other countries an invitation to come and settle among us as members of our rapidly growing family, and for the blessings which we offer them we require of them to look upon our country as their country and to unite with us in the great task of preserving our institutions and thereby perpetuating our liberties. No motive exists for foreign conquest; we desire but to reclaim our almost illimitable wildernesses and to introduce into their depths the lights of civilization. While we shall at all times be prepared to vindicate the national honor, our most earnest desire will be to maintain an unbroken peace.

In presenting the foregoing views I can not withhold the expression of the opinion that there exists nothing in the extension of our Empire over our acknowledged possessions to excite the alarm of the patriot for the safety of our institutions. The federative system, leaving to each State the care of its domestic concerns and devolving on the Federal Government those of general import, admits in safety of the greatest expansion; but at the same time I deem it proper to add that there will be found to exist at all times an imperious necessity for restraining all the functionaries of this Government within the range of their respective powers, thereby preserving a just balance between the powers granted to this Government and those reserved to the States and to the people.

From the report of the Secretary of the Treasury you will perceive that the fiscal means, present and accruing, are insufficient to supply the wants of the Government for the current year. The balance in the Treasury on the 4th day of March last not covered by outstanding drafts, and exclusive of trust funds, is estimated at $860,000. This includes the sum of $215,000 deposited in the Mint and its branches to procure metal for coining and in process of coinage, and which could not be withdrawn without inconvenience, thus leaving subject to draft in the various depositories the sum of $645,000. By virtue of two several acts of Congress the Secretary of the Treasury was authorized to issue on and after the 4th day of March last Treasury notes to the amount of $5,413,000, making an aggregate available fund of $6,058,000 on hand.

But this fund was chargeable, with outstanding Treasury notes redeemable in the current year and interest thereon, to the estimated amount of $5,280,000. There is also thrown upon the Treasury the payment of a large amount of demands accrued in whole or in part in former years, which will exhaust the available means of the Treasury and leave the accruing revenue, reduced as it is in amount, burthened with debt and charged with the current expenses of the Government.

The aggregate amount of outstanding appropriations on the 4th day of March last was $33,429,616.50, of which $24,210,000 will be required during the current year; and there will also be required for the use of the War Department additional appropriations to the amount of, $2,511,132.98, the special objects of which will be seen by reference to the report of the Secretary of War. The anticipated means of the Treasury are greatly inadequate to this demand. The receipts from customs for the last three quarters of the last year and first quarter of the present year amounted to $12,100,000; the receipts for lands for the same time to $2,742,450, shewing an average revenue from both sources of $1,236,870 per month.

A gradual expansion of trade, growing out of a restoration of confidence, together with a reduction in the expenses of collecting and punctuality on the part of collecting officers, may cause an addition to the monthly receipts from the customs. They are estimated for the residue of the year from the 4th of March at $12,000,000. The receipts from the public lands for the same time are estimated at $2,500,000, and from miscellaneous sources at $170,000, making an aggregate of available fund within the year of $15,315,000, which will leave a probable deficit of $11,406,132.98. To meet this some temporary provision is necessary until the amount can be absorbed by the excess of revenues which are anticipated to accrue at no distant day.

There will fall due within the next three months Treasury notes of the issues of 1840, including interest, about $2,850,000. There is chargeable in the same period for arrearages for taking the Sixth Census $294,000, and the estimated expenditures for the current service are about $8,100,000, making the aggregate demand upon the Treasury prior to the 1st of September next about $11,340,000.

The ways and means in the Treasury and estimated to accrue within the above-named period consist of about $694,000 of funds available on the 28th ultimo, an unissued balance of Treasury notes authorized by the act of 1841 amounting to $1,955,000, and estimated receipts from all sources of $3,800,000, making an aggregate of about $6,450,000, and leaving a probable deficit on the 1st of September next of $4,845,000.

In order to supply the wants of the Government, an intelligent constituency, in view of their best interests, will without hesitation submit to all necessary burthens. But it is nevertheless important so to impose them as to avoid defeating the just expectations of the country growing out of preexisting laws. The act of the 2d of March, 1833, commonly called the "compromise act," should not be altered except under urgent necessities, which are not believed at this time to exist. One year only remains to complete the series of reductions provided for by that law, at which time provisions made by the same law, and which then will be brought actively in aid of the manufacturing interests of the Union, will not fail to produce the most beneficial results. Under a system of discriminating duties imposed for purposes of revenue, in unison with the provisions of existing laws, it is to be hoped that our policy will in the future be fixed and permanent, so as to avoid those constant fluctuations which defeat the very objects they have in view. We shall thus best maintain a position which, while it will enable us the more readily to meet the advances of other countries calculated to promote our trade and commerce, will at the same time leave in our own hands the means of retaliating with greater effect unjust regulations.

In intimate connection with the question of revenue is that which makes provision for a suitable fiscal agent, capable of adding increased facilities in the collection and disbursement of the public revenues, rendering more secure their custody, and consulting a true economy in the great, multiplied, and delicate operations of the Treasury Department. Upon such an agent depends in an eminent degree the establishment of a currency of uniform value, which is of so great importance to all the essential interests of society, and on the wisdom to be manifested in its creation much depends.   So intimately interwoven are its operations, not only with the interests of individuals, but of States, that it may be regarded to a great degree as controlling both.   If paper be used as the chief medium of circulation, and the power be vested in the Government of issuing it at pleasure, either in the form of Treasury drafts or any other, or if banks be used as the public depositories, with liberty to regard all surpluses from day to day as so much added to their active capital, prices are exposed to constant fluctuations and industry to severe suffering.   In the one case political considerations directed to party purposes may control, while excessive cupidity may prevail in the other. The public is thus constantly liable to imposition.   Expansions and contractions may follow each other in rapid succession—the one engendering a reckless spirit of adventure and speculation, which embraces States as well as individuals, the other causing a fall in prices and accomplishing an entire change in the aspect of affairs.   Stocks of all sorts rapidly decline, individuals are ruined, and States embarrassed even in their efforts to meet with punctuality the interest on their debts. Such, unhappily, is the condition of things now existing in the United States.   These effects may readily be traced to the causes above referred to.   The public revenues, being removed from the then Bank of the United States, under an order of a late President, were placed in selected State banks, which, actuated by the double motive of conciliating the Government and augmenting their profits to the greatest possible extent, enlarged extravagantly their discounts, thus enabling all other existing banks to do the same; large dividends were declared, which, stimulating the cupidity of capitalists, caused a rush to be made to the legislatures of the respective States for similar acts of incorporation, which by many of the States, under a temporary infatuation, were readily granted, and thus the augmentation of the circulating medium, consisting almost exclusively of paper, produced a most fatal delusion.   An illustration derived from the land sales of the period alluded to will serve best to show the effect of the whole system.   The average sales of the public lands for a period of ten years prior to 1834 had not much exceeded $2,000,000 per annum.   In 1834 they attained in round numbers to the amount of $6,000,000; in the succeeding year of 1835 they reached $16,000,000, and the next year of 1836 they amounted to the enormous sum of $25,000,000, thus crowding into the short space of three years upward of twenty-three years' purchase of the public domain. So apparent had become the necessity of arresting this course of things that the executive department assumed the highly questionable power of discriminating in the funds to be used in payment by different classes of public debtors—a discrimination which was doubtless designed to correct this most ruinous state of things by the exaction of specie in all payments for the public lands, but which could not at once arrest the tide which had so strongly set in.   Hence the demands for specie became unceasing, and corresponding prostration rapidly ensued under the necessities created with the banks to curtail their discounts and thereby to reduce their circulation. I recur to these things with no disposition to censure preexisting Administrations of the Government, but simply in exemplification of the truth of the position which I have assumed. If, then, any fiscal agent which may be created shall be placed, without due restrictions, either in the hands of the administrators of the Government or those of private individuals, the temptation to abuse will prove to be resistless. Objects of political aggrandizement may seduce the first, and the promptings of a boundless cupidity will assail the last. Aided by the experience of the past, it will be the pleasure of Congress so to guard and fortify the public interests in the creation of any new agent as to place them, so far as human wisdom can accomplish it, on a footing of perfect security. Within a few years past three different schemes have been before the country. The charter of the Bank of the United States expired by its own limitations in 1836. An effort was made to renew it, which received the sanction of the two Houses of Congress, but the then President of the United States exercised his *veto* power and the measure was defeated. A regard to truth requires me to say that the President was fully sustained in the course he had taken by the popular voice. His successor to the chair of state unqualifiedly pronounced his opposition to any new charter of a similar institution, and not only the popular election which brought him into power, but the elections through much of his term, seemed clearly to indicate a concurrence with him in sentiment on the part of the people. After the public moneys were withdrawn from the United States Bank they were placed in deposit with the State banks, and the result of that policy has been before the country. To say nothing as to the question whether that experiment was made under propitious or adverse circumstances, it may safely be asserted that it did receive the unqualified condemnation of most of its early advocates, and, it is believed, was also condemned by the popular sentiment. The existing subtreasury system does not seem to stand in higher favor with the people, but has recently been condemned in a manner too plainly indicated to admit of a doubt. Thus in the short period of eight years the popular voice may be regarded as having successively condemned each of the three schemes of finance to which I have adverted. As to the first, it was introduced at a time (1816) when the State banks, then comparatively few in number, had been forced to suspend specie payments by reason of the war which had previously prevailed with Great Britain. Whether if the United States Bank charter, which expired in 1811, had been renewed in due season it would have been enabled to continue specie payments during the war and the disastrous period to the commerce of the country which immediately succeeded is, to say the least, problematical, and whether the United States Bank of 1816 produced a restoration of specie payments or the same was accomplished through the instrumentality of other means was a matter of some difficulty at that time to determine. Certain it is that for the first years of the operation of that bank its course was as disastrous as for the greater part of its subsequent career it became eminently successful. As to the second, the experiment was tried with a redundant Treasury, which continued to increase until it seemed to be the part of wisdom to distribute the surplus revenue among the States, which, operating at the same time with the specie circular and the causes before adverted to, caused them to suspend specie payments and involved the country in the greatest embarrassment. And as to the third, if carried through all the stages of its transmutation from paper and specie to nothing but the precious metals, to say nothing of the insecurity of the public moneys, its injurious effects have been anticipated by the country in its unqualified condemnation. What is now to be regarded as the judgment of the American people on this whole subject I have no accurate means of determining but by appealing to their more immediate representatives. The late contest, which terminated in the election of General Harrison to the Presidency, was decided on principles well known and openly declared, and while the subtreasury received in the result the most decided condemnation, yet no other scheme of finance seemed to have been concurred in. To you, then, who have come more directly from the body of our common constituents, I submit the entire question, as best qualified to give a full exposition of their wishes and opinions. I shall be ready to concur with you in the adoption of such system as you may propose, reserving to myself the ultimate power of rejecting any measure which may, in my view of it, conflict with the Constitution or otherwise jeopardize the prosperity of the country—a power which I could not part with even if I would, but which I will not believe any act of yours will call into requisition.

I can not avoid recurring, in connection with this subject, to the necessity which exists for adopting some suitable measure whereby the unlimited creation of banks by the States may be corrected in future. Such result can be most readily achieved by the consent of the States, to be expressed in the form of a compact among themselves, which they can only enter into with the consent and approbation of this Government—a consent which might in the present emergency of the public demands justifiably be given by Congress in advance of any action by the States, as an inducement to such action, upon terms well defined by the act of tender. Such a measure, addressing itself to the calm reflection of the States, would find in the experience of the past and the condition of the present much to sustain it; and it is greatly to be doubted whether any scheme of finance can prove for any length of time successful while the States shall continue in the unrestrained exercise of the power of creating banking corporations. This power can only be limited by their consent.

With the adoption of a financial agency of a satisfactory character the hope may be indulged that the country may once more return to a state of prosperity. Measures auxiliary thereto, and in some measure inseparably connected with its success, will doubtless claim the attention of Congress. Among such, a distribution of the proceeds of the sales of the public lands, provided such distribution does not force upon Congress the necessity of imposing upon commerce heavier burthens than those contemplated by the act of 1833, would act as an efficient remedial measure by being brought directly in aid of the States. As one sincerely devoted to the task of preserving a just balance in our system of Government by the maintenance of the States in a condition the most free and respectable and in the full possession of all their power, I can no otherwise than feel desirous for their emancipation from the situation to which the pressure on their finances now subjects them. And while I must repudiate, as a measure founded in error and wanting constitutional sanction, the slightest approach to an assumption by this Government of the debts of the States, yet I can see in the distribution adverted to much to recommend it. The compacts between the proprietor States and this Government expressly guarantee to the States all the benefits which may arise from the sales. The mode by which this is to be effected addresses itself to the discretion of Congress as the trustee for the States, and its exercise after the most beneficial manner is restrained by nothing in the grants or in the Constitution so long as Congress shall consult that equality in the distribution which the compacts require. In the present condition of some of the States the question of distribution may be regarded as substantially a question between direct and indirect taxation. If the distribution be not made in some form or other, the necessity will daily become more urgent with the debtor States for a resort to an oppressive system of direct taxation, or their credit, and necessarily their power and influence, will be greatly diminished. The payment of taxes after the most inconvenient and oppressive mode will be exacted in place of contributions for the most part voluntarily made, and therefore comparatively unoppressive. The States are emphatically the constituents of this Government, and we should be entirely regardless of the objects held in view by them in the creation of this Government if we could be indifferent to their good. The happy effects of such a measure upon all the States would immediately be manifested. With the debtor States it would effect the relief to a great extent of the citizens from a heavy burthen of direct taxation, which presses with severity on the laboring classes, and eminently assist in restoring the general prosperity. An immediate advance would take place in the price of the State securities, and the attitude of the States would become once more, as it should ever be, lofty and erect. With States laboring under no extreme pressure from debt, the fund which they would derive from this source would enable them to improve their condition in an eminent degree. So far as this Government is concerned, appropriations to domestic objects approaching in amount the revenue derived from the land sales might be abandoned, and thus a system of unequal, and therefore unjust, legislation would be substituted by one dispensing equality to all the members of this Confederacy.   Whether such distribution should be made directly to the States in the proceeds of the sales or in the form of profits by virtue of the operations of any fiscal agency having those proceeds as its basis, should such measure be contemplated by Congress, would well deserve its consideration.   Nor would such disposition of the proceeds of the sales in any manner prevent Congress from time to time from passing all necessary preemption laws for the benefit of actual settlers, or from making any new arrangement as to the price of the public lands which might in future be esteemed desirable.

I beg leave particularly to call your attention to the accompanying report from the Secretary of War.   Besides the present state of the war which has so long afflicted the Territory of Florida, and the various other matters of interest therein referred to, you will learn from it that the Secretary has instituted an inquiry into abuses, which promises to develop gross enormities in connection with Indian treaties which have been negotiated, as well as in the expenditures for the removal and subsistence of the Indians.   He represents also other irregularities of a serious nature that have grown up in the practice of the Indian Department, which will require the appropriation of upward of $200,000 to correct, and which claim the immediate attention of Congress.

In reflecting on the proper means of defending the country we can not shut our eyes to the consequences which the introduction and use of the power of steam upon the ocean are likely to produce in wars between maritime states.   We can not yet see the extent to which this power may be applied in belligerent operations, connecting itself as it does with recent improvements in the science of gunnery and projectiles; but we need have no fear of being left, in regard to these things, behind the most active and skillful of other nations if the genius and enterprise of our fellow-citizens receive proper encouragement and direction from Government.

True wisdom would nevertheless seem to dictate the necessity of placing in perfect condition those fortifications which are designed for the protection of our principal cities and roadsteads.   For the defense of our extended maritime coast our chief reliance should be placed on our Navy, aided by those inventions which are destined to recommend themselves to public adoption, but no time should be lost in placing our principal cities on the seaboard and the Lakes in a state of entire security from foreign assault.   Separated as we are from the countries of the Old World, and in much unaffected by their policy, we are happily relieved from the necessity of maintaining large standing armies in times of peace.   The policy which was adopted by Mr. Monroe shortly after the conclusion of the late war with Great Britain of preserving a regularly organized staff sufficient for the command of a large military force should a necessity for one arise is founded as well in economy as in true wisdom. Provision is thus made, upon filling up the rank and file, which can readily be done on any emergency, for the introduction of a system of discipline both promptly and efficiently. All that is required in time of peace is to maintain a sufficient number of men to guard our fortifications, to meet any sudden contingency, and to encounter the first shock of war. Our chief reliance must be placed on the militia; they constitute the great body of national guards, and, inspired by an ardent love of country, will be found ready at all times and at all seasons to repair with alacrity to its defense. It will be regarded by Congress, I doubt not, at a suitable time as one of its highest duties to attend to their complete organization and discipline.

The state of the navy pension fund requires the immediate attention of Congress. By the operation of the act of the 3d of March, 1837, entitled "An act for the more equitable administration of the navy pension fund," that fund has been exhausted. It will be seen from the accompanying report of the Commissioner of Pensions that there will be required for the payment of navy pensions on the 1st of July next $88,706.06⅓, and on the 1st of January, 1842, the sum of $69,000. In addition to these sums, about $6,000 will be required to pay arrears of pensions which will probably be allowed between the 1st of July and the 1st of January, 1842, making in the whole $163,706.06⅓. To meet these payments there is within the control of the Department the sum of $28,040, leaving a deficiency of $139,666.06⅓. The public faith requires that immediate provision should be made for the payment of these sums.

In order to introduce into the Navy a desirable efficiency, a new system of accountability may be found to be indispensably necessary. To mature a plan having for its object the accomplishment of an end so important and to meet the just expectations of the country require more time than has yet been allowed to the Secretary at the head of the Department. The hope is indulged that by the time of your next regular session measures of importance in connection with this branch of the public service may be matured for your consideration.

Although the laws regulating the Post-Office Department only require from the officer charged with its direction to report at the usual annual session of Congress, the Postmaster-General has presented to me some facts connected with the financial condition of the Department which are deemed worthy the attention of Congress. By the accompanying report of that officer it appears the existing liabilities of that Department beyond the means of payment at its command can not be less than $500,000. As the laws organizing that branch of the public service confine the expenditure to its own revenues, deficiencies therein can not be presented under the usual estimates for the expenses of Government.

It must therefore be left to Congress to determine whether the moneys now due the contractors shall be paid from the public Treasury or whether that Department shall continue under its present embarrassments. It will be seen by the report of the Postmaster-General that the recent lettings of contracts in several of the States have been made at such reduced rates of compensation as to encourage the belief that if the Department was relieved from existing difficulties its future operations might be conducted without any further call upon the general Treasury.

The power of appointing to office is one of a character the most delicate and responsible. The appointing power is evermore exposed to be led into error. With anxious solicitude to select the most trustworthy for official station, I can not be supposed to possess a personal knowledge of the qualifications of every applicant. I deem it, therefore, proper in this most public manner to invite on the part of the Senate a just scrutiny into the character and pretensions of every person I may bring to their notice in the regular form of a nomination for office. Unless persons every way trustworthy are employed in the public service, corruption and irregularity will inevitably follow. I shall with the greatest cheerfulness acquiesce in the decision of that body, and, regarding it as wisely constituted to aid the executive department in the performance of this delicate duty, I shall look to its "consent and advice" as given only in furtherance of the best interests of the country. I shall also at the earliest proper occasion invite the attention of Congress to such measures as in my judgment will be best calculated to regulate and control the Executive power in reference to this vitally important subject.

I shall also at the proper season invite your attention to the statutory enactments for the suppression of the slave trade, which may require to be rendered more efficient in their provisions. There is reason to believe that the traffic is on the increase. Whether such increase is to be ascribed to the abolition of slave labor in the British possessions in our vicinity and an attendant diminution in the supply of those articles which enter into the general consumption of the world, thereby augmenting the demand from other quarters, and thus calling for additional labor, it were needless to inquire. The highest considerations of public honor as well as the strongest promptings of humanity require a resort to the most vigorous efforts to suppress the trade.

In conclusion I beg to invite your particular attention to the interests of this District; nor do I doubt but that in a liberal spirit of legislation you will seek to advance its commercial as well as its local interests. Should Congress deem it to be its duty to repeal the existing subtreasury law, the necessity of providing a suitable place of deposit of the public moneys which may be required within the District must be apparent to all.

I have felt it due to the country to present the foregoing topics to your consideration and reflection. Others with which it might not seem proper to trouble you at an extraordinary session will be laid before you at a future day. I am happy in committing the important affairs of the country into your hands. The tendency of public sentiment, I am pleased to believe, is toward the adoption, in a spirit of union and harmony, of such measures as will fortify the public interests. To cherish such a tendency of public opinion is the task of an elevated patriotism. That differences of opinion as to the means of accomplishing these desirable objects should exist is reasonably to be expected. Nor can all be made satisfied with any system of measures; but I flatter myself with the hope that the great body of the people will readily unite in support of those whose efforts spring from a disinterested desire to promote their happiness, to preserve the Federal and State Governments within their respective orbits; to cultivate peace with all the nations of the earth on just and honorable grounds; to exact obedience to the laws; to intrench liberty and property in full security; and, consulting the most rigid economy, to abolish all useless expenses.

JOHN TYLER.

SPECIAL MESSAGES.

CITY OF WASHINGTON, *June 2, 1841.*

To the Senate and House of Representatives:

I transmit herewith a report from the Secretary of the Treasury, exhibiting certain transfers of appropriations that have been made in that Department in pursuance of the power vested in the President of the United States by the act of Congress of the 3d of March, 1809, entitled "An act further to amend the several acts for the establishment and regulation of the Treasury, War, and Navy Departments."

JOHN TYLER.

To the Senate of the United States: WASHINGTON, *June 17, 1841.*

I transmit to the Senate the inclosed communication* from the Secretary of State, in answer to a resolution of the Senate of the 12th instant.

JOHN TYLER.

WASHINGTON, *June 17, 1841.*

To the Senate of the United States:

I transmit to the Senate the inclosed communication from the Secretary of State, in answer to a resolution of the Senate of the 12th instant.

JOHN TYLER.

*Relating to the commissioners appointed to investigate the condition of the public works in Washington, D. C., and transmitting copy of the letter of instructions issued to them.

DEPARTMENT OF STATE, *June 15, 1841.*

The PRESIDENT.

SIR: In answer to the resolution of the Senate of the 12th instant, calling for "any orders which may have been issued to the officers of the Army and Navy in relation to political offenses in elections," etc., I inclose a copy of the circular letter addressed, under the direction of the President, by this Department to the heads of the other Departments, and know of no other order to which the resolution can be supposed to have reference.

I have the honor to be, your obedient servant,

DANIEL WEBSTER.

CIRCULAR.

DEPARTMENT OF STATE, *March 20, 1841.*

SIR: The President is of opinion that it is a great abuse to bring the patronage of the General Government into conflict with the freedom of elections, and that this abuse ought to be corrected wherever it may have been permitted to exist, and to be prevented for the future.

He therefore directs that information be given to all officers and agents in your department of the public service that partisan interference in popular elections, whether of State officers or officers of this Government, and for whomsoever or against whomsoever it may be exercised, or the payment of any contribution or assessment on salaries, or official compensation for party or election purposes, will be regarded by him as cause of removal.

It is not intended that any officer shall be restrained in the free and proper expression and maintenance of his opinions respecting public men or public measures, or in the exercise to the fullest degree of the constitutional right of suffrage. But persons employed under the Government and paid for their services out of the public Treasury are not expected to take an active or officious part in attempts to influence the minds or votes of others, such conduct being deemed inconsistent with the spirit of the Constitution and the duties of public agents acting under it; and the President is resolved, so far as depends upon him, that while the exercise of the elective franchise by the people shall be free from undue influences of official station and authority, opinion shall also be free among the officers and agents of the Government.

The President wishes it further to be announced and distinctly understood that from all collecting and disbursing officers promptitude in rendering accounts and entire punctuality in paying balances will be rigorously exacted. In his opinion it is time to return in this respect to the early practice of the Government, and to hold any degree of delinquency on the part of those intrusted with the public money just cause of immediate removal. He deems the severe observance of this rule to be essential to the public service, as every dollar lost to the Treasury by unfaithfulness in office creates a necessity for a new charge upon the people.

I have the honor to be, sir, your obedient servant,

DANIEL WEBSTER.

WASHINGTON, D. C., *June 18, 1841.*

To the Senate of the United States:

I transmit to the Senate a report from the Secretary of the Navy, with accompanying documents,* in answer to their resolution of the 12th instant.

JOHN TYLER.

*Correspondence of the minister in England with the officers of the Mediterranean Squadron, in consequence of which the squadron left that station, and the dispatches of Captain Bolton to the Secretary of the Navy connected with that movement.

To the Senate of the United States: WASHINGTON, *June, 1841.*

I have the honor to transmit to the Senate the accompanying letter*
from the Secretary of the Treasury, in pursuance of its resolution of the
8th instant.

                                        JOHN TYLER.

                             WASHINGTON, *June 22, 1841.*

To the Senate and House of Representatives of the United States:

I have the honor to submit the accompanying correspondence between
myself and the Hon. J. Burnet, J. C. Wright, and others, who arrived
some days ago in this city as a committee on behalf of the people of
Cincinnati for the purpose, with the assent of the family, of removing
the remains of the late President of the United States to North Bend for
interment. I have thought it to be my duty thus to apprise Congress
of the contemplated proceedings.   .   JOHN TYLER.

                         WASHINGTON CITY, *June 16, 1841.*

The PRESIDENT OF THE UNITED STATES.

DEAR SIR: The undersigned were appointed by the citizens and the city council
of Cincinnati and by many of the surviving soldiers of the late war to apply to the
widow and family of our distinguished fellow-citizen, the late President of the United
States, for permission to remove his remains from the city of Washington to the
State of Ohio for interment. They have made the application directed, and have
received permission to perform that sacred trust. They have now the honor of
reporting to you their arrival in this city, and of asking your approbation of the
measure contemplated and your cooperation in carrying it into effect.

We are fully aware of the high estimate you placed on the talents and virtues
of our lamented friend and fellow-citizen, the late Chief Magistrate of the Union,
whose friendship and confidence you possessed many years. We saw the tear fall
from your eye and mingle with the tears of the nation when the inscrutable will of
Heaven removed him from us.

Knowing these things, we approach you with confidence, well assured that you
will justly appreciate our motive for undertaking the mournful duty we have been
deputed to perform, and that the same kind feeling which has marked your course
through life will prompt you on this occasion to afford us your countenance, and, if
necessary, your cooperation.

If it meet your approbation, the committee will do themselves the honor of waiting upon you at the President's house at any hour you may please to designate.

     With high respect, we are, your friends and fellow-citizens,

                               J. BURNET.
                               J. C. WRIGHT.
                               [AND 10 OTHERS.]

                         WASHINGTON, *June 17, 1841.*

J. BURNET, J. C. WRIGHT, AND OTHERS OF THE COMMITTEE.

GENTLEMEN: Your letter of the 16th was duly handed me, and I lose no time in
responding to the feelings and sentiments which you have expressed for yourselves
and those you represent, and which you have correctly ascribed to me in regard to

---

*Relating to allowances since March 4, 1841, of claims arising under the invasion of East Florida
in 1812.

the lamented death of the late President. As a citizen I respected him; as a patriot I honored him; as a friend he was near and dear to me. That the people of Cincinnati should desire to keep watch over his remains by entombing them near their city is both natural and becoming; that the entire West, where so many evidences of his public usefulness are to be found, should unite in the same wish was to have been expected; and that the surviving soldiers of his many battles, led on by him to victory and to glory, should sigh to perform the last melancholy duties to the remains of their old commander is fully in consonance with the promptings of a noble and generous sympathy. I could not, if I was authorized to do so, oppose myself to their wishes. I might find something to urge on behalf of his native State in my knowledge of his continued attachment to her through the whole period of his useful life; in the claims of his relatives there, whose desire it would be that the mortal remains of the illustrious son should sleep under the same turf with those of his distinguished father, one of the signers of the Declaration of Independence; in the wish of the citizens of his native county to claim all that is now left of him for whom they so lately cast their almost unanimous suffrage; to say nothing of my own feelings, allied as I am by blood to many of his near relatives, and with our names so closely associated in much connected with the late exciting political contest. These considerations might present some reasonable ground for opposing your wishes; but the assent which has been given by his respected widow and nearest relatives to the request of the people of Cincinnati admits of no opposition on my part, neither in my individual nor official character.

I shall feel it to be my duty, however, to submit our correspondence to the two Houses of Congress, now in session, but anticipating no effort from that quarter to thwart the wishes expressed by yourselves in consonance with those of the widow and nearest relatives of the late President. I readily promise you my cooperation toward enabling you to fulfill the sacred trust which brought you to this city.

I tender to each of you, gentlemen, my cordial salutations.

JOHN TYLER.

[NOTE.—The remains of the late President of the United States were removed from Washington to North Bend, Ohio, June 26, 1841.]

To the Senate of the United States: WASHINGTON, *June 29, 1841.*

In compliance with the resolution of the Senate of the 14th instant, I have the honor to submit the accompanying reports from the Secretary of State and Secretary of the Treasury, which embrace all the information possessed by the executive department upon that subject.*

JOHN TYLER.

WASHINGTON, *June 30, 1841.*

To the House of Representatives of the United States:

The accompanying memorial in favor of the passage of a bankrupt law, signed by nearly 3,000 of the inhabitants of the city of New York, has been forwarded to me, attended by a request that I would submit it to the consideration of Congress. I can not waive a compliance with a request urged upon me by so large and respectable a number of my fellow-citizens. That a bankrupt law, carefully guarded against fraudulent practices and embracing as far as practicable all classes of society— the failure to do which has heretofore constituted a prominent objection

_____
*Payment or assumption of State stocks by the General Government.

to the measure—would afford extensive relief I do not doubt. The distress incident to the derangements of some years past has visited large numbers of our fellow-citizens with hopeless insolvency, whose energies, both mental and physical, by reason of the load of debt pressing upon them, are lost to the country. Whether Congress shall deem it proper to enter upon the consideration of this subject at its present extraordinary session it will doubtless wisely determine. I have fulfilled my duty to the memorialists in submitting their petition to your consideration.

JOHN TYLER.

WASHINGTON, *July 1, 1841.*

To the Senate of the United States:

I have the honor herewith to submit to the Senate the copy of a letter addressed by myself to Mrs. Harrison in compliance with the resolutions of Congress, and her reply thereto.

JOHN TYLER.

[The same message was sent to the House of Representatives.]

WASHINGTON, *June 13, 1841.*

Mrs. ANNA HARRISON.

MY DEAR MADAM: The accompanying resolutions, adopted by the Senate and House of Representatives of the United States, will convey to you an expression of the deep sympathy felt by the representatives of the States and of the people in the sad bereavement which yourself and the country have sustained in the death of your illustrious husband. It may now be justly considered that the public archives constitute his enduring monument, on which are inscribed in characters not to be effaced the proudest evidences of public gratitude for services rendered and of sorrow for his death. A great and united people shed their tears over the bier of a devoted patriot and distinguished public benefactor.

In conveying to you, my dear madam, the profound respect of the two Houses of Congress for your person and character, and their sincere condolence on the late afflicting dispensation of Providence, permit me to mingle my feelings with theirs and to tender you my fervent wishes for your health, happiness, and long life.

JOHN TYLER.

A RESOLUTION manifesting the sensibility of Congress upon the event of the death of William Henry Harrison, late President of the United States.

The melancholy event of the death of William Henry Harrison, the late President of the United States, having occurred during the recess of Congress, and the two Houses sharing in the general grief and desiring to manifest their sensibility upon the occasion of that public bereavement: Therefore,

Resolved by the Senate and House of Representatives of the United States of America in Congress assembled, That the chairs of the President of the Senate and of the Speaker of the House of Representatives be shrouded in black during the residue of the session, and that the President *pro tempore* of the Senate, the Speaker of the House of Representatives, and the members and officers of both Houses wear the usual badge of mourning for thirty days.

Resolved, That the President of the United States be requested to transmit a copy of these resolutions to Mrs. Harrison, and to assure her of the profound respect of the two Houses of Congress for her person and character, and of their sincere condolence on the late afflicting dispensation of Providence.

NORTH BEND, *June 24, 1841.*

His Excellency JOHN TYLER,
  President United States, Washington City, D. C.

DEAR SIR: I have received with sentiments of deep emotion the resolutions of the Senate and House of Representatives which you have done me the honor of forwarding, relative to the decease of my lamented husband.

I can not sufficiently express the thanks I owe to the nation and its assembled representatives for their condolence, so feelingly expressed, of my individual calamity and the national bereavement; but, mingling my tears with the sighs of the many patriots of the land, pray to Heaven for the enduring happiness and prosperity of our beloved country.

ANNA HARRISON.

WASHINGTON, *July 3, 1841.*

To the Senate of the United States:

In compliance with a resolution of the Senate of the 9th instant [ultimo], I communicate to that body a report from the Secretary of State, conveying copies of the correspondence,* which contains all the information called for by said resolution.

JOHN TYLER.

WASHINGTON, *July 9, 1841.*

To the Senate of the United States:

I transmit a report from the Secretary of State, in answer to the resolution of the Senate of the 2d instant, calling for information as to the progress and actual condition of the commission† under the convention with the Mexican Republic.

JOHN TYLER.

WASHINGTON, *July 14, 1841.*

To the Speaker and Members of the House of Representatives:

In compliance with a resolution of the House of Representatives of the 21st ultimo, I have the honor to submit the accompanying communication‡ from the Secretary of State.

JOHN TYLER.

WASHINGTON, *July 16, 1841.*

To the House of Representatives:

I herewith transmit to the House of Representatives, in reply to their resolution of the 21st ultimo, a report§ from the Secretary of State, with accompanying papers.

JOHN TYLER.

---

*Relating to the duties levied on American tobacco imported into the States composing the German Commercial and Custom-House Union.

†Appointed under the convention of April 11, 1839, for adjusting the claims of citizens of the United States upon the Republic of Mexico.

‡Transmitting correspondence with Great Britain relative to the seizure of American vessels by British armed cruisers under the pretense that they were engaged in the slave trade; also correspondence with N. P. Trist, United States consul at Habana, upon the subject of the slave trade, etc.

§Stating that there is no correspondence in his office showing that any American citizens are British prisoners of state in Van Diemens Land; transmitting correspondence with the British minister on the subject of the detention or imprisonment of citizens of the United States on account of occurrences in Canada, instructions issued to the special agent appointed to inquire into such detention or imprisonment, and report of said special agent.

WASHINGTON, *July 19, 1841.*

To the Senate and House of Representatives of the United States:

The act of Congress of the 10th of March, 1838, entitled "An act supplementary to an act entitled 'An act in addition to the act for the punishment of certain crimes against the United States and to repeal the acts therein mentioned,' approved 20th of April, 1818," expired by its own limitation on the 10th of March, 1840. The object of this act was to make further provision for preventing military expeditions or enterprises against the territory or dominions of any prince or state or of any colony, district, or people conterminous with the United States and with whom they are at peace, contrary to the act of April 20, 1818, entitled "An act in addition to the act for the punishment of certain crimes against the United States and to repeal the acts therein mentioned."

The act of Congress of March 10, 1838, appears to have had a very salutary effect, and it is respectfully recommended to Congress that it be now revived or its provisions be reenacted.

JOHN TYLER.

WASHINGTON, *July 27, 1841.*

To the Senate and House of Representatives of the United States:

I transmit herewith to Congress a communication from the Secretary of State, on the subject of appropriations required for outfits and salaries of diplomatic agents of the United States.

JOHN TYLER.

WASHINGTON, *August 2, 1841.*

To the House of Representatives of the United States:

On the 18th of February, 1832, the House of Representatives adopted a resolution in the following words:

Resolved, That the President of the United States be authorized to employ Horatio Greenough, of Massachusetts, to execute in marble a full-length pedestrian statue of Washington, to be placed in the center of the Rotunda of the Capitol; the head to be a copy of Houdon's Washington, and the accessories to be left to the judgment of the artist.

On the 23d of the same month the Secretary of State, by direction of the President, addressed to Mr. Greenough a letter of instructions for carrying into effect the resolution of the House.

On the 14th of July, 1832, an appropriation of the sum of $5,000 was made "to enable the President of the United States to contract with a skillful artist to execute in marble a pedestrian statue of George Washington, to be placed in the center of the Rotunda of the Capitol," and several appropriations were made at the succeeding sessions in furtherance of the same object.

Mr. Greenough, having been employed upon the work for several years at Florence, completed it some months ago.

By a resolution of Congress of the 27th of May, 1840, it was directed "that the Secretary of the Navy be authorized and instructed to take measures for the importation and erection of the statue of Washington by Greenough." In pursuance of this authority the Navy Department held a correspondence with Commodore Hull, commanding on the Mediterranean station, who entered into an agreement with the owners or master of the ship *Sea* for the transportation of the statue to the United States. This ship, with the statue on board, arrived in this city on the 31st ultimo, and now lies at the navy-yard.

As appropriations have become necessary for the payment of the freight and other expenses, I communicate to Congress such papers as may enable it to judge of the amount required.

JOHN TYLER.

AUGUST 3, 1841.

Hon. JOHN WHITE,
     Speaker of the House of Representatives.

SIR: I herewith transmit a communication* received from the Postmaster-General, to which I would invite the attention of Congress.

JOHN TYLER.

AUGUST 3, 1841.

To the House of Representatives:

I herewith transmit a report from the Secretary of the Treasury, to whom I referred the resolution of the House calling for a communication† addressed to him by the French minister.

JOHN TYLER.

WASHINGTON, *August 6, 1841.*

To the House of Representatives:

In compliance with a resolution of the House of Representatives of the 16th of July, 1841, I communicate reports ‡ from the several Executive Departments, containing the information requested by said resolution.

JOHN TYLER.

WASHINGTON, *August 25, 1841.*

To the Senate of the United States:

I herewith transmit to the Senate, in pursuance of their resolution of the 22d ultimo, copies of the several reports of the commissioners appointed in March last to examine into certain matters connected with the public buildings in this city and the conduct of those employed in their erection.

JOHN TYLER.

---

* Asking for a further appropriation for completing the new General Post-Office building.
† Relating to the commerce and navigation between France and the United States.
‡ Transmitting list of officers deriving their appointments from the nomination of the President and the concurrence of the Senate who were removed from office since March 4, 1841, and also those who were removed from March 4, 1829, to March 4, 1841.

WASHINGTON, *August 27, 1841.*

To the House of Representatives of the United States:

I transmit herewith a letter from the Secretary of the Treasury, bearing date this day, with the accompanying papers, in answer to the resolution of the House of Representatives of the 16th ultimo, relative to removals from office, etc.

These statements should have accompanied those from the other Departments on the same subject transmitted in my message to the House on the 7th ultimo,* but which have been delayed for reasons stated in the letter of the Secretary of the Treasury above referred to.

JOHN TYLER.

WASHINGTON, D. C., *September 1, 1841.*

To the Senate of the United States:

I submit to the Senate, for its consideration and constitutional action, a treaty concluded at Oeyoowasha, on Minneesota (or St. Peters) River, in the Territory of Iowa, on the 31st day of July last, between James Duane Doty, commissioner on the part of the United States, and the Seeseeahto, Wofpato, and Wofpakoota bands of the Dakota (or Sioux) Nation of Indians.

The accompanying communication from the Secretary of War fully sets forth the considerations which have called for the negotiation of this treaty, and which have induced me to recommend its confirmation, with such exceptions and modifications as the Senate may advise.

JOHN TYLER.

DEPARTMENT OF WAR, *August 31, 1841.*

The PRESIDENT OF THE UNITED STATES.

SIR: I transmit herewith a treaty concluded with certain bands of the Dahcota Nation of Indians, commonly called Sioux, which has been received at this Department from His Excellency James D. Doty, governor of Wisconsin, who was appointed a commissioner on the part of the United States for the purpose of negotiating the treaty; and I desire to submit the following facts and opinions inducing me to request its favorable consideration:

It was known on my entering upon the duties of the Department of War that some provision must speedily be made for the Winnebago Indians in the Northwest. By the treaty with those Indians in 1837 it was provided that they should move temporarily upon a narrow strip of country west of the Mississippi River, called the neutral ground, from the object of its purchase in 1830. That strip of country is only 40 miles in width, 20 miles of it having been purchased from the Sac and Fox Indians and 20 miles from the Sioux, the object of the purchase having been to place a barrier between those tribes, which had been for many years at war and parties of which were continually meeting and destroying each other upon or adjacent to the country purchased.

When the delegation of Winnebago chiefs was in Washington negotiating a sale of all their lands east of the Mississippi River, in 1837, a permanent location for those Indians was not fixed upon, and a temporary expedient was adopted, and acceded to

* Not found. Evidently refers to message of August 6, 1841, on preceding page.

by the Indians, by which they agreed, within eight months from the ratification of the treaty, to move upon and occupy a portion of the neutral ground until they should select a permanent home.

Owing to the small extent of country thus temporarily assigned to the Winnebagoes, utterly destitute of all preparation for the reception of them, slenderly supplied with game, and, above all, the circumstance that the Sac and Fox Indians were continually at war with the Sioux, the object of the purchase having utterly failed, the neutral ground, so called, proving literally the fighting ground of the hostile tribes—owing to all these circumstances the Winnebagoes were extremely reluctant to comply with the treaty. It was in part a dictate of humanity to give them more time for removal than that allotted in the treaty, in the hope of effecting their permanent removal beyond the Missouri or elsewhere; but as no steps were taken to select their future home, and as the white settlers in Wisconsin were fast crowding upon the Indians, overrunning the country, as usual, in search of town sites, water privileges, and farming districts, it became absolutely necessary to make some efforts toward carrying the treaty into effect. Owing to the excited state of the Indians and the apprehension of disturbance, the Eighth Regiment of Infantry, in 1840, more than two years, instead of eight months, after the ratification of the treaty, was ordered upon the Winnebago frontier, the greater part of the Fifth Regiment being already there, and in the presence of that force the Indians were required to comply with the treaty. They reluctantly removed from the banks of the Wisconsin River and crossed the Mississippi, but did not go to that portion of the neutral ground agreed upon, which commenced 20 miles from the river, but instead of it they spread themselves along the bank of the Mississippi, some of them recrossing that river and ascending the Chippewa and Black rivers. Only a small portion of the tribe has yet removed to the portion of the neutral ground assigned to them, and it is perhaps fortunate that local attachments have not been formed, since, from the position of the country, it was not and never could have been intended as their permanent home.

After a careful examination of the country in the Northwest the importance of providing for the Winnebago Indians, though immediate, became secondary in a more national and wider prospect of benefits in future years by arrangements which presented themselves to my mind as not only practicable, but of easy accomplishment.

A glance at the map and at the efforts hitherto made in emigration will show an extensive body of Indians accumulated upon the Southwestern frontier, and, looking to the numbers yet to be emigrated from within the circle of territory soon to become States of the American Union, it will appear upon very many considerations to be of the utmost importance to separate the Indians and to interpose a barrier between the masses which are destined to be placed upon the western frontier, instead of accumulating them within limits enabling them to unite and in concert spread desolation over the States of Missouri and Arkansas to, perhaps, the banks of the Mississippi.

Entertaining these views, it was determined to open negotiations with the Sioux Indians north and northwest of the purchase of 1830, the neutral ground, so called, with the purpose of purchasing sufficient territory beyond the reasonable limits of Iowa to provide a resting place for the Winnebagoes, intending to treat also with the Sac and Fox Indians and with the Potawatamies north of the State of Missouri, and thus enable our citizens to expand west of the Missouri River north of the State.

It is difficult to state in a condensed report all the reasons now imperatively urging the adoption of these measures. Besides the absolute necessity of providing a home for the Winnebagoes, the citizens of Iowa and of Missouri are crowding upon the territory of the Sac and Fox Indians and already producing those irritations which in former times have led to bloody wars. It is not to be for a moment concealed that our enterprising and hardy population must and will occupy the territory adjacent to that purchased in 1837 from the Sacs and Foxes, and the only possible mode of its being done in peace is by another purchase from those Indians. But the position of the Potawatamies will then become relatively what that of the Sac and Fox Indians now is, with the difference that access to their country by the Missouri River will hasten its occupancy by our people. The only mode of guarding against future collision, near at hand if not provided against, is by emigrating not only the Sac and Fox Indians, but also the Potawatamies.

Great efforts have been made to induce those Indians, as also the Winnebagoes, to move south of the Missouri, but without effect, their opposition to it being apparently insurmountable, the Potawatamies expressing the most decided aversion to it on being urged to join other bands of Potawatamies on the Marais de Cygne, declaring that they would rather at once go to California, being determined not to unite with those bands, but to maintain an independence of them. By the purchase from the Sioux no doubt is entertained that their prejudices may be advantageously accommodated, for among the objects in contemplation before adverted to it is to my mind of primary importance so to dispose of those Indians as to enable this Government to interpose a State between the Northern and Southern Indians along the Missouri River, and thus, by dividing the Indians on the frontier and separating the divisions, prevent a combination and concert of action which future progress in civilization might otherwise enable them to effect in the prosecution of revenge for real or imagined grievances.

Great importance is attached to this view of the subject, but scarcely less to the means provided by the treaty for inducing the remnants of other Northern tribes to remove to a climate congenial to their habits and disposition.

From the earliest efforts at emigration certain Northern Indians have strenuously objected to a removal south of the Missouri on account of the climate; and where tribes have been induced to dispose of all right to live east of the Mississippi within the United States, many individuals, dreading their southern destination, have wandered to the north and are now living in Canada, annually in the receipt of presents from the British Government, and will be ready without doubt to side with that power in any future conflict with this Government. In this manner considerable numbers of the Delawares and Shawnees and other Indians have disappeared from our settlements—a fact of great importance, and which I apprehend has not been heretofore sufficiently considered. There are many Potawatamies and Ottawas, as also Winnebagoes and Menomonees, who may be easily induced to move into Canada by seductive bribes, in the use of which the British Government has always displayed a remarkable foresight.

Of the Chippewas and Ottawas now in the northern part of Michigan it is believed there are over 5,000 under treaty obligations to remove to the Southwest, the greater portion of whom openly declared their determination to cross the line into Canada and put themselves under the protection of the British Government in preference to a removal to that country. These Indians may be accommodated by the arrangements in contemplation, not only to their own satisfaction, but under circumstances promising the greatest permanent advantages to the United States, and separating them from all inducements and even the possibility of entering the British service. I am not without hope, also, that through this treaty some suitable and acceptable arrangement may be made with the New York Indians by which they may be removed with safety to themselves and benefit to the people of that State. The very peculiar situation of these Indians is well known; that while they are under treaty obligation to remove, the treaty being by the Constitution the supreme law of the land and perfecting in this instance the title of the land they occupy in a private land company, there is yet every reason to sympathize with them and the highest moral inducements for extending every possible relief to them within the legitimate powers of the Government. I have been assured from sources entitled to my fullest confidence that although these Indians have hitherto expressed the most decided aversion to a removal south of the Missouri, there will probably be no difficulty in persuading them to occupy a more northern region in the West. I have every reason for believing that a benevolent interest in their behalf among a portion of our own people, which, it is supposed, has heretofore presented an obstacle to their emigration, will be exerted to effect their removal if a portion of the Sioux country can be appropriated to them.

It will be perceived, therefore, that a multitude of objects thus rest upon the success of this one treaty, now submitted for examination and approbation.

Of the Sioux Indians I will but remark that they occupy an immense country spreading from the Mississippi north of the neutral ground west and northwest, crossing the Missouri River more than 1,200 miles above the city of St. Louis. They are divided into bands, which have various names, the generic name for the whole being the Dahcota Nation. These bands, though speaking a common language, are independent in their occupancy of portions of country, and separate treaties may be made with them. Treaties are already subsisting with some of the bands both on the Mississippi and Missouri. The treaty now submitted is believed to be advantageous, and from its provisions contemplates the reduction of those wandering Indians from their nomadic habits to those of an agricultural people.

If some of the provisions seem not such as might be desired, it will be recollected that many interests have to be accommodated in framing an Indian treaty which can only be fully known to the commissioner, who derives his information directly from the Indians in the country which is the object of the purchase.

It is proper to add that I had instructed the commissioner expressly not to take into consideration what are called traders' claims, in the hope of correcting a practice which, it is believed, has been attended with mischievous consequences; but the commissioner has by a letter of explanations fully satisfied me that in this instance it was absolutely necessary to accommodate those claims as an indispensable means of obtaining the assent of the Indians to the treaty. This results, doubtless, from their dependence upon the traders for articles, in a measure necessaries, which are for the most part furnished without competition, and of the proper value of which the Indians are ignorant.

To compensate in some degree for the article in this treaty providing for the payment of traders' claims, very judicious guards are introduced into the treaty, calculated effectually to exclude that source of interest adverse to the Government in all future time within the purchase under this treaty.

There are other articles in the treaty which I have not been able fully to realize as judicious or necessary, but for reasons already stated they deserve respectful consideration.

Notwithstanding the article stipulating that a rejection of any of the provisions of the treaty should render the whole null and void, I would respectfully recommend such modified acceptance of the treaty as in the wisdom of the Senate may seem just and proper, conditioned upon the assent of the Indians subsequently to be obtained, the Senate making provision for its reference back to the Indians if necessary.

It will be seen that the treaty provides for a power of regulation in the Indian Territory by the United States Government under circumstances not hitherto attempted, presenting an opportunity for an experiment well worthy of mature consideration.

I ought not to dismiss this subject without adverting to one other important consideration connected with the integrity of our Northwest Indians and territory. The Sioux treaty will effectually withdraw from British influence all those who are a party to it by making them stipendiaries of the United States and by operating a change in their wandering habits and establishing them at known and fixed points under the observation of Government agents, and as the British can only have access to that region by the way of Fond du Lac, one or two small military posts in a direction west and south from that point, it is believed, will completely control all intercourse with the Indians in that section of country.

Very respectfully, your obedient servant,

JNO. BELL.

WASHINGTON, *September 8, 1841.*

To the Senate of the United States:

I have the honor, in compliance with the resolution of the Senate of the 8th June, to communicate a letter* from the Secretary of the Treasury and the correspondence accompanying it.

JOHN TYLER.

WASHINGTON, *September 13, 1841.*

To the Senate of the United States:

In compliance with a resolution of the Senate of the 14th July last, I communicate to the Senate a report from the Secretary of State, accompanied by copies of the correspondence† called for by said resolution.

JOHN TYLER.

VETO MESSAGES.

WASHINGTON, *August 16, 1841.*

To the Senate of the United States:

The bill entitled "An act to incorporate the subscribers to the Fiscal Bank of the United States," which originated in the Senate, has been considered by me with a sincere desire to conform my action in regard to it to that of the two Houses of Congress. By the Constitution it is made my duty either to approve the bill by signing it or to return it with my objections to the House in which it originated. I can not conscientiously give it my approval, and I proceed to discharge the duty required of me by the Constitution—to give my reasons for disapproving.

The power of Congress to create a national bank to operate *per se* over the Union has been a question of dispute from the origin of the Government. Men most justly and deservedly esteemed for their high intellectual endowments, their virtue, and their patriotism have in regard to it entertained different and conflicting opinions; Congresses have differed; the approval of one President has been followed by the disapproval of another; the people at different times have acquiesced in decisions both for and against. The country has been and still is deeply agitated

---

*Relating to the deposits of public moneys in banks by disbursing officers and agents.

† Relating to the origin, progress, and conclusion of the treaty of November 26, 1838, between Sardinia and the United States.

by this unsettled question.   It will suffice for me to say that my own opinion has been uniformly proclaimed to be against the exercise of any such power by this Government.   On all suitable occasions during a period of twenty-five years the opinion thus entertained has been unreservedly expressed.   I declared it in the legislature of my native State; in the House of Representatives of the United States it has been openly vindicated by me; in the Senate Chamber, in the presence and hearing of many who are at this time members of that body, it has been affirmed and reaffirmed in speeches and reports there made and by votes there recorded; in popular assemblies I have unhesitatingly announced it, and the last public declaration which I made—and that but a short time before the late Presidential election—I referred to my previously expressed opinions as being those then entertained by me.   With a full knowledge of the opinions thus entertained and never concealed, I was elected by the people Vice-President of the United States.   By the occurrence of a contingency provided for in the Constitution and arising under an impressive dispensation of Providence I succeeded to the Presidential office.   Before entering upon the duties of that office I took an oath that I would ''preserve, protect, and defend the Constitution of the United States.''   Entertaining the opinions alluded to and having taken this oath, the Senate and the country will see that I could not give my sanction to a measure of the character described without surrendering all claim to the respect of honorable men, all confidence on the part of the people, all self-respect, all regard for moral and religious obligations, without an observance of which no government can be prosperous and no people can be happy.   It would be to commit a crime which I would not willfully commit to gain any earthly reward, and which would justly subject me to the ridicule and scorn of all virtuous men.

I deem it entirely unnecessary at this time to enter upon the reasons which have brought my mind to the convictions I feel and entertain on this subject.   They have been over and over again repeated.   If some of those who have preceded me in this high office have entertained and avowed different opinions, I yield all confidence that their convictions were sincere.   I claim only to have the same measure meted out to myself.   Without going further into the argument, I will say that in looking to the powers of this Government to collect, safely keep, and disburse the public revenue, and incidentally to regulate the commerce and exchanges, I have not been able to satisfy myself that the establishment by this Government of a bank of discount in the ordinary acceptation of that term was a necessary means or one demanded by propriety to execute those powers.   What can the local discounts of the bank have to do with the collecting, safe-keeping, and disbursing of the revenue?   So far as the mere discounting of paper is concerned, it is quite immaterial to this question whether the discount is obtained at a State bank or a United States bank.   They are both equally local, both beginning and both ending in a local accommodation. What influence have local discounts granted by any form of bank in the regulating of the currency and the exchanges? Let the history of the late United States Bank aid us in answering this inquiry.

For several years after the establishment of that institution it dealt almost exclusively in local discounts, and during that period the country was for the most part disappointed in the consequences anticipated from its incorporation. A uniform currency was not provided, exchanges were not regulated, and little or nothing was added to the general circulation, and in 1820 its embarrassments had become so great that the directors petitioned Congress to repeal that article of the charter which made its notes receivable everywhere in payment of the public dues. It had up to that period dealt to but a very small extent in exchanges, either foreign or domestic, and as late as 1823 its operations in that line amounted to a little more than $7,000,000 per annum. A very rapid augmentation soon after occurred, and in 1833 its dealings in the exchanges amounted to upward of $100,000,000, including the sales of its own drafts; and all these immense transactions were effected without the employment of extraordinary means. The currency of the country became sound, and the negotiations in the exchanges were carried on at the lowest possible rates. The circulation was increased to more than $22,000,000 and the notes of the bank were regarded as equal to specie all over the country, thus showing almost conclusively that it was the capacity to deal in exchanges, and not in local discounts, which furnished these facilities and advantages. It may be remarked, too, that notwithstanding the immense transactions of the bank in the purchase of exchange, the losses sustained were merely nominal, while in the line of discounts the suspended debt was enormous and proved most disastrous to the bank and the country. Its power of local discount has in fact proved to be a fruitful source of favoritism and corruption, alike destructive to the public morals and to the general weal.

The capital invested in banks of discount in the United States, created by the States, at this time exceeds $350,000,000, and if the discounting of local paper could have produced any beneficial effects the United States ought to possess the soundest currency in the world; but the reverse is lamentably the fact.

Is the measure now under consideration of the objectionable character to which I have alluded? It is clearly so unless by the sixteenth fundamental article of the eleventh section it is made otherwise. That article is in the following words:

The directors of the said corporation shall establish one competent office of discount and deposit in any State in which two thousand shares shall have been subscribed or may be held, whenever, upon application of the legislature of such State, Congress may by law require the same. And the said directors may also establish one or more competent offices of discount and deposit in any Territory or District of the United States, and in any State with the assent of such State, and when established the said office or offices shall be only withdrawn or removed by the said directors prior to the expiration of this charter with the previous assent of Congress: *Provided*, In respect to any State which shall not, at the first session of the legislature thereof held after the passage of this act, by resolution or other usual legislative proceeding, unconditionally assent or dissent to the establishment of such office or offices within it, such assent of the said State shall be thereafter presumed: *And provided, nevertheless*, That whenever it shall become necessary and proper for carrying into execution any of the powers granted by the Constitution to establish an office or offices in any of the States whatever, and the establishment thereof shall be directed by law, it shall be the duty of the said directors to establish such office or offices accordingly.

It will be seen that by this clause the directors are invested with the fullest power to establish a branch in any State which has yielded its assent; and having once established such branch, it shall not afterwards be withdrawn except by order of Congress.   Such assent is to be *implied* and to have the force and sanction of an actually expressed assent, "provided, in respect to any State which shall not, at *the first session* of the legislature thereof held after the passage of this act, by *resolution* or *other usual legislative proceeding*, *unconditionally* assent or dissent to the establishment of such office or offices within it, such assent of said State shall be thereafter presumed."   The assent or dissent is to be expressed *unconditionally at the first session of the legislature, by some formal legislative act;* and if not so expressed its assent is to be *implied*, and the directors are thereupon invested with power, at such time thereafter as they may please, to establish branches, which can not afterwards be withdrawn except by resolve of Congress.   No matter what may be the cause which may operate with the legislature, which either prevents it from speaking or addresses itself to its wisdom, to induce delay, its assent is to be implied.   This iron rule is to give way to no circumstances; it is unbending and inflexible.   It is the language of the master to the vassal; an unconditional answer is claimed forthwith, and delay, postponement, or incapacity to answer produces an implied assent which is ever after irrevocable.   Many of the State elections have already taken place without any knowledge on the part of the people that such a question was to come up.   The representatives may desire a submission of the question to their constituents preparatory to final action upon it, but this high privilege is denied; whatever may be the motives and views entertained by the representatives of the people to induce delay, their assent is to be presumed, and is ever afterwards binding unless their dissent shall be unconditionally expressed at their first session after the passage of this bill into a law.   They may by formal resolution declare the question of assent or dissent to be undecided and postponed, and yet, in opposition to their express declaration to the contrary, their assent is to be implied. Cases innumerable might be cited to manifest the irrationality of such an inference.   Let one or two in addition suffice.   The popular branch of the legislature may express its dissent by an unanimous vote, and its resolution may be defeated by a tie vote of the senate, and yet the assent is to be implied. Both branches of the legislature may concur in a resolution of decided dissent, and yet the governor may exert the *veto* power conferred on him by the State constitution, and their legislative action be defeated, and yet the assent of the legislative authority is implied, and the directors of this contemplated institution are authorized to establish a branch or branches in such State whenever they may find it conducive to the interest of the stockholders to do so; and having once established it they can under no circumstances withdraw it except by act of Congress. The State may afterwards protest against such unjust inference, but its authority is gone. Its assent is implied by its failure or inability to act at its first session, and its voice can never afterwards be heard. To inferences so violent and, as they seem to me, irrational I can not yield my consent. No court of justice would or could sanction them without reversing all that is established in judicial proceeding by introducing presumptions at variance with fact and inferences at the expense of reason. A State in a condition of duress would be *presumed* to speak as an individual manacled and in prison might be presumed to be in the enjoyment of freedom. Far better to say to the States boldly and frankly, Congress wills and submission is demanded.

It may be said that the directors may not establish branches under such circumstances; but this is a question of power, and this bill invests them with full authority to do so. If the legislature of New York or Pennsylvania or any other State should be found to be in such condition as I have supposed, could there be any security furnished against such a step on the part of the directors? Nay, is it not fairly to be presumed that this proviso was introduced for the sole purpose of meeting the contingency referred to? Why else should it have been introduced? And I submit to the Senate whether it can be believed that any State would be likely to sit quietly down under such a state of things. In a great measure of public interest their patriotism may be successfully appealed to, but to infer their assent from circumstances at war with such inference I can not but regard as calculated to excite a feeling at fatal enmity with the peace and harmony of the country. I must therefore regard this clause as asserting the power to be in Congress to establish offices of discount in a State not only without its assent, but against its dissent, and so regarding it I can not sanction it. On general principles the right in Congress to prescribe terms to any State implies a superiority of power and control, deprives the transaction of all pretense to compact between them, and terminates, as we have seen, in the total abrogation of freedom of action on the part of the States. But, further, the State may express, after the most solemn form of legislation, its dissent, which may from time to time thereafter be repeated in full view of its own interest, which can never be separated from the wise and beneficent operation of this Government, and yet Congress may by virtue of the last proviso overrule its law, and upon grounds which to such State will appear to rest on a constructive necessity and propriety and nothing more. I regard the bill as asserting for Congress the right to incorporate a United States bank with power and right to establish offices of discount and deposit in the several States of this Union with or without their consent—a principle to which I have always heretofore been opposed and which can never obtain my sanction; and waiving all other considerations growing out of its other provisions, I return it to the House in which it originated with these my objections to its approval.

JOHN TYLER.

WASHINGTON, *September 9, 1841.*
To the House of Representatives of the United States:

It is with extreme regret that I feel myself constrained by the duty faithfully to execute the office of President of the United States and to the best of my ability to ''preserve, protect, and defend the Constitution of the United States'' to return to the House in which it originated the bill '' to provide for the better collection, safe-keeping, and disbursement of the public revenue by means of a corporation to be styled the Fiscal Corporation of the United States,'' with my written objections.

In my message sent to the Senate on the 16th day of August last, returning the bill ''to incorporate the subscribers to the Fiscal Bank of the United States,'' I distinctly declared that my own opinion had been uniformly proclaimed to be against the exercise ''of the power of Congress to create a national bank to operate *per se* over the Union,'' and, entertaining that opinion, my main objection to that bill was based upon the highest moral and religious obligations of conscience and the Constitution. I readily admit that whilst the qualified *veto* with which the Chief Magistrate is invested should be regarded and was intended by the wise men who made it a part of the Constitution as a great conservative principle of our system, without the exercise of which on important occasions a mere representative majority might urge the Government in its legislation beyond the limits fixed by its framers or might exert its just powers too hastily or oppressively, yet it is a power which ought to be most cautiously exerted, and perhaps never except in a case eminently involving the public interest or one in which the oath of the President, acting under his convictions, both mental and moral, imperiously requires its exercise. In such a case he has no alternative. He must either exert the negative power intrusted to him by the Constitution chiefly for its own preservation, protection, and defense or commit an act of gross moral turpitude. Mere regard to the will of a majority must not in a constitutional republic like ours control this sacred and solemn duty of a sworn officer. The Constitution itself I regard and cherish as the embodied and written will of the whole people of the United States. It is their fixed and fundamental law; which they unanimously prescribe to the public functionaries, their mere trustees and servants. This *their* will and the law which *they* have given us as the rule of our action have no guard, no guaranty of preservation, protection, and defense, but the oaths which it prescribes to the public officers, the sanctity with which they shall religiously observe those oaths, and the patriotism with which the people shall shield it by their own sovereign will, which has made the Constitution supreme. It must be exerted against the will of a mere representative majority or not at all. It is alone in pursuance of that will that any measure can reach the President, and to say that because a majority in Congress have passed a bill he should therefore sanction it is to abrogate the power altogether and to render its insertion in the Constitution a work of absolute supererogation. The duty is to guard the fundamental will of the people themselves from (in this case, I admit, unintentional) change or infraction by a majority in Congress; and in that light alone do I regard the constitutional duty which I now most reluctantly discharge. Is this bill now presented for my approval or disapproval such a bill as I have already declared could not receive my sanction? Is it such a bill as calls for the exercise of the negative power under the Constitution? Does it violate the Constitution by creating a national bank to operate *per se* over the Union? Its title, in the first place, describes its general character. It is "an act to provide for the better collection, safe-keeping, and disbursement of the *public* revenue by means of a *corporation* to be styled the *Fiscal Corporation* of the *United States*." In style, then, it is plainly national in its character. Its powers, functions, and duties are those which pertain to the *collecting*, *keeping*, and *disbursing* the *public* revenue. The means by which these are to be exerted is a *corporation* to be styled the *Fiscal* Corporation of the United States. It is a corporation created by the Congress of the United States, in its character of a national legislature for the whole Union, to perform the *fiscal* purposes, meet the *fiscal* wants and exigencies, supply the *fiscal* uses, and exert the *fiscal* agencies of the Treasury of the United States. Such is its own description of itself. Do its provisions contradict its title? They do not. It is true that by its first section it provides that it shall be established in the District of Columbia; but the amount of its capital, the manner in which its stock is to be subscribed for and held, the persons and bodies, corporate and politic, by whom its stock may be held, the appointment of its directors and their powers and duties, its fundamental articles, especially that to establish agencies in any part of the Union, the corporate powers and business of such agencies, the prohibition of Congress to establish any other corporation with similar powers for twenty years, with express reservation in the same clause to modify or create any bank for the District of Columbia, so that the aggregate capital shall not exceed five millions, without enumerating other features which are equally distinctive and characteristic, clearly show that it can not be regarded as other than a bank of the United States, with powers seemingly more limited than have heretofore been granted to such an institution. It operates *per se* over the Union by virtue of the unaided and, in my view, assumed author-ity of Congress as a national legislature, as distinguishable from a bank created by Congress for the District of Columbia as the local legislature of the District. Every United States bank heretofore created has had power to deal in bills of exchange as well as local discounts. Both were trading privileges conferred, and both were exercised by virtue of the aforesaid power of Congress over the whole Union. The question of power remains unchanged without reference to the extent of privilege granted. If this proposed corporation is to be regarded as a local bank of the District of Columbia, invested by Congress with general powers to operate over the Union, it is obnoxious to still stronger objections. It assumes that Congress may invest a local institution with general or national powers. With the same propriety that it may do this in regard to a bank of the District of Columbia it may as to a State bank. Yet who can indulge the idea that this Government can rightfully, by mak-ing a State bank its fiscal agent, invest it with the absolute and unquali-fied powers conferred by this bill? When I come to look at the details of the bill, they do not recommend it strongly to my adoption. A brief notice of some of its provisions will suffice.

First. It may justify substantially a system of discounts of the most objectionable character. It is to deal in bills of exchange drawn in one State and payable in another without any restraint. The bill of exchange may have an unlimited time to run, and its renewability is nowhere guarded against. It may, in fact, assume the most objection-able form of accommodation paper. It is not required to rest on any actual, real, or substantial exchange basis. A drawer in one place becomes the accepter in another, and so in turn the accepter may become the drawer upon a mutual understanding. It may at the same time indulge in mere local discounts under the name of bills of exchange. A bill drawn at Philadelphia on Camden, N. J., at New York on a border town in New Jersey, at Cincinnati on Newport, in Kentucky, not to multiply other examples, might, for anything in this bill to restrain it, become a mere matter of local accommodation. Cities thus relatively situated would possess advantages over cities otherwise situated of so decided a character as most justly to excite dissatisfaction.

Second. There is no limit prescribed to the premium in the purchase of bills of exchange, thereby correcting none of the evils under which the community now labors, and operating most injuriously upon the agricultural States, in which the irregularities in the rates of exchange are most severely felt. Nor are these the only consequences. A resump-tion of specie payments by the banks of those States would be liable to indefinite postponement; for as the operation of the agencies of the interior would chiefly consist in selling bills of exchange, and the pur-chases could only be made in specie or the notes of banks paying specie, the State banks would either have to continue with their doors closed or exist at the mercy of this national monopoly of brokerage. Nor can it be passed over without remark that whilst the District of Columbia is made the seat of the principal bank, its citizens are excluded from all participation in any benefit it might afford by a positive prohibition on the bank from all discounting within the District.

These are some of the objections which prominently exist against the details of the bill. Others might be urged of much force, but it would be unprofitable to dwell upon them. Suffice it to add that this charter is designed to continue for twenty years without a competitor; that the defects to which I have alluded, being founded on the fundamental law of the corporation, are irrevocable, and that if the objections be well founded it would be overhazardous to pass the bill into a law.

In conclusion I take leave most respectfully to say that I have felt the most anxious solicitude to meet the wishes of Congress in the adoption of a fiscal agent which, avoiding all constitutional objections, should harmonize conflicting opinions. Actuated by this feeling, I have been ready to yield much in a spirit of conciliation to the opinions of others; and it is with great pain that I now feel compelled to differ from Congress a second time in the same session. At the commencement of this session, inclined from choice to defer to the legislative will, I submitted to Congress the propriety of adopting a fiscal agent which, without violating the Constitution, would separate the public money from the Executive control and perform the operations of the Treasury without being burdensome to the people or inconvenient or expensive to the Government. It is deeply to be regretted that this department of the Government can not upon constitutional and other grounds concur with the legislative department in this last measure proposed to attain these desirable objects. Owing to the brief space between the period of the death of my lamented predecessor and my own installation into office, I was, in fact, not left time to prepare and submit a definitive recommendation of my own in my regular message, and since my mind has been wholly occupied in a most anxious attempt to conform my action to the legislative will. In this communication I am confined by the Constitution to my objections simply to this bill, but the period of the regular session will soon arrive, when it will be my duty, under another clause of the Constitution, "to give to Congress information of the state of the Union and recommend to their consideration such measures as" I "shall judge necessary and expedient." And I most respectfully submit, in a spirit of harmony, whether the present differences of opinion should be pressed further at this time, and whether the peculiarity of my situation does not entitle me to a postponement of this subject to a more auspicious period for deliberation. The two Houses of Congress have distinguished themselves at this extraordinary session by the performance of an immense mass of labor at a season very unfavorable both to health and action, and have passed many laws which I trust will prove highly beneficial to the interests of the country and fully answer its just expectations.   It has been my good fortune and pleasure to concur with them in all measures except this.   And why should our difference on this alone be pushed to extremes?   It is my anxious desire that it should not be.   I too have been burdened with extraordinary labors of late, and I sincerely desire time for deep and deliberate reflection on this the greatest difficulty of my Administration.   May we not now pause until a more favorable time, when, with the most anxious hope that the Executive and Congress may cordially unite, some measure of finance may be deliberately adopted promotive of the good of our common country?

I will take this occasion to declare that the conclusions to which I have brought myself are those of a settled conviction, founded, in my opinion, on a just view of the Constitution; that in arriving at it I have been actuated by no other motive or desire than to uphold the institutions of the country as they have come down to us from the hands of our godlike ancestors, and that I shall esteem my efforts to sustain them, even though I perish, more honorable than to win the applause of men by a sacrifice of my duty and my conscience.

JOHN TYLER.

PROCLAMATION.

[From Statutes at Large (Little, Brown & Co.), Vol. XI, p. 796.]

BY THE PRESIDENT OF THE UNITED STATES OF AMERICA.

A PROCLAMATION.

Whereas it has come to the knowledge of the Government of the United States that sundry secret lodges, clubs, or associations exist on the northern frontier; that the members of these lodges are bound together by secret oaths; that they have collected firearms and other military materials and secreted them in sundry places; and that it is their purpose to violate the laws of their country by making military and lawless incursions, when opportunity shall offer, into the territories of a power with which the United States are at peace; and

Whereas it is known that traveling agitators, from both sides of the line, visit these lodges and harangue the members in secret meeting, stimulating them to illegal acts; and

Whereas the same persons are known to levy contributions on the ignorant and credulous for their own benefit, thus supporting and enriching themselves by the basest means; and

Whereas the unlawful intentions of the members of these lodges have already been manifested in an attempt to destroy the lives and property of the inhabitants of Chippewa, in Canada, and the public property of the British Government there being:

Now, therefore, I, John Tyler, President of the United States, do issue this my proclamation, admonishing all such evil-minded persons of the condign punishment which is certain to overtake them; assuring them that the laws of the United States will be rigorously executed against their illegal acts, and that if in any lawless incursion into Canada they fall into the hands of the British authorities they will not be reclaimed as American citizens nor any interference made by this Government in their behalf. And I exhort all well-meaning but deluded persons who may have joined these lodges immediately to abandon them and to have nothing more to do with their secret meetings or unlawful oaths, as they would avoid serious consequences to themselves. And I expect the intelligent and well-disposed members of the community to frown on all these unlawful combinations and illegal proceedings, and to assist the Government in maintaining the peace of the country against the mischievous consequences of the acts of these violators of the law.

Given under my hand, at the city of Washington, the 25th day of September, A. D. 1841, and of the Independence of the United States the sixty-sixth.

[SEAL.]

JOHN TYLER.

By the President:
DANIEL WEBSTER,
Secretary of State.

EXECUTIVE ORDER.

GENERAL ORDERS.

WAR DEPARTMENT,
ADJUTANT-GENERAL'S OFFICE,
Washington, July 5, 1841.

Brevet Major-General Winfield Scott having been appointed by the President, by and with the consent and advice of the Senate, the Major-General of the Army of the United States, he is directed to assume the command and enter upon his duties accordingly.

By command of the President of the United States:

R. JONES,
Adjutant-General.

FIRST ANNUAL MESSAGE.

WASHINGTON, *December 7, 1841.*
To the Senate and House of Representatives of the United States:

In coming together, fellow-citizens, to enter again upon the discharge of the duties with which the people have charged us severally, we find great occasion to rejoice in the general prosperity of the country. We are in the enjoyment of all the blessings of civil and religious liberty, with unexampled means of education, knowledge, and improvement. Through the year which is now drawing to a close peace has been in our borders and plenty in our habitations, and although disease has visited some few portions of the land with distress and mortality, yet in general the health of the people has been preserved, and we are all called upon by the highest obligations of duty to renew our thanks and our devotion to our Heavenly Parent, who has continued to vouchsafe to us the eminent blessings which surround us and who has so signally crowned the year with His goodness. If we find ourselves increasing beyond example in numbers, in strength, in wealth, in knowledge, in everything which promotes human and social happiness, let us ever remember our dependence for all these on the protection and merciful dispensations of Divine Providence.

Since your last adjournment Alexander McLeod, a British subject who was indicted for the murder of an American citizen, and whose case has been the subject of a correspondence heretofore communicated to you, has been acquitted by the verdict of an impartial and intelligent jury, and has under the judgment of the court been regularly discharged.

Great Britain having made known to this Government that the expedition which was fitted out from Canada for the destruction of the steamboat *Caroline* in the winter of 1837, and which resulted in the destruction of said boat and in the death of an American citizen, was undertaken by orders emanating from the authorities of the British Government in Canada, and demanding the discharge of McLeod upon the ground that if engaged in that expedition he did but fulfill the orders of his Government, has thus been answered in the only way in which she could be answered by a government the powers of which are distributed among its several departments by the fundamental law. Happily for the people of Great Britain, as well as those of the United States, the only mode by which an individual arraigned for a criminal offense before the courts of either can obtain his discharge is by the independent action of the judiciary and by proceedings equally familiar to the courts of both countries.

If in Great Britain a power exists in the Crown to cause to be entered a *nolle prosequi*, which is not the case with the Executive power of the United States upon a prosecution pending in a State court, yet *there* no more than *here* can the chief executive power rescue a prisoner from custody without an order of the proper tribunal directing his discharge. The precise stage of the proceedings at which such order may be made is a matter of municipal regulation exclusively, and not to be complained of by any other government. In cases of this kind a government becomes politically responsible only when its tribunals of last resort are shown to have rendered unjust and injurious judgments in matters not doubtful. To the establishment and elucidation of this principle no nation has lent its authority more efficiently than Great Britain. Alexander McLeod, having his option either to prosecute a writ of error from the decision of the supreme court of New York, which had been rendered upon his application for a discharge, to the Supreme Court of the United States, or to submit his case to the decision of a jury, preferred the latter, deeming it the readiest mode of obtaining his liberation; and the result has fully sustained the wisdom of his choice. The manner in which the issue submitted was tried will satisfy the English Government that the principles of justice will never fail to govern the enlightened decision of an American tribunal. I can not fail, however, to suggest to Congress the propriety, and in some degree the necessity, of making such provisions by law, so far as they may constitutionally do so, for the removal at their commencement and at the option of the party of all such cases as may hereafter arise, and which may involve the faithful observance and execution of our international obligations, from the State to the Federal judiciary. This Government, by our institutions, is charged with the maintenance of peace and the preservation of amicable relations with the nations of the earth, and ought to possess without question all the reasonable and proper means of maintaining the one and preserving the other. While just confidence is felt in the judiciary of the States, yet this Government ought to be competent in itself for the fulfillment of the high duties which have been devolved upon it under the organic law by the States themselves.

In the month of September a party of armed men from Upper Canada invaded the territory of the United States and forcibly seized upon the person of one Grogan, and under circumstances of great harshness hurriedly carried him beyond the limits of the United States and delivered him up to the authorities of Upper Canada. His immediate discharge was ordered by those authorities upon the facts of the case being brought to their knowledge—a course of procedure which was to have been expected from a nation with whom we are at peace, and which was not more due to the rights of the United States than to its own regard for justice. The correspondence which passed between the Department of State and the British envoy, Mr. Fox, and with the governor of Vermont, as soon as the facts had been made known to this department, are herewith communicated.

I regret that it is not in my power to make known to you an equally satisfactory conclusion in the case of the *Caroline* steamer, with the circumstances connected with the destruction of which, in December, 1837, by an armed force fitted out in the Province of Upper Canada, you are already made acquainted. No such atonement as was due for the public wrong done to the United States by this invasion of her territory, so wholly irreconcilable with her rights as an independent power, has yet been made. In the view taken by this Government the inquiry whether the vessel was in the employment of those who were prosecuting an unauthorized war against that Province or was engaged by the owner in the business of transporting passengers to and from Navy Island in hopes of private gain, which was most probably the case, in no degree alters the real question at issue between the two Governments. This Government can never concede to any foreign government the power, except in a case of the most urgent and extreme necessity, of invading its territory, either to arrest the persons or destroy the property of those who may have violated the municipal laws of such foreign government or have disregarded their obligations arising under the law of nations. The territory of the United States must be regarded as sacredly secure against all such invasions until they shall voluntarily acknowledge their inability to acquit themselves of their duties to others. And in announcing this sentiment I do but affirm a principle which no nation on earth would be more ready to vindicate at all hazards than the people and Government of Great Britain. If upon a full investigation of all the facts it shall appear that the owner of the *Caroline* was governed by a hostile intent or had made common cause with those who were in the occupancy of Navy Island, then so far as he is concerned there can be no claim to indemnity for the destruction of his boat which this Government would feel itself bound to prosecute, since he would have acted not only in derogation of the rights of Great Britain, but in clear violation of the laws of the United States; but that is a question which, however settled, in no manner involves the higher consideration of the violation of territorial sovereignty and jurisdiction. To recognize it as an admissible practice that each Government in its turn, upon any sudden and unauthorized outbreak which, on a frontier the extent of which renders it impossible for either to have an efficient force on every mile of it, and which outbreak, therefore, neither may be able to suppress in a day, may take vengeance into its own hands, and without even a remonstrance, and in the absence of any pressing or overruling necessity may invade the territory of the other, would inevitably lead to results equally to be deplored by both. When border collisions come to receive the sanction or to be made on the authority of either Government general war must be the inevitable result. While it is the ardent desire of the United States to cultivate the relations of peace with all nations and to fulfill all the duties of good neighborhood toward those who possess territories adjoining their own, that very desire would lead them to deny the right of any foreign power to invade their boundary with an armed force. The correspondence between the two Governments on this subject will at a future day of your session be submitted to your consideration; and in the meantime I can not but indulge the hope that the British Government will see the propriety of renouncing as a rule of future action the precedent which has been set in the affair at Schlosser.

I herewith submit the correspondence which has recently taken place between the American minister at the Court of St. James, Mr. Stevenson, and the minister of foreign affairs of that Government on the right claimed by that Government to visit and detain vessels sailing under the American flag and engaged in prosecuting lawful commerce in the African seas. Our commercial interests in that region have experienced considerable increase and have become an object of much importance, and it is the duty of this Government to protect them against all improper and vexatious interruption. However desirous the United States may be for the suppression of the slave trade, they can not consent to interpolations into the maritime code at the mere will and pleasure of other governments. We deny the right of any such interpolation to any one or all the nations of the earth without our consent. We claim to have a voice in all amendments or alterations of that code, and when we are given to understand, as in this instance, by a foreign government that its treaties with other nations can not be executed without the establishment and enforcement of new principles of maritime police, to be applied without our consent, we must employ a language neither of equivocal import or susceptible of misconstruction. American citizens prosecuting a lawful commerce in the African seas under the flag of their country are not responsible for the abuse or unlawful use of that flag by others; nor can they rightfully on account of any such alleged abuses be interrupted, molested, or detained while on the ocean, and if thus molested and detained while pursuing honest voyages in the usual way and violating no law themselves they are unquestionably entitled to indemnity. This Government has manifested its repugnance to the slave trade in a manner which can not be misunderstood. By its fundamental law it prescribed limits in point of time to its continuance, and against its own citizens who might so far forget the rights of humanity as to engage in that wicked traffic it has long since by its municipal laws denounced the most condign punishment. Many of the States composing this Union had made appeals to the civilized world for its suppression long before the moral sense of other nations had become shocked by the iniquities of the traffic. Whether this Government should now enter into treaties containing mutual stipulations upon this subject is a question for its mature deliberation. Certain it is that if the right to detain American ships on the high seas can be justified on the plea of a necessity for such detention arising out of the existence of treaties between other nations, the same plea may be extended and enlarged by the new stipulations of new treaties to which the United States may not be a party. This Government will not cease to urge upon that of Great Britain full and ample remuneration for all losses, whether arising from detention or otherwise, to which American citizens have heretofore been or may hereafter be subjected by the exercise of rights which this Government can not recognize as legitimate and proper. Nor will I indulge a doubt but that the sense of justice of Great Britain will constrain her to make retribution for any wrong or loss which any American citizen engaged in the prosecution of lawful commerce may have experienced at the hands of her cruisers or other public authorities. This Government, at the same time, will relax no effort to prevent its citizens, if there be any so disposed, from prosecuting a traffic so revolting to the feelings of humanity. It seeks to do no more than to protect the fair and honest trader from molestation and injury; but while the enterprising mariner engaged in the pursuit of an honorable trade is entitled to its protection, it will visit with condign punishment others of an opposite character.

I invite your attention to existing laws for the suppression of the African slave trade, and recommend all such alterations as may give to them greater force and efficacy. That the American flag is grossly abused by the abandoned and profligate of other nations is but too probable. Congress has not long since had this subject under its consideration, and its importance well justifies renewed and anxious attention.

I also communicate herewith the copy of a correspondence between Mr. Stevenson and Lord Palmerston upon the subject, so interesting to several of the Southern States, of the rice duties, which resulted honorably to the justice of Great Britain and advantageously to the United States.

At the opening of the last annual session the President informed Congress of the progress which had then been made in negotiating a convention between this Government and that of England with a view to the final settlement of the question of the boundary between the territorial limits of the two countries. I regret to say that little further advancement of the object has been accomplished since last year, but this is owing to circumstances no way indicative of any abatement of the desire of both parties to hasten the negotiation to its conclusion and to settle the question in dispute as early as possible. In the course of the session it is my hope to be able to announce some further degree of progress toward the accomplishment of this highly desirable end.

The commission appointed by this Government for the exploration and survey of the line of boundary separating the States of Maine and New Hampshire from the conterminous British Provinces is, it is believed, about to close its field labors and is expected soon to report the results of its examinations to the Department of State. The report, when received, will be laid before Congress.

The failure on the part of Spain to pay with punctuality the interest due under the convention of 1834 for the settlement of claims between the two countries has made it the duty of the Executive to call the particular attention of that Government to the subject. A disposition has been manifested by it, which is believed to be entirely sincere, to fulfill its obligations in this respect so soon as its internal condition and the state of its finances will permit. An arrangement is in progress from the result of which it is trusted that those of our citizens who have claims under the convention will at no distant day receive the stipulated payments.

A treaty of commerce and navigation with Belgium was concluded and signed at Washington on the 29th of March, 1840, and was duly sanctioned by the Senate of the United States. The treaty was ratified by His Belgian Majesty, but did not receive the approbation of the Belgian Chambers within the time limited by its terms, and has therefore become void.

This occurrence assumes the graver aspect from the consideration that in 1833 a treaty negotiated between the two Governments and ratified on the part of the United States failed to be ratified on the part of Belgium. The representative of that Government at Washington informs the Department of State that he has been instructed to give explanations of the causes which occasioned delay in the approval of the late treaty by the legislature, and to express the regret of the King at the occurrence.

The joint commission under the convention with Texas to ascertain the true boundary between the two countries has concluded its labors, but the final report of the commissioner of the United States has not been received. It is understood, however, that the meridian line as traced by the commission lies somewhat farther east than the position hitherto generally assigned to it, and consequently includes in Texas some part of the territory which had been considered as belonging to the States of Louisiana and Arkansas.

The United States can not but take a deep interest in whatever relates to this young but growing Republic. Settled principally by emigrants from the United States, we have the happiness to know that the great principles of civil liberty are there destined to flourish under wise institutions and wholesome laws, and that through its example another evidence is to be afforded of the capacity of popular institutions to advance the prosperity, happiness, and permanent glory of the human race. The great truth that government was made for the people and not the people for government has already been established in the practice and by the example of these United States, and we can do no other than contemplate its further exemplification by a sister republic with the deepest interest.

Our relations with the independent States of this hemisphere, formerly under the dominion of Spain, have not undergone any material change within the past year.   The incessant sanguinary conflicts in or between those countries are to be greatly deplored as necessarily tending to disable them from performing their duty as members of the community of nations and rising to the destiny which the position and natural resources of many of them might lead them justly to anticipate, as constantly giving occasion also, directly or indirectly, for complaints on the part of our citizens who resort thither for purposes of commercial intercourse, and as retarding reparation for wrongs already committed, some of which are by no means of recent date.

The failure of the Congress of Ecuador to hold a session at the time appointed for that purpose, in January last, will probably render abortive a treaty of commerce with that Republic, which was signed at Quito on the 13th of June, 1839, and had been duly ratified on our part, but which required the approbation of that body prior to its ratification by the Ecuadorian Executive.

A convention which has been concluded with the Republic of Peru, providing for the settlement of certain claims of citizens of the United States upon the Government of that Republic, will be duly submitted to the Senate.

The claims of our citizens against the Brazilian Government originating from captures and other causes are still unsatisfied.   The United States have, however, so uniformly shown a disposition to cultivate relations of amity with that Empire that it is hoped the unequivocal tokens of the same spirit toward us which an adjustment of the affairs referred to would afford will be given without further avoidable delay.

The war with the Indian tribes on the peninsula of Florida has during the last summer and fall been prosecuted with untiring activity and zeal. A summer campaign was resolved upon as the best mode of bringing it to a close.   Our brave officers and men who have been engaged in that service have suffered toils and privations and exhibited an energy which in any other war would have won for them unfading laurels.   In despite of the sickness incident to the climate, they have penetrated the fastnesses of the Indians, broken up their encampments, and harassed them unceasingly.   Numbers have been captured, and still greater numbers have surrendered and have been transported to join their brethren on the lands elsewhere allotted to them by the Government, and a strong hope is entertained that under the conduct of the gallant officer at the head of the troops in Florida that troublesome and expensive war is destined to a speedy termination.   With all the other Indian tribes we are enjoying the blessings of peace.   Our duty as well as our best interests prompts us to observe in all our intercourse with them fidelity in fulfilling our engagements, the practice of strict justice, as well as the constant exercise of acts of benevolence and kindness.   These are the great instruments of civilization, and through the use of them alone can the untutored child of the forest be induced to listen to its teachings.

The Secretary of State, on whom the acts of Congress have devolved the duty of directing the proceedings for the taking of the sixth census or enumeration of the inhabitants of the United States, will report to the two Houses the progress of that work. The enumeration of persons has been completed, and exhibits a grand total of 17,069,453, making an increase over the census of 1830 of 4,202,646 inhabitants, and showing a gain in a ratio exceeding 32½ per cent for the last ten years.

From the report of the Secretary of the Treasury you will be informed of the condition of the finances. The balance in the Treasury on the 1st of January last, as stated in the report of the Secretary of the Treasury submitted to Congress at the extra session, was $987,345.03. The receipts into the Treasury during the first three quarters of this year from all sources amount to $23,467,072.52; the estimated receipts for the fourth quarter amount to $6,943,095.25, amounting to $30,410,167.77, and making with the balance in the Treasury on the 1st of January last $31,397,512.80. The expenditures for the first three quarters of this year amount to $24,734,346.97. The expenditures for the fourth quarter as estimated will amount to $7,290,723.73, thus making a total of $32,025,070.70, and leaving a deficit to be provided for on the 1st of January next of about $627,557.90.

Of the loan of $12,000,000 which was authorized by Congress at its late session only $5,432,726.88 have been negotiated. The shortness of time which it had to run has presented no inconsiderable impediment in the way of its being taken by capitalists at home, while the same cause would have operated with much greater force in the foreign market. For that reason the foreign market has not been resorted to; and it is now submitted whether it would not be advisable to amend the law by making what remains undisposed of payable at a more distant day.

Should it be necessary, in any view that Congress may take of the subject, to revise the existing tariff of duties, I beg leave to say that in the performance of that most delicate operation moderate counsels would seem to be the wisest. The Government under which it is our happiness to live owes its existence to the spirit of compromise which prevailed among its framers; jarring and discordant opinions could only have been reconciled by that noble spirit of patriotism which prompted conciliation and resulted in harmony. In the same spirit the compromise bill, as it is commonly called, was adopted at the session of 1833. While the people of no portion of the Union will ever hesitate to pay all necessary taxes for the support of Government, yet an innate repugnance exists to the imposition of burthens not really necessary for that object. In imposing duties, however, for the purposes of revenue a right to discriminate as to the articles on which the duty shall be laid, as well as the amount, necessarily and most properly exists; otherwise the Government would be placed in the condition of having to levy the same duties upon all articles, the productive as well as the unproductive. The slightest duty upon some might have the effect of causing their importation to cease, whereas others, entering extensively into the consumption of the country, might bear the heaviest without any sensible diminution in the amount imported. So also the Government may be justified in so discriminating by reference to other considerations of domestic policy connected with our manufactures. So long as the duties shall be laid with distinct reference to the wants of the Treasury no well-founded objection can exist against them. It might be esteemed desirable that no such augmentation of the taxes should take place as would have the effect of annulling the land-proceeds distribution act of the last session, which act is declared to be inoperative the moment the duties are increased beyond 20 per cent, the maximum rate established by the compromise act. Some of the provisions of the compromise act, which will go into effect on the 30th day of June next, may, however, be found exceedingly inconvenient in practice under any regulations that Congress may adopt. I refer more particularly to that relating to the home valuation. A difference in value of the same articles to some extent will necessarily exist at different ports, but that is altogether insignificant when compared with the conflicts in valuation which are likely to arise from the differences of opinion among the numerous appraisers of merchandise. In many instances the estimates of value must be conjectural, and thus as many different rates of value may be established as there are appraisers. These differences in valuation may also be increased by the inclination which, without the slightest imputation on their honesty, may arise on the part of the appraisers in favor of their respective ports of entry. I recommend this whole subject to the consideration of Congress with a single additional remark. Certainty and permanency in any system of governmental policy are in all respects eminently desirable, but more particularly is this true in all that affects trade and commerce, the operations of which depend much more on the certainty of their returns and calculations which embrace distant periods of time than on high bounties or duties, which are liable to constant fluctuations.

At your late session I invited your attention to the condition of the currency and exchanges and urged the necessity of adopting such measures as were consistent with the constitutional competency of the Government in order to correct the unsoundness of the one and, as far as practicable, the inequalities of the other. No country can be in the enjoyment of its full measure of prosperity without the presence of a medium of exchange approximating to uniformity of value. What is necessary as between the different nations of the earth is also important as between the inhabitants of different parts of the same country. With the first the precious metals constitute the chief medium of circulation, and such also would be the case as to the last but for inventions comparatively modern, which have furnished in place of gold and silver a paper circulation. I do not propose to enter into a comparative analysis of the merits of the two systems. Such belonged more properly to the period of the introduction of the paper system. The speculative philosopher might find inducements to prosecute the inquiry, but his researches could only lead him to conclude that the paper system had probably better never have been introduced and that society might have been much happier without it. The practical statesman has a very different task to perform. He has to look at things as they are, to take them as he finds them, to supply deficiencies and to prune excesses as far as in him lies. The task of furnishing a corrective for derangements of the paper medium with us is almost inexpressibly great. The power exerted by the States to charter banking corporations, and which, having been carried to a great excess, has filled the country with, in most of the States, an irredeemable paper medium, is an evil which in some way or other requires a corrective. The rates at which bills of exchange are negotiated between different parts of the country furnish an index of the value of the local substitute for gold and silver, which is in many parts so far depreciated as not to be received except at a large discount in payment of debts or in the purchase of produce. It could earnestly be desired that every bank not possessing the means of resumption should follow the example of the late United States Bank of Pennsylvania and go into liquidation rather than by refusing to do so to continue embarrassments in the way of solvent institutions, thereby augmenting the difficulties incident to the present condition of things. Whether this Government, with due regard to the rights of the States, has any power to constrain the banks either to resume specie payments or to force them into liquidation, is an inquiry which will not fail to claim your consideration. In view of the great advantages which are allowed the corporators, not among the least of which is the authority contained in most of their charters to make loans to three times the amount of their capital, thereby often deriving three times as much interest on the same amount of money as any individual is permitted by law to receive, no sufficient apology can be urged for a long-continued suspension of specie payments. Such suspension is productive of the greatest detriment to the public by expelling from circulation the precious metals and seriously hazarding the success of any effort that this Government can make to increase commercial facilities and to advance the public interests.

This is the more to be regretted and the indispensable necessity for a sound currency becomes the more manifest when we reflect on the vast amount of the internal commerce of the country. Of this we have no statistics nor just data for forming adequate opinions. But there can be no doubt but that the amount of transportation coastwise by sea, and the transportation inland by railroads and canals, and by steamboats and other modes of conveyance over the surface of our vast rivers and immense lakes, and the value of property carried and interchanged by these means form a general aggregate to which the foreign commerce of the country, large as it is, makes but a distant approach.

In the absence of any controlling power over this subject, which, by forcing a general resumption of specie payments, would at once have the effect of restoring a sound medium of exchange and would leave to the country but little to desire, what measure of relief falling within the limits of our constitutional competency does it become this Government to adopt? It was my painful duty at your last session, under the weight of most solemn obligations, to differ with Congress on the measures which it proposed for my approval, and which it doubtless regarded as corrective of existing evils. Subsequent reflection and events since occurring have only served to confirm me in the opinions then entertained and frankly expressed. I must be permitted to add that no scheme of governmental policy unaided by individual exertions can be available for ameliorating the present condition of things. Commercial modes of exchange and a good currency are but the necessary means of commerce and intercourse, not the direct productive sources of wealth. Wealth can only be accumulated by the earnings of industry and the savings of frugality, and nothing can be more ill judged than to look to facilities in borrowing or to a redundant circulation for the power of discharging pecuniary obligations. The country is full of resources and the people full of energy, and the great and permanent remedy for present embarrassments must be sought in industry, economy, the observance of good faith, and the favorable influence of time. In pursuance of a pledge given to you in my last message to Congress, which pledge I urge as an apology for adventuring to present you the details of any plan, the Secretary of the Treasury will be ready to submit to you, should you require it, a plan of finance which, while it throws around the public treasure reasonable guards for its protection and rests on powers acknowledged in practice to exist from the origin of the Government, will at the same time furnish to the country a sound paper medium and afford all reasonable facilities for regulating the exchanges. When submitted, you will perceive in it a plan amendatory of the existing laws in relation to the Treasury Department, subordinate in all respects to the will of Congress directly and the will of the people indirectly, self-sustaining should it be found in practice to realize its promises in theory, and repealable at the pleasure of Congress. It proposes by effectual restraints and by invoking the true spirit of our institutions to separate the purse from the sword, or, more properly to speak, denies any other control to the President over the agents who may be selected to carry it into execution but what may be indispensably necessary to secure the fidelity of such agents, and by wise regulations keeps plainly apart from each other private and public funds. It contemplates the establishment of a board of control at the seat of government, with agencies at prominent commercial points or wherever else Congress shall direct, for the safe-keeping and disbursement of the public moneys, and a substitution at the option of the public creditor of Treasury notes in lieu of gold and silver. It proposes to limit the issues to an amount not to exceed $15,000,000 without the express sanction of the legislative power. It also authorizes the receipt of individual deposits of gold and silver to a limited amount, and the granting certificates of deposit divided into such sums as may be called for by the depositors. It proceeds a step further and authorizes the purchase and sale of domestic bills and drafts resting on a real and substantial basis, payable at sight or having but a short time to run, and drawn on places not less than 100 miles apart, which authority, except in so far as may be necessary for Government purposes exclusively, is only to be exerted upon the express condition that its exercise shall not be prohibited by the State in which the agency is situated. In order to cover the expenses incident to the plan, it will be authorized to receive moderate premiums for certificates issued on deposits and on bills bought and sold, and thus, as far as its dealings extend, to furnish facilities to commercial intercourse at the lowest possible rates and to subduct from the earnings of industry the least possible sum. It uses the State banks at a distance from the agencies as auxiliaries without imparting any power to trade in its name. It is subjected to such guards and restraints as have appeared to be necessary. It is the creature of law and exists only at the pleasure of the Legislature. It is made to rest on an actual specie basis in order to redeem the notes at the places of issue, produces no dangerous redundancy of circulation, affords no temptation to speculation, is attended by no inflation of prices, is equable in its operation, makes the Treasury notes (which it may use along with the certificates of deposit and the notes of specie-paying banks) convertible at the place where collected, receivable in payment of Government dues, and without violating any principle of the Constitution affords the Government and the people such facilities as are called for by the wants of both. Such, it has appeared to me, are its recommendations, and in view of them it will be submitted, whenever you may require it, to your consideration.

I am not able to perceive that any fair and candid objection can be urged against the plan, the principal outlines of which I have thus presented. I can not doubt but that the notes which it proposes to furnish at the voluntary option of the public creditor, issued in lieu of the revenue and its certificates of deposit, will be maintained at an equality with gold and silver everywhere. They are redeemable in gold and silver on demand at the places of issue. They are receivable everywhere in payment of Government dues. The Treasury notes are limited to an amount of one-fourth less than the estimated annual receipts of the Treasury, and in addition they rest upon the faith of the Government for their redemption. If all these assurances are not sufficient to make them available, then the idea, as it seems to me, of furnishing a sound paper medium of exchange may be entirely abandoned.

If a fear be indulged that the Government may be tempted to run into excess in its issues at any future day, it seems to me that no such apprehension can reasonably be entertained until all confidence in the representatives of the States and of the people, as well as of the people themselves, shall be lost.   The weightiest considerations of policy require that the restraints now proposed to be thrown around the measure should not for light causes be removed.   To argue against any proposed plan its liability to possible abuse is to reject every expedient, since everything dependent on human action is liable to abuse.   Fifteen millions of Treasury notes may be issued as the *maximum*, but a discretionary power is to be given to the board of control under that sum, and every consideration will unite in leading them to feel their way with caution. For the first eight years of the existence of the late Bank of the United States its circulation barely exceeded $4,000,000, and for five of its most prosperous years it was about equal to $16,000,000; furthermore, the authority given to receive private deposits to a limited amount and to issue certificates in such sums as may be called for by the depositors may so far fill up the channels of circulation as greatly to diminish the necessity of any considerable issue of Treasury notes.   A restraint upon the amount of private deposits has seemed to be indispensably necessary from an apprehension, thought to be well founded, that in any emergency of trade confidence might be so far shaken in the banks as to induce a withdrawal from them of private deposits with a view to insure their unquestionable safety when deposited with the Government, which might prove eminently disastrous to the State banks.   Is it objected that it is proposed to authorize the agencies to deal in bills of exchange? It is answered that such dealings are to be carried on at the lowest possible premium, are made to rest on an unquestionably sound basis, are designed to reimburse merely the expenses which would otherwise devolve upon the Treasury, and are in strict subordination to the decision of the Supreme Court in the case of the Bank of Augusta against Earle, and other reported cases, and thereby avoids all conflict with State jurisdiction, which I hold to be indispensably requisite.   It leaves the banking privileges of the States without interference, looks to the Treasury and the Union, and while furnishing every facility to the first is careful of the interests of the last.   But above all, it is created by law, is amendable by law, and is repealable by law, and, wedded as I am to no theory, but looking solely to the advancement of the public good, I shall be among the very first to urge its repeal if it be found not to subserve the purposes and objects for which it may be created.   Nor will the plan be submitted in any overweening confidence in the sufficiency of my own judgment, but with much greater reliance on the wisdom and patriotism of Congress. I can not abandon this subject without urging upon you in the most emphatic manner, whatever may be your action on the suggestions which I have felt it to be my duty to submit, to relieve the Chief Executive

Magistrate, by any and all constitutional means, from a controlling power over the public Treasury. If in the plan proposed, should you deem it worthy of your consideration, that separation is not as complete as you may desire, you will doubtless amend it in that particular. For myself, I disclaim all desire to have any control over the public moneys other than what is indispensably necessary to execute the laws which you may pass.

Nor can I fail to advert in this connection to the debts which many of the States of the Union have contracted abroad and under which they continue to labor. That indebtedness amounts to a sum not less than $200,000,000, and which has been retributed to them for the most part in works of internal improvement which are destined to prove of vast importance in ultimately advancing their prosperity and wealth. For the debts thus contracted the States are alone responsible. I can do no more than express the belief that each State will feel itself bound by every consideration of honor as well as of interest to meet its engagements with punctuality. The failure, however, of any one State to do so should in no degree affect the credit of the rest, and the foreign capitalist will have no just cause to experience alarm as to all other State stocks because any one or more of the States may neglect to provide with punctuality the means of redeeming their engagements. Even such States, should there be any, considering the great rapidity with which their resources are developing themselves, will not fail to have the means at no very distant day to redeem their obligations to the uttermost farthing; nor will I doubt but that, in view of that honorable conduct which has evermore governed the States and the people of the Union, they will each and all resort to every legitimate expedient before they will forego a faithful compliance with their obligations.

From the report of the Secretary of War and other reports accompanying it you will be informed of the progress which has been made in the fortifications designed for the protection of our principal cities, roadsteads, and inland frontier during the present year, together with their true state and condition. They will be prosecuted to completion with all the expedition which the means placed by Congress at the disposal of the Executive will allow.

I recommend particularly to your consideration that portion of the Secretary's report which proposes the establishment of a chain of military posts from Council Bluffs to some point on the Pacific Ocean within our limits. The benefit thereby destined to accrue to our citizens engaged in the fur trade over that wilderness region, added to the importance of cultivating friendly relations with savage tribes inhabiting it, and at the same time of giving protection to our frontier settlements and of establishing the means of safe intercourse between the American settlements at the mouth of the Columbia River and those on this side of the Rocky Mountains, would seem to suggest the importance of carrying into effect the recommendations upon this head with as little delay as may be practicable.

The report of the Secretary of the Navy will place you in possession of the present condition of that important arm of the national defense. Every effort will be made to add to its efficiency, and I can not too strongly urge upon you liberal appropriations to that branch of the public service. Inducements of the weightiest character exist for the adoption of this course of policy. Our extended and otherwise exposed maritime frontier calls for protection, to the furnishing of which an efficient naval force is indispensable. We look to no foreign conquests, nor do we propose to enter into competition with any other nation for supremacy on the ocean; but it is due not only to the honor but to the security of the people of the United States that no nation should be permitted to invade our waters at pleasure and subject our towns and villages to conflagration or pillage. Economy in all branches of the public service is due from all the public agents to the people, but parsimony alone would suggest the withholding of the necessary means for the protection of our domestic firesides from invasion and our national honor from disgrace. I would most earnestly recommend to Congress to abstain from all appropriations for objects not absolutely necessary; but I take upon myself, without a moment of hesitancy, all the responsibility of recommending the increase and prompt equipment of that gallant Navy which has lighted up every sea with its victories and spread an imperishable glory over the country.

The report of the Postmaster-General will claim your particular attention, not only because of the valuable suggestions which it contains, but because of the great importance which at all times attaches to that interesting branch of the public service. The increased expense of transporting the mail along the principal routes necessarily claims the public attention, and has awakened a corresponding solicitude on the part of the Government. The transmission of the mail must keep pace with those facilities of intercommunication which are every day becoming greater through the building of railroads and the application of steam power, but it can not be disguised that in order to do so the Post-Office Department is subjected to heavy exactions. The lines of communication between distant parts of the Union are to a great extent occupied by railroads, which, in the nature of things, possess a complete monopoly, and the Department is therefore liable to heavy and unreasonable charges. This evil is destined to great increase in future, and some timely measure may become necessary to guard against it.

I feel it my duty to bring under your consideration a practice which has grown up in the administration of the Government, and which, I am deeply convinced, ought to be corrected. I allude to the exercise of the power which usage rather than reason has vested in the Presidents of removing incumbents from office in order to substitute others more in favor with the dominant party. My own conduct in this respect has been governed by a conscientious purpose to exercise the removing power only in cases of unfaithfulness or inability, or in those in which its exercise appeared necessary in order to discountenance and suppress that spirit of active partisanship on the part of holders of office which not only withdraws them from the steady and impartial discharge of their official duties, but exerts an undue and injurious influence over elections and degrades the character of the Government itself, inasmuch as it exhibits the Chief Magistrate as being a party through his agents in the secret plots or open workings of political parties.

In respect to the exercise of this power nothing should be left to discretion which may safely be regulated by law, and it is of high importance to restrain as far as possible the stimulus of personal interests in public elections. Considering the great increase which has been made in public offices in the last quarter of a century and the probability of further increase, we incur the hazard of witnessing violent political contests, directed too often to the single object of retaining office by those who are in or obtaining it by those who are out. Under the influence of these convictions I shall cordially concur in any constitutional measure for regulating and, by regulating, restraining the power of removal.

I suggest for your consideration the propriety of making without further delay some specific application of the funds derived under the will of Mr. Smithson, of England, for the diffusion of knowledge, and which have heretofore been vested in public stocks until such time as Congress should think proper to give them a specific direction. Nor will you, I feel confident, permit any abatement of the principal of the legacy to be made should it turn out that the stocks in which the investments have been made have undergone a depreciation.

In conclusion I commend to your care the interests of this District, for which you are the exclusive legislators. Considering that this city is the residence of the Government and for a large part of the year of Congress, and considering also the great cost of the public buildings and the propriety of affording them at all times careful protection, it seems not unreasonable that Congress should contribute toward the expense of an efficient police.

JOHN TYLER.

SPECIAL MESSAGES.

WASHINGTON, *December 7, 1841.*

To the Senate of the United States:

I transmit herewith a report from the Secretary of War, in compliance with a resolution of the Senate of the 3d of March last, calling for a comparative statement of the condition of the public defenses, of all the preparations and means of defense, and of the actual and authorized strength of the Army on the 1st of January, 1829, and the 1st of January, 1841.

JOHN TYLER.

WASHINGTON, *December 7, 1841.*

To the Senate of the United States:

I transmit herewith a report from the War Department, in compliance with so much of the resolution of the Senate of March 3, 1841, respecting the military and naval defenses of the country, as relates to the defenses under the superintendence of that Department.

JOHN TYLER.

WASHINGTON, *December 8, 1841.*

To the House of Representatives of the United States:

In answer to the resolution of the House of Representatives of the 4th of September last, requesting information touching the relations between the United States and the Republic of Texas, I transmit a report from the Secretary of State, to whom the resolution was referred.

JOHN TYLER.

WASHINGTON, *December 8, 1841.*

To the House of Representatives of the United States:

I transmit herewith a report from the Secretary of the Treasury, exhibiting certain transfers of appropriations which have been made in that Department in pursuance of the power vested in the President of the United States by the act of Congress of the 3d of March, 1809, entitled "An act further to amend the several acts for the establishment and regulation of the Treasury, War, and Navy Departments."

JOHN TYLER.

WASHINGTON, *December 29, 1841.*

To the Senate of the United States:

I herewith transmit to the Senate a report* from the Secretary of State, in answer to their resolution of the 27th instant.

JOHN TYLER.

WASHINGTON, *January 4, 1842.*

To the House of Representatives of the United States:

I herewith communicate a report and statement from the Secretary of State, in answer to a resolution of the House of the 19th of June, 1841, requesting the aggregate amount of each description of persons within the several districts of the United States by counties and principal towns.

JOHN TYLER.

* Stating that no proposition has been made by either the United States or Great Britain relative to the mutual right of search.

WASHINGTON, *January 10, 1842.*

To the Senate of the United States:

I transmit to the Senate, for its consideration with a view to ratification, a convention between the United States and the Republic of Peru, signed at Lima on the 17th of March last, providing for the adjustment and satisfaction of certain claims of citizens of the United States against the Government of that Republic.

For the purpose of acquainting the Senate with the nature and amount of those demands and with the course of the negotiation, I also communicate a copy of such parts of the correspondence of the agents of the two Governments as relate thereto.

JOHN TYLER.

WASHINGTON, *January 17, 1842.*

To the Senate of the United States:

I transmit to the Senate a report from the Secretary of State, relative to the proceedings and final decision of the commissioners under the convention with the Republic of Texas upon the subject of the boundary between the United States and that Republic.

JOHN TYLER.

[The same message was sent to the House of Representatives.]

WASHINGTON, *January 18, 1842.*

To the House of Representatives:

I transmit to the House of Representatives, in answer to the resolution of the 14th instant, a report* from the Secretary of State and the papers by which it was accompanied.

JOHN TYLER.

WASHINGTON, *January 19, 1842.*

To the Senate of the United States:

I transmit to the Senate herewith a report† from the Secretary of State, with accompanying papers, in answer to their resolution of the 11th instant.

JOHN TYLER.

JANUARY 27, 1842.

To the House of Representatives:

I transmit herewith a report‡ of the Secretary of War, in answer to the resolution of the House of Representatives of the 9th August, 1841.

JOHN TYLER.

---

* Relating to American citizens captured near Santa Fe, Mexico, by the Mexican army.

† Transmitting correspondence relative to the action of the authorities of Nassau, New Providence, in the imprisonment of slaves charged with mutiny and murder, the refusal to surrender them to the United States consul for trial in the United States, and the liberation of slaves, all of said slaves being a part of the cargo of the United States brig *Creole.*

‡ Relating to the origin of the Seminole war, slaves captured during said war by United States troops, etc.

WASHINGTON, *February 5, 1842.*

To the Senate of the United States:

I transmit herewith to the Senate copies of a report and letter from the commissioners appointed by the President for the exploration and survey of the boundary line between the States of Maine and New Hampshire and the conterminous British Provinces, showing the progress made in that work during the past season, and submitting an estimate, to which I invite the attention of Congress, of the funds that will be requisite for completing the surveys yet to be made on the boundary, and the office work consequent thereon, and for completing the maps of surveys already made.

JOHN TYLER.

[The same message was sent to the House of Representatives.]

Hon. DANIEL WEBSTER,   NEW YORK, *January 4, 1842.*
    Secretary of State:

The undersigned, commissioners appointed by the President of the United States for the purpose of exploring and surveying the boundary line between the States of Maine and New Hampshire and the British Provinces in North America, respectfully report—

That in pursuance of the duties of their appointment they have in the course of the late season performed the following surveys and explorations:

1. The meridian line of the monument at the source of the St. Croix has, under the direction of J. D. Graham, been carefully and accurately traced from the station in the vicinity of Houlton where the labors of the year 1840 terminated to a point 4 miles north of the St. John River in the vicinity of the Grand Falls, being a distance of 81 miles from the monument. The timber has been removed along this line to a width necessary for its accurate prolongation and for the requisite astronomical observations at various points upon it, and a correct profile, or vertical section, has also been obtained by means of the spirit level the whole of the distance above mentioned.

Besides the astronomical observations necessary to obtain and continue the due north direction upon this line, numerous magnetic observations have also been made at a number of points upon it, in order to show the physical causes which must operate to produce serious discrepancies between a meridian line properly traced and such a one as has actually separated the jurisdiction of the two Governments since the attempt in the years 1817 and 1818 to define and mark this portion of the boundary under the provisions of the treaty of Ghent, although no portion of that line was ever ratified or made binding upon the parties to the treaty.

Upon this portion of the survey there have been chained, including measured offsets to the old line and to other important points, 85 miles.

Four hundred and fifty-two transit observations of heavenly bodies have been made, aided by three excellent chronometers, for the determination of the true meridian direction, most of which also served for the computation of the correct time.

For the determination of the longitude of this meridian west of the Royal Observatory of Greenwich and the latitudes of four important points upon it there were made eighty-five complete sets of astronomical observations, including altitudes of the sun and stars and the meridian transits of the moon and moon-culminating stars.

The number of barometric observations made upon the line and in its vicinity is 5,767; besides which there were made at Calais, for comparison with the level of mean tide on the St. Croix, 1,336 similar observations.

There have been determined in altitude above or below the level of the monument, by means of the spirit level, 1,716 points, and the altitudes of 1,816 other points have been similarly observed in order to verify the altitude of the monument above the level of mean tide at Calais.

For the determination of the magnetic variation at a number of points on the meridian line, more than 200 observations have been made upon four different needles, and for the determination of the magnetic dip at four principal stations on the same meridian 300 observations have been made upon two different needles.

Under the directions of the same commissioner the line claimed by Great Britain from Mars Hill and that recently chosen by Messrs. Mudge and Featherstonhaugh have been surveyed westward from the meridian line to the highlands near the head waters of the Aroostook, and the necessary data obtained for the construction of a correct map of that portion of country.

Upon this survey, without reckoning the distances traveled for approaching many important points of observation, there have been actually measured with the chain and coursed with proper instruments 267 miles, including the Aroostook River from its mouth to the point where it receives the Lapawmpeag Stream, a profile of the country from the head waters of the Moluncus to the St. John at Fish River, and such other important lines as were necessary for obtaining the correct topography of the country, and the altitudes of many points upon the line claimed by Great Britain as the boundary, in the vicinity of the Aroostook, have been obtained.

Ten principal points have been determined in latitude and longitude by means of 115 sets of astronomical observations, aided by three good chronometers, and seventeen other points have been determined by triangulation with a portable theodolite. Two hundred and five points have been determined in altitude by means of 1,319 barometric observations, and seventeen by means of the theodolite and spirit level. One hundred and ninety-two observations have been made for determining the variation of the magnetic needle at three important points.

The field duties above mentioned are considered to furnish sufficient data for a correct map of the line reported upon by the late British commissioners, Colonel Mudge and Mr. Featherstonhaugh, between the St. John River and the head of the Aroostook, besides some lateral explorations of considerable extent that will have an important bearing upon this branch of the subject. The work accomplished is full as much as could have been properly done in a single season, marked, as the last was, by an unusual drought of long continuance, which rendered it impossible to ascend, even with light canoes, some of the smaller streams, especially those forming the northwesternmost sources of the Aroostook. These might be profitably explored another season.

2. The division under the direction of A. Talcott has, besides verifying a part of the line of 1840 and tracing the course of Indian Stream (a branch of the Connecticut) to its source, explored and surveyed the line of highlands which extends from the Kennebec road to the Temiscouata portage, and so much of the line claimed by Great Britain as extends from the Kennebec road to the eastward as far as the head of the Aroostook River.

In the course of this survey, without counting the lines of approach or ground traveled over more than once, 703 miles have been passed over and such notes taken as will form the basis of a map. Of these 703 miles, 335 are upon the lines respectively claimed as boundaries by the Governments of the United States and Great Britain. In the course of these surveys, in order to the geographical determination of the position of the line, the latitudes of 54 points have been determined by means of 114 sets of altitudes of heavenly bodies, and the sets of subsidiary observations for time and for the determination of longitude by chronometers amount to 245. The number of points at which observations have been made by barometers for the purpose of determining their altitudes is 930, of which 669 are upon the boundaries respectively claimed by the two countries. The number of separate sets of barometric readings made at these points amounts to 1,981, while those made at the fixed stations, with which the former are to be compared, amount to 1,671.

3. The division under the direction of J. Renwick has explored or surveyed the line of highlands from the southeastern extremity of Lake Matapediac to the vicinity of the river Du Loup, where the line of survey has been connected with that of A. Talcott. In this survey a gap is yet left of a few miles on the western side of the valley of the Rimouski near its source.

In the course of the operations of this division 586 miles have been passed over and such notes taken as will form the basis of a map. Of these 586 miles, 275 have been actually measured, 209 are upon the boundary claimed by the United States, and about 30 upon the line pointed out by the proclamation of the King of Great Britain of the 7th of October, 1763, as the southern boundary of the Province of Quebec, making in all 239 miles of the height of land.

In the course of these surveys, in order to the geographical determination of the position of the line, the latitudes of 47 points have been determined by means of 85 sets of altitudes of heavenly bodies, and the sets of subsidiary observations for time and for the determination of longitude by chronometers amount to 130. The number of points at which observations have been made by barometers for the purpose of determining their altitudes is 407, of which 267 are upon the boundary claimed by the United States. The number of separate sets of barometric readings made at these points amounts to 1,153, while those made at the fixed stations amount to 837.

The division of Major Graham not having returned from the field until within a few days, neither the reduction of the astronomical observations nor any of the office work preparatory to a general map has yet been commenced by his division.

The office work of the divisions of A. Talcott and J. Renwick has been steadily carried on since the return of those commissioners from the field in the month of October, and great progress has been made in the calculations and plotting preparatory to the construction of maps, and necessary as materials for a general report.

In this state of the work of the several divisions the undersigned find themselves under the necessity of communicating to the State Department that the further progress of their operations is about to be arrested by the exhaustion of the appropriation, and of stating that unless speedy provision be made for the supply of the necessary funds the report of their operations can not be made up in time to be laid before Congress at its present session.

The position of the finances of the commission may be seen by the following statement:

Of the appropriation of $75,000 there have been drawn—

By J. Renwick..	$21,000
By A. Talcott..	24,200
By J. D. Graham..	25,000
Total drawn..	70,200

Leaving in the Treasury of the United States $4,800.

By a careful estimate it is found that to finish the office work of the several divisions there will be required over and above any balances in the hands of the several commissioners—

For the division of J. Renwick...	$3,000
For the division of A. Talcott...	5,800
For the division of J. D. Graham, including some arrearages due for instruments and to assistant engineers attached to this division.................	6,500

Making in all $15,300, and leaving to be provided for the completion of the work of the late season $10,500.

The undersigned can not refrain from stating that the necessity of applying for further funds was unexpected by each of them individually, as it is painful to them collectively. There are, however, reasons that in their opinion are incontrovertible which have led to an expenditure thus exceeding their estimate submitted to the Secretary of State the 11th of January, 1841:

1. The estimate for the expenses of the division under the direction of Major Graham amounted to $22,500. This referred only, however, to the continuation of the survey of the meridian line; and as the country had been represented by the most authentic maps as generally rising from the monument to the north, it was inferred that the timber to be cut away in opening this line through a dense forest would be of the description generally found upon elevated and dry lands, and the labor supposed to be requisite was estimated accordingly. So far, however, from this being the case, 26 miles out of the 32 between the base of Parks Ridge, near Houlton, and the river Des Chutes (6 miles north of the latitude of Mars Hill) have actually been found to be below the level of the monument and intersected by swamps covered with a thick growth of cedar and other timber common to such land, extremely difficult to cut away. More than double the labor estimated had therefore to be performed in accomplishing this and all similar portions of the work, and a corresponding increase of expense was unavoidable.

In addition to this increased labor upon the meridian line, the division of Major Graham has executed the surveys between that line and the head waters of the Aroostook, already given in detail, the expenses for which were not estimated or included in the sum above mentioned.

The cost of this survey, including the instruments that were required for it, has amounted to $5,500, and while this sum should be added to the original estimate for this division, the expenses of the divisions of the other two commissioners have not in any manner been thereby diminished, for the actual quantity of work performed by them has exceeded what was supposed from the best maps extant to be necessary upon the whole of the lines claimed by the two Governments, respectively, exclusive of the meridian line, as will hereafter be shown.

There was another cause which tended in a great degree to augment the expenses of this division in proportion to the progress of the work, which it was not within the power of human agency to control, and which we should not omit to mention here.

The severe drought which prevailed throughout this region of country during the month of August and the greater part of September caused the fires which are annually set to the fallen timber upon newly cleared lands to spread far and wide into the growing forest, and so rapid was its progress and so serious its ravages as to compel the inhabitants in many cases to fly for the preservation of life. Some check was experienced in the duties along the meridian line from the flames that actually embraced it, but a far more serious one from the dense smoke which filled the atmosphere almost incessantly for six weeks, and so obstructed the view as to render it impossible to fix the stations in advance with the requisite precision.

While the party charged with the astronomical operations was thus deprived of the opportunity of making scarcely any progress for six weeks, the expense of maintaining it could not in any way be diminished, because there was a daily hope that such a change in the weather might occur as would have removed this difficulty.

In order to make amends as far as practicable for so much time unavoidably lost, this division continued to prosecute its field duties north of the forty-seventh degree of latitude until several weeks after the severities of winter had commenced, with no other protection than their tents, the commissioner in charge of it believing that the expectations of the Government and of the country generally would but be fulfilled by the investigations in relation to this important line being pushed to the utmost attainable point. But for this it would have been impossible to have reached the St. John River the late season.

There remains to be surveyed along this meridian line, in order to reach the northwest angle of Nova Scotia as claimed by the United States, about 64 miles, to accomplish which will require another season of active field duty.

2. In the estimate for the work of the divisions of A. Talcott and J. Renwick it was assumed that the length of the boundary remaining on the line claimed by the United States was 320 miles, and upon the lines claimed by Great Britain 170 miles. Of the latter, about one-half was undertaken by Major Graham's division,* leaving for the estimated distance to be surveyed by the divisions of A. Talcott and J. Renwick 405 miles.

It will appear by the statement hereinbefore given that the joint surveys of these two divisions upon the lines of highlands have actually amounted to 574 miles. Upon the principle of their estimate, the probable cost of this would have amounted to $49,746.37, and with the addition for instruments and for the additional cost of the more remote parts of the line to $57,079.70.

The actual cost, including the foregoing estimate for the completion of the work, is $54,000.

It will appear, therefore, that when the increased extent of the work performed over that made the basis of the estimate is considered, the cost of performing it, so far from having exceeded the estimate, has fallen short of it by $3,000.

The reason of the discrepancy between the real extent of the line, as actually measured, and that which formed the basis of the calculation is that the latter was made by reference to the best existing maps, which were considered to be entitled to a certain degree of credit. Upon the close examination which the operations of the late season have afforded, these maps have been ascertained to be exceedingly erroneous. Well-known streams have been found to extend in either direction many miles beyond the points at which their sources have been laid down on the maps, and great rivers and lakes have, as it were, been discovered, of which no delineation had ever been given by geographers. The extent of these errors in remote and difficultly accessible points may be inferred from what has been found to occur in the part of the region which is most accessible, best known, and most frequently traversed.

On the Temiscouata portage, a road traveled weekly by the mail of Her Britannic Majesty, continually passed by the officers of her various services, which had been carefully surveyed by civil engineers preparatory to its reconstruction, and which has been traveled by the surveyors of both countries under the joint commission, it had hitherto been believed, and it was so represented on all maps, both English and American, that the line dividing the waters crossed the road three times. The surveys of the late season show that the boundary claimed by the United States crosses this road five times, and it became necessary to explore the culminating points of the valleys of four streams, instead of two, as had been anticipated. Instances of the same sort, but which do not admit of verbal description, have occurred on every part of the lines of highlands.

The two commissioners whose operations are under consideration no doubt had it in their power to have suspended their operations and returned so soon as the portion of the appropriation placed at their disposal was so far exhausted as to leave no more than would be needed to complete their office work; but they feel satisfied that they would not have been justified in so doing so long as any portion of the line remained unsurveyed or the weather would permit a party to keep the field. Thus, although in the original plan for the partition of the work it was estimated that their lines would probably be connected in the parallel of the river Ouelle, about 30 miles south of Temiscouata portage, when it was found that, from unforeseen delays in the transportation of the party of J. Renwick by sea to their work, and on the river

* It has already been stated that in the survey of the portion of this line allotted to Major Graham there were actually measured upon it, with the chain, 276 miles, and this did not constitute more than one-half the labor and expense incident to all the duties enumerated and performed by his division on his portion, so much did the work required upon this portion of it exceed what was estimated for the whole of it.

St. Lawrence from one station to another, it became doubtful whether he could pass the Temiscouata portage before the woods became impassable, his colleague continued his parties in the field until the junction was effected. In this way, while the expenses of the division of J. Renwick have not been materially diminished, those of the division of A. Talcott have been largely increased; but a portion of the general work has been accomplished which might otherwise have been left incomplete.

The undersigned, in conclusion, beg leave respectfully to urge the importance of a speedy appropriation to enable them to make up their report. A delay of any continuance will be productive of evil, either by enhancing the cost of office work or by rendering it difficult in consequence of the dispersion of the engineers and surveyors by whom the field notes have been taken. Upon the completion only of such a report will it be possible to render apparent how much of the whole task has been accomplished and how much remains to be performed; and the Department will then have it in its power to decide whether the part that has not been completed is of such importance to the question at issue as to require further operations upon it.

All which is respectfully submitted.

JAS. RENWICK,
A. TALCOTT,
J. D. GRAHAM,
Commissioners.

WASHINGTON, *January 25, 1842.*

Hon. DANIEL WEBSTER,
  Secretary of State.

SIR: The undersigned, commissioners appointed by the President of the United States for the purpose of surveying and exploring the boundary line between the States of Maine and New Hampshire and the British Provinces, beg leave, in compliance with your directions, to submit an estimate for the operations of the commission for the ensuing year.

So much of your directions as regards the state of the survey and the amount required to complete the office work preparatory to a report has already been laid before you in their report of the 4th January, 1842, prepared in anticipation of your orders. By reference thereto it will appear that the delineation of the meridian of the source of St. Croix has not, in spite of every effort on the part of the commissioner to whom it was assigned, been pursued farther than 81 miles from the monument. Sixty-four miles, therefore, of the said meridian line remain to be surveyed before this part of their task is completed. The other two commissioners, while they would not have hesitated to join in a final report in case the state of the survey of the meridian line would have permitted it, are aware that the hasty manner in which their work was performed, in anticipation of completing the object of their appointment during the past year, leaves room for a more accurate examination of some parts of the lines they have surveyed. Some portions, also, of the lines intrusted to them, respectively, were not reached; and, in addition, a part of the survey which was contemplated in their original instructions from your predecessor was not included in their estimates for the past year, in consequence of its having only a collateral relation to the main object.

Thus the surveys respectively undertaken by Messrs. Talcott and Graham of the lines claimed on the part of Great Britain and by Messrs. Mudge and Featherstonhaugh, although brought near to each other, have not been united, and a part of the highlands claimed by the United States near the source of the Rimouski was not reached by the parties of Professor Renwick.

The height of a part of the line explored by Captain Talcott in 1840, lying at the source of Arnolds River, was not determined for the want of a barometer.

Two or three miles in length of the line of highlands near the source of the river Du Loup require to be reexamined.

The longitudes of Lake Megantic, Lake Etchemin, the source of the Metjarmette, upon the line of Captain Talcott, and of some one point on the line of Professor Renwick ought to be ascertained with greater precision than the time that could be allowed during the last season would permit.

The instructions of Mr. Forsyth contemplated an exploration of the highlands described in the proclamation of 1763 as beginning on the north shore of the Bay of Chaleurs. The existence of a continuous elevated region from the tide of that bay to the termination of the exploring meridian line has been ascertained in a manner satisfactory to the commission, but the heights have not been measured on that part of it which lies nearest to the Bay of Chaleurs.

Under these circumstances the undersigned are of opinion that as no delay in the presentation of a final report will arise from further explorations of the parts of the territory thus pointed out and the more accurate examination of the uncertain matters, it would add to the confidence which may be placed in their results that a party be employed under the direction of each of the above-named commissioners upon the said work. For this object it is estimated—

1. That $25,000 in all, say $12,500 to be expended under the direction of each of the two above-named commissioners, will suffice. A less sum than this will not keep two parties in the field during the working season; a larger sum could not advantageously be expended on this part of the work.

2. In estimating the amount necessary for completing the delineation of the meridian of the source of the river St. Croix, it will be borne in mind that numerous astronomical observations must be made in aid of the operations with the transit instrument, in order constantly to preserve the true north direction, a condition of the utmost consequence, not alone as affecting the extent of territory that will be embraced by it, but more particularly because the character and position of the highlands alluded to in the treaty of 1783 would be exhibited in a very different light as encountered by a line running *due north*, as is required by the treaty, and by one varying even in a slight degree from that direction. This principle has already been exhibited in a striking manner by the trace of the meridian line as far as it has now progressed, for instead of encountering highlands in the latitude of Mars Hill having a claim to be considered those described in the treaty as the intended boundary between the two countries, the line as recently traced actually passes that latitude at an elevation of less than 10 feet above the level of the monument, and the greatest elevation encountered by this line in passing over any spur connected with Mars Hill is 63 feet above the level of the monument. In advance of this spur the line becomes again depressed below the level of the monument at several points before it reaches the Aroostook.

These, however, are only a few of the many facts that might be adduced from the surveys already made to show how important it is to the question at issue that every necessary means to avail of the aids of science should be adopted in order to preserve scrupulously the direction specified in the treaty while tracing this line. It must also be remembered that in the further prosecution of this duty a wilderness has to be traversed, totally uninhabited and totally without roads. The only means of progressing through it and of transporting the necessary provisions and the instruments indispensable to accuracy will be by means of canoes, for supplying two or three depots at points where Grand River and the waters of the Restigouche intersect the line, leaving the whole transportation along the meridian to be performed by packmen, or men carrying burdens on their backs. That the usual avenue to give an unimpeded view along the line must be opened through a dense forest, which in the neighborhood of all streams crossing it will still be found to consist of that swampy growth described in the report from the undersigned of the 4th of January instant as requiring so much labor to cut through it.

With all these circumstances in view. the following estimate for the completion of the survey of the meridian line and for some further surveys between that line and the source of the Aroostook is submitted; and it is intended to embrace the expense of completing both the field and the office work that will require to be done in order to a final accomplishment of the duties:

Estimate for the meridian line.

1. Pay of 4 assistant engineers from May 1, 1842, to March 31, 1843, being 304 days, at $4 per day each.. $4, 864.00
2. Pay of 3 other assistant engineers from May 1, 1842, to December 31, 1842, being 275 days, at $3 per day each.. 2, 475.00
3. Hire of 30 men as axmen, and for preparing, constructing, and erecting stations and signals in advance, from June 1 to November 30, 1842, being 183 days, at $1 each per day.. 5, 490.00
4. Hire of 30 other men as instrument carriers, chain bearers, canoe men, and packmen for 183 days, as above, at $1 per day each.......................... 5, 490.00
5. Hire of 1 carpenter and 2 cooks 183 days, as above, at $1.25 per day each..... 686.25
6. Subsistence of 1 commissioner, 7 assistant engineers, 1 carpenter, 2 cooks, and 60 men, as above, being in all 71 persons, while in the field, 183 days, at 50 cents per day each, including transportation of provisions to Grand Falls of St. John, or first depot... 6, 496.50
7. Purchase of barometers and repairs of instruments heretofore used.......... 800.00
8. Salary of commissioner... 3, 000.00
9. Contingencies, including stationery, office rent, and fuel, and transportation of engineers and commissioner to and from the field.................. 1,500.00

Total required for the meridian line.................................... 30, 801.75

That is to say, $30,801.75, making the whole amount for the work yet to be performed in the field on all parts of the boundary and for the office work that will be consequent from the said field work $55,801.75

All which is respectfully submitted.

JAS. RENWICK,⎫
A. TALCOTT, ⎬ *Commissioners.*
J. D. GRAHAM, ⎭

RECAPITULATION.

1. Amount of estimate for completing the surveys yet required to be made on the boundary, as above stated.. $55, 801.75
2. Amount of estimate rendered with report of January 4, 1842, for completing maps of surveys already made, etc..................................... 10, 500.00

Aggregate amount required 66, 301.75

WASHINGTON, *February 9, 1842.*

To the House of Representatives:

In answer to a resolution of the House of Representatives of the 7th of February, 1842, in the following words—

Resolved, That the President of the United States inform this House under what authority the commission, consisting of George Poindexter and others, for the investigation of the concerns of the New York custom-house was raised; what were the purposes and objects of said commission; how many persons have in any way been connected with it, and the compensation received or to be received by each; and the aggregate amount of every description of said commission, and out of what fund the said expenditures have been or are to be paid—

I have to state that the authority for instituting the commission mentioned in said resolution is the authority vested in the President of the United States to "take care that the laws be faithfully executed, and to give to Congress from time to time information on the state of the Union, and to recommend to their consideration such measures as he shall judge necessary and expedient."

The expediency, if not the necessity, of inquiries into the transactions of our custom-houses, especially in cases where abuses and malpractices are alleged, must be obvious to Congress, and that investigations of this kind were expected to be made appears from the provision in the twenty-first section of the act of 1799, "which enjoins collectors of the customs to submit their books, papers, and accounts to the inspection of such persons as shall be appointed for that purpose."

The purposes and objects of the commission will be explained by the commission itself, a copy of which, together with information on the other subjects mentioned in the resolution, will at the proper time be laid before Congress.

JOHN TYLER.

WASHINGTON, *February 11, 1842.*

To the Senate of the United States:

In compliance with the request of the governor of the Territory of Iowa, I have the honor to submit the accompanying memorials* and joint resolutions* of the council and house of representatives of that Territory to your consideration.

JOHN TYLER.

WASHINGTON, *February 14, 1842.*

To the House of Representatives of the United States:

In compliance with a resolution of the House of Representatives of the 3d instant, I transmit herewith a report† from the Secretary of State, with copies of the papers requested by the resolution.

JOHN TYLER.

WASHINGTON, *February 16, 1842.*

To the House of Representatives:

I transmit herewith a communication addressed to me by the Secretary of War, in relation to certain contracts entered into by a board of medical officers appointed for that purpose for the purchase of sites on the western waters for the erection of marine hospitals; and concurring fully in his views of the subject, I recommend that either an appropriation of $44,721 be made for the purpose of satisfying the claims of the individuals with whom the contracts were made or that the Department of War be authorized to reconvey to them their lands and annul the contracts.

JOHN TYLER.

WASHINGTON, *February 18, 1842.*

To the Senate and House of Representatives of the United States:

I have the honor to invite the attention of Congress to the accompanying letter, addressed to me by the Secretary of State. You will doubtless

*Asking an appropriation to defray the expenses growing out of the dispute between the United States, within the Territory of Iowa, and the State of Missouri relative to the southern boundary line, an appropriation to defray the expenses of a convention for the formation of a State constitution, etc.

†Relating to letters written in March, 1841, by Andrew Stevenson, United States minister at the Court of Great Britain, to Isaac Hull, commander of the United States squadron in the Mediterranean, which caused a part of that squadron to return to the United States.

perceive the importance of furnishing a uniform rule for the guidance of the public officers in the matter referred to in the Secretary's letter.*

JOHN TYLER.

WASHINGTON, *February 19, 1842.*
To the House of Representatives:

In compliance with the resolution of the House of Representatives of the 8th instant, I have the honor to submit the accompanying communication† from the Secretary of State and the correspondence on the subject referred to by the resolution of the House.

JOHN TYLER.

WASHINGTON, *February 21, 1842.*
To the Senate of the United States:

I transmit to the Senate herewith a report from the Secretary of State, with an accompanying paper,‡ in answer to their resolution of the 18th instant.

JOHN TYLER.

WASHINGTON, *February 26, 1842.*
To the House of Representatives:

The resolution of the House of Representatives of the 21st instant, requesting the President of the United States to communicate to that body, "if not incompatible with the public interest, the state of the negotiation between the United States and the Government of Great Britain in relation to the northeastern boundary of the State of Maine, and also all correspondence on that subject between the two Governments not hitherto communicated," has been transmitted to me. Desirous always to lay before Congress and the public everything affecting the state of the country to the fullest extent consistent with propriety and prudence, I have to inform the House of Representatives that in my judgment no communication could be made by me at this time on the subject of its resolution without detriment or danger to the public interests.

JOHN TYLER.

WASHINGTON, *February 28, 1842.*
To the House of Representatives:

I have the honor to submit copies of the correspondence§ and other documents called for by the resolution of the House of Representatives of the 2d February.

---

*Relating to the mode of paying salaries, etc., of ministers and other diplomatic agents of the United States at the several Courts of Europe.

†Relating to the colonial history of New York.

‡Extract of a letter from the Department of State to the United States minister at London relative to the case of the brig *Creole*.

§Relating to an act of the legislature of South Carolina providing for the imprisonment of free negroes found on board vessels entering any of the ports of that State, complaints of the British Government relative to the operation of said act, etc.

I am not informed of the existence of any official opinion of the late Judge Johnson on the unconstitutionality of the act or acts of the State of South Carolina upon the subject referred to in the resolution.

JOHN TYLER.

WASHINGTON, *March 8, 1842.*

To the House of Representatives:

I feel it to be my duty to invite your attention to the accompanying communication from the Secretary of the Treasury, in relation to the probable demands which will be made upon the Treasury for the present quarter. It will be seen that, without arresting the requisitions which will be made by the War and Navy Departments for the months of March, April, and May, there will be an unprovided-for deficit of upward of three millions.

I can not bring myself, however, to believe that it will enter into the view of any department of the Government to arrest works of defense now in progress of completion or vessels under construction or preparation for sea. Having due regard to the unsettled condition of our foreign relations and the exposed situation of our inland and maritime frontier, I should feel myself wanting in my duty to the country if I could hesitate in urging upon Congress all necessary appropriations for placing it in an attitude of strength and security. Such recommendation, however, has heretofore been made in full reliance as well on Congress as on the well-known patriotism of the people, their high sense of national honor, and their determination to defend our soil from the possibility, however remote, of a hostile invasion.

The diminution in the revenue arising from the great diminution of duties under what is commonly called the compromise act necessarily involves the Treasury in embarrassments, which have been for some years palliated by the temporary expedient of issuing Treasury notes— an expedient which, affording no permanent relief, has imposed upon Congress from time to time the necessity of replacing the old by a new issue. The amount outstanding on the 4th of March, 1840, varies in no great degree from the amount which will be outstanding on the 1st of January next, while in the interim the new issues are rendered equivalent to the redemption of the old, and at the end of the fiscal year leave an augmented pressure on the finances by the accumulation of interest.

The contemplated revision of the tariff of duties may, and doubtless will, lead in the end to a relief of the Treasury from these constantly recurring embarrassments, but it must be obvious that time will be necessary to realize the full anticipations of financial benefit from any modification of the tariff laws. In the meantime I submit to Congress the suggestions made by the Secretary, and invite its prompt and speedy action.

JOHN TYLER.

WASHINGTON, *March 8, 1842.*

To the Senate and House of Representatives:

In my message of the 7th of December I suggested to Congress the propriety, and in some degree the necessity, of making proper provisions by law within the pale of the Constitution for the removal at their commencement and at the option of the party of all such cases as might arise in State courts involving national questions or questions touching the faithful observance and discharge of the international obligations of the United States from such State tribunal to the Federal judiciary. I am urged to repeat at this time this recommendation by the receipt of intelligence, upon which I can rely, that a subject of Great Britain residing in Upper Canada has been arrested upon a charge of connection with the expedition fitted out by the Canadian authorities by which the *Caroline* was destroyed, and will in all probability be subjected to trial in the State courts of New York. It is doubtful whether in this state of things, should his discharge be demanded by the British Government, this Government is invested with any control over the subject until the case shall have reached the court of final resort of the State of New York and been decided in that court; and although such delay ought not, in a national point of view to give cause of umbrage to Great Britain, yet the prompt and instant rendering of justice to foreign nations should be placed among our highest duties. I can not, therefore, in consideration of what properly becomes the United States, and in anticipation of any demand from a foreign government for the discharge of one of its subjects, forego the duty of repeating my recommendation to Congress for the immediate adoption of some suitable legislative provision on this subject.

JOHN TYLER.

WASHINGTON, *March 11, 1842.*

To the House of Representatives:

In compliance with a resolution of the House of Representatives of the 23d ultimo, I communicate to that body a report from the Secretary of State, conveying copies of the correspondence* which contains the information called for by said resolution.

JOHN TYLER.

WASHINGTON, *March 12, 1842.*

To the Senate of the United States:

I have reason to think that the rejection of Silas Reed as surveyor-general of Illinois and Missouri on the evening of the last day of the session of the Senate at the last session of Congress was founded in a misapprehension of facts, which, while it deprived the public of the services

* Relating to complaints of Spain and Portugal that the operation of the revenue act of September 11, 1841, infringed treaty stipulations.

of a useful officer, left him to suffer a considerable degree of injustice in his reputation. After mature reflection upon all the circumstances of his case, and particularly of facts which have become known since his rejection, I have felt it my duty to submit his nomination for the same office anew to the Senate for its advice and consent.

I therefore nominate Silas Reed to be surveyor-general of Illinois and Missouri, in place of Joseph C. Brown, removed.

JOHN TYLER.

MARCH 15, 1842.

To the Senate of the United States:

I take the earliest moment to correct an error into which I inadvertently fell in my message of the 12th instant, nominating Silas Reed to be surveyor-general for Illinois and Missouri. In that message I represent the nominee as being rejected by the Senate on the evening of the last day of the last session of Congress, when upon a more accurate inquiry I find that he was rejected on the 14th of August, 1841, and his successor nominated on the 23d August and confirmed on the 13th September, which was the last day of the last session of Congress, and which fact had become identified in my memory, upon which I drew when I wrote the message, with the fact of his rejection.

I hasten to make the correction, not deeming it, however, of much moment in regard to the real merits of the nomination; for whether the rejection occurred on the last or any other day of the session, if done under a misapprehension or mistake of the facts, the Senate, I doubt not, will take equal pleasure in correcting the error.

JOHN TYLER.

WASHINGTON, *March 17, 1842.*

To the Senate of the United States:

In answer to the resolution of the Senate of the 2d ultimo, requesting information in regard to the demarcation of the boundary line between the United States and the Republic of Texas, I transmit a report from the Secretary of State and the papers by which it was accompanied.

JOHN TYLER.

WASHINGTON, *March 17, 1842.*

To the Senate of the United States:

I have the honor to submit the accompanying report and documents* from the Postmaster-General, in compliance with the resolution of the Senate of the 16th February.

JOHN TYLER.

*Statements of the quantity and cost of labor and materials for the new public buildings in Washington, D. C., etc.

WASHINGTON, *March 23, 1842.*

To the House of Representatives of the United States:

A resolution adopted by the House of Representatives on the 16th instant, in the following words, viz, "*Resolved,* That the President of the United States and the heads of the several Departments be requested to communicate to the House of Representatives the names of such of the members (if any) of the Twenty-sixth and Twenty-seventh Congresses who have been applicants for office, and for what offices, distinguishing between those who have applied in person and those whose applications were made by friends, whether in person or by writing," has been transmitted to me for my consideration.

If it were consistent with the rights and duties of the executive department, it would afford me great pleasure to furnish in this, as in all cases in which proper information is demanded, a ready compliance with the wishes of the House of Representatives. But since, in my view, general considerations of policy and propriety, as well as a proper defense of the rights and safeguards of the executive department, require of me as the Chief Magistrate to refuse compliance with the terms of this resolution, it is incumbent on me to urge, for the consideration of the House of Representatives, my reasons for declining to give the desired information.

All appointments to office made by a President become from the date of their nomination to the Senate official acts, which are matter of record and are at the proper time made known to the House of Representatives and to the country. But applications for office, or letters respecting appointments, or conversations held with individuals on such subjects are not official proceedings, and can not by any means be made to partake of the character of official proceedings unless after the nomination of such person so writing or conversing the President shall think proper to lay such correspondence or such conversations before the Senate. Applications for office are in their very nature confidential, and if the reasons assigned for such applications or the names of the applicants were communicated, not only would such implied confidence be wantonly violated, but, in addition, it is quite obvious that a mass of vague, incoherent, and personal matter would be made public at a vast consumption of time, money, and trouble without accomplishing or tending in any manner to accomplish, as it appears to me, any useful object connected with a sound and constitutional administration of the Government in any of its branches.

But there is a consideration of a still more effective and lofty character which is with me entirely decisive of the correctness of the view that I have taken of this question. While I shall ever evince the greatest readiness to communicate to the House of Representatives all proper information which the House shall deem necessary to a due discharge of its constitutional obligations and functions, yet it becomes me, in defense of the Constitution and laws of the United States, to protect the executive department from all encroachment on its powers, rights, and duties. In my judgment a compliance with the resolution which has been transmitted to me would be a surrender of duties and powers which the Constitution has conferred exclusively on the Executive, and therefore such compliance can not be made by me nor by the heads of Departments by my direction. The appointing power, so far as it is bestowed on the President by the Constitution, is conferred without reserve or qualification. The reason for the appointment and the responsibility of the appointment rest with him alone. I can not perceive anywhere in the Constitution of the United States any right conferred on the House of Representatives to hear the reasons which an applicant may urge for an appointment to office under the executive department, or any duty resting upon the House of Representatives by which it may become responsible for any such appointment.

Any assumption or misapprehension on the part of the House of Representatives of its duties and powers in respect to appointments by which it encroaches on the rights and duties of the executive department is to the extent to which it reaches dangerous, impolitic, and unconstitutional.

For these reasons, so perfectly convincing to my mind, I beg leave respectfully to repeat, in conclusion, that I can not comply with the request contained in the above resolution.

JOHN TYLER.

WASHINGTON, *March 25, 1842.*

To the Senate and House of Representatives of the United States:

Notwithstanding the urgency with which I have on more than one occasion felt it my duty to press upon Congress the necessity of providing the Government with the means of discharging its debts and maintaining inviolate the public faith, the increasing embarrassments of the Treasury impose upon me the indispensable obligation of again inviting your most serious attention to the condition of the finances. Fortunately for myself in thus bringing this important subject to your view for a deliberate and comprehensive examination in all its bearings, and I trust I may add for a final adjustment of it to the common advantage of the whole Union, I am permitted to approach it with perfect freedom and candor. As few of the burdens for which provision is now required to be made have been brought upon the country during my short administration of its affairs, I have neither motive nor wish to make them a matter of crimination against any of my predecessors. I am disposed to regard, as I am bound to treat, them *as facts* which can not now be undone, and as deeply interesting to us all, and equally imposing upon all the most solemn duties; and the only use I would make of the errors of the past is by a careful examination of their causes and character to avoid if possible the repetition of them in future. The condition of the country, indeed, is such as may well arrest the conflict of parties.

The conviction seems at length to have made its way to the minds of all that the disproportion between the public responsibilities and the means provided for meeting them is no casual nor transient evil. It is, on the contrary, one which for some years to come, notwithstanding a resort to all reasonable retrenchments and the constant progress of the country in population and productive power, must continue to increase under existing laws, unless we consent to give up or impair all our defenses in war and peace. But this is a thought which I am persuaded no patriotic mind would for a moment entertain. Without affecting an alarm, which I do not feel, in regard to our foreign relations, it may safely be affirmed that they are in a state too critical and involve too many momentous issues to permit us to neglect in the least, much less to abandon entirely, those means of asserting our rights without which negotiation is without dignity and peace without security.

In the report of the Secretary of the Treasury submitted to Congress at the commencement of the present session it is estimated that after exhausting all the probable resources of the year there will remain a deficit of about $14,000,000. With a view partly to a permanent system of revenue and partly to immediate relief from actual embarrassment, that officer recommended, together with a plan for establishing a Government exchequer, some expedients of a more temporary character, viz, the issuing of Treasury notes and the extension of the time for which the loan authorized to be negotiated by the act of the last session should be taken. Congress accordingly provided for an issue of Treasury notes to the amount of $5,000,000, but subject to the condition that they should not be paid away below par.

No measure connected with the last of the two objects above mentioned was introduced until recently into the House of Representatives. Should the loan bill now pending before that body pass into a law for its present amount, there would still remain a deficit of $2,500,000. It requires no argument to show that such a condition of the Treasury is incompatible not only with a high state of public credit, but with anything approaching to efficiency in the conduct of public affairs. It must be obvious even to the most inexperienced minds that, to say nothing of any particular exigency, actual or imminent, there should be at all times in the Treasury of a great nation, with a view to contingencies of ordinary occurrence, a surplus at least equal in amount to the above deficiency. But that deficiency, serious as it would be in itself, will, I am compelled to say, rather be increased than diminished without the adoption of measures adequate to correct the evil at once. The stagnation of trade and business, in some degree incident to the derangement of the national finances and the state of the revenue laws, holds out but little prospect of relief, in the ordinary course of things, for some time to come.

Under such circumstances I am deeply impressed with the necessity of meeting the crisis with a vigor and decision which it imperatively demands at the hands of all intrusted with the conduct of public affairs. The gravity of the evil calls for a remedy proportioned to it. No slight palliatives or occasional expedients will give the country the relief it needs. Such measures, on the contrary, will in the end, as is now manifest to all, too surely multiply its embarrassments. Relying, as I am bound to do, on the representatives of a people rendered illustrious among nations by having paid off its whole public debt, I shall not shrink from the responsibility imposed upon me by the Constitution of pointing out such measures as will in my opinion insure adequate relief. I am the more encouraged to recommend the course which necessity exacts by the confidence which I have in its complete success. The resources of the country in everything that constitutes the wealth and strength of nations are so abundant, the spirit of a most industrious, enterprising, and intelligent people is so energetic and elastic, that the Government will be without the shadow of excuse for its delinquency if the difficulties which now embarrass it be not speedily and effectually removed.

From present indications it is hardly doubtful that Congress will find it necessary to lay additional duties on imports in order to meet the ordinary current expenses of the Government. In the exercise of a sound discrimination having reference to revenue, but at the same time necessarily affording incidental protection to manufacturing industry, it seems equally probable that duties on some articles of importation will have to be advanced above 20 per cent. In performing this important work of revising the tariff of duties, which in the present emergency would seem to be indispensable, I can not too strongly recommend the cultivation of a spirit of mutual harmony and concession, to which the Government itself owes its origin, and without the continued exercise of which jarring and discord would universally prevail.

An additional reason for the increase of duties in some instances beyond the rate of 20 per cent will exist in fulfilling the recommendations already made, and now repeated, of making adequate appropriations for the defenses of the country.

By the express provision of the act distributing the proceeds of the sales of the public lands among the States its operation is *ipso facto* to cease so soon as the rate of the duties shall exceed the limits prescribed in the act.

In recommending the adoption of measures for distributing the proceeds of the public lands among the States at the commencement of the last session of Congress such distribution was urged by arguments and considerations which appeared to me then and appear to me now of great weight, and was placed on the condition that it should not render necessary any departure from the act of 1833. It is with sincere regret that I now perceive the necessity of departing from that act, because I am well aware that expectations justly entertained by some of the States will be disappointed by any occasion which shall withhold from them the proceeds of the lands. But the condition was plainly expressed in the message and was inserted in terms equally plain in the law itself, and amidst the embarrassments which surround the country on all sides and beset both the General and the State Governments it appears to me that the object first and highest in importance is to establish the credit of this Government and to place it on durable foundations, and thus afford the most effectual support to the credit of the States, equal at least to what it would receive from a direct distribution of the proceeds of the sales of the public lands.

When the distribution law was passed there was reason to anticipate that there soon would be a real surplus to distribute. On that assumption it was in my opinion a wise, a just, and a beneficent measure. But to continue it in force while there is no such surplus to distribute and when it is manifestly necessary not only to increase the duties, but at the same time to borrow money in order to liquidate the public debt and disembarrass the public Treasury, would cause it to be regarded as an unwise alienation of the best security of the public creditor, which would with difficulty be excused and could not be justified.

Causes of no ordinary character have recently depressed American credit in the stock market of the world to a degree quite unprecedented. I need scarcely mention the condition of the banking institutions of some of the States, the vast amount of foreign debt contracted during a period of wild speculation by corporations and individuals, and, above all, the doctrine of repudiation of contracts solemnly entered into by States, which, although as yet applied only under circumstances of a peculiar character and generally rebuked with severity by the moral sense of the community, is yet so very licentious and, in a Government depending wholly on opinion, so very alarming that the impression made by it to our disadvantage as a people is anything but surprising. Under such circumstances it is imperatively due from us to the people whom we represent that when we go into the money market to contract a loan we should tender such securities as to cause the money lender, as well at home as abroad, to feel that the most propitious opportunity is afforded him of investing profitably and judiciously his capital. A government which has paid off the debts of two wars, waged with the most powerful nation of modern times, should not be brought to the necessity of chaffering for terms in the money market. Under such circumstances as I have adverted to our object should be to produce with the capitalist a feeling of entire confidence, by a tender of that sort of security which in all times past has been esteemed sufficient, and which for the small amount of our proposed indebtedness will unhesitatingly be regarded as amply adequate. While a pledge of all the revenues amounts to no more than is implied in every instance when the Government contracts a debt, and although it ought in ordinary circumstances to be entirely satisfactory, yet in times like these the capitalist would feel better satisfied with the pledge of a specific fund, ample in magnitude to the payment of his interest and ultimate reimbursement of his principal. Such is the character of the land fund. The most vigilant money dealer will readily perceive that not only will his interest be secure on such a pledge, but that a debt of $18,000,000 or $20,000,000 would by the surplus of sales over and above the payment of the interest be extinguished within any reasonable time fixed for its redemption. To relieve the Treasury from its embarrassments and to aid in meeting its requisitions until time is allowed for any new tariff of duties to become available, it would seem to be necessary to fund a debt approaching to $15,000,000; and in order to place the negotiation of the loan beyond a reasonable doubt I submit to Congress whether the proceeds of the sales of the public lands should not be pledged for the payment of the interest, and the Secretary of the Treasury be authorized out of the surplus of the proceeds of such sales to purchase the stock, when it can be procured on such terms as will render it beneficial in that way, to extinguish the debt and prevent the accumulation of such surplus while its distribution is suspended.

No one can doubt that were the Federal Treasury now as prosperous as it was ten years ago and its fiscal operations conducted by an efficient agency of its own, coextensive with the Union, the embarrassments of the States and corporations in them would produce, even if they continued as they are (were that possible), effects far less disastrous than those now experienced. It is the disorder here, at the heart and center of the system, that paralyzes and deranges every part of it. Who does not know the permanent importance, not to the Federal Government alone, but to every State and every individual within its jurisdiction, even in their most independent and isolated individual pursuits, of the preservation of a sound state of public opinion and a judicious administration here? The sympathy is instantaneous and universal. To attempt to remedy the evil of the deranged credit and currency of the States while the disease is allowed to rage in the vitals of this Government would be a hopeless undertaking.

It is the full conviction of this truth which emboldens me most earnestly to recommend to your early and serious consideration the measures now submitted to your better judgment, as well as those to which your attention has been already invited. The first great want of the country, that without answering which all attempts at bettering the present condition of things will prove fruitless, is a complete restoration of the credit and finances of the Federal Government. The source and foundation of all credit is in the confidence which the Government inspires, and just in proportion as that confidence shall be shaken or diminished will be the distrust among all classes of the community and the derangement and demoralization in every branch of business and all the interests of the country. Keep up the standard of good faith and punctuality in the operations of the General Government, and all partial irregularities and disorders will be rectified by the influence of its example; but suffer that standard to be debased or disturbed, and it is impossible to foresee to what a degree of degradation and confusion all financial interests, public and private, may sink. In such a country as this the representatives of the people have only to will it, and the public credit will be as high as it ever was.

My own views of the measures calculated to effect this great and desirable object I have thus frankly expressed to Congress under circumstances which give to the entire subject a peculiar and solemn interest. The Executive can do no more. If the credit of the country be exposed to question, if the public defenses be broken down or weakened, if the whole administration of public affairs be embarrassed for want of the necessary means for conducting them with vigor and effect, I trust that this department of the Government will be found to have done all that was in its power to avert such evils, and will be acquitted of all just blame on account of them.

JOHN TYLER.

WASHINGTON, *March 25, 1842.*

To the Senate of the United States:

I have the honor herewith to submit a report * from the Secretary of the Navy, in compliance with your resolution of the 18th February, 1842.

JOHN TYLER.

WASHINGTON, *March 30, 1842.*

To the House of Representatives of the United States:

I transmit to the House of Representatives two extracts from a note of the chargé d'affaires of the Republic of Texas accredited to this Government to the Department of State, one suggesting in behalf of his Government such modifications of the existing laws of the United States as will impart greater facility to the trade between the two countries, particularly to that which passes across their frontier, and the other expressing a desire for some regulation on the part of this Government by means of which the communication by post between the United States and Texas may be improved.

As the wishes of the Texan Government in relation to those subjects can only be gratified by means of laws to be passed by Congress, they are accordingly referred to the consideration of the two Houses.

JOHN TYLER.

[The same message was sent to the Senate.]

* Transmitting list of agents, etc., employed by the Navy Department without express authority of law, etc.

To the Senate: WASHINGTON, *April 1, 1842.*

In part compliance with a resolution of the Senate of the 20th of July, 1841, I transmit herewith a report * from the Department of War.

JOHN TYLER.

WASHINGTON, *April 1, 1842.*

To the House of Representatives of the United States:

In compliance with your resolution of the 21st of March, I have the honor to submit the accompanying communication † from the Secretary of the Navy.

JOHN TYLER.

WASHINGTON, *April 4, 1842.*

To the House of Representatives of the United States:

In part compliance with a resolution of the House of Representatives of the 21st March, 1842, I herewith communicate a report ‡ from the Secretary of State.

JOHN TYLER.

WASHINGTON, *April 7, 1842.*

To the House of Representatives of the United States:

I herewith transmit to the House of Representatives copies of a letter addressed to the Secretary of State by the chairman of the board of commissioners appointed to explore and survey the boundary line between the States of Maine and New Hampshire and the adjoining British Provinces, together with the report of the operations of that commission to the 31st ultimo, and a profile of the meridian line from the source of the St. Croix River as far as surveyed, illustrative of the report.

JOHN TYLER.

[The same message was sent to the Senate.]

DEPARTMENT OF STATE,
Washington, March 31, 1842.

Hon. DANIEL WEBSTER,

          Secretary of State.

SIR: By directions of the board of commissioners for exploring and surveying the northeastern boundary, I have handed you the papers hereinafter specified, viz:

1. The report of the operations of the commission up to the present date.

2. A profile of the meridian line of the source of the St. Croix as far as surveyed, intended to illustrate the report.

3. A portfolio of drawings intended for the same purpose.

---

*Transmitting list of removals from and appointments to office in the Department of War from March 4, 1829, to September 30, 1841.

† Relating to appointments to office in the Navy and Marine Corps since April 4, 1841.

‡ Transmitting list of appointments by the President or Secretary of State since April 4, 1841.

4. A roll marked Appendix No. 1, containing the narrative of the field operations of the division of Professor Renwick.

5. A tin case containing the detail of the surveys of the division of Professor Renwick.

In reply to your inquiry in relation to the disposition of the said papers, I am directed respectfully to suggest that all which it is absolutely necessary to lay before Congress are the items 1 and 2, which, with a general map now in preparation, will contain all that will be of any general public interest.

The portfolio (No. 3) and the box of maps and profiles (No. 5) should remain on file in the Department; and while a part of the drawings in the former may be useful for illustration, the latter will be superseded by the general map, in which will be embodied all that they contain of importance to the question at issue.

Appendix No. 1, specified as No. 4 in the above list, will probably be demanded hereafter to give authenticity to the conclusions of the report (No. 1). It ought not, however, to be communicated until the Appendices Nos. 2 and 3, containing the operations of the divisions of Messrs. Graham and Talcott, are handed in; and of the three no more than a limited number of copies will be useful.

I have the honor to be, with much respect, your most obedient servant,

JAS. RENWICK,
Chairman.

Report of the commissioners appointed by the President of the United States for the purpose of surveying and exploring the boundary line between the States of Maine and New Hampshire and the British Provinces.

WASHINGTON, *March 28, 1842.*

Hon. DANIEL WEBSTER,
Secretary of State.

SIR: The duties assigned to the undersigned by the instructions of your predecessor were twofold:

First. To explore and survey the lines respectively claimed by the Governments of the United States and Great Britain.

Second. To examine and report upon the arguments contained in the report of Messrs. Featherstonhaugh and Mudge addressed to the secretary of state of Her Britannic Majesty for foreign affairs under date of 16th April, 1840.

In order to the more exact and successful performance of the duties included under the first of the above heads, the boundary line was divided by their instructions into three separate portions, one of which was assigned to each of the commissioners; and while they were instructed to assemble in a board for the purpose of comparing their respective surveys, in view of the performance of the duties included in the second of the above divisions their explorations have been separately conducted. Each of the commissioners has employed the methods and course of action most appropriate in his opinion to the successful fulfillment of his appointed task, and the nature of the surveys assigned to one of them has been of a character widely different from those of his colleagues. The commissioners, therefore, while uniting in a general report of the progress made up to this time in the duties of their appointment, beg leave to submit, in the form of appendices, the narrative of their several operations, with so much of the records of their observations and calculations as they have severally judged necessary to authenticate the conclusions at which they have arrived.

The progress which has been made in the labors of the commissioners enables them at this time to lay before you—

1. A description of the physical features of the disputed territory.

2. A comparison of the heights of the line claimed by the United States with those of the line styled the "axis of maximum elevation" by Messrs. Featherston-haugh and Mudge. In laying the latter before you they have, in order to avoid delay, made use in part of the published results obtained by those gentlemen, and although they have already detected errors in their inferences they do not consider that by accepting them for the moment as the basis of comparison they can be accused of exhibiting the line claimed by Great Britain in an unfavorable light.

1.—DESCRIPTION OF THE DISPUTED TERRITORY.

The seacoast of the State of Maine is rugged and hilly. The primitive rocks of which its geological structure is chiefly composed are broken into ridges which run parallel to the great streams, and therefore in a direction from north to south. These ridges terminate in an irregular line, which to the east of the Penobscot may be identified nearly with the military road to Houlton. From the northern summit of these ridges an extensive view of the disputed territory can in many places be obtained. This is the case at the military post at Houlton, whence a wide extent of country may be seen. A still more perfect view may be obtained from the summit of Parks Hill, at a point about 400 yards south of the road from Houlton to Wood-stock and about half a mile east of the exploring meridian line. At the time when that line was run by the British and American surveyors, under the fifth article of the treaty of Ghent, the top of this hill was covered with wood, and they were obliged to content themselves with the view from Park's barn, which is at least 200 feet beneath the summit. At the present moment the latter is cleared, and the view from west-southwest to northeast is unimpeded except by a single clump of trees, which cuts off the view for a few degrees in the northwest direction; but by a change of position every part of the horizon between these points is to be seen. Toward the west are seen ridges parallel to the Penobscot, over which Katahdin towers to a great height, bearing by compass N. 85° W. In a direction N. 75° W. are seen two distant peaks, one of which was identified as the Traveller. All of these eminences lie south of the line claimed by Great Britain. In the north-northwest direction there appear two ridges of comparatively small elevation, which were pointed out as the Aroostook Mountains, but have since been ascertained to lie near the sources of the Meduxnikeag. These lie in the line claimed by Great Britain in 1817.

Between these and the other mountains there is evidently no connection, and the rest of the country, as seen from the hill, bears the aspect of a wooded plain. It will be sufficient to refer to this view to be satisfied that all the impressions which have been circulated of a continuous chain of elevations extending along the line claimed by Great Britain are utterly fallacious.

Toward the north the country exhibits the same general features. One vast and apparently unbroken plain extends to the utmost limits of the visible horizon. In the midst of this, and at a distance of nearly 30 miles, Mars Hill alone breaks the monotonous prospect, and from its isolated position assumes to the eye an importance to which its altitude of less than 1,800 feet would not otherwise entitle it. No other eminences are to be seen in this direction, except a round peak bearing a few degrees west of north and some distant ridges about an equal distance to the east. The first of these has been ascertained by the surveys of Major Graham to be an isolated hill near the peak known as Quaquajo. The eastern ridges are probably those measured between the Tobique and the Bay of Chaleurs by the British commissioners. A sketch of this view from Parks Hill is annexed to the report, and lest any doubt be entertained of its accuracy it is proper to state that the unassisted vision was not relied upon, but that the outlines were carefully delineated by means of the camera lucida.

From this view it might be inferred that the northern part of the admitted possessions of the United States to the east of the Penobscot and the disputed territory as far as visible constitute a vast table-land slightly inclined toward the southeast.

On descending into the valley of the St. John the appearances change. The table-land is cut to a great depth by that stream, and from its bed the broken edges of the great plain look like ridges whose height is exaggerated to the senses in consequence of their being densely clothed with wood. The same is the case with all the branches of this river, which also cut the table-land to greater or less depths according to their distance from the stream into which they discharge themselves.

The want of a true highland or mountainous character in this region is obvious from the aspect it presents in the two different points of view. Mountainous regions are most imposing when seen from a distance and from heights. On a nearer approach, and from the valleys which intersect them, the elevations, so important in the distant view, are hidden by their own slopes or lose the appearance of relative elevation in consequence of the absolute heights of the valleys themselves. In conformity with this character, the line claimed by the United States for the most part presents, when seen at a distance, the appearance of lofty and deeply serrated ridges, while to one who traverses it it is a labyrinth of lakes, morasses, and short but steep elevations which hide its peaks from the valleys and streams.

The line claimed by Great Britain, on the other hand, when seen from a distance is as level as the surface of the ocean, with no greater appearance of elevation and depression than would represent its billows; while, seen from its own valleys, the heights assume an importance which their elevation above the valleys when actually measured does not warrant. The characteristics of the region through which the line of Messrs. Mudge and Featherstonhaugh passes are therefore the opposite of those usually remarked in highland countries, while those of the line claimed by the United States are the same as are always observed in such regions.

This character of a table-land deeply cut by streams is well exhibited in the section of their "axis of maximum elevation" by the British commissioners. In that will be seen the mountains near the source of the Aroostook, Alleguash, and Penobscot on the one hand, and of the Tobique on the other, while the intervening space is occupied by a curve resembling an inverted arch, of which the St. John occupies the keystone. In a country of this character any line whatever would present the appearance of a succession of eminences, and might by as liberal a construction of the term as has been made by Messrs. Mudge and Featherstonhaugh be called highlands.

The sameness of this general character is broken only by a single chain of hills.* This is a prolongation of Mars Hill toward the north, and, being both of less height and breadth than that mountain, is hidden by it from the view of a spectator on Parks Hill. Mars Hill is itself an isolated eminence, and is in fact nearly an island, for the Presque Isle and Gissiguit rivers, running the one to the north and the other to the south of it, have branches which take their rise in the same swamp on its northwestern side. To the north of the Des Chutes the ground again rises, and although cut by several streams, and particularly by the Aroostook, the chain is prolonged by isolated eminences as far as the White Rapids, below the Grand Falls of the St. John, where it crosses that river. It may thence be traced in a northern direction to the Sugar Loaf Mountain, on the Wagansis portage, where it terminates.

To this broken chain belongs the elevation of 918 feet given by Messrs. Mudge and Featherstonhaugh to an eminence in the neighborhood of the Aroostook Falls. An accurate profile of so many of these eminences as fall in the line of the connected meridian is herewith submitted. This chain of eminences is not prolonged to the westward, as it is entirely unconnected with any other height aspiring to the name of mountain in that direction.

* A chain is made up of mountains whose bases touch each other.—BALBI.

It is not in any sense a dividing ridge, being cut by all the streams in the country, and in particular to a great depth by the St. John and the Aroostook.

A section of this line was given in a report to the British commissioner under the fifth article of the treaty of Ghent by Colonel Bouchette, the surveyor-general of the Province of Canada. His heights were determined by the barometer, and estimated from the assumed level of the monument at the source of the St. Croix.

It would now appear that the section of Colonel Bouchette is very inaccurate, and that the heights as reported by him are not only much beyond the truth, but that the continually ascending slope ascribed by him to the country from the monument at the source of the St. Croix to the point where the due north line crosses the St. John is entirely erroneous. He, however, adroitly availed himself of this inaccurate section to attempt to prove the existence of a continuous chain of mountains from Katahdin to the Great Falls of the St. John, and thence around the southwestern branches of the Restigouche until it met the heights rising from the north shore of the Bay of Chaleurs. For this reason his view taken from Park's barn and that made by Mr. Odell from the same point were urged for admission as evidence on oath by the British agent, and the map of Mr. Johnson, which contradicted this evidence, was carefully excluded. It can not be concealed that could Colonel Bouchette's idea founded on erroneous premises have been established by indisputable facts it would have been the most fatal argument that has ever been adduced against the American claim, for he would have argued that the meridian line of the St. Croix would at Mars Hill have first intersected highlands which, rising from the north shore of the Bay of Chaleurs, would have appeared to divide until within a few miles of the Grand Falls of the St. John waters which fall into the St. Lawrence from those which fall into the Atlantic, and would have been the south boundary of the Province of Quebec.

Mars Hill would then have appeared to be in truth as well as in claim the north-west angle of the Province of Nova Scotia; and although the rest of the line would not have fulfilled the conditions, the United States might by an arbitrator have been compelled to accept this point as the beginning of their boundary. Nor, in the unexplored state of the country, is it by any means certain that the American agent, who does not seem to have seen the drift of the proceedings of Colonel Bouchette, would have been prepared with the adverse facts, which are now known to be undeniable. It may therefore be considered fortunate for the claim of the United States that the survey was afterwards intrusted to a surveyor who, in pursuit of the double object of encroachment on the United States and the enlargement of his native Province at the expense of Canada, signally failed in the proof of either of his positions.

The knowledge now acquired shows that the idea of Colonel Bouchette is unsupported by the facts of the case, for the highlands which rise from the north shore of the Bay of Chaleurs do not meet those in which the most southerly branch of the Restigouche takes its rise.

The British commissioners, although they give a profile of this ridge, do not pretend to have examined it except at Mars Hill, near the Aroostook, and at the Grand Falls of the St. John. It must be remarked that these profiles (the original one of Colonel Bouchette and that exhibited by themselves) are contrasted—one British authority with another—for the purpose of invalidating the ground on which the American claim is founded.

It is not our business to reconcile these conflicting authorities, but it is our duty to recall the recollections of the fact that no part of the American argument laid before the King of the Netherlands was founded on this or any other estimate of heights. Many elevations, indeed, were measured with great pains on the part of the Americans as well as of Great Britain.

On behalf of the United States Captain Partridge made many barometric observations, while Mr. Johnson took an extensive series of vertical and horizontal angles.

His operations were performed in the presence of Mr. Odell, the surveyor on behalf of Great Britain, who doubtless made similar ones, as he visited the same stations with a better instrument and for the same avowed purpose. Mr. Odell's observations were not presented by the British agent, and those of Mr. Johnson were objected to. If received, they would have set aside the pretensions that a continuous ridge of mountains existed between the Metjarmette portage and Mars Hill. They are, however, superseded by the operations of the undersigned, which have yielded satisfactory evidence that no chain of highlands in the sense of the British commissioners, or even an "axis of maximum elevation," exists where it is laid down on their map. Nor can it be doubted that the operations of Mr. Johnson had a decided advantage in point of probable accuracy over theirs. The exploring meridian line used as a base was measured with a tolerable degree of accuracy, and from the three heights chosen by him the whole country is visible.

On the other hand, the course of Messrs. Mudge and Featherstonhaugh being confined, except where they ascended Mars Hill, to the valleys of the streams, they were for the most part excluded from a prospect. In describing the view from Mars Hill, however, they have pictured in most accurate terms the true features of the country:

"The character of the country may be well discerned and understood from this insulated hill. It presents to the eye one mass of dark and gloomy forest to the utmost limits of sight, covering by its umbrageous mantle the principal rivers, minor streams, and scanty vestiges of the habitation of man."

This description can only agree with that of a vast table-land into which the streams cut so deep and form such narrow valleys as to be invisible.

But if a chain of highlands, or even an "axis of maximum elevation," had existed as they lay it down, within 20 miles, it would have been visible, and it need not be said that they would not have failed to describe it. The inconsistency between their map and this true and forcible description of the features of the country is apparent.

The same general character of table-land is found to the north of the St. John above the Grand Falls. Its first important northern tributary is the Grand River. In ascending this stream the level of the table-land is soon reached. The river runs between banks of very moderate elevation and on a regular slope, and although running with great rapidity upon a pebbly bed it is yet so tortuous that while its distance from its mouth to the Wagansis portage in a straight line is no more than 13 miles the meanders of its channel amount to 30.

On the Wagansis portage the table-land is terminated by a ridge whose summit is elevated 264 feet above the wagansis* of Grand River. It was at first believed that this, although of small elevation, was a dividing ridge, and that it might correspond to one construction which has, although inaccurately, been put on the treaty of 1783. This belief was speedily removed, for the rivulet on its northern side was found to be cut off from the Restigouche by the Sugar Loaf Mountain, and is therefore a branch either of the Grand River or of the stream which falls into the St. John immediately above the Grand Falls. The height of land which divides this rivulet from the wagan of the Restigouche is not elevated above the former more than 117 feet. There is, in fact, at this place a gap 5 or 6 miles in breadth in the great system of mountains which extend from the Gulf of St. Lawrence at the Bay des Chaleurs to the river St. Lawrence near the Temiscouata portage. At the northern verge of the table-land which has been described, and near the mouth of Green River, rises to the height of about 1,600 feet a mountain known from the name of that stream. This is, like Mars Hill, isolated, and affords an extensive view. To the north and west the prospect is bounded by a continuous line of horizon, which, instead of being

* Wagan is a term in the Abenaki language signifying way. Sis is a diminutive particle. Wagansis is therefore the little way; and it seems probable that the name of Grand River, the usual epithet for the St. John, has been improperly applied to the small stream which bears it on the map.

obviously below the level of the eye, as in the view of the disputed territory from Mars Hill, is evidently of even greater height than the Green River Mountain itself.

On entering into this region from the south by any of the navigable streams which traverse it, it presents a more decidedly mountainous character than the country to the south. The Grande Fourche of Restigouche is bordered by two continuous chains of mountains, rising when it first issues from them to the height of a thousand feet above its surface. The stream having a rapid fall, the relative elevation becomes less until, in the neighborhood of the lake in which its north branch first collects its waters, the relative elevation is not more than four or five hundred feet.

On traversing this elevated country it presents a different aspect from what is seen either from a distance or where it is entered from the rivers. Frequent ridges are crossed; the tops of these are often occupied by swamps filled with a thick growth of cedars. Deep and small basins occur, which are occupied by lakes that give rise to rivers flowing to the St. Lawrence or to the St. John. These are intermingled with thickets of dwarf spruce, and the streams are sometimes bordered by marshes covered by low alders, and sometimes cut deep into rocky channels. In this apparent labyrinth one positive circumstance marks the line of division, or the true height of land: The streams which run to the St. John are all of the first description—sluggish—while those which discharge themselves into the St. Lawrence are rapid, and have the character of torrents.

On the western side of the disputed territory are ridges of rocky hills running nearly north and south, and thus tending toward the St. Lawrence, which they in some places reach and shut out the view of the interior.

It thus becomes difficult to find a station whence the heights of land can be viewed and its character exhibited. It has therefore been hitherto possible for those who have argued in support of the claims of Great Britain to represent without meeting with contradiction that the streams which fall into the St. John had their rise in a country possessed of none of that mountainous character which they urged was essential to the epithet of highlands. There are, however, points where a different character is apparent, and some of these are easy of access. Thus, on the main mail road, along the Southeast Branch of the St. Lawrence a mile northeast of the church of L'Islette, a rocky eminence is passed, whence may be seen a bold group of mountains which have been identified with the sources of the Ouelle, the Kamouraska, and Black rivers. A view of this group is herewith presented.

From the height to the east of river Du Loup a view may be seen on a clear day extending round 137° of the horizon, beginning with the highlands of Bic, bearing N. 58° E., and terminating in a conical mountain bearing S. 15° W.

The nearest and more conspicuous of these highlands (named those of St. Andre) are on the river Fourche, a branch of the river Du Loup, whose waters they divide from those of the St. Francis. A view of these is also submitted herewith.

A similar view of the same panorama of highlands is obtained from Hare Island, in the St. Lawrence, an outline of which, taken with the camera lucida, is likewise submitted. About a quarter of a mile to the south of the point where the Temiscouata portage crosses Mount Biort the highlands may be seen at the head of Rimouski, bearing nearly east, thence extending round by the north to the mountains of St. Andre, bearing nearly west, forming about one-half of the entire horizon. The entire panorama from the latter point, taken with the camera lucida, along with copies of some daguerreotypes made at the same place, are herewith submitted. Of the part of the line which extends to the northeast from the source of the Etchemin for a distance of many miles, a view may be almost constantly seen from the citadel of Quebec and from the tops of the houses in that city. One still more satisfactory may be obtained from the road between Quebec and the Falls of Montmorency, in the neighborhood of the village of Belport. The latter views are in particular referred to, as they are within the reach of numerous civil and military officers of the British Government, who must assent to the evidence of their own senses, which will prove that this region, the position of the path pursued during the present year by Captain Talcott's parties, is to all intents a range of highlands.

The boundary presents from these positions the aspect of a continuous and deeply serrated ridge.

The geological character of the country can not be admitted as having any bearing upon the subject under consideration. It never entered into the views of the framers of the treaty of 1783, and therefore could afford no illustrations of their intentions.

Were it admissible, however, it might be cited as an additional argument that the dividing height which incloses the waters of the Connecticut continues unchanged in its features until it is cut off by the deep channel of the St. Lawrence.

Opportunities for observations of this character were most frequent on the Temiscouata portage and on the banks of the St. Lawrence itself. It was only on the former place that the relative geological heights of the rocks could be observed by means of their outcrop.

The whole of the portage passes over stratified rocks dipping rapidly to the southeast. They were found to be alternate groups of common and talcose slate and of a rock made up principally of angular fragments of white quartz (grauwacke). These are in all respects identical with rocks which have been observed by one of the commissioners in place in Berkshire County, Mass., and in Columbia and Rensselaer counties, N. Y., and the description of geologists at various intervening points, as well as the observations of Captain Talcott's parties, would tend to establish the fact that the formations are continuous.

From these data it would appear probable that the rocks are a prolongation of the western slope of the great range called by Mr. Featherstonhaugh, in his report as United States geologist, the Atlantic ridge. This formation, which is but a few miles in width where it crosses the Hudson, appears gradually to widen as it proceeds to the north, and was on the St. Lawrence found to prevail both at the river Du Loup and at Grand Metis, dipping in the two places in opposite directions and covered in the interval by the thick diluvial deposits which form the valley of the Trois Pistoles. To render the analogy more complete, in the valley of the outlet of the Little Lake (Temiscouata) was found a vein of metalliferous quartz charged with peroxide of iron, evidently arising from the decomposition of pyrites, being in fact the same as the matrix of the gold which has been traced in the talcose slate formation from Georgia to Vermont; and on the western shore of the Temiscouata Lake, about a mile to the south of Fort Ingall, lie great masses of granular carbonate of lime, identically resembling the white marbles of Pennsylvania, Westchester County, N. Y., and Berkshire County, Mass.

If the latter be in place, which, although probable, was not ascertained beyond all question, the primitive carbonate of lime has exactly the same relation to the slaty rocks which it bears in the latter locality.

The formations which have been spoken of appear to occupy the whole extent of the country explored by the parties of Professor Renwick. Everywhere the streams were found cutting through rocks of slate. On the summits of many of the hills were found weathered masses of angular quartz rocks, showing that while the slate had yielded to the action of the elements, the harder and less friable rock had kept its place. The ridges which intervene between the St. Lawrence at the river Du Loup and Lake Temiscouata have the character, so well described by Élie de Beaumont, of mountains elevated by some internal force.

To the eastward of Lake Temiscouata, on the other hand, the country has the aspect of having once been a table-land, elevated on the average about 1,700 feet above the level of the sea, and of having been washed by some mighty flood, which, wearing away the softer rocks, had cut it into valleys, forming a complex system incapable of being described in words and only to be understood by inspection of a map.

2.—COMPARISON OF THE ELEVATIONS OF THE BOUNDARY LINE CLAIMED BY THE UNITED STATES WITH THOSE OF THE "AXIS OF MAXIMUM ELEVATION" OF MESSRS. FEATHERSTONHAUGH AND MUDGE.

For the purpose of exhibiting the relative claims of the two lines to the exclusive epithet of "the highlands" in the most clear and definite manner, each of them will be considered as divided into three portions, which will be contrasted with each other by pairs. The first portion of each of the lines is that which lies nearest to the point of bifurcation; the residue of the American line is divided at the source of the Ouelle; the remainder of the line of Messrs. Featherstonhaugh and Mudge at that of the Aroostook. Metjarmette portage is taken as the point of bifurcation, whence waters run to the Penobscot, the St. John, and the St. Lawrence.

On the American line from the Metjarmette portage to Lake Etchemin—	Feet.
The maximum height is	1,718
The minimum height is	1,218

The minimum measured height is that of Lake Etchemin, which is lower than the actual source of that stream, and whose omission as not upon the dividing ridge would make the minimum greater. This height was determined by the parties of A. Talcott, esq., by two distinct and separate sets of observations, one of which was continued hourly for several days; and no doubt can exist that it is as accurate a measure as the barometer is capable of affording. In the report of Messrs. Featherstonhaugh and Mudge this height is set down as no more than 957 feet, but it is determined from a single observation. That it is erroneous must be considered as demonstrated. In the map presented by those gentlemen they have made use of this erroneous determination for a purpose which, even were it correct, would not be warranted, for they on its authority leave out all the symbols by which heights are represented, and substitute therefor a dotted line with the inscription "Fictitious hills of Mr. Burnham's map." The actual character of this part of the American line is an undulating country.

On the line of Messrs. Featherstonhaugh and Mudge between the Metjarmette portage and the Cocumgamoc Mountains—	Feet.
The maximum elevation is	2,302
The minimum elevation is	987

This part of the line of Messrs. Featherstonhaugh and Mudge derives its apparent advantage from the fact that it crosses the summit and occupies the eastern slope of the highlands claimed by the United States. Notwithstanding this, the difference in their elevation is not such as to give it any decided superiority in its highland character.

On the American line from Lake Etchemin to the river Ouelle—	Feet.
The maximum height is	2,854
The minimum height is	1,306
On the line of Messrs. Featherstonhaugh and Mudge from the Cocumgamoc Mountains to the head waters of the Aroostook—	
The maximum height is	1,268
The minimum height is	880

On the parts of the line thus contrasted the maximum height of that claimed by Great Britain is less elevated than the lowest gap of that claimed by the United States.

On the third portion of the American line:	
From the head of the Ouelle to the Temiscouata portage—	Feet.
The maximum height is	2,231
The minimum height is	853
From the point where the line first crosses the Temiscouata portage to Mount Paradis—	
The maximum height is	1,983
The minimum height is	906

On the third portion of the American line (continued):

	Feet.
From the Temiscouata portage to the head of the Abagusquash—	
The maximum height is	1,510
The minimum height is	676
From Abagusquash to the Rimouski Lake—	
The maximum height is	1,824
The minimum height is	651
From the Rimouski Lake to the northwest angle—	
The maximum height is	1,841
The minimum height is	1,014
The greatest elevation of the whole of the third part of the American line, therefore, is	2,231
The minimum is	651

The termination of the exploring meridian line falls into this part of the American line. Its height of 1,519 feet was determined by two separate observations, compared with others taken on Lake Johnson. The height of the latter was calculated at 1,007 feet from a series of observations continued for seventeen days, and is believed to be as accurate as the method of the barometer is susceptible of.

This height of the termination of that line is estimated by Messrs. Featherstonhaugh and Mudge at no more than 388 feet, and that of the lake at no more than 363. In this estimate they reject the indications of their own barometers, because the results of them would have contradicted the previous impressions which seem to have governed all their operations, viz, that the point claimed by the United States as the northwest angle of Nova Scotia is not in an elevated region of country.*

On the third part of the British line from the sources of the Aroostook to the Grand Falls of the St. John no height is reported as measured by the British commissioners which exceeds 1,050 feet, while the greatest height on their profile is 1,150 feet. The minimum height on their profile, excluding the Aroostook at its mouth and its intersection with the meridian line, is 243 feet, and the mean of the numbers entered by them both on their map and profile is 665 feet.

It will therefore appear that if the profile of Messrs. Featherstonhaugh and Mudge be correct the lowest gap on the third part of the American line is about as high as the mean elevation of the part of the British line with which it is compared.

The line claimed by the United States therefore possesses throughout in a preeminent degree the highland character according to the sense at one time contended for in the argument of Great Britain, and is, to use the term of the British commissioners, "the axis of maximum elevation," the mean of all the heights measured upon it being 1,459 feet, while that of those measured on the line of Messrs. Featherstonhaugh and Mudge is no more than 1,085 feet.

It is regretted that the computations of the barometric and other observations for the determination of the heights of that portion of the country between the valley of the St. John and the sources of the Aroostook, explored by the division of Major Graham, could not be completed in time to be made use of for this report in the description of that portion of the line claimed for Great Britain by Messrs. Featherstonhaugh and Mudge. This delay has been solely caused by a want of reasonable time to complete this portion of the work, the commissioner having direction of the division charged with it having only returned from the field in the month of January.

Sufficient information is known, however, to have been derived from those surveys to justify the assertion that, instead of the strongly marked range of highlands represented by the British commissioners as constituting a part of their "axis of

---

*A continuous line of leveling was carried by one of the parties of Major Graham's division, by means of two spirit levels checking one another, from tide water at Calais, in Maine, to the monument at the source of the St. Croix, and thence along the true meridian line to its intersection with the river St. John. The surface of the St. John at this point of intersection was thus found to be 419½ feet above the level of mean tide at Calais. The basin of the river immediately above the Grand Falls may be stated as of the same elevation in round numbers, as there is very little current in the river between those two points.

maximum elevation," the country in the vicinity of the Aroostook lying between its sources and the valley of the St. John is devoid of the character they have attributed to it. When properly represented upon a map it will appear as an extended undulating surface of moderate elevation above the level of the Aroostook River, sparsely interspersed with occasional detached elevations rising to heights of 600 to 900 and 1,400 feet above the level of the sea, but forming no continuous or connected chain whatever in the direction represented by the British commissioners, or that could be construed into the character of highlands such as are described in the treaty of 1783.*

In addition to the surveys upon the boundary line claimed by the United States, an exploring line was run under the direction of Professor Renwick, as is more particularly described in Appendix No. 1. This line extended to an eminence on the eastern side of Lake Matapediac, elevated 1,743 feet above the level of the sea. The views obtained from this eminence established the fact that a chain of highlands extended thence to the north shore of the Bay des Chaleurs. They are believed to terminate in an eminence, which from its imposing appearance has been called by the Scotch settlers at its foot Ben Lomond. This was measured during the operations of the summer of 1840, and found to rise from the tide of the bay to the height of 1,024 feet. This exploring line, coupled with the more accurate surveys, appears to establish the fact of the existence of a continuous chain of eminences entitled to

*NOTE.—Since the above was written Major Graham's map and the computations of the barometric heights above alluded to have been completed.

This map exhibits in their proper positions the numerous altitudes which were determined throughout the country watered by the Aroostook and its principal tributaries, extending laterally to the heights which bound the basin of that river on either side; along the due west line traced in the year 1835 by Captain Yule, of the royal engineers, between Mars Hill and a point near the forks of the Great Machias River; along and in the vicinity of the road recently opened by the State of Maine from Lewis's (a point in latitude 46° 12′ 20″, between the head branches of the Meduxnikeag and the Masardis or St. Croix of the Aroostook) to the mouth of Fish River, in latitude 47° 15′ 13″, being a distance, actually measured, of 79 miles; and along the new military road, embracing 40½ miles of the distance from Fort Fairfield to Houlton and including the adjacent heights on either side.

The number of elevations within the territory watered by the Aroostook and claimed by Great Britain that have thus been carefully measured amounts to upward of 200.

This survey shows that although the prominent eminences which occur along that portion of the "axis of maximum elevation" of Messrs. Mudge and Featherstonhaugh which lies between the mouth and the source of the Aroostook correspond very nearly in height and position by our measurements with those reported by themselves, yet these eminences are separated one from another by spaces of comparatively low and very often swampy country, so extended as to preclude the idea of a continuous range of highlands in the direction represented upon the map of those commissioners.

If a range or chain of highlands is to be made to appear by drawing a strongly marked line over widely extended valleys or districts of comparatively low country so as to reach and connect the most prominent eminences which may fall within the assumed direction, then such a range or chain of highlands may here be made as plausibly in any other direction as in that chosen by Messrs. Mudge and Featherstonhaugh, for the detached elevated peaks are so distributed as under such a principle to favor any one direction as much as another, and might thus be made to subserve in an equal degree whatever conflicting theories the object in view might cause to be originated.

We may also refer, in further illustration of the character of the country through which a portion of this pretended "axis of maximum elevation" is made to pass, to a panorama view taken in October, 1841, by one of Major Graham's assistants from the summit of Blue Hill, where crossed by the true meridian of the monument, at the source of the St. Croix. This position is 1,100 feet above the level of the sea and 47½ miles north of the monument. It commands a most satisfactory view of the whole country embraced within a radius of 40 to 60 miles, including, as the landscape shows, Parks Hill to the south; Katahdin, the Traveller, and Mars Hill to the southwest; Quaquajo, the Horseback, the Haystack, and one or two peaks beyond the Aroostook to the west; the heights upon the Fish River and the southern margin of the Eagle Lakes to the northwest, and those south of the St. John (except a small angle obstructed by the Aroostook Hill) to the north.

The character of the great basin of the Aroostook, dotted with the detached peaks which rise abruptly from it at intervals of many miles apart, is here exhibited through at least two-thirds of its extent in so satisfactory a manner as in itself to preclude the idea of an "axis of maximum elevation" composed of anything like a connected or continuous chain in this region of country.

MAY 1, 1842.

the epithet of highlands from the north shore of the Bay des Chaleurs at its western extremity to the sources of the Connecticut River. Returning from the latter point, they exhibit the aspect of well-marked ranges of mountains as far as the sources of the Metjarmette. Thence to the sources of the Etchemin extends an undulating country whose mean height is 1,300 or 1,500 feet above the level of the sea. The boundary line is thence prolonged to the Temiscouata portage over well-defined ridges to the eastern side of Lake Temiscouata. At the sources of two of the streams which run into this lake the minimum heights of 651 feet and 676 feet have been observed.

With these exceptions, the sources of the streams which rise to the north of the Temiscouata portage and between the lake of that name and Lake Matapediac average more than 900 feet above the level of the sea. For the purpose of describing this portion of the line claimed by the United States, we may take this height of 900 feet as the elevation of a horizontal plane or base. On this are raised knolls, eminences, and short ridges whose heights above this assumed base vary from 300 to 1,300 feet. The more elevated of these are universally designated by the hunters who occasionally visit the country and the lumberers who search it for timber as mountains clothed to the summit with wood, which, in consequence of the rigor of the climate, attains but a feeble growth. They have an aspect of much greater altitude than they in reality possess, but their character as highlands is indisputable. This term, which the first English visitors ascribed without hesitation to the hills of New Jersey,* whose altitude is about 300 feet above the level of the sea, is much better merited by a group of eminences rising from 300 to 1,300 feet above a base itself 900 feet in height, and which exceed in elevation the well-known highlands of the Hudson River.

Not to rest merely on instances drawn from the language of those of English birth who first settled or traded on the coast of the present United States, there are in the immediate vicinity of the region in question a range of eminences the highest of which is no more than 1,206 feet above the level of the sea. These, on the authority of a distinguished officer of Her Britannic Majesty's navy,† are named the "highlands of Bic," and have long been thus known by all the navigators of the St. Lawrence who use the English tongue.

To sum up the results of the field operations of the commissioners:

(1) The meridian has been traced by astronomic observations from the monument, established by the consent of both nations in 1798, at the source of the St. Croix to a point 4 miles beyond the left bank of the St. John in the neighborhood of the Grand Falls. In the course of this not only has no highland dividing waters which run into the St. Lawrence from those which run into the Atlantic been reached, but no common source or reservoir of two streams running in opposite directions.‡ No place has, therefore, been found which by any construction proposed or attempted to be put on the words of the treaty of 1783 can be considered as the northwest angle of Nova Scotia. This point must, in consequence, lie in the further prolongation of the meridian line to the north.

(2) The streams whose title to the name of the northwesternmost head of the Connecticut River is in dispute have been explored, and the line of the highlands has been traced from their sources to the point at which the lines respectively claimed by the two nations diverge from each other.

(3) The line claimed by Messrs. Featherstonhaugh and Mudge, on the part of Great Britain, has been in a great measure explored.

* The highlands of Neversink.
† Captain Byfield.
‡ The levelings carried along this meridian line by means of spirit levels, alluded to in the note at bottom of page 121, passed Mars Hill at a depression of 12 feet *below* the level of the base of the monument which stands (except at seasons of extreme drought) in the water at the source of the St. Croix.

(4) The line of highlands claimed by the United States has, with some small exceptions, been thoroughly examined, and its prolongation as far as the north shore of the Bay of Chaleurs reconnoitered. The parts of the line which have not been actually reached have been seen from a distance, and streams flowing from them crossed and leveled. From the former indication it is probable that the average height of those parts exceeds that of the neighboring parts of the line. From the heights of the streams it is certain that the lowest gaps in the unexplored portion of the line can not be less elevated than 1,000 feet above the level of the sea.

That part of this line of highlands which lies east of the sources of the Rimouski fulfills to the letter the words of the royal proclamation of 1763 and the contemporaneous commission of Governor Wilmot. The first of those instruments defines the mouth of the river St. Lawrence by a line drawn from Cape Rozier to the St. John River (on the Labrador coast), and therefore all to the eastward of that line is "the sea." The height of land thus traced by the commission, rising from the north shore of the Bay des Chaleurs at its western extremity, divides waters which fall into the river St. Lawrence from those which fall into the sea, and is the southern boundary of the Province established by the proclamation of 1763 under the name of Quebec. The identity of the line defined in the proclamation of 1763 and the boundary of the United States in the treaty of 1783 has been uniformly maintained on the part of the United States, and is not merely admitted but strenuously argued for in the report of Messrs. Featherstonhaugh and Mudge.

The undersigned therefore report that they have explored and in a great measure surveyed and leveled a line of highlands in which the northwest angle of Nova Scotia lies, and which in their opinion is the true boundary between the States of Maine and New Hampshire and the British Provinces.

II.—EXAMINATION OF THE ARGUMENT CONTAINED IN THE REPORT OF MESSRS. MUDGE AND FEATHERSTONHAUGH.

The progress which has been made in the first portion of the duties of the commissioners has been set forth in the preceding part of this report.

Although, as will be there seen, the task of running the meridian line of the monument marking the source of the St. Croix and of exploring and surveying the lines of highlands respectively claimed by the Governments of the United States and Great Britain has not been completed, yet enough has been done to furnish materials for an examination of the argument preferred by Messrs. Mudge and Featherstonhaugh in support of the novel form in which the claim of Great Britain has been presented by them.

In the surveys made by direction of the commissioners under the fifth article of the treaty of Ghent the difficult character of the country had prevented any other method of exploration than that of ascending rivers to their sources. It was believed on the part of the United States that the determination of the position of these sources was sufficient for the demarcation of the line of highlands in relation to which the controversy exists, and no attempt was made to meet the British argument by the exhibition of the fact that the lines joining these sources run in some cases along ridges and in other cases pass over elevations to which in any sense of the term the epithet of "highlands" may be justly applied. The denial of this mode of determining the line of highlands by Great Britain has made it important that both the lines claimed by Great Britain and by the United States should be explored and leveled—a task which until recently had not been attempted on either part. The examination of the lines claimed by the two nations, respectively, has been in a great measure accomplished, as will be seen from the reports of the field operations of the commission, while such of these determinations as have a direct bearing on the argument will be cited in their proper place in this report.

It is to be regretted that the document now under consideration exhibits many instances of an unfriendly spirit. Charges of direct and implied fraud are made, and language is used throughout that is irritating and insulting. It is fondly hoped that these passages do not express the sentiments of the British nation, as in a state of feeling such as this report indicates little hope could be entertained of an amicable adjustment of this question. Any inference to be drawn from the language of the report under consideration is contradicted by the official declarations of the British Government, and may therefore be considered as the individual act of the authors, not as the deliberate voice of the nation by which they were employed.

It might have been easy to have retorted similar charges, and thus have excited in the Government of Great Britain feelings of irritation similar to those which pervaded the whole population of the United States on the reception of that report. While, however, it is due to the honor of the United States to declare that no desire of undue aggrandizement has been felt, no claim advanced beyond what a strict construction of their rights will warrant, it is trusted that the pretensions of Great Britain, however unfounded in fact or principle, have been advanced with a like disregard to mere extension of territory, and urged with the same good faith which has uniformly characterized the proceedings of the United States.

It is not to be wondered that the claims of Great Britain have been urged with the utmost pertinacity and supported by every possible form of argument. The territory in question is of great value to her, by covering the only mode of communication which can exist for nearly six months in the year, not only between two valuable colonies, but between the most important of all her possessions and the mother country. The time is not long past when the use of this very communication was not an unimportant part of the means by which that colony was restrained from an attempt to assert its independence. It is not, therefore, surprising that the feelings of British statesmen and of those who desired to win their favor have been more obvious in the several arguments which have appeared on that side of the question than a sober view of the true principles, on which alone a correct opinion of the case can be founded.

To the United States in their collective capacity the territory in dispute is, on the other hand, of comparatively little moment. No other desire is felt throughout the greater part of the Union than that the question should be settled upon just principles. No regret could, therefore, be widely felt if it should be satisfactorily shown that the title of Great Britain to this region is indisputable. But should it be shown, as is beyond all question the fact, that the title is in truth in the United States, national honor forbids that this title should be abandoned. To the States of Maine and Massachusetts, who are the joint proprietors of the unseated lands, the territory is of a certain importance from the value of the land and timber, and to the latter, within whose jurisdiction it falls, as a future means of increasing her relative importance in the Union, and a just and proper feeling on the part of their sister States must prevent their yielding to any unfounded claim or the surrender of any territory to which a title can be established without an equivalent satisfactory to those States.

To show the basis on which the title rests—

It is maintained on the part of the United States that the territory they held on the continent of North America prior to the purchase of Louisiana and the Floridas was possessed by a title derived from their own Declaration of Independence on the 4th of July, 1776, the assertion of that independence in a successful war, and its acknowledgment by Great Britain as a preliminary to any negotiation for a treaty of peace. It is admitted on the part of Great Britain that a territory designated by certain limits was *granted* to the United States in the treaty of 1783. As a matter of national pride, the question whether the territory of the original United States was held by the right of war or by virtue of a grant from the British Crown is not unimportant; as a basis of title it has not the least bearing on the subject. From the date of the treaty of 1783 all pretensions of the British Crown to jurisdiction or property within the limits prescribed by the provisions of that instrument ceased, and when a war arose in 1812 between the two nations it was terminated by the treaty of Ghent, in which the original boundaries were confirmed and acknowledged on both sides.

The treaty of 1783, therefore, is, in reference to this territory, the only instrument of binding force upon the two parties; nor can any other document be with propriety brought forward in the discussion except for the purpose of explaining and rendering definite such of the provisions of that treaty as are obscure or apparently uncertain.

The desire of full and ample illustration, which has actuated both parties, has led to the search among neglected archives for documents almost innumerable, and their force and bearing upon the question have been exhibited in arguments of great ability. Such has been the talent shown in this task of illustration and so copious have been the materials employed for the purpose that the great and only important question, although never lost sight of by the writers themselves, has to the eye of the casual observer been completely hidden. In the report under consideration this distinction between treaties of binding force and documents intended for mere illustration has not been regarded, and the vague as well as obviously inaccurate delineations of a French or a Venetian map maker are gravely held forth as of equal value for a basis of argument as the solemn and ratified acts of the two nations.

In pursuance of this desire of illustration, every known document which could in any form support either claim has been advanced and set forth in the statements laid before His Majesty the King of the Netherlands when acting as umpire under the fifth article of the treaty of Ghent. If not yet given entire to the public,* they are in the possession of both Governments in a printed form, together with the opinion of the arbiter in respect to them; and although it is necessary that the arguments then adduced in favor of the American claim should be in part repeated, and although new illustrations of the correctness of that argument have since been brought to light, the present document will be confined as closely as possible to the provisions of the treaty itself, and will adduce no more of illustration than is barely sufficient to render the terms of that treaty certain and definite.

The boundaries of the United States are described in the treaty of 1783 in the following words:†

"And that *all disputes which might arise in future on the subject of the boundaries of the said United States may be prevented* it is hereby agreed and declared that the following are and shall be their boundaries, viz: *From the northwest angle of Nova Scotia*, viz, *that angle which is formed by a line drawn due north from the source of St. Croix River to the highlands; along the said highlands which divide those rivers that empty themselves into the river St. Lawrence from those which fall into the Atlantic Ocean* to the *northwesternmost* head of Connecticut River; *thence* down along the middle of that river to the forty-fifth degree of north latitude; from thence by a line due west on said latitude until it strikes the river Iroquois, or Cataraquy; thence along the middle of said river into Lake Ontario; through the middle of said lake until it strikes the communication by water between that lake and Lake Erie; thence along the middle of said communication into Lake Erie through the middle of said lake until it arrives at the water communication between that lake and Lake Huron; thence along the middle of said water communication into the Lake Huron; thence through the middle of said lake to the water communication between that

---

*A considerable part of the papers, together with the argument, has been published by Mr. Gallatin in his Right of the United States to the Northeastern Boundary. New York, 1840. 8 vo. pp. 180.

† The words here appearing in italics are not italicized in the original treaty.

lake and Lake Superior; thence through Lake Superior northward of the Isles Royal and Phelipeaux to the Long Lake; thence through the middle of said Long Lake and the water communication between it and the Lake of the Woods to the said Lake of the Woods; thence through the said lake to the most northwestern point thereof, and from thence on a due west course to the river Mississippi; thence by a line to be drawn along the middle of the said river Mississippi until it shall intersect the north-ernmost part of the thirty-first degree of north latitude; south by a line to be drawn due east from the determination of the line last mentioned in the latitude of 31° north of the equator to the middle of the river Apalachicola, or Catahouche; thence along the middle thereof to its junction with the Flint River; thence straight to the head of St. Marys River, and thence down along the middle of St. Marys River to the Atlantic Ocean; east *by a line to be drawn along the middle of the river St. Croix from its mouth in the Bay of Fundy to its source* and from its source *directly north* to the aforesaid highlands which divide the rivers that fall into the Atlantic Ocean from those which fall into the river St. Lawrence; comprehending all islands within 20 leagues of any part of the shores of the United States and lying between lines to be drawn due east from the points where the aforesaid boundaries between Nova Scotia on the one part and East Florida on the other shall respectively touch the Bay of Fundy and the Atlantic Ocean, excepting such islands as now are or heretofore have been within the limits of the said Province of Nova Scotia."

So far as the present question is concerned, five points of discussion are presented by this article of the treaty of 1783:

I. What stream is to be understood by the name of the river St. Croix?

II. The determination of the line due north from the source of that river.

III. What is the position of the northwest angle of Nova Scotia?

IV. The delineation of the line passing through the highlands from that angle to the northwest head of Connecticut River.

V. What is to be considered as the northwestern head of Connecticut River?

I.—RIVER ST. CROIX.

Doubts in respect to the particular river intended to be understood by the name of the St. Croix having arisen, an article was inserted in the treaty of commerce signed in London in November, 1794, by Lord Grenville on the part of Great Britain and by John Jay on the part of the United States.* This article, the fifth of that treaty, pro-vided for the appointment of a joint commission with full powers to decide that ques-tion. This commission was constituted in conformity, and the award was accepted by both Governments.† The river designated in this award became thenceforth the true St. Croix, however erroneous may have been the grounds on which it was decided so to be. When, therefore, in the fourth article of the treaty of Ghent it is declared that the due north line from the source of the St. Croix has not been sur-veyed, and when in this and the other articles of the same treaty all other uncertain parts of the boundary are recited, the validity of the decision of the commissioners under the fifth article of Jay's treaty is virtually acknowledged. Nay, more; the acknowledgment is completed by the stipulation in the second article of the treaty of Ghent that "all territory, places, and possessions taken by either party during the war," with certain exceptions, shall be forthwith restored to their previous possessors.‡ The only exceptions are the islands in Passamaquoddy Bay; and had it been believed that any uncertainty in respect to the adjacent territory existed it would not have been neglected. Nay, more; all the settlements lying within the line claimed by Great Britain before the commission created by the treaty of 1794 had been taken, and were in her actual possession at the time the treaty of Ghent took effect, and were forthwith restored to the jurisdiction of the United States.

*See Note I, pp. 141, 142.   †See Note II, p. 142.   ‡See Note III, pp. 142, 143.

When, also, it became necessary to proceed to the investigation of the second point of the discussion, the agents and surveyors of both parties proceeded as a matter of course to the point marked in 1798 as the source of the St. Croix.* This point is therefore fixed and established beyond the possibility of cavil, and the faith of both Governments is pledged that it shall not be disturbed.

II.—DUE NORTH LINE FROM THE SOURCE OF THE ST. CROIX.

The treaty of 1783 provides that the boundary from the source of the St. Croix shall be drawn "directly north." In relation to this expression no possible doubt can arise. It is neither susceptible of more than a single meaning nor does it require illustration from any extrinsic source. The undersigned, therefore, do not consider that so much of the argument of Messrs. Mudge and Featherstonhaugh as attempts to show that this line ought to be drawn in any other direction than due north requires any reply on the part of the United States. Admitting that the words had been originally used as a mistranslation of terms in the Latin grant of James I to Sir William Alexander, the misconception was equally shared by both parties to the treaty of 1783; and it will be shown hereafter that this misconception, if any, had its origin in British official papers. Were it capable of proof beyond all possibility of denial that the limit of the grant to Sir William Alexander was intended to be a line drawn toward the northwest instead of the north it would not affect the question. So far as that grant was used by American negotiators to illustrate the position of the northwest angle of Nova Scotia it would have failed to fulfill the object, but such failure in illustration does not involve the nullity of the treaty itself.

That the translation which has hitherto been universally received as correct of the terms in the grant to Sir William Alexander is the true one, and that the new construction which is now attempted to be put upon it is inaccurate, will be shown in another place,† where will also be exhibited an error committed in rendering the sense of another part of that instrument. The consideration of the correctness or incorrectness of the several translations can form no part of the present argument. While, therefore, it is denied that Messrs. Mudge and Featherstonhaugh have succeeded in showing that the grant to Sir William Alexander has been mistranslated, it is maintained that an error in the translation of this document can have no effect in setting aside the simple and positive terms of the treaty of 1783. That treaty and its confirmation in the treaty of Ghent must be admitted to be null and void before that line can be drawn in any other direction than "due north."

III.—NORTHWEST ANGLE OF NOVA SCOTIA.

The term northwest angle of Nova Scotia was used in the secret instructions of Congress and is adopted in the treaty of 1783. In the instructions it is named without any explanation, as if it were a point perfectly well known. In one sense it was so, for although it never had been marked by a monument, nor perhaps visited by the foot of man, its position could be laid down upon a map; nay, was so on many existing maps, and the directions for finding it on the ground were clear and explicit. These directions are to be found in the royal proclamation of October, 1763, and in the commission to Montague Wilmot, governor of Nova Scotia, of cotemporaneous date. Any uncertainty in regard to the position of this angle which may have existed in relation to the meaning of the first of these instruments is removed by the act of Parliament of 1774, commonly called the Quebec act.

Before citing these instruments it will be proper to refer to the circumstances under which the two first were issued.

Great Britain, after a successful war, found herself in possession of the whole

---

* See Note IV, p. 143.   † See Note V, pp. 143–147.

eastern side of the continent of North America. So much of this as lay to the south of the St. Lawrence and the forty-fifth parallel of north latitude had been previously made the subject of charters from the British Crown under a claim of right from priority of discovery.* The possession of this wide tract was not uncontested, and various other European nations had attempted to found settlements within the limits of the British charters. In such cases it was held as a matter of law that where the occupation or defense of the territory granted had been neglected the right had ceased, and the country, when recovered by conquest or restored by treaty, was again vested in the Crown, to be made the subject of new grants or governed as a royal colony. Thus, when the settlements made by the Dutch and Swedes, which by the fortune of war had become wholly vested in Holland, were reduced, the Crown exercised its rights by conveying them to the Duke of York, although covered in a great part, if not wholly, by previous charters; and when these countries were again occupied by the Dutch and restored by the treaty of Breda it was thought necessary that the title of the Duke of York should be restored by a fresh grant. In both of these charters to that prince was included the Province of Sagadahock, within whose chartered limits was comprised the territory at present in dispute. This Province, confined on the sea between the rivers St. Croix and Kennebec, had for its opposite limits the St. Lawrence, or, as the grant expresses it, "extending from the river of Kenebeque and so upward by the shortest course to the river Canada northward." The shortest course from the source of the Kennebec to the St. Lawrence is by the present Kennebec road. This grant therefore covered the whole space along the St. Lawrence from about the mouth of the Chaudiere River† to the eastern limit of the grant to Sir William Alexander. By the accession of James II, or, as some maintain, by the act of attainder, it matters not which, this Province reverted to the Crown, and was by it granted, in 1691, to the colony of Massachusetts. In the same charter Nova Scotia also was included. This has been called a war grant, as in fact it was, and the colony of Massachusetts speedily availed themselves of it by conquering the whole of the territory conveyed except the island of Cape Breton. The latter, too, fell before the unassisted arms of the New England Provinces in 1745, at a time when Great Britain was too deeply engaged in the contest of a civil war to give aid either in money or in men to her transatlantic possessions.

The colony of Massachusetts, therefore, could not be charged with any want of energy in asserting her chartered rights to the territory in question. It is, in fact, due to her exertions that both Nova Scotia and New Brunswick came at so early a period into the possession of the British Crown. In 1654 the French settlements as far as Port Royal, at the head of the Bay of Fundy, were reduced by Major Sedgwick, but by the treaty of Breda they were restored to France.

In 1690 Sir William Phips, governor of Massachusetts, with a force of 700 men, raised in that colony, again conquered the country, and although on his return the French dislodged the garrison possession was forthwith resumed by an expedition under Colonel Church. Acadie, however, or Nova Scotia, was ceded again to France by the treaty of Ryswick. After several spirited but unsuccessful attempts during the War of the Succession, General Nicholson, with a force of five regiments, four of which were levied in Massachusetts, reduced Port Royal, and by its capitulation the present Provinces of Nova Scotia and New Brunswick were permanently annexed to the British Crown.‡ Finally the militia of Massachusetts, during the War of 1776, took possession of the territory, and occupied it until the date of the treaty of

---

* Sebastian Cabot, in the employ of Henry VII, discovered the continent of North America 24th June, 1497, and explored it from Hudsons Bay to Florida in 1498. Columbus discovered South America 1st August, 1498, while the voyage of Vespucci, whose name has been given to the conti. nent, was not performed until 1499.—HUMBOLDT.

† See Note VI, p. 147.

‡ Haliburton's History, Vol. I, pp. 83-87.

1783. This occupation was not limited by the St. Croix, or even by the St. John, but included the whole of the southern part of New Brunswick, while the peninsula of Nova Scotia was only preserved to Great Britain by the fortification of the isthmus which unites it to the mainland.*

The recession of Acadie, or Nova Scotia, to France by the treaty of Ryswick divested Massachusetts only of the territory granted her in the charter of 1691 under the latter name. Her war title to Sagadahock was confirmed by a conquest with her own unaided arms; and even the cession of Nova Scotia was a manifest injustice to her, as she was at the moment in full possession of it. It, however, suited the purpose of Great Britain to barter this part of the conquest of that colony for objects of more immediate interest.

Admitting that England did convey a part or the whole of Sagadahock to France under the vague name of Acadie or Nova Scotia,† the conquest by Massachusetts in 1710 renewed her rights to this much at least, and although the Crown appropriated to itself the lion's share of the spoils by making Nova Scotia a royal province, it did not attempt to disturb her possession of Sagadahock. So far from so doing, the commission of the royal governors was limited to the west by the St. Croix, although it was stated in a saving clause that the Province of Nova Scotia extended of right to the Penobscot. From that time until the breaking out of the Revolutionary War, a space of more than sixty years, the Province of Sagadahock was left in the undisturbed possession of Massachusetts under the charter of 1691.

In defiance of this charter the French proceeded to occupy the right bank of the St. Lawrence, which at the time of the capture of Quebec and the cession in the treaty of 1763 was partially held by settlements of Canadians. The Crown therefore acted upon the principle that the right of Massachusetts to the right bank of the St. Lawrence had thus become void, and proceeded by proclamation to form the possessions of France on both banks of the St. Lawrence into a royal colony under the name of the Province of Quebec.

This was not done without a decided opposition on the part of Massachusetts, but any decision in respect to her claims was rendered needless by the breaking out of the War of Independence. It is only proper to remark that this opposition was in fact made and that her claim to the right bank of the St. Lawrence was only abandoned by the treaty of 1783. The country of which it was intended to divest her by the proclamation of 1763 is described in a letter of her agent, Mr. Mauduit, to the general court of that colony as "the narrow tract of land which lies beyond the sources of all your rivers and is watered by those which run into the St. Lawrence."

It is assigned by him as a reason why the Province of Massachusetts should assent to the boundary assigned to the Province of Quebec by the proclamation that "it would not be of any great consequence to you" (Massachusetts), "but is absolutely necessary to the Crown to preserve the continuity of the Province of Quebec." The part of the Province of Quebec whose continuity with the rest of that colony was to be preserved is evidently the district of Gaspe, of which Nova Scotia, a royal colony, was divested by the same proclamation. For this continuity no more was necessary than a road along the St. Lawrence itself, and the reason would have been absurd if applied to any country lying beyond the streams which fall into that river, for up to the present day no communication between parts of Canada exists through any part of the disputed territory. The narrow territory thus advised to be relinquished extends, according to the views of Messrs. Mudge and Featherstonhaugh, from the Great Falls of the St. John to Quebec, a distance in a straight line of 160 miles. It has a figure not far from triangular, of which this line is the perpendicular and the shore of the St. Lawrence from the Chaudiere to the Metis the base. It contains about 16,000 square miles. It would have been a perversion of language in Mr.

*Haliburton's History, Vol. I, pp. 244-289.   †See Note VII, pp. 147, 148.

Mauduit to describe this to his employers as a narrow tract. But the space whose cession he really intended to advise is in every sense a narrow tract, for its length along the St. Lawrence is about 200 miles, and its average breadth to the sources of the streams 30. It contains 6,000 square miles, and is described by him in a manner that leaves no question as to its extent being "watered by streams" which "run into the St. Lawrence." It therefore did not include any country watered by streams which run into the St. John.

It is believed that this is the first instance in which the term *narrow* has ever been applied to a triangle almost right angled and nearly isosceles, and it is not a little remarkable that this very expression was relied upon in the statement to the King of the Netherlands as one of the strongest proofs of the justice of the American claim.

Admitting, however, for the sake of argument, that the Crown did demand this territory, and that the mere advice of an agent without powers was binding on Massachusetts, the fact would have no direct bearing upon the point under consideration. The relinquishment by Massachusetts of the whole of the territory west of the meridian of the St. Croix would not have changed the position of the northwest angle of Nova Scotia, nor the title of the United States collectively under the treaty of 1783 to a boundary to be drawn from that angle, however it might have affected the right of property of that State to the lands within it.

And here it is to be remarked that the Government of the United States is twofold—that of the individual States and that of the Federal Union. It would be possible, therefore, that all right of property in unseated lands within a State's jurisdiction might be in the General Government, and this is in fact the case in all the new States. Even had Massachusetts divested herself of the title (which she has not) the treaty of 1783 would have vested it in the Confederation. She had at least a color of title, under which the Confederation claimed to the boundaries of Nova Scotia on the east and to the southern limits of the Province of Quebec on the north, and this claim was allowed by Great Britain in the treaty of 1783 in terms which are at least admitted to be identical in meaning with those of the proclamation creating the latter Province.*

To illustrate the subject further:

Of the seventeen British colonies in North America, thirteen succeeded in asserting their independence; the two Floridas were conquered and ceded to Spain; while of her magnificent American domain only Quebec and Nova Scotia were left to Great Britain. The thirteen colonies, now independent States, claimed all that part of the continent to the eastward of the Mississippi and north of the bounds of Florida which was not contained within the limits of the last-named colonies, and this claim was fully admitted by the boundary agreed to in the treaty of 1783. Within the limits thus assigned it was well known that there were conflicting claims to parts which had more than once been covered by royal charters; it was even possible that there were portions of the wide territory the right to which was asserted by the United States and admitted by Great Britain that had not been covered by any royal grant; but the jurisdiction in respect to disputed rights and the title to land not conveyed forever ceased to be in the British Crown—first by a successful assertion of independence in arms, and finally by the positive terms of a solemn treaty.

If it should be admitted, for argument's sake, that the claim of Massachusetts, as inherited by the State of Maine, to the disputed territory is unfounded, it is a circumstance that can not enter into a discussion between Great Britain and the United States of America. Massachusetts did claim, under at least the color of a title, not merely to "the highlands," but to the St. Lawrence itself, and the claim was admitted as far as the former by the treaty of 1783. If it should hereafter appear that this claim can not be maintained, the territory which is not covered by her

* Report of Messrs. Featherstonhaugh and Mudge, p. 6.

title, if within the boundary of the treaty of 1783, can not revert to Great Britain, which has ceded its rights to the thirteen independent States, but to the latter in their confederate capacity, and is thus the property of the whole Union.   As well might Great Britain set up a claim to the States of Alabama and Mississippi, which, although claimed by the State of Georgia, were found not to be covered by its royal charter, as to any part of the territory contained within the line defined by the treaty of 1783, under pretense that the rights of Massachusetts are not indefeasible.

While, therefore, it is maintained that whether the title of Massachusetts be valid or not is immaterial to the present question, it may be further urged that not even the shadow of a pretense existed for divesting her of her rights by the proclamation of 1763, except to territory which by neglect she had permitted France to occupy. On this point the French are the best authority, for it can not be pretended that the Crown of England intended in forming the Province of Quebec to go beyond the utmost limits of the claim of France to her colony of Canada.   The assertions on the part of France in the argument preceding the War of 1756 were:

First. That both banks of the St. Lawrence are included in Canada.

Second. That with the exception of Miscou and Cape Breton, her grants extended 10 leagues from the river.

Third. That the commissions of the governors of Canada in the most formal and precise manner extended their jurisdiction to the sources of the rivers which discharge themselves into the St. Lawrence.

Now the distance of 10 French leagues and that of the sources of the rivers, on an average, are nearly identical, and this narrow tract, of which alone the Crown could with any shadow of justice assume the right of disposing, is that of which Massachusetts was intended to be divested by the proclamation of 1763.

It was because Great Britain held that these claims on the part of France were too extensive that the War of 1756 was waged.   In this war at least one-half of the force which under Wolfe took Louisburg and reduced Quebec, and under Amherst forced the French armies in Canada to a capitulation, was raised and paid by the colonies. The creation of the Province of Quebec, covering a part of their chartered limits, was therefore a just subject of complaint.

The bounds assigned to the new Province of Quebec to the south by the proclamation of 7th October, 1763, are as follows:

"The line, crossing the river St. Lawrence and the Lake Champlain in 45° of north latitude, passes along the highlands which divide the rivers that empty themselves into the St. Lawrence from those which fall into the sea, and also along the north coast of the Bay des Chaleurs and the Gulf of St. Lawrence to Cape Rosieres," etc.

In the same month of October, 1763, the limits of the royal Province of Nova Scotia are fixed, in the commission to Governor Wilmot, on the west "by the said river St. Croix to its source, and by a line drawn due north from thence to the southern boundary of our Province of Quebec; to the northward, by the same boundary, as far as the western extremity of the Bay des Chaleurs."

Here, then, we find the first mention in an English dress of the line to be drawn due north from the source of the St. Croix.   There is no evidence that it was a translation of the terms in the grant to Sir William Alexander, but if it were it was made not by Americans, but by Englishmen; and not only made, but set forth under the high authority of the royal sign manual and authenticated by the great seal of the United Kingdom of England and Scotland.

The due north line from the source of the St. Croix, meeting the south bounds of the Province of Quebec, forms two angles.   One of these was the northeast angle of the Province of Sagadahock; the other is the northwest angle of Nova Scotia.   It might be debated which of the streams that fall into Passamaquoddy Bay was the true St. Croix, but such a question could be settled by reference to evidence, and has been thus settled by the award of the commissioners under the fifth article of

Jay's treaty. Among the many branches of a stream it may for a moment be doubted which is to be considered as its principal source, but this can be ascertained by proper methods, and it has been ascertained and marked with a monument by the same commissioners. The tracing of a meridian line may be a difficult operation in practical surveying, but it can be effected by proper instruments and adequate skill, and this task has in fact been performed by one of the present commissioners, after being attempted by the surveyors under the fifth article of the treaty of Ghent. The highlands are defined in the commission of Governor Wilmot and the proclamation of 1763 beyond the possibility of doubt. They are on the north shore of the Bay of Chaleurs as described in the one instrument, and on the western extremity of that bay as described by the other. They can therefore be found, and they have been found.

The Congress of 1779 and the framers of the treaty of 1783 were therefore warranted in speaking of the northwest angle of Nova Scotia as if it were a known point. It could have been laid down with precision on any good map; it could be discovered by the use of adequate methods and the expenditure of a sufficient appropriation; it was, in fact, as well known as the forty-fifth and thirty-second parallels of latitude, which are named in the same article of the treaty, or as the boundaries of very many of the States which had united in the Confederation. These were defined by the course and sources of rivers—by parallels of latitude and circles of longitude, either of indefinite extent or setting out from some prescribed point whose position was to be determined. At the time of making these grants, as in the case before us, many of the boundaries had never been visited by civilized men. Some of these lines had, indeed, been sought and traced upon the ground in pursuance of orders from the privy council of Great Britain or the high court of chancery, and the recollection of the operation was fresh in the memory of both parties. Thus in 1750 it was ordered by the latter tribunal that the boundary on the lower counties on the Delaware (now the State of that name) and the Province of Maryland should be marked out. The boundary was an arc of a circle described around the town of Newcastle, with a given radius, and a meridian line tangent thereto. This was a far more difficult operation than to draw a meridian line from a given point, such as the source of a river. It was thought in 1763 worthy of the attention of the first assistant in the Royal Observatory at Greenwich, and the American Rittenhouse was associated with him. This operation was not only of great contemporary fame, but is still quoted in English books among the data whence we derive our knowledge of the magnitude and figure of the earth. So also the same astronomer (Mason) had but a few years before the War of Independence commenced the tracing of a parallel of latitude from the former line to the westward, thus marking the respective limits of Pennsylvania, Maryland, and Virginia. With such examples before them the framers of the treaty of 1783 were warranted in considering the northwest angle of Nova Scotia as a point sufficiently definite to be made not merely one of the landmarks of the new nation, but the corner at which the description of its boundaries should begin. It has been well remarked by one of the commentators* on the report of Messrs. Featherstonhaugh and Mudge that if the treaty of 1783 be a grant the grantors are bound by rule of law to mark out that corner of their *own land* whence the description of the grant commences. The British Government therefore ought, if it be, as it is maintained on its part, a grant, to have traced the line of highlands dividing their Provinces of Nova Scotia and Canada. Had this been done in conformity with the proclamation of 1763 and the commission to Governor Wilmot, the northwest angle of Nova Scotia would be given by the trace of the meridian of the St. Croix. So far from doing this, the question has been complicated by the denial that the boundaries defined in that proclamation and in the treaty of 1783 were intended to be identical. The argument on this point was so ingenious that the arbiter under the fifth article of the treaty of

* Hon. John Holmes, of Maine.

Ghent did not consider the American case as made out,* and this doubt was the principal ground on which his decision rested. It is therefore an earnest of a more favorable state of feeling that the sophistry with which this fact had been veiled, at least in part, is now withdrawn, and that the commission whose report is under consideration frankly admit this identity.† This admission being made, it is obvious that the origin of the highlands of the treaty must be sought on the north shore of the Bay des Chaleurs and at its western extremity, and it follows that the point where this line of highlands is cut by the meridian of the monument at the source of the St. Croix is the northwest angle of Nova Scotia of the treaty of 1783, and must lie to the north of the Restigouche, or in the very spot claimed by the United States.

The British Government has not only failed in marking out the corner of their territory at which the boundary of the United States begins, but has in practice adopted a very different point as the northwest angle of the Province of New Brunswick, which now occupies the place of ancient Nova Scotia in its contiguity to the American lines. Up to the time of the discussion before the King of the Netherlands the commissions of the governors of New Brunswick had been, so far as the western and northern boundaries are concerned, copies of that to Governor Wilmot. The undersigned have no means of ascertaining when or how the form of these commissions was changed, but it was found during the exploration of the country that the jurisdiction of New Brunswick, limited at least to the north of the St. John by the exploring meridian line, did not leave the Bay of Chaleurs at its western extremity and follow thence the old bounds of the Province of Quebec. It, on the contrary, was ascertained that it was limited by the Restigouche as far as the confluence of its southwestern branch, formerly known by the name of Chacodi, and thence followed the latter up to the point where it is crossed by the exploring meridian line. On all the territory thus severed from the ancient domain of Nova Scotia permits to cut timber were found to have been issued by Canadian authorities, and the few settlers derived their titles to land from the same source.

Although this demarcation involves a double deviation from the proclamation of 1763 (first, in following a river instead of highlands; second, in taking a small branch instead of pursuing the main supply of the Bay of Chaleurs), the northwest angle of Nova Scotia may be considered as at last fixed by British authority at a point many miles north of the point claimed to be such in the statements laid before the King of the Netherlands on the part of Great Britain, and 48 miles to the north of where the line of "abraded highlands" of Messrs. Featherstonhaugh and Mudge crosses the St. John. Were it not that the American claim would be weakened by any change in the strong ground on which it has always rested, it might be granted that this is in fact the long-lost northwest angle of Nova Scotia, and the highlands allowed to be traced from that point through the sources of the branches of the St. John and the St. Lawrence.

In proof of the position now assigned to this angle of New Brunswick, and consequently of ancient Nova Scotia, in the absence of documents which the archives of Great Britain alone can furnish, the map published by the Society for the Encouragement of Useful Knowledge, the several maps of the surveyor-general of the Province of Canada, and the most recent map of the Provinces of Nova Scotia and New Brunswick, by John Wyld, geographer to the Queen of Great Britain, may be cited.

It may therefore be concluded that the northwest angle of Nova Scotia is no longer an unknown point. It can be found by a search conducted in compliance with the proclamation of 1763 and the contemporaneous commission of Governor Wilmot, and the researches of the present commission show that it can not be far distant from the point originally assigned to it in the exploring meridian line. The identity of the first of these documents with the boundary of the treaty of 1783 is admitted,

---

* See Note VIII, p. 148.

† Report of Messrs. Featherstonhaugh and Mudge, pp. 6, 23.

and the latter is word for word the same with the description of the eastern boundary of the United States in the same treaty. Moreover, a northwest angle has been assigned to the Province of New Brunswick by British authority, which, did it involve no dereliction of principle, might without sensible loss be accepted on the part of the United States.

IV.—HIGHLANDS OF THE TREATY OF 1783.

The highlands of the treaty of 1783 are described as those "which divide those rivers that empty themselves into the river St. Lawrence from those which fall into the Atlantic Ocean." It has been uniformly and consistently maintained on the part of the United States that by the term "highlands" was intended what is in another form of the same words called the height of land. The line of highlands in this sense was to be sought by following the rivers described in the treaty to their source and drawing lines between these sources in such manner as to divide the surface waters. It was believed that the sources of such rivers as the Connecticut and the St. John must lie in a country sufficiently elevated to be entitled to the epithet of highlands, although it should appear on reaching it that it had the appearance of a plain. Nay, it was even concluded, although, as now appears, incorrectly—and it was not feared that the conclusion would weaken the American argument—that the line from the northwest angle of Nova Scotia, at least as far as the sources of Tuladi, did pass through a country of that description. Opposite ground was taken in the argument of Great Britain by her agent, but however acute and ingenious were the processes of reasoning by which this argument was supported, it remained in his hands without application, for the line claimed by him on the part of his Government was one having the same physical basis for its delineation as that claimed by the agent of the United States, namely, one joining the culminating points of the valleys in which streams running in opposite directions took their rise. The argument appears to have been drawn while he hoped to be able to include Katahdin and the other great mountains in that neighborhood in his claimed boundary, and he does not appear to have become aware how inapplicable it was in every sense to the line by which he was, for want of a better, compelled to abide. The British Government, however, virtually abandoned the construction of their agent in the convention signed in London the 27th September, 1827.*

In this it was stipulated that Mitchell's and Map A should be admitted to the exclusion of all others "as the only maps that shall be considered as evidence" of the topography of the country, and in the latter of these maps, constructed under the joint direction of the British and American negotiators by the astronomer of the British Government, it was agreed that nothing but the water courses should be represented. Finally, it was admitted in the report of Messrs. Featherstonhaugh and Mudge that the terms highlands and height of land are identical. The decision of the King of the Netherlands, to which Great Britain gave her assent in the first instance, recognizes the correctness of the views entertained in the American statements.† All discussion on this subject is, however, rendered unnecessary by the knowledge which the undersigned have obtained of the country. The line surveyed by them not only divides rivers, but possesses in a preeminent degree the character by which in the British argument highlands are required to be distinguished.

It is sufficient for the present argument that the identity of the lines pointed out by the proclamation of 1763 and the act of 1774 with the boundary of the treaty of 1783 be admitted. Such has been the uniform claim of the Government of the United States and the State of Massachusetts, and such is the deliberate verdict of the British commissioners.‡ The words of the proclamation of 1763 have already

---

* See Note IX, p. 148.   † See Note X, pp. 148, 149.
‡ Report of Featherstonhaugh and Mudge, pp. 6, 23.

been cited. By reference to them it will be seen that the origin of "the highlands" is to be sought on the *north* shore of the Bay of Chaleurs. If they are not to be found there, a gap exists in the boundary of the proclamation, which it is evident could not have been intended. It has been thought by some that the gap did actually exist, but this idea was founded on an imperfect knowledge of the country. The Bay of Chaleurs seems, in fact, to have been better known to the framers of the proclamation of 1763 and the act of 1774 than to any subsequent authorities, whether British or American. Researches made in the year 1840 show that at the head of the tide of the Bay of Chaleurs a mountain rises immediately on the northern bank, which from its imposing appearance has been called by the Scotch settlers at its foot Ben Lomond. This, indeed, has by measurement been found to be no more than 1,024 feet in height, but no one can deny its title to the name of a highland. From this a continuous chain of heights has been ascertained to exist, bounding in the first instance the valley of the Matapediac to the sources of that stream, which they separate from those of the Metis. The height of land then passes between the waters of Metis and Restigouche, and, bending around the sources of the latter to the sources of the Rimouski, begins there to separate waters which fall into the St. Lawrence from those which fall into the St. John, which they continue to do as far as the point where they merge in the line admitted by both parties.

These highlands have all the characteristics necessary to constitute them the highlands of the treaty. Throughout their whole northern and western slopes flow streams which empty themselves into the St. Lawrence. Beginning at the Bay of Chaleurs, they in the first place divide, as it is necessary they should, waters which fall into that bay; they next separate the waters of Restigouche from those of Metis; they then make a great detour to the south and inclose the valley of Rimouski, separating its waters from those of Matapediac and Restigouche, the Green River of St. John and Tuladi; they next perform a circuit around Lake Temiscouata, separating its basin from those of the Otty and Trois Pistoles, until they reach the Temiscouata portage at Mount Paradis. This portage they cross five times, and finally, bending backward to the north, inclose the stream of the St. Francis, whose waters they divide from those of Trois Pistoles, Du Loup, and the Green River of the St. Lawrence. Leaving the Temiscouata portage at the sixteenth milepost, a region positively mountainous is entered, which character continues to the sources of the Etchemin. It there assumes for a short space the character of a rolling country, no point in which, however, is less than 1,200 feet above the level of the sea. It speedily resumes a mountainous character, which continues unaltered to the sources of the Connecticut.

Now it is maintained that all the streams and waters which have been named as flowing from the southern and eastern sides of this line are in the intended sense of the treaty of 1783 rivers which empty themselves into the Atlantic. The first argument adduced in support of this position is that the framers of that treaty, having, as is admitted, Mitchell's map before them, speak only of two classes of rivers—those which discharge themselves into the St. Lawrence River and those which fall into the Atlantic Ocean; yet upon this map were distinctly seen the St. John and the Restigouche. The latter, indeed, figures twice—once as a tributary to the Bay of Miramichi and once as flowing to the Bay of Chaleurs.* It can not reasonably be pretended that men honestly engaged in framing an article to prevent "all disputes which might arise in future" should have intentionally passed over and left undefined these important rivers, when by the simplest phraseology they might have described them had they believed that in any future time a question could have arisen whether they were included in one or the other of the two classes of rivers they named. Had it been intended that the due north line should have stopped short of the St. John, the highlands must have been described as those which divide rivers

*See Note XI, p. 149.

which fall into the St. Lawrence *and the St. John* from those which fall into the Atlantic Ocean. The mouth of the St. Lawrence had been defined in the proclamation of 1763 by a line drawn from the river St. John (on the Labrador coast) to Cape Rozier. If, then, it had been intended that the meridian line should not have crossed the Restigouche, the phraseology must have been highlands which divide rivers which fall into the river *and* Gulf of St. Lawrence from those which fall into the Atlantic Ocean. Where such obvious modes of expressing either of these intentions existed, it is not to be believed that they would have been omitted; but had they been proposed to be introduced the American negotiators would have been compelled by their instructions to refuse them. Such expressions would have prescribed a boundary different not only in fact, but in terms, from that of the proclamation of 1763 and the contemporaneous commission to Governor Wilmot. Either, then, the British plenipotentiaries admitted the American claim to its utmost extent or they fraudulently assented to terms with the intention of founding upon them a claim to territory which if they had openly asked for must have been denied them. The character of the British ministry under whose directions that treaty was made forbids the belief of the latter having been intended. The members of that ministry had been when in opposition the constant advocates of an accommodation with the colonies or of an honorable peace after all hopes of retaining them in their allegiance had ceased. They showed on coming into power a laudable anxiety to put an end to the profitless effusion of human blood, and they wisely saw that it would be of more profit to their country to convert the new nation into friends by the free grant of terms which sooner or later must have been yielded than to widen the breach of kindred ties by an irritating delay. The debates which ensued in the British Parliament when the terms of the treaty were made known show the view which the party that had conducted the war entertained of this question. The giving up of the very territory now in dispute was one of the charges made by them against their successors, and that it had been given up by the treaty was not denied. Nay, the effect of this admission was such as to leave the administration in a minority in the House of Commons, and thus became at least one of the causes of the resignation of the ministry * by which the treaty had been made. At this very moment more maps than one were published in London which exhibit the construction then put upon the treaty by the British public. The boundary exhibited upon these maps is identical with that which the United States now claim and have always claimed.

The full avowal that the boundary of the treaty of 1783 and of the proclamation of 1763 and act of 1774 are identical greatly simplifies the second argument. It has been heretofore maintained on the part of Great Britain that the word "sea" of the two latter-named instruments was not changed in the first to "Atlantic Ocean" without an obvious meaning. All discussion on this point is obviated by the admission. But it is still maintained that the Bay of Fundy is not a part of the Atlantic Ocean because it happens to be named in reference to the St. Croix in the same article of the treaty. To show the extent to which such an argument, founded on a mere verbal quibble, may be carried, let it be supposed that at some future period two nations on the continent of North America shall agree on a boundary in the following terms: By a line drawn through the Mississippi from its mouth in the Gulf of Mexico to its source; thence a parallel of latitude until it meet the highlands which divide the waters that empty themselves into the Pacific Ocean from those which fall into the Atlantic. Could it be pretended that because the mouth of the Mississippi is said to be in the Gulf of Mexico the boundary must be transferred from the Rocky Mountains to the Alleghanies? Yet this would be as reasonable as the pretensions so long set up by the British agents and commissioners.

It can not be denied that the line claimed by the United States fulfills at least one

* Hansard's Parliamentary Register for 1783.

of the conditions. The streams which flow from one side of it fall without exception into the river St. Lawrence. The adverse line claimed by Great Britain in the reference to the King of the Netherlands divides until within a few miles of Mars Hill waters which fall into the St. John from those of the Penobscot and Kennebec. The latter do not discharge their waters directly into the ocean, but Sagadahock and Penobscot bays intervene, and the former falls into the Bay of Fundy; hence, according to the argument in respect to the Bay of Fundy, this line fulfills neither condition.

The line of Messrs. Featherstonhaugh and Mudge is even less in conformity to the terms of the treaty. In order to find mountains to form a part of it they are compelled to go south of the source of branches of the Penobscot; thence from mountains long well known, at the sources of the Alleguash, well laid down on the rejected map of Mr. Johnson, it becomes entangled in the stream of the Aroostook, which it crosses more than once. In neither part does it divide waters at all. It then, as if to make its discrepancy with the line defined in the proclamation of 1763 apparent, crosses the St. John and extends to the *south* shore of the Bay of Chaleurs, although that instrument fixes the boundary of the Province of Quebec on the north shore of the bay. In this part of its course it divides waters which fall into the said bay from those which fall into the St. John. But the proclamation with whose terms this line is said to be identical directs that the highlands shall divide waters which fall into the St. Lawrence from those which fall into the sea. If the branches of the Bay of Chaleurs fulfill the first condition, which, however, is denied, the St. John must fulfill the latter. It therefore falls into the Atlantic Ocean, and as the identity of the boundary of the treaty with that of the proclamation of 1763 and act of 1774 is admitted, then is the St. John an Atlantic river, and the line claimed by the United States fulfills both conditions, and is the only line to the west of the meridian of the St. Croix which can possibly do so.

The choice of a line different from that presented to the choice of the King of the Netherlands is no new instance of the uncertainty which has affected all the forms in which Great Britain has urged her claim.

In fact, nothing shows more conclusively the weakness of the ground on which the British claim rests than the continual changes which it has been necessary to make in order to found any feasible argument upon it.* In the discussion of 1798 it was maintained on the part of Great Britain that the meridian line must cross the St. John River; in the argument before the commissioners under the fifth article of the treaty of Ghent it was denied that it ever could have been the intention of the framers of the treaty of 1783 that it should. Yet the mouthpiece by which both arguments were delivered was one and the same person. The same agent chose as the termination of what he attempted to represent as a continuous range of hills an isolated mountain, Mars Hill; and the commissioners whose report is under consideration place a range of abraded highlands, "the maximum axis of elevation," in a region over which British engineers have proposed to carry a railroad as the most level and lowest line which exists between St. Andrews and Quebec.†

On the other hand, the American claim, based on the only practicable interpretation of the treaty of 1783, has been consistent throughout: "Let the meridian line be extended until it meets the southern boundary of the Province of Quebec, as defined by the proclamation of 1763 and the act of Parliament of 1774."

No argument can be drawn against the American claim from the secret instructions of Congress dated August, 1779. All that is shown by these instructions is the willingness to accept a more convenient boundary—one defined by a great natural feature, and which would have rendered the difficult operation of tracing the line

---

* See Note XII, p. 149.
† Prospectus of St. Andrews and Quebec Railroad, 1836; and Survey of Captain Yule, 1835.

of highlands and that of determining the meridian of the St. Croix by astronomic methods unnecessary. The words of the instructions are:

"And east by a line to be drawn along the middle of the St. John from its source to its mouth in the Bay of Fundy, *or* by a line to be settled and adjusted between that part of the State of Massachusetts Bay formerly called the Province of Maine and the colony of Nova Scotia, agreeably to their respective rights, comprehending all islands within 20 leagues of the shores of the United States and lying between lines to be drawn due east from the points where the aforesaid boundaries between Nova Scotia on the one part and East Florida on the other part shall respectively touch the Bay of Fundy and the Atlantic Ocean."

The proposal in the first alternative was to appearance a perfectly fair one. From an estimate made by Dr. Tiarks, the astronomer of Great Britain under the fifth article of the treaty of Ghent, in conformity with directions from Colonel Barclay, the British commissioner, it was ascertained that the whole disputed territory contained 10,705 square miles; that the territory bounded by the St. John to its mouth contained 707 square miles less, or 9,998 square miles. The difference at the time was probably believed to be insensible. The first alternative was, however, rejected by Great Britain, and obviously on grounds connected with a difference in supposed advantage between the two propositions. The American commissioners were satisfied that they could urge no legal claim along the coast beyond the river St. Croix; they therefore treated on the other alternative in their instructions—the admitted limits between Massachusetts and Nova Scotia. Even in the former alternative, Nova Scotia would still have had a northwest angle, for the very use of the term shows that by the St. John its northwestern and not the southwestern branch was intended.

At that moment, when the interior of the country was unknown, the adoption of the St. John as the boundary, even admitting that the Walloostook, its southwestern branch, is the main stream, would have given to the United States a territory of more immediate value than that they now claim. For this very reason the proposition was instantly rejected by Great Britain, and the State of Massachusetts was forced to be contented with the distant region now in debate—a region then believed to be almost inaccessible and hardly fit for human habitation.

Even now, were there not vested private rights on both sides which might render such a plan difficult of application, the undersigned would not hesitate to recommend that this line should be accepted in lieu of the one which is claimed under the treaty of 1783.

It is finally obvious, from the most cursory inspection of any of the maps of the territory in question, that the line claimed for Great Britain in the argument before the King of the Netherlands fulfills no more than one of the two conditions, while that of Messrs. Featherstonhaugh and Mudge fulfills neither; and as the line claimed on the part of the United States is denied to be capable of meeting the terms of the treaty of 1783 by Great Britain, there is no line that, in conformity with the British argument, can be drawn within the disputed territory or its vicinity that will comply with either of the conditions. This is as well and as distinctly shown in the map of Mitchell as in the map of the British commission. It would therefore appear, if these views be correct, that the framers of the treaty of 1783 went through the solemn farce of binding their respective Governments to a boundary which they well knew did not and could not exist.

V.—NORTHWEST HEAD OF CONNECTICUT RIVER.

The true mode of determining the most northwesterly of any two given points need no longer be a matter of discussion. It has already been a matter adjudicated and assented to by both Governments, in the case of the Lake of the Woods. The point to be considered as most to the northwest is that which a ruler laid on a map drawn according to Mercator's projection in a direction northeast and southwest and moved parallel to itself toward the northwest would last touch. In this view of the subject the Eastern Branch of the Connecticut, which forms the lake of that name, is excluded, for its source, so far from lying to the northwest of those of the other two branches which have been explored, actually lies to the south of the source of the Indian Stream. The question must therefore lie between the two others, and it is as yet impossible to decide which of them is best entitled to the epithet, as their sources lie very nearly in the same northeast and southwest rhomb line. Another circumstance would, however, render the decision between them easy. The forty-fifth parallel of latitude, as laid out by the surveyors of the Provinces of Quebec and New York in conformity with the proclamation of 1763, crosses Halls Stream above its junction with the united current of the other two. In this case the latter is the Connecticut River of the treaty of 1783, and Halls Stream, which has not yet joined it, must be excluded. The parallel, as corrected by the united operations of the British and American astronomers under the fifth article of the treaty of Ghent, does not touch Halls Stream, and the Connecticut River, to which it is produced, is the united current of the three streams. If, then, the corrected parallel should become the boundary between the United States and the British Provinces, Halls Stream must become one of those the claim of whose source to the title of the north-westernmost head of Connecticut River is to be examined. And here it may be suggested, although with the hesitation that is natural in impeaching such high authority, that the commissioners under the fifth article of the treaty of Ghent in all probability misconstrued that instrument when they reopened the question of the forty-fifth parallel. It can not be said that the forty-fifth degree of latitude had "*not been surveyed*," when it is notorious that it had been traced and marked throughout the whole extent from St. Regis to the bank of the Connecticut River.

In studying, for the purpose of illustration, the history of this part of the boundary line it will be found that a change was made in it by the Quebec act of 1774. The proclamation of 1763 directs the forty-fifth parallel to be continued only until it meets highlands, while in that bill the Connecticut River is made the boundary of the Province of Quebec. Now the earlier of these instruments was evidently founded upon the French claim to extend their possession of Canada 10 leagues from the St. Lawrence River, and from the citadel of Quebec, looking to the south, are seen mountains whence rivers flow to the St. Lawrence. On their opposite slope there was a probability that streams might flow to the Atlantic. These mountains, however, are visibly separated from those over which the line claimed by the United States runs by a wide gap. This is the valley of the Chaudiere; and the St. Francis also rises on the southeastern side of these mountains and makes its way through them. It is not, therefore, in any sense a dividing ridge. Yet under the proclamation of 1763 the Provinces of New York and New Hampshire claimed and were entitled to the territory lying behind it, which is covered by their royal charters. The Quebec act, it would appear, was intended to divest them of it, and according to the construction of the treaty of 1783 now contended for the United States acquiesced in this diminution of the territory of those members of the Union. If, however, it be true, as maintained by Messrs. Featherstonhaugh and Mudge, that the highlands seen to the south of Quebec are a portion of the ridge seen from southeast to northeast, and if, as they maintain, so deep and wide a valley as that of the St. John is no disruption of the continuity of highlands, it would be possible to show that the highlands of the treaty of 1783 are made up of these two ridges of mountains and that the United States is entitled to the whole of the eastern townships. This range of highlands would coincide with the terms of the proclamation of 1763 by terminating on the north shore of the Bay of Chaleurs, while the abraded highlands of Messrs. Featherstonhaugh and Mudge terminate on its south shore. In fact, there is no step in their argument which might not be adduced to support this claim, nor any apparent absurdity in preferring it which would not find its parallel in one or other of the positions they assume.

In this view of the history of this part of the line it becomes evident, however, that in divesting the Provinces of New York and New Hampshire by the Quebec act of territory admitted to belong to them in the proclamation of 1763 the British Parliament must have intended to make the encroachment as small as possible, and the first important branch of the Connecticut met with in tracing the forty-fifth parallel must have been intended. This intention is fully borne out by the words of the treaty of 1783, which chose from among the branches of the Connecticut that whose source is farthest to the northwest.

It has therefore been shown in the foregoing statement—

1. That the river to be considered as the St. Croix and its true source have been designated by a solemn act, to which the good faith of the majesty of Great Britain and of the people of the United States is pledged, and can not now be disturbed.

2. That the boundary line must, in compliance with the provisions of the treaty of 1783, be drawn due north from the source of that river, and in no other direction whatever.

3. That the northwest angle of Nova Scotia was a point sufficiently known at the date of the treaty of 1783 to be made the starting point of the boundary of the United States; that it was both described in the treaty and defined, without being named in previous official acts of the British Government, in so forcible a manner that no difficulty need have existed in finding it.

4. That the line of highlands claimed by the United States is, as the argument on the part of Great Britain has maintained it ought to be, in a mountainous region, while that proposed by Messrs. Featherstonhaugh and Mudge does not possess this character; that it is also, in the sense uniformly maintained by the United States, the height of land, which that of Messrs. Featherstonhaugh and Mudge is not; that it fulfills in every sense the conditions of the proclamation of 1763, the Quebec act of 1774, and the treaty of 1783, which no other line that can possibly be drawn in the territory in question can perform.

5. That as far as the Indian Stream and that flowing through Lake Connecticut are concerned, the source of the former must in the sense established by the assent of both parties be considered as the northwestern source of the Connecticut River, but that if the old demarcation of the forty-fifth parallel be disturbed the question must lie between the sources of Halls and of Indian streams.

All which is respectfully submitted.

> JAS. RENWICK,
> JAMES D. GRAHAM,
> A. TALCOTT,
> *Commissioners.*

Note I.

[Treaty of 1794, Article V.]

Whereas doubts have arisen what river was truly intended under the name of the river St. Croix mentioned in the said treaty of peace, and forming a part of the boundary therein described, that question shall be referred to the final decision of commissioners to be appointed in the following manner, viz:

One commissioner shall be named by His Majesty and one by the President of the United States, by and with the advice and consent of the Senate thereof, and the said two commissioners shall agree on the choice of a third, or, if they can not so agree, they shall each propose one person, and of the two names so proposed one shall be drawn by lot in the presence of the two original commissioners; and the three commissioners so appointed shall be sworn impartially to examine and decide the said question according to such evidence as shall respectively be laid before them on the part of the British Government and of the United States. The said commissioners shall meet at Halifax, and shall have power to adjourn to such other place or places as they shall think fit. They shall have power to appoint a secretary and to employ such surveyors or other persons as they shall judge necessary. The said commissioners shall, by a declaration under their hands and seals, decide what river is the river St. Croix intended by the treaty. The said declaration shall contain a description of the said river and shall particularize the latitude and longitude of its mouth and of its source. Duplicates of this declaration and of the statements of their accounts and of the journal of their proceedings shall be delivered by them to the agent of His Majesty and to the agent of the United States who may be respectively appointed and authorized to manage the business on behalf of the respective Governments. And both parties agree to consider such decision as final and conclusive, so as that the same shall never thereafter be called into question or made the subject of dispute or difference between them.

Note II.

Declaration of the commissioners under the fifth article of the treaty of 1794 between the United States and Great Britain, respecting the true river St. Croix, by Thomas Barclay, David Howell, and Egbert Benson, commissioners appointed in pursuance of the fifth article of the treaty of amity, commerce, and navigation between His Britannic Majesty and the United States of America finally to decide the question "What river was truly intended under the name of the river St. Croix mentioned in the treaty of peace between His Majesty and the United States, and forming a part of the boundary therein described?"

DECLARATION.

We, the said commissioners, having been sworn impartially to examine and decide the said question according to such evidence as should respectively be laid before us on the part of the British Government and of the United States, respectively, appointed and authorized to manage the business on behalf of the respective Governments, have decided, and hereby do decide, the river hereinafter particularly described and mentioned to be the river truly intended under the name of the river St. Croix in the said treaty of peace, and forming a part of the boundary therein described; that is to say, the mouth of the said river is in Passamaquoddy Bay at a point of land called Joes Point, about 1 mile northward from the northern part of St. Andrews Island, and in the latitude of 45° 5′ and 5″ north, and in the longitude of 67° 12′ and 30″ west from the Royal Observatory at Greenwich, in Great Britain, and 3° 54′ and 15″ east from Harvard College, in the University of Cambridge, in the State of Massachusetts; and the course of the said river up from its said mouth is northerly to a point of land called the Devils Head; then, turning the said point, is westerly to where it divides into two streams, the one coming from the westward and the other from the northward, having the Indian name of Cheputnatecook, or Chebuitcook, as the same may be variously spelt; then up the said stream so coming from the northward to its source, which is at a stake near a yellow-birch tree hooped with iron and marked S. T. and J. H., 1797, by Samuel Titcomb and John Harris, the surveyors employed to survey the above-mentioned stream coming from the northward.

Note III.

[Article V of the treaty of Ghent, 1814.]

Whereas neither that point of the highlands lying due north from the source of the river St. Croix, and designated in the former treaty of peace between the two powers as the northwest angle of Nova Scotia, nor the northwesternmost head of Connecticut River has yet been ascertained; and whereas that part of the boundary line between the dominions of the two powers which extends from the source of the river St. Croix directly north to the above-mentioned northwest angle of Nova Scotia; thence along the said highlands which divide those rivers that empty themselves into the river St. Lawrence from those which fall into the Atlantic Ocean, to the northwesternmost head of Connecticut River; thence down along the middle of that river to the forty-fifth degree of north latitude; thence by a line due west on said latitude until it strikes the river Iroquois, or Cataraquy, has not yet been surveyed, it is agreed that for these several purposes two commissioners shall be appointed, sworn, and authorized to act exactly in the manner directed with respect to those mentioned in the next preceding article, unless otherwise specified in the present article. The said commissioners shall meet at St. Andrews, in the Province of New Brunswick, and shall have power to adjourn to such other place or places as they shall think fit. The said commissioners shall have power to ascertain and determine the points above mentioned in conformity with the provisions of the said treaty of peace of 1783, and shall cause the boundary aforesaid, from the source of the river St. Croix to the river Iroquois, or Cataraquy, to be surveyed and marked according to the said provisions. The said commissioners shall make a map of the said boundary, and annex to it a declaration under their hands and seals certifying it to be the true map of the said boundary, and particularizing the latitude and longitude of the northwest angle of Nova Scotia, of the northwesternmost head of Connecticut River, and of such other points of the said boundary as they may deem proper; and both parties agree to consider such map and declaration as finally and conclusively fixing the said boundary. And in the event of the said two commissioners differing, or both or either of them refusing, declining, or willfully omitting to act, such reports, declarations, or statements shall be made by them or either of them, and such reference to a friendly sovereign or state shall be made in all respects as in the latter part of the fourth article is contained, and in as full a manner as if the same was herein repeated.

Note IV.

The point originally chosen by the commissioners in 1798 as the source of the St. Croix was to all appearance the act of an umpire who wished to reconcile two contending claims by giving to each party about half the matter in dispute. No one who compares Mitchell's map with that of Messrs. Featherstonhaugh and Mudge can fail to recognize in the St. Croix of the former the Magaguadavic of the latter. That this was the St. Croix intended by the framers of the treaty of 1783 was maintained, and, it may be safely asserted, proved on the American side. On the other hand, it was ascertained that the river called St. Croix by De Monts was the Schoodiac; and the agent of Great Britain insisted that the letter of the instrument was to be received as the only evidence, no matter what might have been the intentions of the framers. The American argument rested on the equity of the case, the British on the strict legal interpretation of the document. The commissioners were divided in opinion, each espousing the cause of his country. In this position of things the umpire provided for in the treaty of 1794 was chosen, and in the United States it has always been believed unfortunately for her pretensions. A lawyer of eminence, who had reached the seat of a judge, first of a State court and then of a tribunal of the General Government, he prided himself on his freedom from the influence of feeling in his decisions. As commissioner for the settlement of the boundary between the States of New York and Vermont, he had offended the former, of which he was a native, by admitting the claim of the latter in its full extent, and it was believed that he would rather encounter the odium of his fellow-citizens than run the risk of being charged with partiality toward them. Colonel Barclay, the British commissioner, who concurred in choosing him as umpire, had been his schoolfellow and youthful associate, and it is believed in the United States that he concurred in, if he did not prompt, the nomination from a knowledge of this feature of character. Had he, as is insinuated by Messrs. Featherstonhaugh and Mudge, been inclined to act with partiality toward his own country, he had most plausible grounds for giving a verdict in her favor, and that he did not found his decisions upon them is evidence of a determination to be impartial, which his countrymen have said was manifested in a leaning to the opposite side. Those who suspect him of being biased by improper motives must either be ignorant of the circumstances of the case or else incapable of estimating the purity of the character of Egbert Benson. His award, however, has nothing to do with the question, as it was never acted upon. Both parties were dissatisfied with the conclusions at which he arrived, and in consequence a conventional line in which both concurred was agreed upon, and the award of the commissioners was no more than a formal act to make this convention binding.

If, then, both Governments should think it expedient to unsettle the vested rights which have arisen out of the award of 1798, there is a strong and plausible ground on which the United States may claim the Magaguadavic as their boundary, and the meridian line of its source will throw the valley of the St. John from Woodstock to the Grand Falls within the limits of the State of Maine. While, therefore, it is maintained that it would violate good faith to reopen the question, there is good reason to hope that an impartial umpire would decide it so as to give the United States the boundary formerly claimed.

Note V.

The angle made by the southern boundary of the Province of Quebec with the due north line from the source of the St. Croix first appeared in an English dress in the commission to Governor Wilmot. This was probably intended to be identical in its meaning with the terms in the Latin grant to Sir William Alexander, although there is no evidence to that effect. If, therefore, it were a false translation, the error has been committed on the side of Great Britain, and not on that of the United States. But it is not a false translation, as may be shown to the satisfaction of the merest tyro in classical literature.

The words of the grant to Sir William Alexander, as quoted by Messrs. Featherstonhaugh and Mudge, are as follows, viz:

"Omnes et singulas terras continentis ac insulas situatas et jacentes in America intra caput seu promontorium communiter *Cap de Sable* appellat, jacen. prope latitudinem quadraginta trium graduum aut eo circa ab equinoctiali linea versus septentrionem, a quo promontorio versus littus maris tenden. ad occidentem ad stationem Sanctæ Mariæ navium vulgo *Sanctmareis Bay.* Et deinceps, versus septentrionem per directam lineam introitum sive ostium magnæ illius stationis navium trajicien. quæ excurrit in terræ orientalem plagam inter regiones Suriquorum et Etcheminorum vulgo *Suriquois* et *Etchemines* ad fluvium vulgo nomine *Sanctæ Crucis* appellat. Et ad scaturiginem remotissimam sive fontem ex occidentali parte ejusdem qui se primum predicto fluvio immiscet. Unde per imaginariam directam lineam quæ pergere per terram seu currere versus septentrionem concipietur ad proximam navium stationem, fluvium, vel scaturiginem in magno fluvio de Canada sese exonerantem. Et ab eo pergendo versus orientem per maris oris littorales ejusdem fluvii de Canada ad fluvium, stationem navium, portum, aut littus communiter nomine de Gathepe vel Gaspee notum et appellatum."

The authentic Latin copy of the grant to Sir William Alexander, as communicated officially by the British Government, contains no commas, and would read as follows:

"Omnes et singulas terras continentis ac insulas situatas et jacentes in America intra caput seu promontorium communiter Cap de Sable appellat. Jacen. prope latitudinem quadraginta trium graduum aut eo circa ab equinoctiali linea versus septentrionem a quo promontorio versus littus maris tenden. ad occidentem ad stationem Sanctæ Mariæ navium vulgo Sanctmareis Bay. Et deinceps versus septentrionem per directam lineam introitum sive ostium magnæ illius stationis navium trajicien. quæ excurrit in terræ orientalem plagam inter regiones Suriquorum et Etcheminorum vulgo Suriquois et Etechemines ad fluvium vulgo nomine Sanctæ Crucis appellat. Et ad scaturiginem remotissimam sive fontem ex occidentali parte ejusdem qui se primum predicto fluvio immiscet. Unde per imaginariam directam lineam quæ pergere per terram seu currere versus septentrionem concipietur ad proximam navium stationem fluvium vel scaturiginem in magno fluvio de Canada sese exonerantem. Et ab eo pergendo versus orientem per maris oris littorales ejusdem fluvii de Canada ad fluvium stationem navium portum aut littus communiter nomine de Gathepe vel Gaspee notum et appellatum."

The translation of Messrs. Mudge and Featherstonhaugh is as follows:

"All and each of the lands of the continent and the islands situated and lying in America within the headland or promontory commonly called Cape Sable, lying near the forty-third degree of latitude from the equinoctial line or thereabout; from which promontory stretching westwardly toward the north by the seashore to the naval station of St. Mary, commonly called St. Marys Bay; from thence passing toward the north by a straight line, the entrance or mouth of that great naval station which penetrates the interior of the eastern shore betwixt the countries of the Suriquois and Etchemins, to the river commonly called the St. Croix, and to the most remote source or spring of the same on the western side which first mingles itself with the aforesaid river; from whence, by an imaginary straight line, which may be supposed (concipietur) to advance into the country or to run toward the north to the nearest naval station, river, or spring discharging itself into the great river of Canada and from thence advancing toward the east by the gulf shores of the said river of Canada to the river, naval station, port, or shore commonly known or called by the name of Gathepe or Gaspe."

The only American translations which have ever been presented in argument are as follows:

[Translation of Messrs. Gallatin and Preble, who were employed to prepare the statement laid before the King of the Netherlands.]

"Beginning at Cape Sable, in 43° north latitude or thereabout; extending thence westwardly along the seashore to the road commonly called St. Marys Bay; thence toward the north by a direct line, crossing the entrance or mouth of that great ship road which runs into the eastern tract of land between the territories of the Suriquois and of the Etchemins (Bay of Fundy), to the river commonly called St. Croix, and to the most remote spring or source which from the western part thereof first mingles itself with the river aforesaid; and from thence, by an imaginary direct line, which may be conceived to stretch through the land or to run toward the north, to the nearest road, river, or spring emptying itself into the great river de Canada (river St. Lawrence); and from thence, proceeding eastwardly along the seashores of the said river de Canada, to the river, road, port, or shore commonly known and called by the name of Gathepe or Gaspe."

[Translation of Mr. Bradley, the American agent under the fifth article of the treaty of Ghent.]

"By the tenor of this our present charter we do give, grant, and convey to the said Sir William Alexander, his heirs or assigns, all and singular the lands of the continent and islands situated and lying in America within the headland or promontory commonly called Cape Sable, lying near the latitude of 43° or thereabout, from the equinoctial line toward the north; from which promontory stretching toward the shore of the sea to the west to the road of ships commonly called St. Marys Bay, and then toward the north by a direct line, crossing the entrance or mouth of that great road of ships which runs into the eastern tract of land between the territories of the Souriquois and the Etchemins, to the river called by the name of St. Croix, and to the most remote spring or fountain from the western part thereof which first mingles itself with the river aforesaid; whence, by an imaginary direct line, which may be conceived to go through or run toward the north, to the nearest road of ships, river, or spring emptying itself into the great river of Canada; and from thence proceeding toward the east by the shores of the sea of the said river of Canada to the river, road of ships, or shore commonly known and called by the name of Gachepe or Gaspe."

But the translations of the Americans were merely for form's sake, as the original Latin, in a copy furnished from a British public office, was laid before the King of the Netherlands; and no fear need have been felt that the umpire would not have been able to judge whether the translations were true or not. It was rather to be inferred that he, in examining a question submitted in a language foreign to him, would have found the Latin quite as intelligible as the English. This examination, however, is wholly superfluous.

From whatever source the negotiators of the treaty of 1783 derived their view of the boundary, that instrument directs that it shall be a due north line from the source of the river St. Croix. This expression is too definite to require explanation or illustration, and it is only for those purposes that any other instrument can be permitted to be quoted.

In the passages referred to the words "versus septentrionem" occur three times, and in two of the instances are qualified by the context in such manner as to leave no possible doubt as to the meaning. The first time they occur the words of the passage are, "prope latitudinem quadraginta trium graduum aut eo circa versus septentrionem." The free translation into modern idiom is beyond doubt, "near the forty-third degree of north latitude or thereabout;" and the direction toward the north must be along a meridian line on which latitude is measured, or due north. Messrs. Mudge and Featherstonhaugh, instead of connecting in their translation the words "versus septentrionem" with the words "prope latitudinem," etc., with which they stand in juxtaposition in the Latin text which they quote, connect them with the words "ad occidentem tendentem," which occur in the next clause of the sentence, even according to their own punctuation. We note this as a false translation, although it does not touch the point in dispute. They have, indeed, attempted to use it in their argument; but even if the use they make of it had been successful their inferences fall, because drawn from erroneous premises.

The second clause in which the words occur is as follows: "Ad stationem navium Sanctæ Mariæ vulgo St. Marys Bay, et deinceps versus septentrionem per directam lineam introitum sive ostium magnæ illius stationis navium trajicientem," etc., "ad fluvium vulgo nomine Sanctæ Crucis appellatum." Here the line, although directed to be drawn toward the north, is also directed to be drawn between two given points, and it is clear that under the double direction, if they should differ from each other, the position of the given points must govern, and the line be traced from one of them to the other, no matter what may be their bearings.

The last time the words occur is after the direction that the line shall pass up the St. Croix and to the most remote western spring or fountain of that stream, "unde per imaginariam lineam directam quæ pergere per terram seu currere versus septentrionem concipietur." Here alone can any doubt exist as to the meaning of the terms, and that is easily solved.

The boundary pointed out in the instrument is "such as may be conceived to go or run toward the north by (per) a direct (directam) line." Now a direct line toward the north can be no other than a meridian line. Had it been merely a straight line of vague northerly direction which was meant, *rectum*, the usual expression for a mathematical straight line, would have been used instead of *directam*. It is, moreover, to be considered that the Romans had names both for the northeast and northwest points of the compass, and that the expression "versus septentrionem" in its most vague application could not possibly have admitted of a deviation of more than two points on either hand. Had the direction intended deviated more than that amount from the true north, the Latin term corresponding to northeast or northwest must have been used. Nor is this a matter of mere surmise, for in a passage immediately following that which has been quoted the direction through the Gulf of St. Lawrence toward Cape Breton is denoted by the term "versus Euronotum," leaving no possibility of doubt that had the line directed to be drawn from the source of the St. Croix been intended to have a northwestern bearing the appropriate Latin words would have been employed.

It is, besides, to be recollected that the instrument was drawn by a person using habitually and thinking in a modern idiom, and that in translating the English words due north into Latin no other possible expression could suggest itself than the one employed. Such, then, was the sense appropriately given to the Latin words, first in the commission of Governor Wilmot and his successors, governors of Nova Scotia, and subsequently in the commission of all the governors of New Brunswick from the time that it was erected into a province until the question was referred to the King of the Netherlands. In this reference, although a translation was given in the American argument, it was not as quoted by Messrs. Featherstonhaugh and Mudge, but was in the words which have already been cited.

Connected with this subject, although, like it, wholly irrelevant, is another conclusion which Messrs. Mudge and Featherstonhaugh attempt to draw from the same grant to Sir William Alexander. That charter directs the line "versus septentrionem" to be produced "ad proximam navium stationem, fluvium, vel scaturiginem in magno fluvio de Canada sese exonerantem." It can hardly be credited that, although a literal translation of this passage is given, including the whole of the three terms naval station, river, or spring, that it is attempted to limit the meaning to the first expression only, and to infer that as Quebec, in their opinion, is the first naval station above Gaspe on the St. Lawrence, the line "versus septentrionem" was intended to be drawn toward that place, but that as "spring" is also mentioned the line must stop at the source of the Chaudiere. Now it has been uniformly maintained by British authorities, and most strongly in the discussion which preceded the War of 1756, that Nova Scotia extended to the St. Lawrence. The boundary of Sir William Alexander's grant was therefore to be changed from a geographical line to a water course as soon as it met with one, and the apparently useless verbiage was introduced to meet every possible contingency. Supposing, however, that it did not extend so far, the northwest angle of his Nova Scotia will be where the meridian line of the St. Croix crosses the Beaver Stream running into Lake Johnson, only a mile to the north of the point maintained by the American claim to be such.

The map of L'Escarbot, quoted by Messrs. Mudge and Featherstonhaugh, illustrates both this point and the second instance in which the term "versus septentrionem" is employed. On that map, due north of the Bay of St. Marys, a deep inlet of the Bay of Fundy is represented, and, continuing in the same direction, a deep inlet of the St. Lawrence is figured. The latter does not exist, but this map shows that it was believed to exist at the time of the grant, and must be the "statio navium" of that instrument.

This inlet of the Bay of Fundy occupies the position of the St. John, which is almost due north by the most recent determination from St. Marys Bay, and is so represented on their own map. That the St. John was by mistake arising from this cause taken for the St. Croix in the charter to Alexander is obvious from its being described as lying between the territories of the Etchemin and Souriquois. Now Etchemin, or canoe men, is the name given by the Micmac Indians to the race of the Abenakis, from their skill in the management of the canoe; and this race has always inhabited the river, whence one of their tribes is still called St. John's Indians. The language of this tribe, although they have lived apart for many years, is still perfectly intelligible by the Indians of the Penobscot, and those in the service of the commission conversed with perfect ease with the Indians of Tobique. Massachusetts, then, was right in claiming to the St. John as the eastern limit of the grant to Sir William Alexander, being the stream understood and described in it under the name of St. Croix, and wholly different from the river known to the French under that name. If, therefore, Great Britain should insist that the question in relation to the St. Croix shall be reopened, the United States would be able to maintain in the very terms of the original grant to Alexander (on which the British argument in 1797 rested) that the St. John is the St. Croix, and the boundary will be that river to its most northwestern source, the Asherbish, which flows into the upper end of Lake Temiscouata. Nova Scotia will then have recovered her lost northwest angle, which can not be found in any of the many shapes under which the British argument has been presented, although it forms the place of beginning of what is called a grant to the United States.

Note VI.

The fact that a line drawn from the source of the Kennebec to the mouth of the Chaudiere or thereabout must be one of the boundary lines of the grant to the Duke of York has not escaped the notice of Messrs. Featherstonhaugh and Mudge; but they have not derived the true result from this discovery. The Kennebec being the western limit of the grant, the line in question bounds the territory on the southwest, while they infer that it bounds it on the northeast. In making this inference they appear to have forgotten that the St. Croix is the eastern boundary of the grant. By their argument the grant to the Duke of York is blotted wholly from the map, or, rather, becomes a mathematical line which is absurd.

Note VII.

No name which has ever been applied to any part of North America is as vague as that of Acadie. The charter to De Monts in 1604 extended from the fortieth to the forty-sixth degree of north latitude; that is to say, from Sandy Hook, at the mouth of the Hudson, to the peninsula of Nova Scotia. It therefore included New York, parts of New Jersey and Pennsylvania, and all the New England States, but excluded the disputed territory. His settlement was at the mouth of the St. Croix, but was speedily removed to Port Royal. The latter place was soon after destroyed by an expedition from Virginia under Argall. Under the title derived from this conquest it would appear probable that the celebrated grant to Sir William Stirling was made; but when his agents attempted to make settlements in the country they found that the French had preoccupied it. Although the son of Alexander succeeded in conquering the country granted to his father, and even beyond it to the Penobscot, it was restored to France by the treaty of St. Germains in 1634, and the Alexanders were indemnified for the loss by the Crown of England.

In the subsequent cessions to France after its occupations by the arms of Massachusetts, and in its final cession to Great Britain by the treaty of Utrecht in 1713, the country ceded is described as Acadie or Nova Scotia, with its ancient bounds (*cum finibus antiquis*). The uncertainty arising from this vague description became in 1750 a subject of controversy between France and England, and was one of the causes which led to the war of 1756. In this discussion both parties admitted that the names Acadie and Nova Scotia were convertible terms. England maintained that the territory thus named extended to the St. Lawrence; France, on the other hand, insisted that their Acadie had never extended more than 10 leagues from the Bay of Fundy; while by geographers, as quoted by the British commissioners, the name was limited to the peninsula which forms the present Province of Nova Scotia.* If Acadie had been limited to the north by the forty-sixth degree of north latitude, as expressed in the charter of De Monts, that parallel is to the south of Mars Hill. The British Government, therefore, derives no title to the disputed territory from this source, as the title of Massachusetts and of Maine as her successor is admitted to all country south of that parallel.†

It is very easy to tell what country was actually settled by the French as Acadie. Its chief town was Port Royal, now Annapolis, at the head of the Bay of Fundy. Nearly all the settlements of the Acadians were in that vicinity, and for the most part within the peninsula.

From these seats they were removed in 1756 by Great Britain, and to them a remnant was permitted to return. The most western settlement of Acadians was on the St. John River near the present site of Fredericton, and no permanent occupation was ever made by them of country west of the St. Croix. It is even doubtful whether the settlement near Fredericton was a part of French Acadie, for it seems to have been formed by persons who escaped from the general seizure and transportation of their countrymen.

This settlement was broken up in 1783, and its inhabitants sought refuge at Madawaska; but it can not be pretended that this forced removal of Acadians subsequent to the treaty of 1783 was an extension of the name of their country. The whole

---

* Report of Featherstonhaugh and Mudge, p. 8.
† It can not be seriously pretended that when by the treaty of St. Germains, in 1632, Acadie was restored to France the intention was to cede to her the colonies already settled in New England Yet the language of the British commissioners would imply that this was the case were it not that they evidently consider the forty-sixth parallel as the southern boundary of the grant to De Monts, whereas it is the northern.

argument in favor of the British claim founded on the limits of ancient Acadie therefore fails:

First. Because of the inherent vagueness of the term, on which no settled understanding was ever had, although England held it to be synonymous with Nova Scotia and France denied that it extended more than 10 leagues from the Bay of Fundy.

Second. Because by its original definition in the grant to De Monts it excludes the whole disputed territory on the one side; and

Third. Because in its practical sense, as a real settlement, it is wholly to the east of the meridian of the St. Croix, and this excludes the whole of the disputed territory on the other.

The portion of the territory granted to the Duke of York, and which is now the subject of dispute, therefore can not be claimed as a part of Acadie, as it never fell within its limits either by charter or by occupation.

Note VIII.

[Extract from the award of the King of the Netherlands.]

Considering that in 1763, 1765, 1773, and 1782 it was established that Nova Scotia should be bounded at the north as far as the western extremity of the Bay des Chaleurs by the southern boundary of the Province of Quebec; that this delimitation is again found with respect to the Province of Quebec in the commission of the Governor-General of Quebec of 1786, wherein the language of the proclamation of 1763 and of the Quebec act of 1774 has been used, as also in the commissions of 1786 and others of subsequent dates of the governors of New Brunswick, with respect to the last-mentioned Province, as well as in a great number of maps anterior and posterior to the treaty of 1783; and that the first article of the said treaty specifies by name the States whose independence is acknowledged; but that this mention does not imply (*implique*) the entire coincidence of the boundaries between the two powers, as settled by the following article, with the ancient delimitation of the British Provinces, whose preservation is not mentioned in the treaty of 1783, and which, owing to its continual changes and the uncertainty which continued to exist respecting it, created from time to time differences between the provincial authorities.

Note IX.

[Article IV of the convention of 1827.]

The map called Mitchell's map, by which the framers of the treaty of 1783 are acknowledged to have regulated their joint and official proceedings, and the Map A, which has been agreed on by the contracting parties as a delineation of the water courses, and of the boundary lines in reference to the said water courses, as contended for by each party, respectively, and which has accordingly been signed by the above-named plenipotentiaries at the same time with this convention, shall be annexed to the statements of the contracting parties and be the only maps that shall be considered as evidence mutually acknowledged by the contracting parties of the topography of the country.

It shall, however, be lawful for either party to annex to its respective first statement, for the purposes of general illustration, any of the maps, surveys, or topographical delineations which were filed with the commissioners under the fifth article of the treaty of Ghent, any engraved map heretofore published, and also a transcript of the above-mentioned Map A or of a section thereof, in which transcript each party may lay down the highlands or other features of the country as it shall think fit, the water courses and the boundary lines as claimed by each party remaining as laid down in the said Map A. But this transcript, as well as all the other maps, surveys, or topographical delineations, other than the Map A and Mitchell's map, intended to be thus annexed by either party to the respective statements, shall be communicated to the other party, in the same manner as aforesaid, within nine months after the exchange of the ratifications of this convention, and shall be subject to such objections and observations as the other contracting party may deem it expedient to make thereto, and shall annex to his first statement, either in the margin of such transcript, map or maps, or otherwise.

Note X.

[Extract from the award of the King of the Netherlands.]

Considering that, according to the instances alleged, the term highlands applies not only to a hilly or elevated country, but also to land which, without being hilly, divides waters flowing in different directions, and that thus the character, more or less hilly and elevated, of the country through which are drawn the two lines respectively claimed at the north and at the south of the river St. John can not form the basis of a choice between them.

Note XI.

The reason of the double delineation of the Restigouche on the map of Mitchell and several others of ancient date is obvious. A mistake was common to them all by which the Bay of Chaleurs was laid down too far to the north. The main branch, or Grande Fourche, of Restigouche (Katawamkedgwick) has been reached by parties setting out from the banks of the St. Lawrence at Metis, and was known to fall into the Bay of Chaleurs, while the united stream had also been visited by persons crossing the wagansis of Grand River and descending the Southwestern Branch. The map makers could not, in consequence of the error in latitude, make their plat meet, and therefore considered the part of the united streams reached in the two different directions as different bodies of water, and without authority sought an outlet for that which they laid down as the southernmost of the two in another bay of the Gulf of St. Lawrence. On many of the maps, however, the small stream which modern geographers improperly call Restigouche is readily distinguishable under the name of Chacodi.

Note XII.

In the argument of the British commissioners under Jay's treaty the following points were maintained, and, being sanctioned by the decision of the umpire, became the grounds of an award acceded to by both Governments:

First. That the limits of Nova Scotia had been altered from the southern bank of the St. Lawrence to the highlands described in the treaty of peace.

Second. That if the river Schoodiac were the true St. Croix the northwest angle of Nova Scotia could be formed by the western and northern boundaries (the meridian line and the highlands).

Third. That the territory of Acadie, or Nova Scotia, was the same territory granted to Sir William Alexander.

Fourth. That the sea and Atlantic Ocean were used as convertible terms.

Fifth. That from the date of the treaty of Utrecht the boundary between Massachusetts and Nova Scotia was that of the patent to Sir William Alexander.

Sixth. That the Provinces of Quebec and Nova Scotia belonged to and were in possession of His Britannic Majesty in 1783, and that he had an undoubted right to cede to the United States such part of them as he might think fit.

Seventh. That the due north line from the source of the St. Croix must of necessity cross the St. John.

It has since been maintained on the part of Great Britain:

First. That the limits of Nova Scotia never did extend to the St. Lawrence.

Second. That the northwest angle of Nova Scotia was unknown in 1783.

Third. That Acadie extended south to the forty-sixth degree of north latitude, and was not the same with Nova Scotia.

Fourth. That the sea and the Atlantic Ocean were different things.

Fifth. That the claims and rights of Massachusetts did not extend to the western bounds of the grant to Sir William Alexander.

Sixth. That this being the case the cession of territory not included within her limits is void.

Seventh. That it could never have been intended that the meridian line should cross the St. John.

Note XIII.

It has been pretended that the grant of the fief of Madawaska in 1683 can be urged as a bar to the claim of Massachusetts. That fief, indeed, was among the early grants of the French governors of Canada, but it is not included in the claim which the French themselves set up. It was therefore covered by the Massachusetts charter, because the grant had never been acted upon. Even up to the present day this fief can hardly be said to be settled or occupied except by the retainers of the garrison of Fort Ingall, and from all the evidence which could be found on the spot it appeared that no settlement had ever been made upon it until the establishment of a posthouse some time between the date of the treaties of 1783 and 1794. It therefore was not at the time the charter of Massachusetts was granted (1691) "actually possessed or inhabited by any other Christian prince or state."

An argument has also been attempted to be drawn from the limits given on Greenleaf's map to a purchase made from the State of Massachusetts by Watkins and Flint. This purchase is, however, by the patent extended to the highlands, and the surveyors who laid it out crossed the Walloostook in search of them. Here they met, at a short distance from that stream, with waters running to the north, which they conceived to be waters of the St. Lawrence, and they terminated their survey. The lines traced on Greenleaf's map are therefore incorrect, either as compared with the grant or the actual survey, and although from a want of knowledge of the country the surveyors stopped at waters running into Lake Temiscouata instead of the St. Lawrence, the very error shows the understanding they had of the true design of the patent, and this transaction, so far from being an available argument against the American claim, is an act of possession at an early date within the limits of the disputed territory.

WASHINGTON, *April 8, 1842.*

To the Senate of the United States:

In compliance with your resolution of the 31st March, 1842, I have the honor to submit the accompanying document and report * from the Commissioner of the General Land Office.

JOHN TYLER.

WASHINGTON, *April 9, 1842.*

To the House of Representatives of the United States:

I transmit herewith to the House of Representatives a report from the Secretary of State, with a copy of the correspondence † requested by their resolution of the 7th instant.

JOHN TYLER.

WASHINGTON, *April 11, 1842.*

To the Senate of the United States:

I herewith transmit a memorial ‡ which I have received from the Choctaw tribe of Indians and citizens of the State of Mississippi, with a request that I should communicate the same to Congress. This I do not feel myself at liberty to decline, inasmuch as I think that some action by Congress is called for by justice to the memorialists and in compliance with the plighted national faith.

JOHN TYLER.

WASHINGTON, *April 12, 1842.*

To the Senate of the United States:

In further compliance with the resolution of the Senate of the 2d of February last, requesting information touching the demarcation of the boundary line between the United States and the Republic of Texas, I transmit a report from the Secretary of State and the accompanying documents.

JOHN TYLER.

* Relating to surveys and sales of the public lands during 1841 and 1842, etc.
† With Great Britain relative to an international copyright law.
‡ Relating to an alleged violation by the United States of the treaty of Dancing Rabbit Creek.

WASHINGTON, *April 13, 1842.*

To the Senate of the United States:

In compliance with a resolution of the Senate of the 24th of July last, I communicate to that body a report from the Secretary of State, conveying copies of the correspondence * which contains the information called for by that resolution.

JOHN TYLER.

WASHINGTON, *April 13, 1842.*

To the Senate of the United States:

In compliance with a resolution of the Senate of the 29th July last, I communicate to that body a report from the Secretary of State, conveying copies of the correspondence † which contains the information called for by said resolution.

In communicating these papers to the Senate I call their particular attention to that portion of the report of the Secretary of State in which he suggests the propriety of not making public certain parts of the correspondence which accompanied it.

JOHN TYLER.

WASHINGTON, *April 18, 1842.*

To the Senate of the United States:

I have the honor to transmit herewith the report ‡ of the Secretary of State, in compliance with the resolution of the Senate of the 18th February, 1842.

JOHN TYLER.

WASHINGTON, *April 19, 1842.*

To the Senate of the United States:

I transmit herewith, in part compliance with a resolution of the Senate of February 18, a report from the Secretary of War, inclosing a list of all officers, agents, and commissioners employed under the War Department who are not such by express provision of law, with other information required by the resolution.

JOHN TYLER.

WASHINGTON, *April 19, 1842.*

To the House of Representatives:

I transmit herewith a report from the Secretary of War, containing a list of appointments to office made in that Department since the 4th day of April, 1841, in part compliance with the resolution of the House of Representatives of the 21st ultimo.

JOHN TYLER.

---

*Of the diplomatic agent and minister of the United States at the Court of Austria relative to the commercial interests of the United States.

† Between the Department of State and Belgium relative to the rejection by that Government of the treaty ratified by the Senate February 9, 1833, and the causes of the delay in exchanging the ratifications of the treaty ratified by the Senate December 31, 1840.

‡ Transmitting names of agents employed by the State Department without express provision of law.

WASHINGTON, *April 20, 1842.*

To the Senate and House of Representatives of the United States:

I submit to Congress a report from the Secretary of State, accompanied by documents relating to an application by the captain and owners of the Spanish ship *Sabina,** which is recommended to their favorable consideration.

JOHN TYLER.

WASHINGTON, *April 28, 1842.*

To the Senate of the United States:

I submit to the Senate, for the constitutional action of that body, a treaty concluded on the 11th day of August last with the Minda Wankanton bands of the Dakota or Sioux Nation of Indians, with the papers necessary to an understanding of the subject.

JOHN TYLER.

WASHINGTON, *April 28, 1842.*

To the Senate of the United States:

I submit to the Senate, for the constitutional action of that body, a treaty concluded with the half-breeds of the Dakota or Sioux Nation on the 31st day of July last, together with the papers referred to in the accompanying communication from the Secretary of War as necessary to a full view of the whole subject.

JOHN TYLER.

WASHINGTON, *April 30, 1842.*

To the House of Representatives of the United States:

In compliance with your resolution of the 29th instant, I have the honor to transmit the reports of Messrs. Kelley and Steuart, two of the commissioners originally appointed, along with Mr. Poindexter, to investigate the affairs of the custom-house of New York, together with all the correspondence and testimony accompanying the same, and also the report of Mr. Poindexter, to which is annexed two letters, subscribed by Mr. Poindexter and Mr. Bradley. The last-named gentleman was substituted in the place of Mr. Kelley, whose inclinations and duties called him to his residence in Ohio after the return of the commissioners to this city, about the last of August. One of the letters just mentioned was addressed to the Secretary of the Treasury and bears date the 12th of April instant, and the other to myself, dated the 20th of this month. From the former you will learn that a most interesting portion of the inquiry instituted by this Department (viz, that relating to light-houses, buoys, beacons, revenue cutters, and revenue boats) is proposed to be made the subject of a further report by Messrs. Bradley and Poindexter. You will also learn, through the accompanying letter from Mr. Steuart,

---

* For compensation for rescuing and supporting the captain, supercargo, and 17 officers and men of the American ship *Courier*, of New York, which foundered at sea, and landing them safely at the Cape of Good Hope.

the reasons which have delayed him in making a supplemental and additional report to that already made by himself and Mr. Kelley, embracing his views and opinions upon the developments made subsequent
to the withdrawal of Mr. Kelley from the commission and the substitution of Mr. Bradley in his place. I also transmit two documents
furnished by Mr. Steuart, and which were handed by him to the Secretary of the Treasury on the 7th instant, the one being "memoranda
of proceedings," etc., marked No. 1, and the other "letters accompanying memoranda," etc., marked No. 2.

The commission was instituted for the purpose of ascertaining existing
defects in the custom-house regulations, to trace to their true causes past
errors, to detect abuses, and by wholesome reforms to guard in future
not only against fraud and peculation, but error and mismanagement.
For these purposes a selection was made of persons of acknowledged
intelligence and industry, and upon this task they have been engaged
for almost an entire year, and their labors remain yet to be completed.
The character of those labors may be estimated by the extent of Messrs.
Kelley and Steuart's report, embracing about 100 pages of closely written
manuscript, the voluminous memoranda and correspondence of Mr.
Steuart, the great mass of evidence accompanying Messrs. Kelley and
Steuart's report, and the report of Mr. Poindexter, extending over 394
pages, comprised in the volume accompanying this, and additional reports
still remaining to be made, as before stated.

I should be better pleased to have it in my power to communicate
the entire mass of reports made and contemplated to be made at one
and the same time, and still more should I have been gratified if time
could have been allowed me, consistently with the apparent desire of the
House of Representatives to be put into immediate possession of these
papers, to have compared or even to have read with deliberation the views
presented by the commissioners as to proposed reforms in the revenue
laws, together with the mass of documentary evidence and information
by which they have been explained and enforced and which do not admit
of a satisfactory comparison until the whole circle of reports be completed.
Charges of malfeasance against some of those now in office will devolve
upon the Executive a rigid investigation into their extent and character,
and will in due season claim my attention. The readiness, however,
with which the House proposes to enter upon the grave and difficult
subjects which these papers suggest having anticipated that consideration of them by the Executive which their importance demands, it only
remains for me, in lieu of specific recommendations, which under other
circumstances it would have been my duty to make, to urge upon Congress the importance and necessity of introducing the earliest reforms
in existing laws and usages, so as to guard the country in future against
frauds in the collection of the revenues and the Treasury against peculation, to relieve trade and commerce from oppressive regulations, and to
guard law and morality against violation and abuse.

. As from their great volume it has been necessary to transmit the original papers to the House, I have to suggest the propriety of the House taking order for their restoration to the Treasury Department at such time as may comport with its pleasure.

JOHN TYLER.

WASHINGTON, *May 2, 1842.*

To the House of Representatives of the United States:

I have this day received and now transmit to the House of Representatives the accompanying communication from Benjamin F. Butler, having relation to the reports of the commissioners appointed by me to examine into the affairs connected with the New York custom-house. As the whole subject is in possession of the House, I deem it also proper to communicate Mr. Butler's letter.

JOHN TYLER.

WASHINGTON, *May 10, 1842.*

To the Senate and House of Representatives:

The season for active hostilities in Florida having nearly terminated, my attention has necessarily been directed to the course of measures to be pursued hereafter in relation to the few Indians yet remaining in that Territory. Their number is believed not to exceed 240, of whom there are supposed to be about 80 warriors, or males capable of bearing arms. The further pursuit of these miserable beings by a large military force seems to be as injudicious as it is unavailing. The history of the last year's campaign in Florida has satisfactorily shown that notwithstanding the vigorous and incessant operations of our troops (which can not be exceeded), the Indian mode of warfare, their dispersed condition, and the very smallness of their number (which increases the difficulty of finding them in the abundant and almost inaccessible hiding places of the Territory) render any further attempt to secure them by force impracticable except by the employment of the most expensive means. The exhibition of force and the constant efforts to capture or destroy them of course places them beyond the reach of overtures to surrender. It is believed by the distinguished officer in command there that a different system should now be pursued to attain the entire removal of all the Indians in Florida, and he recommends that hostilities should cease unless the renewal of them be rendered necessary by new aggressions; that communications should be opened by means of the Indians with him to insure them a peaceful and voluntary surrender, and that the military operations should hereafter be directed to the protection of the inhabitants.

These views are strengthened and corroborated by the governor of the Territory, by many of its most intelligent citizens, and by numerous officers of the Army who have served and are still serving in that region. Mature reflection has satisfied me that these recommendations are sound and just; and I rejoice that consistently with duty to Florida I may indulge my desire to promote the great interests of humanity and extend the reign of peace and good will by terminating the unhappy warfare that has so long been carried on there, and at the same time gratify my anxiety to reduce the demands upon the Treasury by curtailing the extraordinary expenses which have attended the contest. I have therefore authorized the colonel in command there as soon as he shall deem it expedient to declare that hostilities against the Indians have ceased, and that they will not be renewed unless provoked and rendered indispensable by new outrages on their part, but that neither citizens nor troops are to be restrained from any necessary and proper acts of self-defense against any attempts to molest them. He is instructed to open communications with those yet remaining, and endeavor by all peaceable means to persuade them to consult their true interests by joining their brethren at the West; and directions have been given for establishing a cordon or line of protection for the inhabitants by the necessary number of troops.

But to render this system of protection effectual it is essential that settlements of our citizens should be made within the line so established, and that they should be armed, so as to be ready to repel any attack. In order to afford inducements to such settlements, I submit to the consideration of Congress the propriety of allowing a reasonable quantity of land to the head of each family that shall permanently occupy it, and of extending the existing provisions on that subject so as to permit the issue of rations for the subsistence of the settlers for one year; and as few of them will probably be provided with arms, it would be expedient to authorize the loan of muskets and the delivery of a proper quantity of cartridges or of powder and balls. By such means it is to be hoped that a hardy population will soon occupy the rich soil of the frontiers of Florida, who will be as capable as willing to defend themselves and their houses, and thus relieve the Government from further anxiety or expense for their protection.

JOHN TYLER.

WASHINGTON, *May 13, 1842.*

To the House of Representatives of the United States:

I transmit herewith a report* from the Postmaster-General, made in pursuance of the resolution of the House of Representatives of the 21st of March last, together with the accompanying documents.

JOHN TYLER.

WASHINGTON, *May 16, 1842.*

To the Senate:

Having directed hostilities in Florida to cease, the time seems to have arrived for distinguishing with appropriate honors the brave army that have so long encountered the perils of savage warfare in a country presenting every imaginable difficulty and in seasons and under a climate

---

* Transmitting lists of postmasters and others appointed by the President and Post-Office Department from April 4, 1841, to March 21, 1842.

fruitful of disease. The history of the hardships which our soldiers have endured, of the patience and perseverance which have enabled them to triumph over obstacles altogether unexampled, and of the gallantry which they have exhibited on every occasion which a subtle and skulking foe would allow them to improve is so familiar as not to require repetition at my hands. But justice to the officers and men now in Florida demands that their privations, sufferings, and dauntless exertions during a summer's campaign in such a climate, which for the first time was witnessed during the last year, should be specially commended. The foe has not been allowed opportunity either to plant or to cultivate or to reap. The season, which to him has usually been one of repose and preparation for renewed conflict, has been vigorously occupied by incessant and harassing pursuit, by penetrating his hiding places and laying waste his rude dwellings, and by driving him from swamp to swamp and from everglade to everglade. True, disease and death have been encountered at the same time and in the same pursuit, but they have been disregarded by a brave and gallant army, determined on fulfilling to the uttermost the duties assigned them, however inglorious they might esteem the particular service in which they were engaged.

To all who have been thus engaged the executive department, responding to the universal sentiment of the country, has already awarded the meed of approbation. There must, however, in all such cases be some who, availing themselves of the occasions which fortune afforded, have distinguished themselves for "gallant actions and meritorious conduct" beyond the usual high gallantry and great merit which an intelligent public opinion concedes to the whole Army. To express to these the sense which their Government cherishes of their public conduct and to hold up to their fellow-citizens the bright example of their courage, constancy, and patriotic devotion would seem to be but the performance of the very duty contemplated by that provision of our laws which authorizes the issuing of brevet commissions.

Fortunately for the country, a long peace, interrupted only by difficulties with Indians at particular points, has afforded few occasions for the exercise of this power, and it may be regarded as favorable to the encouragement of a proper military spirit throughout the Army that an opportunity is now given to evince the readiness of the Government to reward unusual merit with a peculiar and lasting distinction.

I therefore nominate to the Senate the persons whose names are contained in the accompanying list* for brevet commissions for services in Florida. That the number is large is evidence only of the value of the services rendered during a contest that has continued nearly as long as the War of the Revolution. The difficulty has been to reduce the number as much as possible without injustice to any, and to accomplish this great and mature consideration has been bestowed on the case of every officer who has served in Florida.

JOHN TYLER.

*Omitted.

WASHINGTON, *May 24, 1842.*

To the Senate of the United States:

I transmit herewith to the Senate a treaty recently concluded with the Wyandott tribe of Indians, and request the advice and consent of the Senate to the ratification of the same as proposed to be modified by the War Department.

JOHN TYLER.

WASHINGTON, *June 1, 1842.*

To the Senate of the United States:

I herewith transmit a report from the Acting Commissioner of the General Land Office and the documents accompanying the same (from No. 1 to No. 7), in relation to the conduct of N. P. Taylor, present register and former clerk in the land office at St. Louis, in compliance with your resolution of the 9th May.

JOHN TYLER.

WASHINGTON, *June 10, 1842.*

To the Senate of the United States:

I submit herewith a treaty concluded at Buffalo Creek on the 20th day of May last between the United States and the Seneca Nation of Indians, for your advice and consent to its ratification, together with a report on the subject from the War Department.

JOHN TYLER.

WASHINGTON, *June 13, 1842.*

To the Senate of the United States:

In compliance with a resolution of the Senate of the 2d of March last, requesting information touching proceedings under the convention of the 11th of April, 1839, between the United States and the Mexican Republic, I transmit a report from the Secretary of State, with the accompanying documents.

JOHN TYLER.

WASHINGTON, *June 15, 1842.*

To the Senate of the United States:

In compliance with the resolution of the Senate of the 29th of March last, calling for information touching the relations between the United States and the Mexican Republic, I transmit a report from the Secretary of State, with the accompanying documents.*

JOHN TYLER.

WASHINGTON, *June 17, 1842.*

To the House of Representatives:

I herewith transmit a report from the Secretary of the Treasury, which, accompanied by copies of certain letters of Mr. Ewing, late Secretary of

* Correspondence respecting certain citizens of the United States captured with the Texan expedition to Santa Fe, and held in confinement in Mexico.

the Treasury, and a statement* from the Treasury Department, completes the answer, a part of which has heretofore been furnished, to your resolution of the 7th of February last, and complies also with your resolution of the 3d instant.

JOHN TYLER.

WASHINGTON, *June 20, 1842.*

To the House of Representatives:

A resolution of the House of Representatives of the 13th instant has been communicated to me, requesting, "so far as may be compatible with the public interest, a copy of the quintuple treaty between the five powers of Europe for the suppression of the African slave trade, and also copies of any remonstrance or protest addressed by Lewis Cass, envoy extraordinary and minister plenipotentiary of the United States at the Court of France, to that Government, against the ratification by France of the said treaty, and of all correspondence between the Governments of the United States and of France, and of all communications from the said Lewis Cass to his own Government and from this Government to him relating thereto."

In answer to this request I have to say that the treaty mentioned therein has not been officially communicated to the Government of the United States, and no authentic copy of it, therefore, can be furnished. In regard to the other papers requested, although it is my hope and expectation that it will be proper and convenient at an early day to lay them before Congress, together with others connected with the same subjects, yet in my opinion a communication of them to the House of Representatives at this time would not be compatible with the public interest.

JOHN TYLER.

WASHINGTON, *June 22, 1842.*

To the Senate of the United States:

In compliance with a resolution of the Senate of the 15th of April last, I communicate to the Senate a report from the Secretary of State, accompanying copies of the correspondence † called for by said resolution.

JOHN TYLER.

WASHINGTON, *June 24, 1842.*

To the Senate of the United States:

I transmit herewith to the Senate the translation of a letter ‡ addressed by the minister of France at Washington to the Secretary of State of the United States and a copy of the answer given thereto by my direction, and invite to the subject of the minister's letter all the consideration due

---

* Of expenses of the commission to investigate the New York custom-house, etc.
† Relating to the conduct and character of William B. Hodgson (nominated to be consul at Tunis) while dragoman at Constantinople.
‡ Relating to the establishment of a line of steamers between Havre and New York.

to its importance and to a proposition originating in a desire to promote mutual convenience and emanating from a Government with which it is both our interest and our desire to maintain the most amicable relations.

JOHN TYLER.

[The same message was sent to the House of Representatives.]

WASHINGTON, *June 24, 1842.*

To the Senate of the United States:

In compliance with the resolution of the Senate of the 16th of February last, I herewith transmit a letter* from the Secretary of State and the papers in that Department called for by the resolution aforesaid.

JOHN TYLER.

WASHINGTON, *June 25, 1842.*

To the House of Representatives:

I have this day approved and signed an act, which originated in the House of Representatives, entitled "An act for an apportionment of Representatives among the several States according to the Sixth Census," and have caused the same to be deposited in the office of the Secretary of State, accompanied by an exposition of my reasons for giving to it my sanction.

JOHN TYLER.

[Transmitted to the House of Representatives by the Secretary of State in compliance with a resolution of that body.]

WASHINGTON, *June 25, 1842.*

A BILL entitled "An act for an apportionment of Representatives among the several States according to the Sixth Census," approved June 25, 1842.

In approving this bill I feel it due to myself to say, as well that my motives for signing it may be rightly understood as that my opinions may not be liable to be misconstrued or quoted hereafter erroneously as a precedent, that I have not proceeded so much upon a *clear and decided opinion of my own* respecting the constitutionality or policy of the entire act as from respect to the declared will of the two Houses of Congress.

In yielding *my doubts* to the matured opinion of Congress I have followed the advice of the first Secretary of State to the first President of the United States and the example set by that illustrious citizen upon a memorable occasion.

When I was a member of either House of Congress I acted under the conviction that *to doubt* as to the constitutionality of a law was sufficient to induce me to give my vote against it; but I have not been able to bring myself to believe that *a doubtful opinion* of the Chief Magistrate ought to outweigh the solemnly pronounced opinion of the representatives of the people and of the States.

One of the prominent features of the bill is that which purports to be mandatory on the States to form districts for the choice of Representatives to Congress, in single districts. That Congress itself has power by law to alter State regulations respecting the manner of holding elections for Representatives is clear, but its power to command the States to make new regulations or alter their existing regulations is the question upon which I have felt deep and strong doubts. I have yielded those

* Transmitting names and compensation of employees and witnesses in connection with the commission of inquiry relative to the public buildings in Washington, D. C.

doubts, however, to the opinion of the Legislature, giving effect to their enactment as far as depends on my approbation, and leaving questions which may arise here-after, if unhappily such should arise, to be settled by full consideration of the several provisions of the Constitution and the laws and the authority of each House to judge of the elections, returns, and qualifications of its own members.

Similar considerations have operated with me in regard to the representation of fractions above a moiety of the representative number, and where such moiety exceeds 30,000—a question on which a diversity of opinion has existed from the foundation of the Government. The provision recommends itself from its nearer approxima-tion to equality than would be found in the application of a common and simple divisor to the entire population of each State, and corrects in a great degree those inequalities which are destined at the recurrence of each succeeding census so greatly to augment.

In approving the bill I flatter myself that a disposition will be perceived on my part to concede to the opinions of Congress in a matter which may conduce to the good of the country and the stability of its institutions, upon which my own opinion is not clear and decided. But it seemed to me due to the respectability of opin-ion against the constitutionality of the bill, as well as to the real difficulties of the subject, which no one feels more sensibly than I do, that the reasons which have determined me should be left on record.

JOHN TYLER.

WASHINGTON, *July 1, 1842.*

To the Senate of the United States:

In pursuance of the suggestions contained in the accompanying letter from the Secretary of the Navy and of my own convictions of their pro-priety, I transmit to the Senate the report made by Lieutenant Wilkes, commander of the exploring expedition, relative to the Oregon Terri-tory. Having due regard to the negotiations now pending between this Government and the Government of Great Britain through its special envoy, I have thought it proper to communicate the report confidentially to the Senate.

JOHN TYLER.

WASHINGTON, *July 2, 1842.*

To the Senate and House of Representatives of the United States:

I submit to Congress the printed copy of certain resolutions of the legislature of the State of Louisiana, accompanied by a letter from the Senators and Representatives from that State, and also a letter from the Solicitor of the Treasury and Commissioner of the General Land Office, requesting and recommending that a suit in ejectment may be authorized and directed in order to test the validity of a grant made on the 20th of June, 1797, by the Baron de Carondelet, Governor-General of Louisiana, to the Marquis de Maison Rouge.

The magnitude of this claim renders it highly desirable that a speedy termination should be put to all contest concerning it, and I therefore recommend that Congress shall authorize such proceedings as may be best calculated to bring it to a close.

JOHN TYLER.

WASHINGTON, *July 9, 1842.*
To the House of Representatives of the United States:

In compliance with the resolution of the House of Representatives of the 21st ultimo, requesting information relative to proceedings of this Government in the case of George Johnson, a citizen of the United States aggrieved by acts of authorities of the Republic of Uruguay, I transmit a report from the Secretary of State, with the accompanying papers.

JOHN TYLER.

WASHINGTON, *July 14, 1842.*
To the House of Representatives of the United States:

In answer to the resolution of the House of Representatives of the 12th instant, requesting copies of papers upon the subject of the relations between the United States and the Mexican Republic, I transmit a report from the Secretary of State and the documents by which it was accompanied.

JOHN TYLER.

WASHINGTON, *July 14, 1842.*
To the Senate of the United States:

In compliance with the resolution of the Senate of the 11th instant, calling for the recent correspondence between the Republic of Mexico and this Government in relation to Texas, I transmit a report from the Secretary of State, with the accompanying documents.

JOHN TYLER.

WASHINGTON, *July 20, 1842.*
To the House of Representatives of the United States:

In further compliance with the resolution of the House of Representatives of the 29th of April last, I transmit herewith a supplemental and additional report of William M. Steuart, one of the commissioners appointed to investigate the affairs of the New York custom-house, which has recently been received, and which, like the reports of the commissioners heretofore communicated to the House, I have not had an opportunity to examine. For the reason stated in my message to the House of the 30th of April last, I shall abstain, as I have done hitherto, from recommending any specific measures which might be suggested by an examination of the various reports on the subject.

JOHN TYLER.

WASHINGTON, *July 22, 1842.*
To the House of Representatives of the United States:

In answer to the resolution of the House of Representatives of the 13th instant, upon the subject of the relations between the United States and the Republic of Texas, I transmit a report from the Secretary of State. My last communication to Congress relating to that Republic was my message of the 30th of March last, suggesting the expediency of legislative provisions for improving the trade and facilitating the intercourse by post between the United States and Texas. The report of the Secretary of State is accompanied by a copy of all the correspondence between the two Governments since that period which it would be compatible with the public interest to communicate to the House of Representatives at this time.

JOHN TYLER.

WASHINGTON, *August 8, 1842.*

To the Senate of the United States:

In the communication made to the Senate on the 13th of June, in answer to its resolution of the 2d of March last, there appears to have been, among other papers, sundry letters addressed to the Department of State by certain claimants or their agents containing reflections upon the character of the umpire appointed by His Prussian Majesty pursuant to the convention between the United States and the Mexican Republic of the 11th of April, 1839. As the call was for all communications which had been addressed to the Department of State by any of the claimants under that convention relative to the proceedings and progress of the mixed commission, the copies were prepared and submitted without attracting the attention either of the head of the Department or myself. If those letters had been noticed, their transmission to the Senate, if transmitted at all, would have been accompanied by a disclaimer on the part of the Executive of any intention to approve such charges. The Executive has no complaint to make against the conduct or decisions of the highly respectable person appointed by his sovereign umpire between the American and Mexican commissioners.

JOHN TYLER.

WASHINGTON, *August 10, 1842.*

To the Senate of the United States:

In compliance with your resolution of the 18th July, I herewith transmit a letter from the Acting Secretary of the Treasury and a report from the Commissioner of Public Buildings, together with the accompanying documents.*

JOHN TYLER.

WASHINGTON, *August 11, 1842.*

To the Senate of the United States:

I have the satisfaction to communicate to the Senate the results of the negotiations recently had in this city with the British minister, special and extraordinary.

---

*Relating to the macadamizing of Pennsylvania avenue, Washington, D. C.

These results comprise—

First. A treaty to settle and define the boundaries between the territories of the United States and the possessions of Her Britannic Majesty in North America, for the suppression of the African slave trade, and the surrender of criminals fugitive from justice in certain cases.

Second. A correspondence on the subject of the interference of the colonial authorities of the British West Indies with American merchant vessels driven by stress of weather or carried by violence into the ports of those colonies.

Third. A correspondence upon the subject of the attack and destruction of the steamboat *Caroline*.

Fourth. A correspondence on the subject of impressment.

If this treaty shall receive the approbation of the Senate, it will terminate a difference respecting boundary which has long subsisted between the two Governments, has been the subject of several ineffectual attempts at settlement, and has sometimes led to great irritation, not without danger of disturbing the existing peace. Both the United States and the States more immediately concerned have entertained no doubt of the validity of the American title to all the territory which has been in dispute, but that title was controverted and the Government of the United States had agreed to make the dispute a subject of arbitration. One arbitration had been actually had, but had failed to settle the controversy, and it was found at the commencement of last year that a correspondence had been in progress between the two Governments for a joint commission, with an ultimate reference to an umpire or arbitrator with authority to make a final decision. That correspondence, however, had been retarded by various occurrences, and had come to no definite result when the special mission of Lord Ashburton was announced. This movement on the part of England afforded in the judgment of the Executive a favorable opportunity for making an attempt to settle this long-existing controversy by some agreement-or treaty without further reference to arbitration.

It seemed entirely proper that if this purpose were entertained consultation should be had with the authorities of the States of Maine and Massachusetts. Letters, therefore, of which copies are herewith communicated, were addressed to the governors of those States, suggesting that commissioners should be appointed by each of them, respectively, to repair to this city and confer with the authorities of this Government on a line by agreement or compromise, with its equivalents and compensations. This suggestion was met by both States in a spirit of candor and patriotism and promptly complied with. Four commissioners on the part of Maine and three on the part of Massachusetts, all persons of distinction and high character, were duly appointed and commissioned and lost no time in presenting themselves at the seat of the Government of the United States. These commissioners have been in correspondence with this Government during the period of the discussions; have enjoyed its confidence and freest communications; have aided the general object with their counsel and advice, and in the end have unanimously signified their assent to the line proposed in the treaty.

Ordinarily it would be no easy task to reconcile and bring together such a variety of interests in a matter in itself difficult and perplexed, but the efforts of the Government in attempting to accomplish this desirable object have been seconded and sustained by a spirit of accommodation and conciliation on the part of the States concerned, to which much of the success of these efforts is to be ascribed.

Connected with the settlement of the line of the northeastern boundary, so far as it respects the States of Maine and Massachusetts, is the continuation of that line along the highlands to the northwesternmost head of Connecticut River. Which of the sources of that stream is entitled to this character has been matter of controversy and of some interest to the State of New Hampshire. The King of the Netherlands decided the main branch to be the northwesternmost head of the Connecticut. This did not satisfy the claim of New Hampshire. The line agreed to in the present treaty follows the highlands to the head of Halls Stream and thence down that river, embracing the whole claim of New Hampshire and establishing her title to 100,000 acres of territory more than she would have had by the decision of the King of the Netherlands.

By the treaty of 1783 the line is to proceed down the Connecticut River to the forty-fifth degree of north latitude, and thence west by that parallel till it strikes the St. Lawrence. Recent examinations having ascertained that the line heretofore received as the true line of latitude between those points was erroneous, and that the correction of this error would not only leave on the British side a considerable tract of territory heretofore supposed to belong to the States of Vermont and New York, but also Rouses Point, the site of a military work of the United States, it has been regarded as an object of importance not only to establish the rights and jurisdiction of those States up to the line to which they have been considered to extend, but also to comprehend Rouses Point within the territory of the United States. The relinquishment by the British Government of all the territory south of the line heretofore considered to be the true line has been obtained, and the consideration for this relinquishment is to inure by the provisions of the treaty to the States of Maine and Massachusetts.

The line of boundary, then, from the source of the St. Croix to the St. Lawrence, so far as Maine and Massachusetts are concerned, is fixed by their own consent and for considerations satisfactory to them, the chief of these considerations being the privilege of transporting the lumber and agricultural products grown and raised in Maine on the waters of the St. Johns and its tributaries down that river to the ocean free from imposition or disability. The importance of this privilege, perpetual in its terms, to a country covered at present by pine forests of great value, and much of it capable hereafter of agricultural improvement, is not a matter upon which the opinion of intelligent men is likely to be divided.

So far as New Hampshire is concerned, the treaty secures all that she requires, and New York and Vermont are quieted to the extent of their claim and occupation. The difference which would be made in the northern boundary of these two States by correcting the parallel of latitude may be seen on Tanner's maps (1836), new atlas, maps Nos. 6 and 9.

From the intersection of the forty-fifth degree of north latitude with the St. Lawrence and along that river and the lakes to the water communication between Lake Huron and Lake Superior the line was definitively agreed on by the commissioners of the two Governments under the sixth article of the treaty of Ghent; but between this last-mentioned point and the Lake of the Woods the commissioners acting under the seventh article of that treaty found several matters of disagreement, and therefore made no joint report to their respective Governments. The first of these was Sugar Island, or St. Georges Island, lying in St. Marys River, or the water communication between Lakes Huron and Superior. By the present treaty this island is embraced in the territories of the United States. Both from soil and position it is regarded as of much value.

Another matter of difference was the manner of extending the line from the point at which the commissioners arrived, north of Isle Royale, in Lake Superior, to the Lake of the Woods. The British commissioner insisted on proceeding to Fond du Lac, at the southwest angle of the lake, and thence by the river St. Louis to the Rainy Lake. The American commissioner supposed the true course to be to proceed by way of the Dog River. Attempts were made to compromise this difference, but without success. The details of these proceedings are found at length in the printed separate reports of the commissioners.

From the imperfect knowledge of this remote country at the date of the treaty of peace, some of the descriptions in that treaty do not harmonize with its natural features as now ascertained. "Long Lake" is nowhere to be found under that name. There is reason for supposing, however, that the sheet of water intended by that name is the estuary at the mouth of Pigeon River. The present treaty therefore adopts that estuary and river, and afterwards pursues the usual route across the height of land by the various portages and small lakes till the line reaches Rainy Lake, from which the commissioners agreed on the extension of it to its termination in the northwest angle of the Lake of the Woods. The region of country on and near the shore of the lake between Pigeon River on the north and Fond du Lac and the river St. Louis on the south and west, considered valuable as a mineral region, is thus included within the United States. It embraces a territory of

4,000,000 acres northward of the claim set up by the British commissioner under the treaty of Ghent.   From the height of land at the head of Pigeon River westerly to the Rainy Lake the country is understood to be of little value, being described by surveyors and marked on the map as a region of rock and water.

From the northwest angle of the Lake of the Woods, which is found to be in latitude 45° 23′ 55″ north, existing treaties require the line to be run due south to its intersection with the forty-fifth parallel, and thence along that parallel to the Rocky Mountains.

After sundry informal communications with the British minister upon the subject of the claims of the two countries to territory west of the Rocky Mountains, so little probability was found to exist of coming to any agreement on that subject at present that it was not thought expedient to make it one of the subjects of formal negotiation to be entered upon between this Government and the British minister as part of his duties under his special mission.

By the treaty of 1783 the line of division along the rivers and lakes from the place where the forty-fifth parallel of north latitude strikes the St. Lawrence to the outlet of Lake Superior is invariably to be drawn through the middle of such waters, and not through the middle of their main channels.   Such a line, if extended according to the literal terms of the treaty, would, it is obvious, occasionally intersect islands.   The manner in which the commissioners of the two Governments dealt with this difficult subject may be seen in their reports.   But where the line thus following the middle of the river or water course did not meet with islands, yet it was liable sometimes to leave the only practicable navigable channel altogether on one side.   The treaty made no provision for the common use of the waters by the citizens and subjects of both countries.

It has happened, therefore, in a few instances that the use of the river in particular places would be greatly diminished to one party or the other if in fact there was not a choice in the use of channels and passages. Thus at the Long Sault, in the St. Lawrence—a dangerous passage, practicable only for boats—the only safe run is between the Long Sault Islands and Barnharts Island (all which belong to the United States) on one side and the American shore on the other.   On the other hand, by far the best passage for vessels of any depth of water from Lake Erie into the Detroit River is between Bois Blanc, a British island, and the Canadian shore.   So again, there are several channels or passages, of different degrees of facility and usefulness, between the several islands in the river St. Clair at or near its entry into the lake of that name.   In these three cases the treaty provides that all the several passages and channels shall be free and open to the use of the citizens and subjects of both parties.

The treaty obligations subsisting between the two countries for the suppression of the African slave trade and the complaints made to this Government within the last three or four years, many of them but too well founded, of the visitation, seizure, and detention of American vessels on that coast by British cruisers could not but form a delicate and highly important part of the negotiations which have now been held.

The early and prominent part which the Government of the United States has taken for the abolition of this unlawful and inhuman traffic is well known. By the tenth article of the treaty of Ghent it is declared that the traffic in slaves is irreconcilable with the principles of humanity and justice, and that both His Majesty and the United States are desirous of continuing their efforts to promote its entire abolition; and it is thereby agreed that both the contracting parties shall use their best endeavors to accomplish so desirable an object. The Government of the United States has by law declared the African slave trade piracy, and at its suggestion other nations have made similar enactments. It has not been wanting in honest and zealous efforts, made in conformity with the wishes of the whole country, to accomplish the entire abolition of the traffic in slaves upon the African coast, but these efforts and those of other countries directed to the same end have proved to a considerable degree unsuccessful. Treaties are known to have been entered into some years ago between England and France by which the former power, which usually maintains a large naval force on the African station, was authorized to seize and bring in for adjudication vessels found engaged in the slave trade under the French flag.

It is known that in December last a treaty was signed in London by the representatives of England, France, Russia, Prussia, and Austria having for its professed object a strong and united effort of the five powers to put an end to the traffic. This treaty was not officially communicated to the Government of the United States, but its provisions and stipulations are supposed to be accurately known to the public. It is understood to be not yet ratified on the part of France.

No application or request has been made to this Government to become party to this treaty, but the course it might take in regard to it has excited no small degree of attention and discussion in Europe, as the principle upon which it is founded and the stipulations which it contains have caused warm animadversions and great political excitement.

In my message at the commencement of the present session of Congress I endeavored to state the principles which this Government supports respecting the right of search and the immunity of flags. Desirous of maintaining those principles fully, at the same time that existing obligations should be fulfilled, I have thought it most consistent with the honor and dignity of the country that it should execute its own laws and perform its own obligations by its own means and its own power.

The examination or visitation of the merchant vessels of one nation by the cruisers of another for any purpose except those known and acknowledged by the law of nations, under whatever restraints or regulations it may take place, may lead to dangerous results. It is far better by other means to supersede any supposed necessity or any motive for such examination or visit. Interference with a merchant vessel by an armed cruiser is always a delicate proceeding, apt to touch the point of national honor as well as to affect the interests of individuals. It has been thought, therefore, expedient, not only in accordance with the stipulations of the treaty of Ghent, but at the same time as removing all pretext on the part of others for violating the immunities of the American flag upon the seas, as they exist and are defined by the law of nations, to enter into the articles now submitted to the Senate.

The treaty which I now submit to you proposes no alteration, mitigation, or modification of the rules of the law of nations. It provides simply that each of the two Governments shall maintain on the coast of Africa a sufficient squadron to enforce separately and respectively the laws, rights, and obligations of the two countries for the suppression of the slave trade.

Another consideration of great importance has recommended this mode of fulfilling the duties and obligations of the country. Our commerce along the western coast of Africa is extensive, and supposed to be increasing. There is reason to think that in many cases those engaged in it have met with interruptions and annoyances caused by the jealousy and instigation of rivals engaged in the same trade. Many complaints on this subject have reached the Government. A respectable naval force on the coast is the natural resort and security against further occurrences of this kind.

The surrender to justice of persons who, having committed high crimes, seek an asylum in the territories of a neighboring nation would seem to be an act due to the cause of general justice and properly belonging to the present state of civilization and intercourse. The British Provinces of North America are separated from the States of the Union by a line of several thousand miles, and along portions of this line the amount of population on either side is quite considerable, while the passage of the boundary is always easy.

Offenders against the law on the one side transfer themselves to the other. Sometimes, with great difficulty, they are brought to justice, but very often they wholly escape. A consciousness of immunity from the power of avoiding justice in this way instigates the unprincipled and reckless to the commission of offenses, and the peace and good neighborhood of the border are consequently often disturbed.

In the case of offenders fleeing from Canada into the United States, the governors of States are often applied to for their surrender, and questions of a very embarrassing nature arise from these applications. It has been thought highly important, therefore, to provide for the whole case by a proper treaty stipulation. The article on the subject in the proposed treaty is carefully confined to such offenses as all mankind agree to regard as heinous and destructive of the security of life and property. In this careful and specific enumeration of crimes the object has been to exclude all political offenses or criminal charges arising from wars or intestine commotions. Treason, misprision of treason, libels, desertion from military service, and other offenses of similar character are excluded.

And lest some unforeseen inconvenience or unexpected abuse should arise from the stipulation rendering its continuance in the opinion of one or both of the parties not longer desirable, it is left in the power of either to put an end to it at will.

The destruction of the steamboat *Caroline* at Schlosser four or five years ago occasioned no small degree of excitement at the time, and became the subject of correspondence between the two Governments. That correspondence, having been suspended for a considerable period, was renewed in the spring of the last year, but no satisfactory result having been arrived at, it was thought proper, though the occurrence had ceased to be fresh and recent, not to omit attention to it on the present occasion. It has only been so far discussed in the correspondence now submitted as it was accomplished by a violation of the territory of the United States. The letter of the British minister, while he attempts to justify that violation upon the ground of a pressing and overruling necessity, admitting, nevertheless, that even if justifiable an apology was due for it, and accompanying this acknowledgment with assurances of the sacred regard of his Government for the inviolability of national territory, has seemed to me sufficient to warrant forbearance from any further remonstrance against what took place as an aggression on the soil and territory of the country. On the subject of the interference of the British authorities in the West Indies, a confident hope is entertained that the correspondence which has taken place, showing the grounds taken by this Government and the engagements entered into by the British minister, will be found such as to satisfy the just expectation of the people of the United States.

The impressment of seamen from merchant vessels of this country by British cruisers, although not practiced in time of peace, and therefore not at present a productive cause of difference and irritation, has, nevertheless, hitherto been so prominent a topic of controversy and is so likely to bring on renewed contentions at the first breaking out of a European war that it has been thought the part of wisdom now to take it into serious and earnest consideration. The letter from the Secretary of State to the British minister explains the ground which the Government has assumed and the principles which it means to uphold. For the defense of these grounds and the maintenance of these principles the most perfect reliance is placed on the intelligence of the American people and on their firmness and patriotism in whatever touches the honor of the country or its great and essential interests.

JOHN TYLER.

[The following are inserted because they pertain to the treaty transmitted with the message of President Tyler immediately preceding.]

DEPARTMENT OF STATE,
Washington, August 3, 1848.

To the Senate of the United States:

The Secretary of State has the honor to transmit to the Senate, in compliance with a resolution adopted by it on the 29th ultimo, a copy of the *joint report* of the commissioners under the treaty of Washington of August 9, 1842, together with a copy of the report of the American commissioner transmitting the same to the State Department.

JAMES BUCHANAN.

Mr. Smith to Mr. Buchanan.

WASHINGTON, *April 20, 1848.*

SIR: In presenting to you the joint report of the commissioners appointed under the treaty of Washington of August 9, 1842, to survey and mark the line of boundary between the United States and the British Provinces, which I have the honor herewith most respectfully to submit, I have to perform the painful duty of informing you that the maps of that line and of the adjacent country, which had been elaborately constructed by the scientific corps on the part of the United States, and contained upon 100 sheets of drawing paper of the largest size, together with the tables of the survey, have been destroyed by the conflagration of the building in which they were contained. This house had been occupied by Major James D. Graham, the head of the scientific corps and principal astronomer of the American commission, as his office until his departure for Mexico. All the maps, drawings, and tables had been completed and duly authenticated by the joint commissioners, and were ready to be deposited with their joint report under their hands and seals in the archives of this Government. Of this I had the honor to inform you in my letter of the 24th ultimo.

I can hardly express the pain which this unfortunate event has occasioned me. But I can not perceive that any imputation of blame can properly be attached to any officer of the commission. The care and custody of all the work of the United States scientific corps were properly placed in charge of Major Graham, as the head of that corps, who had had the immediate direction and superintendence of it from the first organization of the commission. He required the maps and tables at his office for reference and revision in the progress of the astronomical work. Upon his departure for Mexico he placed Lieutenant A. W. Whipple in his rooms with an injunction to guard with the utmost care the valuable property of the commission. On the day after he left the city, and when for the first time informed of the fact, I called upon Lieutenant Whipple and requested him to have all the maps, drawings, and tables ready to be turned over to the State Department on the following day. On the 24th ultimo I acquainted you with that fact.

No censure can possibly be attributed to Lieutenant Whipple, whose great care and attention to all his duties have been on all occasions highly distinguished. He escaped from the fire with scarcely an article of his dress, and his loss in money and clothing is at least $1,000. Major Graham has lost his valuable library, together with personal effects to a large amount. The fire was communicated from the basement of the house, and by no effort could anything be saved.

There are tracings of the maps upon "tissue paper," without the topography, in the State of Maine, but they are not signed by the commissioners.

The field books of the engineers were, fortunately, not in Major Graham's office, and are preserved.

Duplicates of the maps, duly authenticated, have been placed in the British archives at London, which, although they have not the topography of the country so fully laid down upon them as it was upon our own, represent with equal exactness the survey of the boundary itself. Should it be deemed expedient by this Government to procure copies of them, access to those archives for that purpose would undoubtedly be permitted, and the object accomplished at small expense, and when completed these copies could be authenticated by the joint commissioners in accordance with the provisions of the treaty.

I have the honor to be, with great respect, your obedient and humble servant,

ALBERT SMITH.

Report of the joint commission of boundary appointed under the treaty of Washington of August 9, 1842.

The undersigned, commissioners appointed under the treaty of Washington to trace and mark the boundary, as directed by that treaty, between the British possessions in North America and the United States—that is to say, James Bucknall Bucknall Estcourt, lieutenant-colonel in the British army, appointed commissioner by Her Britannic Majesty, and Albert Smith, appointed commissioner by the President of the United States—having accomplished the duty assigned to them, do now, in accordance with the directions of the said treaty, submit the following report and the accompanying maps, jointly signed, to their respective Governments.

In obedience to the terms of the treaty, the undersigned met at Bangor, in the State of Maine, on the 1st day of May, 1843, where they produced and verified the authority under which they each were respectively to act. They then adjourned, because the weather was not sufficiently open for taking the field, to the 1st of the following month (June), and agreed to meet again at that time at Houlton.

Accordingly, they did meet at that place, and began their operations.

It may be desirable to state at the outset that for the sake of convenience the whole line of boundary marked by the undersigned has been divided in the mention made of the different portions into the following grand divisions, viz:

"North line," from the source of the St. Croix to the intersection of the St. John.

"River St. John," from the intersection of the north line to the mouth of the St. Francis.

"River St. Francis," from its mouth to the outlet of Lake Pohenagamook.

"Southwest line," from the outlet of Lake Pohenagamook to the Northwest Branch of the St. John.

"South line," from the Northwest Branch to the parallel of latitude 46° 25′ on the Southwest Branch.

"Southwest Branch," from the parallel 46° 25′ to its source.

"Highlands," from the source of the Southwest Branch of the St. John to the source of Halls Stream.

"Halls Stream," from its source to the intersection of the line of Valentine and Collins.

"West line," from Halls Stream to the St. Lawrence near St. Regis, along the line of Valentine and Collins.

To return to the narration of operations:

The exploring line of Colonel Bouchette and Mr. Johnson, as directed by the treaty, was traced from the monument at the source of the St. Croix to the intersection of the St. John.

The monument found at the source of the St. Croix, as described in the report of Colonel Bouchette and Mr. Johnson, and the course of their exploring line, was traced by blazes or marks upon the trees.

An old line, cut out by the assistant surveyors of Colonel Bouchette and Mr. Johnson, was also found, which terminated about half a mile north of the South Branch of the Meduxnikeag, where, by records to which the undersigned referred, they ascertained that it had been abandoned because of its deviation from the exploring line of Colonel Bouchette and Mr. Johnson.

After the exploration and re-marking of the north line it was cut out 30 feet wide. The same was afterwards done in all parts where the boundary passed through woodland. After thus opening the north line it was surveyed, and iron posts were erected at intervals to mark it.

The general bearing of the line was rather to the west of the meridian of the monument at the source of the St. Croix. The precise line laid down by the undersigned was determined by successive courses, of which each was made to be as long as was convenient, provided it did not pass out of the opening of 30 feet.

At each angle of deflection an iron monument was erected, and placed anglewise with the line. Other monuments were erected at the crossing of roads, rivers, and at every mile, commencing from the source of the St. Croix. Those which were not intended to mark angles of deflection were placed square with the line.

At the intersection of the St. John by the north line the river is deep and broad. The boundary runs up the middle of the channel of the river, as indicated by the maps, dividing the islands as follows:

No. 1.	Ryan's Island	United States.
No. 2.	King's Island	United States.
No. 3.	Les Trois Isles	United States.
No. 4.	La Septieme Isle	United States.
No. 5.	Quissibis	Great Britain.
No. 6.	La Grand Isle	United States.
No. 7.	Thibideau's Islands	United States.
No. 8.	Madawaska Islands	Great Britain.
No. 9.	Joseph Michaud's three islands	United States.
No. 10.	Pine Island	Great Britain.
No. 11.	Baker's, Turtle, Dagle's, Fourth, Fifth } islands	Great Britain.
No. 12.	Kennedy's Island	Great Britain.
No. 13.	Crock's, Cranberry, Gooseberry } islands	Great Britain.
No. 14.	Savage's Island	United States.
No. 15.	Wheelock's Island	United States.
No. 16.	Caton's Island	United States.
No. 17.	Honeywell's Island	United States.
No. 18.	Savage and Johnson's Island	United States.
No. 19.	Grew's Island	United States.
No. 20.	Kendall's Island	Great Britain.

The islands were distributed to Great Britain or to the United States, as they were found to be on the right or left of the deep channel. There was but one doubtful case, La Septieme Isle, and that was apportioned to the United States because the majority of the owners were ascertained to reside on the United States side of the river.

Monuments were erected upon the islands, marking them for Great Britain or the United States, as the case may have been.

After leaving the St. John the boundary enters the St. Francis, dividing the islands at the mouth of that river in the manner shown in the maps. It then runs up the

St. Francis, through the middle of the lakes upon it, to the outlet of Lake Pohenaga-mook, the third large lake from the mouth of the river. At the outlet a large monument has been erected.

In order to determine the point on the Northwest Branch to which the treaty directed that a straight line should be run from the outlet of Lake Pohenagamook, a survey of that stream was made, and also of the main St. John in the neighborhood of the mouth of the Northwest Branch, and a line was cut between the St. John and the point on the Northwest Branch ascertained by the survey to be 10 miles in the nearest direction from it, and the distance was afterwards verified by chaining.

It was ascertained also, in accordance with the provisions of the treaty, by a triangulation of the country toward the highlands dividing the waters of the St. Lawrence and of the St. John, that more than 7 miles intervened between the point selected on the Northwest Branch and the crest of the dividing ridge. A large iron monument was afterwards erected on the point thus selected, and the space around was cleared and sown with grass seed. It is a short distance below the outlet of Lake Ishaganalshegeck.

The outlet of Lake Pohenagamook and the point on the Northwest Branch designated by the treaty having been thus ascertained and marked, in the spring of 1844 a straight line was run between them. Along that line, which passes entirely through forest, monuments were erected at every mile, at the crossings of the principal streams and rivers, and at the tops of those hills where a transit instrument had been set up to test the straightness of the line.

As soon as the parallel of latitude 46° 25′ had been determined on the Southwest Branch, in the early part of the summer of 1844, a straight line was drawn from the boundary point on the Northwest Branch to a large monument erected on the left bank of the Southwest Branch where it is intersected by the parallel of latitude 46° 25′. The line so drawn crosses the Southwest Branch once before it reaches the parallel of latitude 46° 25′, and at about half a mile distance from that parallel. There also a large monument has been set up on the left bank.

From the intersection of the parallel 46° 25′ the boundary ascends the Southwest Branch, passes through a lake near its head, and so up a small stream which falls into the lake from the west to the source of that stream, which has been selected as the source of the Southwest Branch.

On the Southwest Branch there are two principal forks, at each of which two monuments have been erected, one on each bank of the river immediately above the forks and upon the branch established as the boundary. The maps point out their positions. At the mouth of the small stream selected as the source of the Southwest Branch a monument has been erected upon a delta formed by two small outlets. Above those outlets three other monuments have been placed at intervals upon the same stream.

Upon the crest of the dividing ridge, very close to the source of the Southwest Branch, a large monument has been erected. It is the first point in the highlands, and from it the boundary runs along the crest in a southerly direction, passing near to the southeastern shore of the Portage Lake, and so on to a large monument erected on a small eminence on the east side of the Kennebec road. Thence it passes through a dwelling house called Tachereau's, which was standing there at the time the line was run; so, by a tortuous course, it runs to the top of Sandy Stream Mountain; thence, inclining to the southwest, it runs over Hog Back the First, as shown in the maps; thence toward Hog Back the Second, which it leaves on the north side. Further on, at the head of Leech Lake, there is a stream which divides its waters and flows both into Canada and into the United States. The boundary has been made to run up that stream a short distance from the fork where the waters divide to a second fork; thence between the streams which unite to form that fork, and then to ascend again the dividing ridge. A monument has been erected at the fork first mentioned, where the waters divide.

As the boundary approaches the valley of Spider River it bends to the southeast, and, by a wide circuit over high and steep hills, it turns the head of Spider River; thence it bends to the northwest until it approaches within about 4 miles of Lake Megantic; thence it turns again south, having the valley of Arnolds River on the right and of Dead River on the left. It leaves Gasford Mountain in Canada, threads its way over very high ground between the head of Arnolds River and the tributaries of the Magalloway; inclines then to the north, so to the west, over very rocky, mountainous, and difficult country, leaving Gipps Peak in the United States, and turns by a sharp angle at Saddle Back to the south. After that it again inclines to the west, and then to the south, and again to the west, and passes the head of the Connecticut. About 3 miles and a half east of the head of the Connecticut there is a division of waters similar to that described near Leech Lake. The boundary runs down a stream from near its source to the fork where it divides, and then again follows the dividing ridge. The spot is noted on the map.

After the boundary has passed the head of the Connecticut it runs to the northwest, descending into very low, swampy ground between the heads of Indian Stream and the tributaries of the St. Francis. Thus it passes on, bending again to the south of west, over a high hill, to the source of Halls Stream.

Iron monuments have been erected at intervals along the highlands from the source of the Southwest Branch of the St. John to the source of Halls Stream, the position of each of which is shown upon the maps.

From the source of Halls Stream the boundary descends that river, dividing the islands, which are, however, merely unimportant alluvial deposits, in the manner indicated by the maps until it reaches the intersection of that stream by the line formerly run by Valentine and Collins as the forty-fifth degree of north latitude.

At that point a large monument has been erected on the right and a small one on the left bank of the stream. Monuments have also been erected along the bank of this stream, as indicated on the maps.

The line of Valentine and Collins was explored and found by the blazes still remaining in the original forest.

Upon cutting into those blazes it was seen that deep seated in the tree there was a scar, the surface of the original blaze, slightly decayed, and upon counting the rings (which indicate each year's growth of the tree) it was found that the blazes dated back to 1772, 1773, and 1774. The line of Valentine and Collins was run in 1771, 1772, 1773, and 1774. The coincidence of the dates of the blazes with those of the above line, confirmed by the testimony of the people of the country, satisfied the undersigned that the line they had found was that mentioned in the treaty. Along this portion of the boundary, which is known as the forty-fifth degree of Valentine and Collins, and which extends from Halls Stream to St. Regis, there are several interruptions to the blazes in those parts where clearings have been made, and there the authentic marks of the precise situation of the old line have been lost. In those cases the undersigned have drawn the boundary line straight from the original blazes on the one side of a clearing to the original blazes on the other side of the same clearing.

It can not be positively stated that the line as it has been traced through those clearings precisely coincides with the old line, but the undersigned believe that it does not differ materially from it; nor have they had the means of determining a nearer or a surer approximation.

Along this line, at every point of deflection, an iron monument has been erected; also at the crossing of rivers, lakes, and roads. Those which mark deflections are placed, as on the "north line," anglewise with the line; all the others are placed square with it. The maps show the position of each.

On the eastern shore of Lake Memphremagog an astronomical station was established, and on a large flat rock of granite, which happened to lie between the astronomical station and the boundary, was cut the following inscription:

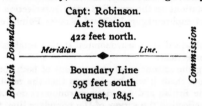

Capt: Robinson.
Ast: Station
422 feet north.

Meridian ◆ *Line.*

Boundary Line
595 feet south
August, 1845.

A mark was cut upon the stone, as indicated by the dot upon the meridian line above, from which these measurements were made.

At Rouses Point a monument of wrought stone was set up at the intersection of the boundary by the meridian of the transit instrument used there by Major Graham, and an inscription was cut upon it stating the latitude and longitude, the names of the observer and his assistant, the names of the commissioners, and the territories divided.

To mark the position of the instruments used at the following astronomical stations along the west line, two monuments within a few feet of each other have been erected at each station, and they have been placed on the boundary line due north or south of the instrument, as the case may have been.

The stations are: Lake Memphremagog, Richford, John McCoy's, Trout River.

The boundary along the west line, though very far from being a straight line, is generally about half a mile north of the true parallel of latitude 45° from Halls Stream to Rouses Point. At about 28 miles west of Rouses Point it, however, crosses that parallel to the south until it reaches Chateaugay River, where it bends northward, and, crossing the parallel again about 4 miles east of St. Regis, it strikes the St. Lawrence 151 feet north of 45°. At that point a large monument has been erected on the bank of the St. Lawrence. Two large monuments have also been erected, one on either side of the river Richelieu near Rouses Point.

No marks of the old line were to be found about St. Regis. It was therefore agreed to run a line due west from the last blaze which should be found in the woods on the east side of St. Regis. That blaze occurred about 1 mile east of the St. Regis River.

The maps, which exhibit the boundary on a scale of 4 inches to 1 statute mile, consist of 62 consecutive sheets of antiquarian paper as constructed by the British and of 61 as constructed by the American commission. A general map has also been constructed on a scale of 8 miles to 1 inch by the British and of 10 miles to 1 inch by the American commission, upon which the before-mentioned sheets are represented.

The following portions of the boundary have been laid down by the British commission, on detached maps, on a scale of 12 inches to 1 mile, which have been signed by both commissioners:

Grand Falls of the St. John, including the intersection of that river by the north line; islands of the St. John; the outlet of Lake Pohenagamook; the turning point of the boundary on the Northwest Branch of the St. John; the intersection of the Southwest Branch by the parallel of latitude 46° 25'; the source of the Southwest Branch; the source of Halls Stream; the intersection of Halls Stream by the west line; Rouses Point; St. Regis; Derby.

But similar maps have not been prepared by the American commission, because during the interval between the finishing of the maps of the British commission and those of the American it was thought that the maps already constructed upon a scale of 4 inches to 1 mile represented the boundary with sufficient clearness and accuracy.

The astronomical observations were begun at the Grand Falls early in June, 1843, and were carried up the St. John River to the Northwest Branch by a chain of stations, which, together with the results obtained, are tabulated in the appendix accompanying this report.

From the valley of the St. John an astronomical connection was made with Quebec, and thence to Montreal, and so to Rouses Point. From Rouses Point a connection was obtained with Cambridge University, near Boston.

The astronomical stations on the west line were: Intersection of Halls Stream by the west line, Lake Memphremagog, Richford, Rouses Point, John McCoy's, Trout River, St. Regis.

Latitude was also obtained at an astronomical station established for the purpose at the head of the Connecticut.

Volumes containing the astronomical observations of both commissions are herewith submitted. From them it will be observed that the results for absolute longitude obtained by the British and American astronomers do not agree. It being a difference in no way affecting the survey of the boundary line, the undersigned do not feel called upon to attempt to reconcile it. The data upon which those results are based may be seen in the volumes of observations accompanying this report.

In the appendix will be found, in a tabular form, the following:

An abstract of the survey of the boundary along the north line; an abstract of the survey of the boundary along the southwest line; an abstract of the survey of the boundary along the south line; an abstract of the survey of the boundary along the highlands; an abstract of the survey of the boundary along the west line; the position of the monuments erected on the Southwest Branch of the St. John and on Halls Stream; the distribution of the islands of the St. John and the monuments on them; the guide lines and offsets run by each commission for the survey of the highlands; the azimuths of verification for the survey of the highlands; the latitudes and longitudes obtained from the astronomical observations; the comparative longitudes obtained, and the methods used for the purpose.

Upon comparing the maps of the two commissions it will be seen that the American commission numbers two monuments more than the British. Those are to be found, one on the "Fourth Island," in the river St. John, and the other on the highlands between the source of the Southwest Branch of the river St. John and the Kennebec road.

On the maps of the British commission representing the "west line" the name of the town of "*Derby*" has been improperly placed north of the line instead of south of it. Also, on the same maps the direction of Salmon River, near the western extremity of the "west line," has been incorrectly laid down from the boundary line northward. A direction has been given to it northeasterly instead of northwesterly.

The above two corrections the British commissioner is authorized to make on his maps after his return to England.

To avoid unnecessary delay in making their joint report, the undersigned have attached their signatures to the maps, although the lettering of some of the astronomical stations upon the maps of the American commission, as well as the alterations before mentioned in the maps of the British commission, are yet to be made; but in the maps of both the boundary has been laid down accurately and definitively, and the undersigned engage that it shall not be altered in any respect.

In conclusion the undersigned have the honor to report that the line of boundary described in the foregoing statement has been run, marked, and surveyed, and the accompanying maps faithfully constructed from that survey.

The undersigned take leave to add that the most perfect harmony has subsisted between the two commissions from first to last, and that no differences have arisen between the undersigned in the execution of the duties intrusted to them.

Signed and sealed in duplicate, at the city of Washington, this 28th day of June, A. D. 1847.

J. B. BUCKNALL ESTCOURT, [SEAL.]
Lieutenant-Colonel, Her Britannic Majesty's Commissioner.
ALBERT SMITH, [SEAL.]
United States Commissioner.

NOTE.—The astronomical computations of the American commission not being completed, and it being unnecessary to defer the signing of the report on that account, the American commissioner engages to transmit them, with any other papers or tables not yet finished, as soon as they shall be so, to the British commissioner, through the American minister resident in London, to whom, upon delivery of the documents, the British commissioner will give a receipt, to be transmitted to the American commissioner.

J. B. BUCKNALL ESTCOURT,
Lieutenant-Colonel, H. B. M. Commissioner of Boundary.

ALBERT SMITH,
United States Commissioner.

WASHINGTON, *August 18, 1842.*
To the Senate of the United States:

I transmit to the Senate, for its consideration with a view to its ratification, a treaty of amity, commerce, and navigation with the Republic of Texas, negotiated at the seat of Government of the United States between the Secretary of State, duly empowered for that purpose, and the chargé d'affaires of that Republic.

In forming the first commercial treaty between the two Governments an anxious desire has been felt to introduce such provisions as should promote the interests of both countries. The immediate proximity of Texas to the United States and the consequent facility of intercourse, the nature of its principal agricultural production, and the relations which both countries bear to several large rivers which are boundaries between them, and which in some part of their course run within the territories of both, have caused peculiarities of condition and interests which it has been necessary to guard.

The treaty provides that Texas shall enjoy a right of deposit for such of her productions as may be introduced into the United States for exportation, but upon the condition that the Executive of the United States may prescribe such regulations as may be necessary for the proper enjoyment of the privilege within our territory. It was thought no more than reasonable to grant this facility to the trade of Texas, under such conditions as seem best calculated to guard against abuse or inconvenience.

The treaty further provides that raw cotton may be imported from either country into the other free of duties. In general it is not wise to enter into treaty stipulations respecting duties of import; they are usually much better left to the operation of general laws. But there are circumstances existing in this case which have been thought to justify a departure from the general rule, and the addition of it to the number of instances, not large, in which regulations of duties of imports have been made the subject of national compact.

The United States consume large quantities of raw cotton, but they are exporters of the article to a still greater extent. Texas, for the present at least, exports her whole crop. These exportations are, in general, to the same foreign markets, and it is supposed to be of no considerable importance to the American producer whether he meets the Texan product at home or abroad.

On the other hand, it is thought that a useful commercial intercourse would be promoted in several ways by receiving the raw cotton of Texas at once into the United States free of duty. The tendency of such a measure is to bring to the United States, in the first instance, Texan cotton ultimately destined to European markets. The natural effect of this, it is supposed, will be to increase the business of the cities of the United States to the extent of this importation and exportation, and to secure a further degree of employment to the navigation of the country. But these are by no means all the benefits which may be reasonably expected from the arrangement. Texas, at least for a considerable time to come, must import all the manufactured articles and much of the supplies and provisions necessary for her use and consumption. These commodities she will be likely to obtain, if to be had, in the markets of the country in which she disposes of her main annual product. The manufactures of the North and East, therefore, and the grain and provisions of the Western States are likely to find in Texas a demand, increased by whatever augments intercourse between the two countries, and especially by whatever tends to give attraction to the cities of the United States as marts for the sale of her great and principal article of export.

As a security, however, against unforeseen results or occurrences, it has been thought advisable to give this article of the treaty a limitation of five years.

JOHN TYLER.

WASHINGTON, *August 23, 1842.*

To the Senate of the United States:

A resolution of the Senate of the 21st of June last requested the President to communicate to the Senate, so far as he might deem it compatible with the public interests, what measures, if any, had been taken to obtain the recognition by the Mexican Government of such claims of American citizens as were laid before the late joint commission, but were not finally acted on by it, and the satisfaction of such claims as were admitted by said commission; also whether any facts had come to his knowledge calculated to induce a belief that any such claims had been rejected in consequence of the evidence thereof having been withheld by the Mexican Government, its officers or agents, and any other information which he might deem it expedient to communicate relative to said claims; and another resolution of the 6th instant requested the President, so far as he might deem it compatible with the public service, to communicate to the Senate the measures taken to obtain the performance of the stipulations contained in the convention with Mexico in relation to the awards made by the commissioners and umpire under said convention.

In the present state of the correspondence and of the relations between the two Governments on these important subjects it is not deemed consistent with the public interest to communicate the information requested. The business engages earnest attention, and will be made the subject of a full communication to Congress at the earliest practicable period.

JOHN TYLER.

WASHINGTON, *August 24, 1842.*

To the Senate of the United States:

On the 15th day of April, 1842, in virtue of the sentence of a court-martial regularly convened under orders from the Secretary of the Navy, which received my approval, John H. Clack, who was a captain in the Navy, was dismissed the service. Since the confirmation of that sentence a letter has been addressed by Mr. Paulding, late Secretary of the Navy, to Captain Clack, which leads to the belief that he had analyzed the charges made against Captain Clack, and for reasons which appeared to him satisfactory and which, according to his letter, he indorsed on the charges, disposed of the case by refusing to submit it to a court-martial.

Notwithstanding a diligent search has been made for this document, none such can be found; but the only paper in the office having reference to this subject is a letter addressed by Mr. Paulding to Lieutenant Buchanan, a copy of which, together with the original of that of Mr. P. to Captain C., is herewith communicated. I felt it, however, every way due to the high character of Mr. Paulding to consider the fact stated by him to be as well sustained by his declaration to that effect as if the record was found, and as the court-martial would not have been ordered by the present Secretary with the knowledge of the fact stated by Mr. Paulding, since it would have been improper to have reopened a case once finally disposed of, I have felt that it was alike due to the general service of the Navy as to Mr. Clack to nominate him for reappointment to the service.

I therefore nominate John H. Clack to be a captain in the Navy of the United States.

JOHN TYLER.

WASHINGTON, *August 25, 1842.*

To the House of Representatives of the United States:

In answer to the resolution of the House of Representatives of the 11th of June last, upon the subject of claims of citizens of the United States against the Government of the Mexican Republic, I transmit a report from the Secretary of State and a copy of the report of the commissioners on the part of the United States under the late convention between the United States and that Republic.

JOHN TYLER.

VETO MESSAGES.

WASHINGTON, *June 29, 1842.*

To the House of Representatives of the United States:

I return the bill, which originated in the House of Representatives, entitled "An act to extend for a limited period the present laws for laying and collecting duties on imports," with the following objections:

It suspends—in other words, abrogates for the time—the provision of the act of 1833, commonly called the "compromise act." The only ground on which this departure from the solemn adjustment of a great and agitating question seems to have been regarded as expedient is the alleged necessity of establishing by legislative enactments rules and regulations for assessing the duties to be levied on imports after the 30th June according to the home valuation, and yet the bill expressly provides that "if before the 1st of August there be no further legislation upon the subject, the laws for laying and collecting duties shall be the same as though this act had not been passed." In other words, that the act of 1833, imperfect as it is considered, shall in that case continue to be and to be executed under such rules and regulations as previous statutes had prescribed or had enabled the executive department to prescribe for that purpose, leaving the supposed chasm in the revenue laws just as it was before.

I am certainly far from being disposed to deny that additional legislation upon the subject is very desirable; on the contrary, the necessity, as well as difficulty, of establishing uniformity in the appraisements to be made in conformity with the true intention of that act was brought to the notice of Congress in my message to Congress at the opening of its present session. But however sensible I may be of the embarrassments to which the Executive, in the absence of all aid from the superior wisdom of the Legislature, will be liable in the enforcement of the existing laws, I have not, with the sincerest wish to acquiesce in its expressed will, been able to persuade myself that the exigency of the occasion is so great as to justify me in signing the bill in question with my present views of its character and effects. The existing laws, as I am advised, are sufficient to authorize and enable the collecting officers, under the directions of the Secretary of the Treasury, to levy the duties imposed by the act of 1833.

That act was passed under peculiar circumstances, to which it is not necessary that I should do more than barely allude. Whatever may be, in theory, its character, I have always regarded it as importing the highest moral obligation. It has now existed for nine years unchanged in any essential particular, with as general acquiescence, it is believed, of the whole country as that country has ever manifested for any of her wisely established institutions. It has insured to it the repose which always flows from truly wise and moderate counsels—a repose the more striking because of the long and angry agitations which preceded it. This salutary law proclaims in express terms the principle which, while it led to the abandonment of a scheme of indirect taxation founded on a false basis and pushed to dangerous excess, justifies any enlargement of duties that may be called for by the real exigencies of the public service. It provides "that duties shall be laid for the purpose of raising such revenue as may be necessary to an economical administration of the Government." It is therefore in the power of Congress to lay duties as high as its discretion may dictate for the necessary uses of the Government without infringing upon the objects of the act of 1833. I do not doubt that the exigencies of the Government do require an increase of the tariff of duties above 20 per cent, and I as little doubt that Congress may, above as well as below that rate, so discriminate as to give incidental protection to manufacturing industry, thus to make the burdens which it is compelled to impose upon the people for the purposes of Government productive of a double benefit. This most of the reasonable opponents of protective duties seem willing to concede, and, if we may judge from the manifestations of public opinion in all quarters, this is all that the manufacturing interests really require. I am happy in the persuasion that this double object can be most easily and effectually accomplished at the present juncture without any departure from the spirit and principle of the statute in question. The manufacturing classes have now an opportunity which may never occur again of permanently identifying their interests with those of the whole country, and making them, in the highest sense of the term, a national concern. The moment is propitious to the interests of the whole country in the introduction of harmony among all its parts and all its several interests. The same rate of imposts, and no more, as will most surely reestablish the public credit will secure to the manufacturer all the protection he ought to desire, with every prospect of permanence and stability which the hearty acquiescence of the whole country on a reasonable system can hold out to him.

But of this universal acquiescence, and the harmony and confidence and the many other benefits that will certainly result from it, I regard the suspension of the law for distributing the proceeds of the sales of the public lands as an indispensable condition. This measure is, in my judgment, called for by a large number, if not a great majority, of the people of the United States; by the state of the public credit and finances; by the critical posture of our various foreign relations; and, above all, by that most sacred of all duties—public faith. The act of September last, which provides for the distribution, couples it inseparably with the condition that it shall cease—first, in case of war; second, as soon and so long as the rate of duties shall for any reason whatever be raised above 20 per cent. Nothing can be more clear, express, or imperative than this language. It is in vain to allege that a deficit in the Treasury was known to exist and that means were taken to supply this deficit by loan when the act was passed. It is true that a loan was authorized at the same session during which the distribution law was passed, but the most sanguine of the friends of the two measures entertained no doubt but that the loan would be eagerly sought after and taken up by capitalists and speedily reimbursed by a country destined, as they hoped, soon to enjoy an overflowing prosperity. The very terms of the loan, making it redeemable *in three years*, demonstrate this beyond all cavil. Who at the time foresaw or imagined the possibility of the present real state of things, when a nation that has paid off her whole debt since the last peace, while all the other great powers have been increasing theirs, and whose resources, already so great, are yet but in the infancy of their development, should be compelled to haggle in the money market for a paltry sum not equal to one year's revenue upon her economical system? If the distribution law is to be indefinitely suspended, according not only to its own terms, but by universal consent, in the case of war, wherein are the actual exigencies of the country or the moral obligation to provide for them less under present circumstances than they could be were we actually involved in war? It appears to me to be the indispensable duty of all concerned in the administration of public affairs to see that a state of things so humiliating and so perilous should not last a moment longer than is absolutely unavoidable. Much less excusable should we be in parting with any portion of our available means, at least until the demands of the Treasury are fully supplied. But besides the urgency of such considerations, the fact is undeniable that the distribution act could not have become a law without the guaranty in the proviso of the act itself.

This connection, thus meant to be inseparable, is severed by the bill presented to me. The bill violates the principle of the acts of 1833 and September, 1841, by suspending the first and rendering for a time the last inoperative. Duties above 20 per cent are proposed to be levied, and yet the *proviso* in the distribution act is disregarded. The proceeds of the sales are to be distributed on the 1st of August, so that, while the duties proposed to be enacted exceed 20 per cent, no suspension of the distribution to the States is permitted to take place. To abandon the principle for a month is to open the way for its total abandonment. If such is not meant, why postpone at all? Why not let the distribution take place on the 1st of July if the law so directs (which, however, is regarded as questionable)? But why not have limited the provision to that effect? Is it for the accommodation of the Treasury? I see no reason to believe that the Treasury will be in better condition to meet the payment on the 1st of August than on the 1st of July.

The bill assumes that a distribution of the proceeds of the public lands is, by existing laws, to be made on the 1st day of July, 1842, notwithstanding there has been an imposition of duties on imports exceeding 20 per cent up to that day, and directs it to be made on the 1st of August next. It seems to me very clear that this conclusion is equally erroneous and dangerous, as it would divert from the Treasury a fund sacredly pledged for the general purposes of the Government in the event of a rate of duty above 20 per cent being found necessary for an economical administration of the Government.

The bill under consideration is designed only as a temporary measure; and thus a temporary measure, passed merely for the convenience of Congress, is made to affect the vital principle of an important act. If the proviso of the act of September, 1841, can be suspended for the whole period of a temporary law, why not for the whole period of a permanent law? In fact, a doubt may be well entertained, according to strict legal rules, whether the condition, having been thus expressly suspended by this bill and rendered inapplicable to a case where it would otherwise have clearly applied, will not be considered as ever after satisfied and gone. Without expressing any decided opinion on this point, I see enough in it to justify me in adhering to the law as it stands in preference to subjecting a condition so vitally affecting the peace of the country, and so solemnly enacted at a momentous crisis, and so steadfastly adhered to ever since, and so replete, if adhered to, with good to every interest of the country, to doubtful or captious interpretation.

In discharging the high duties thus imposed on me by the Constitution I repeat to the House my entire willingness to cooperate in all financial measures, constitutional and proper, which in its wisdom it may judge necessary and proper to reestablish the credit of the Government. I believe that the proceeds of the sales of the public lands being restored to the Treasury—or, more properly speaking, the proviso of the act of September, 1841, being permitted to remain in full force—a tariff of duties may easily be adjusted, which, while it will yield a revenue sufficient to maintain the Government in vigor by restoring its credit, will afford ample protection and infuse a new life into all our manufacturing establishments. The condition of the country calls for such legislation, and it will afford me the most sincere pleasure to cooperate in it.

JOHN TYLER.

WASHINGTON, *August 9, 1842.*

To the House of Representatives of the United States:

It is with unfeigned regret that I find myself under the necessity of returning to the House of Representatives with my objections a bill entitled "An act to provide revenue from imports, and to change and modify existing laws imposing duties on imports, and for other purposes." Nothing can be more painful to any individual called upon to perform the Chief Executive duties under our limited Constitution than to be constrained to withhold his assent from an important measure adopted by the Legislature. Yet he would neither fulfill the high purposes of his station nor consult the true interests or the solemn will of the people—the common constituents of both branches of the Government—by yielding his well-considered, most deeply fixed, and repeatedly declared opinions on matters of great public concernment to those of a coordinate department without requesting that department seriously to reexamine the subject of their difference. The exercise of some independence of judgment in regard to all acts of legislation is plainly implied in the responsibility of approving them. At all times a duty, it becomes a peculiarly solemn and imperative one when the subjects passed upon by Congress happen to involve, as in the present instance, the most momentous issues, to affect variously the various parts of a great country, and to have given rise in all quarters to such a conflict of opinion as to render it impossible to conjecture with any certainty on which side the majority really is. Surely if the pause for reflection intended by the wise authors of the Constitution by referring the subject back to Congress for reconsideration be ever expedient and necessary it is precisely such a case as the present.

On the subject of distributing the proceeds of the sales of the public lands in the existing state of the finances it has been my duty to make known my settled convictions on various occasions during the present session of Congress. At the opening of the extra session, upward of twelve months ago, sharing fully in the general hope of returning prosperity and credit, I recommended such a distribution, but that recommendation was even then expressly coupled with the condition that the duties on imports should not exceed the rate of 20 per cent provided by the compromise act of 1833. These hopes were not a little encouraged and these views strengthened by the report of Mr. Ewing, then Secretary of the Treasury, which was shortly thereafter laid before Congress, in which he recommended the imposition of duties at the rate of 20 per cent *ad valorem* on all free articles, with specified exceptions, and stated "if this measure be adopted there will be received in the Treasury from customs in the last quarter of the present year (1841) $5,300,000; in all of the year 1842, about $22,500,000; and in the year 1843, after the final reduction under the act of March 2, 1833, about $20,800,000;" and adds:

It is believed that after the heavy expenditures required by the public service in the present year shall have been provided for, the revenues which will accrue from that or a nearly approximate rate of duty will be sufficient to defray the expenses of the Government and leave a surplus to be annually applied to the gradual payment of the national debt, leaving the proceeds of *the public lands* to be disposed of as Congress shall see fit.

I was most happy that Congress at the time seemed entirely to concur in the recommendations of the Executive, and, anticipating the correctness of the Secretary's conclusions, and in view of an actual surplus, passed the distribution act of the 4th September last, wisely limiting its operation by two conditions having reference, both of them, to a possible state of the Treasury different from that which had been anticipated by the Secretary of the Treasury and to the paramount necessities of the public service. It ordained that "if at any time during the existence of that act there should be an imposition of duties on imports inconsistent with the provision of the act of the 2d March, 1833, and beyond the rate of duties fixed by that act, to wit, 20 per cent on the value of such imports or any of them, then the distribution should be suspended, and should continue so suspended until that cause should be removed." By a previous clause it had, in a like spirit of wise and cautious patriotism, provided for another case, in which all are even now agreed, that the proceeds of the sales of the public lands should be used for the defense of the country. It was enacted that the act should continue and be in force until otherwise provided by law, unless the United States should become involved in war with any foreign power, in which event, from the commencement of hostilities, the act should be suspended until the cessation of hostilities.

Not long after the opening of the present session of Congress the unprecedented and extraordinary difficulties that have recently embarrassed the finances of the country began to assume a serious aspect. It soon became quite evident that the hopes under which the act of 4th September was passed, and which alone justified it in the eyes either of Congress who imposed or of the Executive who approved, the first of the two conditions just recited were not destined to be fulfilled. Under the pressure, therefore, of the embarrassments which had thus unexpectedly arisen it appeared to me that the course to be pursued had been clearly marked out for the Government by that act itself. The condition contemplated in it as requiring a suspension of its operation had occurred. It became necessary in the opinions of all to raise the rate of duties upon imports above 20 per cent; and with a view both to provide available means to meet present exigencies and to lay the foundation for a successful negotiation of a loan, I felt it incumbent on me to urge upon Congress to raise the duties accordingly, imposing them in a spirit of a wise discrimination for the twofold object of affording ample revenue for the Government and incidental protection to the various branches of domestic industry. I also pressed, in the most emphatic but respectful language I could employ, the necessity of making the land sales available to the Treasury, as the basis of public credit. I did not think that I could stand excused, much less justified, before the people of the United States, nor could I reconcile it to myself to recommend the imposition of additional taxes upon them without at the same time urging the employment of all the legitimate means of the Government toward satisfying its wants. These opinions were communicated in advance of any definitive action of Congress on the subject either of the tariff or land sales, under a high sense of public duty and in compliance with an express injunction of the Constitution, so that if a collision, extremely to be deprecated, as such collisions always are, has seemingly arisen between the executive and legislative branches of the Government, it has assuredly not been owing to any capricious interference or to any want of a plain and frank declaration of opinion on the part of the former.   Congress differed in its views with those of the Executive, as it had undoubtedly a right to do, and passed a bill virtually for a time repealing the proviso of the act of the 4th September, 1841.   The bill was returned to the House in which it originated with my objections to its becoming a law.   With a view to prevent, if possible, an open disagreement of opinion on a point so important, I took occasion to declare that I regarded it as an indispensable prerequisite to an increase of duties above 20 per cent that the act of the 4th September should remain unrepealed in its provisions.   My reasons for that opinion were elaborately set forth in the message which accompanied the return of the bill, which no constitutional majority appears to have been found for passing into a law.

The bill which is now before me proposes in its twenty-seventh section the total repeal of one of the provisos in the act of September, and, while it increases the duties above 20 per cent, directs an unconditional distribution of the land proceeds.   I am therefore subjected a second time in the period of a few days to the necessity of either giving my approval to a measure which, in my deliberate judgment, is in conflict with great public interests or of returning it to the House in which it originated with my objections.   With all my anxiety for the passage of a law which would replenish an exhausted Treasury and furnish a sound and healthy encouragement to mechanical industry, I can not consent to do so at the sacrifice of the peace and harmony of the country and the clearest convictions of public duty.

For some of the reasons which have brought me to this conclusion I refer to my previous messages to Congress, and briefly subjoin the following:

1. The bill unites two subjects which, so far from having any affinity to one another, are wholly incongruous in their character.   It is both a revenue and an appropriation bill.   It thus imposes on the Executive, in the first place, the necessity of either approving that which he would reject or rejecting that which he might otherwise approve.   This is a species of constraint to which the judgment of the Executive ought not, in my opinion, to be subjected.   But that is not my only objection to the act in its present form.   The union of subjects wholly dissimilar in their character in the same bill, if it grew into a practice, would not fail to lead to consequences destructive of all wise and conscientious legislation.   Various measures, each agreeable only to a small minority, might by being thus united—and the more the greater chance of success—lead to

the passing of laws of which no single provision could if standing alone command a majority in its favor.

2. While the Treasury is in a state of extreme embarrassment, requiring every dollar which it can make available, and when the Government has not only to lay additional taxes, but to borrow money to meet pressing demands, the bill proposes to give away a fruitful source of revenue—which is the same thing as raising money by loan and taxation—not to meet the wants of the Government, but for distribution—a proceeding which I must regard as highly impolitic, if not unconstitutional.

A brief review of the present condition of the public finances will serve to illustrate the true condition of the Treasury and exhibit its actual necessities:

On the 5th of August (Friday last) there was in the Treasury, in round numbers..		$2,150,000
Necessary to be retained to meet trust funds........................	$360,000	
Interest on public debt due in October.............................	80,000	
To redeem Treasury notes and pay the interest.....................	100,000	
Land distribution under the act of the 4th of September, 1841........	640,000	
		1,180,000
Leaving an available amount of...		970,000

The Navy Department had drawn requisitions on the Treasury at that time to meet debts actually due, among which are bills under protest for $1,414,000, thus leaving an actual deficit of $444,000.

There was on hand about $100,000 of unissued Treasury notes, assisted by the accruing revenue (amounting to about $150,000 per week, exclusive of receipts on unpaid bonds), to meet requisitions for the Army and the demands of the civil list.

The withdrawal of the sum of $640,000 to be distributed among the States, so soon as the statements and accounts can be made up and completed, by virtue of the provisions of the act of the 4th of September last (of which nearly a moiety goes to a few States, and only about $383,000 is to be divided among all the States), while it adds materially to the embarrassments of the Treasury, affords to the States no decided relief.

No immediate relief from this state of things is anticipated unless (what would most deeply be deplored) the Government could be reconciled to the negotiation of loans already authorized by law at a rate of discount ruinous in itself and calculated most seriously to affect the public credit. So great is the depression of trade that even if the present bill were to become a law and prove to be productive some time would elapse before sufficient supplies would flow into the Treasury, while in the meantime its embarrassments would be continually augmented by the semiannual distribution of the land proceeds.

Indeed, there is but too much ground to apprehend that even if this bill were permitted to become a law—alienating, as it does, the proceeds of the land sales—an actual deficit in the Treasury would occur, which would more than probably involve the necessity of a resort to direct taxation.

Let it be also remarked that $5,500,000 of the public debt becomes redeemable in about two years and a half, which at any sacrifice must be met, while the Treasury is always liable to demands for the payment of outstanding Treasury notes. Such is the gloomy picture which our financial department now presents, and which calls for the exercise of a rigid economy in the public expenditures and the rendering available of all the means within the control of the Government. I most respectfully submit whether this is a time to give away the proceeds of the land sales when the public lands constitute a fund which of all others may be made most useful in sustaining the public credit. Can the Government be generous and munificent to others when every dollar it can command is necessary to supply its own wants? And if Congress would not hesitate to suffer the provisions of the act of 4th September last to remain unrepealed in case the country was involved in war, is not the necessity for such a course now just as imperative as it would be then?

3. A third objection remains to be urged, which would be sufficient in itself to induce me to return the bill to the House with my objections. By uniting two subjects so incongruous as tariff and distribution it inevitably makes the fate of the one dependent upon that of the other in future contests of party. Can anything be more fatal to the merchant or manufacturer than such an alliance? What they most of all require is a system of moderate duties so arranged as to withdraw the tariff question, as far as possible, completely from the arena of political contention. Their chief want is permanency and stability. Such an increase of the tariff I believe to be necessary in order to meet the economical expenditures of Government. Such an increase, made in the spirit of moderation and judicious discrimination, would, I have no doubt, be entirely satisfactory to the great majority of the American people. In the way of accomplishing a measure so salutary and so imperatively demanded by every public interest, the legislative department will meet with a cordial cooperation on the part of the Executive. This is all that the manufacturer can desire, and it would be a burden readily borne by the people. But I can not too earnestly repeat that in order to be beneficial it must be permanent, and in order to be permanent it must command general acquiescence. But can such permanency be justly hoped for if the tariff question be coupled with that of distribution, as to which a serious conflict of opinion exists among the States and the people, and which enlists in its support a bare majority, if, indeed, there be a majority, of the two Houses of Congress? What permanency or stability can attach to a measure which, warring upon itself, gives away a fruitful source of revenue at the moment it proposes a large increase of taxes on the people? Is the manufacturer prepared to stake himself and his interests upon such an issue?

I know that it is urged (but most erroneously, in my opinion) that instability is just as apt to be produced by retaining the public lands as a source of revenue as from any other cause, and this is ascribed to a constant fluctuation, as it is said, in the amount of sales. If there were anything in this objection, it equally applies to every imposition of duties on imports. The amount of revenue annually derived from duties is constantly liable to change.˙ The regulations of foreign governments, the varying productiveness of other countries, periods of excitement in trade, and a great variety of other circumstances are constantly arising to affect the state of commerce, foreign and domestic, and, of consequence, the revenue levied upon it. The sales of the public domain in ordinary times are regulated by fixed laws which have their basis in a demand increasing only in the ratio of the increase of population. In recurring to the statistics connected with this subject it will be perceived that for a period of ten years preceding 1834 the average amount of land sales did not exceed $2,000,000. For the increase which took place in 1834, 1835, and 1836 we are to look to that peculiar condition of the country which grew out of one of the most extraordinary excitements in business and speculation that has ever occurred in the history of commerce and currency. It was the fruit of a wild spirit of adventure engendered by a vicious system of credits, under the evils of which the country is still laboring, and which it is fondly hoped will not soon recur. Considering the vast amount of investments made by private individuals in the public lands during those three years, and which equaled $43,000,000 (equal to more than twenty years' purchase), taking the average of sales of the ten preceding years, it may be safely asserted that the result of the public-land sales can hold out nothing to alarm the manufacturer with the idea of instability in the revenues and consequently in the course of the Government.

Under what appears to me, therefore, the soundest considerations of public policy, and in view of the interests of every branch of domestic industry, I return you the bill with these my objections to its becoming a law.

I take occasion emphatically to repeat my anxious desire to cooperate with Congress in the passing of a law which, while it shall assist in supplying the wants of the Treasury and reestablish public credit, shall afford to the manufacturing interests of the country all the incidental protection they require.

After all, the effect of what I do is substantially to call on Congress to reconsider the subject. If on such reconsideration a majority of two-thirds of both Houses should be in favor of this measure, it will become a law notwithstanding my objections. In a case of clear and manifest error on the part of the President the presumption of the Constitution is that such majorities will be found. Should they be so found in this case, having conscientiously discharged my own duty I shall cheerfully acquiesce in the result.

JOHN TYLER.

PROTEST.*

WASHINGTON, *August 30, 1842.*

To the House of Representatives:

By the Constitution of the United States it is provided that "every bill which shall have passed the House of Representatives and the Senate shall before it become a law be presented to the President of the United States; *if he approve*, he *shall* sign it; but if *not*, he *shall* return it with his objections to that House in which it shall have originated, who shall enter the objections at large upon the Journal and proceed to reconsider it."

In strict compliance with the positive obligation thus imposed upon me by the Constitution, not having been able to bring myself to approve a bill which originated in the House of Representatives entitled "An act to provide revenue from imports, and to change and modify existing laws imposing duties on imports, and for other purposes," I returned the same to the House with my objections to its becoming a law. These objections, which had entirely satisfied my own mind of the great impolicy, if not unconstitutionality, of the measure, were presented in the most respectful and even deferential terms. I would not have been so far forgetful of what was due from one department of the Government to another as to have intentionally employed in my official intercourse with the House any language that could be in the slightest degree offensive to those to whom it was addressed. If in assigning my objections to the bill I had so far forgotten what was due to the House of Representatives as to impugn its motives in passing the bill, I should owe, not only to that House, but to the country, the most profound apology. Such departure from propriety is, however, not complained of in any proceeding which the House has adopted. It has, on the contrary, been expressly made a subject of remark, and almost of complaint, that the language in which my dissent was couched was studiously guarded and cautious.

Such being the character of the official communication in question, I confess I was wholly unprepared for the course which has been pursued in regard to it. In the exercise of its power to regulate its own proceedings the House for the first time, it is believed, in the history of the Government thought proper to refer the message to a select committee of its own body for the purpose, as my respect for the House would have compelled me to infer, of deliberately weighing the objections urged against the bill by the Executive with a view to its own judgment upon the question of the final adoption or rejection of the measure.

Of the temper and feelings in relation to myself of some of the members selected for the performance of this duty I have nothing to say.

*The House of Representatives ordered that it be not entered on the Journal.

That was a matter entirely within the discretion of the House of Representatives. But that committee, taking a different view of its duty from that which I should have supposed had led to its creation, instead of confining itself to the objections urged against the bill availed itself of the occasion formally to arraign the motives of the President for others of his acts since his induction into office. In the absence of all proof and, as I am bound to declare, against all law or precedent in parliamentary proceedings, and at the same time in a manner which it would be difficult to reconcile with the comity hitherto sacredly observed in the intercourse between independent and coordinate departments of the Government, it has assailed my whole official conduct without the shadow of a pretext for such assault, and, stopping short of impeachment, has charged me, nevertheless, with offenses declared to deserve impeachment.

Had the extraordinary report which the committee thus made to the House been permitted to remain without the sanction of the latter, I should not have uttered a regret or complaint upon the subject. But unaccompanied as it is by any particle of testimony to support the charges it contains, without a deliberate examination, almost without any discussion, the House of Representatives has been pleased to adopt it as its own, and thereby to become my accuser before the country and before the world. The high character of such an accuser, the gravity of the charges which have been made, and the judgment pronounced against me by the adoption of the report upon a distinct and separate vote of the House leave me no alternative but to enter my solemn protest against this proceeding as unjust to myself as a man, as an invasion of my constitutional powers as Chief Magistrate of the American people, and as a violation in my person of rights secured to every citizen by the laws and the Constitution. That Constitution has intrusted to the House of Representatives the sole power of impeachment. Such impeachment is required to be tried before the most august tribunal known to our institutions. The Senate of the United States, composed of the representatives of the sovereignty of the States, is converted into a hall of justice, and in order to insure the strictest observance of the rules of evidence and of legal procedure the Chief Justice of the United States, the highest judicial functionary of the land, is required to preside over its deliberations. In the presence of such a judiciary the voice of faction is presumed to be silent, and the sentence of guilt or innocence is pronounced under the most solemn sanctions of religion, of honor, and of law. To such a tribunal does the Constitution authorize the House of Representatives to carry up its accusations against any chief of the executive department whom it may believe to be guilty of high crimes and misdemeanors. Before that tribunal the accused is confronted with his accusers, and may demand the privilege, which the justice of the common law secures to the humblest citizen, of a full, patient, and impartial inquiry into the facts, upon the testimony of witnesses rigidly cross-examined and deposing in the face of day. If such a proceeding had been adopted toward me, unjust as I should certainly have regarded it, I should, I trust, have met with a becoming constancy a trial as painful as it would have been undeserved. I would have manifested by a profound submission to the laws of my country my perfect faith in her justice, and, relying on the purity of my motives and the rectitude of my conduct, should have looked forward with confidence to a triumphant refutation in the presence of that country and by the solemn judgment of such a tribunal not only of whatever charges might have been formally preferred against me, but of all the calumnies of which I have hitherto been the unresisting victim. As it is, I have been accused without evidence and condemned without a hearing. As far as such proceedings can accomplish it, I am deprived of public confidence in the administration of the Government and denied even the boast of a good name—a name transmitted to me from a patriot father, prized as my proudest inheritance, and carefully preserved for those who are to come after me as the most precious of all earthly possessions.   I am not only subjected to imputations affecting my character as an individual, but am charged with offenses against the country so grave and so heinous as to deserve public disgrace and disfranchisement. I am charged with violating pledges which I never gave, and, because I execute what I believe to be the law, with usurping powers not conferred by law, and, above all, with using the powers conferred upon the President by the Constitution from corrupt motives and for unwarrantable ends.   And these charges are made without any particle of evidence to sustain them, and, as I solemnly affirm, without any foundation in truth.

Why is a proceeding of this sort adopted at this time? Is the occasion for it found in the fact that having been elected to the second office under the Constitution by the free and voluntary suffrages of the people, I have succeeded to the first according to the express provisions of the fundamental law of the same people? It is true that the succession of the Vice-President to the Chief Magistracy has never occurred before and that all prudent and patriotic minds have looked on this new trial of the wisdom and stability of our institutions with a somewhat anxious concern. I have been made to feel too sensibly the difficulties of my unprecedented position not to know all that is intended to be conveyed in the reproach cast upon a President without a party. But I found myself placed in this most responsible station by no usurpation or contrivance of my own. I was called to it, under Providence, by the supreme law of the land and the deliberately declared will of the people. It is by these that I have been clothed with the high powers which they have seen fit to confide to their Chief Executive and been charged with the solemn responsibility under which those powers are to be exercised. It is to them that I hold myself answerable as a moral agent for a free and conscientious discharge of the duties which they have imposed upon me. It is not as an individual merely that I am now called upon to resist the encroachments of unconstitutional power. I represent the executive authority of the people of the United States, and it is in their name, whose mere agent and servant I am, and whose will declared in their fundamental law I dare not, even were I inclined, to disobey, that I protest against every attempt to break down the undoubted constitutional power of this department without a solemn amendment of that fundamental law.

I am determined to uphold the Constitution in this as in other respects to the utmost of my ability and in defiance of all personal consequences. What may happen to an individual is of little importance, but the Constitution of the country, or any one of its great and clear principles and provisions, is too sacred to be surrendered under any circumstances whatever by those who are charged with its protection and defense. Least of all should he be held guiltless who, placed at the head of one of the great departments of the Government, should shrink from the exercise of its unquestionable authority on the most important occasions and should consent without a struggle to efface all the barriers so carefully erected by the people to control and circumscribe the powers confided to their various agents. It may be desirable, as the majority of the House of Representatives has declared it is, that no such checks upon the will of the Legislature should be suffered to continue. This is a matter for the people and States to decide, but until they shall have decided it I shall feel myself bound to execute, without fear or favor, the law as it has been written by our predecessors.

I protest against this whole proceeding of the House of Representatives as *ex parte* and extrajudicial. I protest against it as subversive of the common right of all citizens to be condemned only upon a fair and impartial trial, according to law and evidence, before the country. I protest against it as destructive of all the comity of intercourse between the departments of this Government, and destined sooner or later to lead to conflicts fatal to the peace of the country and the integrity of the Constitution. I protest against it in the name of that Constitution which is not only my own shield of protection and defense, but that of every American citizen. I protest against it in the name of the people, by whose will I stand where I do, by whose authority I exercised the power which I am charged with having usurped, and to whom I am responsible for a firm and faithful discharge according to my own convictions of duty of the high stewardship confided to me by them. I protest against it in the name of all regulated liberty and all limited government as a proceeding tending to the utter destruction of the checks and balances of the Constitution and the accumulating in the hands of the House of Representatives, or a bare majority of Congress for the time being, an uncontrolled and despotic power. And I respectfully ask that this my protest may be entered upon the Journal of the House of Representatives as a solemn and formal declaration for all time to come against the injustice and unconstitutionality of such a proceeding.

JOHN TYLER.

SECOND ANNUAL MESSAGE.

WASHINGTON, *December 6, 1842.*

To the Senate and House of Representatives of the United States:

We have continued reason to express our profound gratitude to the Great Creator of All Things for numberless benefits conferred upon us as a people. Blessed with genial seasons, the husbandman has his garners filled with abundance, and the necessaries of life, not to speak of its luxuries, abound in every direction. While in some other nations steady and industrious labor can hardly find the means of subsistence, the greatest evil which we have to encounter is a surplus of production beyond the home demand, which seeks, and with difficulty finds, a partial market in other regions. The health of the country, with partial exceptions, has for the past year been well preserved, and under their free and wise institutions the United States are rapidly advancing toward the consummation of the high destiny which an overruling Providence seems to have marked out for them. Exempt from domestic convulsion and at peace with all the world, we are left free to consult as to the best means of securing and advancing the happiness of the people. Such are the circumstances under which you now assemble in your respective chambers and which should lead us to unite in praise and thanksgiving to that great Being who made us and who preserves us as a nation.

I congratulate you, fellow-citizens, on the happy change in the aspect of our foreign affairs since my last annual message. Causes of complaint at that time existed between the United States and Great Britain which, attended by irritating circumstances, threatened most seriously the public peace. The difficulty of adjusting amicably the questions at issue between the two countries was in no small degree augmented by the lapse of time since they had their origin. The opinions entertained by the Executive on several of the leading topics in dispute were frankly set forth in the message at the opening of your late session. The appointment of a special minister by Great Britain to the United States with power to negotiate upon most of the points of difference indicated a desire on her part amicably to adjust them, and that minister was met by the Executive in the same spirit which had dictated his mission. The treaty consequent thereon having been duly ratified by the two Governments, a copy, together with the correspondence which accompanied it, is herewith communicated. I trust that whilst you may see in it nothing objectionable, it may be the means of preserving for an indefinite period the amicable relations happily existing between the two Governments. The question of peace or war between the United States and Great Britain is a question of the deepest interest, not only to themselves, but to the civilized world, since it is scarcely possible that a war could exist between them without endangering the peace of Christendom. The immediate effect of the treaty upon ourselves will be felt in the security afforded to mercantile enterprise, which, no longer apprehensive of interruption, adventures its speculations in the most distant seas, and, freighted with the diversified productions of every land, returns to bless our own. There is nothing in the treaty which in the slightest degree compromits the honor or dignity of either nation. Next to the settlement of the boundary line, which must always be a matter of difficulty between states as between individuals, the question which seemed to threaten the greatest embarrassment was that connected with the African slave trade.

By the tenth article of the treaty of Ghent it was expressly declared that—

Whereas the traffic in slaves is irreconcilable with the principles of humanity and justice, and whereas both His Majesty and the United States are desirous of continuing their efforts to promote its entire abolition, it is hereby agreed that both the contracting parties shall use their best endeavors to accomplish so desirable an object.

In the enforcement of the laws and treaty stipulations of Great Britain a practice had threatened to grow up on the part of its cruisers of subjecting to visitation ships sailing under the American flag, which, while it seriously involved our maritime rights, would subject to vexation a branch of our trade which was daily increasing, and which required the fostering care of Government. And although Lord Aberdeen in his correspondence with the American envoys at London expressly disclaimed all right to detain an American ship on the high seas, even if found with a cargo of slaves on board, and restricted the British pretension to a mere claim to visit and inquire, yet it could not well be discerned by the Executive of the United States how such visit and inquiry could be made without detention on the voyage and consequent interruption to the trade. It was regarded as the right of search presented only in a new form and expressed in different words, and I therefore felt it to be my duty distinctly to declare in my annual message to Congress that no such concession could be made, and that the United States had both the will and the ability to enforce their own laws and to protect their flag from being used for purposes wholly forbidden by those laws and obnoxious to the moral censure of the world. Taking the message as his letter of instructions, our then minister at Paris felt himself required to assume the same ground in a remonstrance which he felt it to be his duty to present to Mr. Guizôt, and through him to the King of the French, against what has been called the "quintuple treaty;" and his conduct in this respect met with the approval of this Government. In close conformity with these views the eighth article of the treaty was framed, which provides "that each nation shall keep afloat in the African seas a force not less than 80 guns, to act separately and apart, under instructions from their respective Governments, and for the enforcement of their respective laws and obligations.'' From this it will be seen that the ground assumed in the message has been fully maintained at the same time that the stipulations of the treaty of Ghent are to be carried out in good faith by the two countries, and that all pretense is removed for interference with our commerce for any purpose whatever by a foreign government. While, therefore, the United States have been standing up for the freedom of the seas, they have not thought proper to make that a pretext for avoiding a fulfillment of their treaty stipulations or a ground for giving countenance to a trade reprobated by our laws. A similar arrangement by the other great powers could not fail to sweep from the ocean the slave trade without the interpolation of any new principle into the maritime code. We may be permitted to hope that the example thus set will be followed by some if not all of them. We thereby also afford suitable protection to the fair trader in those seas, thus fulfilling at the same time the dictates of a sound policy and complying with the claims of justice and humanity.

It would have furnished additional cause for congratulation if the treaty could have embraced all subjects calculated in future to lead to a misunderstanding between the two Governments. The Territory of the United States commonly called the Oregon Territory, lying on the Pacific Ocean north of the forty-second degree of latitude, to a portion of which Great Britain lays claim, begins to attract the attention of our fellow-citizens, and the tide of population which has reclaimed what was so lately an unbroken wilderness in more contiguous regions is preparing to flow over those vast districts which stretch from the Rocky Mountains to the Pacific Ocean. In advance of the acquirement of individual rights to these lands, sound policy dictates that every effort should be resorted to by the two Governments to settle their respective claims. It became manifest at an early hour of the late negotiations that any attempt for the time being satisfactorily to determine those rights would lead to a protracted discussion, which might embrace in its failure other more pressing matters, and the Executive did not regard it as proper to waive all the advantages of an honorable adjustment of other difficulties of great magnitude and importance because this, not so immediately pressing, stood in the way. Although the difficulty referred to may not for several years to come involve the peace of the two countries, yet I shall not delay to urge on Great Britain the importance of its early settlement. Nor will other matters of commercial importance to the two countries be overlooked, and I have good reason to believe that it will comport with the policy of England, as it does with that of the United States, to seize upon this moment, when most of the causes of irritation have passed away, to cement the peace and amity of the two countries by wisely removing all grounds of probable future collision.

With the other powers of Europe our relations continue on the most amicable footing. Treaties now existing with them should be rigidly observed, and every opportunity compatible with the interests of the United States should be seized upon to enlarge the basis of commercial intercourse. Peace with all the world is the true foundation of our policy, which can only be rendered permanent by the practice of equal and impartial justice to all. Our great desire should be to enter only into that rivalry which looks to the general good in the cultivation of the sciences, the enlargement of the field for the exercise of the mechanical arts, and the spread of commerce—that great civilizer—to every land and sea. Carefully abstaining from interference in all questions exclusively referring themselves to the political interests of Europe, we may be permitted to hope an equal exemption from the interference of European Governments in what relates to the States of the American continent.

On the 23d of April last the commissioners on the part of the United States under the convention with the Mexican Republic of the 11th of April, 1839, made to the proper Department a final report in relation to the proceedings of the commission. From this it appears that the total amount awarded to the claimants by the commissioners and the umpire appointed under that convention was $2,026,079.68. The arbiter having considered that his functions were required by the convention to terminate at the same time with those of the commissioners, returned to the board, undecided for want of time, claims which had been allowed by the American commissioners to the amount of $928,620.88. Other claims, in which the amount sought to be recovered was $3,336,837.05, were submitted to the board too late for its consideration. The minister of the United States at Mexico has been duly authorized to make demand for payment of the awards according to the terms of the convention and the provisions of the act of Congress of the 12th of June, 1840. He has also been instructed to communicate to that Government the expectations of the Government of the United States in relation to those claims which were not disposed of according to the provisions of the convention, and all others of citizens of the United States against the Mexican Government. He has also been furnished with other instructions, to be followed by him in case the Government of Mexico should not find itself in a condition to make present payment of the amount of the awards in specie or its equivalent.

I am happy to be able to say that information which is esteemed favorable both to a just satisfaction of the awards and a reasonable provision for other claims has been recently received from Mr. Thompson, the minister of the United States, who has promptly and efficiently executed the instructions of his Government in regard to this important subject.

The citizens of the United States who accompanied the late Texan expedition to Santa Fe, and who were wrongfully taken and held as prisoners of war in Mexico, have all been liberated.

A correspondence has taken place between the Department of State and the Mexican minister of foreign affairs upon the complaint of Mexico that citizens of the United States were permitted to give aid to the inhabitants of Texas in the war existing between her and that Republic. Copies of this correspondence are herewith communicated to Congress, together with copies of letters on the same subject addressed to the diplomatic corps at Mexico by the American minister and the Mexican secretary of state.

Mexico has thought proper to reciprocate the mission of the United States to that Government by accrediting to this a minister of the same rank as that of the representative of the United States in Mexico. From the circumstances connected with his mission favorable results are anticipated from it. It is so obviously for the interest of both countries as neighbors and friends that all just causes of mutual dissatisfaction should be removed that it is to be hoped neither will omit or delay the employment of any practicable and honorable means to accomplish that end.

The affairs pending between this Government and several others of the States of this hemisphere formerly under the dominion of Spain have again within the past year been materially obstructed by the military revolutions and conflicts in those countries.

The ratifications of the treaty between the United States and the Republic of Ecuador of the 13th of June, 1839, have been exchanged, and that instrument has been duly promulgated on the part of this Government. Copies are now communicated to Congress with a view to enable that body to make such changes in the laws applicable to our intercourse with that Republic as may be deemed requisite.

Provision has been made by the Government of Chile for the payment of the claim on account of the illegal detention of the brig *Warrior* at Coquimbo in 1820. This Government has reason to expect that other claims of our citizens against Chile will be hastened to a final and satisfactory close.

The Empire of Brazil has not been altogether exempt from those convulsions which so constantly afflict the neighboring republics. Disturbances which recently broke out are, however, now understood to be quieted. But these occurrences, by threatening the stability of the governments, or by causing incessant and violent changes in them or in the persons who administer them, tend greatly to retard provisions for a just indemnity for losses and injuries suffered by individual subjects or citizens of other states. The Government of the United States will feel it to be its duty, however, to consent to no delay not unavoidable in making satisfaction for wrongs and injuries sustained by its own citizens. Many years having in some cases elapsed, a decisive and effectual course of proceeding will be demanded of the respective governments against whom claims have been preferred.

The vexatious, harassing, and expensive war which so long prevailed with the Indian tribes inhabiting the peninsula of Florida has happily been terminated, whereby our Army has been relieved from a service of the most disagreeable character and the Treasury from a large expenditure. Some casual outbreaks may occur, such as are incident to the close proximity of border settlers and the Indians, but these, as in all other cases, may be left to the care of the local authorities, aided when occasion may require by the forces of the United States. A sufficient number of troops will be maintained in Florida so long as the remotest apprehensions of danger shall exist, yet their duties will be limited rather to the garrisoning of the necessary posts than to the maintenance of active hostilities. It is to be hoped that a territory so long retarded in its growth will now speedily recover from the evils incident to a protracted war, exhibiting in the increased amount of its rich productions true evidences of returning wealth and prosperity. By the practice of rigid justice toward the numerous Indian tribes residing within our territorial limits and the exercise of a parental vigilance over their interests, protecting them against fraud and intrusion, and at the same time using every proper expedient to introduce among them the arts of civilized life, we may fondly hope not only to wean them from their love of war, but to inspire them with a love for peace and all its avocations. With several of the tribes great progress in civilizing them has already been made. The schoolmaster and the missionary are found side by side, and the remnants of what were once numerous and powerful nations may yet be preserved as the builders up of a new name for themselves and their posterity.

The balance in the Treasury on the 1st of January, 1842, exclusive of the amount deposited with the States, trust funds, and indemnities, was $230,483.68. The receipts into the Treasury during the three first quarters of the present year from all sources amount to $26,616,593.78, of which more than fourteen millions were received from customs and about one million from the public lands. The receipts for the fourth quarter are estimated at nearly eight millions, of which four millions are expected from customs and three millions and a half from loans and Treasury notes. The expenditures of the first three quarters of the present year exceed twenty-six millions, and those estimated for the fourth quarter amount to about eight millions; and it is anticipated there will be a deficiency of half a million on the 1st of January next, but that the amount of outstanding warrants (estimated at $800,000) will leave an actual balance of about $224,000 in the Treasury. Among the expenditures of this year are more than eight millions for the public debt and about $600,000 on account of the distribution to the States of the proceeds of sales of the public lands.

The present tariff of duties was somewhat hastily and hurriedly passed near the close of the late session of Congress. That it should have defects can therefore be surprising to no one. To remedy such defects as may be found to exist in any of its numerous provisions will not fail to claim your serious attention. It may well merit inquiry whether the exaction of all duties in cash does not call for the introduction of a system which has proved highly beneficial in countries where it has been adopted. I refer to the warehousing system. The first and most prominent effect which it would produce would be to protect the market alike against redundant or deficient supplies of foreign fabrics, both of which in the long run are injurious as well to the manufacturer as the importer. The quantity of goods in store being at all times readily known, it would enable the importer with an approach to accuracy to ascertain the actual wants of the market and to regulate himself accordingly. If, however, he should fall into error by importing an excess above the public wants, he could readily correct its evils by availing himself of the benefits and advantages of the system thus established. In the storehouse the goods imported would await the demand of the market and their issues would be governed by the fixed principles of demand and supply. Thus an approximation would be made to a steadiness and uniformity of price, which if attainable would conduce to the decided advantage of mercantile and mechanical operations.

The apprehension may be well entertained that without something to ameliorate the rigor of cash payments the entire import trade may fall into the hands of a few wealthy capitalists in this country and in Europe. The small importer, who requires all the money he can raise for investments abroad, and who can but ill afford to pay the lowest duty, would have to subduct in advance a portion of his funds in order to pay the duties, and would lose the interest upon the amount thus paid for all the time the goods might remain unsold, which might absorb his profits. The rich capitalist, abroad as well as at home, would thus possess after a short time an almost exclusive monopoly of the import trade, and laws designed for the benefit of all would thus operate for the benefit of a few—a result wholly uncongenial with the spirit of our institutions and antirepublican in all its tendencies. The warehousing system would enable the importer to watch the market and to select his own time for offering his goods for sale. A profitable portion of the carrying trade in articles entered for the benefit of drawback must also be most seriously affected without the adoption of some expedient to relieve the cash system. The warehousing system would afford that relief, since the carrier would have a safe recourse to the public storehouses and might without advancing the duty reship within some reasonable period to foreign ports. A further effect of the measure would be to supersede the system of drawbacks, thereby effectually protecting the Government against fraud, as the right of debenture would not attach to goods after their withdrawal from the public stores.

In revising the existing tariff of duties, should you deem it proper to do so at your present session, I can only repeat the suggestions and recommendations which upon several occasions I have heretofore felt it to be my duty to offer to Congress. The great primary and controlling interest of the American people is union—union not only in the mere forms of government, forms which may be broken, but union founded in an attachment of States and individuals for each other. This union in sentiment and feeling can only be preserved by the adoption of that course of policy which, neither giving exclusive benefits to some nor imposing unnecessary burthens upon others, shall consult the interests of all by pursuing a course of moderation and thereby seeking to harmonize public opinion, and causing the people everywhere to feel and to know that the Government is careful of the interests of all alike. Nor is there any subject in regard to which moderation, connected with a wise discrimination, is more necessary than in the imposition of duties on imports. Whether reference be had to revenue, the primary object in the imposition of taxes, or to the incidents which necessarily flow from their imposition, this is entirely true. Extravagant duties defeat their end and object, not only by exciting in the public mind an hostility to the manufacturing interests, but by inducing a system of smuggling on an extensive scale and the practice of every manner of fraud upon the revenue, which the utmost vigilance of Government can not effectually suppress. An opposite course of policy would be attended by results essentially different, of which every interest of society, and none more than those of the manufacturer, would reap important advantages. Among the most striking of its benefits would be that derived from the general acquiescence of the country in its support and the consequent permanency and stability which would be given to all the operations of industry. It can not be too often repeated that no system of legislation can be wise which is fluctuating and uncertain. No interest can thrive under it. The prudent capitalist will never adventure his capital in manufacturing establishments, or in any other leading pursuit of life, if there exists a state of uncertainty as to whether the Government will repeal to-morrow what it has enacted to-day. Fitful profits, however high, if threatened with a ruinous reduction by a vacillating policy on the part of Government, will scarcely tempt him to trust the money which he has acquired by a life of labor upon the uncertain adventure. I therefore, in the spirit of conciliation, and influenced by no other desire than to rescue the great interests of the country from the vortex of political contention, and in the discharge of the high and solemn duties of the place which I now occupy, recommend moderate duties, imposed with a wise discrimination as to their several objects, as being not only most likely to be durable, but most advantageous to every interest of society.

The report of the Secretary of the War Department exhibits a very full and satisfactory account of the various and important interests committed to the charge of that officer. It is particularly gratifying to find that the expenditures for the military service are greatly reduced in amount—that a strict system of economy has been introduced into the service and the abuses of past years greatly reformed. The fortifications on our maritime frontier have been prosecuted with much vigor, and at many points our defenses are in a very considerable state of forwardness. The suggestions in reference to the establishment of means of communication with our territories on the Pacific and to the surveys so essential to a knowledge of the resources of the intermediate country are entitled to the most favorable consideration. While I would propose nothing inconsistent with friendly negotiations to settle the extent of our claims in that region, yet a prudent forecast points out the necessity of such measures as may enable us to maintain our rights. The arrangements made for preserving our neutral relations on the boundary between us and Texas and keeping in check the Indians in that quarter will be maintained so long as circumstances may require. For several years angry contentions have grown out of the disposition directed by law to be made of the mineral lands held by the Government in several of the States. The Government is constituted the landlord, and the citizens of the States wherein lie the lands are its tenants. The relation is an unwise one, and it would be much more conducive of the public interest that a sale of the lands should be made than that they should remain in their present condition. The supply of the ore would be more abundantly and certainly furnished when to be drawn from the enterprise and the industry of the proprietor than under the present system.

The recommendations of the Secretary in regard to the improvements of the Western waters and certain prominent harbors on the Lakes merit, and I doubt not will receive, your serious attention. The great importance of these subjects to the prosperity of the extensive region referred to and the security of the whole country in time of war can not escape observation. The losses of life and property which annually occur in the navigation of the Mississippi alone because of the dangerous obstructions in the river make a loud demand upon Congress for the adoption of efficient measures for their removal.

The report of the Secretary of the Navy will bring you acquainted with that important branch of the public defenses. Considering the already vast and daily increasing commerce of the country, apart from the exposure to hostile inroad of an extended seaboard, all that relates to the Navy is calculated to excite particular attention. Whatever tends to add to its efficiency without entailing unnecessary charges upon the Treasury is well worthy of your serious consideration. It will be seen that while an appropriation exceeding by more than a million the appropriations of the current year is asked by the Secretary, yet that in this sum is proposed to be included $400,000 for the purchase of clothing, which when once expended will be annually reimbursed by the sale of the clothes, and will thus constitute a perpetual fund without any new appropriation to the same object. To this may also be added $50,000 asked to cover the arrearages of past years and $250,000 in order to maintain a competent squadron on the coast of Africa; all of which when deducted will reduce the expenditures nearly within the limits of those of the current year. While, however, the expenditures will thus remain very nearly the same as of the antecedent year, it is proposed to add greatly to the operations of the marine, and in lieu of only 25 ships in commission and but little in the way of building, to keep with the same expenditure 41 vessels afloat and to build 12 ships of a small class.

A strict system of accountability is established and great pains are taken to insure industry, fidelity, and economy in every department of duty. Experiments have been instituted to test the quality of various materials, particularly copper, iron, and coal, so as to prevent fraud and imposition.

It will appear by the report of the Postmaster-General that the great point which for several years has been so much desired has during the current year been fully accomplished. The expenditures of the Department for current service have been brought within its income without lessening its general usefulness. There has been an increase of revenue equal to $166,000 for the year 1842 over that of 1841, without, as it is believed, any addition having been made to the number of letters and newspapers transmitted through the mails. The post-office laws have been honestly administered, and fidelity has been observed in accounting for and paying over by the subordinates of the Department the moneys which have been received. For the details of the service I refer you to the report.

I flatter myself that the exhibition thus made of the condition of the public administration will serve to convince you that every proper attention has been paid to the interests of the country by those who have been called to the heads of the different Departments. The reduction in the annual expenditures of the Government already accomplished furnishes a sure evidence that economy in the application of the public moneys is regarded as a paramount duty.

At peace with all the world, the personal liberty of the citizen sacredly maintained and his rights secured under political institutions deriving all their authority from the direct sanction of the people, with a soil fertile almost beyond example and a country blessed with every diversity of climate and production, what remains to be done in order to advance the happiness and prosperity of such a people? Under ordinary circumstances this inquiry could readily be answered. The best that probably could be done for a people inhabiting such a country would be to fortify their peace and security in the prosecution of their various pursuits by guarding them against invasion from without and violence from within. The rest for the greater part might be left to their own energy and enterprise. The chief embarrassments which at the moment exhibit themselves have arisen from overaction, and the most difficult task which remains to be accomplished is that of correcting and overcoming its effects. Between the years 1833 and 1838 additions were made to bank capital and bank issues, in the form of notes designed for circulation, to an extent enormously great. The question seemed to be not how the best currency could be provided, but in what manner the greatest amount of bank paper could be put in circulation. Thus a vast amount of what was called money—since for the time being it answered the purposes of money—was thrown upon the country, an overissue which was attended, as a necessary consequence, by an extravagant increase of the prices of all articles of property, the spread of a speculative mania all over the country, and has finally ended in a general indebtedness on the part of States and individuals, the prostration of public and private credit, a depreciation in the market value of real and personal estate, and has left large districts of country almost entirely without any circulating medium. In view of the fact that in 1830 the whole banknote circulation within the United States amounted to but $61,323,898, according to the Treasury statements, and that an addition had been made thereto of the enormous sum of $88,000,000 in seven years (the circulation on the 1st of January, 1837, being stated at $149,185,890), aided by the great facilities afforded in obtaining loans from European capitalists, who were seized with the same speculative *mania* which prevailed in the United States, and the large importations of funds from abroad—the result of stock sales and loans—no one can be surprised at the apparent but unsubstantial state of prosperity which everywhere prevailed over the land; and as little cause of surprise should be felt at the present prostration of everything and the ruin which has befallen so many of our fellow-citizens in the sudden withdrawal from circulation of so large an amount of bank issues since 1837—exceeding, as is believed, the amount added to the paper currency for a similar period antecedent to 1837—it ceases to be a matter of astonishment that such extensive shipwreck should have been made of private fortunes or that difficulties should exist in meeting their engagements on the part of the debtor States; apart from which, if there be taken into account the immense losses sustained in the dishonor of numerous banks, it is less a matter of surprise that insolvency should have visited many of our fellow-citizens than that so many should have escaped the blighting influences of the times.

In the solemn conviction of these truths and with an ardent desire to meet the pressing necessities of the country, I felt it to be my duty to cause to be submitted to you at the commencement of your last session the plan of an exchequer, the whole power and duty of maintaining which in purity and vigor was to be exercised by the representatives of the people and the States, and therefore virtually by the people themselves. It was proposed to place it under the control and direction of a Treasury board to consist of three commissioners, whose duty it should be to see that the law of its creation was faithfully executed and that the great end of supplying a paper medium of exchange at all times convertible into gold and silver should be attained. The board thus constituted was given as much permanency as could be imparted to it without endangering the proper share of responsibility which should attach to all public agents. In order to insure all the advantages of a well-matured experience, the commissioners were to hold their offices for the respective periods of two, four, and six years, thereby securing at all times in the management of the exchequer the services of two men of experience; and to place them in a condition to exercise perfect independence of mind and action it was provided that their removal should only take place for actual incapacity or infidelity to the trust, and to be followed by the President with an exposition of the causes of such removal, should it occur. It was proposed to establish subordinate boards in each of the States, under the same restrictions and limitations of the power of removal, which, with the central board, should receive, safely keep, and disburse the public moneys. And in order to furnish a sound paper medium of exchange the exchequer should retain of the revenues of the Government a sum not to exceed $5,000,000 in specie, to be set apart as required by its operations, and to pay the public creditor at his own option either in specie or Treasury notes of denominations not less than $5 nor exceeding $100, which notes should be redeemed at the several places of issue, and to be receivable at all times and everywhere in payment of Government dues, with a restraint upon such issue of bills that the same should not exceed the *maximum* of $15,000,000. In order to guard against all the hazards incident to fluctuations in trade, the Secretary of the Treasury was invested with authority to issue $5,000,000 of Government stock, should the same at any time be regarded as necessary in order to place beyond hazard the prompt redemption of the bills which might be thrown into circulation; thus in fact making the issue of $15,000,000 of exchequer bills rest substantially on $10,000,000, and keeping in circulation never more than one and one-half dollars for every dollar in specie. When to this it is added that the bills are not only everywhere receivable in Government dues, but that the Government itself would be bound for their ultimate redemption, no rational doubt can exist that the paper which the exchequer would furnish would readily enter into general circulation and be maintained at all times at or above par with gold and silver, thereby realizing the great want of the age and fulfilling the wishes of the people. In order to reimburse the Government the expenses of the plan, it was proposed to invest the exchequer with the limited authority to deal in bills of exchange (unless prohibited by the State in which an agency might be situated) having only thirty days to run and resting on a fair and *bona fide* basis. The legislative will on this point might be so plainly announced as to avoid all pretext for partiality or favoritism. It was furthermore proposed to invest this Treasury agent with authority to receive on deposit to a limited amount the specie funds of individuals and to grant certificates therefor to be redeemed on presentation, under the idea, which is believed to be well founded, that such certificates would come in aid of the exchequer bills in supplying a safe and ample paper circulation. Or if in place of the contemplated dealings in exchange the exchequer should be authorized not only to exchange its bills for actual deposits of specie, but, for specie or its equivalent, to sell drafts, charging therefor a small but reasonable premium, I can not doubt but that the benefits of the law would be speedily manifested in the revival of the credit, trade, and business of the whole country. Entertaining this opinion, it becomes my duty to urge its adoption upon Congress by reference to the strongest considerations of the public interests, with such alterations in its details as Congress may in its wisdom see fit to make.

I am well aware that this proposed alteration and amendment of the laws establishing the Treasury Department has encountered various objections, and that among others it has been proclaimed a Government bank of fearful and dangerous import. It is proposed to confer upon it no extraordinary power. It purports to do no more than pay the debts of the Government with the redeemable paper of the Government, in which respect it accomplishes precisely what the Treasury does daily at this time in issuing to the public creditors the Treasury notes which under law it is authorized to issue. It has no resemblance to an ordinary bank, as it furnishes no profits to private stockholders and lends no capital to individuals. If it be objected to as a Government bank and the objection be available, then should all the laws in relation to the Treasury be repealed and the capacity of the Government to collect what is due to it or pay what it owes be abrogated.

This is the chief purpose of the proposed exchequer, and surely if in the accomplishment of a purpose so essential it affords a sound circulating medium to the country and facilities to trade it should be regarded as no slight recommendation of it to public consideration. Properly guarded by the provisions of law, it can run into no dangerous evil, nor can any abuse arise under it but such as the Legislature itself will be answerable for if it be tolerated, since it is but the creature of the law and is susceptible at all times of modification, amendment, or repeal at the pleasure of Congress. I know that it has been objected that the system would be liable to be abused by the Legislature, by whom alone it could be abused, in the party conflicts of the day; that such abuse would manifest itself in a change of the law which would authorize an excessive issue of paper for the purpose of inflating prices and winning popular favor. To that it may be answered that the ascription of such a motive to Congress is altogether gratuitous and inadmissible. The theory of our institutions would lead us to a different conclusion. But a perfect security against a proceeding so reckless would be found to exist in the very nature of things. The political party which should be so blind to the true interests of the country as to resort to such an expedient would inevitably meet with final overthrow in the fact that the moment the paper ceased to be convertible into specie or otherwise promptly redeemed it would become worthless, and would in the end dishonor the Government, involve the people in ruin and such political party in hopeless disgrace. At the same time, such a view involves the utter impossibility of furnishing any currency other than that of the precious metals; for if the Government itself can not forego the temptation of excessive paper issues what reliance can be placed iñ corporations upon whom the temptations of individual aggrandizement would most strongly operate? The people would have to blame none but themselves for any injury that might arise from a course so reckless, since their agents would be the wrongdoers and they the passive spectators.

There can be but three kinds of public currency—first, gold and silver; second, the paper of State institutions; or, third, a representative of the precious metals provided by the General Government or under its authority. The subtreasury system rejected the last in any form, and as it was believed that no reliance could be placed on the issues of local institutions for the purposes of general circulation it necessarily and unavoidably adopted specie as the exclusive currency for its own use; and this must ever be the case unless one of the other kinds be used. The choice in the present state of public sentiment lies between an exclusive specie currency on the one hand and Government issues of some kind on the other. That these issues can not be made by a chartered institution is supposed to be conclusively settled. They must be made, then, directly by Government agents. For several years past they have been thus made in the form of Treasury notes, and have answered a valuable purpose. Their usefulness has been limited by their being transient and temporary; their ceasing to bear interest at given periods necessarily causes their speedy return and thus restricts their range of circulation, and being used only in the disbursements of Government they can not reach those points where they are most required. By rendering their use permanent, to the moderate extent already mentioned, by offering no inducement for their return and by exchanging them for coin and other values, they will constitute to a certain extent the general currency so much needed to maintain the internal trade of the country. And this is the exchequer plan so far as it may operate in furnishing a currency.

I can not forego the occasion to urge its importance to the credit of the Government in a financial point of view. The great necessity of resorting to every proper and becoming expedient in order to place the Treasury on a footing of the highest respectability is entirely obvious. The credit of the Government may be regarded as the very soul of the Government itself—a principle of vitality without which all its movements are languid and all its operations embarrassed. In this spirit the Executive felt itself bound by the most imperative sense of duty to submit to Congress at its last session the propriety of making a specific pledge of the land fund as the basis for the negotiation of the loans authorized to be contracted. I then thought that such an application of the public domain would without doubt have placed at the command of the Government ample funds to relieve the Treasury from the temporary embarrassments under which it labored. American credit has suffered a considerable shock in Europe from the large indebtedness of the States and the temporary inability of some of them to meet the interest on their debts. The utter and disastrous prostration of the United States Bank of Pennsylvania had contributed largely to increase the sentiment of distrust by reason of the loss and ruin sustained by the holders of its stock, a large portion of whom were foreigners and many of whom were alike ignorant of our political organization and of our actual responsibilities.

It was the anxious desire of the Executive that in the effort to negotiate the loan abroad the American negotiator might be able to point the money lender to the fund mortgaged for the redemption of the principal and interest of any loan he might contract, and thereby vindicate the Government from all suspicion of bad faith or inability to meet its engagements. Congress differed from the Executive in this view of the subject. It became, nevertheless, the duty of the Executive to resort to every expedient in its power to do so.

After a failure in the American market a citizen of high character and talent was sent to Europe, with no better success; and thus the mortifying spectacle has been presented of the inability of this Government to obtain a loan so small as not in the whole to amount to more than one-fourth of its ordinary annual income, at a time when the Governments of Europe, although involved in debt and with their subjects heavily burthened with taxation, readily obtained loans of any amount at a greatly reduced rate of interest. It would be unprofitable to look further into this anomalous state of things, but I can not conclude without adding that for a Government which has paid off its debts of two wars with the largest maritime power of Europe, and now owing a debt which is almost next to nothing when compared with its boundless resources—a Government the strongest in the world, because emanating from the popular will and firmly rooted in the affections of a great and free people, and whose fidelity to its engagements has never been questioned—for such a Government to have tendered to the capitalists of other countries an opportunity for a small investment in its stock, and yet to have failed, implies either the most unfounded distrust in its good faith or a purpose to obtain which the course pursued is the most fatal which could have been adopted. It has now become obvious to all men that the Government must look to its own means for supplying its wants, and it is consoling to know that these means are altogether adequate for the object. The exchequer, if adopted, will greatly aid in bringing about this result. Upon what I regard as a well-founded supposition that its bills would be readily sought for by the public creditors and that the issue would in a short time reach the maximum of $15,000,000, it is obvious that $10,000,000 would thereby be added to the available means of the Treasury without cost or charge. Nor can I fail to urge the great and beneficial effects which would be produced in aid of all the active pursuits of life. Its effects upon the solvent State banks, while it would force into liquidation those of an opposite character through its weekly settlements, would be highly beneficial; and with the advantages of a sound currency the restoration of confidence and credit would follow with a numerous train of blessings. My convictions are most strong that these benefits would flow from the adoption of this measure; but if the result should be adverse there is this security in connection with it—that the law creating it may be repealed at the pleasure of the Legislature without the slightest implication of its good faith.

I recommend to Congress to take into consideration the propriety of reimbursing a fine imposed on General Jackson at New Orleans at the time of the attack and defense of that city, and paid by him. Without designing any reflection on the judicial tribunal which imposed the fine, the remission at this day may be regarded as not unjust or inexpedient. The voice of the civil authority was heard amidst the glitter of arms and obeyed by those who held the sword, thereby giving additional luster to a memorable military achievement. If the laws were offended, their majesty was fully vindicated; and although the penalty incurred and paid is worthy of little regard in a pecuniary point of view, it can hardly be doubted that it would be gratifying to the war-worn veteran, now in retirement and in the winter of his days, to be relieved from the circumstances in which that judgment placed him. There are cases in which public functionaries may be called on to weigh the public interest against their own personal hazards, and if the civil law be violated from praiseworthy motives or an overruling sense of public danger and public necessity punishment may well be restrained within that limit which asserts and maintains the authority of the law and the subjection of the military to the civil power. The defense of New Orleans, while it saved a city from the hands of the enemy, placed the name of General Jackson among those of the greatest captains of the age and illustrated one of the brightest pages of our history. Now that the causes of excitement existing at the time have ceased to operate, it is believed that the remission of this fine and whatever of gratification that remission might cause the eminent man who incurred and paid it would be in accordance with the general feeling and wishes of the American people.

I have thus, fellow-citizens, acquitted myself of my duty under the Constitution by laying before you as succinctly as I have been able the state of the Union and by inviting your attention to measures of much importance to the country. The executive will most zealously unite its efforts with those of the legislative department in the accomplishment of all that is required to relieve the wants of a common constituency or elevate the destinies of a beloved country.

JOHN TYLER.

SPECIAL MESSAGES.

WASHINGTON CITY, *December 13, 1842.*

To the Senate of the United States:

I hereby communicate to the Senate a letter from the Secretary of the Navy, with accompanying documents.*

JOHN TYLER.

[The same message was sent to the House of Representatives.]

WASHINGTON, *December 14, 1842.*

To the Senate of the United States:

I transmit to the Senate a treaty recently concluded with the Chippewa Indians of the Mississippi and Lake Superior, with communications from the War Department in relation thereto, and ask the advice and consent of the Senate to the ratification of the said treaty.

JOHN TYLER.

WASHINGTON, *December 14, 1842.*

To the Senate of the United States:

I transmit to the Senate a treaty recently concluded with the Sac and Fox Indians, with communications from the War Department in relation thereto, and ask the advice and consent of the Senate to the ratification of the said treaty.

JOHN TYLER.

WASHINGTON, *December 23, 1842.*

To the Senate of the United States:

I have received the resolution of the 22d instant, requesting me "to inform the Senate of the nature and extent of 'the informal communications' which took place between the American Secretary of State and the British special minister during the late negotiations in Washington City upon the subject of the claims of the United States and Great Britain to the territory west of the Rocky Mountains," and also to inform the Senate what were the reasons which prevented "any agreement upon the subject at present" and which made it "inexpedient to include that subject among the subjects of formal negotiation."

In my message to Congress at the commencement of the present session, in adverting to the territory of the United States on the Pacific Ocean north of the forty-second degree of north latitude, a part of which

*Communication from Commodore Charles W. Morgan, commanding the United States naval forces in the Mediterranean, relative to the adjustment of differences with Morocco; translation of a letter from the Emperor of Morocco, etc.

is claimed by Great Britain, I remarked that "in advance of the acquirement of individual rights to these lands sound policy dictates that every effort should be resorted to by the two Governments to settle their respective claims," and also stated that I should not delay to urge on Great Britain the importance of an early settlement. Measures have been already taken in pursuance of the purpose thus expressed, and under these circumstances I do not deem it consistent with the public interest to make any communication on the subject.

JOHN TYLER.

WASHINGTON, *December 23, 1842.*

To the Senate of the United States:

I herewith communicate to the Senate a report * from the Secretary of State, in answer to a resolution of the Senate adopted on the 22d instant.

JOHN TYLER.

WASHINGTON, *December 29, 1842.*

To the Senate of the United States:

I herewith transmit to the Senate a report † from the Secretary of State, with accompanying papers, in answer to their resolution of the 27th instant.

JOHN TYLER.

WASHINGTON, *December 30, 1842.*

To the Senate of the United States:

In reply to the resolution of the Senate of the 14th December, I transmit herewith the accompanying letter ‡ from the Secretary of the Navy and the statement thereto appended from the Bureau of Equipment and Construction.

JOHN TYLER.

WASHINGTON, *December 30, 1842.*

To the Senate and House of Representatives of the United States:

I communicate herewith to Congress copies of a correspondence which has recently taken place between certain agents of the Government of the Hawaiian or Sandwich Islands and the Secretary of State.

The condition of those islands has excited a good deal of interest, which

---

* Stating that the special minister from Great Britain to the United States made no proposition, informal or otherwise, to the negotiator on the part of the United States for the assumption or guaranty of the State debts by the Government of the United States to the holders of said debts.

† Transmitting correspondence between the United States minister at London and the British Government in relation to certain slaves taken from the wreck of the schooner *Hermosa* and liberated by the authorities at Nassau, New Providence.

‡ Relating to the strength and expense of maintaining the African Squadron under the late British treaty, the number of guns it is expected to have afloat in the United States Navy during 1843, and the estimated expense of the naval establishment for 1843.

is increasing by every successive proof that their inhabitants are making progress in civilization and becoming more and more competent to maintain regular and orderly civil government. They lie in the Pacific Ocean, much nearer to this continent than the other, and have become an important place for the refitment and provisioning of American and European vessels.

Owing to their locality and to the course of the winds which prevail in this quarter of the world, the Sandwich Islands are the stopping place for almost all vessels passing from continent to continent across the Pacific Ocean. They are especially resorted to by the great number of vessels of the United States which are engaged in the whale fishery in those seas. The number of vessels of all sorts and the amount of property owned by citizens of the United States which are found in those islands in the course of the year are stated probably with sufficient accuracy in the letter of the agents.

Just emerging from a state of barbarism, the Government of the islands is as yet feeble, but its dispositions appear to be just and pacific, and it seems anxious to improve the condition of its people by the introduction of knowledge, of religious and moral institutions, means of education, and the arts of civilized life.

It can not but be in conformity with the interest and wishes of the Government and the people of the United States that this community, thus existing in the midst of a vast expanse of ocean, should be respected and all its rights strictly and conscientiously regarded; and this must also be the true interest of all other commercial states. Far remote from the dominions of European powers, its growth and prosperity as an independent state may yet be in a high degree useful to all whose trade is extended to those regions; while its near approach to this continent and the intercourse which American vessels have with it, such vessels constituting five-sixths of all which annually visit it, could not but create dissatisfaction on the part of the United States at any attempt by another power, should such attempt be threatened or feared, to take possession of the islands, colonize them, and subvert the native Government. Considering, therefore, that the United States possesses so large a share of the intercourse with those islands, it is deemed not unfit to make the declaration that their Government seeks, nevertheless, no peculiar advantages, no exclusive control over the Hawaiian Government, but is content with its independent existence and anxiously wishes for its security and prosperity. Its forbearance in this respect under the circumstances of the very large intercourse of their citizens with the islands would justify this Government, should events hereafter arise to require it, in making a decided remonstrance against the adoption of an opposite policy by any other power. Under the circumstances I recommend to Congress to provide for a moderate allowance to be made out of the Treasury to the consul residing there, that in a Government so new and a country so remote

American citizens may have respectable authority to which to apply for redress in case of injury to their persons and property, and to whom the Government of the country may also make known any acts committed by American citizens of which it may think it has a right to complain.

Events of considerable importance have recently transpired in China. The military operations carried on against that Empire by the English Government have been terminated by a treaty, according to the terms of which four important ports hitherto shut against foreign commerce are to be open to British merchants, viz, Amoy, Foo-Choo-Foo, Ningpo, and Chinghai. It can not but be interesting to the mercantile interest of the United States, whose intercourse with China at the single port of Canton has already become so considerable, to ascertain whether these other ports now open to British commerce are to remain shut, nevertheless, against the commerce of the United States. The treaty between the Chinese Government and the British commissioner provides neither for the admission nor the exclusion of the ships of other nations. It would seem, therefore, that it remains with every other nation having commercial intercourse with China to seek to make proper arrangements for itself with the Government of that Empire in this respect.

The importations into the United States from China are known to be large, having amounted in some years, as will be seen by the annexed tables, to $9,000,000. The exports, too, from the United States to China constitute an interesting and growing part of the commerce of the country. It appears that in the year 1841, in the direct trade between the two countries, the value of the exports from the United States amounted to $715,000 in domestic produce and $485,000 in foreign merchandise. But the whole amount of American produce which finally reaches China and is there consumed is not comprised in these tables, which show only the direct trade. Many vessels with American products on board sail with a primary destination to other countries, but ultimately dispose of more or less of their cargoes in the port of Canton.

The peculiarities of the Chinese Government and the Chinese character are well known. An Empire supposed to contain 300,000,000 subjects, fertile in various rich products of the earth, not without the knowledge of letters and of many arts, and with large and expensive accommodations for internal intercourse and traffic, has for ages sought to exclude the visits of strangers and foreigners from its dominions, and has assumed for itself a superiority over all other nations. Events appear likely to break down and soften this spirit of nonintercourse and to bring China ere long into the relations which usually subsist between civilized states. She has agreed in the treaty with England that correspondence between the agents of the two Governments shall be on equal terms—a concession which it is hardly probable will hereafter be withheld from other nations.

It is true that the cheapness of labor among the Chinese, their ingenuity in its application, and the fixed character of their habits and pursuits may discourage the hope of the opening of any great and sudden demand for the fabrics of other countries.   But experience proves that the productions of western nations find a market to some extent among the Chinese; that that market, so far as respects the productions of the United States, although it has considerably varied in successive seasons, has on the whole more than doubled within the last ten years; and it can hardly be doubted that the opening of several new and important ports connected with parts of the Empire heretofore seldom visited by Europeans or Americans would exercise a favorable influence upon the demand for such productions.

It is not understood that the immediate establishment of correspondent embassies and missions or the permanent residence of diplomatic functionaries with full powers of each country at the Court of the other is contemplated between England and China, although, as has been already observed, it has been stipulated that intercourse between the two countries shall hereafter be on equal terms.   An ambassador or envoy extraordinary and minister plenipotentiary can only be accredited, according to the usages of western nations, to the head or sovereign of the state, and it may be doubtful whether the Court of Pekin is yet prepared to conform to these usages so far as to receive a minister plenipotentiary to reside near it.

Being of opinion, however, that the commercial interests of the United States connected with China require at the present moment a degree of attention and vigilance such as there is no agent of this Government on the spot to bestow, I recommend to Congress to make appropriation for the compensation of a commissioner to reside in China to exercise a watchful care over the concerns of American citizens and for the protection of their persons and property, empowered to hold intercourse with the local authorities, and ready, under instructions from his Government, should such instructions become necessary and proper hereafter, to address himself to the high functionaries of the Empire, or through them to the Emperor himself.

It will not escape the observation of Congress that in order to secure the important object of any such measure a citizen of much intelligence and weight of character should be employed on such agency, and that to secure the services of such an individual a compensation should be made corresponding with the magnitude and importance of the mission.

JOHN TYLER.

WASHINGTON, *December 31, 1842.*

To the House of Representatives:

In compliance with your resolution of the 12th of February, 1841, requesting me to communicate to the House of Representatives the documents and other information in the possession of the Executive regarding claims of citizens of the United States on the Government of Hayti, I now transmit a letter from the Secretary of State and the accompanying documents.

JOHN TYLER.

WASHINGTON, *January 9, 1843.*

To the Senate of the United States:

I have received a resolution of the Senate of the 27th of December, in the following terms:

Resolved, That the President be requested to inform the Senate, if compatible with the public interest, whether the quintuple treaty for the suppression of the slave trade has been communicated to the Government of the United States in any form whatever, and, if so, by whom, for what purpose, and what answer may have been returned to such communication. Also to communicate to the Senate all the information which may have been received by the Government of the United States going to show that the "*course which this Government might take in relation to said treaty has excited no small degree of attention and discussion in Europe.*" Also to inform the Senate how far the "*warm animadversions*" and the "*great political excitement*" which this treaty has caused in Europe have any application or reference to the United States. Also to inform the Senate what danger there was that "*the laws and the obligations*" of the United States in relation to the suppression of the slave trade would be "*executed by others,*" if we did not "*remove the pretext and motive for violating our flag and executing our laws*" by entering into the stipulations for the African squadron and the remonstrating embassies which are contained in the eighth and ninth articles of the late British treaty. Also that the President be requested to communicate to the Senate all the correspondence with our ministers abroad relating to the foregoing points of inquiry. Also that the President be requested to communicate to the Senate all such information upon the negotiation of the African squadron articles as will show the origin of such articles and the history and progress of their formation.

I informed the Senate, in the message transmitting the treaty with England of the 9th of August last, that no application or request had been made to this Government to become a party to the quintuple treaty. Agents of the Government abroad, regarding the signature of that treaty as a political occurrence of some importance, obtained, unofficially, copies of it, and transmitted those copies to the Department of State, as other intelligence is communicated for the information of the Government. The treaty has not been communicated to the Government of the United States from any other quarter, in any other manner, or for any other purpose.

The next request expressed in the resolution is in these words:

Also to communicate to the Senate all the information which may have been received by the Government of the United States going to show that the "course which this Government might take in relation to said treaty has excited no small degree of attention and discussion in Europe." Also to inform the Senate how far the "warm animadversions" and the "great political excitement" which this treaty has caused in Europe have any application or reference to the United States.

The words quoted in this part of the resolution appear to be taken from my message above mentioned. In that communication I said:

No application or request has been made to this Government to become a party to this treaty, but the course it might take in regard to it has excited no small degree of attention and discussion in Europe, as the principle upon which it is founded and the stipulations which it contains have caused warm animadversions and great political excitement.

In my message at the commencement of the present session of Congress I endeavored to state the principles which this Government supports respecting the right of search and the immunity of flags. Desirous of maintaining those principles fully, at the same time that existing obligations should be fulfilled, I have thought it most consistent with the honor and dignity of the country that it should execute its own laws and perform its own obligations by its own means and its own power. The examination or visitation of the merchant vessels of one nation by the cruisers of another for any purposes except those known and acknowledged by the law of nations, under whatever restraints or regulations it may take place, may lead to dangerous results. It is far better by other means to supersede any supposed necessity or any motive for such examination or visit. Interference with a merchant vessel by an armed cruiser is always a delicate proceeding, apt to touch the point of national honor as well as to affect the interests of individuals. It has been thought, therefore, expedient, not only in accordance with the stipulations of the treaty of Ghent, but at the same time as removing all pretext on the part of others for violating the immunities of the American flag upon the seas as they exist and are defined by the law of nations, to enter into the articles now submitted to the Senate.

The treaty which I now submit to you proposes no alteration, mitigation, or modification of the rules of the law of nations. It provides simply that each of the two Governments shall maintain on the coast of Africa a sufficient squadron to enforce, separately and respectively, the laws, rights, and obligations of the two countries for the suppression of the slave trade.

These opinions were expressed by me officially upon the occasion of making to the Senate a communication of very great importance. It is not perceived how the accuracy of this general statement can be doubted by those who are acquainted with the debates of public bodies in Europe, the productions of the press, and the other modes by which public opinion is manifested in an enlightened age. It is not to be supposed that excited attention to public and national transactions or general political discussions in Europe on subjects open to all the world are known only in consequence of private information communicated to the Government, and feeling a strong persuasion that it would be improper in the Executive to go into any discussion or argument upon such a subject with the Senate, I have no further remarks to make upon this part of the inquiry.

The third inquiry is:

What danger there was that "the laws and the obligations" of the United States in relation to the suppression of the slave trade would be "executed by others" if we do not "remove the pretext and motive for violating our flag and executing our laws."

I have already quoted from the message the entire paragraph to a part of which this portion of the inquiry is supposed to refer.

As to the danger there was that the laws and the obligations of the

United States in relation to the suppression of the slave trade would be executed by others if we did not remove the pretext and motive for violating our flag and provide for executing our laws, I might say that this depends upon notorious facts and occurrences, of which the evidence has been in various forms before the country and all the branches of the Government.

When I came to occupy the Executive chair I could not be ignorant of the numerous complaints which had been made on account of alleged interruptions of American vessels engaged in lawful commerce on the coast of Africa by British cruisers on the ground of their being engaged in the slave trade. I could not be ignorant, at the same time, of the well-grounded suspicions which pervaded the country that some American vessels were engaged in that odious and unlawful traffic. There were two dangers, then, to be guarded against—the one, that this traffic would continue to be carried on in American ships, and perhaps much increased, unless some new and vigorous effort should be made for its suppression; the other, that acquiescence in the capture of American vessels, notorious slave dealers, by British cruisers might give countenance to seizures and detentions of vessels lawfully employed on light or groundless suspicions. And cases had arisen under the administration of those who preceded me well calculated to show the extent and magnitude of this latter danger; and believing that very serious consequences might in time grow out of the obvious tendency and progress of things, I felt it to be my duty to arrest that progress, to rescue the immunity of the American flag from the danger which hung over it, and to do this by recommending such a provision for the execution of our own laws as should remove all pretense for the interference of others.

Among the occurrences to which I have alluded, it may be useful to particularize one case.

The schooner *Catharine*, an American vessel owned by citizens of the United States, was seized on the coast of Africa by the British cruiser called the *Dolphin* and brought into the port of New York in the summer of 1839. Upon being brought into port, Benjamin F. Butler, esq., district attorney of the United States for the southern district of New York, appeared in the district court of the United States for that district and in the name and behalf of the United States libeled the schooner, her apparel and furniture, for a violation of the several acts of Congress passed for the suppression of the slave trade. The schooner being arrested by the usual process in such cases and possession taken of her from the hands of the British captors by officers of the United States, the cause proceeded, and by a decree of the circuit court in December, 1840, a forfeiture was pronounced. From this decree an appeal was taken, which is now pending in the Supreme Court of the United States.

It is true that in another case, that of the *Tigris*, of like general character, soon after arising, the then Secretary of State, on the 1st of March,

1841, informed Mr. Fox, the British minister, that "however strong and unchangeable may be the determination of this Government to punish any citizens of the United States who violate the laws against the African slave trade, it will not permit the exercise of any authority by foreign armed vessels in the execution of those laws."

But it is evident that this general declaration did not relieve the subject from its difficulties. Vessels of the United States found engaged in the African slave trade are guilty of piracy under the acts of Congress. It is difficult to say that such vessels can claim any interference of the Government in their behalf, into whosesoever hands they may happen to fall, any more than vessels which should turn general pirates. Notorious African slave traders can not claim the protection of the American character, inasmuch as they are acting in direct violation of the laws of their country and stand denounced by those laws as pirates. In case of the seizure of such a vessel by a foreign cruiser, and of her being brought into a port of the United States, what is to be done with her? Shall she be libeled, prosecuted, and condemned as if arrested by a cruiser of the United States? If this is to be done, it is clear that the agency of a foreign power has been instrumental in executing the laws of the United States. Or, on the other hand, is the vessel, with all her offenses flagrant upon her, to be released on account of the agency by which she was seized, discharged of all penalties, and left at liberty to renew her illegal and nefarious traffic?

It appeared to me that the best, if not the only, mode of avoiding these and other difficulties was by adopting such a provision as is contained in the late treaty with England.

The Senate asks me for the reasons for entering into the stipulations for the "remonstrating embassies" contained in the late treaty. Surely there is no stipulation in the treaty for any "remonstrating embassies," or any other embassies, nor any reference or allusion to any such thing. In this respect all that the treaty provides is in the ninth article and is in these words:

The parties to this treaty agree that they will unite in all becoming representations and remonstrances with any and all powers within whose dominions such markets [for African slaves] are allowed to exist, and that they will urge upon all such powers the propriety and duty of closing such markets effectually, at once and forever.

It always gives me sincere pleasure to communicate to both Houses of Congress anything in my power which may aid them in the discharge of their high duties and which the public interest does not require to be withheld. In transmitting the late treaty to the Senate everything was caused to accompany it which it was supposed could enlighten the judgment of the Senate upon its various provisions. The views of the Executive, in agreeing to the eighth and ninth articles, were fully expressed, and pending the discussion in the Senate every call for further information was promptly complied with, and nothing kept back which the

Senate desired.   Upon this information and upon its own knowledge of the subject the Senate made up and pronounced its judgment upon its own high responsibility, and as the result of that judgment the treaty was ratified, as the Journal shows, by a vote of 39 to 9.   The treaty has thus become the law of the land by the express advice of the Senate, given in the most solemn manner known to its proceedings.

The fourth request is—

That the President be requested to communicate to the Senate all the correspondence with our ministers abroad relating to the foregoing points of inquiry.

If this branch of the resolution were more definite, some parts of it might perhaps be met without prejudice to the public interest by extracts from the correspondence referred to.   At a future day a communication may be expected to be made as broad and general as a proper regard to these interests will admit, but at present I deem any such communication not to be consistent with the public interest.

The fifth and last is—

That the President be requested to communicate to the Senate all such information upon the negotiation of the African squadron articles as will show the origin of such articles and the history and progress of their formation.

These articles were proposed to the British minister by the Secretary of State under my express sanction and were acceded to by him and have since been ratified by both Governments.   I might without disrespect speak of the novelty of inquiring by the Senate into the history and progress of articles of a treaty through a negotiation which has terminated, and as the result of which these articles have become the law of the land by the constitutional advice of the Senate itself.   But I repeat that those articles had their origin in a desire on the part of the Government of the United States to fulfill its obligations, entered into by the treaty of Ghent, to do its utmost for the suppression of the African slave trade, and to accomplish this object by such means as should not lead to the interruption of the lawful commerce of the United States or any derogation from the dignity and immunity of their flag.   And I have the satisfaction to believe that both the Executive, in negotiating the treaty of which these articles form part, and the Senate, in advising to its ratification, have effected an object important to the Government and satisfactory to the people.

In conclusion I hope I may be permitted to observe that I have, out of a profound respect for the Senate, been induced to make this communication in answer to inquiries some of which at least are believed to be without precedent in the history of the relations between that body and the executive department.   These inquiries were particularly unexpected to me at the present moment.   As I had been so fortunate as to find my own views of the expediency of ratifying the late treaty with England confirmed by a vote of somewhat more than four-fifths of the Senators present, I have hitherto flattered myself that the motives which influenced my conduct had been fully appreciated by those who advised and approved it, and that if a necessity should ever arise for any special explanation or defense in regard to those motives it could scarcely be in that assembly itself.   JOHN TYLER.

WASHINGTON, *January 18, 1843.*

To the House of Representatives:

In compliance with the resolution of the House of Representatives of the 27th ultimo, I now transmit the letter and pamphlet* which accompanies this.   JOHN TYLER.

WASHINGTON, *January 23, 1843.*

To the Senate of the United States:

I herewith transmit to the Senate, in answer to their resolution of the 19th instant, reports† from the State and War Departments.

JOHN TYLER.

WASHINGTON, *January 23, 1843.*

To the Senate of the United States:

I transmit to the Senate herewith, in answer to their resolution of the 5th instant, a report‡ from the Secretary of State, with accompanying documents.   JOHN TYLER.

WASHINGTON, *January 31, 1843.*

To the House of Representatives:

In compliance with a resolution of the House of Representatives of the 24th instant, requesting me to communicate answers to certain queries therein contained respecting instructions given to the commissioners appointed to adjudicate claims arising under the Cherokee treaty of 1835, I transmit herewith a report from the War Department, accompanied by a copy of the instructions referred to.   JOHN TYLER.

WASHINGTON, *January 31, 1843.*

To the House of Representatives:

At the last session of Congress a resolution was passed by the House of Representatives requesting me to cause to be communicated to the

---

*Entitled "Acts and Resolutions of the Legislative Council of the Territory of Florida," passed at its twentieth session, January 3 to March 5, 1842.

†Relating to a grant of land in Oregon Territory to the Hudsons Bay Company by the British Government

‡Transmitting correspondence with Great Britain relative to the destruction of the steamboat *Caroline* at Schlosser, N. Y., December 29, 1837.

House "the several reports made to the Department of War by Lieutenant-Colonel Hitchcock relative to the affairs of the Cherokee Indians, together with all information communicated by him concerning the frauds he was charged to investigate; also all facts in the possession of the Executive relating to the subject."

A resolution of the same import had been passed by the House of Representatives on the 18th of May last, requiring the Secretary of War to communicate to the House the same reports and matters. After consultation with me and under my directions, the Secretary of War informed the House that the reports referred to relative to the affairs of the Cherokees contained information and suggestions in reference to the matters which it was supposed would become the subject of a negotiation between that Department and the delegates of the Cherokee Nation. It was stated by him that the nature and subject of the report, in the opinion of the President and the Department, rendered its publication at that time inconsistent with the public interest. The negotiation referred to subsequently took place, and embraced the matters upon which Lieutenant-Colonel Hitchcock had communicated his views. That negotiation terminated without the conclusion of any arrangement. It may, and in all probability will, be renewed. All the information communicated by Lieutenant-Colonel Hitchcock respecting the Cherokees—their condition as a nation and their relations to other tribes—is herewith transmitted. But his suggestions and projects respecting the anticipated propositions of the delegates and his views of their personal characters can not in any event aid the legislation of Congress, and in my opinion the promulgation of them would be unfair and unjust to him and inconsistent with the public interest, and they are therefore not transmitted.

The Secretary of War further stated in his answer to the resolution that the other report referred to in it, relating to the alleged frauds which Lieutenant-Colonel Hitchcock was charged to investigate, contained such information as he (Colonel Hitchcock) was enabled to obtain by *ex parte* inquiries of various persons whose statements were necessarily without the sanction of an oath, and which the persons implicated had had no opportunity to contradict or explain. He expressed the opinion that to promulgate those statements at that time would be grossly unjust to those persons and would be calculated to defeat rather than promote the objects of the inquiry, and he remarked that sufficient opportunity had not been given to the Department to pursue the investigation or to call upon the parties affected for explanations or to determine on the measures proper to be adopted. And he hoped these reasons would be satisfactory for not transmitting to the House at that time the reports referred to in its resolution.

It would appear from the report of the Committee on Indian Affairs, to whom the communication of the Secretary of War was referred, and which report has been transmitted to me, together with the resolutions of the House adopted on the recommendation of the committee, and from those resolutions, that the reasons given by the Secretary were not deemed satisfactory and that the House of Representatives claims the right to demand from the Executive and heads of Departments such information as may be in their possession relating to "subjects of the deliberations of the House and within the sphere of its legitimate powers," and that in the opinion of the House the reports and facts called for by its resolution of the 18th of May related to subjects of its deliberations and were within the sphere of its legitimate powers, and should have been communicated.

If by the assertion of this claim of right to call upon the Executive for all the information in its possession relating to any subject of the deliberation of the House, and within the sphere of its legitimate powers, it is intended to assert also that the Executive is bound to comply with such call without the authority to exercise any discretion on its part in reference to the nature of the information required or to the interests of the country or of individuals to be affected by such compliance, then do I feel bound, in the discharge of the high duty imposed upon me "to preserve, protect, and defend the Constitution of the United States," to declare in the most respectful manner my entire dissent from such a proposition. The instrument from which the several departments of the Government derive their authority makes each independent of the other in the discharge of their respective functions. The injunction of the Constitution that the President "shall take care that the laws be faithfully executed" necessarily confers an authority commensurate with the obligation imposed to inquire into the manner in which all public agents perform the duties assigned to them by law. To be effective these inquiries must often be confidential. They may result in the collection of truth or of falsehood, or they may be incomplete and may require further prosecution. To maintain that the President can exercise no discretion as to the time in which the matters thus collected shall be promulgated or in respect to the character of the information obtained would deprive him at once of the means of performing one of the most salutary duties of his office. An inquiry might be arrested at its first stage and the officers whose conduct demanded investigation may be enabled to elude or defeat it. To require from the Executive the transfer of this discretion to a coordinate branch of the Government is equivalent to the denial of its possession by him and would render him dependent upon that branch in the performance of a duty purely executive.

Nor can it be a sound position that all papers, documents, and information of every description which may happen by any means to come into the possession of the President or of the heads of Departments must necessarily be subject to the call of the House of Representatives *merely* because they relate to a subject of the deliberations of the House, although that subject may be within the sphere of its legitimate powers.

It can not be that the only test is whether the information relates to a legitimate subject of deliberation. The Executive Departments and the citizens of this country have their rights and duties as well as the House of Representatives, and the maxim that the rights of one person or body are to be so exercised as not to impair those of others is applicable in its fullest extent to this question. Impertinence or malignity may seek to make the Executive Departments the means of incalculable and irremediable injury to innocent parties by throwing into them libels most foul and atrocious. Shall there be no discretionary authority permitted to refuse to become the instruments of such malevolence?

And although information comes through a proper channel to an executive officer it may often be of a character to forbid its being made public. The officer charged with a confidential inquiry, and who reports its result under the pledge of confidence which his appointment implies, ought not to be exposed individually to the resentment of those whose conduct may be impugned by the information he collects. The knowledge that such is to be the consequence will inevitably prevent the performance of duties of that character, and thus the Government will be deprived of an important means of investigating the conduct of its agents.

It is certainly no new doctrine in the halls of judicature or of legislation that certain communications and papers are privileged, and that the general authority to compel testimony must give way in certain cases to the paramount rights of individuals or of the Government. Thus no man can be compelled to accuse himself, to answer any question that tends to render him infamous, or to produce his own private papers on any occasion. The communications of a client to his counsel and the admissions made at the confessional in the course of religious discipline are privileged communications. In the courts of that country from which we derive our great principles of individual liberty and the rules of evidence it is well settled—and the doctrine has been fully recognized in this country—that a minister of the Crown or the head of a department can not be compelled to produce any papers or disclose any transactions relating to the executive functions of the Government which he declares are confidential or such as the public interest requires should not be divulged; and the persons who have been the channels of communication to officers of the State are in like manner protected from the disclosure of their names. Other instances of privileged communications might be enumerated if it were deemed necessary. These principles are as applicable to evidence sought by a legislature as to that required by a court.

The practice of the Government since its foundation has sanctioned the principle that there must necessarily be a discretionary authority in reference to the nature of the information called for by either House of Congress.

The authority was claimed and exercised by General Washington in 1796. In 1825 President Monroe declined compliance with a resolution of the House of Representatives calling for the correspondence between the Executive Departments of this Government and the officers of the United States Navy and others at or near the ports of South America on the Pacific Ocean. In a communication made by the Secretary of War in 1832 to the Committee of the House on the Public Lands, by direction of President Jackson, he denies the obligation of the Executive to furnish the information called for and maintains the authority of the President to exercise a sound discretion in complying with calls of that description by the House of Representatives or its committees. Without multiplying other instances, it is not deemed improper to refer to the refusal of the President at the last session of the present Congress to comply with a resolution of the House of Representatives calling for the names of the members of Congress who had applied for offices. As no further notice was taken in any form of this refusal, it would seem to be a fair inference that the House itself admitted that there were cases in which the President had a discretionary authority in respect to the transmission of information in the possession of any of the Executive Departments.

Apprehensive that silence under the claim supposed to be set up in the resolutions of the House of Representatives under consideration might be construed as an acquiescence in its soundness, I have deemed it due to the great importance of the subject to state my views, that a compliance in part with the resolution may not be deemed a surrender of a necessary authority of the Executive.

Many of the reasons which existed at the date of the report of the Secretary of War of June 1, 1842, for then declining to transmit the report of Lieutenant-Colonel Hitchcock concerning the frauds which he was charged to investigate have ceased to operate. It has been found wholly impracticable to pursue the investigation in consequence of the death and removal out of the country of those who would be called upon to testify, and in consequence of the want of adequate authority or means to render it effectual. It could not be conducted without expense. Congress at its last session prohibited the payment of any account or charge whatever growing out of or in any way connected with any commission or inquiry, except military and naval courts-martial and courts of inquiry, unless special appropriations should be made for the payment of such accounts and charges. Of the policy of that provision of law it does not become me to speak, except to say that the institution of inquiries into the conduct of public agents, however urgent the necessity for such inquiry may be, is thereby virtually denied to the Executive, and that if evils of magnitude shall arise in consequence of the law I take to myself no portion of the responsibility.

In relation to the propriety of directing prosecutions against the contractors to furnish Indians rations who are charged with improper conduct, a correspondence has been had between the War Department and the Solicitor of the Treasury, which is herewith transmitted in a conviction that such prosecution would be entirely ineffectual.

Under these circumstances I have thought proper to direct that the report of Lieutenant-Colonel Hitchcock concerning the frauds which he was charged to investigate be transmitted to the House of Representatives, and it accordingly accompanies this message. At the same time, I have to request the House to consider it so far confidential as not to direct its publication until the appropriate committee shall have examined it and expressed their opinion whether a just regard to the character and rights of persons apparently implicated, but who have not had an opportunity to meet the imputations on them, does not require that portions at least of the report should not at present be printed.

This course is adopted by me from a desire to render justice to all and at the same time avoid even the appearance of a desire to screen any, and also to prevent the exaggerated estimate of the importance of the information which is likely to be made from the mere fact of its being withheld.

The resolution of the House also calls for "all facts in the possession of the Executive, from any source, relating to the subject." There are two subjects specified in the resolution—one "relative to the affairs of the Cherokee Indians," and another "concerning the frauds he [Lieutenant-Colonel Hitchcock] was charged to investigate."

All the papers in the War Department or its bureaus relating to the affairs of the Cherokee Indians, it is believed, have been from time to time communicated to Congress and are contained in the printed documents, or are now transmitted, with the exception of those portions of Lieutenant-Colonel Hitchcock's report hereinbefore mentioned, and excepting the correspondence with the Cherokee delegates in the negotiations which took place during the last summer, which are not supposed to be within the intent of the resolution of the House. For the same reason a memorial from the Old Settlers, or Western Cherokees, as they term themselves, recently presented, is not transmitted. If these or any other public documents should be desired by the House, a specification of them will enable me to cause them to be furnished if it should be found proper.

All the papers in the War Office or its bureaus known or supposed to have any relation to the alleged frauds which Lieutenant-Colonel Hitchcock was charged to investigate are herewith transmitted.

JOHN TYLER.

WASHINGTON, *February 8, 1843.*

To the House of Representatives of the United States:

I herewith transmit to the House of Representatives, in answer to their resolution of the 28th ultimo, a report* from the Secretary of State.

JOHN TYLER.

* Stating that no information is in possession of the Government of any negotiation of a treaty, or of any overtures to treat, for a cession of California by Mexico to England.

WASHINGTON, *February 9, 1843.*

To the House of Representatives:

In order to enable Congress to approve or disapprove the selection of a site for a Western-armory made by the board of commissioners appointed by me for that purpose pursuant to the act of September 9, 1841, I transmit herewith their report and proceedings, as required by that act.

JOHN TYLER.

WASHINGTON, *February 13, 1843.*

To the House of Representatives:

I herewith transmit to the House of Representatives a report made to me on the 9th instant by the Secretary of the Treasury, on the subject of the present and prospective condition of the finances.

You will perceive from it that even if the receipts from the various sources of revenue for the current year shall prove not to have been overrated and the expenditures be restrained within the estimates, the Treasury will be exhausted before the close of the year, and that this will be the case although authority should be given to the proper Department to reissue Treasury notes. But the state of facts existing at the present moment can not fail to awaken a doubt whether the amount of the revenue for the respective quarters of the year will come up to the estimates, nor is it entirely certain that the expenditures which will be authorized by Congress may not exceed the aggregate sum which has hitherto been assumed as the basis of the Treasury calculations.

Of all the duties of the Government, none is more sacred and imperative than that of making adequate and ample provision for fulfilling with punctuality its pecuniary engagements and maintaining the public credit inviolate. Any failure in this respect not produced by unforeseen causes could only be regarded by our common constituents as a serious neglect of the public interests. I feel it, therefore, to be an indispensable obligation, while so much of the session yet remains unexpired as to enable Congress to give to the subject the consideration which its great importance demands, most earnestly to call its attention to the propriety of making further provision for the public service of the year.

The proper objects of taxation are peculiarly within the discretion of the Legislature, while it is the duty of the Executive to keep Congress duly advised of the state of the Treasury and to admonish it of any danger which there may be ground to apprehend of a failure in the means of meeting the expenditures authorized by law.

I ought not, therefore, to dissemble my fears that there will be a serious falling off in the estimated proceeds both of the customs and the public lands. I regard the evil of disappointment in these respects as altogether too great to be risked if by any possibility it may be entirely obviated.

While I am far from objecting, under present circumstances, to the recommendation of the Secretary that authority be granted him to reissue Treasury notes as they shall be redeemed, and to other suggestions which he has made on this subject, yet it appears to me to be worthy of grave consideration whether more permanent and certain supplies ought not to be provided. The issue of one note in redemption of another is not the payment of a debt, which must be made in the end by some form of public taxation.

I can not forbear to add that in a country so full of resources, of such abundant means if they be but judiciously called out, the revenues of the Government, its credit, and its ability to fulfill all its obligations ought not to be made dependent on temporary expedients or on calculations of an uncertain character. The public faith in this or in all things else ought to be placed beyond question and beyond contingency.

The necessity of further and full provision for supplying the wants of the Treasury will be the more urgent if Congress at this present session should adopt no plan for facilitating the financial operations of the Government and improving the currency of the country. By the aid of a wise and efficient measure of that kind not only would the internal business and prosperity of the country be revived and invigorated, but important additions to the amount of revenue arising from importations might also be confidently expected. Not only does the present condition of things in relation to the currency and commercial exchanges produce severe and distressing embarrassments in the business and pursuits of individuals, but its obvious tendency is to create also a necessity for the imposition of new burdens of taxation in order to secure the Government and the country against discredit from the failure of means to fulfill the public engagements.

JOHN TYLER.

WASHINGTON, *February 18, 1843.*

To the House of Representatives of the United States:

A resolution has been communicated to me, which was adopted by the House of Representatives on the 2d instant, in the following terms:

Resolved, That the President of the United States be requested to inform this House by what authority and under whose instructions Captain Thomas ap Catesby Jones, commander of the squadron of the United States in the Pacific Ocean, did, on or about the 19th of October last, invade in warlike array the territories of the Mexican Republic, take possession of the town of Monterey, and declare himself the commander of the naval and military expedition for the occupation of the Californias.

Resolved, That the President of the United States be requested to communicate to this House copies of all the instructions given by him or under his authority to the said Captain Jones from the time of his appointment to the command of the said squadron; also copies of all communications received from him relating to his expedition for the occupation of the Californias; and also to inform this House whether orders have been dispatched to the said Captain Jones recalling him from his command.

The proceeding of Captain Jones in taking possession of the town of Monterey, in the possessions of Mexico, was entirely of his own authority, and not in consequence of any orders or instructions of any kind given to him by the Government of the United States. For that proceeding he has been recalled, and the letter recalling him will be found among the papers herewith communicated.

The resolution of the House of Representatives asks for "copies of all the instructions given to Captain Jones from the time of his appointment to the command of the said squadron, also copies of all communications received from him relating to his expedition for the occupation of the Californias," without confining the request to such instructions and correspondence as relate to the transactions at Monterey, and without the usual reservation of such portions of the instructions or correspondence as in the President's judgment could not be made public without prejudice or danger to the public interests.

It may well be supposed that cases may arise even in time of peace in which it would be highly injurious to the country to make public at a particular moment the instructions under which a commander may be acting on a distant and foreign service. In such a case, should it arise, and in all similar cases the discretion of the Executive can not be controlled by the request of either House of Congress for the communication of papers. The duties which the Constitution and the laws devolve on the President must be performed by him under his official responsibility, and he is not at liberty to disregard high interests or thwart important public objects by untimely publications made against his own judgment, by whomsoever such publications may be requested. In the present case, not seeing that any injury is likely to arise from so doing, I have directed copies of all the papers asked for to be communicated; and I avail of the opportunity of transmitting also copies of sundry letters, as noted below.

JOHN TYLER.

WASHINGTON, *February 20, 1843.*

To the House of Representatives:

I transmit to the House of Representatives a report from the Secretary of State, accompanied by a copy of the correspondence* requested by their resolution of the 29th of December last.

JOHN TYLER.

WASHINGTON, *February 20, 1843.*

To the Senate of the United States:

I transmit to the Senate a report† from the Secretary of State, in answer to their resolution of the 14th instant.

JOHN TYLER.

---

*Between the consul-general of the United States at Tangier and the Government of Morocco.
†Communicating a copy of the commission and instructions issued to Daniel Webster, Secretary of State, to treat with Lord Ashburton, special minister from Great Britain to the United States.

WASHINGTON, *February 24, 1843.*

To the Senate of the United States:

I transmit to the Senate, in answer to their resolutions of the 20th of December and of the 9th instant, the inclosed copies of papers* from the Department of State, with an accompanying list.

JOHN TYLER.

WASHINGTON, *February 27, 1843.*

To the House of Representatives:

In compliance with the resolution of the House of Representatives of the 22d instant, requesting me to communicate to the House "whatever correspondence or communication may have been received from the British Government respecting the President's construction of the late British treaty concluded at Washington as it concerns an alleged right to visit American vessels," I herewith transmit a report made to me by the Secretary of State.

I have also thought proper to communicate copies of Lord Aberdeen's letter of the 20th December, 1841, to Mr. Everett, Mr. Everett's letter of the 23d December in reply thereto, and extracts from several letters of Mr. Everett to the Secretary of State.

I can not forego the expression of my regret at the apparent purport of a part of Lord Aberdeen's dispatch to Mr. Fox. I had cherished the hope that all possibility of misunderstanding as to the true construction of the eighth article of the treaty lately concluded between Great Britain and the United States was precluded by the plain and well-weighed language in which it is expressed. The desire of both Governments is to put an end as speedily as possible to the slave trade, and that desire, I need scarcely add, is as strongly and as sincerely felt by the United States as it can be by Great Britain. Yet it must not be forgotten that the trade, though now universally reprobated, was up to a late period prosecuted by all who chose to engage in it, and there were unfortunately but very few Christian powers whose subjects were not permitted, and even encouraged, to share in the profits of what was regarded as a perfectly legitimate commerce. It originated at a period long before the United States had become independent and was carried on within our borders in opposition to the most earnest remonstrances and expostulations of some of the colonies in which it was most actively prosecuted. Those engaged in it were as little liable to inquiry or interruption as any others. Its character, thus fixed by common consent and general practice, could only be changed by the positive assent of each and every nation, expressed either in the form of municipal law or conventional arrangement. The United States led the way in efforts to suppress it. They claimed no right to dictate to others, but they resolved, without waiting for the

---

*Correspondence with the United States minister to France relative to the quintuple treaty of December 20, 1841, and the Ashburton treaty of August 9, 1842.

cooperation of other powers, to prohibit it to their own citizens and to visit its perpetration by them with condign punishment. I may safely affirm that it never occurred to this Government that any new maritime right accrued to it from the position it had thus assumed in regard to the slave trade. If before our laws for its suppression the flag of every nation might traverse the ocean unquestioned by our cruisers, this freedom was not, in our opinion, in the least abridged by our municipal legislation.

Any other doctrine, it is plain, would subject to an arbitrary and ever-varying system of maritime police, adopted at will by the great naval power for the time being, the trade of the world in any places or in any articles which such power might see fit to prohibit to its own subjects or citizens. A principle of this kind could scarcely be acknowledged without subjecting commerce to the risk of constant and harassing vexations.

The attempt to justify such a pretension from the right to visit and detain ships upon reasonable suspicion of piracy would deservedly be exposed to universal condemnation, since it would be an attempt to convert an established rule of maritime law, incorporated as a principle into the international code by the consent of all nations, into a rule and principle adopted by a single nation and enforced only by its assumed authority. To seize and detain a ship upon suspicion of piracy, with probable cause and in good faith, affords no just ground either for complaint on the part of the nation whose flag she bears or claim of indemnity on the part of the owner. The universal law sanctions and the common good requires the existence of such a rule. The right under such circumstances not only to visit and detain but to search a ship is a perfect right and involves neither responsibility nor indemnity. But, with this single exception, no nation has in time of peace any authority to detain the ships of another upon the high seas on any pretext whatever beyond the limits of her territorial jurisdiction. And such, I am happy to find, is substantially the doctrine of Great Britain herself in her most recent official declarations, and even in those now communicated to the House. These declarations may well lead us to doubt whether the apparent difference between the two Governments is not rather one of definition than of principle. Not only is the right of *search*, properly so called, disclaimed by Great Britain, but even that of mere visit and inquiry is asserted with qualifications inconsistent with the idea of a perfect right.

In the dispatch of Lord Aberdeen to Mr. Everett of the 20th of December, 1841, as also in that just received by the British minister in this country made to Mr. Fox, his lordship declares that if in spite of all the precaution which shall be used to prevent such occurrences an American ship, by reason of any visit or detention by a British cruiser, "should suffer loss and injury, it would be followed by prompt and ample remuneration;" and in order to make more manifest her intentions in this respect, Lord Aberdeen in the dispatch of the 20th December makes known to Mr. Everett the nature of the instructions given to the British cruisers. These are such as, if faithfully observed, would enable the British Government to approximate the standard of a fair indemnity. That Government has in several cases fulfilled her promises in this particular by making adequate reparation for damage done to our commerce. It seems obvious to remark that a right which is only to be exercised under such restrictions and precautions and risk, in case of any assignable damage to be followed by the consequences of a trespass, can scarcely be considered anything more than a privilege asked for and either conceded or withheld on the usual principles of international comity.

The principles laid down in Lord Aberdeen's dispatches and the assurances of indemnity therein held out, although the utmost reliance was placed on the good faith of the British Government, were not regarded by the Executive as a sufficient security against the abuses which Lord Aberdeen admitted might arise in even the most cautious and moderate exercise of their new maritime police, and therefore in my message at the opening of the last session I set forth the views entertained by the Executive on this subject, and substantially affirmed both our inclination and ability to enforce our own laws, protect our flag from abuse, and acquit ourselves of all our duties and obligations on the high seas. In view of these assertions the treaty of Washington was negotiated, and upon consultation with the British negotiator as to the quantum of force necessary to be employed in order to attain these objects, the result to which the most deliberate estimate led was embodied in the eighth article of the treaty.

Such were my views at the time of negotiating that treaty, and such, in my opinion, is its plain and fair interpretation. I regarded the eighth article as removing all possible pretext on the ground of mere necessity to visit and detain our ships upon the African coast because of any alleged abuse of our flag by slave traders of other nations. We had taken upon ourselves the burden of preventing any such abuse by stipulating to furnish an armed force regarded by both the high contracting parties as sufficient to accomplish that object.

Denying as we did and do all color of right to exercise any such general police over the flags of independent nations, we did not demand of Great Britain any formal renunciation of her pretension; still less had we the idea of yielding anything ourselves in that respect. We chose to make a practical settlement of the question. This we owed to what we had already done upon this subject. The honor of the country called for it; the honor of its flag demanded that it should not be used by others to cover an iniquitous traffic. This Government, I am very sure, has both the inclination and the ability to do this; and if need be it will not content itself with a fleet of eighty guns, but sooner than any foreign government shall exercise the province of executing its laws and fulfilling its obligations, the highest of which is to protect its flag alike from abuse or insult, it would, I doubt not, put in requisition for that purpose its whole naval power. The purpose of this Government is faithfully to fulfill the treaty on its part, and it will not permit itself to doubt that Great Britain will comply with it on hers. In this way peace will best be preserved and the most amicable relations maintained between the two countries.

JOHN TYLER.

WASHINGTON, *February 27, 1843.*

To the House of Representatives:

I transmit to Congress sundry letters which have passed between the Department of State and the Chevalier d'Argaïz, envoy extraordinary and minister plenipotentiary of Spain near the Government of the United States, on the subject of the schooner *Amistad* since the last communication of papers connected with that case. This correspondence will show the general grounds on which the Spanish minister expresses dissatisfaction with the decision of the Supreme Court in that case and the answers which have been made to his complaints by the Department of State.

In laying these papers before Congress I think it proper to observe that the allowance of salvage on the cargo does not appear to have been a subject of discussion in the Supreme Court. Salvage had been denied in the court below and from that part of the decree no appeal had been claimed.

The ninth article of the treaty between the United States and Spain provides that "all ships and merchandise of what nature soever which shall be rescued out of the hands of any pirates or robbers on the high seas shall be brought into some port of either State and shall be delivered to the custody of the officers of that port in order to be taken care of and restored entire to the true proprietor as soon as due and sufficient proof shall be made concerning the property thereof." The case of the *Amistad*, as was decided by the court, was not a case of piracy, and therefore not within the terms of the treaty; yet it was a case in which the authority of the master, officers, and crew of the vessel had been divested by force, and in that condition the vessel, having been found on the coast, was brought into a port of the United States; and it may deserve consideration that the salvors in this case were the officers and seamen of a public ship.

It is left to Congress to consider, under these circumstances, whether, although in strictness salvage may have been lawfully due, it might not yet be wise to make provision to refund it, as a proof of the entire good faith of the Government and of its disposition to fulfill all its treaty stipulations to their full extent under a fair and liberal construction.

JOHN TYLER.

WASHINGTON, *February 28, 1843.*

To the Senate of the United States:

I transmit to the Senate, for its consideration with a view to ratification, a convention further to provide for the payment of awards in favor of claimants under the convention between the United States and the Mexican Republic of the 11th of April, 1839, signed in the City of Mexico on the 30th day of last month. A copy of the instructions from the Department of State to the minister of the United States at Mexico relative to the convention and of the dispatches of that minister to the Department is also communicated. By adverting to the signatures appended to the original draft of the convention as transmitted from the Department of State to General Thompson it will be seen that the convention as concluded was substantially approved by the representatives of a large majority in value of the parties immediately interested.

JOHN TYLER.

WASHINGTON, *February 28, 1843.*

To the House of Representatives:

I communicate to the House of Representatives a report from the Secretary of State, which, with the documents* accompanying it, furnishes the information requested by their resolution of the 18th instant.

JOHN TYLER.

WASHINGTON, *March 3, 1843.*

To the Senate of the United States:

In submitting the name of Henry A. Wise to the Senate for the mission to France, I was led to do so by considerations of his high talent, his exalted character, and great moral worth. The country, I feel assured, would be represented at Paris in the person of Mr. Wise by one wholly unsurpassed in exalted patriotism and well fitted to be the representative of his country abroad. His rejection by the Senate has caused me to reconsider his qualifications, and I see no cause to doubt that he is eminently qualified for the station. I feel it, therefore, to be my duty to renominate him.

I nominate Henry A. Wise, of Virginia, to be envoy extraordinary and minister plenipotentiary to the Court of His Majesty the King of the French, in place of Lewis Cass, resigned.

JOHN TYLER.

MARCH 3, 1843.

To the Senate of the United States:

In submitting to you the name of Caleb Cushing as Secretary of the Treasury, I did so in full view of his consummate abilities, his unquestioned patriotism and full capacity to discharge with honor to himself

---

*Correspondence between the representatives of foreign governments and the United States relative to the operation of the tariff laws on treaties existing with foreign governments.

and advantage to the country the high and important duties appertaining to that Department of the Government. The respect which I have for the wisdom of the Senate has caused me again, since his rejection, to reconsider his merits and his qualifications. That review has satisfied me that I could not have a more able adviser in the administration of public affairs or the country a more faithful officer. I feel it, therefore, to be my duty to renominate him.

I nominate Caleb Cushing to be Secretary of the Treasury, in the place of Walter Forward, resigned.

JOHN TYLER.

WASHINGTON, *March 3, 1843.*

To the House of Representatives of the United States:

I herewith transmit to the House of Representatives copies of the final report and appendices of the joint commission appointed to explore and survey the boundary line between the States of Maine and New Hampshire and the adjoining British Provinces, together with a general map showing the results of their labors.

JOHN TYLER.

*Report of the commissioners appointed by the President of the United States for the purpose of exploring and surveying the boundary line between the States of Maine and New Hampshire and the British Provinces.**

Hon. DANIEL WEBSTER,
    Secretary of State.

WASHINGTON, *January 27, 1843.*

SIR: The operations of the divisions under the direction of the several commissioners during the past season have been as follows, viz:

I.

The work remaining to be performed by the division under the direction of the chairman of the board was as follows:

1. The completion of the survey of the line of highlands around the sources of the Rimouski, filling up the gap left in former surveys in the line of boundary claimed by the United States.

2. The survey of the line of highlands rising from the northern side of the Bay of Chaleurs at its western extremity from the point visited and measured in 1840 to its connection with the line surveyed in 1841 in the vicinity of Lake Metis.

3. The astronomical determination of the longitude of one or more points in the surveyed lines, in order to the compilation of a geographical map of undeniable accuracy.

The party, which was dispatched at the earliest possible period, having been recalled by a special messenger as soon as the signature of the treaty of Washington was made known to the commissioner, no more than the first of these objects was attempted, and some of the observations that would have been considered necessary to make

---

* This report proper and Appendix No. 1 are the only portions of the original final report which can be found filed with the archives of the commission. The copy of the report which was transmitted to the House of Representatives is missing from the files of the House. A careful search in the Government libraries of Washington warrants me in asserting that the report has never been printed.—COMPILER.

this survey useful as evidence in case of a further discussion of the subject of boundary were not completed. The expedition has, however, obtained for its results an
accurate survey of the Green River of St. John from its mouth to the portage between it and the South Branch of the Katawamkedgwick, a survey of that portage,
and a careful chain and compass survey of the highlands surrounding the sources
of Rimouski. The first of these is connected with the survey of the river St. John
made by Major Graham; the last was united at its two extremities with stations of
the survey of 1841. Throughout the whole of the surveys the latitudes were carefully
determined, by the methods employed during the former years, at a sufficient number of points. The longitudes have been estimated by the use of chronometers, but
the sudden recall of the party left the latter part of the task incomplete. Any defect
arising from the latter cause may be considered as in a great degree compensated by
the connections referred to with the work of Major Graham and the surveys of the
previous years.

The party left Portland to take the field on the 18th June, and reached the Grand
Falls of the St. John on its return on the 25th August.

The surplus stores, with the boats and camp equipage, were stored there, and were
afterwards transferred to the parties of the two other commissioners.

A map of the operations of this division was placed on file in the State Department
on the 27th December.

The distance surveyed along Green River from its mouth to the portage is 57
miles, the length of the portage 5½ miles, the distance measured in exploration
of the remaining portion of the boundary claimed by the United States 61½ miles,
making in all 124 miles.

II.

The parties under the direction of A. Talcott entered upon their field duties about
the middle of September, and completed that branch of the service by the 5th of
November.

During that period the following rivers and streams were surveyed:

1. The "main St. John River" from the mouth of the "Alleguash" to the Forks.
2. The "Southwest Branch" to its source at the Metjarmette portage.
3. The "South Branch," or "Wool-as-ta-qua-guam," to 5 miles above Bakers
Lake and near to the exploring line of 1841 along the highlands claimed by Great
Britain.
4. The "West Branch," or "Mat-ta-wa-quam," to its source in the highlands.
5. The "Northwest Branch" to its source in the highlands.
6. The "Big Black River," or "Chim-pas-a-ooc-ten," to its source.
7. The "Little Black River," or "Pas-a-ooc-ten."
8. The "Chim-mem-ti-cook River" as far as navigable.

The character of all these streams is the same—slack water of moderate depth
alternating with rapids. They can never be navigated by anything larger than a
bateau.

The method of survey was to trace the course of each stream by compass, estimating distances by the eye, or by pacing when the nature of the margin of the river
would permit.

The average distance coursed per day was about 9 miles, and at the camps formed
at night astronomical observations north and south of the zenith were made to determine their position in latitude, and observations for the local time to ascertain their
differences of longitude.

Meridian observations of the sun were also made at a point intermediate to the
camps whenever they could be obtained.

Thirty-three of these points have been used in the correction of the paced and
estimated distances.

Tables exhibiting these observations, their calculation and results, will accompany the detailed maps.

With a view to facilitate the operations of the joint commission it was conceived to be important that the intersection of the parallel of 46° 25′ with the Southwest Branch should be ascertained, as also the point on the Northwest Branch (10 miles from the main St. John) where the boundary line from the outlet of Lake Pohenaga-mook intersects the said branch.

It is believed that these points are projected on the map which accompanies this report so near to their true position that the line indicating the boundary as drawn on the map may be considered to substantially exhibit the division of territory as effected by the late treaty.

The more thorough knowledge acquired through these explorations of the charac-ter of the territory which has been relinquished by the United States fully confirms the opinion previously entertained of its little value, either for its timber growth or for purposes of agriculture.

Bordering on the "Big Black" and "Little Black" rivers the growth of pine is large and apparently of good quality, and it is believed that most of the smaller streams falling into the St. John below the "Seven Islands" will be found fringed with pine, but it is quite certain that very little will be found included between the lines of boundary and the highlands as claimed by the United States to the westward of St. Francis River.

The office work of this party is nearly completed, all the calculations arising from the astronomical observations have been made, and the detailed maps (five in num-ber) drawn to the scale of 1:50,000 (or nearly 1¼ inches to 1 mile), exhibiting the result of the surveys in 1840, 1841, and 1842, are in such a state of forwardness as to insure their completion by the middle of February.

These explorations and surveys embrace—

1. The highlands as claimed by the United States, extending from the northwest-ernmost head of the Connecticut River to the portage road which leads from the St. Lawrence River to Lake Temiscouata.

2. The highlands as claimed by Great Britain from the Metjarmette portage to the source of the Aroostook River.

3. All the principal heads or branches of the Connecticut River north of the forty-fifth degree of latitude.

4. The St. John and all its principal branches or tributaries west of the Alleguash River.

III.

The division under the direction of Major Graham has been employed during the past season in making the following surveys, viz:

1. In prolonging the meridian of the monument at the source of the river St. Croix.

2. In making a survey of the Little Madawaska River, a tributary to the Aroostook, from its mouth to its source in the Madawaska Lakes.

3. In surveying the group of lakes lying northwest of the Madawaska Lakes, known by the appellation of the Eagle Lakes, or sometimes by the aboriginal one of the Cheaplawgan Lakes, and especially to ascertain if those lakes, or any of them, emptied their waters into the river St. John by any other outlet than Fish River.

4. A survey of the portion of Fish River included between the outlet of Lake Winthrop and the river St. John.

5. A survey of the river St. John between the Grand Falls and the mouth of the Alleguash.

6. A survey of the Alleguash from its mouth to its source.

7. A survey of the river St. Francis from its mouth to the outlet of Lake St. Francis.

8. In making astronomical observations for the latitude and longitude of the Grand

Falls and the mouths of the Grand, the Green, Madawaska, Fish, and St. Francis rivers.

Early in July a party under the direction of an officer of Topographical Engineers was sent into the field and directed to occupy the most northern astronomical station fixed the preceding year upon the true meridian of the monument at the source of the river St. Croix, with the view of being prepared to complete its trace to the northwest angle of Nova Scotia before the termination of the season in case the pending negotiations for a conventional boundary should fail.

The true meridian was in this way prolonged to a point 19 miles north of the station alluded to of last year, or 13½ miles north of its intersection with the river St. John, reaching to the summit of the height immediately south of Grand River, where a permanent station was fixed. The point thus fixed is 90¼ miles north of the monument at the source of the St. Croix.

This portion of the work was performed by the 15th of August, at which period it was considered inexpedient to incur the expense of continuing it any farther.

A party under the direction of another officer of Topographical Engineers, which took the field also in July was charged with the surveys of the Little Madawaska River, the Eagle or Cheaplawgan Lakes, the portion of Fish River from the outlet of Lake Winthrop—one of the Eagle group—to its débouché into the St. John, of the river St. John, thence to the meridian of the source of the St. Croix, and finally of the Alleguash from its mouth to its source.

The Little Madawaska was ascended in bateaux from its mouth to its source, which is found in the Madawaska Lakes, and a trace of the river was made by coursing with a compass and estimating the distances, which were checked by astronomical observations for latitude and longitude.

The position of its mouth had been fixed by the surveys of the preceding year, and observations for latitude and longitude were made at a point intermediate between its mouth and its source and also at the junction of the two lakes which form its source. The trace of the river was corrected so as to agree with the results of these observations before being laid down upon the map.

A portage of 5¼ miles was cut from the Madawaska to the Eagle Lakes, which are only 4¼ miles apart in a direct line. The party transported their baggage and boats by this portage and launched them on Lake Sedgwick, the most southern and largest of the Eagle group.

This group, which is composed of the Winthrop, Sedgwick, Preble, Bear, and Cleveland lakes, being all connected one with another by water communications between them, was carefully surveyed by triangulating them and coursing their shores with the chain and compass, except those parts which were so straight as to render the work sufficiently accurate by sketching those portions between consecutive points of triangulation of no great distance apart. They were also sounded so far as to obtain their general depths.

The survey was continued from the outlet of Lake Winthrop down Fish River to its mouth, which was found to be the only outlet from this group to the river St. John.

Lake Cleveland, the most northern and deepest of the group, was connected in position with the river St. John at a point 2 miles below the upper chapel of the Madawaska settlement, by a chained and coursed line following the portage represented on the map 5⅙ miles long.

The Alleguash was ascended in the month of October in bateaux and canoes from its mouth to its source in Lake Telos, a distance of about 94 miles. The river and its lakes were coursed by a compass, the distances estimated, and the projection resulting therefrom corrected before being placed upon the map by means of astronomical observations at eight intermediate points between its mouth and its source. The lakes were triangulated by means of magnetic bearings as far as was practicable, in order to obtain their widths and general contour. In the vicinity of Chamberlain Lake use has also been made of a recent survey of Mr. Parrott, a surveyor in the employ of the State of Maine, to whom we acknowledge ourselves indebted for the aid which this portion of his valuable labors furnished us.

Between the head of Lake Telos and Webster Pond, one of the sources of the East Branch of the Penobscot, there is a portage of only 1 mile and a half. This, together with a small cut or canal, made in 1841 to connect the waters of Lake Telos with those of Webster Pond, enabled the party which made this survey to proceed with their boats and baggage down the Penobscot to Bangor, where they and their surplus stores were disposed of.

A survey of the river St. John was made in the month of September with the chain and compass from the mouth of Fish River to the intersection of the meridian of the monument at the source of the St. Croix with the St. John. This survey was afterwards extended eastward to the Grand Falls, in order to connect with the astronomical station established there, and westward to the mouth of the Alleguash, embracing a distance of 87 miles. The islands were all surveyed, and the channels on either side of them sounded.

The commissioner, having had other duties assigned him in reference to the question of boundary, did not take the field in person until September. Between the middle of that month and the middle of December he was occupied in performing the field duties assigned him by the Department of State.

The party conducted by him in person made the astronomical observations for the determination of the latitude and longitude of the Grand Falls of the St. John, and of the mouths of the Grand, Green, Madawaska, Fish, and St. Francis rivers, all tributary to the St. John.

The same party also made a survey of the river St. Francis from its mouth to the outlet of Lake St. Francis, a distance of 81 miles.

This river was coursed by means of a compass, and whenever the nature of the shores would permit the distances from bend to bend were either measured with a chain or paced. Through the greater part of the stream, however, the impediments offered by the thick and small growth near the shores rendered this degree of minuteness impracticable and a resort to estimating the distances by the eye, well practiced by previous actual measurements, became necessary.

Before putting the trace of the river thus derived upon the map it was adjusted to correspond with the results of astronomical observations for latitude and longitude at twelve intermediate points between its mouth and the outlet of Lake St. Francis. Its three principal lakes, viz, Pettiquaggamas, Petteiquaggamak, and Pohenagamook, were triangulated and sounded as exhibited by the maps of detail yet to be handed in of the operations of this division.

A profile of the river, exhibiting the slope of the country through which it flows, was obtained by barometric observations made at fifteen points between its mouth and the bridge where it is intersected by the Grand portage road.

A connection was made with Long Lake, a tributary to Lake Temiscouata, by a chained line from a point on the St. Francis 2 miles below the mouth of Blue River to the western shore of Long Lake, by which it was ascertained that the shore of this lake approached within 2¼ miles of the river St. Francis.

The outlet of Lake Pohenagamook was reached in a distance of 49¼ miles from the mouth of the St. Francis following the sinuosities of the river on the 18th of October.

A camp was established on the southwest shore of the lake at its outlet for the purpose of making the necessary astronomical observations to determine the latitude and longitude of this position. Ten days were spent here for this object, out of which we had only three nights that were favorable for observation. These were improved as far as possible, and the results obtained, combined with those obtained by Captain

Talcott's parties on the Northwest and Southwest branches of the St. John, have furnished the elements for laying down upon the general map the straight lines which show the boundary as it is required to run between the highlands and the river St. John under the treaty of 1842. These furnish data for an accurate exhibition of the extent of territory included by this portion of the boundary as fixed by that treaty.

The south shore of Lake Pohenagamook forms an angle of about 100° with the direction of the stream which flows from it, and marks with great certainty the point at which, according to the late treaty, the straight line is to be commenced in running the boundary southwestward to the Northwest Branch of the river St. John.

The work of this division was connected with that of Captain Talcott's division of the preceding year by noting the position of a common point on the western shore of Lake Pohenagamook near its head.

The commissioner and his party reached the Grand portage, or British military road, where it crosses the river St. Francis on the 2d of November, and connected their work with that of Professor Renwick's division of the preceding year at the bridge near Fournier's house.

Observations were also made at this bridge for the latitude and longitude, when the weather was favorable, between the nights of the 2d and 5th of November, and a connection was made in longitude with the meridian of Quebec by comparisons of the local time with three chronometers transported from the first to the last mentioned place between the 6th and 10th of November.

This comparison was repeated on the return of the commissioner by observing again at the St. Francis bridge before mentioned on the night of the 10th of December, with the thermometer ranging during these observations from 11 to 15° below zero of Fahrenheit's scale, there being then near 4 feet of snow upon the ground. The commissioner then proceeded by the Grand portage road, and the road which pursues the margin of Temiscouata Lake and the valleys of the Madawaska and St. John rivers, to the mouth of Green River, where on the night of the 12th of December he again observed at the same point where his observations of the 29th of September were made while ascending the St. John. These completed, he proceeded to the Grand Falls, and on the 14th of December discharged his party, which terminated his field duties for the season.

The distance surveyed along the new line of boundary by this division the past season is—

	Miles.
1. Along the river St. John from the meridian of the monument of the source of the St. Croix to the mouth of the river St. Francis.	71½
2. Along the river St. Francis from its mouth to the outlet of Lake Pohenagamook.	49¾
Total	121¼

IV.

A map marked **L′**, on a scale of 1:400,000, exhibiting the lines respectively claimed by the two nations under the treaty of 1783, as well as that adopted by the treaty of 1842, is herewith presented. By reference thereto the operations of the several divisions during the present and previous years will be better understood.

For a more particular view of the surveys and explorations made under the direction of each of the commissioners, including descriptions of the face of the country, navigation of streams, etc., the undersigned respectfully refer to their respective narratives hereto appended, and to the maps of detail deposited by each in the Department of State.

All which is respectfully submitted.

JAS. RENWICK,
A. TALCOTT,
JAMES D. GRAHAM,
Commissioners.

APPENDIX No. 1.

OPERATIONS OF THE DIVISION UNDER THE DIRECTION OF JAMES RENWICK, LL. D., CHAIRMAN OF THE BOARD.

I.—*Operations during the year 1841.*

1. At as early a period as there was any probability of the country being accessible two engineers were dispatched from the city of New York for the purpose of exploring the Rimouski River. This had been crossed by the commissioner late in the previous season. It had been ascertained that it took its source much farther to the south than was represented on any map, and that at its head would be the greatest difficulty in the intended researches. It was, besides, considered necessary that skillful boatmen and practiced woodsmen should be engaged in Canada. These it was believed could be found in Quebec, and the chief of this detachment, with an appointment as acting commissioner, was directed to perform this duty on his route.

This detachment accordingly left New York on the 22d May. On reaching Quebec it was found that the proper persons could only be engaged at Trois Rivieres. A delay was thus occasioned before this part of the duty could be performed. The detachment, however, reached Rimouski 4th June, where the snow was still found upon the ground and the river barely fit for the access of boats. No time had therefore been lost, and the reconnoissance of the river was successfully performed. The detachment, after passing all the establishments of lumberers, extended its explorations beyond the remotest Indian paths, and leaving its boats penetrated on foot several miles to the south of the highest point of the stream in which boats could float. In this progress through unexplored ground a lake wholly unknown was discovered. The results of this expedition were embodied in a map, which on examination by parties furnished with better means was found accurate.

It was found by this party that the Rimouski presented difficulties which would forbid its ascent by a party provided with stores and instruments for the prosecution of a survey along the height of land, and that it would be impracticable even to make it the route of an expedition to reach its own source. The little knowledge which was possessed of its upper course and the fact that it had probably never been explored even by Indian hunters were accounted for by its difficulty of access, which would forbid the carriage of a sufficient supply of provisions for consumption during its ascent and descent. On other streams difficulties of this sort had been and were afterwards overcome by the use of the bateaux of the Penobscot, of greater burthen and strength than the birch canoes, but the continual repetition of portages on the Rimouski forbade the use of any vessel heavier than the latter.

2. The main body of engineers, etc., was ordered to assemble in New York on the 15th May, for which time a vessel was chartered for the purpose of conveying them, with stores sufficient for an expedition of five months and the necessary instruments and camp equipage, to Metis, on the St. Lawrence. The experience of the former season had shown that the country was so poor as to furnish little for the support of a numerous party, and it was believed that even game and fish would be found scarce at the points where supplies would be most needed. It was therefore to be chosen between laying in the supplies in New York or in Quebec, and while the great advantage of conveying all the important instruments by sea turned the scale in favor of the former place, it has been ascertained that the decision was in other respects correct, for the dangers and difficulties of navigating the St. Lawrence might have frustrated altogether, and would certainly have materially delayed, the commencement of the main survey.

The sailing of the vessel was delayed, in expectation of the arrival of instruments from Europe, until the 30th of May, when a sufficient supply for beginning the operations arrived.

In the meantime Mr. Lally, one of the first assistants, was directed to proceed to Bangor, in Maine, for the purpose of procuring boats and men to manage them. These were obtained and brought down the Penobscot to Castine, where they were on the 8th June embarked in the vessel which carried the rest of the party, and which had orders to call at that port for the purpose. The experience of the previous year had manifested the great superiority of the bateaux of the Penobscot over all other vessels in the navigation of shallow and rapid rivers. The physical energy and enterprise of the boatmen of that river had also been known. It was believed that it was not only essential that a considerable proportion of the laboring force should be American citizens, but that much good would result from emulation between the boatmen of the Penobscot and the Canadian voyageurs. This expectation was in a great degree confirmed by the result, for although it must be stated with regret that it became necessary at an early period to discharge some of the Americans, the remainder were models of intelligence, sobriety, industry, and perseverance, and entered into the work, not with the feelings of hired laborers, but with those of men who felt that the interest of their country was at stake.

3. The commissioner did not leave New York until 30th of June, being delayed in expectation of more instruments. A part of these only had arrived, but further delay might have been injurious. Proper instructions had been given for setting the party in motion in case it could be organized before he joined it, but these were rendered nugatory by the length of the vessel's passage. This did not reach Metis till 7th July, so that the commissioner, arriving on the 9th, was in time to direct the first operations in person. The stores, boats, and instruments had been landed and partially carried to a camp on the river above the falls. A heavy rain on the 10th July rendered the roads almost impassable, and it was not till the morning of the 12th that the first detachment could be embarked. This was comprised of Dr. O. Goodrich, the assistant commissary, two surveyors, and an assistant engineer. The first was in charge of stores sufficient for six weeks' consumption. The surveyors had orders to survey the river for the purpose of connecting it with the line of exploration, and the latter was directed to make barometric observations. The commissioner and the remaining engineers were detained at Metis by the necessary astronomic observations. These being completed, the instruments, camp equipage, and a portion of the stores were embarked, and the main body proceeded up the river about noon on the 15th July.

4. The river was found to be still swollen by the melting of the snows on the highlands near its source, and, being at all times rapid, the progress of the party was attended both with difficulty and danger. One of the birch canoes, although managed by a skillful voyageur, was twice upset, and one of the heavily loaded bateaux filled with water in a rapid. The result of the first accident was unimportant, except as respected the personal comfort of one of the party, who lost his clothing when it could not be replaced; the second accident caused the loss of some valuable stores. A guide had been procured in the person of a Canadian who was said to have acted in the same capacity to Captain Broughton, who had descended the river by order of the commissioners of Great Britain in 1840. So long as the services of the guide were unimportant he was found intelligent and acquainted with the country, but on passing beyond the region usually visited by lumbering parties he manifested a very scanty knowledge. It had been the intention of the commissioner to ascend to Lake Metis and thence proceed to the height of land by an old portage said to have existed from that lake to the one at the head of the Grande Fourche of the Restigouche, which had been explored by the commissioner in 1840. Lake Metis was chosen because all former accounts, and particularly those of the surveyors of the joint commission under the fifth article of the treaty of Ghent, represented this

as the body of water seen to the northwest of the termination of the exploring meridian line. The guide appeared to confirm this impression, and held out inducements that led to the belief that he was acquainted with the portage in question. The nearer, however, it was approached the less seemed to be his confidence. When there appeared to be some reason to doubt his competency or his will, a place in the river was reached where it divided into two branches of nearly equal magnitude. On inquiry from the guide it was ascertained that the easternmost of these was the main Metis, the other the Mistigougeche (Riviere au Foin). Although the latter appeared to be the most direct course to the boundary, it was still believed, and nothing could be learned from him to the contrary, that the former led to the termination of the exploring meridian line. The party of Dr. Goodrich had gone up the Metis, and it was necessary to communicate with it before any change in plan could be made. The commissioner therefore entered the main Metis, and in the evening overtook the surveyors, who had been unable to keep the survey up with the progress of the boats. An express was therefore sent forward to stop the boats, and, the party encamping, astronomic observations were made for the solution of the difficulty in which it appeared to be enveloped. A detachment was also sent out to explore to the eastward of the Metis. This reached the Lake of the Little Red River, and from its banks took bearings to what appeared to be the greatest mountain of the country. This is known by the name of Paganet, and lies to the southwest of Lake Matapediac, forming a part of the highlands which are so obviously described as the boundary of the Province of Quebec in the proclamation of 1763. Its height was reported to be probably 3,000 feet, but as it has appeared in the course of the survey that heights in that region may easily be overestimated, it can not be safely taken at more than 2,500 feet. The result of the astronomic observations seemed to show that the main stream would lead too far to the eastward, and after mature deliberation it was resolved that the course should be retraced and the Mistigougeche ascended. The first part of the operation was attended with little delay. Half an hour sufficed for reaching the forks, whence the party had been six hours in mounting. The guide also stated that the Mistigougeche was a much less difficult stream than Metis. Of the comparative facility, except for a few miles of the latter, no opportunity for judging was obtained; but these were so difficult as to confirm his statement. On the other hand, the former was found to be much worse than it had been represented by him. His knowledge, in fact, was limited to its state in winter, for it appeared from a subsequent interview with Captain Broughton to be doubtful whether he had served in the employ of that officer; and it can be well imagined that the river when locked up in ice should present an aspect of far less rapidity than when rushing with its springtide violence. The Mistigougeche was found to be intercepted by a fall of a few feet, which could not be passed by the boats when loaded, although the Penobscot men boldly and successfully carried theirs up when empty, in which feat they were imitated by the voyageurs, who had at first deemed it impossible. The loads of the boats were carried over a portage, and in this operation the chronometers were found to deviate from each other, showing a manifest change of rate in some or all of them. This may be ascribed to a change in the mode of transportation, but was more than could be reasonably anticipated, considering the shortness of the portage (2,000 yards) and the great care that was taken in conveying them. At some distance above the falls a lake of moderate size was reached, embosomed in hills and embarrassed at its upper end with grass. From the last feature it was ascertained that both lake and river take their epithet of Grassy (Riviere au Foin, and, in Indian, of Mistigougeche, or Grassy Lake). At this lake the party of the commissioner was in advance of the loaded boats. A halt was therefore made and a party sent out to explore to the westward. This party reached an eminence whence a lake was seen, which the guide stated to be the head of a branch of the Rimouski, far distant, as he averred, from any waters of the Restigouche. Subsequent examination has shown that this party had actually reached the height of land and that the survey of the boundary might have been advantageously commenced from this point.

On leaving the lake the river was found to have a gentle current for a few miles. It was then interrupted by a bed of timber, after passing which it became as rapid as ever. In a short time, however, a noble sheet of water was reached, surrounded by lofty hills, and of great depth. At the upper end of this a place was chosen for a stationary camp, and preparations were made for proceeding to the land survey. While these were going forward with as much dispatch as possible, Mr. Lally, one of the first assistants, was detached to reconnoiter the inlet of the lake. During his absence observations were taken and the rates of the chronometers worked up. Of the four instruments with which the expedition was furnished, two had varied from the other two on the portage. All were of good reputation, and no means existed of determining on which pair reliance could be placed. From the rates of two of them it appeared that the camp was situated 12 miles to the northwest of the tree chosen by the American surveyors in 1818 as marking the northwest angle of Nova Scotia. Actual survey has shown that the distance is about 10 miles. The result given by the chronometers was speedily confirmed by the return of Mr. Lally, who reported that he had actually reached the marked tree, well known to him by his visit to it the year before, and that he had pursued for a couple of miles the line cut out subsequently by Captain Broughton.

6. The preparations being completed, Messrs. H. B. Renwick and Lally were sent out, each at the head of a sufficient party, with instructions to proceed together to the west until they reached waters running to the Restigouche and then to divide, Mr. Lally proceeding to the northwest angle and Mr. Renwick toward Rimouski. Each was directed to pursue as far as possible the height of land and to remain in the field as long as the supplies which the men could carry would permit. They were also ordered to mark their path in order to insure a safe return, as well as all the stations of their barometric observations. Each of the laborers was loaded with 56 pounds besides his own baggage and ax, and the engineers and surveyors carried their own baggage and instruments. The commissioner, with one assistant, remained in the stationary camp for the purpose of determining the longitude accurately and of making corresponding barometric observations.

7. In this place it will be proper to state that the lake which was thus reached was ascertained with certainty to be that seen by the surveyors of the joint commission in 1818, and which was by them supposed to be Lake Metis. As it has no name yet assigned to it, it has been called upon our maps Lake Johnson, in honor of the American surveyor by whom it was first visited. It is 1,007 feet above the level of the sea, being more than twice as much as the total fall assigned to the waters of the Metis in the report of Messrs. Mudge and Featherstonhaugh. So great an elevation in so short a course is sufficient to account for the great rapidity of the stream. To illustrate this rapidity in an obvious manner, the birch canoes, which on the waters of the St. John are easily managed by one man, are never intrusted on those of the Metis to less than two. Our departure from Metis in boats so deeply loaded, as was afterwards learned, was considered there as a desperate attempt, and although but one of them sustained injury, this is to be ascribed to the great skill of the boatmen; and to show the velocity of the stream in a still stronger light, it is to be recollected that, after deducting the loss of time on the Metis, nine days of incessant labor were spent in taking up the loaded boats, while the assistant commissary whom it became necessary to send to Metis left the stationary camp at 2 o'clock in the morning of the 28th July and reached the mouth of the river before sunset of the same day, after making two portages, one of 2,000 yards and the other of 2 miles.

8. The first day of the operations of Messrs. H. B. Renwick and Lally was attended with an accident which had an injurious effect. The surveyor of Mr. Lally's party, Mr. W. G. Waller, fell from a tree laid as a bridge across a stream and lamed himself

to such a degree as to be incapable either of proceeding with the party or of returning to the stationary camp. It became necessary, therefore, to leave him, with a man to attend him, in the woods, and it was a week before he was sufficiently recovered to be able to walk. Intelligence was immediately sent to the commissioner, by whom the assistant he had retained in camp to aid in astronomic observations was sent to take the place of the surveyor. Two days were thus lost, and the intended astronomic observations were far less numerous than they might have been with the aid of a competent assistant.

The two parties, proceeding together, reached Katawamkedgwick Lake. That under the direction of Mr. H. B. Renwick immediately crossed it, while that of Mr. Lally proceeded along the eastern bank for the purpose of reaching the source of the stream. This being attained, the party of Mr. L. pursued the height of land as nearly as possible and reached the exploring meridian line. Crossing this, some progress was made to the eastward, when a failure of provisions compelled a return to camp. The party of Mr. H. B. Renwick, proceeding until the Rimouski was seen, turned to the south and finally reached the southeasterly source of that river, a point probably never before pressed by human foot, for it was found to consist in a series of beaver ponds, in which that animal was residing in communities and without any appearance of having been ever disturbed. The low state of provisions in this instance also called the party back, but not before every anticipated result had been obtained.

9. The party of Mr. H. B. Renwick having returned first, immediate preparations were made for descending the stream. Before they were completed Mr. Lally also came in, and both were assembled at Metis on the 14th, whence the commissioner set out instantly for the river Du Loup, which had been chosen as the base of further operations.

The circumstances of the operations up the Metis and Metis and Mistigougeche had been upon the whole favorable. With the exception of a single thundershower, no rain had been experienced; the country was still sufficiently moist to insure a supply of water even upon the ridges. The sun was observed daily for time and latitude, and the nights admitted of observations of the pole star for latitude at almost every camp. At the stationary camp, however, the mists rising from the lake obscured the horizon and rendered the eclipses of Jupiter's satellites invisible; nor was it possible to observe the only occultation of a star which calculation rendered probable during the period in question. Much, however, had been accomplished. A river little known had been carefully surveyed some miles beyond its junction with a branch unheard of by geographers. This branch had been explored, its course and length determined; a path nearly coinciding with the boundary line for an extent of 86 miles had been measured and leveled, and regions before unseen visited. One accident of a serious character had occurred, and one of the laboring men, although an *homme du nord*, seasoned in the service of the Hudsons Bay Company, had been rendered unfit by fatigue for further duty in the service; but with these exceptions the health and strength of the party were unimpaired. All augured well for a speedy and successful completion of the task in a manner as perfect as had been anticipated.

10. Instructions had been transmitted to the commissary, as soon as it was found that a portage to Katawamkedgwick and thence to Rimouski was impracticable, to have a vessel ready at Metis to transport the stores to the river Du Loup. One was in consequence chartered, but, being neaped in the harbor of Rimouski, did not reach Metis till the 19th August. When loaded, her sailing was delayed by an unfavorable wind, and its continuance prevented her from reaching the river Du Loup before the 29th August. An entire week of very favorable weather was thus lost for field operations, and it was not even possible to employ it to advantage in observations, as all the chronometers but one and the larger instruments, in order to expose them as little as possible to change of rate or injury, had been forwarded from Metis in the vessel. With the one chronometer and the reflecting repeating circle numerous observations were, however, made for the latitude of the river Du Loup.

11. During the time the main body was engaged in ascending the Metis and in the other operations which have been mentioned an engineer was directed to proceed

from Metis along the Kempt road for the purpose of exploring along the dividing ridge between the waters of the Bay of Chaleurs in the vicinity of Lake Matapediac and the St. Lawrence. This line forms the continuation of that claimed by the United States, and is important in its connection with the proclamation of 1763; but as it falls without the ground which is the subject of dispute, it was not considered necessary to survey it. The heights which could be reached were therefore measured with the barometer, and the position of the points at which the observations were taken referred to existing maps without any attempt to correct their errors.

In the course of this reconnoissance an eminence 1,743 feet in height, lying to the southeast of Lake Matapediac, was ascended. Thence was had the view of a wide, open valley extending toward the southeast to the Bay of Chaleurs and bounded on the northeast and southwest by highlands. The former were pointed out by the guide as the Chic Choc Mountains, in the district of Gaspe; the latter, it appeared beyond question, extended to the Bay of Chaleurs, and strike it below the Matapediac. At the latter place a party detached down the Restigouche in 1840 had measured the height of Ben Lomond, a highland rising abruptly from the western termination of the Bay of Chaleurs, and found it to be 1,024 feet. Thus it appears beyond the possibility of doubt that a chain of eminences well entitled to the name of highlands, both as dividing waters and rising to the character of mountains, depart from "*the northern shore of the Bay of Chaleurs at its western extremity*," bound the valley of the Matapediac to the northeast, and, bending around the lake of that name, separate its waters from those of the Metis. These are deeply cut by valleys, whose direction appears from the map of the reconnoissance and from the course of the tributary streams which occupy their lines of maximum slope to run from southwest to northeast, or at right angles to the general course of the highlands themselves. These highlands are obviously those defined in the proclamation of 1763 and the commission of Governor Wilmot.

12. As soon as the necessary instruments arrived from Metis at the river Du Loup a party was detached to survey the Temiscouata portage, a line known to be of great importance to the subsequent operations, but whose interest has been increased from the unexpected frequency with which the line dividing the waters touches or crosses it. Stores for a month's service were transported with all possible dispatch to Lake Temiscouata, along with the boats and camp equipage.

Two separate parties were now formed, the one to proceed up Temiscouata Lake, the other to ascend the Tuladi. The embarkation of both was completed at noon on the 4th September.

13. Mr. H. B. Renwick, with the party under his command, was directed if possible to ascend the middle or main branch of Tuladi and form a stationary camp at the highest point of that stream which could be reached by boats.

Mr. Lally had orders to enter and follow the river Asherbish, which enters Lake Temiscouata at its head, until the progress of his boats should be interrupted. The first party was directed to operate in the first place toward the west, the second toward the east, upon the height of land until they should meet each other's marks. The party of Mr. H. B. Renwick was directed, therefore, to proceed from the head of Tuladi and reach if possible the head of Rimouski, thus forming a connection with the line explored from the head of Mistigougeche; that of Mr. Lally to proceed from the head of Asherbish along the height of land to the Temiscouata portage. The commissary was then moved up with a large amount of stores and halted on the summit of Mount Biort, to be within reach of both the parties in case of a demand for new supplies, and to receive them on their return.

14. The party of Mr. H. B. Renwick, having passed through Tuladi Lake, entered the main stream of that name on the 5th September. The head of it had been seen by that gentleman in September, 1840, and held out the promise of abundance of water for navigation. This promise did not fail, but it was found that the stream

had probably never before been ascended, and was therefore embarrassed with drift-wood. After cutting through several rafts with great labor, a place was reached where the stream spread out to a great width over beds of gravel, and all further progress in boats became impossible. It was therefore determined to fall down the stream and ascend the western branch, well known under the name of Abagusquash, and which had been fully explored in 1840. The resolution to return was taken on the 6th, and on the evening of the 9th the beaver pond at the head of Abagusquash was reached; here a stationary camp was established. One of the men had wounded himself with an ax and three more were so ill as to be unfit for service. The numbers were yet sufficient for short expeditions, and one was immediately fitted out for the head of Tuladi with provisions to form a cache for future operations. This expedition explored so much of the height of land as would otherwise have been thrown out of the regular order in consequence of the failure to ascend the main branch of Tuladi.

15. In the meantime Mr. Lally proceeded up Lake Temiscouata and entered the Asherbish. This stream was also found very difficult, and on the evening of the 7th no more than 7 miles had been accomplished on it. At this point a stationary camp was fixed and a detachment sent out to explore the neighborhood. On the 10th Mr. Lally set out to the eastward, and struck the lower end of Abagusquash Lake on the afternoon of the 11th September. Being obviously too far to the south, he ascended that stream and reached H. B. Renwick's camp on the evening of the 12th. The next morning he proceeded to the height of land, and after twice crossing it reached his stationary camp on Asherbish at noon on the 21st September.

On this expedition two out of three barometers were broken, and an assistant was therefore sent to seek a fresh supply from the stores.

16. The expedition sent out by H. B. Renwick to the head of the Tuladi returned on the 13th September. One of the men came in severely wounded, and those left sick and wounded in camp were still unfit for service; others also were taken sick. Of the laborers of the party, one-half were thus lost for the present to the service. The engineer in command, who had finished the observations for which he had remained in the stationary camp, determined, therefore, to proceed to Mount Biort in order to obtain men. Previous to his departure on the 15th September he fitted out a second expedition with all the disposable strength for the purpose of operating between the head of Tuladi and the point in the height of land where Mr. Lally's line diverged to the southwest. The newly engaged hands and the detachment on its return both reached the camp on the Abagusquash on the 19th of September. On the 21st, all arrangements having been completed, Mr. H. B. Renwick, leaving the assistant commissary with only one man in the stationary camp, set off toward the head of Rimouski. This course was pursued for six days, when it became necessary to return for want of provisions, and the stationary camp was reached on the 2d October. On this expedition the line of exploration made in June up the Rimouski was intersected and the ground traversed in July and August seen and connected with the survey, but it was found impossible to penetrate along the height of land on the western side of Rimouski to its head. On reaching the camp snow began to fall, and the thermometer marked 18° in the morning. All further operations for the season in this direction were therefore at an end. A portion of the line which divides the waters falling into the St. John from those falling into the St. Lawrence remained in consequence unsurveyed. It can not, however, be said to be absolutely unexplored, for it was seen from the eastern side of Rimouski, presenting the appearance of a range of hills at least as elevated as any on the boundary.

18. Mr. Lally, having received a fresh supply of barometers on the evening of the 23d, resumed his survey of the height of land on the 25th September, and reached the camp of the commissary on Mount Biort on the 2d October, having surveyed and leveled the intermediate dividing ridge. The party of H. B. Renwick descended the Abagusquash and Tuladi, and, crossing Lake Temiscouata, reached the same

rendezvous on the 5th October. The interval was spent by Mr. Lally's party in clearing a space for a panoramic view on the summit of Mount Biort.

19. The commissioner, having superintended in person the equipment and embarkation of the parties of Messrs. H. B. Renwick and Lally on Lake Temiscouata, returned to the river Du Loup for the purpose of making astronomic observations. These being completed, he visited and conferred with the parties of his colleague, A. Talcott, esq., on their way to the height of land southeast of Kamouraska. Here he made arrangements for the junction of the two lines on the Temiscouata portage. He then proceeded to the camp of the commissary on Mount Biort, and there made provision for the completion of the residue of the line in the vicinity of the portage. He also selected points of view for the use of the daguerreotype and camera lucida, and, being unable to do any more on the ground for the furtherance of the objects of his appointment, returned to New York, taking with him the earlier records of the field operations for the purpose of organizing the office work.

20. Under the direction of Mr. H. B. Renwick, a party led by Mr. Lally set off from Mount Biort on the 7th October, and, proceeding westward along the portage road to the ridge of Mount Paradis, turned to the south along the dividing ridge. This being pursued led them back to the portage at a point about 21½ miles from the river Du Loup on the 10th. The dividing ridge was now found for some distance to coincide nearly with the portage road and to pass over the summit of the Grande Fourche Mountain, a fact which had not before been suspected. The source of the Grande Fourche of Trois Pistoles having been headed, the party reached a station which the commissary had now established at the river St. Francis on the 13th October. Departing from this, the basin of the St. Francis to the north of the portage road was explored, and the survey finished on the 17th October.

Operating from the St. Lawrence as a base, and within reach of a cultivated country, whence numerous roads are cut to the height of land, it would have been possible to have kept the field for perhaps a fortnight longer. The plans and estimates of the division had been made with this view, and it was anticipated that the height of land might have been surveyed 30 miles to the south of the Temiscouata portage. Although this would have been practicable, it would have been a service of hardship. The necessity for this was obviated by the progress of the parties of A. Talcott, esq., which completed their surveys up to the portage on the same day that the surveys of this division were finished.

22. The circumstances under which the latter part of the survey was performed from the time of leaving the river Du Loup, on the 3d September, were far less favorable than had been experienced on the Metis and its branches. The continual drought had at the beginning of this part of the duty affected the streams and springs in such a way as to render navigation difficult and water for drinking scarce on the heights of land to which the survey was necessarily directed. On the eastern side of Lake Temiscouata a large fire had extended itself into the woods. On the Temiscouata portage the persons in charge of that road had set fire to the brush and wood cut in opening it out to an increased breadth, and a belt of flame 30 miles in length was at each change of wind carried in some new direction into the dry forest. The camp and collection of stores on Mount Biort were thus threatened for several days, and only saved by great exertions. Serious apprehensions were entertained lest the return of the parties in the field might be obstructed by the spreading of their own fires. The smoke of this vast extent of combustion obscured the heavens and rendered astronomic observations difficult or prevented it altogether. Finally, a season of unprecedented drought was closed on the 24th of September by the setting in of the equinoctial storm, and from this day until that on which the survey terminated few hours elapsed without rain, sleet, or snow. In spite of these obstacles, it is believed that the State Department will have no reason to be dissatisfied with the results of the campaign.

23. The results of the operations of this division are embodied in a map and profiles, which are herewith presented. The degree of reliance to be placed on this map will be best understood from a detail of the methods employed in preparing it.

The river Metis and its branch, the Mistigougeche, were surveyed by an azimuth compass of Smallcaldus construction, and the distances measured by a micrometric telescope by Ertil, of Munich. The courses of the rest of the lines were determined by compasses of similar construction, and the distances measured by chains of 100 feet constructed by Dollond, of London, and Brown, of New York. An exception to this general rule exists in the survey of the eastern side of Rimouski. The courses and distances thus measured, and corrected for the variation of the compass, were compared with astronomic observations for latitude and with longitudes deduced from chronometers. For this reason, as the line on the east side of Rimouski is almost in the direction of the meridian, it was not considered necessary to lose time in measuring it when the latitude of the several camps, determined by observations of the pole star, were taken nightly.

The latitudes of the courses under the direction of Mr. H. B. Renwick were determined by a reflecting repeating circle of Dollond; those on Mr. Lally's by a good sextant. The latitudes and times at Grand Metis, the river Du Loup, and the stationary camp on Mistigougeche and Abagusquash were principally determined from observations made with the Dollond circle. Lunar transits were taken at the river Du Loup, and distances of the moon for longitude at several places on the line. The reliance for the longitudes was, however, principally upon timekeepers, and of these the party was furnished with one box and two pocket chronometers by Parkinson & Trodsham, one pocket chronometer by Molyneux, one by French, one by Barraud, and one by Morrice. Thus, while several could be retained at the station, each party in the field was furnished with two, and the measured distance furnished a check, which, in case of discrepancy, that on which greatest reliance could be placed might be ascertained. It is sufficient to say that the deductions have been in general satisfactory, although the rough motion to which these instruments were subjected in passing through pathless woods, embarrassed by fallen trees and morasses in which the bearers often sunk to the middle, caused changes of rate and even sudden variations. Uncertainty arising from these causes was rendered less to be dreaded from its being possible to refer, as a base of operations, to the excellent survey of the St. Lawrence River by Captain Byfield, of the British navy. With the geographical positions given in his charts our own observations agreed so closely as materially to confirm the respective accuracy of both.

24. The point which in this part of the survey has been kept in view as most important is the determination of the heights. For this purpose the party of Professor Renwick was furnished with the following barometers:

Two loaned by the Superintendent of the Coast Survey, of his own construction; two portable and one standard, by Neurnan; three of the siphon form, by Buntin, of Paris; one by Traughton & Simms; one by Forlin, of Paris; three of siphon form, by Roach & Warner, of New York; two by Tagliabue, of New York, originally on the plan of Durand, but which had been advantageously altered by Roach & Warner in such manner as to admit of the adjustment of the level of the mercury in the cistern.

The stations at which the lower barometers were placed were Grand Metis until the return of the expedition up the river of that name, and the river Du Loup from that time until the close of the survey. At these places all the barometers not actually in the field were suspended and registered at the hours most likely to correspond with the observations of a traveling party, say at 6, 7, 8, and 9 in the morning, noon, 1, 5, and 6 in the afternoon, until as the season advanced and the days became short the earliest and latest of these hours were omitted. Although several barometers were thus constantly observed, no other use of these was made but to determine their comparisons with each other, except one of the barometers of Mr. Hassler,

Superintendent of the Coast Survey. This, from its superior simplicity, being, in fact, no more than the original Tonicillean experiment, with a well-divided scale and adjustment of its 0° to the surface of the mercury in the cistern, was found to be most certain in its results. All the barometers used by the parties in the field were therefore reduced to this by their mean differences.

The stations at the two above-mentioned places were near the St. Lawrence. At Metis the height of the cistern of the standard barometer was determined by a spirit level. At the river Du Loup the height of the station was determined by two sets of observations of barometers, taken with different instruments by different observers, and at an interval of a week from each other. The results of the two several sets, which were calculated separately, differ no more than 0.5 of a foot from each other.

On reaching the highest accessible points of the streams on which the parties proceeded toward the height of land, stationary camps were established, as has been already stated. At these series of observations were made at the same hours as at the river stations. The height of the former was then calculated from a series of observations taken at noon and at 1 p. m. for the whole of the time the camp was occupied. The heights of the points at which observations were made by the traveling party were then deduced from a comparison with the nearest contemporaneous observations at the stationary camp. An exception to this rule was made in the observations to the westward of Temiscouata Lake, which were referred directly to those made at the river Du Loup, which was sufficiently near for the purpose.

The height of the stationary camp at Mount Biort having been determined by observations continued for several days, the level of Lake Temiscouata was thence determined by using a set of levels taken with a theodolite by Breithaupt, of Cassel, in 1840. The height of the lake thus deduced is greater than it would appear to be from the barometric observations taken in December, 1840. It had been imagined that a difference in level might exist between the St. Lawrence at Metis and at the river Du Loup. Four days of contemporaneous observations were therefore made at each with a view to the solution of this question. The idea of a difference of level was not sustained by the operation.

The heights of the river stations were measured in each case to the highest mark left by spring tides, and half the fall of that tide as given by Captain Byfield has been added in all cases as a reduction to the mean level of the sea. Opportunities were offered in a few instances for testing the accuracy of the method by different barometers used by different observers at different days on the same point. No discrepancy greater than 7 feet has been thus discovered. In other cases the same observer returned and observed at the same places, and here a similar congruity of result has been found to exist.

The whole of the calculations have been made by the formulæ and tables of Bailey. Before adopting these their results were compared in one or two instances with those of a more exact formula. The differences, however, were found so small as to be of no importance, amounting in the height of Lake Johnson to no more than 5 feet in 1,007. The original record of the barometric observations, each verified by the initials of the observer, have been deposited in the State Department.

25. The paths pursued by the traveling parties were marked by blazing trees. The position of the barometer at each place of observation was also marked. The operation was a search for the boundary line in an unknown country, hence it rarely happened that the path of the parties has pursued the exact dividing line of the waters of the St. Lawrence and the Atlantic, but has been continually crossing it. The maps herewith submitted and the marks by which the line of the survey has been perpetuated would have enabled a party sent out for that especial purpose to trace the boundary on the ground without difficulty other than that arising from the inaccessible character of the country.

26. The commissioner can not speak in too high terms of the industry and perseverance manifested by the engineers and surveyors employed on this division, and in particular of the skill and intelligence of the two first assistants. Circumstances had prevented the receipt of portable astronomic instruments which had been ordered from Paris and Munich, and an instrument formed by the adaptation of a vertical circle to the lower part of an excellent German theodolite by Draper, of Philadelphia, was found on its being opened at Metis to have received an injury which rendered its accuracy doubtful. The whole reliance for the greatest accuracy was thus thrown on the repeating circle of Dollond. Such, however, was the address and skill of the engineer to whom it was intrusted that he not only fulfilled the object for which it was intended, of determining the position of the points visited by the traveling parties, but accomplished the same object at the stationary camps and at the river stations, without delaying for an hour the operations of the survey.

The duty which these gentlemen performed was arduous in the extreme. It has been seen that on the expedition up the Metis a seasoned voyageur had been worn out by the severity of his labors; on the Tuladi half the men were sick at a time; and of Mr. Lally's party two Penobscot Indians of herculean frame were compelled to return by extreme fatigue. The engineers, while in the field, were even more exposed to fatigue than the laborers, for they carried their own baggage and instruments, and were engaged nightly in observation and calculation, while the workmen could repose.

27. The commissioner to whom the survey of the northern division of the boundary line was intrusted has to express his acknowledgments for the politeness and good offices of the authorities of Her Britannic Majesty. In compliance with his request, permission was granted by the late lamented Governor-General for the admission of a vessel and the entry of the stores, camp equipage, and instruments of the party at one or more ports on the St. Lawrence. Letters were addressed by the principal secretary of the colony of Canada to all the officers and magistrates, directing them to give every facility to the operations, and these directions were obeyed, not as mere matters of form, but with a truly hospitable spirit. To the officers of the Sixty-eighth Regiment, forming the garrison of Fort Ingall and occupying the post of the river Du Loup, as well as to the officers of the commissariat on duty at those places, acknowledgments are due for numerous attentions.

II.—*Operations of the year 1842.*

1. Of the task originally assigned in the instructions for this division there remained to be completed—

(1) A portion of the boundary claimed by the United States around the head waters of the river Rimouski.

(2) The line of highlands forming the south bounds of the Province of Quebec, extending from the north shore of the Bay of Chaleurs at its western extremity.

2. Experience had shown that the portion of the boundary which remained unsurveyed could not be reached with any hope of completing the survey by any of the streams running into the St. Lawrence nor from the waters of Lake Temiscouata. The Green River (of St. John) was therefore chosen as the line of operation. It was known that a portage existed between its boatable waters and those of the Grande Fourche of Restigouche. The plan for the work of the season was therefore laid as follows:

To proceed up Green River with a party, thence to cross to the Bell Kedgwick by the portage, and having, by expeditions from the banks of that stream, surveyed the remainder of the claimed boundary, to fall down the stream to the Bay of Chaleurs, and, ascending the highland measured in 1840, to proceed along the heights in order to reach if possible the northwest angle of Nova Scotia.

The work being the most remote and difficult of access of any on the whole boundary, it was necessary to take measures early, and, it being apparent that if they were not vigorously pressed the whole summer's work would be frustrated, permission was granted by the Secretary of State to prepare stores and provisions, and the party was sent forward toward its line of operations. Care was, however, taken, in conformity with his instructions, to secure means of communication.

3. The transportation of stores, equipage, and instruments was rendered unexpectedly easy by a steamboat running from Portland to St. John, and by the politeness of the British consul at Portland and the collector of Her Britannic Majesty's customs at St. John free entrance was permitted at the latter port. These articles were shipped from Portland the 19th of June and under the charge of the Hon. Albert Smith reached the Grand Falls of St. John July ——.

4. Mr. Lally, first assistant engineer, with the surveyor, was dispatched by the way of Bangor and Houlton to the same point of rendezvous on 18th June for the purpose of procuring boats and engaging laborers. Mr. H. B. Renwick, first assistant, with Mr. F. Smith, second assistant, were placed in charge of the chronometers and the necessary astronomic instruments, with instructions to observe on the meridian of the St. Croix at Houlton, and again at its intersection with the river St. John, for the purpose of ascertaining the rate taken by the chronometers when carried. These preliminary operations being successfully performed, the party was completely organized at the Grand Falls of the St. John on the 2d July. The energy and activity of the persons intrusted with these several duties was such that this date of complete preparation for the field duties was at least a week earlier than any calculation founded on the experience of former years rendered probable. The commissioner, advised of the negotiation in progress, had made his arrangements to reach the Grand Falls of the St. John on the 10th July. Being directed by the State Department to remain in New York, he sent orders by mail to the party to halt until further instructions.

5. These orders were not received, for the party, being fully organized, left the Grand Falls in three different detachments on the 4th, 6th, and 8th of July. The first detachment was composed of the surveyor, Mr. Bell, and an engineer having instructions to make a survey of Green River. The second was in charge of the assistant commissary, and was composed of three bateaux and fourteen pirogues, carrying stores and equipage for three months' service. The third was formed by the two first assistants, who, after performing the necessary astronomic observations at the Grand Falls and at two points on Green River, passed the surveying party and reached the portage between Green and Kedgwick rivers on the evening of the 13th July.

6. Green River has a fall and rapids near its junction with the St. John, which are passed by a portage of 1½ miles. At 15 miles from its mouth is a second fall, which is passed by a portage of 82 yards. The stream for this distance and for 5 miles above the second fall is very rapid, its bed being in some reaches almost filled with rocks. For the next 10 miles it has deep still reaches, alternating with gravel beds, or else the river flows over ledges of rock. It is then interrupted by a third fall, requiring a portage of 176 yards. Thence to the second fork of the lakes it has the same character as for the last 10 miles, except that in some places it flows with a gentle current between low banks covered with alder. From the second fork of the lakes to the southern end of the Green River and Kedgwick portage the stream is very narrow and may be styled one continuous rapid. It is upon the whole the most difficult of navigation of all the streams running into the St. John from its northern side, and approaches in its character of a torrent to the waters on the St. Lawrence side of the highlands.

7. The portage from Green River to the South Branch of Kedgwick is 5¼ miles in length, and passes over the summits of two of the highest mountains in the ceded

district, as well as several ridges. No vessel heavier than a birch canoe had ever before been carried over it. It therefore became necessary to clear it out before the bateaux and other heavy articles could be transported. Fifteen extra laborers, who had been engaged, with their pirogues, to carry some of the stores from the St. John, were retained to aid in making this portage, which swelled the number to twenty-seven. This large force was industriously engaged for eight days in carrying the stores and equipage over the portage, with the boats and canoes required for the future operations of the party. In the meantime the portage was surveyed, and a great number of observations were made, by which the latitude of the southern end of the portage and its difference in longitude from that of the meridian line were determined with great accuracy. In addition to the other labors of the party, a storehouse and observatory were erected.

8. The commissioner, learning that the party had left the Grand Falls before his letter could have reached that place, addressed fresh orders to the engineer in command. These were sent under cover to the British postmaster at Lake Temiscouata, who was requested to send them up Green River by an express. By these he was directed to stop the progress of the party and to proceed himself to the river Du Loup, there to await fresh instructions.

These orders did not arrive in time to prevent the party intended for the survey of the boundary from setting out. The engineer who had hitherto been in command returned to the St. John in pursuance of his original instructions and met the express on his way down Green River. The commissioner, being advised on the 13th July that the treaty had been signed, immediately dispatched a special messenger, who joined the chief of the division at the mouth of Green River on the 24th July. Measures were now taken for the recall and return of the party in the woods, and the whole division was assembled at the stationary camp at the north end of the portage on the 11th of August.

9. The party engaged in the survey of the remaining part of the boundary line had before the orders of recall reached them successfully accomplished that duty, having connected their survey with points in the survey of the previous year and thoroughly explored the culminating points of the valley of Rimouski. As had been anticipated from the level of the streams seen in 1841, this portion of the boundary claimed by the United States is more elevated than any other portion of that line between the Temiscouata portage and the northwest angle of Nova Scotia. This survey would therefore have added an important link to the argument of the United States had not the question been settled by treaty.

The party having received its orders of recall, all the articles of equipment which could not be carried in the boats which had been launched on the waters of the Restigouche were transported to the other end of the portage and embarked in pirogues sent up Green River for that purpose under the direction of the assistant commissary. The engineers then set out on their return by the Bell Kedgwick, the Grande Fourche, and the Southwest Branch of Restigouche. Ascending the latter stream, this party reached the Wagansis portage on the 21st August, and arrived at the Grand Falls on the 25th August.

The descent of the Bell Kedgwick was attended with great difficulties in consequence of the low state of the waters. Until its junction with Katawamkedgwick, to form the Grande Fourche of Restigouche, it was necessary to drag the boats by hand.

10. The detailed map of the surveys of this division, exhibiting the more important points whose altitudes were determined by the barometer, has already been lodged in the Department of State under date of 27th December.

Although the interest of this survey to the United States has now passed away, yet, as it is probable that many years may elapse before this country shall be again explored, and as it may still possess some interest to the nation into whose undisputed possession it has now fallen, it may not be improper to state the methods employed in the survey, for the purpose of showing to what degree of faith it is entitled.

The latitude and longitude of the mouth of Green River were furnished by Major Graham. The three portages on that river were surveyed by chain and compass. The courses on the navigable parts of the river were taken with a compass and the distances measured by a micrometrical telescope by Ertil, of Munich. This instrument, which had given satisfactory results on Metis and Mistigougeche in 1841, was still more accurate in the present survey. The latitude of the south end of the Kedgwick portage as given by the plot of Green River on the original projection differed no more than 5″ from that given by numerous astronomic observations, an agreement so close that it might be almost considered as arising from happy accident. This survey therefore required but little correction, which was applied from the observations already cited and from those at two intermediate points.

The survey of Kedgwick portage was performed with chain and compass. In the woods between the Bell Kedgwick and the boundary and along the whole line of survey the same method was used, observations for time and latitude being also taken whenever the weather permitted. As the lines intersected those of the last year, it can now be stated that every part of the boundary claimed by the United States, from the height of land on the Temiscouata portage which divides the waters of the Green River of the St. Lawrence from those of the St. Francis to the northwest angle of Nova Scotia, as well as its connections with the St. Lawrence and Lake Temiscouata by the Temiscouata portage, and with the St. Lawrence a second time by the Metis and Mistigougeche, and with the St. John by Green River, has been actually surveyed. This result is one that neither the Department in its original instructions nor the commissioner on his first view of the country had contemplated. In stating this the commissioner feels it his duty to acknowledge his obligations to the untiring zeal and energy of the gentlemen who have acted under his orders, and especially to his two first assistants, who, entering upon duties of an entirely novel character, not only to themselves, but to the country, have in the course of the operations of two years accumulated under the most disadvantageous circumstances a stock of observations which for number and accuracy may compare with those taken with every convenience at hand by the most practiced astronomers.

In addition to the latitude of numerous points determined astronomically by the party engaged in surveying the line through the woods, the latitude of a point near the southern end of Green River and Kedgwick has been determined by eighty-six altitudes of sun and stars taken with a repeating and reflecting circle.

The whole number of altitudes of sun and stars taken during the expedition for time and latitude was 806.

III.

1. The operations of this division during the three seasons which it has been engaged in field duties have given a view of nearly every part of the country which has now been ceded to Great Britain to the north of the St. John River and the Temiscouata portage. During the year 1840 the commissioner proceeded in person by the wagansis of Grand River to the waters of the Bay of Chaleurs, ascended the Grande Fourche of the Restigouche to Lake Kedgwick, and then traversed the country from that lake to the Tuladi by a route never before explored. In 1841 the Rimouski and Metis were both ascended—the first to the limits of its navigation by canoes, the latter to the lake in which the waters of its western branch are first collected. From this lake lines of survey repeatedly crossing the boundary claimed by the United States were extended to a great distance in both directions. The operations of the year were closed by a survey of so much of the boundary as incloses the basin of Lake Temiscouata and intersects so frequently the great portage. These latter surveys covered in some degree the explorations of one of the parties in 1840,

which, therefore, are not quoted as a part of the work of that year. In 1842 the valley of Green River was explored, that stream was carefully surveyed, and the remainder of the boundary line dividing the sources of Rimouski from those of Green River and the eastern branches of Tuladi run out with chain and compass.

In these surveys and explorations the character of the country, its soil, climate, and natural productions, have been thoroughly examined, and may be stated with full confidence in the accuracy of the facts.

2. Beginning on the southern side of the ceded territory, the left bank of the St. John is for a few miles above the Grand Falls uncultivated and apparently barren. Thence to the confluence of the Madawaska it presents a continued settlement upon land of good quality, producing large crops of potatoes and grass. It also yields wheat, oats, and barley, but the crops are neither abundant nor certain. The Madawaska River presents but few attempts at settlement on either of its banks. Its left bank is represented to be generally barren, but some good land is said to exist on its southwestern side. The shores of Lake Temiscouata are either rocky or composed of a light, gravelly soil, which is so poor that it will not repay the labor of cultivation, even when newly cleared, without the aid of manure. Some tolerable meadows are found, which are at the moment highly valued in consequence of a demand for forage by the British troops. The valley of Green River has in some places upon its banks intervals of level alluvium which might be improved as meadows, and it has been represented as being in general fertile. A close examination has not confirmed this impression.

Mr. Lally reports that—

"In the valley of Green River there are some tracts of land capable of cultivation, but the greater portion of it is a hard, rocky soil, covered with a growth of poplar and trees of that description. Some of the most desirable spots for farms had been formerly taken up by settlers from the Madawaska settlement, but although the land is as good as that on the river St. John, they were obliged to abandon their clearings on account of the early frosts and the black flies. It can hardly be conceived that the latter would be a sufficient cause for leaving valuable land to waste, but such is the fact, as I have been informed by some of those who made the attempt to settle, and I can well believe it from my own experience there."

3. The explorations of 1840, in which the ground lying between the western sources of Green River and Squattuck, a branch of Tuladi, was traversed, showed a considerable extent of better land than any other in the ceded territory. The commissioner traveled for a part of two days along a table-land of no great elevation, covered with rock, maple, and a thick undergrowth of moosewood, both said to be signs of good soil; of this there may be from seven to ten thousand acres, and it is a far larger body of tillable land than is to be found in any other part of the country north of the settlements on the St. John.

4. By far the greater portion of the territory in question is composed of the highlands in which the streams that flow to the St. Lawrence and the Atlantic take their rise. With but three exceptions no part of this is less than 1,000 feet above the level of the sea. It is a perfect labyrinth of small lakes, cedar and alder swamps, and ridges covered with a thick but small growth of fir and spruce, or, more rarely, of birch. No portion of it appears to be fit for tillage.

5. In respect to timber, it was found that the pine, the only tree considered of any value, ceased to grow in rising from the St. Lawrence at less than 1,000 feet above the level of the sea. Only one extensive tract of pine was seen by any of the parties; this lies around the sources of the St. Francis, and may cover three or four thousand acres. This river, however, discharges itself from Lake St. Francis through a bed of bowlders, and is sometimes wholly lost to the view. This tract, therefore, although repeatedly examined by the proprietors of sawmills on the St. Lawrence and the St. John, has been hitherto found inaccessible. The pine timber on the seigniory of

Temiscouata has been in a great degree cut off or burnt by fires in the woods. There is still some timber on the waters of Squattuck, but it has been diminished by two or three years of active lumbering, while that around Tuladi, if it were ever abundant, has disappeared. It would, however, appear from report that on the waters of the North Branch of Restigouche to the eastward of the exploring meridian there is some valuable timber. This is the only portion of the district which has not been explored.

6. As to the valley of Green River, the engineer who has already been quoted reports as follows:

"This river has had the reputation of having on it large quantities of pine timber, but as far as I have been able to judge it is small and rather sparsely scattered along the slopes of the ridges. Above the third falls of the river, which are rather more than 30 miles from its mouth, there is scarcely any to be seen. Some of the Madawaska settlers, who have explored nearly every tributary of the river, report that there is good timber on some of them. Judging from the language that they used in relation to some that I saw myself, I infer that what they call good would not be so considered by the lumbermen of the Penobscot. The people who lumber in this vicinity do it on a small scale when compared with the operators in Maine. They rarely use more than two horses to draw their lumber to the stream, so that a tract which would not afford more than a month's work to an extensive operator would keep one of these people employed for years."

7. As respects climate, the country would be considered unfit for habitation by those accustomed to the climates even of the southern parts of Maine and of New Hampshire. Frosts continue on the St. John until late in May, and set in early in September. In 1840 ice was found on the Grand River on the 12th of that month, and snow fell in the first week of October on Lake Temiscouata. In the highland region during the last week of July, although the thermometer rose above 80°, and was once above 90°, white frost was formed every clear night. Upon the whole, therefore, it may be concluded that there is little in this country calculated to attract either settlers or speculators in lumber. The former were driven to it under circumstances of peculiar hardship and of almost paramount necessity. Their industry and perseverance under adverse circumstances is remarkable, but they would have been hardly able to overcome them had not the very question of the disputed boundary led to an expenditure of considerable money among them.

VETO MESSAGE.*

WASHINGTON, *December 14, 1842.*

To the House of Representatives:

Two bills were presented to me at the last session of Congress, which originated in the House of Representatives, neither of which was signed by me; and both having been presented within ten days of the close of the session, neither has become a law.

The first of these was a bill entitled "An act to repeal the proviso of the sixth section of the act entitled 'An act to appropriate the proceeds of the sales of the public lands and to grant preemption rights,' approved September 4, 1841."

* Pocket veto.

This bill was presented to me on Tuesday, the 30th August, at twenty-four minutes after 4 o'clock in the afternoon. For my opinions relative to the provisions contained in this bill it is only necessary that I should refer to previous communications made by me to the House of Representatives.

The other bill was entitled "An act regulating the taking of testimony in cases of contested elections, and for other purposes." This bill was presented to me at a quarter past 1 o'clock on Wednesday, the 31st day of August. The two Houses, by concurrent vote, had already agreed to terminate the session by adjournment at 2 o'clock on that day—that is to say, within three-quarters of an hour from the time the bill was placed in my hands. It was a bill containing twenty-seven sections, and, I need not say, of an important nature.

On its presentment to me its reading was immediately commenced, but was interrupted by so many communications from the Senate and so many other causes operating at the last hour of the session that it was impossible to read the bill understandingly and with proper deliberation before the hour fixed for the adjournment of the two Houses; and this, I presume, is a sufficient reason for neither signing the bill nor returning it with my objections.

The seventeenth joint rule of the two Houses of Congress declares that " no bill or resolution that shall have passed the House of Representatives and the Senate shall be presented to the President of the United States for his approbation on the last day of the session."

This rule was evidently designed to give to the President a reasonable opportunity of perusing important acts of Congress and giving them some degree of consideration before signing or returning the same.

It is true that the two Houses have been in the habit of suspending this rule toward the close of the session in relation to particular bills, and it appears by the printed Journal that by concurrent votes of the two Houses passed on the last day of the session the rule was agreed to be suspended so far as the same should relate to all such bills as should have been passed by the two Houses at 1 o'clock on that day. It is exceedingly to be regretted that a necessity should ever exist for such suspension in the case of bills of great importance, and therefore demanding careful consideration.

As the bill has failed under the provisions of the Constitution to become a law, I abstain from expressing any opinions upon its several provisions, keeping myself wholly uncommitted as to my ultimate action on any similar measure should the House think proper to originate it *de novo*, except so far as my opinion of the unqualified power of each House to decide for itself upon the elections, returns, and qualifications of its own members has been expressed by me in a paper lodged in the Department of State at the time of signing an act entitled "An act for the apportionment of Representatives among the several States according to the Sixth Census," approved June 22, 1842, a copy of which is in possession of the House.

JOHN TYLER.

THIRD ANNUAL MESSAGE.

WASHINGTON, *December, 1843.*

To the Senate and House of Representatives of the United States:

If any people ever had cause to render up thanks to the Supreme Being for parental care and protection extended to them in all the trials and difficulties to which they have been from time to time exposed, we certainly are that people. From the first settlement of our forefathers on this continent, through the dangers attendant upon the occupation of a savage wilderness, through a long period of colonial dependence, through the War of the Revolution, in the wisdom which led to the adoption of the existing forms of republican government, in the hazards incident to a war subsequently waged with one of the most powerful nations of the earth, in the increase of our population, in the spread of the arts and sciences, and in the strength and durability conferred on political institutions emanating from the people and sustained by their will, the superintendence of an overruling Providence has been plainly visible. As preparatory, therefore, to entering once more upon the high duties of legislation, it becomes us humbly to acknowledge our dependence upon Him as our guide and protector and to implore a continuance of His parental watchfulness over our beloved country. We have new cause for the expression of our gratitude in the preservation of the health of our fellow-citizens, with some partial and local exceptions, during the past season, for the abundance with which the earth has yielded up its fruits to the labors of the husbandman, for the renewed activity which has been imparted to commerce, for the revival of trade in all its departments, for the increased rewards attendant on the exercise of the mechanic arts, for the continued growth of our population and the rapidly reviving prosperity of the whole country. I shall be permitted to exchange congratulations with you, gentlemen of the two Houses of Congress, on these auspicious circumstances, and to assure you in advance of my ready disposition to concur with you in the adoption of all such measures as shall be calculated to increase the happiness of our constituents and to advance the glory of our common country.

Since the last adjournment of Congress the Executive has relaxed no effort to render indestructible the relations of amity which so happily exist between the United States and other countries. The treaty lately concluded with Great Britain has tended greatly to increase the good understanding which a reciprocity of interests is calculated to encourage, and it is most ardently to be hoped that nothing may transpire to interrupt the relations of amity which it is so obviously the policy of both nations to cultivate. A question of much importance still remains to be adjusted between them. The territorial limits of the two countries in relation to what is commonly known as the Oregon Territory still remain in dispute. The United States would be at all times indisposed to aggrandize itself at the expense of any other nation; but while they would be restrained by principles of honor, which should govern the conduct of nations as well as that of individuals, from setting up a demand for territory which does not belong to them, they would as unwillingly consent to a surrender of their rights. After the most rigid and, as far as practicable, unbiased examination of the subject, the United States have always contended that their rights appertain to the entire region of country lying on the Pacific and embraced within 42° and 54° 40' of north latitude. This claim being controverted by Great Britain, those who have preceded the present Executive—actuated, no doubt, by an earnest desire to adjust the matter upon terms mutually satisfactory to both countries—have caused to be submitted to the British Government propositions for settlement and final adjustment, which, however, have not proved heretofore acceptable to it. Our minister at London has, under instructions, again brought the subject to the consideration of that Government, and while nothing will be done to compromit the rights or honor of the United States, every proper expedient will be resorted to in order to bring the negotiation now in the progress of resumption to a speedy and happy termination. In the meantime it is proper to remark that many of our citizens are either already established in the Territory or are on their way thither for the purpose of forming permanent settlements, while others are preparing to follow; and in view of these facts I must repeat the recommendation contained in previous messages for the establishment of military posts at such places on the line of travel as will furnish security and protection to our hardy adventurers against hostile tribes of Indians inhabiting those extensive regions. Our laws should also follow them, so modified as the circumstances of the case may seem to require. Under the influence of our free system of government new republics are destined to spring up at no distant day on the shores of the Pacific similar in policy and in feeling to those existing on this side of the Rocky Mountains, and giving a wider and more extensive spread to the principles of civil and religious liberty.

I am happy to inform you that the cases which have from time to time arisen of the detention of American vessels by British cruisers on the coast of Africa under pretense of being engaged in the slave trade have been placed in a fair train of adjustment. In the case of the *William and Francis* full satisfaction will be allowed. In the cases of the *Tygris* and *Seamew* the British Government admits that satisfaction is due. In the case of the *Jones* the sum accruing from the sale of that vessel and cargo will be paid to the owners, while I can not but flatter myself that full indemnification will be allowed for all damages sustained by the detention of the vessel; and in the case of the *Douglas* Her Majesty's Government has expressed its determination to make indemnification.

Strong hopes are therefore entertained that most, if not all, of these cases will be speedily adjusted. No new cases have arisen since the ratification of the treaty of Washington, and it is confidently anticipated that the·slave trade, under the operation of the eighth article of that treaty, will be altogether suppressed.

The occasional interruption experienced by our fellow-citizens engaged in the fisheries on the neighboring coast of Nova Scotia has not failed to claim the attention of the Executive. Representations upon this subject have been made, but as yet no definitive answer to those representations has been received from the British Government.

Two other subjects of comparatively minor importance, but nevertheless of too much consequence to be neglected, remain still to be adjusted between the two countries. By the treaty between the United States and Great Britain of July, 1815, it is provided that no higher duties shall be levied in either country on articles imported from the other than on the same articles imported from any other place. In 1836 rough rice by act of Parliament was admitted from the coast of Africa into Great Britain on the payment of a duty of 1 penny a quarter, while the same article from all other countries, including the United States, was subjected to the payment of a duty of 20 shillings a quarter. Our minister at London has from time to time brought this subject to the attention of the British Government, but so far without success. He is instructed to renew his representations upon it.

Some years since a claim was preferred against the British Government on the part of certain American merchants for the return of export duties paid by them on shipments of woolen goods to the United States after the duty on similar articles exported to other countries had been repealed, and consequently in contravention of the commercial convention between the two nations securing to us equality in such cases. The principle on which the claim rests has long since been virtually admitted by Great Britain, but obstacles to a settlement have from time to time been interposed, so that a large portion of the amount claimed has not yet been refunded. Our minister is now engaged in the prosecution of the claim, and I can not but persuade myself that the British Government will no longer delay its adjustment.

I am happy to be able to say that nothing has occurred to disturb in any degree the relations of amity which exist between the United States and France, Austria, and Russia, as well as with the other powers of Europe, since the adjournment of Congress. Spain has been agitated with internal convulsions for many years, from the effects of which, it is hoped, she is destined speedily to recover, when, under a more liberal system of commercial policy on her part, our trade with her may again fill its old and, so far as her continental possessions are concerned, its almost forsaken channels, thereby adding to the mutual prosperity of the two countries.

The Germanic Association of Customs and Commerce, which since its establishment in 1833 has been steadily growing in power and importance, and consists at this time of more than twenty German States, and embraces a population of 27,000,000 people united for all the purposes of commercial intercourse with each other and with foreign states, offers to the latter the most valuable exchanges on principles more liberal than are offered in the fiscal system of any other European power. From its origin the importance of the German union has never been lost sight of by the United States. The industry, morality, and other valuable qualities of the German nation have always been well known and appreciated. On this subject I invite the attention of Congress to the report of the Secretary of State, from which it will be seen that while our cotton is admitted free of duty and the duty on rice has been much reduced (which has already led to a greatly increased consumption), a strong disposition has been recently evinced by that great body to reduce, upon certain conditions, their present duty upon tobacco. This being the first intimation of a concession on this interesting subject ever made by any European power, I can not but regard it as well calculated to remove the only impediment which has so far existed to the most liberal commercial intercourse between us and them. In this view our minister at Berlin, who has heretofore industriously pursued the subject, has been instructed to enter upon the negotiation of a commercial treaty, which, while it will open new advantages to the agricultural interests of the United States and a more free and expanded field for commercial operations, will affect injuriously no existing interest of the Union. Should the negotiation be crowned with success, its results will be communicated to both Houses of Congress.

I communicate herewith certain dispatches received from our minister at Mexico, and also a correspondence which has recently occurred between the envoy from that Republic and the Secretary of State. It must but be regarded as not a little extraordinary that the Government of Mexico, in anticipation of a public discussion (which it has been pleased to infer from newspaper publications as likely to take place in Congress, relating to the annexation of Texas to the United States), should have so far anticipated the result of such discussion as to have announced its determination to visit any such anticipated decision by a formal declaration of war against the United States. If designed to prevent Congress from introducing that question as a fit subject for its calm deliberation and final judgment, the Executive has no reason to doubt that it will entirely fail of its object. The representatives of a brave and patriotic people will suffer no apprehension of future consequences to embarrass them in the course of their proposed deliberations, nor will the executive department of the Government fail for any such cause to discharge its whole duty to the country.

The war which has existed for so long a time between Mexico and

Texas has since the battle of San Jacinto consisted for the most part of predatory incursions, which, while they have been attended with much of suffering to individuals and have kept the borders of the two countries in a state of constant alarm, have failed to approach to any definitive result. Mexico has fitted out no formidable armament by land or by sea for the subjugation of Texas. Eight years have now elapsed since Texas declared her independence of Mexico, and during that time she has been recognized as a sovereign power by several of the principal civilized states. Mexico, nevertheless, perseveres in her plans of reconquest, and refuses to recognize her independence. The predatory incursions to which I have alluded have been attended in one instance with the breaking up of the courts of justice, by the seizing upon the persons of the judges, jury, and officers of the court and dragging them along with unarmed, and therefore noncombatant, citizens into a cruel and oppressive bondage, thus leaving crime to go unpunished and immorality to pass unreproved. A border warfare is evermore to be deprecated, and over such a war as has existed for so many years between these two States humanity has had great cause to lament. Nor is such a condition of things to be deplored only because of the individual suffering attendant upon it. The effects are far more extensive. The Creator of the Universe has given man the earth for his resting place and its fruits for his subsistence. Whatever, therefore, shall make the first or any part of it a scene of desolation affects injuriously his heritage and may be regarded as a general calamity. Wars may sometimes be necessary, but all nations have a common interest in bringing them speedily to a close. The United States have an immediate interest in seeing an end put to the state of hostilities existing between Mexico and Texas. They are our neighbors, of the same continent, with whom we are not only desirous of cultivating the relations of amity, but of the most extended commercial intercourse, and to practice all the rites of a neighborhood hospitality. Our own interests are involved in the matter, since, however neutral may be our course of policy, we can not hope to escape the effects of a spirit of jealousy on the part of both of the powers. Nor can this Government be indifferent to the fact that a warfare such as is waged between those two nations is calculated to weaken both powers and finally to render them—and especially the weaker of the two—the subjects of interference on the part of stronger and more powerful nations, who, intent only on advancing their own peculiar views, may sooner or later attempt to bring about a compliance with terms as the condition of their interposition alike derogatory to the nation granting them and detrimental to the interests of the United States. We could not be expected quietly to permit any such interference to our disadvantage. Considering that Texas is separated from the United States by a mere geographical line; that her territory, in the opinion of many, down to a late period formed a portion of the territory of the United

States; that it is homogeneous in its population and pursuits with the adjoining States, makes contributions to the commerce of the world in the same articles with them, and that most of her inhabitants have been citizens of the United States, speak the same language, and live under similar political institutions with ourselves, this Government is bound by every consideration of interest as well as of sympathy to se:. that she shall be left free to act, especially in regard to her domestic affairs, unawed by force and unrestrained by the policy or views of other countries. In full view of all these considerations, the Executive has not hesitated to express to the Government of Mexico how deeply it deprecated a continuance of the war and how anxiously it desired to witness its termination. I can not but think that it becomes the United States, as the oldest of the American Republics, to hold a language to Mexico upon this subject of an unambiguous character. It is time that this war had ceased. There must be a limit to all wars, and if the parent state after an eight years' struggle has failed to reduce to submission a portion of its subjects standing out in revolt against it, and who have not only proclaimed themselves to be independent, but have been recognized as such by other powers, she ought not to expect that other nations will quietly look on, to their obvious injury, upon a protraction of hostilities. These United States threw off their colonial dependence and established independent governments, and Great Britain, after having wasted her energies in the attempt to subdue them for a less period than Mexico has attempted to subjugate Texas, had the wisdom and justice to acknowledge their independence, thereby recognizing the obligation which rested on her as one of the family of nations. An example thus set by one of the proudest as well as most powerful nations of the earth it could in no way disparage Mexico to imitate. While, therefore, the Executive would deplore any collision with Mexico or any disturbance of the friendly relations which exist between the two countries, it can not permit that Government to control its policy, whatever it may be, toward Texas, but will treat her—as by the recognition of her independence the United States have long since declared they would do—as entirely independent of Mexico. The high obligations of public duty may enforce from the constituted authorities of the United States a policy which the course persevered in by Mexico will have mainly contributed to produce, and the Executive in such a contingency will with confidence throw itself upon the patriotism of the people to sustain the Government in its course of action.

Measures of an unusual character have recently been adopted by the Mexican Government, calculated in no small degree to affect the trade of other nations with Mexico and to operate injuriously to the United States. All foreigners, by a decree of the 23d day of September, and after six months from the day of its promulgation, are forbidden to carry on the business of selling by retail any goods within the confines of Mexico. Against this decree our minister has not failed to remonstrate.

The trade heretofore carried on by our citizens with Santa Fe, in which much capital was already invested and which was becoming of daily increasing importance, has suddenly been arrested by a decree of virtual prohibition on the part of the Mexican Government. Whatever may be the right of Mexico to prohibit any particular course of trade to the citizens or subjects of foreign powers, this late procedure, to say the least of it, wears a harsh and unfriendly aspect.

The installments on the claims recently settled by the convention with Mexico have been punctually paid as they have fallen due, and our minister is engaged in urging the establishment of a new commission in pursuance of the convention for the settlement of unadjusted claims.

With the other American States our relations of amity and good will have remained uninterrupted. Our minister near the Republic of New Granada has succeeded in effecting an adjustment of the claim upon that Government for the schooner *By Chance*, which had been pending for many years. The claim for the brig *Morris*, which had its origin during the existence of the Republic of Colombia, and indemnification for which since the dissolution of that Republic has devolved upon its several members, will be urged with renewed zeal.

I have much pleasure in saying that the Government of Brazil has adjusted the claim upon that Government in the case of the schooner *John S. Bryan*, and that sanguine hopes are entertained that the same spirit of justice will influence its councils in arriving at an early decision upon the remaining claims, thereby removing all cause of dissension between two powers whose interests are to some extent interwoven with each other.

Our minister at Chili has succeeded in inducing a recognition by that Government of the adjustment effected by his predecessor of the first claim in the case of the *Macedonian*. The first installment has been received by the claimants in the United States.

Notice of the exchange of ratifications of the treaty with Peru, which will take place at Lima, has not yet reached this country, but is shortly expected to be received, when the claims upon that Republic will doubtless be liquidated and paid.

In consequence of a misunderstanding between this Government and that of Buenos Ayres, occurring several years ago, this Government has remained unrepresented at that Court, while a minister from it has been constantly resident here. The causes of irritation have in a great measure passed away, and it is in contemplation, in view of important interests which have grown up in that country, at some early period during the present session of Congress, with the concurrence of the Senate, to restore diplomatic relations between the two countries.

Under the provisions of an act of Congress of the last session a minister was dispatched from the United States to China in August of the present year, who, from the latest accounts we have from him, was at Suez, in Egypt, on the 25th of September last, on his route to China.

In regard to the Indian tribes residing within our jurisdictional limits, the greatest vigilance of the Government has been exerted to preserve them at peace among themselves and to inspire them with feelings of confidence in the justice of this Government and to cultivate friendship with the border inhabitants. This has happily succeeded to a great extent, but it is a subject of regret that they suffer themselves in some instances to be imposed upon by artful and designing men, and this notwithstanding all efforts of the Government to prevent it.

The receipts into the Treasury for the calendar year 1843, exclusive of loans, were little more than $18,000,000, and the expenditures, exclusive of the payments on the public debt, will have been about $23,000,000. By the act of 1842 a new arrangement of the fiscal year was made, so that it should commence on the 1st day of July in each year. The accounts and estimates for the current fiscal year will show that the loans and Treasury notes made and issued before the close of the last Congress to meet the anticipated deficiency have not been entirely adequate. Although on the 1st of October last there was a balance in the Treasury, in consequence of the provisions thus made, of $3,914,082.77, yet the appropriations already made by Congress will absorb that balance and leave a probable deficiency of $2,000,000 at the close of the present fiscal year. There are outstanding Treasury notes to about the amount of $4,600,000, and should they be returned upon the Treasury during the fiscal year they will require provision for their redemption. I do not, however, regard this as probable, since they have obviously entered into the currency of the country and will continue to form a portion of it if the system now adopted be continued. The loan of 1841, amounting to $5,672,976.88, falls due on the 1st day of January, 1845, and must be provided for or postponed by a new loan; and unless the resources of revenue should be materially increased by you there will be a probable deficiency for the service of the fiscal year ending June 30, 1845, of upward of $4,000,000.

The delusion incident to an enormously excessive paper circulation, which gave a fictitious value to everything and stimulated adventure and speculation to an extravagant extent, has been happily succeeded by the substitution of the precious metals and paper promptly redeemable in specie; and thus false values have disappeared and a sounder condition of things has been introduced. This transition, although intimately connected with the prosperity of the country, has nevertheless been attended with much embarrassment to the Government in its financial concerns. So long as the foreign importers could receive payment for their cargoes in a currency of greatly less value than that in Europe, but fully available here in the purchase of our agricultural productions (their profits being immeasurably augmented by the operation), the shipments were large and the revenues of the Government became superabundant. But the change in the character of the circulation from a nominal and apparently real value in the first stage of its existence to an obviously depreciated value in its second, so that it no longer answered the purposes of exchange or barter, and its ultimate substitution by a sound metallic and paper circulation combined, has been attended by diminished importations and a consequent falling off in the revenue. This has induced Congress, from 1837, to resort to the expedient of issuing Treasury notes, and finally of funding them, in order to supply deficiencies. I can not, however, withhold the remark that it is in no way compatible with the dignity of the Government that a public debt should be created in time of peace to meet the current expenses of the Government, or that temporary expedients should be resorted to an hour longer than it is possible to avoid them. The Executive can do no more than apply the means which Congress places in its hands for the support of Government, and, happily for the good of the country and for the preservation of its liberties, it possesses no power to levy exactions on the people or to force from them contributions to the public revenue in any form. It can only recommend such measures as may in its opinion be called for by the wants of the public service to Congress, with whom alone rests the power to "lay and collect taxes, duties, imposts, and excises." This duty has upon several occasions heretofore been performed. The present condition of things gives flattering promise that trade and commerce are rapidly reviving, and, fortunately for the country, the sources of revenue have only to be opened in order to prove abundant.

While we can anticipate no considerable increase in the proceeds of the sales of the public lands, for reasons perfectly obvious to all, for several years to come, yet the public lands can not otherwise than be regarded as the foundation of the public credit. With so large a body of the most fertile lands in the world under the control and at the disposal of this Government, no one can reasonably doubt the entire ability to meet its engagements under every emergency. In seasons of trial and difficulty similar to those through which we are passing the capitalist makes his investments in the Government stocks with the most assured confidence of ultimate reimbursement; and whatever may be said of a period of great financial prosperity, such as existed for some years after 1833, I should regard it as suicidal in a season of financial embarrassment either to alienate the lands themselves or the proceeds arising from their sales. The first and paramount duty of those to whom may be intrusted the administration of public affairs is to guard the public credit. In reestablishing the credit of this central Government the readiest and most obvious mode is taken to restore the credit of the States. The extremities can only be made sound by producing a healthy action in the central Government, and the history of the present day fully establishes the fact that an increase in the value of the stocks of this Government will in a great majority of instances be attended by an increase in the value of the stocks of the States. It should therefore be a matter of general congratulation that amidst all the embarrassments arising from surrounding circumstances the credit of the Government should have been so fully restored that it has been enabled to effect a loan of $7,000,000 to redeem that amount of Treasury notes on terms more favorable than any that have been offered for many years. And the 6 per cent stock which was created in 1842 has advanced in the hands of the holders nearly 20 per cent above its par value. The confidence of the people in the integrity of their Government has thus been signally manifested. These opinions relative to the public lands do not in any manner conflict with the observance of the most liberal policy toward those of our fellow-citizens who press forward into the wilderness and are the pioneers in the work of its reclamation. In securing to all such their rights of preemption the Government performs but an act of retributive justice for sufferings encountered and hardships endured, and finds ample remuneration in the comforts which its policy insures and the happiness which it imparts.

Should a revision of the tariff with a view to revenue become necessary in the estimation of Congress, I doubt not you will approach the subject with a just and enlightened regard to the interests of the whole Union. The principles and views which I have heretofore had occasion to submit remain unchanged. It can, however, never be too often repeated that the prominent interest of every important pursuit of life requires for success permanency and stability in legislation. These can only be attained by adopting as the basis of action moderation in all things, which is as indispensably necessary to secure the harmonious action of the political as of the animal system. In our political organization no one section of the country should desire to have its supposed interests advanced at the sacrifice of all others, but union, being the great interest, equally precious to all, should be fostered and sustained by mutual concessions and the cultivation of that spirit of compromise from which the Constitution itself proceeded.

You will be informed by the report from the Treasury Department of the measures taken under the act of the last session authorizing the reissue of Treasury notes in lieu of those then outstanding. The system adopted in pursuance of existing laws seems well calculated to save the country a large amount of interest, while it affords conveniences and obviates dangers and expense in the transmission of funds to disbursing agents. I refer you also to that report for the means proposed by the Secretary to increase the revenue, and particularly to that portion of it which relates to the subject of the warehousing system, which I earnestly urged upon Congress at its last session and as to the importance of which my opinion has undergone no change.

In view of the disordered condition of the currency at the time and the high rates of exchange between different parts of the country, I felt it to be incumbent on me to present to the consideration of your predecessors a proposition conflicting in no degree with the Constitution or with the rights of the States and having the sanction (not in detail, but in principle) of some of the eminent men who have preceded me in the Executive office. That proposition contemplated the issuing of Treasury notes of denominations of not less than $5 nor more than $100, to be employed in the payment of the obligations of the Government in lieu of gold and silver at the option of the public creditor, and to an amount not exceeding $15,000,000. It was proposed to make them receivable everywhere and to establish at various points depositories of gold and silver to be held in trust for the redemption of such notes, so as to insure their convertibility into specie. No doubt was entertained that such notes would have maintained a par value with gold and silver, thus furnishing a paper currency of equal value over the Union, thereby meeting the just expectations of the people and fulfilling the duties of a parental government. Whether the depositories should be permitted to sell or purchase bills under very limited restrictions, together with all its other details, was submitted to the wisdom of Congress and was regarded as of secondary importance. I thought then and think now that such an arrangement would have been attended with the happiest results. The whole matter of the currency would have been placed where by the Constitution it was designed to be placed—under the immediate supervision and control of Congress. The action of the Government would have been independent of all corporations, and the same eye which rests unceasingly on the specie currency and guards it against adulteration would also have rested on the paper currency, to control and regulate its issues and protect it against depreciation. The same reasons which would forbid Congress from parting with the power over the coinage would seem to operate with nearly equal force in regard to any substitution for the precious metals in the form of a circulating medium. Paper when substituted for specie constitutes a standard of value by which the operations of society are regulated, and whatsoever causes its depreciation affects society to an extent nearly, if not quite, equal to the adulteration of the coin. Nor can I withhold the remark that its advantages contrasted with a bank of the United States, apart from the fact that a bank was esteemed as obnoxious to the public sentiment as well on the score of expediency as of constitutionalty, appeared to me to be striking and obvious. The relief which a bank would afford by an issue of $15,000,000 of its notes, judging from the experience of the late United States Bank, would not have occurred in less than fifteen years, whereas under the proposed arrangement the relief arising from the issue of $15,000,000 of Treasury notes would have been consummated in one year, thus furnishing in one-fifteenth part of the time in which a bank could have accomplished it a paper medium of exchange equal in amount to the real wants of the country at par value with gold and silver. The saving to the Government would have been equal to all the interest which it has had to pay on Treasury notes of previous as well as subsequent issues, thereby relieving the Government and at the same time affording relief to the people.   Under all the responsibilities attached to the station which I occupy, and in redemption of a pledge given to the last Congress at the close of its first session, I submitted the suggestion to its consideration at two consecutive sessions.   The recommendation, however, met with no favor at its hands.   While I am free to admit that the necessities of the times have since become greatly ameliorated and that there is good reason to hope that the country is safely and rapidly emerging from the difficulties and embarrassments which everywhere surrounded it in 1841, yet I can not but think that its restoration to a sound and healthy condition would be greatly expedited by a resort to the expedient in a modified form.

The operations of the Treasury now rest upon the act of 1789 and the resolution of 1816, and those laws have been so administered as to produce as great a quantum of good to the country as their provisions are capable of yielding.   If there had been any distinct expression of opinion going to show that public sentiment is averse to the plan, either as heretofore recommended to Congress or in a modified form, while my own opinion in regard to it would remain unchanged I should be very far from again presenting it to your consideration.   The Government has originated with the States and the people, for their own benefit and advantage, and it would be subversive of the foundation principles of the political edifice which they have reared to persevere in a measure which in their mature judgments they had either repudiated or condemned. The will of our constituents clearly expressed should be regarded as the light to guide our footsteps, the true difference between a monarchical or aristocratical government and a republic being that in the first the will of the few prevails over the will of the many, while in the last the will of the many should be alone consulted.

The report of the Secretary of War will bring you acquainted with the condition of that important branch of the public service.   The Army may be regarded, in consequence of the small number of the rank and file in each company and regiment, as little more than a nucleus around which to rally the military force of the country in case of war, and yet its services in preserving the peace of the frontiers are of a most important nature.   In all cases of emergency the reliance of the country is properly placed in the militia of the several States, and it may well deserve the consideration of Congress whether a new and more perfect organization might not be introduced, looking mainly to the volunteer companies of the Union for the present and of easy application to the great body of the militia in time of war.

The expenditures of the War Department have been considerably reduced in the last two years.   Contingencies, however, may arise which would call for the filling up of the regiments with a full complement of men and make it very desirable to remount the corps of dragoons, which by an act of the last Congress was directed to be dissolved.

I refer you to the accompanying report of the Secretary for information in relation to the Navy of the United States. While every effort has been and will continue to be made to retrench all superfluities and lop off all excrescences which from time to time may have grown up, yet it has not been regarded as wise or prudent to recommend any material change in the annual appropriations. The interests which are involved are of too important a character to lead to the recommendation of any other than a liberal policy. Adequate appropriations ought to be made to enable the Executive to fit out all the ships that are now in a course of building or that require repairs for active service in the shortest possible time should any emergency arise which may require it. An efficient navy, while it is the cheapest means of public defense, enlists in its support the feelings of pride and confidence which brilliant deeds and heroic valor have heretofore served to strengthen and confirm.

I refer you particularly to that part of the Secretary's report which has reference to recent experiments in the application of steam and in the construction of our war steamers, made under the superintendence of distinguished officers of the Navy. In addition to other manifest improvements in the construction of the steam engine and application of the motive power which has rendered them more appropriate to the uses of ships of war, one of those officers has brought into use a power which makes the steamship most formidable either for attack or defense. I can not too strongly recommend this subject to your consideration and do not hesitate to express my entire conviction of its great importance.

I call your particular attention also to that portion of the Secretary's report which has reference to the act of the late session of Congress which prohibited the transfer of any balance of appropriation from other heads of appropriation to that for building, equipment, and repair. The repeal of that prohibition will enable the Department to give renewed employment to a large class of workmen who have been necessarily discharged in consequence of the want of means to pay them—a circumstance attended, especially at this season of the year, with much privation and suffering.

It gives me great pain to announce to you the loss of the steamship the *Missouri* by fire in the Bay of Gibraltar, where she had stopped to renew her supplies of coal on her voyage to Alexandria, with Mr. Cushing, the American minister to China, on board. There is ground for high commendation of the officers and men for the coolness and intrepidity and perfect submission to discipline evinced under the most trying circumstances. Surrounded by a raging fire, which the utmost exertions could not subdue, and which threatened momentarily the explosion of her well-supplied magazines, the officers exhibited no signs of fear and the men obeyed every order with alacrity. Nor was she abandoned until the last gleam of hope of saving her had expired. It is well worthy of your consideration whether the losses sustained by the officers and crew in this unfortunate affair should not be reimbursed to them.

I can not take leave of this painful subject without adverting to the aid rendered upon the occasion by the British authorities at Gibraltar and the commander, officers, and crew of the British ship of the line the *Malabar*, which was lying at the time in the bay. Everything that generosity or humanity could dictate was promptly performed. It is by such acts of good will by one to another of the family of nations that fraternal feelings are nourished and the blessings of permanent peace secured.

The report of the Postmaster-General will bring you acquainted with the operations of that Department during the past year, and will suggest to you such modifications of the existing laws as in your opinion the exigencies of the public service may require. The change which the country has undergone of late years in the mode of travel and transportation has afforded so many facilities for the transmission of mail matter out of the regular mail as to require the greatest vigilance and circumspection in order to enable the officer at the head of the Department to restrain the expenditures within the income. There is also too much reason to fear that the franking privilege has run into great abuse. The Department, nevertheless, has been conducted with the greatest vigor, and has attained at the least possible expense all the useful objects for which it was established.

In regard to all the Departments, I am quite happy in the belief that nothing has been left undone which was called for by a true spirit of economy or by a system of accountability rigidly enforced. This is in some degree apparent from the fact that the Government has sustained no loss by the default of any of its agents. In the complex, but at the same time beautiful, machinery of our system of government, it is not a matter of surprise that some remote agency may have failed for an instant to fulfill its desired office; but I feel confident in the assertion that nothing has occurred to interrupt the harmonious action of the Government itself, and that, while the laws have been executed with efficiency and vigor, the rights neither of States nor individuals have been trampled on or disregarded.

In the meantime the country has been steadily advancing in all that contributes to national greatness. The tide of population continues unbrokenly to flow into the new States and Territories, where a refuge is found not only for our native-born fellow-citizens, but for emigrants from all parts of the civilized world, who come among us to partake of the blessings of our free institutions and to aid by their labor to swell the current of our wealth and power.

It is due to every consideration of public policy that the lakes and rivers of the West should receive all such attention at the hands of Congress as the Constitution will enable it to bestow. Works in favorable and proper situations on the Lakes would be found to be as indispensably necessary, in case of war, to carry on safe and successful naval operations as fortifications on the Atlantic seaboard. The appropriation made by the last Congress for the improvement of the navigation of the Mississippi River has been diligently and efficiently applied.

I can not close this communication, gentlemen, without recommending to your most favorable consideration the interests of this District. Appointed by the Constitution its exclusive legislators, and forming in this particular the only anomaly in our system of government—of the legislative body being elected by others than those for whose advantage they are to legislate—you will feel a superadded obligation to look well into their condition and to leave no cause for complaint or regret. The seat of Government of our associated republics can not but be regarded as worthy of your parental care.

In connection with its other interests, as well as those of the whole country, I recommend that at your present session you adopt such measures in order to carry into effect the Smithsonian bequest as in your judgment will be best calculated to consummate the liberal intent of the testator.

When, under a dispensation of Divine Providence, I succeeded to the Presidential office, the state of public affairs was embarrassing and critical. To add to the irritation consequent upon a long-standing controversy with one of the most powerful nations of modern times, involving not only questions of boundary (which under the most favorable circumstances are always embarrassing), but at the same time important and high principles of maritime law, border controversies between the citizens and subjects of the two countries had engendered a state of feeling and of conduct which threatened the most calamitous consequences. The hazards incident to this state of things were greatly heightened by the arrest and imprisonment of a subject of Great Britain, who, acting (as it was alleged) as a part of a military force, had aided in the commission of an act violative of the territorial jurisdiction of the United States and involving the murder of a citizen of the State of New York. A large amount of claims against the Government of Mexico remained unadjusted and a war of several years' continuance with the savage tribes of Florida still prevailed, attended with the desolation of a large portion of that beautiful Territory and with the sacrifice of many valuable lives. To increase the embarrassments of the Government, individual and State credit had been nearly stricken down and confidence in the General Government was so much impaired that loans of a small amount could only be negotiated at a considerable sacrifice. As a necessary consequence of the blight which had fallen on commerce and mechanical industry, the ships of the one were thrown out of employment and the operations of the other had been greatly diminished. Owing to the condition of the currency, exchanges between different parts of the country had become ruinously high and trade had to depend on a depreciated paper currency in conducting its transactions. I shall be permitted to congratulate the country that under an overruling Providence peace was preserved without a sacrifice of the national honor; the war in Florida was brought · to a speedy termination; a large portion of the claims on Mexico have been fully adjudicated and are in a course of payment, while justice has been rendered to us in other matters by other nations; confidence between man and man is in a great measure restored and the credit of this Government fully and perfectly reestablished; commerce is becoming more and more extended in its operations and manufacturing and mechanical industry once more reap the rewards of skill and labor honestly applied; the operations of trade rest on a sound currency and the rates of exchange are reduced to their lowest amount.

In this condition of things I have felt it to be my duty to bring to your favorable consideration matters of great interest in their present and ultimate results; and the only desire which I feel in connection with the future is and will continue to be to leave the country prosperous and its institutions unimpaired.

JOHN TYLER.

SPECIAL MESSAGES. ·

CITY OF WASHINGTON, December 8, 1843.

To the House of Representatives of the United States:

I transmit herewith a report from the Secretary of the Treasury, exhibiting certain transfers of appropriations which have been made in that Department in pursuance of the power vested in the President of the United States by the act of Congress of the 3d March, 1809, entitled "An act further to amend the several acts for the establishment and regulation of the Treasury, War, and Navy Departments."

JOHN TYLER.

WASHINGTON, December 12, 1843.

To the Senate of the United States:

I transmit herewith to the Senate, for their consideration in reference to its ratification, a convention for the surrender of criminals between the United States of America and His Majesty the King of the French, signed at this place on the 9th day of November last by the Secretary of State and the minister plenipotentiary *ad interim* from the French Government to the United States.

JOHN TYLER.

WASHINGTON, December 16, 1843.

To the House of Representatives:

The two Houses of Congress at their last session passed a joint resolution, which originated in the House of Representatives, "presenting the thanks of Congress to Samuel T. Washington for the service sword of George Washington and the staff of Benjamin Franklin, presented by him to Congress.'' This resolution (in consequence, doubtless, of a merely accidental omission) did not reach me until after the adjournment of Congress, and therefore did not receive my approval and signature, which it would otherwise promptly have received. I nevertheless felt myself at liberty and deemed it entirely proper to communicate a copy of the resolution to Mr. Washington, as is manifested by the accompanying copy of the letter which I addressed to him. The joint resolution, together with a copy of the letter, is deposited in the Department of State, and can be withdrawn and communicated to the House if it see cause to require them.

JOHN TYLER.

[From Miscellaneous Letters, Department of State.]

SAMUEL T. WASHINGTON, Esq. WASHINGTON, *April 27.*

DEAR SIR: I send you a copy of a joint resolution of the two Houses of Congress expressive of the estimate which they place upon the presents which you recently made to the United States of the sword used by your illustrious relative, George Washington, in the military career of his early youth in the Seven Years' War, and throughout the War of our National Independence, and of the staff bequeathed by the patriot, statesman, and sage Benjamin Franklin to the same leader of the armies of freedom in the Revolutionary War, George Washington.

These precious relics have been accepted in the name of the nation, and have been deposited among its archives.

I avail myself of the opportunity afforded in the performance of this pleasing task to tender you assurances of my high respect and esteem.

JOHN TYLER.

[From Pocketed Laws, Department of State.]

JOINT RESOLUTION presenting the thanks of Congress to Samuel T. Washington for the service sword of George Washington and the staff of Benjamin Franklin, presented by him to Congress.

Resolved unanimously by the Senate and House of Representatives of the United States of America in Congress assembled, That the thanks of this Congress be presented to Samuel T. Washington, of Kanawha County, Va., for the present of the sword used by his illustrious relative, George Washington, in the military career of his early youth in the Seven Years' War, and throughout the War of our National Independence, and of the staff bequeathed by the patriot, statesman, and sage Benjamin Franklin to the same leader of the armies of freedom in the Revolutionary War, George Washington.

That these precious relics are hereby accepted in the name of the nation; that they be deposited for safe-keeping in the Department of State of the United States; and that a copy of this resolution, signed by the President of the Senate and the Speaker of the House of Representatives, be transmitted to the said Samuel T. Washington.

JOHN WHITE,
Speaker of the House of Representatives.
WILLIE P. MANGUM,
President of the Senate pro tempore.

WASHINGTON, *December 26, 1843.*

To the Senate of the United States:

I transmit herewith a communication from the War Department, containing all the information and correspondence in that Department "on the subject of the 'mountain howitzer' taken by Lieutenant Fremont on the expedition to the Oregon" [Territory], as requested by the resolution of the Senate of the 18th instant.

                              JOHN TYLER.

WASHINGTON, D. C., *December 27, 1843.*

To the Senate of the United States:

I lay before the Senate a convention for the settlement of the claims of the citizens and Government of the Mexican Republic against the Government of the United States and of the citizens and Government of the United States against the Government of the Mexican Republic, signed in the City of Mexico on the 20th of last month.

I am happy to believe that this convention provides as fully as is practicable for the adjustment of all claims of our citizens on the Government of Mexico. That Government has thus afforded a gratifying proof of its promptness and good faith in observing the stipulation of the sixth article of the convention of the 30th of January last.

                              JOHN TYLER.

WASHINGTON, *January 8, 1844.*

To the Senate of the United States:

I herewith transmit a report* made by the Secretary of the Navy in pursuance of the provisions of the act of the 3d March, 1843.

                              JOHN TYLER.

WASHINGTON, *January 10, 1844.*

To the House of Representatives:

I transmit the accompanying letter† from the Secretary of State, and copy of a correspondence between that officer and the minister from Portugal near this Government, to which I invite the attention of Congress.

                              JOHN TYLER.

WASHINGTON, *January 16, 1844.*

To the House of Representatives of the United States:

In answer to the resolution of the House of Representatives of the 10th instant, requesting the President to communicate to that body "copies of all correspondence with any foreign government relative to the title, boundary, discovery, and settlement of the Territory of Oregon," I have

---

*Transmitting abstracts of proposals made to the Navy Department and its several bureaus.
†Relating to the duties levied on the wines of Portugal and its possessions by tariff acts of the United States in violation of the treaty of August 26, 1840.

to state that the information called for by the House has been already from time to time transmitted to Congress, with the exception of such correspondence as has been held within the last few months between the Department of State and our minister at London; that there is a prospect of opening a negotiation on the subject of the northwestern boundary of the United States immediately after the arrival at Washington of the newly appointed British minister, now daily expected; and that under existing circumstances it is deemed inexpedient, with a view to the public interest, to furnish a copy of the correspondence above mentioned.

JOHN TYLER.

WASHINGTON CITY, *January 17, 1844.*

To the Senate of the United States:

In compliance with the resolution of the Senate of the 26th ultimo, I transmit herewith a report of the Secretary of War, with a copy of the proceedings of the court-martial in the case of Second Lieutenant D. C. Buell, Third Infantry, and of all orders and papers in relation thereto.

It will be perceived that at the date of the resolution the final action of the Executive was not had upon the case. That action having since taken place, it is communicated with the papers.

JOHN TYLER.

WASHINGTON, D. C., *January 19, 1844.*

To the House of Representatives:

In compliance with your resolution of the 15th December, 1843, requesting "such information as may be on file in any of the Departments relative to the formation of a junction between the Atlantic and Pacific oceans," I transmit herewith a letter from the Secretary of State, with accompanying documents, in relation thereto.

JOHN TYLER.

WASHINGTON, *January 24, 1844.*

To the House of Representatives:

I communicate to the House of Representatives a report from the Secretary of State, under date of the 7th ultimo, accompanied by a copy of a note from the Chevalier de Argaïz, on the subject of the schooner *Amistad.*

JOHN TYLER.

WASHINGTON, *January 26, 1844.*

To the House of Representatives:

I transmit herewith a report of the Secretary of War and accompanying papers, containing the information respecting the Indians remaining at present in Florida, requested by a resolution of the House of Representatives of the 10th instant.

JOHN TYLER.

WASHINGTON, *January 30, 1844.*

To the Senate of the United States:

I transmit a report* of the War Department, prepared under a resolution of the Senate of the 4th instant.

JOHN TYLER.

WASHINGTON, *February 6, 1844.*

To the House of Representatives:

In compliance with the resolution of the House of Representatives of the 22d January, I herewith transmit a letter† from the Secretary of the Navy, containing all the information in the possession of that Department on the subject to which the resolution refers.

JOHN TYLER.

WASHINGTON, *February 7, 1844.*

To the Senate of the United States:

I transmit to the Senate of the United States, in answer to their resolution of the 9th of January last, a report‡ from the Secretary of State and a report§ from the Secretary of War.

JOHN TYLER.

WASHINGTON, *February 9, 1844.*

To the Senate of the United States:

In compliance with the resolution of the Senate of the 31st January, I herewith transmit the accompanying letter|| from the Secretary of the Navy.

JOHN TYLER.

WASHINGTON, *February 12, 1844.*

To the Senate of the United States:

I herewith transmit to the Senate articles of agreement between the Delawares and Wyandots, by which the Delawares propose to convey to the Wyandots certain lands therein mentioned, for the ratification and approval of the Senate, together with the accompanying documents, marked A and B.

My mind is not clear of doubt as to the power of the Executive to act in the matter, but being opposed to the assumption of any doubtful power, I have considered it best to submit the agreement to your consideration.

JOHN TYLER.

*Relating to the proceedings and conduct of the Choctaw commission, sitting in the State of Mississippi, under the Dancing Rabbit Creek treaty.
†Relating to appointments of masters' mates and the postponement of the sailing of the frigate *Raritan*.
‡Stating that there has been no correspondence with the British Government relative to presents, etc., by that Government to Indians in the United States.
§Transmitting a letter from the Commissioner of Indian Affairs relative to presents, etc., to Indians in the United States by the British Government.
||Relating to a proposed extension of the duties of the Home Squadron.

WASHINGTON, *February 12, 1844.*
To the Senate of the United States:

I transmit herewith a letter from the governor of Iowa, accompanied by a memorial from the legislative assembly of that Territory, asking admission as an independent State into the Union.

JOHN TYLER.

WASHINGTON, *February 12, 1844.*
To the Senate of the United States:

I transmit herewith the copy of a report made by Captain R. F. Stockton, of the United States Navy, relative to the vessel of war the *Princeton*, which has been constructed under his supervision and direction, and recommend the same to the attentive consideration of Congress.

JOHN TYLER.

To the Senate of the United States: FEBRUARY 15, 1844.

I communicate herewith a letter from the Secretary of the Treasury, submitting a report from the Commissioner of the General Land Office and accompanying papers, in answer to a resolution adopted by the Senate on the 6th instant, requesting certain information respecting the receipt by local land officers of fees not authorized by law and the measures which have been adopted in reference thereto.

JOHN TYLER.

WASHINGTON, D. C., *February 15, 1844.*
To the Senate and House of Representatives of the United States:

In compliance with the request contained in the accompanying letter from the governor of the State of Kentucky, I herewith transmit certain resolutions* adopted by the legislature of that State, in relation to a digest of the decisions of the Supreme Court of the United States.

JOHN TYLER.

WASHINGTON, *February 20, 1844.*
To the House of Representatives of the United States:

I transmit herewith a report† from the Secretary of War, containing the information requested in the resolution of the House of Representatives of the 29th ultimo.

In order to a full understanding of the matter I have deemed it proper to transmit with the information requested a copy of the reply of the Adjutant-General to Brevet Major-General Gaines, with the documents to which it refers.

JOHN TYLER.

---

*Asking the publication and distribution of a digest of the decisions of the Supreme Court of the United States.

†Relating to the settlement of the accounts of Major-General Gaines, etc.

WASHINGTON, *February 20, 1844.*

To the Senate of the United States:

I transmit to the Senate a report* from the Secretary of State, with accompanying documents, in answer to their resolution of the 31st of January last.

JOHN TYLER.

WASHINGTON, *February 21, 1844.*

To the House of Representatives of the United States:

I herewith transmit to the House of Representatives, in answer to their resolution of the 16th instant, a report† from the Secretary of State, with the correspondence therein referred to.

JOHN TYLER.

WASHINGTON, *February 23, 1844.*

To the House of Representatives:

I transmit herewith a communication from the Secretary of the Navy, to which I invite the particular attention of Congress. The act entitled "An act to authorize the President of the United States to direct transfers of appropriation in the naval service under certain circumstances" has this day met with my approval, under no expectation that it can be rendered available to the present wants of the service, but as containing an exposition of the views of Congress as to the entire policy of transfers from one head of appropriation to any other in the naval service and as a guide to the Executive in the administration of the duties of that Department. The restrictions laid upon the power to transfer by the latter clauses of the act have rendered its passage of no avail at the present moment.

It will, however, be perceived by the document accompanying the report of the Secretary that there has been realized by recent sales of old iron, copper, and other materials the sum of $116,922.79. These sales were ordered for the express purpose of enabling the Executive to complete certain ships now on the stocks, the completion of which is called for by the economical wants of the service; and the doubt existing as to the power of the Government to apply this sum to the objects contemplated proceeds from the fact that the late Secretary of the Navy directed them to be placed in the Treasury, although in doing so he had no intention of diverting them from their intended head of expenditure. The Secretary of the Treasury, however, has brought himself to the opinion that they could only be entered under the head of miscellaneous receipts, and therefore can only be withdrawn by authority of an express act of Congress. I would suggest the propriety of the passage of such an act without delay.

As intimately associated with the means of public defense, I can not

* Relating to slaves committing crimes and escaping from the United States to the British dominions since the ratification of the treaty of 1842, and the refusal of the British authorities to give them up, and to the construction which the British Government puts upon the article of said treaty relative to slaves committing crimes in the United States and taking refuge in the British dominions.

† Relating to a demand upon the British Government for the surrender of certain fugitive criminals from Florida under the provisions of the tenth article of the treaty of Washington.

forbear urging upon you the importance of constructing, upon the principles which have been brought into use in the construction of the *Princeton*, several ships of war of a larger class, better fitted than that ship to the heavy armament which should be placed on board of them. The success which has so eminently crowned this first experiment should encourage Congress to lose no time in availing the country of all the important benefits so obviously destined to flow from it. Other nations will speedily give their attention to the subject, and it would be criminal in the United States, the first to apply to practical purposes the great power which has been brought into use, to permit others to avail themselves of our improvements while we stood listlessly and supinely by. In the number of steam vessels of war we are greatly surpassed by other nations, and yet to Americans is the world indebted for that great discovery of the means of successfully applying steam power which has in the last quarter century so materially changed the condition of the world. We have now taken another and even bolder step, the results of which upon the affairs of nations remain still to be determined, and I can not but flatter myself that it will be followed up without loss of time to the full extent of the public demands. The Secretary of the Navy will be instructed to lay before you suitable estimates of the cost of constructing so many ships of such size and dimensions as you may think proper to order to be built.

The application of steam power to ships of war no longer confines us to the seaboard in their construction. The urgent demands of the service for the Gulf of Mexico and the substitution of iron for wood in the construction of ships plainly point to the establishment of a navy-yard at some suitable place on the Mississippi. The coal fields and iron mines of the extensive region watered by that noble river recommend such an establishment, while high considerations of public policy would lead to the same conclusion.

One of the complaints of the Western States against the actual operation of our system of government is that while large and increasing expenditures of public money are made on the Atlantic frontier the expenditures in the interior are comparatively small. The time has now arrived when this cause of complaint may be in a great measure removed by adopting the legitimate and necessary policy which I have indicated, thereby throwing around the States another bond of union.

I could not forego the favorable opportunity which has presented itself, growing out of the communication from the Secretary of the Navy, to urge upon you the foregoing recommendations.

JOHN TYLER.

WASHINGTON, *February 29, 1844.*

To the Senate and House of Representatives of the United States:

I have to perform the melancholy duty of announcing to the two Houses of Congress the death of the Hon. Abel P. Upshur, late Secretary of State, and the Hon. Thomas W. Gilmer, late Secretary of the Navy.

This most lamentable occurrence transpired on board the United States ship of war the *Princeton* on yesterday at about half past 4 o'clock in the evening, and proceeded from the explosion of one of the large guns of that ship.

The loss which the Government and the country have sustained by this deplorable event is heightened by the death at the same time and by the same cause of several distinguished persons and valuable citizens.

I shall be permitted to express my great grief at an occurrence which has thus suddenly stricken from my side two gentlemen upon whose advice I so confidently relied in the discharge of my arduous task of administering the office of the executive department, and whose services at this interesting period were of such vast importance.

In some relief of the public sorrow which must necessarily accompany this most painful event, it affords me much satisfaction to say that it was produced by no carelessness or inattention on the part of the officers and crew of the *Princeton*, but must be set down as one of those casualties which to a greater or less degree attend upon every service, and which are invariably incident to the temporal affairs of mankind. I will also add that it in no measure detracts from the value of the improvement contemplated in the construction of the *Princeton* or from the merits of her brave and distinguished commander and projector.

JOHN TYLER.

WASHINGTON, *March 7, 1844.*

To the House of Representatives of the United States:

I transmit to the House of Representatives a report* from the Secretary of State, with documents, containing the information requested by their resolution of the 26th ultimo.

JOHN TYLER.

WASHINGTON, *March 8, 1844.*

To the House of Representatives:

In compliance with a resolution of the House of Representatives of the 10th of January last, I communicate to that body a report † from the Secretary of State *ad interim*, which embraces the information called for by said resolution.

JOHN TYLER.

WASHINGTON, *March 8, 1844.*

To the Senate of the United States:

I communicate to the Senate a report,‡ with the documents accompanying it, from the Secretary of State, in answer to a resolution of that body of the 25th of January, 1844.

JOHN TYLER.

*Relating to the colony of Liberia, in Africa.
† Relating to the production, growth, and trade in tobacco.
‡ Transmitting names, returns, etc., of consuls and commercial agents of the United States.

WASHINGTON, *March 9, 1844.*

To the Senate of the United States:

I transmit to the Senate, in answer to their resolution of the 21st ultimo, a report * from the Secretary of State, with accompanying papers.

JOHN TYLER.

WASHINGTON, *March 11, 1844.*

To the House of Representatives:

In compliance with your resolution of the 26th ultimo, I herewith transmit a report † from the Secretary of the Navy.

JOHN TYLER.

WASHINGTON, *March 12, 1844.*

To the House of Representatives:

I transmit herewith a report ‡ of the Secretary of War, prepared in compliance with a resolution of the House of Representatives of the 26th ultimo. JOHN TYLER.

WASHINGTON, D. C., *March 18, 1844.*

To the House of Representatives:

I transmit herewith a report § from the Secretary of State, in answer to the resolution of the House of Representatives of the 18th of January last. JOHN TYLER.

WASHINGTON, *March 19, 1844.*

To the Senate of the United States:

I transmit herewith a letter ‖ from the Secretary of State and certain documents accompanying the same, in answer to the resolution of the Senate of the 8th instant. JOHN TYLER.

WASHINGTON, *March 20, 1844.*

To the Senate of the United States:

I transmit to the Senate a report from the Secretary of State, with documents, containing the information ** requested by their resolution of the 23d ultimo. JOHN TYLER.

* Relating to the abuse of the United States flag in subservience to the African slave trade, and to the taking away of slaves the property of Portuguese subjects in vessels owned or employed by citizens of the United States.

† Transmitting list of officers appointed in the Navy since June 1, 1843.

‡ Transmitting list of officers appointed in the Army since June 1, 1843.

§ Transmitting list of persons employed by the Department of State without express authority of law, etc., from March 4, 1837, to December 31, 1843, inclusive.

‖ Transmitting the commission appointing Caleb Cushing a representative of the Government of the United States in China; papers, etc., concerning the payment of $40,000, appropriated for sending a commissioner, etc., to China.

** Relating to the interpretation of the tenth article of the treaty of August 9, 1842, between the United States and Great Britain.

WASHINGTON, *March 20, 1844*

To the House of Representatives:

I transmit herewith to the House of Representatives a copy of the convention concluded on the 17th day of March, 1841, between the United States and the Republic of Peru, which has been duly ratified and of which the ratifications have been exchanged.

The communication of this treaty is now made to the end that suitable measures may be adopted to give effect to the first article thereof, which provides for the distribution among the claimants of the sum of $300,000, thereby stipulated to be paid.   JOHN TYLER.

[The same message was sent to the Senate.]

WASHINGTON CITY, *March 26, 1844.*

To the Senate of the United States:

I transmit herewith copies of the report and papers* referred to in a resolution of the Senate of the 20th of February last.

JOHN TYLER.

WASHINGTON, *March 26, 1844.*

To the House of Representatives of the United States:

I submit for the consideration of Congress the accompanying communication from A. Pageot, minister plenipotentiary *ad interim* of the King of the French, upon the subject of the tonnage duties levied on French vessels coming into the ports of the United States from the islands of St. Pierre and Miquelon, and proposing to place our commercial intercourse with those islands upon the same footing as now exists with the islands of Martinique and Guadaloupe, as regulated by the acts of the 9th of May, 1828, and of the 13th of July, 1832.   No reason is perceived for the discrimination recognized by the existing law, and none why the provisions of the acts of Congress referred to should not be extended to the commerce of the islands in question.   JOHN TYLER.

To the Senate: WASHINGTON, *March 27, 1844.*

I transmit herewith a communication from the Secretary of the Treasury, to whom I had referred the resolution of the Senate of the 27th December last, showing that the information† called for by that resolution can not be furnished from authentic data.

JOHN TYLER.

---

* Relating to the survey of the harbor of St. Louis.

† Statement of the expenditures of the Government each year from its organization up to the present period, and when and for what purpose these expenditures were made.

WASHINGTON, D. C., *April 9, 1844.*

To the House of Representatives:

In compliance with a resolution of the House of Representatives of the 23d of March last, requesting the President to lay before the House "the authority and the true copies of all requests and applications upon which he deemed it his duty to interfere with the naval and military forces of the United States on the occasion of the recent attempt of the people of Rhode Island to establish a free constitution in the place of the old charter government of that State; also copies of the instructions to and statements of the charter commissioners sent to him by the then existing authorities of the State of Rhode Island; also copies of the correspondence between the Executive of the United States and the charter government of the State of Rhode Island, and all the papers and documents connected with the same; also copies of the correspondence, if any, between the heads of Departments and said charter government or any person or persons connected with the said government, and of any accompanying papers and documents; also copies of all orders issued by the Executive of the United States, or any of the Departments, to military officers for the movement or employment of troops to or in Rhode Island; also copies of all orders to naval officers to prepare steam or other vessels of the United States for service in the waters of Rhode Island; also copies of all orders to the officers of revenue cutters for the same service; also copies of any instructions borne by the Secretary of War to Rhode Island on his visit in 1842 to review the troops of the charter government; also copies of any order or orders to any officer or officers of the Army or Navy to report themselves to the charter government; and that he be requested to lay before this House copies of any other papers or documents in the possession of the Executive connected with this subject not above specifically enumerated," I have to inform the House that the Executive did not deem it his "duty to interfere with the naval and military forces of the United States" in the late disturbances in Rhode Island; that no orders were issued by the Executive or any of the Departments to military officers for the movement or employment of troops to or in Rhode Island other than those which accompany this message and which contemplated the strengthening of the garrison at Fort Adams, which, considering the extent of the agitation in Rhode Island, was esteemed necessary and judicious; that no orders were issued to naval officers to prepare steam or other vessels of the United States for service in the waters of Rhode Island; that no orders were issued "to the officers of the revenue cutters for said service;" that no instructions were borne by "the Secretary of War to Rhode Island on his visit in 1842 *to review the troops of the charter government;*" that no orders were given to any officer or officers of the Army or Navy to report themselves to the charter government; that "requests and applications" were made to the Executive to fulfill the guaranties of the Constitution which impose on the Federal Government the obligation to protect and defend each State of the Union against ''domestic violence and foreign invasion,'' but the Executive was at no time convinced that the *casus fœderis* had arisen which required the interposition of the military or naval power in the controversy which unhappily existed between the people of Rhode Island. I was in no manner prevented from so interfering by the inquiry whether Rhode Island existed as an independent State of the Union under a charter granted at an early period by the Crown of Great Britain or not. It was enough for the Executive to know that she was recognized as a sovereign State by Great Britain by the treaty of 1783; that at a later day she had in common with her sister States poured out her blood and freely expended her treasure in the War of the Revolution; that she was a party to the Articles of Confederation; that at an after period she adopted the Constitution of the United States as a free, independent, and republican State; and that in this character she has always possessed her full quota of representation in the Senate and House of Representatives; and that up to a recent day she has conducted all her domestic affairs and fulfilled all her obligations as a member of the Union, in peace and war, under her *charter government*, as it is denominated by the resolution of the House of the 23d March. I must be permitted to disclaim entirely and unqualifiedly the right on the part of the Executive to make any real or supposed defects existing in any State constitution or form of government the pretext for a failure to enforce the laws or the guaranties of the Constitution of the United States in reference to any such State. I utterly repudiate the idea, in terms as emphatic as I can employ, that those laws are not to be enforced or those guaranties complied with because *the President* may believe that the right of suffrage or any other great popular right is either too restricted or too broadly enlarged. I also with equal strength resist the idea that it falls within the Executive competency to decide in controversies of the nature of that which existed in Rhode Island on which side is the majority of the people or as to the extent of the rights of a mere numerical majority. For the Executive to assume such a power would be to assume a power of the most dangerous character. Under such assumptions the States of this Union would have no security for peace or tranquillity, but might be converted into the mere instruments of Executive will. Actuated by selfish purposes, he might become the great agitator, fomenting assaults upon the State constitutions and declaring the majority of to-day to be the minority of to-morrow, and the minority, in its turn, the majority, before whose decrees the established order of things in the State should be subverted. Revolution, civil commotion, and bloodshed would be the inevitable consequences. The provision in the Constitution intended for the security of the States would thus be turned into the instrument of their destruction. The President would become, in fact, the great *constitution maker* for the States, and all power would be vested in his hands.

When, therefore, the governor of Rhode Island, by his letter of the 4th of April, 1842, made a requisition upon the Executive for aid to put down the late disturbances, I had no hesitation in recognizing the obligations of the Executive to furnish such aid upon the occurrence of the contingency provided for by the Constitution and laws. My letter of the 11th of April, in reply to the governor's letter of the 4th, is herewith communicated, together with all correspondence which passed at a subsequent day and the letters and documents mentioned in the schedule hereunto annexed. From the correspondence between the Executive of the United States and that of Rhode Island, it will not escape observation that while I regarded it as my duty to announce the principles by which I should govern myself in the contingency of an armed interposition on the part of this Government being necessary to uphold the rights of the State of Rhode Island and to preserve its domestic peace, yet that the strong hope was indulged and expressed that all the difficulties would disappear before an enlightened policy of conciliation and compromise. In that spirit I addressed to Governor King the letter of the 9th of May, 1842, marked "private and confidential," and received his reply of the 12th of May of the same year. The desire of the Executive was from the beginning to bring the dispute to a termination without the interposition of the military power of the United States, and it will continue to be a subject of self-congratulation that this leading object of policy was finally accomplished. The Executive resisted all entreaties, however urgent, to depart from this line of conduct. Information from private sources had led the Executive to conclude that little else was designed by Mr. Dorr and his adherents than mere menace with a view to intimidation; nor was this opinion in any degree shaken until the 22d of June, 1842, when it was strongly represented from reliable sources, as will be seen by reference to the documents herewith communicated, that preparations were making by Mr. Dorr, with a large force in arms, to invade the State, which force had been recruited in the neighboring States and had been already preceded by the collection of military stores in considerable quantities at one or two points. This was a state of things to which the Executive could not be indifferent. Mr. Dorr speedily afterwards took up his headquarters at Chepachet and assumed the command of what was reported to be a large force, drawn chiefly from voluntary enlistments made in neighboring States. The Executive could with difficulty bring itself to realize the fact that the citizens of other States should have forgotten their duty to themselves and the Constitution of the United States and have entered into the highly reprehensible and indefensible course of interfering so far in the concerns of a sister State as to have entered into plans of invasion, conquest, and revolution; but the Executive felt it to be its duty to look minutely into the matter, and therefore the Secretary of War was dispatched to Rhode Island with instructions (a copy of which is herewith transmitted), and was authorized, should a requisition be made upon the Executive by the government of Rhode Island in pursuance of law, and the invaders should not abandon their purposes, to call upon the governors of Massachusetts and Connecticut for a sufficient number of militia at once to arrest the invasion and to interpose such of the regular troops as could be spared from Fort Adams for the defense of the city of Providence in the event of its being attacked, as was strongly represented to be in contemplation. Happily there was no necessity for either issuing the proclamation or the requisition or for removing the troops from Fort Adams, where they had been properly stationed. Chepachet was evacuated and Mr. Dorr's troops dispersed without the necessity of the interposition of any military force by this Government, thus confirming me in my early impressions that nothing more had been designed from the first by those associated with Mr. Dorr than to excite fear and apprehension and thereby to obtain concessions from the constituted authorities which might be claimed as a triumph over the existing government.

With the dispersion of Mr. Dorr's troops ended all difficulties. A convention was shortly afterwards called, by due course of law, to amend the fundamental law, and a new constitution, based on more liberal principles than that abrogated, was proposed, and adopted by the people. Thus the great American experiment of a change in government under the influence of opinion and not of force has been again crowned with success, and the State and people of Rhode Island repose in safety under institutions of their own adoption, unterrified by any future prospect of necessary change and secure against domestic violence and invasion from abroad. I congratulate the country upon so happy a termination of a condition of things which seemed at one time seriously to threaten the public peace. It may justly be regarded as worthy of the age and of the country in which we live.

JOHN TYLER.

The PRESIDENT OF THE UNITED STATES. PROVIDENCE, *April 4, 1842.*

SIR: The State of Rhode Island is threatened with domestic violence. Apprehending that the legislature can not be convened in sufficient season to apply to the Government of the United States for effectual protection in this case, I hereby apply to you, as the executive of the State of Rhode Island, for the protection which is required by the Constitution of the United States. To communicate more fully with you on this subject, I have appointed John Whipple, John Brown Francis, and Elisha R. Potter, esqs., three of our most distinguished citizens, to proceed to Washington and to make known to you in behalf of this State the circumstances which call for the interposition of the Government of the United States for our protection.

I am, sir, very respectfully, your obedient servant,

SAM. W. KING,
Governor of Rhode Island.

The PRESIDENT OF THE UNITED STATES. PROVIDENCE, *April 4, 1842.*

SIR: For nearly a year last past the State of Rhode Island has been agitated by revolutionary movements, and is now threatened with domestic violence.

The report* of a joint committee of both branches of the legislature of this State, with an act* and resolutions* accompanying the same, herewith communicated, were passed unanimously by the senate, and by a vote of 60 to 6 in the house of representatives. The legislature adjourned to the first Tuesday of May next.

It has become my duty by one of these resolutions to adopt such measures as in my opinion may be necessary in the recess of the legislature to execute the laws and preserve the State from domestic violence.

The provisions of the said act "in relation to offenses against the sovereign power of this State" have created much excitement among that portion of the people who have unequivocally declared their intention to set up another government in this State and to put down the existing government, and they threaten, individually and collectively, to resist the execution of this act. The numbers of this party are sufficiently formidable to threaten seriously our peace, and in some portions of the State, and in this city particularly, may constitute a majority of the physical force, though they are a minority of the people of the State.

Under the dangers which now threaten us, I have appointed John Whipple, John Brown Francis, and Elisha R. Potter, esqs., three of our most distinguished citizens, to proceed to Washington and consult with you in behalf of this State, with a view that such precautionary measures may be taken by the Government of the United States as may afford us that protection which the Constitution of the United States requires. There is but little doubt that a proclamation from the President of the United States and the presence here of a military officer to act under the authority of the United States would destroy the delusion which is now so prevalent, and convince the deluded that in a contest with the government of this State they would be involved in a contest with the Government of the United States, which could only eventuate in their destruction.

As no State can keep troops in time of peace without the consent of Congress, there is the more necessity that we should be protected by those who have the means of protection. We shall do all we can for ourselves. The Government of the United States has the power to *prevent* as well as to defend us from violence. The protection provided by the Constitution of the United States will not be effectual unless such precautionary measures may be taken as are necessary to prevent lawless men from breaking out into violence, as well as to protect the State from further violence after it has broken out. Preventive measures are the most prudent and safe, and also the most merciful.

The protective power would be lamentably deficient if "the beginning of strife," which "is like the letting out of waters," can not be prevented, and no protection can be afforded the State until to many it would be too late.

The above-named gentlemen are fully authorized to act in behalf of the State of Rhode Island in this emergency, and carry with them such documents and proof as will, no doubt, satisfy you that the interposition of the authority of the Government of the United States will be salutary and effectual.

I am, sir, very respectfully, your obedient servant,

SAM. W. KING,
Governor of Rhode Island.

APRIL 9, 1842.

MY DEAR SIR:† Will you do me the favor to see the committee from Rhode Island as soon after the meeting of the Cabinet as may suit your convenience?

I regret to learn from Mr. Francis that the leaning of your mind was decidedly against any expression of opinion upon the subject, upon the ground that *free suffrage* must *prevail*. Undoubtedly it will. That is not the question. The freeholders of Rhode Island have yielded that point, and the *only* question is between their constitution, providing for an extension of suffrage, and ours, containing *substantially*

---

*Omitted.
†Addressed to the President of the United States.

the *same* provision—whether their constitution shall be carried out by *force of arms without* a majority, or the present government be supported *until* a constitution can be agreed upon that will command a majority. Neither their constitution nor ours has as yet received a majority of the free white males over 21 years of age. *There is no doubt upon that subject*, and I very much regret that your mind should have been influenced (if it has) by the paper called the Express. Nearly all the leaders who are professional men have abandoned them, on the ground that a majority is not in favor of their constitution. I *know* this to be true. I do hope that you will reconsider this vital question and give us a full hearing before you decide.

With great respect, very truly and sincerely, yours,

JOHN WHIPPLE.

His Excellency JOHN TYLER,
    President of the United States:

The undersigned, having been deputed by Samuel W. King, the governor of the State of Rhode Island, to lay before you the present alarming condition in which the people of that State are placed, and to request from you the adoption of such prudential measures as in your opinion may tend to prevent domestic violence, beg leave most respectfully to state the following among the leading facts, to which your attention is more particularly invited:

That the people of Rhode Island have no fundamental law except the charter of King Charles II, granted in 1663, and the usage of the legislature under it. Legislative usage under their charters has been decided by the Supreme Court of the United States to be the fundamental law both in Connecticut and Rhode Island.

That from the date of the Rhode Island charter down to the year 1841, a period of nearly two hundred years, no person has been allowed to vote for town or State offices unless possessed of competent estates and admitted free in the several towns in which they resided.

That since the statute of 1728 no person could be admitted a freeman of any town unless he owned a freehold estate of the value fixed by law (now $134) or was the eldest son of such a freeholder.

That until the past year no attempt has been made, to our knowledge, to establish any other fundamental law, by force, than the one under which the people have lived for so long a period.

That at the January session of the legislature in 1841 a petition signed by five or six hundred male inhabitants, praying for such an extension of suffrage as the legislature might in their wisdom deem expedient to propose, was presented.

That, influenced by that petition, as well as by other considerations, the legislature at that session requested the qualified voters, or freemen, as they are called with us, to choose delegates at their regular town meetings to be holden in August, 1841, for a convention to be holden in November, 1841, to frame a written constitution.

That the result of the last meeting of this legal convention in February, 1842, was the constitution * accompanying this statement, marked ——, which, in case of its adoption by the people, would have been the supreme law of the State.

Most of the above facts are contained in the printed report of a numerous committee of the legislature at their session in March, 1842, which report was adopted by the legislature.

That in May, 1841, after said legal convention had been provided for by the legislature, and before the time appointed for the choice of delegates by the qualified voters (August, 1841), a mass meeting was held by the friends of an extension of suffrage at Newport, at which meeting a committee was appointed, called the State committee, who were authorized by said mass meeting to take measures for calling a convention to frame a constitution.

* Omitted.

That this committee, thus authorized, issued a request for a meeting of the male citizens in the several towns to appoint delegates to the proposed convention.

That meetings (of unqualified voters principally, as we believe) were accordingly holden in the several towns, unauthorized by law, and contrary to the invariable custom and usage of the State from 1663 down to that period; that the aggregate votes appointing the delegates to that convention were, according to their own estimate, about 7,200, whereas the whole number of male citizens over 21 years of age, after making a deduction for foreigners, paupers, etc., was, according to their own estimate, over 22,000.

That this convention, thus constituted, convened in Providence in October, 1841, and the constitution called the "people's constitution" was the result of their deliberations.

That at subsequent meetings of portions of the people in December, 1841, by the authority of this convention alone (elected, as its delegates had been, by about one-third of the voters, according to their own standard of qualification), all males over 21 years of age were admitted to vote for the adoption of the people's constitution; that these meetings were not under any presiding officer whose legal right or duty it was to interpose any check or restraint as to age, residence, property, or color.

By the fourteenth article of this constitution it was provided that "this constitution shall be submitted to the people for their adoption or rejection on Monday, the 27th of December next, and on the two succeeding days;" "and every person entitled to vote as aforesaid who from sickness or *other causes* may be unable to attend and vote in the town or ward meetings assembled for voting upon said constitution on the days aforesaid is requested to write his name on a ticket, and to obtain the signature upon the back of the same of a person who has given in his vote, as a witness thereto, and the moderator or clerk of any town or ward meeting convened for the purpose aforesaid shall receive such vote on either of the three days next succeeding the three days before named for voting for said constitution."

During the first three days about 9,000 votes were received from the hands of the voters in the open meetings. By the privilege granted to any and all friends of the constitution of *bringing into* their meetings the *names* of voters during the three following days 5,000 votes more were obtained, making an aggregate of about 14,000 votes.

This constitution, thus originating and thus formed, was subsequently declared by this convention to be the supreme law of the land. By its provisions a government is to be organized under it, by the choice of a governor, lieutenant-governor, senators and representatives, on the Monday preceding the third Wednesday in April, 1842.

By the provisions of the "landholder's constitution," as the legal constitution is called, every white native citizen possessing the freehold qualification, and over 21 years of age, may vote upon a residence of *one* year, and without any freehold may vote upon a residence of *two* years, except in the case of votes for town taxes, in which case the voter must possess the freehold qualification *or* be taxed for other property of the value of $150.

By the "people's constitution" "every white male citizen of the United States of the age of 21 years who has resided in this State for *one* year and in the town where he votes for six months" shall be permitted to vote, with the same exception as to voting for town taxes as is contained in the other constitution.

The provision, therefore, in relation to the great subject in dispute—the elective franchise—is substantially the same in the two constitutions.

On the 21st, 22d, and 23d March last the legal constitution, by an act of the legislature, was submitted to all the persons who by its provisions would be entitled to vote under it after its adoption, for their ratification. It was rejected by a majority of 676 votes, the number of votes polled being over 16,000. It is believed that many freeholders voted against it because they were attached to the old form of government and were against any new constitution whatever. Both parties used uncommon exertions to bring all their voters to the polls, and the result of the vote was, under the scrutiny of opposing interests in legal town meetings, that the friends of the people's constitution brought to the polls probably not over 7,000 to 7,500 votes. The whole vote against the legal constitution was about 8,600. If we allow 1,000 as the number of freeholders who voted against the legal constitution because they are opposed to any constitution, it would leave the number of the friends of the people's constitution 7,600, or about one-third of the voters of the State under the new qualification proposed by either constitution.

It seems incredible that there can be 14,000 friends of the people's constitution in the State, animated as they are by a most extraordinary and enthusiastic feeling; and yet upon this trial, in the usual open and fair way of voting, they should have obtained not over 7,600 votes.

The unanimity of the subsequent action of the legislature, comprehending as it did both the great political parties—the house of representatives giving a vote of 60 in favor of maintaining the existing government of the State and only 6 on the other side, with a unanimous vote in the senate—the unanimous and decided opinion of the supreme court declaring this extraordinary movement to be illegal in all its stages (see ——*), a majority of that court being of the Democratic party, with other facts of a similar character, have freed this question of a mere party character and enabled us to present it as a great constitutional question.

Without presuming to discuss the elementary and fundamental principles of government, we deem it our duty to remind you of the fact that the existing government of Rhode Island is *the* government that adopted the Constitution of the United States, became a member of this Confederacy, and has ever since been represented in the Senate and House of Representatives. It is at this moment the existing government of Rhode Island, both *de facto* and *de jure*, and is the only government in that State entitled to the protection of the Constitution of the United States.

It is that government which now calls upon the General Government for its interference; and even if the legal effect of there being an ascertained majority of unqualified voters against the existing government was as is contended for by the opposing party, yet, upon their own principle, ought not that majority in point of fact to be clearly ascertained, not by assertion, but by proof, in order to justify the General Government in withdrawing its legal and moral influence to prevent domestic violence?

That a domestic war of the most furious character will speedily ensue unless prevented by a prompt expression of opinion here can not be doubted. In relation to this, we refer to the numerous resolutions passed at meetings of the friends of the people's constitution, and more especially to the Cumberland resolutions* herewith presented, and the affidavits,* marked ——, and to repeated expressions of similar reliance upon the judgment of the Chief Magistrate of the nation.

All which is respectfully submitted by—

> JOHN WHIPPLE.
> JOHN BROWN FRANCIS.
> ELISHA R. POTTER.

WASHINGTON, *April 11, 1842.*

His Excellency the GOVERNOR OF RHODE ISLAND.

SIR: Your letter dated the 4th instant was handed me on Friday by Mr. Whipple, who, in company with Mr. Francis and Mr. Potter, called upon me on Saturday and placed me, both verbally and in writing, in possession of the prominent facts which have led to the present unhappy condition of things in Rhode Island—a state of things which every lover of peace and good order must deplore. I shall not adventure the expression of an opinion upon those questions of domestic policy which

* Omitted.

seem to have given rise to the unfortunate controversies between a portion of the citizens and the existing government of the State. They are questions of municipal regulation, the adjustment of which belongs exclusively to the people of Rhode Island, and with which this Government can have nothing to do. For the regulation of my conduct in any interposition which I may be called upon to make between the government of a State and any portion of its citizens who may assail it with domestic violence, or may be in actual insurrection against it, I can only look to the Constitution and laws of the United States, which plainly declare the obligations of the executive department and leave it no alternative as to the course it shall pursue.

By the fourth section of the fourth article of the Constitution of the United States it is provided that "the United States shall guarantee to every State in this Union a republican form of government, and shall protect each of them against invasion, and, on application of the legislature or executive (when the legislature can not be convened), *against domestic violence.*" And by the act of Congress approved on the 28th February, 1795, it is declared "that in case of an insurrection in any State *against the government thereof* it shall be lawful for the President of the United States, upon application of the legislature of such State or by the executive (when the legislature can not be convened), to call forth such numbers of the militia of any other State or States as may be applied for, as he may judge sufficient to suppress such insurrection." By the third section of the same act it is provided "that whenever it may be necessary, in the judgment of the President, to use the military force hereby directed to be called forth, the President shall forthwith, by proclamation, command such insurgents to disperse and retire peaceably to their respective abodes within a reasonable time." By the act of March 3, 1807, it is provided "that in all cases of insurrection or obstruction to the laws, either of the United States or of any individual State or Territory where it is lawful for the President of the United States to call forth the militia for the purpose of suppressing such insurrection or of causing the laws to be duly executed, it shall be lawful for him to employ for the same purposes such part of the land or naval force of the United States as shall be judged necessary, having first observed all the prerequisites of the law in that respect."

This is the first occasion, so far as the government of a State and its people are concerned, on which it has become necessary to consider of the propriety of exercising those high and most important of constitutional and legal functions.

By a careful consideration of the above-recited acts of Congress your excellency will not fail to see that no power is vested in the Executive of the United States to anticipate insurrectionary movements against the government of Rhode Island so as to sanction the interposition of the military authority, but that there must be an actual insurrection, manifested by lawless assemblages of the people or otherwise, to whom a proclamation may be addressed and who may be required to betake themselves to their respective abodes. I have, however, to assure your excellency that should the time arrive—and my fervent prayer is that it may never come—when an insurrection shall exist *against the government* of Rhode Island, and a requisition shall be made upon the Executive of the United States to furnish that protection which is guaranteed to each State by the Constitution and laws, I shall not be found to shrink from the performance of a duty which, while it would be the most painful, is at the same time the most imperative. I have also to say that in such a contingency the Executive could not look into real or supposed defects of the existing government in order to ascertain whether some other plan of government proposed for adoption was better suited to the wants and more in accordance with the wishes of any portion of her citizens. To throw the Executive power of this Government into any such controversy would be to make the President the armed arbitrator between the people of the different States and their constituted authorities, and might lead to a usurped power dangerous alike to the stability of the State governments and the liberties of the people. It will be my duty, on the contrary, to respect the requisitions of that government which has been recognized as the existing government of the State through all time past until I shall be advised in regular manner that it has been altered and abolished and another substituted in its place by legal and peaceable proceedings adopted and pursued by the authorities and people of the State. Nor can I readily bring myself to believe that any such contingency will arise as shall render the interference of this Government at all necessary. The people of the State of Rhode Island have been too long distinguished for their love of order and of regular government to rush into revolution in order to obtain a redress of grievances, real or supposed, which a government under which their fathers lived in peace would not in due season redress. No portion of her people will be willing to drench her fair fields with the blood of their own brethren in order to obtain a redress of grievances which their constituted authorities can not for any length of time resist if properly appealed to by the popular voice. None of them will be willing to set an example, in the bosom of this Union, of such frightful disorder, such needless convulsions of society, such danger to life, liberty, and property, and likely to bring so much discredit on the character of popular governments. My reliance on the virtue, intelligence, and patriotism of her citizens is great and abiding, and I will not doubt but that a spirit of conciliation will prevail over rash councils, that all actual grievances will be promptly redressed by the existing government, and that another bright example will be added to the many already prevailing among the North American Republics of change without revolution and a redress of grievances without force or violence.

I tender to your excellency assurances of my high respect and consideration.

JOHN TYLER.

NEWPORT, R. I., *May 4, 1842.*

His Excellency JOHN TYLER,
     President of the United States.

SIR: I transmit herewith certain resolutions passed by the general assembly of this State at their session holden at Newport on the first Wednesday of May instant.

You are already acquainted with some of the circumstances which have rendered necessary the passage of these resolutions. Any further information that may be desired will be communicated by the bearers, the Hon. Richard K. Randolph, speaker of the house of representatives, and Elisha R. Potter, esq., a member of the senate of this State.

I can not allow myself to doubt but that the assistance to which this State is entitled under the Constitution of the United States, to protect itself against domestic violence, will be promptly rendered by the General Government of the Union.

With great respect, I am, Your Excellency's humble servant,

SAM. W. KING,
Governor of Rhode Island.

STATE OF RHODE ISLAND AND PROVIDENCE PLANTATIONS,
In General Assembly, May Session, 1842.

Whereas a portion of the people of this State, for the purpose of subverting the laws and existing government thereof, have framed a pretended constitution, and for the same unlawful purposes have met in lawless assemblages and elected officers for the future government of this State; and

Whereas the persons so elected in violation of law, but in conformity to the said pretended constitution, have, on the 3d day of May instant, organized themselves into executive and legislative departments of government, and under oath assumed the duties and exercise of said powers; and

Whereas in order to prevent the due execution of the laws a strong military force was called out and did array themselves to protect the said unlawful organization of government and to set at defiance the due enforcement of law: Therefore,

Resolved by the general assembly, That there now exists in this State an insurrection against the laws and constituted authorities thereof, and that, in pursuance of the Constitution and laws of the United States, a requisition be, and hereby is, made by this legislature upon the President of the United States forthwith to interpose the authority and power of the United States to suppress such insurrectionary and lawless assemblages, to support the existing government and laws, and protect the State from domestic violence.

Resolved, That his excellency the governor be requested immediately to transmit a copy of these resolutions to the President of the United States.

True copy.

Witness:

HENRY BOWEN,
Secretary of State.

WASHINGTON, *May 7, 1842.*

The GOVERNOR OF THE STATE OF RHODE ISLAND.

SIR: Your letter of the 4th instant, transmitting resolutions of the legislature of Rhode Island, informing me that there existed in that State "certain lawless assemblages of a portion of the people" "for the purpose of subverting the laws and overthrowing the existing government," and calling upon the Executive "forthwith to interpose the authority and power of the United States to suppress such insurrectionary and lawless assemblages and to support the existing government and laws and protect the State from domestic violence," was handed me on yesterday by Messrs. Randolph and Potter.

I have to inform your excellency in reply that my opinions as to the duties of this Government to protect the State of Rhode Island against domestic violence remain unchanged. Yet, from information received by the Executive since your dispatches came to hand I am led to believe that the lawless assemblages to which reference is made have already dispersed and that the danger of domestic violence is hourly diminishing, if it has not wholly disappeared. I have with difficulty brought myself at any time to believe that violence would be resorted to or an exigency arise which the unaided power of the State could not meet, especially as I have from the first felt persuaded that your excellency and others associated with yourself in the administration of the government would exhibit a temper of conciliation as well as of energy and decision. To the insurgents themselves it ought to be obvious, when the excitement of the moment shall have passed away, that changes achieved by regular and, if necessary, repeated appeals to the constituted authorities, in a country so much under the influence of public opinion, and by recourse to argument and remonstrance, are more likely to insure lasting blessings than those accomplished by violence and bloodshed on one day, and liable to overthrow by similar agents on another.

I freely confess that I should experience great reluctance in employing the military power of this Government against any portion of the people; but however painful the duty, I have to assure your excellency that if resistance be made to the execution of the laws of Rhode Island by such force as the *civil power* shall be unable to overcome, it will be the duty of this Government to enforce the constitutional guaranty— a guaranty given and adopted mutually by all the original States, of which number Rhode Island was one, and which in the same way has been given and adopted by each of the States since admitted into the Union; and if an exigency of lawless violence shall actually arise the executive government of the United States, on the application of your excellency under the authority of the resolutions of the legislature already transmitted, will stand ready to succor the authorities of the State in their efforts to maintain a due respect for the laws. I sincerely hope, however, that no such exigency may occur, and that every citizen of Rhode Island will manifest his love of peace and good order by submitting to the laws and seeking a redress of grievances by other means than intestine commotions.

I tender to your excellency assurances of my distinguished consideration.

JOHN TYLER.

JOHN TYLER,
   President of the United States.

SIR: As requested by the general assembly, I have the honor of transmitting to you, under the seal of the State, the accompanying resolutions.

And I am, very respectfully, your obedient servant,

THOMAS W. DORR,
   Governor of the State of Rhode Island and Providence Plantations.

STATE OF RHODE ISLAND AND PROVIDENCE PLANTATIONS,
General Assembly, May Session, in the City of Providence, A. D. 1842.

Resolved, That the governor be requested to inform the President of the United States that the government of this State has been duly elected and organized under the constitution of the same, and that the general assembly are now in session and proceeding to discharge their duties according to the provisions of said constitution.

Resolved, That the governor be requested to make the same communication to the President of the Senate and to the Speaker of the House of Representatives, to be laid before the two Houses of the Congress of the United States.

Resolved, That the governor be requested to make the same communication to the governors of the several States, to be laid before the respective legislatures.

A true copy.

Witness:

[L. S.]

WM. H. SMITH,
   Secretary of State.

MAY 9, 1842.

Governor KING, *of Rhode Island.*

SIR: Messrs. Randolph and Potter will hand you an official letter, but I think it important that you should be informed of my views and opinions as to the best mode of settling all difficulties. I deprecate the use of force except in the last resort, and I am persuaded that measures of conciliation will at once operate to produce quiet. *I am well advised*, if the general assembly would authorize you to announce a general amnesty and pardon for the past, without making any exception, upon the condition of a return to allegiance, and follow it up by a call for a new convention upon somewhat liberal principles, that all difficulty would at once cease. And why should not this be done? A government never loses anything by mildness and forbearance to its own citizens, more especially when the consequences of an opposite course may be the shedding of blood. In your case the one-half of your people are involved in the consequences of recent proceedings. Why urge matters to an extremity? If you succeed by the bayonet, you succeed against your own fellow-citizens and by the shedding of kindred blood, whereas by taking the opposite course you will have shown a paternal care for the lives of your people. My own opinion is that the adoption of the above measures will give you peace and insure you harmony. A resort to force, on the contrary, will engender for years to come feelings of animosity.

I have said that I *speak advisedly*. Try the experiment, and if it fail then your justification in using force becomes complete.

Excuse the freedom I take, and be assured of my respect.

JOHN TYLER.

PROVIDENCE, R. I., *May 12, 1842.*

His Excellency the PRESIDENT OF UNITED STATES.

MY DEAR SIR: I have had the honor to receive your communication of 9th instant by Mr. Randolph, and assure you it has given me much satisfaction to know that your views and opinions as to the course proper to be pursued by the government of this State in the present unhappy condition of our political affairs is so much in conformity with my own.

Our legislature will undoubtedly at their session in June next adopt such measures as will be necessary to organize a convention for the formation of a new constitution of government, by which all the evils now complained of may be removed.

It has already been announced as the opinion of the executive that such of our citizens as are or have been engaged in treasonable and revolutionary designs against the State will be pardoned for the past on the condition only that they withdraw themselves from such enterprise and signify their return to their allegiance to the government.

With high consideration and respect, your obedient and very humble servant,

SAM. W. KING.

KINGSTON, R. I., *May 15, 1842.*

His Excellency JOHN TYLER,
President of the United States.

DEAR SIR: We arrived at Newport on Wednesday morning in time to attend the meeting of our legislature.

The subject of calling a convention immediately, and upon a liberal basis as to the right of voting for the delegates, was seriously agitated amongst us. The only objection made was that they did not wish to concede while the *people's party* continued *their threats.* All allowed that the concession must be made, and the only difference of opinion was as to time.

For my own part, I fear we shall never see the time when concession could have been made with better grace or with better effect than now. If two or three *noisy* folks among the suffrage party could only have their mouths stopped for a week or two, a reconciliation could be brought about at any time, or if Mr. Dorr would allow himself to be arrested peaceably and give bail no one could then object. But the supporters of the government say it is wrong to give up so long as Mr. Dorr threatens actual resistance to the laws in case he is arrested. If this could be done, they would then consider that they had sufficiently shown their determination to support the laws, and the two measures which you proposed to us in conversation at Washington—a convention and then a *general* amnesty—would succeed beyond a doubt.

Allow me to suggest that if Mr. Wickliffe, or someone who you might think would have most influence, would address a letter to Governor Fenner on the subject of conciliation it might be of great service. Governor F. is the father-in-law of General Mallett and a member of our senate.

Our assembly adjourned to the third Monday of June, but it is in the power of the governor to call it sooner, which can be done in a day at any time. Unless, however, there is a little more *prudence* in the *leaders* on both sides, we shall then be farther from reconciliation than now. The great mass of both parties I believe to be sincerely anxious for a settlement.

I do not know whether a letter addressed to the President upon a subject of this nature would of course be considered as public and liable to inspection. Few would write freely if that were the case. If private, I will cheerfully communicate from time to time any information that may be in my power and which might be of any service.

I am, sir, very respectfully, your obedient servant,

ELISHA R. POTTER.

Mr. Dorr returned to Providence this (Monday) morning with an armed escort.

ELISHA R. POTTER, Esq.

DEAR SIR: You have my thanks for your favor of the 16th [15th] instant, and I have to request that you will write to me without reserve whenever anything of importance shall arise. My chief motives for desiring the adoption of the measures suggested to you, viz, a general amnesty and a call of a convention, were, first, because I felt convinced that peace and harmony would follow in their train, and, secondly, if in this I was disappointed the insurgents would have had no longer a pretense for an appeal to the public sympathies in their behalf. I saw nothing to degrade or to give rise to injurious reflections against the government of the State for resorting to every proper expedient in order to quiet the disaffection of any portion of her own people. Family quarrels are always the most difficult to appease, but everybody will admit that those of the family who do most to reconcile them are entitled to the greatest favor. Mr. Dorr's recent proceedings have been of so extravagant a character as almost to extinguish the last hope of a peaceable result, and yet I can not but believe that much is meant for effect and for purposes of intimidation merely. I certainly hope that such may be the case, though the recent proceedings in New York may have excited new feelings and new desires. This mustering of the clans may place Governor King in a different situation from that which he occupied when I had the pleasure of seeing you. *Then* he might have yielded with grace; whether he can do so now is certainly a question of much difficulty and one on which I can not venture to express an opinion at this distance from the scene of action.

I shall be always most happy to hear from you, and your letters will never be used to your prejudice.

Accept assurances of my high respect.

JÓHN TYLER.

PROVIDENCE, *May 16, 1842.*
The PRESIDENT OF THE UNITED STATES.

SIR: At the request of Governor King, I inclose to you an extra of the Providence Daily Express of this morning, containing the proclamation of Thomas W. Dorr to the people of this State.

It states definitely the position assumed by him and his faction against the government of this State and of the United States.

His excellency tenders to you the highest respect and consideration.

Respectfully, yours,

THOS. A. JENCKES,
Private Secretary.

STATE OF RHODE ISLAND AND PROVIDENCE PLANTATIONS.

A PROCLAMATION.

BY THOMAS W. DORR, GOVERNOR AND COMMANDER IN CHIEF OF THE SAME.

FELLOW-CITIZENS: Shortly after the adjournment of the general assembly and the completion of indispensable executive business I was induced by the request of the most active friends of our cause to undertake the duty (which had been previously suggested) of representing in person the interests of the people of Rhode Island in other States and at the seat of the General Government. By virtue of a resolution of the general assembly, I appointed Messrs. Pearce and Anthony commissioners for the same purpose.

Of the proposed action of the Executive in the affairs of our State you have been already apprised. In case of the failure of the civil posse (which expression was intended by the President, as I have been informed, to embrace the military power) to execute any of the laws of the charter assembly, including their law of pains and penalties and of treason, as it has been for the first time defined, the President intimates an intention of resorting to the forces of the United States to check the movements of the people of this State in support of their republican constitution recently adopted.

From a decision which conflicts with the right of sovereignty inherent in the people of this State and with the principles which lie at the foundation of a democratic republic an appeal has been taken to the people of our country. They understand our cause; they sympathize in the injuries which have been inflicted upon us; they disapprove the course which the National Executive has adopted toward this State, and they assure us of their disposition and intention to interpose a barrier between the supporters of the people's constitution and the hired soldiery of the United States. The democracy of the country are slow to move in any matter which involves an issue so momentous as that which is presented by the controversy in Rhode Island, but when they have once put themselves in motion they are not to be easily diverted from their purposes. They believe that the people of Rhode Island are in the right; that they are contending for equal justice in their political system; that they have properly adopted a constitution of government for themselves, as they were entitled to do, and they can not and will not remain indifferent to any act, from whatever motive it may proceed, which they deem to be an invasion of the sacred right of self-government, of which the people of the respective States can not be divested.

As your representative I have been everywhere received with the utmost kindness and cordiality. To the people of the city of New York, who have extended to us the hand of a generous fraternity, it is impossible to overrate our obligation at this most important crisis.

It has become my duty to say that so soon as a soldier of the United States shall be set in motion, by whatever direction, to act against the people of this State in aid of the charter government I shall call for that aid to oppose all such force, which, I am fully authorized to say, will be immediately and most cheerfully tendered to the service of the people of Rhode Island from the city of New York and from other places. The contest will then become national, and our State the battle ground of American freedom.

As a Rhode Island man I regret that the constitutional question in this State can not be adjusted among our own citizens, but as the minority have asked that the sword of the National Executive may be thrown into the scale against the people, it is imperative upon them to make the same appeal to their brethren of the States—an appeal which they are well assured will not be made in vain. They who have been the first to ask assistance from abroad can have no reason to complain of any consequences which may ensue.

No further arrests under the law of pains and penalties, which was repealed by the general assembly of the people at their May session, will be permitted. I hereby direct the military, under their respective officers, promptly to prevent the same and to release all who may be arrested under said law.

As requested by the general assembly, I enjoin upon the militia forthwith to elect their company officers; and I call upon volunteers to organize themselves without delay. The military are directed to hold themselves in readiness for immediate service.

Given under my hand and the seal of the State, at the city of Providence, this 6th day of May, A. D. 1842.

[L. S.]
THOMAS W. DORR,
Governor and Commander in Chief of the State of
Rhode Island and Providence Plantations.

By the governor's command:
WILLIAM H. SMITH,
Secretary of State.

PROVIDENCE, R. I., *May 25, 1842.*

The PRESIDENT OF THE UNITED STATES.

SIR: Since my last communication the surface of things in this city and State has been more quiet. The complete dispersing of the insurgents and flight of their leader on Wednesday last, 18th instant, seem to have broken their strength and prevented them from making head openly in any quarter.

But another crisis now appears to be approaching. By the private advices received by myself and the council from our messengers in the neighboring States we learn that Dorr and his agents are enlisting men and collecting arms for the purpose of again attempting to subvert, by open war, the government of this State. Those who have assisted him at home in his extreme measures are again holding secret councils and making preparations to rally on his return. Companies of men pledged to support him have met and drilled in the north part of this State during the present week.

From the forces which he can collect among our own citizens we have nothing to fear. Our own military strength has once scattered them, and could as easily do so a second time. But if the bands which are now organizing in Massachusetts, Connecticut, and New York should make the incursion which they threaten, with Dorr at their head, we have reason to apprehend a civil war of the most destructive and vindictive character. Our own forces might be sufficient to repel them, but having little discipline and no officer of military experience to lead them, they could not do it without the loss of many valuable lives.

For the evidence that such forces are organizing in other States, I refer Your Excellency to a letter from Governor Seward, of New York, and to a statement made by one of our messengers to the council, which will be handed you. Other messengers confirm to the fullest extent the same intelligence.

In this posture of affairs I deem it my duty to call upon Your Excellency for the support guaranteed by the Constitution and laws of the United States to this government. I would submit to Your Excellency whether a movement of a sufficient body of troops to this quarter, to be stationed at Fort Adams, and to be subject to the requisitions of the executive of this State whenever in his opinion the exigency should arise to require their assistance, would not be the best measure to insure peace and respect for the laws and to deter invasions.

You will see by the statement* of the secret agent of the government that the time set for this incursion is very near. The mustering of the insurgents and their movement upon the city will probably be with the greatest expedition when once commenced—in a time too short for a messenger to reach Washington and return with aid. I therefore make this application before any movement of magnitude on their part, in order that we may be prepared at the briefest notice to quell domestic insurrection and repel invasion.

SAM. W. KING,
Governor of Rhode Island.

EXECUTIVE DEPARTMENT,
Albany, May 22, 1842.

His Excellency SAMUEL WARD KING,
        Governor of Rhode Island.

SIR: In compliance with your excellency's requisition, I have this day issued a warrant for the arrest of Thomas Wilson Dorr, esq., charged in Rhode Island with the crime of treason. The warrant will be delivered to a police officer of this city, who will attend Colonel Pitman and be advised by him in regard to the arrest of the fugitive should he be found in this State.

May I be allowed to suggest to your excellency that a detention of the accused in

* Omitted.

this State would be liable to misapprehension, and if it should be in a particular region of this State might, perhaps, result in an effort to rescue him. Therefore it seems to be quite important that your excellency should without delay designate, by a communication to me, an agent to receive the fugitive and convey him to Rhode Island.

I have the honor to be, with very high respect and consideration, your excellency's obedient servant, WILLIAM H. SEWARD.

His Excellency Governor KING. WASHINGTON CITY, *May 28, 1842.*

SIR: I have received your excellency's communication of the 25th instant, informing me of efforts making by Mr. Dorr and others to embody a force in the contiguous States for the invasion of the State of Rhode Island, and calling upon the Executive of the United States for military aid.

In answer I have to inform your excellency that means have been taken to ascertain the extent of the dangers of any armed invasion by the citizens of other States of the State of Rhode Island, either to put down her government or to disturb her peace. The apparent improbability of a violation so flagrant and unprecedented of all our laws and institutions makes me, I confess, slow to believe that any serious attempts will be made to execute the designs which some evil-minded persons may have formed.

But should the necessity of the case require the interposition of the authority of the United States it will be rendered in the manner prescribed by the laws.

In the meantime I indulge a confident expectation, founded upon the recent manifestations of public opinion in your State in favor of law and order, that your own resources and means will be abundantly adequate to preserve the public peace, and that the difficulties which have arisen will be soon amicably and permanently adjusted by the exercise of a spirit of liberality and forbearance. JOHN TYLER.

The Secretary of War will issue a private order to Colonel Bankhead, commanding at Newport, to employ, if necessary, a private and confidential person or persons to go into all such places and among all such persons as he may have reason to believe to be likely to give any information touching Rhode Island affairs, and to report with the greatest dispatch, if necessary, to the President. He will also address a letter to General Wool conveying to him the fears entertained of a hostile invasion contemplated to place Dorr in the chair of state of Rhode Island by persons in the States of Connecticut and New York, and also to General Eustis, at Boston, of a similar character, with instructions to adopt such inquiries (to be secretly made) as they may deem necessary, and to report with the greatest dispatch all information which from time to time they may acquire.

(Indorsed: "President's instructions, May 28, 1842.")

Colonel BANKHEAD, WAR DEPARTMENT, *May 28, 1842.*
    Newport, R. I.

SIR: The governor of Rhode Island has represented to the President that preparations are making by Mr. Dorr and some of his adherents to recruit men in the neighboring States for the purpose of supporting his usurpation of the powers of government, and that he has provided arms and camp equipage for a large number of men. It is very important that we should have accurate information on this subject, and particularly in relation to the movements made in other States. I have therefore to desire you to employ proper persons to go to the places where it may be supposed such preparations are making to possess themselves fully of all that is doing and in contemplation, and report frequently to you. It is said that Mr. Dorr's principal headquarters are at the town of Thompson, in the State of Connecticut. It may be well for you to communicate personally with Governor King and ascertain from him the points and places at which any preparations for embodying men are supposed to be making, and to direct your inquiries accordingly.

It is important that you should select persons on whose integrity and accuracy the fullest reliance can be placed. They should not be partisans on either side, although to effect the object it will of course be necessary that some of them should obtain (if they do not already possess) the confidence of the friends of Mr. Dorr. You will please communicate directly to me all the information you obtain, and your own views of it.

It is scarcely necessary to say that this communication is of the most private and confidential character, and is not to be made known to anyone.

Respectfully, your obedient servant,

J. C. SPENCER.

Brigadier-General EUSTIS,
      Boston.

WAR DEPARTMENT, *May 29, 1842.*

SIR: The governor of Rhode Island has represented to the President that preparations are making in other States (particularly in Massachusetts) for an armed invasion of that State to support the usurpations of Mr. Dorr and his friends and foment domestic insurrection. It is very important that we should have accurate information on this subject, and I have to desire you to take all necessary means to acquire it, and communicate directly to me as speedily and frequently as possible. It is said that 1,000 stand of arms have been procured in Boston, some pieces of artillery, and a large quantity of camp equipage for the use of the insurgents. Your attention to this is particularly desired to ascertain its truth or falsehood. It is also said that there are 200 men enrolled and embodied in a town upon the borders of Rhode Island, the name of which has escaped me. Please inquire into this. If it becomes necessary to employ confidential persons to discover what is doing, you will do so, being careful to select those only that are entirely trustworthy; and it will be desirable to avoid heated partisans on either side. Their inquiries should be conducted quietly and privately.

I desire you to communicate fully and freely what you may learn and your views concerning it for the information of the President and the Department. •

It is scarcely necessary to say that this communication is strictly private and confidential.

Respectfully, your obedient servant,

[J. C. SPENCER.]

The PRESIDENT.

NEW YORK, *June 3, 1842.*

MY DEAR SIR: I came to this city yesterday, having taken a severe cold on the Sound, and am now just out of my bed. I transmit herewith a letter from ———, a friend appointed by me, as you requested, to look into the Rhode Island business. Mr. ——— has had access to authentic sources in Governor Dorr's party, and I have no doubt his account of the whole matter is perfectly just. I supposed I should receive the foreign mail here, but I shall not wait for it if I should feel well enough to travel to-morrow.

Yours, truly,

DANL. WEBSTER.

Hon. DANIEL WEBSTER,
      Secretary of State.

NEW YORK, *June 3, 1842.*

DEAR SIR: In pursuance of the arrangement made when you were in Boston, I have visited the State of Rhode Island, and, so far as could be done, possessed myself of a knowledge of the existing state of things there. I had a full and free interview with Governor King and his council, as well as with several other gentlemen upon each side of the matter in controversy. All agree that, so far as the people of Rhode Island are concerned, there is no danger of any further armed resistance to the legitimate authorities of the State. It was never intended, probably, by the majority of those called the suffrage party to proceed in any event to violence, and when they found themselves pushed to such an extremity by their leaders they deserted their leaders and are now every day enrolling themselves in the volunteer companies which are being organized in every part of the State for the suppression of any further insurrectionary movements that may be made. A large majority of those elected or appointed to office under the people's constitution (so called) have resigned their places and renounced all allegiance to that constitution and the party which supports it, so that the insurgents are now without any such organization as would enable them to carry out their original purposes if they otherwise had the power.

Governor King and his council alone, of all the intelligent persons with whom I consulted, fear an irruption upon them of an armed force to be collected in other States, and this is the only difficulty of which they now have any apprehension. This fear is excited by the boasts frequently made by the few who still avow their determination to adhere to the constitution that they have at their control large bodies of armed men, as well as camp equipage, provisions, money, and munitions of war, which have been provided for them in Massachusetts, Connecticut, and New York. The supposition that Rhode Island is to be invaded by a foreign force, when that force would neither be led nor followed by any considerable number of the people of the State, does not seem, to say the least, to be a very reasonable one. If those who think they are suffering injustice are not disposed to make an effort to redress their supposed wrongs, they would hardly expect the work to be done by others.

The ostensible object of the insurgents now is not the real one. They meditate no further forcible proceedings. They bluster and threaten for several reasons:

First. Because they suppose they shall thus break their fall a little and render their retreat a little less inglorious than it would be if they should beat it at once.

Second. They believe that if they keep up a shew of opposition to the existing government they shall be more likely to revolutionize it by peaceable measures; and

Third. They think they can make their influence so far felt as to operate favorably upon those who are now under arrest for treason or who may be hereafter arrested for the same offense.

That these are the views and purposes of the insurgents I am confidentially assured by the notorious individual from whom I told you I could learn their plans and designs; and no one has better means of knowing than he, having been himself one of Mr. Dorr's confidential advisers from the beginning.

The meeting at Woonsocket on the 1st did not amount to much, being but thinly attended. The projected fortifications at that place have been abandoned. It is said they will be thrown up in some other spot to be designated hereafter, but this is not believed.

Mr. Dorr is now understood to be lurking in this city. Warrants have been issued for his arrest both by the governor of this State and the governor of Massachusetts, but he moves so privately and shifts his whereabouts so often that he eludes his pursuers.

Under all the circumstances I think you will come to the opinion entertained by seven-eighths of all the people of Providence (the scene of his operations thus far) that, deserted by his followers at home and disgraced in the estimation of those who sympathized with him abroad, Mr. Dorr has it not in his power to do any further serious mischief.

Yours, very truly,

PROVIDENCE, R. I., *June 22, 1842.*

Hon. J. C. SPENCER,
       Secretary of War.

SIR: When I last had the honor to write to you I felt confident that there would be no further disturbance of the peace in this State. Governor King was of the same opinion. But I now fear, from strong indications, that Mr. Dorr and his party are determined to enter the State in force, and that in a few days serious difficulties will arise.

On my arrival here this morning from Newport, on my way to New York, I learnt from undoubted authority that several large boxes of muskets, supposed to contain about eighty, were received the evening before last at Woonsocket from New York; that several mounted cannon had been also received there and forwarded on to Chepachet; that a number of men, not citizens of the State, with arms, were in and about Woonsocket and Chepachet; that forty-eight kegs of powder were stolen on Sunday night last from a powder house in this neighborhood, and that Dorr, with about twenty men, landed last evening at Norwich.

An unsuccessful attempt was made two nights ago to steal the guns of the artillery company at Warren, and at several other places where guns had been deposited by the State, by some of Dorr's men, one of whom has been identified and arrested.

It has been observed for several days past that many of the suffrage party and residents of this city have been sending off their families and effects. The inhabitants of the city are seriously alarmed and in a state of much excitement. An express to convey the above intelligence to Governor King at Newport will be immediately sent down by the mayor of the city.

I shall be in New York early to-morrow morning ready to receive any instructions you may think proper to honor me with.

I have been compelled to write this in haste.

I am, sir, with great respect, your obedient servant,

JAS. BANKHEAD,
Colonel Second Regiment Artillery.

CITY OF PROVIDENCE, MAYOR'S OFFICE,
June 23, 1842.

SIR:* Governor King, having gone to Newport this afternoon, has requested me to forward his letter to Your Excellency, with such depositions as I could procure concerning the state of affairs in the north part of the State. These documents will be taken on by the Hon. William Sprague, our Senator, who intends leaving to-night for Washington. Should any accident prevent Mr. Sprague from going, I shall forward them to be put in the mail. I inclose the depositions† of Messrs. Samuel W. Peckham and Charles I. Harris. Messrs. Keep and Shelley, whom I sent out, have just returned. If I can get their depositions in time, I shall also forward them.

About 11 a. m. this day a body marched from Woonsocket to Chepachet amounting to 90 men, and other small bodies are marching in that direction, so that I suppose that about 400 will be concentrated at Chepachet this evening.

In this city there is much excitement, but no symptoms as yet of men gathering with arms. There are many who I fear will be ready to join in any mischief should Dorr's forces approach us. Up to 8 o'clock this morning Mr. Dorr was in Connecticut, but a gentleman from Chepachet informs me his friends expect him this day.

I remain, with great respect, your obedient servant,

THOS. M. BURGESS,
Mayor.

*Addressed to the President of the United States.
†Omitted.

EXECUTIVE DEPARTMENT,
Providence, June 23, 1842.

His Excellency JOHN TYLER,
  President of the United States.

SIR: After my last communication the excitement and military operations of the insurgents against the government of this State appeared to subside, and I indulged hopes that no open violence would be attempted, but that they were disposed to await the action of the general assembly, now in session at Newport. I regret that I am obliged to inform Your Excellency that within a few days past appearances have become more alarming. Several iron cannon have been stolen from citizens of Providence, and during the night of the 19th a powder house, owned by a merchant of Providence, was broken open and about 1,200 pounds of powder stolen therefrom. Yesterday the military operations of the insurgents became more decided in their character. At Woonsocket and Chepachet there were gatherings of men in military array, pretending to act under the authority of Thomas W. Dorr. They established a kind of martial law in those villages, stopped peaceable citizens in the highways, and at Chepachet four citizens of Providence were seized by an armed force, pinioned, and compelled to march about 10 miles under a guard of about forty men to Woonsocket, where they were cruelly treated under pretense of being spies. The insurgents are provided with cannon, tents, ammunition, and stores.

It is ascertained that Thomas W. Dorr has returned from the city of New York to the State of Connecticut, and I have reason to believe he will be at Chepachet this day, where he will concentrate what forces he has already under arms with such others as he can collect. Those already assembled are composed of citizens of other States as well as of our own, and are variously estimated at 500 to 1,000 men.

I have this morning had an interview with Colonel Bankhead, who will communicate to the War Department such facts as have come to his knowledge. I would further state to Your Excellency that in those villages and their vicinity the civil authority is disregarded and paralyzed.

Under these circumstances I respectfully submit to Your Excellency that the crisis has arrived when the aid demanded by the legislature of the State from the Federal Government is imperatively required to furnish that protection to our citizens from domestic violence which is guaranteed by the Constitution and laws of the United States.

I confidently trust that Your Excellency will adopt such measures as will afford us prompt and efficient relief.

I remain, with great consideration, your obedient servant,

SAM. W. KING.

WASHINGTON, *June 25, 1842.*

Governor KING.

SIR: Your letter of the 23d instant was this day received by the hands of Governor Sprague, together with the documents accompanying the same. Your excellency has unintentionally overlooked the fact that the legislature of Rhode Island is now in session. The act of Congress gives to the Executive of the United States no power to summon to the aid of the State the military force of the United States unless an application shall be made by the legislature if in session; and that the State executive can not make such application except when the legislature can not be convened. (See act of Congress, February 28, 1795.)

I presume that your excellency has been led into the error of making this application (the legislature of the State being in session at the date of your dispatch) from a misapprehension of the true import of my letter of 7th May last. I lose no time in correcting such misapprehension if it exist.

Should the legislature of Rhode Island deem it proper to make a similar application to that addressed to me by your excellency, their communication shall receive all the attention which will be justly due to the high source from which such application shall emanate.

I renew to your excellency assurances of high consideration.

J. TYLER.

PROVIDENCE, R. I., *June 23, 1842.*

Hon. JOHN C. SPENCER,
    Secretary of War.

SIR: I addressed you yesterday afternoon in great haste, that my letter might go by the mail (then about being closed), to inform you of the sudden change in the aspect of affairs in this State, and also to inform you that I should be this morning at Governors Island, New York.

At the urgent solicitation of Governor King, who crossed over from Newport to Stonington to intercept me on the route, I returned last night to this place from Stonington, having proceeded so far on my way to New York.

In addition to what I stated in my letter yesterday, I learn from Governor King (who has just called on me) that four citizens of this city who had gone to Chepachet to ascertain what was going on there were arrested as spies by the insurgents, bound, and sent last night to Woonsocket, where they were confined when his informer left there at 8 o'clock this morning; also that martial law had been proclaimed by the insurgents at Woonsocket and Chepachet, and no one was allowed to enter or depart from either place without permission.

The citizens of this city are in a state of intense excitement.

I shall return to-morrow to Newport to await any instructions you may be pleased to favor me with.

    I have the honor to be, sir, with great respect, your obedient servant,

JAS. BANKHEAD,
Colonel Second Regiment Artillery.

PROVIDENCE, R. I., *June 23, 1842.*

Brigadier-General R. JONES,
    Adjutant-General United States Army.

SIR: I left Newport yesterday morning to return to Fort Columbus, with the belief that my presence could no longer be necessary for the purpose I had been ordered there for. The legislature was in session, and, as I was well assured, determined honestly and faithfully to adopt measures to meet the wishes of the citizens of this State to form a constitution on such liberal principles as to insure full satisfaction to all patriotic and intelligent men who had any interest in the welfare of the State. The well-known intention of the legislature in this respect would, I hoped and believed, reconcile the factious and produce tranquillity. But the aspect of affairs has suddenly become more threatening and alarming. There is an assemblage of men at Woonsocket and Chepachet, two small villages (say 15 miles distant hence) on the borders of Connecticut, composed principally of strangers or persons from other States. They have recently received 75 muskets from Boston and 80 from New York, in addition to former supplies. They have also several mounted cannon and a large quantity of ammunition, 48 kegs of which they stole from a powder house not far distant from this, the property of a manufacturer of powder. Dorr, it is supposed, joined his party at one of the above-named places the night before last; he has certainly returned from New York and passed through Norwich. His *concentrated* forces are variously estimated at from 500 to 1,000 men.

I had proceeded thus far yesterday afternoon on my return to New York, and had taken my seat in the cars for Stonington, when an express from Governor King, who was at Newport, overtook me, to request that I would not leave the State; too late, however, for me then to stop here, as the cars were just moving off. On getting to Stonington I there found Governor King, who had crossed over from Newport to intercept me, and at his solicitation I at once returned with him last night in an extra car to this place. Not then having a moment's time to write you, as the steamboat left immediately on the arrival of the cars at Stonington, I sent my adjutant on in the boat with directions to report to you the fact and the cause of my return.

I had written thus far when the governor called on me, and has informed me that four citizens of this State, who had gone to Chepachet to ascertain the exact state of affairs there, were arrested as spies, bound, and sent last night to Woonsocket, where two hours ago they were still in confinement. Martial law has been declared in Chepachet and Woonsocket, and no one allowed to enter or depart without permission. I yesterday afternoon wrote to the Secretary of War (as I had been directed), in great haste, however, to send by the mail, to inform him of the sudden change in the aspect of affairs here; in which letter I stated that I should be at Governors Island this morning. As I, of course, then did not contemplate to the contrary, I beg you will do me the favor to acquaint him with the cause of my return.

I can only add that the citizens of this place are in a state of intense anxiety and excitement. I remain here to-day at the special request of several who have just left me. To-morrow I shall return to Newport to await any communication from you.

I am, sir, very respectfully, your obedient servant,

JAS. BANKHEAD,
Colonel Second Regiment Artillery.

PROVIDENCE, R. I., *June 27, 1842.*

SIR:[*] As there was no mail yesterday from this, I could make no report to the Major-General Commanding of the military movements in this quarter up to that time. Since my last letter to you most of the volunteers and other military companies called out by the governor have assembled here to the amount of about 2,000 men. The force of the insurgents under the immediate direction of Mr. Dorr, and concentrated at Chepachet, is estimated at from 800 to 1,000 men armed with muskets, about 1,500 without arms, and 10 or 12 cannon mounted.

It seems to be impossible to avoid a conflict between the contending parties without the interposition of a strong regular force.

The State force here can defend this city, and it might successfully attack the insurgent force at Chepachet; but there would be danger in leaving the city without adequate means of protection to it, as there is doubtless a large number within the city with concealed arms ready to commence hostilities.

The position taken by Dorr's troops at Chepachet is naturally strong, and has been much strengthened by intrenchments, etc. It would therefore be highly imprudent to make the attack, even if no secret foes were left behind within the city, without a positive certainty of success; and with the aid of a few disciplined troops a defeat there would be ruinous and irreparable.

A force of 300 regular troops would insure success, and probably without bloodshed.

I am, sir, very respectfully, your obedient servant,

JAS. BANKHEAD,
Colonel Second Regiment Artillery.

The PRESIDENT OF THE UNITED STATES.   WASHINGTON, *June 27, 1842.*

SIR: The intelligence from Rhode Island since the call was made on you by the Senators from that State is of a character still more serious and urgent than that then communicated to you by Mr. Sprague, who was charged with communications to Your Excellency from Governor King. We are informed that a requisition was made upon the Government of the United States by the governor of Rhode Island, pursuant to resolutions passed by the general assembly of that State when in session in May last, calling for a proclamation against those engaged in an armed rebellion against the government of Rhode Island and for military aid in suppressing the same; that Your Excellency replied to Governor King that in the opinion of the

[*] Addressed to Brigadier-General R. Jones, Adjutant-General United States Army.

Executive the force arrayed against the government of the State was not then such as to warrant immediate action on his part, but that Your Excellency in your reply proceeded to say: "If an exigency of lawless violence shall actually arise, the executive government of the United States, on the application of your excellency under the authority of the resolutions of the legislature already submitted, will stand ready to succor the authorities of the State in their efforts to maintain a due respect for the laws." Whereby it was understood that in the event of the assembling of such an armed force as would require the interference contemplated by the Constitution and laws of the United States the Executive of the United States, upon being duly notified of the fact by the governor of the State, would act upon the requisition already made by the legislature without further action on the part of that body.

We understand that upon this notice being given through the communications handed you by Mr. Sprague on Saturday, containing proof of the existence and array of a large body of armed men within the State of Rhode Island, who had already committed acts of lawless violence, both by depredating largely upon property in various parts of the State and by capturing and confining citizens, as well as owning and manifesting a determination to attack the constituted authorities, you considered that it was desirable that this communication should have been accompanied with a further resolution of the general assembly authorizing the governor to act in this instance, from the fact that the assembly was then in session by adjournment.

It is the purpose of this communication respectfully to state that we conceive the existing circumstances call for the immediate action of the Executive upon the information and papers now in its possession.

The meeting of the legislature during the last week was by adjournment. It is in law regarded as the May session of the general assembly, and can be regarded in no other light than if it had been a continuous session of that body held from day to day by usual adjournments. Had this last been the case, it can not be conceived that new action on its part would have been required to give notice of any movements of hostile forces engaged in the same enterprise which was made known to the Executive by its resolutions of May last.

Our intelligence authorizes us to believe that a multitude of lawless and violent men, not citizens of Rhode Island, but inhabitants of other States, wickedly induced by pay and by hopes of spoil, and perhaps instigated also by motives arising from exasperation on the part of their instigators and of themselves at the course heretofore indicated in this matter by the executive government of the Union, have congregated themselves and are daily increasing their numbers within the borders of our State, organized, armed, and arrayed in open war upon the State authorities, and ready to be led, and avowedly about to be led, to the attack of the principal city of the State as part of the same original plan to overthrow the government, and that in the prosecution of this plan our citizens have reason to apprehend the most desperate and reckless assaults of ruffianly violence upon their property, their habitations, and their lives.

We beg leave to refer you, in addition, to a letter which we understand was received yesterday by General Scott from Colonel Bankhead, detailing some information in his possession.

We therefore respectfully request an immediate compliance on the part of the Executive with the requisition communicated in the papers from Governor King, as the most effectual, and, in our opinion, the only measure that can now prevent the effusion of blood and the calamities of intestine violence, if each has not already occurred.

We are, with the highest respect, Your Excellency's obedient servants,

JAMES F. SIMMONS.
WM. SPRAGUE.
JOSEPH L. TILLINGHAST.

The SECRETARY OF WAR.   WASHINGTON, *June 29, 1842.*

SIR: From the official communication of Colonel Bankhead to you, this day laid before me, it is evident that the difficulties in Rhode Island have arrived at a crisis which may require a prompt interposition of the Executive of the United States to prevent the effusion of blood. From the correspondence already had with the governor of Rhode Island I have reason to expect that a requisition will be immediately made by the government of that State for the assistance guaranteed by the Constitution to protect its citizens from domestic violence. With a view to ascertain the true condition of things and to render the assistance of this Government (if any shall be required) as prompt as may be, you are instructed to proceed to Rhode Island, and, in the event of a requisition being made upon the President in conformity with the laws of the United States, you will cause the proclamation herewith delivered to be published. And should circumstances in your opinion render it necessary, you will also call upon the governors of Massachusetts and Connecticut, or either of them, for such number and description of the militia of their respective States as may be sufficient to terminate at once the insurrection in Rhode Island. And in the meantime the troops in the vicinity of Providence may with propriety be placed in such positions as will enable them to defend that city from assault.

JOHN TYLER.

BY THE PRESIDENT OF THE UNITED STATES·OF AMERICA.

A PROCLAMATION.

Whereas the legislature of the State of Rhode Island has applied to the President of the United States setting forth the existence of a dangerous insurrection in that State, composed partly of deluded citizens of the State, but chiefly of intruders of dangerous and abandoned character coming from other States, and requiring the immediate interposition of the constitutional power vested in him to be exercised in such cases, I do issue this my proclamation, according to law, hereby commanding all insurgents and all persons connected with said insurrection to disperse and retire peaceably to their respective abodes within twenty-four hours from the time when this proclamation shall be made public in Rhode Island.

In testimony whereof I have caused the seal of the United States to be hereunto affixed, and signed the same with my hand.

Done at the city of Washington this —— day of ——, A. D. 1842, and of the Independence of the United States the sixty-sixth.

[L. S.]   JOHN TYLER.

By the President:

DANL. WEBSTER,
Secretary of State.

WASHINGTON, *April 22, 1844.*

To the Senate of the United States:

I transmit herewith, for your approval and ratification, a treaty which I have caused to be negotiated between the United States and Texas, whereby the latter, on the conditions therein set forth, has transferred and conveyed all its right of separate and independent sovereignty and jurisdiction to the United States. In taking so important a step I have been influenced by what appeared to me to be the most controlling considerations of public policy and the general good, and in having accomplished it, should it meet with your approval, the Government will have succeeded in reclaiming a territory which formerly constituted a portion, as it is confidently believed, of its domain under the treaty of cession of 1803 by France to the United States.

The country thus proposed to be annexed has been settled principally by persons from the United States, who emigrated on the invitation of both Spain and Mexico, and who carried with them into the wilderness which they have partially reclaimed the laws, customs, and political and domestic institutions of their native land. They are deeply indoctrinated in all the principles of civil liberty, and will bring along with them in the act of reassociation devotion to our Union and a firm and inflexible resolution to assist in maintaining the public liberty unimpaired—a consideration which, as it appears to me, is to be regarded as of no small moment. The country itself thus obtained is of incalculable value in an agricultural and commercial point of view. To a soil of inexhaustible fertility it unites a genial and healthy climate, and is destined at a day not distant to make large contributions to the commerce of the world. Its territory is separated from the United States in part by an imaginary line, and by the river Sabine for a distance of 310 miles, and its productions are the same with those of many of the contiguous States of the Union. Such is the country, such are its inhabitants, and such its capacities to add to the general wealth of the Union. As to the latter, it may be safely asserted that in the magnitude of its productions it will equal in a short time, under the protecting care of this Government, if it does not surpass, the combined production of many of the States of the Confederacy. A new and powerful impulse will thus be given to the navigating interest of the country, which will be chiefly engrossed by our fellow-citizens of the Eastern and Middle States, who have already attained a remarkable degree of prosperity by the partial monopoly they have enjoyed of the carrying trade of the Union, particularly the coastwise trade, which this new acquisition is destined in time, and that not distant, to swell to a magnitude which can not easily be computed, while the addition made to the boundaries of the home market thus secured to their mining, manufacturing, and mechanical skill and industry will be of a character the most commanding and important. Such are some of the many advantages which will accrue to the Eastern and Middle States by the ratification of the treaty—advantages the extent of which it is impossible to estimate with accuracy or properly to appreciate. Texas, being adapted to the culture of cotton, sugar, and rice, and devoting most of her energies to the raising of these productions, will open an extensive market to the Western States in the important articles of beef, pork, horses, mules, etc., as well as in breadstuffs. At the same time, the Southern and Southeastern States will find in the fact of annexation protection and security to their peace and tranquillity, as well against all domestic as foreign efforts to disturb them, thus consecrating anew the union of the States and holding out the promise of its perpetual duration.

Thus, at the same time that the tide of public prosperity is greatly swollen, an appeal of what appears to the Executive to be of an imposing, if not of a resistless, character is made to the interests of every portion of the country. Agriculture, which would have a new and extensive market opened for its produce; commerce, whose ships would be freighted with the rich productions of an extensive and fertile region; and the mechanical arts, in all their various ramifications, would seem to unite in one universal demand for the ratification of the treaty. But important as these considerations may appear, they are to be regarded as but secondary to others. Texas, for reasons deemed sufficient by herself, threw off her dependence on Mexico as far back as 1836, and consummated her independence by the battle of San Jacinto in the same year, since which period Mexico has attempted no serious invasion of her territory, but the contest has assumed features of a mere border war, characterized by acts revolting to humanity. In the year 1836 Texas adopted her constitution, under which she has existed as a sovereign power ever since, having been recognized as such by many of the principal powers of the world; and contemporaneously with its adoption, by a solemn vote of her people, embracing all her population but ninety-three persons, declared her anxious desire to be admitted into association with the United States as a portion of their territory. This vote, thus solemnly taken, has never been reversed, and now by the action of her constituted authorities, sustained as it is by popular sentiment, she reaffirms her desire for annexation. This course has been adopted by her without the employment of any sinister measures on the part of this Government. No intrigue has been set on foot to accomplish it. Texas herself wills it, and the Executive of the United States, concurring with her, has seen no sufficient reason to avoid the consummation of an act esteemed to be so desirable by both. It can not be denied that Texas is greatly depressed in her energies by her long-protracted war with Mexico. Under these circumstances it is but natural that she should seek for safety and repose under the protection of some stronger power, and it is equally so that her people should turn to the United States, the land of their birth, in the first instance in the pursuit of such protection. She has often before made known her wishes, but her advances have to this time been repelled. The Executive of the United States sees no longer any cause for pursuing such a course. The hazard of now defeating her wishes may be of the most fatal tendency. It might lead, and most probably would, to such an entire alienation of sentiment and feeling as would inevitably induce her to look elsewhere for aid, and force her either to enter into dangerous alliances with other nations, who, looking with more wisdom to their own interests, would, it is fairly to be presumed, readily adopt such expedients; or she would hold out the proffer of discriminating duties in trade and commerce in order to secure the necessary assistance. Whatever step she might adopt looking to this object would prove disastrous in the highest degree to the interests of the whole Union. To say nothing of the impolicy of our permitting the carrying trade and home market of such a country to pass out of our hands into those of a commercial rival, the Government, in the first place, would be certain to suffer most disastrously in its revenue by the introduction of a system of smuggling upon an extensive scale, which an army of custom-house officers could not prevent, and which would operate to affect injuriously the interests of all the industrial classes of this country. Hence would arise constant collisions between the inhabitants of the two countries, which would evermore endanger their peace. A large increase of the military force of the United States would inevitably follow, thus devolving upon the people new and extraordinary burdens in order not only to protect them from the danger of daily collision with Texas herself, but to guard their border inhabitants against hostile inroads, so easily excited on the part of the numerous and warlike tribes of Indians dwelling in their neighborhood. Texas would undoubtedly be unable for many years to come, if at any time, to resist unaided and alone the military power of the United States; but it is not extravagant to suppose that nations reaping a rich harvest from her trade, secured to them by advantageous treaties, would be induced to take part with her in any conflict with us, from the strongest considerations of public policy. Such a state of things might subject to devastation the territory of contiguous States, and would cost the country in a single campaign more treasure, thrice told over, than is stipulated to be paid and reimbursed by the treaty now proposed for ratification. I will not permit myself to dwell on this view of the subject. Consequences of a fatal character to the peace of the Union, and even to the preservation of the Union itself, might be dwelt upon. They will not, however, fail to occur to the mind of the Senate and of the country. Nor do I indulge in any vague conjectures of the future. The documents now transmitted along with the treaty lead to the conclusion, as inevitable, that if the boon now tendered be rejected Texas will seek for the friendship of others. In contemplating such a contingency it can not be overlooked that the United States are already almost surrounded by the possessions of European powers. The Canadas, New Brunswick, and Nova Scotia, the islands in the American seas, with Texas trammeled by treaties of alliance or of a commercial character differing in policy from that of the United States, would complete the circle. Texas voluntarily steps forth, upon terms of perfect honor and good faith to all nations, to ask to be annexed to the Union. As an independent sovereignty her right to do this is unquestionable. In doing so she gives no cause of umbrage to any other power; her people desire it, and there is no slavish transfer of her sovereignty and independence. She has for eight years maintained her independence against all efforts to subdue her. She has been recognized as independent by many of the most prominent of the family of nations, and that recognition, so far as they are concerned, places her in a position, without giving any just cause of umbrage to them, to surrender her sovereignty at her own will and pleasure. The United States, actuated evermore by a spirit of justice, has desired by the stipulations of the treaty to render justice to all. They have made provision for the payment of the public debt of Texas. We look to her ample and fertile domain as the certain means of accomplishing this; but this is a matter between the United States and Texas, and with which other Governments have nothing to do. Our right to receive the rich grant tendered by Texas is perfect, and this Government should not, having due respect either to its own honor or its own interests, permit its course of policy to be interrupted by the interference of other powers, even if such interference were threatened. The question is one purely American. In the acquisition, while we abstain most carefully from all that could interrupt the public peace, we claim the right to exercise a due regard to our own. This Government can not consistently with its honor permit any such interference. With equal, if not greater, propriety might the United States demand of other governments to surrender their numerous and valuable acquisitions made in past time at numberless places on the surface of the globe, whereby they have added to their power and enlarged their resources.

To Mexico the Executive is disposed to pursue a course conciliatory in its character and at the same time to render her the most ample justice by conventions and stipulations not inconsistent with the rights and dignity of the Government. It is actuated by no spirit of unjust aggrandizement, but looks only to its own security. It has made known to Mexico at several periods its extreme anxiety to witness the termination of hostilities between that country and Texas. Its wishes, however, have been entirely disregarded. It has ever been ready to urge an adjustment of the dispute upon terms mutually advantageous to both. It will be ready at all times to hear and discuss any claims Mexico may think she has on the justice of the United States and to adjust any that may be deemed to be so on the most liberal terms. There is no desire on the part of the Executive to wound her pride or affect injuriously her interest, but at the same time it can not compromit by any delay in its action the essential interests of the United States. Mexico has no right to ask or expect this of us; we deal rightfully with Texas as an independent power. The war which has been waged for eight years has resulted only in the conviction with all others than herself that Texas can not be reconquered. I can not but repeat the opinion expressed in my message at the opening of Congress that it is time it had ceased. The Executive, while it could not look upon its longer continuance without the greatest uneasiness, has, nevertheless, for all past time preserved a course of strict neutrality. It could not be ignorant of the fact of the exhaustion which a war of so long a duration had produced. Least of all was it ignorant of the anxiety of other powers to induce Mexico to enter into terms of reconciliation with Texas, which, affecting the domestic institutions of Texas, would operate most injuriously upon the United States and might most seriously threaten the existence of this happy Union. Nor could it be unacquainted with the fact that although foreign governments might disavow all design to disturb the relations which exist under the Constitution between these States, yet that one, the most powerful amongst them, had not failed to declare its marked and decided hostility to the chief feature in those relations and its purpose on all suitable occasions to urge upon Mexico the adoption of such a course in negotiating with Texas as to produce the obliteration of that feature from her domestic policy as one of the conditions of her recognition by Mexico as an independent state. The Executive was also aware of the fact that formidable associations of persons, the subjects of foreign powers, existed, who were directing their utmost efforts to the accomplishment of this object. To these conclusions it was inevitably brought by the documents now submitted to the Senate. I repeat, the Executive saw Texas in a state of almost hopeless exhaustion, and the question was narrowed down to the simple proposition whether the United States should accept the boon of annexation upon fair and even liberal terms, or, by refusing to do so, force Texas to seek refuge in the arms of some other power, either through a treaty of alliance, offensive and defensive, or the adoption of some other expedient which might virtually make her tributary to such power and dependent upon it for all future time. The Executive has full reason to believe that such would have been the result without its interposition, and that such will be the result in the event either of unnecessary delay in the ratification or of the rejection of the proposed treaty.

In full view, then, of the highest public duty, and as a measure of security against evils incalculably great, the Executive has entered into the negotiation, the fruits of which are now submitted to the Senate. Independent of the urgent reasons which existed for the step it has taken, it might safely invoke the fact (which it confidently believes) that there exists no civilized government on earth having a voluntary tender made it of a domain so rich and fertile, so replete with all that can add to national greatness and wealth, and so necessary to its peace and safety that would reject the offer. Nor are other powers, Mexico inclusive, likely in any degree to be injuriously affected by the ratification of the treaty. The prosperity of Texas will be equally interesting to all; in the increase of the general commerce of the world that prosperity will be secured by annexation.

But one view of the subject remains to be presented. It grows out of the proposed enlargement of our territory. From this, I am free to confess, I see no danger. The federative system is susceptible of the greatest extension compatible with the ability of the representation of the most distant State or Territory to reach the seat of Government in time to participate in the functions of legislation and to make known the wants of the constituent body. Our confederated Republic consisted originally of th:. en members. It now consists of twice that number, while appli-ᵧ⁻ .ᵤs are before Congress to permit other additions. This addition of new States has served to strengthen rather than to weaken the Union. New interests have sprung up, which require the united power of all, through the action of the common Government, to protect and defend upon the high seas and in foreign parts. Each State commits with perfect security to that common Government those great interests growing out of our relations with other nations of the world, and which equally involve the good of all the States. Its domestic concerns are left to its own exclusive management. But if there were any force in the objec-. tion it would seem to require an immediate abandonment of territorial possessions which lie in the distance and stretch to a far-off sea, and yet no one would be found, it is believed, ready to recommend such an abandonment. Texas lies at our very doors and in our immediate vicinity.

Under every view which I have been able to take of the subject, I think that the interests of our common constituents, the people of all the States, and a love of the Union left the Executive no other alternative than to negotiate the treaty. The high and solemn duty of ratifying or rejecting it is wisely devolved on the Senate by the Constitution of the United States.

JOHN TYLER.

WASHINGTON, *April 22, 1844.*

To the Senate of the United States:

I transmit herewith an additional article to the treaty of extradition lately concluded between the Governments of France and the United States, for your approval and ratification. The reason upon which it is founded is explained on the face of the article and in the letter from Mr. Pageot which accompanies this communication.

JOHN TYLER.

WASHINGTON, *April 26, 1844.*

To the Senate of the United States:

In compliance with the resolution of the Senate of the 22d instant, requesting the President to communicate to that body any communication, papers, or maps in possession of this Government specifying the southern, southwestern, and western boundaries of Texas, I transmit a map of Texas and the countries adjacent, compiled in the Bureau of Topographical Engineers, under the direction of Colonel J. J. Abert, by Lieutenant U. E. Emory, of that Corps, and also a memoir upon the subject by the same officer.

JOHN TYLER.

To the Senate of the United States:

In my annual message at the commencement of the present session of Congress I informed the two Houses that instructions had been given by the Executive to the United States envoy at Berlin to negotiate a commercial treaty with the States composing the Germanic Customs Union for a reduction of the duties on tobacco and other agricultural productions of the United States, in exchange for concessions on our part in relation to certain articles of export the product of the skill and industry of those countries. I now transmit a treaty which proposes to carry into effect the views and intentions thus previously expressed and declared, accompanied by two dispatches from Mr. Wheaton, our minister at Berlin. This is believed to be the first instance in which the attempt has proved successful to obtain a reduction of the heavy and onerous duties to which American tobacco is subject in foreign markets, and, taken in connection with the greatly reduced duties on rice and lard and the free introduction of raw cotton, for which the treaty provides, I can not but anticipate from its ratification important benefits to the great agricultural, commercial, and navigating interests of the United States. The concessions on our part relate to articles which are believed not to enter injuriously into competition with the manufacturing interest of the United States, while a country of great extent and embracing a population of 28,000,000 human beings will more thoroughly than heretofore be thrown open to the commercial enterprise of our fellow-citizens.

Inasmuch as the provisions of the treaty come to some extent in conflict with existing laws, it is my intention, should it receive your approval and ratification, to communicate a copy of it to the House of Representatives, in order that that House may take such action upon it as it may deem necessary to give efficiency to its provisions.

JOHN TYLER.

APRIL 29, 1844.

WASHINGTON, *April 29, 1844.*

To the Senate of the United States:

I herewith transmit to the Senate, with reference to my message of the 22d instant, the copy of a recent correspondence* between the Department of State and the minister of Her Britannic Majesty in this country.

JOHN TYLER.

WASHINGTON, *April 29, 1844.*

To the Senate of the United States:

I transmit to the Senate a report of the Secretary of War, prepared in compliance with the request contained in a resolution of the 10th instant.†

JOHN TYLER.

* With reference to the annexation of Texas.
† Proceedings under act of March 3, 1843, for the relief of the Stockbridge tribe of Indians in the Territory of Wisconsin.

WASHINGTON, *May 1, 1844.*

To the Senate of the United States:

I transmit herewith a dispatch from the British minister, addressed to the Secretary of State, bearing date the 30th April, in reply to the letter of the Secretary of State of the 27th April, which has already been communicated to the Senate, having relation to the Texas treaty.

JOHN TYLER.

WASHINGTON, *May 3, 1844.*

To the Senate of the United States:

In answer to the resolution of the Senate of the 29th ultimo, requesting a copy of additional papers upon the subject of the relations between the United States and the Republic of Texas, I transmit a report from the Secretary of State and the documents by which it was accompanied.

JOHN TYLER.

WASHINGTON, *May 6, 1844.*

To the Senate of the United States:

I herewith transmit the accompanying correspondence, relating to the treaty recently concluded by the minister of the United States at Berlin with the States comprising the Zollverein.

JOHN TYLER.

To the House of Representatives: WASHINGTON, *May 6, 1844.*

I transmit to the House of Representatives a report* of the Secretary of War, prepared as requested by the resolution of the House of the 18th of January last.

JOHN TYLER.

To the House of Representatives: WASHINGTON, *May 6, 1844.*

I transmit herewith a report and accompanying documents from the Secretary of War, containing all the information that can be now furnished by that Department, in answer to the resolution of the House of Representatives of the 18th of January, respecting the allowance of claims previously rejected.

JOHN TYLER.

WASHINGTON, *May 7, 1844.*

To the Senate of the United States:

I transmit to the Senate, for its consideration with a view to ratification, a postal convention between the United States and the Republic of New Granada, signed in the city of Bogota on the 6th of March last.

---

* Transmitting lists of persons employed by the War Department since March 4, 1837, without express authority of law, etc.

In order that the Senate may better understand the objects of the convention and the motives which have made those objects desirable on the part of the United States, I also transmit a copy of a correspondence between the Department of State and the chairman of the Committee on Commerce in the Senate, and between the same Department and Mr. Blackford, the chargé d'affaires of the United States at Bogota, who concluded the convention on the part of this Government.

JOHN TYLER.

WASHINGTON, *May 10, 1844.*

To the Senate of the United States:

I deem it proper to transmit the accompanying dispatch, recently received from the United States envoy at London, having reference to the treaty now before the Senate lately negotiated by Mr. Wheaton, our envoy at Berlin, with the Zollverein.

I will not withhold the expression of my full assent to the views expressed by Mr. Everett in his conference with Lord Aberdeen.

JOHN TYLER.

To the House of Representatives: WASHINGTON, *May 10, 1844.*

I communicate to Congress a letter from the Imaum of Muscat and a translation of it, together with sundry other papers, by which it will be perceived that His Highness has been pleased again to offer to the United States a present of Arabian horses. These animals will be in Washington in a short time, and will be disposed of in such manner as Congress may think proper to direct.

JOHN TYLER.

WASHINGTON, *May 11, 1844.*

To the Senate of the United States:

I herewith communicate to the Senate, for its consideration, two conventions concluded by the minister of the United States at Berlin—the one with the Kingdom of Wurtemberg, dated on the 10th day of April, and the other with the Grand Duchy of Hesse, dated on the 26th day of March, 1844—for the mutual abolition of the *droit d'aubaine* and the *droit de detraction* between those Governments and the United States, and I communicate with the conventions copies of the correspondence necessary to explain the reasons for concluding them.

JOHN TYLER.

WASHINGTON, *May 15, 1844.*

To the Senate of the United States:

In answer to the resolution of the Senate of the 13th instant, requesting to be informed "whether, since the commencement of the negotiations

which resulted in the treaty now before the Senate for the annexation
of Texas to the United States, any military preparation has been made
or ordered by the President for or in anticipation of war, and, if so, for
what cause, and with whom was such war apprehended, and what are
the preparations that have been made or ordered; has any movement
or assemblage or disposition of any of the military or naval forces of the
United States been made or ordered with a view to such hostilities; and
to communicate to the Senate copies of all orders or directions given
for any such preparation or for any such movement or disposition or for
the future conduct of such military or naval forces,'' I have to inform the
Senate that, in consequence of the declaration of Mexico communicated
to this Government and by me laid before Congress at the opening of its
present session, announcing the determination of Mexico to regard as a
declaration of war against her by the United States the definitive ratification of any treaty with Texas annexing the territory of that Republic to
the United States, and the hope and belief entertained by the Executive
that the treaty with Texas for that purpose would be speedily approved
and ratified by the Senate, it was regarded by the Executive to have
become emphatically its duty to concentrate in the Gulf of Mexico and
its vicinity, as a precautionary measure, as large a portion of the home
squadron, under the command of Captain Conner, as could well be drawn
together, and at the same time to assemble at Fort Jesup, on the borders
of Texas, as large a military force as the demands of the service at other
encampments would authorize to be detached. For the number of ships
already in the Gulf and the waters contiguous thereto and such as are
placed under orders for that destination, and of troops now assembled
upon the frontier, I refer you to the accompanying reports from the Secretaries of the War and Navy Departments. It will also be perceived by
the Senate, by referring to the orders of the Navy Department which are
herewith transmitted, that the naval officer in command of the fleet is
directed to cause his ships to perform all the duties of a fleet of observation and to apprise the Executive of any indication of a hostile design
upon Texas on the part of any nation pending the deliberations of the
Senate upon the treaty, with a view that the same should promptly be
submitted to Congress for its mature deliberation. At the same time, it
is due to myself that I should declare it as my opinion that the United
States having by the treaty of annexation acquired a title to Texas which
requires only the action of the Senate to perfect it, no other power could
be permitted to invade and by force of arms to possess itself of any portion of the territory of Texas pending your deliberations upon the treaty
without placing itself in an hostile attitude to the United States and
justifying the employment of any military means at our disposal to drive
back the invasion. At the same time, it is my opinion that Mexico or
any other power will find in your approval of the treaty no just cause of
war against the United States, nor do I believe that there is any serious

hazard of war to be found in the fact of such approval.   Nevertheless, every proper measure will be resorted to by the Executive to preserve upon an honorable and just basis the public peace by reconciling Mexico, through a liberal course of policy, to the treaty.

JOHN TYLER.

WASHINGTON, *May 15, 1844.*

To the Senate of the United States:

In answer to the resolution of the Senate of the 13th instant, requesting to be informed ''whether a messenger has been sent to Mexico with a view to obtain her consent to the treaty with Texas, and, if so, to communicate to the Senate a copy of the dispatches of which he is bearer and a copy of the instructions given to said messenger; and also to inform the Senate within what time said messenger is expected to return,'' I have to say that no messenger has been sent to Mexico in order to obtain her assent to the treaty with Texas, it not being regarded by the Executive as in any degree requisite to obtain such consent in order (should the Senate ratify the treaty) to perfect the title of the United States to the territory thus acquired, the title to the same being full and perfect without the assent of any third power.   The Executive has negotiated with Texas as an independent power of the world, long since recognized as such by the United States and other powers, and as subordinate in all her rights of full sovereignty to no other power.   A messenger has been dispatched to our minister at Mexico as bearer of the dispatch already communicated to the Senate, and which is to be found in the letter addressed to Mr. Green, and forms a part of the documents ordered confidentially to be printed for the use of the Senate.   That dispatch was dictated by a desire to preserve the peace of the two countries by denying to Mexico all pretext for assuming a belligerent attitude to the United States, as she had threatened to do, in the event of the annexation of Texas to the United States, by the dispatch of her Government which was communicated by me to Congress at the opening of its present session.   The messenger is expected to return before the 15th of June next, but he may be detained to a later day.   The recently appointed envoy from the United States to Mexico will be sent so soon as the final action is had on the question of annexation, at which time, and not before, can his instructions be understandingly prepared.

JOHN TYLER.

WASHINGTON, *May 16, 1844.*

To the Senate of the United States:

In my message communicating the treaty with Texas I expressed the opinion that if Texas was not now annexed it was probable that the opportunity of annexing it to the United States would be lost forever.   Since then the subject has been much agitated, and if an opinion may be formed of the chief ground of the opposition to the treaty, it is not that Texas ought not at some time or other to be annexed, but that the present is not the proper time. It becomes, therefore, important, in this view of the subject, and is alike due to the Senate and the country, that I should furnish any papers in my possession which may be calculated to impress the Senate with the correctness of the opinion thus expressed by me. With this view I herewith transmit a report from the Secretary of State, accompanied by various communications on the subject. These communications are from private sources, and it is to be remarked that a resort must in all such cases be had chiefly to private sources of information, since it is not to be expected that any government, more especially if situated as Texas is, would be inclined to develop to the world its ulterior line of policy.

Among the extracts is one from a letter from General Houston to General Andrew Jackson, to which I particularly invite your attention, and another from General Jackson to a gentleman of high respectability, now of this place. Considering that General Jackson was placed in a situation to hold the freest and fullest interview with Mr. Miller, the private and confidential secretary of President Houston, who, President Houston informed General Jackson, "knows all his actions and understands all his motives," and who was authorized to communicate to General Jackson the views of the policy entertained by the President of Texas, as well applicable to the present as the future; that the declaration made by General Jackson in his letter "that the present golden moment to obtain Texas must not be lost, or Texas might from necessity be thrown into the arms of England and be forever lost to the United States," was made with a full knowledge of all circumstances, and ought to be received as conclusive of what will be the course of Texas should the present treaty fail—from this high source, sustained, if it requires to be sustained, by the accompanying communications, I entertain not the least doubt that if annexation should now fail it will in all human probability fail forever. Indeed, I have strong reasons to believe that instructions have already been given by the Texan Government to propose to the Government of Great Britain, forthwith on the failure, to enter into a treaty of commerce and an alliance offensive and defensive.

JOHN TYLER.

WASHINGTON, *May 17, 1844.*

To the Senate of the United States:

In answer to the resolution of the Senate of the 13th instant, relating to a supposed armistice between the Republics of Mexico and Texas, I transmit a report from the Secretary of State and the papers by which it was accompanied.

JOHN TYLER.

WASHINGTON, *May 18, 1844.*

To the Senate of the United States:

In answer to the resolution of the Senate of the 29th ultimo, upon the subject of unpublished correspondence in regard to the purchase of or title to Texas, I transmit a report from the Secretary of State and the documents by which it was accompanied.

JOHN TYLER.

WASHINGTON, *May 18, 1844.*

To the House of Representatives of the United States:

In answer to a resolution of the House of Representatives of the 3d of January last, requesting the President of the United States "to cause to be communicated to that House copies of all the instructions given to the commanding officers of the squadron stipulated by the treaty with Great Britain of 9th of August, 1842, to be kept on the coast of Africa for the suppression of the slave trade," and also copies of the "instructions given by the British Government to their squadron stipulated by the same, if such instructions have been communicated to this Government," I have to inform the House of Representatives that in my opinion it would be incompatible with the public interests to communicate to that body at this time copies of the instructions referred to.

JOHN TYLER.

To the House of Representatives:

WASHINGTON, *May 20, 1844.*

In compliance with a resolution of the House of Representatives of the 22d ultimo, I communicate a report * from the Secretary of State, which embraces the information called for by said resolution.

JOHN TYLER.

To the House of Representatives:

WASHINGTON, *May 20, 1844.*

I herewith transmit a letter from the Secretary of the Navy, accompanied by a report from the Bureau of Construction and Equipment and a communication from Lieutenant Hunter, of the Navy, prepared at the request of the Secretary, upon the subject of a plan for the establishment in connection with the Government of France of a line of steamers between the ports of Havre and New York, with estimates of the expense which may be necessary to carry the said plan into effect.

JOHN TYLER.

WASHINGTON, *May 23, 1844.*

To the Senate of the United States:

Your resolution of the 18th instant, adopted in *executive* session, addressed to the Secretary of the Treasury *ad interim*, has been commu-

---

* Relating to indemnity from Denmark for three ships and their cargoes sent by Commodore John Paul Jones in 1779 as prizes into Bergen, and there surrendered by order of the Danish King to the British minister, in obedience to the demand of that minister.

nicated to me by that officer. While I can not recognize this call thus made on the head of a Department as consistent with the constitutional rights of the Senate when acting in its executive capacity, which in such case can only properly hold correspondence with the President of the United States, nevertheless, from an anxious desire to lay before the Senate all such information as may be necessary to enable it with full understanding to act upon any subject which may be before it, I herewith transmit communications* which have been made to me by the Secretaries of the War and Navy Departments, in full answer to the resolution of the Senate.

JOHN TYLER.

WASHINGTON CITY, D. C., *May 24, 1844.*

To the House of Representatives of the United States:

I transmit herewith a report † from the Secretary of the Navy, in compliance with the resolution of the House of Representatives of the 18th of January last.

JOHN TYLER.

WASHINGTON, *May 31, 1844.*

To the Senate of the United States:

In answer to the resolution of the Senate of the 22d instant, requesting information in regard to any promise by the President of military or other aid to Texas in the event of an agreement on the part of that Republic to annex herself to the United States, I transmit a report from the Secretary of State and the documents by which it was accompanied.

In my message to the Senate of the 15th of this month I adverted to the duty which, in my judgment, the signature of the treaty for the annexation of Texas had imposed upon me, to repel any invasion of that country by a foreign power while the treaty was under consideration by the Senate, and I transmitted reports from the Secretaries of War and of the Navy, with a copy of the orders which had been issued from those Departments for the purpose of enabling me to execute that duty. In those orders General Taylor was directed to communicate directly with the President of Texas upon the subject, and Captain Conner was instructed to communicate with the chargé d'affaires of the United States accredited to that Government. No copy of any communication which either of those officers may have made pursuant to those orders has yet been received at the Departments from which they emanated.

JOHN TYLER.

---

*Relating to money drawn from the Treasury to carry into effect orders of the War and Navy Departments made since April 12, 1844, for stationing troops or increasing the military force upon the frontiers of Texas and the Gulf of Mexico and for placing a naval force in the Gulf of Mexico, etc.

† Transmitting list of persons employed by the Navy Department without express authority of law from March 4, 1837, to January 18, 1844, etc.

WASHINGTON, *June 1, 1844.*

To the Senate of the United States:

I transmit herewith to the Senate a copy of a letter dated the 25th of August, 1829, addressed by Mr. Van Buren, Secretary of State, to Mr. Poinsett, envoy extraordinary and minister plenipotentiary of the United States to Mexico, which letter contains, it is presumed, the instructions a copy of which was requested by the resolution of the Senate of the 28th ultimo in executive session.

JOHN TYLER.

WASHINGTON, *June 3, 1844.*

To the Senate of the United States:

In answer to the resolution of the Senate of the 28th ultimo, upon the subject of a "private letter" quoted in the instruction from the late Mr. Upshur to the chargé d'affaires of the United States in Texas, dated the 8th of August last, I transmit a report from the Secretary of State, to whom the resolution was referred.

JOHN TYLER.

WASHINGTON, *June 4, 1844.*

To the Senate of the United States:

In answer to the resolution of the Senate of yesterday in executive session, requesting a copy of a note supposed to have been addressed to the Secretary of State by the diplomatic agents of the Republic of Texas accredited to this Government, I transmit a report from the Secretary of State, to whom the resolution was referred.

JOHN TYLER.

WASHINGTON, *June 5, 1844.*

To the Senate of the United States:

I herewith transmit to the Senate, with reference to previous Executive communications to that body relating to the same subject, the copy of a letter* recently received at the Department of State from the minister of the United States in London.

JOHN TYLER.

WASHINGTON, *June 7, 1844.*

To the House of Representatives of the United States:

I herewith transmit to the House of Representatives the copy of a letter recently addressed to the Secretary of State by the British minister at Washington, with the view of ascertaining "whether it would be agreeable to this Government that an arrangement should be concluded for the transmission through the United States of the mails to and from

---

* Relating to the treaty of annexation with Texas.

Canada and England, which are now landed at Halifax and thence forwarded through the British dominions to their destination.''

It will be perceived that this communication has been referred to the Postmaster-General, and his opinion respecting the proposition will accordingly be found in his letter to the Department of State of the 5th instant, a copy of which is inclosed. I lose no time in recommending the subject to the favorable consideration of the House and in bespeaking for it early attention.

JOHN TYLER.

To the House of Representatives: WASHINGTON, *June 8, 1844.*

In compliance with a resolution of the House of Representatives of the 29th of April last, I communicate to that body a report* from the Secretary of State, which embraces the information called for by that resolution.

JOHN TYLER.

WASHINGTON, *June 10, 1844.*

To the House of Representatives of the United States:

The treaty negotiated by the Executive with the Republic of Texas, without a departure from any form of proceeding customarily observed in the negotiations of treaties for the annexation of that Republic to the United States, having been rejected by the Senate, and the subject having excited on the part of the people no ordinary degree of interest, I feel it to be my duty to communicate, for your consideration, the rejected treaty, together with all the correspondence and documents which have heretofore been submitted to the Senate in its executive sessions. The papers communicated embrace not only the series already made public by orders of the Senate, but others from which the veil of secrecy has not been removed by that body, but which I deem to be essential to a just appreciation of the entire question. While the treaty was pending before the Senate I did not consider it compatible with the just rights of that body or consistent with the respect entertained for it to bring this important subject before you. The power of Congress is, however, fully competent in some other form of proceeding to accomplish everything that a formal ratification of the treaty could have accomplished, and I therefore feel that I should but imperfectly discharge my duty to yourselves or the country if I failed to lay before you everything in the possession of the Executive which would enable you to act with full light on the subject if you should deem it proper to take any action upon it.

I regard the question involved in these proceedings as one of vast magnitude and as addressing itself to interests of an elevated and enduring character. A Republic coterminous in territory with our own, of

*Transmitting correspondence from 1816 to 1820, inclusive, between United States ministers to Spain and the Department of State, between those ministers and Spanish secretaries of state, and between the Department of State and the Spanish ministers accredited to the United States.

immense resources, which require only to be brought under the influence of our confederate and free system in order to be fully developed, promising at no distant day, through the fertility of its soil, nearly, if not entirely, to duplicate the exports of the country, thereby making an addition to the carrying trade to an amount almost incalculable and giving a new impulse of immense importance to the commercial, manufacturing, agricultural, and shipping interests of the Union, and at the same time affording protection to an exposed frontier and placing the whole country in a condition of security and repose; a territory settled mostly by emigrants from the United States, who would bring back with them in the act of reassociation an unconquerable love of freedom and an ardent attachment to our free institutions—such a question could not fail to interest most deeply in its success those who under the Constitution have become responsible for the faithful administration of public affairs. I have regarded it as not a little fortunate that the question involved was no way sectional or local, but addressed itself to the interests of every part of the country and made its appeal to the glory of the American name.

It is due to the occasion to say that I have carefully reconsidered the objections which have been urged to immediate action upon the subject without in any degree having been struck by their force. It has been objected that the measure of annexation should be preceded by the consent of Mexico. To preserve the most friendly relations with Mexico; to concede to her, not grudgingly, but freely, all her rights; to negotiate fairly and frankly with her as to the question of boundary; to render her, in a word, the fullest and most ample recompense for any loss she might convince us she had sustained, fully accords with the feelings and views the Executive has always entertained.

But negotiation in advance of annexation would prove not only abortive, but might be regarded as offensive to Mexico and insulting to Texas. Mexico would not, I am persuaded, give ear for a moment to an attempt at negotiation in advance except for the whole territory of Texas. While all the world beside regards Texas as an independent power, Mexico chooses to look upon her as a revolted province. Nor could we negotiate with Mexico for Texas without admitting that our recognition of her independence was fraudulent, delusive, or void. It is only after acquiring Texas that the question of boundary can arise between the United States and Mexico—a question purposely left open for negotiation with Mexico as affording the best opportunity for the most friendly and pacific arrangements. The Executive has dealt with Texas as a power independent of all others, both *de facto* and *de jure*. She was an independent State of the Confederation of Mexican Republics. When by violent revolution Mexico declared the Confederation at an end, Texas owed her no longer allegiance, but claimed and has maintained the right for eight years to a separate and distinct position. During that period no army has invaded her with a view to her reconquest; and if she has not yet established her right to be treated as a nation independent *de facto* and *de jure*, it would be difficult to say at what period she will attain to that condition.

Nor can we by any fair or any legitimate inference be accused of violating any treaty stipulations with Mexico. The treaties with Mexico give no guaranty of any sort and are coexistent with a similar treaty with Texas. So have we treaties with most of the nations of the earth which are equally as much violated by the annexation of Texas to the United States as would be our treaty with Mexico. The treaty is merely commercial and intended as the instrument for more accurately defining the rights and securing the interests of the citizens of each country. What bad faith can be implied or charged upon the Government of the United States for successfully negotiating with an independent power upon any subject not violating the stipulations of such treaty I confess my inability to discern.

The objections which have been taken to the enlargement of our territory were urged with much zeal against the acquisition of Louisiana, and yet the futility of such has long since been fully demonstrated. Since that period a new power has been introduced into the affairs of the world, which has for all practical purposes brought Texas much nearer to the seat of Government than Louisiana was at the time of its annexation. Distant regions are by the application of the steam engine brought within a close proximity.

With the views which I entertain on the subject, I should prove faithless to the high trust which the Constitution has devolved upon me if I neglected to invite the attention of the representatives of the people to it at the earliest moment that a due respect for the Senate would allow me so to do. I should find in the urgency of the matter a sufficient apology, if one was wanting, since annexation is to encounter a great, if not certain, hazard of final defeat if something be not *now* done to prevent it. Upon this point I can not too impressively invite your attention to my message of the 16th of May and to the documents which accompany it, which have not heretofore been made public. If it be objected that the names of the writers of some of the private letters are withheld, all that I can say is that it is done for reasons regarded as altogether adequate, and that the writers are persons of the first respectability and citizens of Texas, and have such means of obtaining information as to entitle their statements to full credit. Nor has anything occurred to weaken, but, on the contrary, much to confirm, my confidence in the statements of General Jackson, and my own statement, made at the close of that message, in the belief, amounting almost to certainty, ''that instructions have already been given by the Texan Government to propose to the Government of Great Britain, forthwith on the failure [of the treaty], to enter into a treaty of commerce and an alliance offensive and defensive.''

I also particularly invite your attention to the letter from Mr. Everett, our envoy at London, containing an account of a conversation in the House of Lords which lately occurred between Lord Brougham and Lord Aberdeen in relation to the question of annexation. Nor can I do so without the expression of some surprise at the language of the minister of foreign affairs employed upon the occasion. That a Kingdom which is made what it now is by repeated acts of annexation—beginning with the time of the heptarchy and concluding with the annexation of the Kingdoms of Ireland and Scotland—should perceive any principle either novel or serious in the late proceedings of the American Executive in regard to Texas is well calculated to excite surprise. If it be pretended that because of commercial or political relations which may exist between the two countries neither has a right to part with its sovereignty, and that no third power can change those relations by a voluntary treaty of union or annexation, then it would seem to follow that an annexation to be achieved by force of arms in the prosecution of a just and necessary war could in no way be justified; and yet it is presumed that Great Britain would be the last nation in the world to maintain any such doctrine. The commercial and political relations of many of the countries of Europe have undergone repeated changes by voluntary treaties, by conquest, and by partitions of their territories without any question as to the right under the public law. The question, in this view of it, can be considered as neither "serious" nor "novel." I will not permit myself to believe that the British minister designed to bring himself to any such conclusion, but it is impossible for us to be blind to the fact that the statements contained in Mr. Everett's dispatch are well worthy of serious consideration. The Government and people of the United States have never evinced nor do they feel any desire to interfere in public questions not affecting the relations existing between the States of the American continent. We leave the European powers exclusive control over matters affecting their continent and the relations of their different States; the United States claim a similar exemption from any such interference on their part. The treaty with Texas was negotiated from considerations of high public policy, influencing the conduct of the two Republics. We have treated with Texas as an independent power solely with a view of bettering the condition of the two countries. If annexation in any form occur, it will arise from the free and unfettered action of the people of the two countries; and it seems altogether becoming in me to say that the honor of the country, the dignity of the American name, and the permanent interests of the United States would forbid acquiescence in any such interference. No one can more highly appreciate the value of peace to both Great Britain and the United States and the capacity of each to do injury to the other than myself, but peace can best be preserved by maintaining firmly the rights which belong to us as an independent community.

So much have I considered it proper for me to say; and it becomes me only to add that while I have regarded the annexation to be accomplished by treaty as the most suitable form in which it could be effected, should Congress deem it proper to resort to any other expedient compatible with the Constitution and likely to accomplish the object I stand prepared to yield my most prompt and active cooperation.

The great question is not as to the manner in which it shall be done, but whether it shall be accomplished or not.

The responsibility of deciding this question is now devolved upon you.

JOHN TYLER.

WASHINGTON, *June 10, 1844.*

To the Senate of the United States:

In answer to the resolution of the Senate of the 7th instant, upon the subject of the supposed employment of Mr. Duff Green in Europe by the Executive of the United States, I transmit a report from the Secretary of State, to whom the resolution was referred.

JOHN TYLER.

WASHINGTON, *June 12, 1844.*

To the Senate of the United States:

In compliance with the resolution of the Senate of the 4th instant, calling for a correspondence* between the late minister of the United States in Mexico and the minister for foreign affairs of that Republic, I transmit a report from the Secretary of State and the documents by which it was accompanied.

JOHN TYLER.

To the Senate of the United States: WASHINGTON, *June, 1844.*

The resolution of the Senate of the 3d instant, requesting the President to lay before that body, confidentially, "a copy of any instructions which may have been given by the Executive to the American minister in England on the subject of the title to and occupation of the Territory of Oregon since the 4th of March, 1841; also a copy of any correspondence which may have passed between this Government and that of Great Britain in relation to the subject since that time," has been received.

In reply I have to state that in the present state of the subject-matter to which the resolution refers it is deemed inexpedient to communicate the information requested by the Senate.

JOHN TYLER.

* On the subject of an order issued by the Mexican Government expelling all natives of the United States from Upper California and other departments of the Mexican Republic, and of the order prohibiting foreigners the privilege of the retail trade in Mexico.

WASHINGTON, *June 15, 1844.*

To the House of Representatives of the United States:

I herewith transmit to the House of Representatives, in answer to their resolution of the 4th instant, a report from the Secretary of State, with the correspondence * therein referred to. JOHN TYLER.

WASHINGTON, *June 17, 1844.*

The PRESIDENT OF THE SENATE:

I transmit herewith a report from the Secretary of State, in answer to a resolution of the 12th instant. Although the contingent fund for foreign intercourse has for all time been placed at the disposal of the President, to be expended for the purposes contemplated by the fund without any requisition upon him for a disclosure of the names of persons employed by him, the objects of their employment, or the amount paid to any particular person, and although any such disclosures might in many cases disappoint the objects contemplated by the appropriation of that fund, yet in this particular instance I feel no desire to withhold the fact that Mr. Duff Green was employed by the Executive to collect such information, from private or other sources, as was deemed important to assist the Executive in undertaking a negotiation then contemplated, but afterwards abandoned, upon an important subject, and that there was paid to him through the hands of the Secretary of State $1,000, in full for all such service. It is proper to say that Mr. Green afterwards presented a claim for an additional allowance, which has been neither allowed nor recognized as correct. JOHN TYLER.

WASHINGTON, *June 17, 1844.*

To the Senate:

I have learned that the Senate has laid on the table the nomination, heretofore made, of Reuben H. Walworth to be an associate justice of the Supreme Court, in the place of Smith Thompson, deceased. I am informed that a large amount of business has accumulated in the second district, and that the immediate appointment of a judge for that circuit is essential to the administration of justice. Under these circumstances I feel it my duty to withdraw the name of Mr. Walworth, whose appointment the Senate by their action seems not now prepared to confirm, in the hope that another name may be more acceptable.

The circumstances under which the Senate heretofore declined to advise and consent to the nomination of John C. Spencer have so far changed as to justify me in my again submitting his name to their consideration.

I therefore nominate John C. Spencer, of New York, to be appointed an associate justice of the Supreme Court, in the place of Smith Thompson, deceased. JOHN TYLER.

* With Great Britain relative to the duties exacted by that Government on rough rice exported from the United States, contrary to the treaty of 1815.

VETO MESSAGES.*

WASHINGTON, *December 18, 1843.*

To the House of Representatives:

I received within a few hours of the adjournment of the last Congress a resolution "directing payment of the certificates or awards issued by the commissioners under the treaty with the Cherokee Indians." Its provisions involved principles of great importance, in reference to which it required more time to obtain the necessary information than was allowed.

The balance of the fund provided by Congress for satisfying claims under the seventeenth article of the Cherokee treaty, referred to in the resolution, is wholly insufficient to meet the claims still pending. To direct the payment, therefore, of the whole amount of those claims which happened to be first adjudicated would prevent a ratable distribution of the fund among those equally entitled to its benefits. Such a violation of the individual rights of the claimants would impose upon the Government the obligation of making further appropriations to indemnify them, and thus Congress would be obliged to enlarge a provision, liberal and equitable, which it had made for the satisfaction of all the demands of the Cherokees. I was unwilling to sanction a measure which would thus indirectly overturn the adjustment of our differences with the Cherokees, accomplished with so much difficulty, and to which time is reconciling those Indians.

If no such indemnity should be provided, then a palpable and very gross wrong would be inflicted upon the claimants who had not been so fortunate as to have their claims taken up in preference to others. Besides, the fund having been appropriated by law to a specific purpose, in fulfillment of the treaty, it belongs to the Cherokees, and the authority of this Government to direct its application to particular claims is more than questionable.

The direction in the joint resolution, therefore, to pay the awards of the commissioners to the amount of $100,000 seemed to me quite objectionable, and could not be approved.

The further direction that the certificates required to be issued by the treaty, and in conformity with the practice of the board heretofore, shall be proper and sufficient vouchers, upon which payments shall be made at the Treasury, is a departure from the system established soon after the adoption of the Constitution and maintained ever since. That system requires that payments under the authority of any Department shall be made upon its requisition, countersigned by the proper Auditor and Comptroller. The greatest irregularity would ensue from the mode of payment prescribed by the resolution.

* The first is a pocket veto.

I have deemed it respectful and proper to lay before the House of Representatives these reasons for having withheld my approval of the above-mentioned joint resolution.

JOHN TYLER.

WASHINGTON, *June 11, 1844.*

To the House of Representatives of the United States:

I return to the House of Representatives, in which it originated, the bill entitled "An act making appropriations for the improvement of certain harbors and rivers," with the following objections to its becoming a law:

At the adoption of the Constitution each State was possessed of a separate and independent sovereignty and an exclusive jurisdiction over all streams and water courses within its territorial limits. The Articles of Confederation in no way affected this authority or jurisdiction, and the present Constitution, adopted for the purpose of correcting the defects which existed in the original Articles, expressly reserves to the States all powers not delegated. No such surrender of jurisdiction is made by the States to this Government by any express grant, and if it is possessed it is to be deduced from the clause in the Constitution which invests Congress with authority "to make all laws which are necessary and proper for carrying into execution" the granted powers. There is, in my view of the subject, no pretense whatever for the claim to power which the bill now returned substantially sets up. The inferential power, in order to be legitimate, must be clearly and plainly incidental to some granted power and necessary to its exercise. To refer it to the head of convenience or usefulness would be to throw open the door to a boundless and unlimited discretion and to invest Congress with an unrestrained authority. The power to remove obstructions from the water courses of the States is claimed under the granted power "to regulate commerce with foreign nations, *among the several States*, and with the Indian tribes;" but the plain and obvious meaning of this grant is that Congress may adopt rules and regulations prescribing the terms and conditions on which the citizens of the United States may carry on commercial operations with foreign states or kingdoms, and on which the citizens or subjects of foreign states or kingdoms may prosecute trade with the United States or either of them. And so the power to regulate commerce *among the several States* no more invests Congress with jurisdiction over the water courses of the States than the first branch of the grant does over the water courses of foreign powers, which would be an absurdity.

The right of common use of the people of the United States to the navigable waters of each and every State arises from the express stipulation contained in the Constitution that "the citizens of each State shall be entitled to all privileges and immunities of citizens in the several States." While, therefore, the navigation of any river in any State is by the laws of such State allowed to the citizens thereof, the same is also secured by the Constitution of the United States on the same terms and conditions to the citizens of every other State; and so of any other privilege or immunity.

The application of the revenue of this Government, if the power to do so was admitted, to improving the navigation of the rivers by removing obstructions or otherwise would be for the most part productive only of local benefit. The consequences might prove disastrously ruinous to as many of our fellow-citizens as the exercise of such power would benefit. I will take one instance furnished by the present bill—out of no invidious feeling, for such it would be impossible for me to feel, but because of my greater familiarity with locations—in illustration of the above opinion: Twenty thousand dollars are proposed to be appropriated toward improving the harbor of Richmond, in the State of Virginia. Such improvement would furnish advantages to the city of Richmond and add to the value of the property of its citizens, while it might have a most disastrous influence over the wealth and prosperity of Petersburg, which is situated some 25 miles distant on a branch of James River, and which now enjoys its fair portion of the trade. So, too, the improvement of James River to Richmond and of the Appomattox to Petersburg might, by inviting the trade to those two towns, have the effect of prostrating the town of Norfolk. This, too, might be accomplished without adding a single vessel to the number now engaged in the trade of the Chesapeake Bay or bringing into the Treasury a dollar of additional revenue. It would produce, most probably, the single effect of concentrating the commerce now profitably enjoyed by three places upon one of them. This case furnishes an apt illustration of the effect of this bill in several other particulars.

There can not, in fact, be drawn the slightest discrimination between the improving the streams of a State under the power to regulate commerce and the most extended system of internal improvements on land. The excavating a canal and paving a road are equally as much incidents to such claim of power as the removing obstructions from water courses; nor can such power be restricted by any fair course of reasoning to the mere fact of making the improvement. It reasonably extends also to the right of seeking a return of the means expended through the exaction of tolls and the levying of contributions. Thus, while the Constitution denies to this Government the privilege of acquiring a property in the soil of any State, even for the purpose of erecting a necessary fortification, without a grant from such State, this claim to power would invest it with control and dominion over the waters and soil of each State without restriction. Power so incongruous can not exist in the same instrument.

The bill is also liable to a serious objection because of its blending appropriations for numerous objects but few of which agree in their general features. This necessarily produces the effect of embarrassing Executive action. Some of the appropriations would receive my sanction if separated from the rest, however much I might deplore the reproduction of a system which for some time past has been permitted to sleep with apparently the acquiescence of the country. I might particularize the Delaware Breakwater as an improvement which looks to the security from the storms of our extended Atlantic seaboard of the vessels of all the country engaged either in the foreign or the coastwise trade, as well as to the safety of the revenue; but when, in connection with that, the same bill embraces improvements of rivers at points far in the interior, connected alone with the trade of such river and the exertion of mere local influences, no alternative is left me but to use the qualified veto with which the Executive is invested by the Constitution, and to return the bill to the House in which it originated for its ultimate reconsideration and decision.

In sanctioning a bill of the same title with that returned, for the improvement of the Mississippi and its chief tributaries and certain harbors on the Lakes, if I bring myself apparently in conflict with any of the principles herein asserted it will arise on my part exclusively from the want of a just appreciation of localities. The Mississippi occupies a footing altogether different from the rivers and water courses of the different States. No one State or any number of States can exercise any other jurisdiction over it than for the punishment of crimes and the service of civil process. It belongs to no particular State or States, but of common right, by express reservation, to all the States. It is reserved as a great common highway for the commerce of the whole country. To have conceded to Louisiana, or to any other State admitted as a new State into the Union, the exclusive jurisdiction, and consequently the right to make improvements and to levy tolls on the segments of the river embraced within its territorial limits, would have been to have disappointed the chief object in the purchase of Louisiana, which was to secure the free use of the Mississippi to all the people of the United States. Whether levies on commerce were made by a foreign or domestic government would have been equally burdensome and objectionable. The United States, therefore, is charged with its improvement for the benefit of all, and the appropriation of governmental means to its improvement becomes indispensably necessary for the good of all.

As to the harbors on the Lakes, the act originates no new improvements, but makes appropriations for the continuance of works already begun.

It is as much the duty of the Government to construct good harbors, without reference to the location or interests of cities, for the shelter of the extensive commerce of the Lakes as to build breakwaters on the Atlantic coast for the protection of the trade of that ocean. These great inland seas are visited by destructive storms, and the annual loss of ships and cargoes, and consequently of revenue to the Government, is immense. If, then, there be any work embraced by that act which is not required in order to afford shelter and security to the shipping against the tempests which so often sweep over those great inland seas, but has, on the contrary, originated more in a spirit of speculation and local interest than in one of the character alluded to, the House of

Representatives will regard my approval of the bill more as the result of misinformation than any design to abandon or modify the principles laid down in this message. Every system is liable to run into abuse, and none more so than that under consideration; and measures can not be too soon taken by Congress to guard against this evil.

JOHN TYLER.

EXECUTIVE ORDERS.

CIRCULAR.*

DEPARTMENT OF STATE,
Washington, February 29, 1844.

SIR: It has become my most painful duty to announce to you the sudden and violent death of the Hon. Abel P. Upshur, late Secretary of State of the United States. This afflicting dispensation occurred on the afternoon of yesterday, from the bursting of one of the great guns on board the Government steamship *Princeton*, near Alexandria, on her return from an excursion of pleasure down the river Potomac. By this most unfortunate accident several of our distinguished citizens, amongst whom were the Secretaries of State and of the Navy, were immediately killed, and many other persons mortally wounded or severely injured. It is the wish of the President that the diplomatic and consular agents of the United States, and all other officers connected with the State Department, either at home or abroad, shall wear the usual badge of mourning, in token of their grief and of respect for the memory of Mr. Upshur, during thirty days from the time of receiving this order.

In consequence of this event, the President has been pleased to charge me *ad interim* with the direction of the Department of State, and I have accordingly this day entered upon the duties of this appointment.

I have the honor to be, with great respect, sir, your obedient servant,

JNO. NELSON.

GENERAL ORDERS.

WAR DEPARTMENT, *February 29, 1844.*

In the deepest grief the President of the United States has instructed the undersigned to announce to the Army that from the accidental explosion of a gun yesterday on board the United States steamship *Princeton* the country and its Government lost at the same moment the Secretary of State, the Hon. A. P. Upshur, and the Secretary of the Navy, the Hon. T. W. Gilmer.

Called but a few days since to preside over the administration of the War Department, it is peculiarly painful to the undersigned that his first official communication to the Army should be the announcement of a

---

* Sent to all diplomatic and consular officers of the United States.

calamity depriving the country of the public services of two of our most accomplished statesmen and popular and deeply esteemed fellow-citizens. Their virtues, talents, and patriotic services will ever be retained in the grateful recollection of their countrymen and perpetuated upon the pages of the history of our common country.

Deep as may be the gloom which spreads over the community, it has pleased the Almighty Disposer of Events to add another shade to it by blending in this melancholy catastrophe the deaths of an eminent citizen, Virgil Maxcy, esq., lately chargé d'affaires to Belgium; a gallant and meritorious officer of the Navy, a chief of a bureau, Captain B. Kennon, and a private citizen of New York of high and estimable character, besides others, citizens and sailors, either killed or wounded.

As appropriate honors to the memory of these distinguished Secretaries, half-hour guns will be fired at every military post furnished with the proper ordnance the day after the receipt of this order from sunrise to sunset. The national flag will be displayed at half-staff during the same time. And all officers of the Army will wear for three months the customary badge of mourning.

WM. WILKINS,
Secretary of War.

GENERAL ORDER.

NAVY DEPARTMENT, *February 29, 1844.*

As a mark of respect to the memory of the late Hon. Thomas W. Gilmer, Secretary of the Navy, whose career at his entrance upon the duties of his office, would have been nobly maintained by that ability and vigor of which his whole previous life had been the guaranty, the flags of all vessels in commission, navy-yards, and stations are to be hoisted at half-mast on the day after the receipt of this order, minute guns to the number of seventeen are to be fired between sunrise and sunset, and crape is to be worn on the left arm and upon the sword for the space of three months.

By command of the President:

L. WARRINGTON,
Secretary of the Navy ad interim.

FOURTH ANNUAL MESSAGE.

WASHINGTON, *December 3, 1844.*

To the Senate and House of Representatives of the United States:

We have continued cause for expressing our gratitude to the Supreme Ruler of the Universe for the benefits and blessings which our country, under His kind providence, has enjoyed during the past year. Notwithstanding the exciting scenes through which we have passed, nothing has occurred to disturb the general peace or to derange the harmony of our political system. The great moral spectacle has been exhibited of a nation approximating in number to 20,000,000 people having performed the high and important function of electing their Chief Magistrate for the term of four years without the commission of any acts of violence or the manifestation of a spirit of insubordination to the laws. The great and inestimable right of suffrage has been exercised by all who were invested with it under the laws of the different States in a spirit dictated alone by a desire, in the selection of the agent, to advance the interests of the country and to place beyond jeopardy the institutions under which it is our happiness to live. That the deepest interest has been manifested by all our countrymen in the result of the election is not less true than highly creditable to them. Vast multitudes have assembled from time to time at various places for the purpose of canvassing the merits and pretensions of those who were presented for their suffrages, but no armed soldiery has been necessary to restrain within proper limits the popular zeal or to prevent violent outbreaks. A principle much more controlling was found in the love of order and obedience to the laws, which, with mere individual exceptions, everywhere possesses the American mind, and controls with an influence far more powerful than hosts of armed men. We can not dwell upon this picture without recognizing in it that deep and devoted attachment on the part of the people to the institutions under which we live which proclaims their perpetuity. The great objection which has always prevailed against the election by the people of their chief executive officer has been the apprehension of tumults and disorders which might involve in ruin the entire Government. A security against this is found not only in the fact before alluded to, but in the additional fact that we live under a Confederacy embracing already twenty-six States, no one of which has power to control the election. The popular vote in each State is taken at the time appointed by the laws, and such vote is announced by the electoral college without reference to the decision of other States. The right of suffrage and the mode of conducting the election are regulated by the laws of each State, and the election is distinctly federative in all its prominent features. Thus it is that, unlike what might be the results under a consolidated system, riotous proceedings, should they prevail, could only affect the elections in single States without disturbing to any dangerous extent the tranquillity of others. The great experiment of a political confederation each member of which is supreme as to all matters appertaining to its local interests and its internal peace and happiness, while by a voluntary compact with others it confides to the united power of all the protection of its citizens in matters not domestic has been so far crowned with complete success. The world has witnessed its rapid growth in wealth and population, and under the guide and direction of a superintending Providence the developments of the past may be regarded but as the shadowing forth of the mighty future. In the bright prospects of that future we shall find, as patriots and philanthropists, the highest inducements to cultivate and cherish a love of union and to frown down every measure or effort which may be made to alienate the States or the people of the States in sentiment and feeling from each other. A rigid and close adherence to the terms of our political compact and, above all, a sacred observance of the guaranties of the Constitution will preserve union on a foundation which can not be shaken, while personal liberty is placed beyond hazard or jeopardy. The guaranty of religious freedom, of the freedom of the press, of the liberty of speech, of the trial by jury, of the habeas corpus, and of the domestic institutions of each of the States, leaving the private citizen in the full exercise of the high and ennobling attributes of his nature and to each State the privilege (which can only be judiciously exerted by itself) of consulting the means best calculated to advance its own happiness—these are the great and important guaranties of the Constitution which the lovers of liberty must cherish and the advocates of union must ever cultivate. Preserving these and avoiding all interpolations by forced construction under the guise of an imagined expediency upon the Constitution, the influence of our political system is destined to be as actively and as beneficially felt on the distant shores of the Pacific as it is now on those of the Atlantic Ocean. The only formidable impediments in the way of its successful expansion (time and space) are so far in the progress of modification by the improvements of the age as to render no longer speculative the ability of representatives from that remote region to come up to the Capitol, so that their constituents shall participate in all the benefits of Federal legislation. Thus it is that in the progress of time the inestimable principles of civil liberty will be enjoyed by millions yet unborn and the great benefits of our system of government be extended to now distant and uninhabited regions. In view of the vast wilderness yet to be reclaimed, we may well invite the lover of freedom of every land to take up his abode among us and assist us in the great work of advancing the standard of civilization and giving a wider spread to the arts and refinements of cultivated life. Our prayers should evermore be offered up to the Father of the Universe for His wisdom to direct us in the path of our duty so as to enable us to consummate these high purposes.

One of the strongest objections which has been urged against confederacies by writers on government is the liability of the members to be tampered with by foreign governments or the people of foreign states, either in their local affairs or in such as affected the peace of others or endangered the safety of the whole confederacy. We can not hope to be entirely exempt from such attempts on our peace and safety. The United States are becoming too important in population and resources not to attract the observation of other nations. It therefore may in the progress of time occur that opinions entirely abstract in the States in which they may prevail and in no degree affecting their domestic institutions may be artfully but secretly encouraged with a view to undermine the Union. Such opinions may become the foundation of political parties, until at last the conflict of opinion, producing an alienation of friendly feeling among the people of the different States, may involve in general destruction the happy institutions under which we live. It should ever be borne in mind that what is true in regard to individuals is equally so in regard to states. An interference of one in the affairs of another is the fruitful cause of family dissensions and neighborhood disputes, and the same cause affects the peace, happiness, and prosperity of states. It may be most devoutly hoped that the good sense of the American people will ever be ready to repel all such attempts should they ever be made.

There has been no material change in our foreign relations since my last annual message to Congress. With all the powers of Europe we continue on the most friendly terms. Indeed, it affords me much satisfaction to state that at no former period has the peace of that enlightened and important quarter of the globe ever been, apparently, more firmly established. The conviction that peace is the true policy of nations would seem to be growing and becoming deeper amongst the enlightened everywhere, and there is no people who have a stronger interest in cherishing the sentiments and adopting the means of preserving and giving it permanence than those of the United States. Amongst these, the first and most effective are, no doubt, the strict observance of justice and the honest and punctual fulfillment of all engagements. But it is not to be forgotten that in the present state of the world it is no less necessary to be ready to enforce their observance and fulfillment in reference to ourselves than to observe and fulfill them on our part in regard to others.

Since the close of your last session a negotiation has been formally entered upon between the Secretary of State and Her Britannic Majesty's minister plenipotentiary and envoy extraordinary residing at Washington relative to the rights of their respective nations in and over the Oregon Territory. That negotiation is still pending. Should it during your session be brought to a definitive conclusion, the result will be promptly communicated to Congress. I would, however, again call your attention to the recommendations contained in previous messages designed to protect and facilitate emigration to that Territory. The establishment of military posts at suitable points upon the extended line of land travel would enable our citizens to emigrate in comparative safety to the fertile regions below the Falls of the Columbia, and make the provision of the existing convention for the joint occupation of the territory by subjects of Great Britain and the citizens of the United States more available than heretofore to the latter. These posts would constitute places of rest for the weary emigrant, where he would be sheltered securely against the danger of attack from the Indians and be enabled to recover from the exhaustion of a long line of travel. Legislative enactments should also be made which should spread over him the ægis of our laws, so as to afford protection to his person and property when he shall have reached his distant home. In this latter respect the British Government has been much more careful of the interests of such of her people as are to be found in that country than the United States. She has made necessary provision for their security and protection against the acts of the viciously disposed and lawless, and her emigrant reposes in safety under the panoply of her laws. Whatever may be the result of the pending negotiation, such measures are necessary. It will afford me the greatest pleasure to witness a happy and favorable termination to the existing negotiation upon terms compatible with the public honor, and the best efforts of the Government will continue to be directed to this end.

It would have given me the highest gratification in this my last annual communication to Congress to have been able to announce to you the complete and entire settlement and adjustment of other matters in difference between the United States and the Government of Her Britannic Majesty, which were adverted to in a previous message. It is so obviously the interest of both countries, in respect to the large and valuable commerce which exists between them, that all causes of complaint, however inconsiderable, should be with the greatest promptitude removed that it must be regarded as cause of regret that any unnecessary delays should be permitted to intervene. It is true that in a pecuniary point of view the matters alluded to are altogether insignificant in amount when compared with the ample resources of that great nation, but they nevertheless, more particularly that limited class which arise under seizures and detentions of American ships on the coast of Africa upon the mistaken supposition indulged in at the time the wrong was committed of their being engaged in the slave trade, deeply affect the sensibilities of this Government and people. Great Britain, having recognized her responsibility to repair all such wrongs by her action in other cases, leaves nothing to be regretted upon the subject as to all cases arising prior to the treaty of Washington than the delay in making suitable reparation in such of them as fall plainly within the principle of others which she has long since adjusted. The injury inflicted by delays in the settlement of these claims falls with severity upon the individual claimants and makes a strong appeal to her magnanimity and sense of justice for a speedy settlement. Other matters arising out of the construction of existing treaties also remain unadjusted, and will continue to be urged upon her attention.

The labors of the joint commission appointed by the two Governments to run the dividing line established by the treaty of Washington were, unfortunately, much delayed in the commencement of the season by the failure of Congress at its last session to make a timely appropriation of funds to meet the expenses of the American party, and by other causes.

The United States commissioner, however, expresses his expectation that by increased diligence and energy the party will be able to make up for lost time.

We continue to receive assurances of the most friendly feelings on the part of all the other European powers, with each and all of whom it is so obviously our interest to cultivate the most amicable relations; nor can I anticipate the occurrence of any event which would be likely in any degree to disturb those relations. Russia, the great northern power, under the judicious sway of her Emperor, is constantly advancing in the road of science and improvement, while France, guided by the counsels of her wise Sovereign, pursues a course calculated to consolidate the general peace. Spain has obtained a breathing spell of some duration from the internal convulsions which have through so many years marred her prosperity, while Austria, the Netherlands, Prussia, Belgium, and the other powers of Europe reap a rich harvest of blessings from the prevailing peace.

I informed the two Houses of Congress in my message of December last that instructions had been given to Mr. Wheaton, our minister at Berlin, to negotiate a treaty with the Germanic States composing the Zollverein if it could be done, stipulating, as far as it was practicable to accomplish it, for a reduction of the heavy and onerous duties levied on our tobacco and other leading articles of agricultural production, and yielding in return on our part a reduction of duties on such articles the product of their industry as should not come into competition, or but a limited one, with articles the product of our manufacturing industry. The Executive in giving such instructions considered itself as acting in strict conformity with the wishes of Congress as made known through several measures which it had adopted, all directed to the accomplishment of this important result. The treaty was therefore negotiated, by which essential reductions were secured in the duties levied by the Zollverein on tobacco, rice, and lard, accompanied by a stipulation for the admission of raw cotton free of duty; in exchange for which highly important concessions a reduction of duties imposed by the laws of the United States on a variety of articles, most of which were admitted free of all duty under the act of Congress commonly known as the compromise law, and but few of which were produced in the United States, was stipulated for on our part. This treaty was communicated to the Senate at an early day of its last session, but not acted upon until near its close, when, for the want (as I am bound to presume) of full time to consider it, it was laid upon the table. This procedure had the effect of virtually rejecting it, in consequence of a stipulation contained in the treaty that its ratifications should be exchanged on or before a day which has already passed. The Executive, acting upon the fair inference that the Senate did not intend its absolute rejection, gave instructions to our minister at Berlin to reopen the negotiation so far as to obtain an extension of time for the exchange of ratifications. I regret, however, to say that his efforts in this respect have been unsuccessful. I am nevertheless not without hope that the great advantages which were intended to be secured by the treaty may yet be realized.

I am happy to inform you that Belgium has, by an *"arrêté royale"* issued in July last, assimilated the flag of the United States to her own, so far as the direct trade between the two countries is concerned. This measure will prove of great service to our shipping interest, the trade having heretofore been carried on chiefly in foreign bottoms. I flatter myself that she will speedily resort to a modification of her system relating to the tobacco trade, which would decidedly benefit the agriculture of the United States and operate to the mutual advantage of both countries.

No definitive intelligence has yet been received from our minister of the conclusion of a treaty with the Chinese Empire, but enough is known to induce the strongest hopes that the mission will be crowned with success.

With Brazil our relations continue on the most friendly footing. The commercial intercourse between that growing Empire and the United States is becoming daily of greater importance to both, and it is to the interest of both that the firmest relations of amity and good will should continue to be cultivated between them.

The Republic of New Granada still withholds, notwithstanding the most persevering efforts have been employed by our chargé d'affaires, Mr. Blackford, to produce a different result, indemnity in the case of the brig *Morris;* and the Congress of Venezuela, although an arrangement has been effected between our minister and the minister of foreign affairs of that Government for the payment of $18,000 in discharge of its liabilities in the same case, has altogether neglected to make provision for its payment. It is to be hoped that a sense of justice will soon induce a settlement of these claims.

Our late minister to Chili, Mr. Pendleton, has returned to the United States without having effected an adjustment in the second claim of the *Macedonian*, which is delayed on grounds altogether frivolous and untenable. Mr. Pendleton's successor has been directed to urge the claim in the strongest terms, and, in the event of a failure to obtain a prompt adjustment, to report the fact to the Executive at as early a day as possible, so that the whole matter may be communicated to Congress.

At your last session I submitted to the attention of Congress the convention with the Republic of Peru of the 17th March, 1841, providing for the adjustment of the claims of citizens of the United States against that Republic, but no definitive action was taken upon the subject. I again invite to it your attention and prompt action.

In my last annual message I felt it to be my duty to make known to Congress, in terms both plain and emphatic, my opinion in regard to the war which has so long existed between Mexico and Texas, which since the battle of San Jacinto has consisted altogether of predatory incursions, attended by circumstances revolting to humanity. I repeat now what I then said, that after eight years of feeble and ineffectual efforts to reconquer Texas it was time that the war should have ceased. The United States have a direct interest in the question. The contiguity of the two nations to our territory was but too well calculated to involve our peace. Unjust suspicions were engendered in the mind of one or the other of the belligerents against us, and as a necessary consequence American interests were made to suffer and our peace became daily endangered; in addition to which it must have been obvious to all that the exhaustion produced by the war subjected both Mexico and Texas to the interference of other powers, which, without the interposition of this Government, might eventuate in the most serious injury to the United States. This Government from time to time exerted its friendly offices to bring about a termination of hostilities upon terms honorable alike to both the belligerents. Its efforts in this behalf proved unavailing. Mexico seemed almost without an object to persevere in the war, and no other alternative was left the Executive but to take advantage of the well-known dispositions of Texas and to invite her to enter into a treaty for annexing her territory to that of the United States.

Since your last session Mexico has threatened to renew the war, and has either made or proposes to make formidable preparations for invading Texas. She has issued decrees and proclamations, preparatory to the commencement of hostilities, full of threats revolting to humanity, and which if carried into effect would arouse the attention of all Christendom. This new demonstration of feeling, there is too much reason to believe, has been produced in consequence of the negotiation of the late treaty of annexation with Texas. The Executive, therefore, could not be indifferent to such proceedings, and it felt it to be due as well to itself as to the honor of the country that a strong representation should be made to the Mexican Government upon the subject. This was accordingly done, as will be seen by the copy of the accompanying dispatch from the Secretary of State to the United States envoy at Mexico. Mexico has no right to jeopard the peace of the world by urging any longer a useless and fruitless contest. Such a condition of things would not be tolerated on the European continent. Why should it be on this? A war of desolation, such as is now threatened by Mexico, can not be waged without involving our peace and tranquillity. It is idle to believe that such a war could be looked upon with indifference by our own citizens inhabiting adjoining States; and our neutrality would be violated in despite of all efforts on the part of the Government to prevent it. The country is settled by emigrants from the United States under invitations held out to them by Spain and Mexico. Those emigrants have left behind them friends and relatives, who would not fail to sympathize with them in their difficulties, and who would be led by those sympathies to participate in their struggles, however energetic the action of the Government to prevent it.   Nor would the numerous and formidable bands of Indians—the most warlike to be found in any land—which occupy the extensive regions contiguous to the States of Arkansas and Missouri, and who are in possession of large tracts of country within the limits of Texas, be likely to remain passive.   The inclinations of those numerous tribes lead them invariably to war whenever pretexts exist.

Mexico had no just ground of displeasure against this Government or people for negotiating the treaty.   What interest of hers was affected by the treaty?   She was despoiled of nothing, since Texas was forever lost to her.   The independence of Texas was recognized by several of the leading powers of the earth.   She was free to treat, free to adopt her own line of policy, free to take the course which she believed was best calculated to secure her happiness.

Her Government and people decided on annexation to the United States, and the Executive saw in the acquisition of such a territory the means of advancing their permanent happiness and glory.   What principle of good faith, then, was violated?   What rule of political morals trampled under foot?   So far as Mexico herself was concerned, the measure should have been regarded by her as highly beneficial.   Her inability to reconquer Texas had been exhibited, I repeat, by eight (now nine) years of fruitless and ruinous contest.   In the meantime Texas has been growing in population and resources.   Emigration has flowed into her territory from all parts of the world in a current which continues to increase in strength.   Mexico requires a permanent boundary between that young Republic and herself.   Texas at no distant day, if she continues separate and detached from the United States, will inevitably seek to consolidate her strength by adding to her domain the contiguous Provinces of Mexico.   The spirit of revolt from the control of the central Government has heretofore manifested itself in some of those Provinces, and it is fair to infer that they would be inclined to take the first favorable opportunity to proclaim their independence and to form close alliances with Texas.   The war would thus be endless, or if cessations of hostilities should occur they would only endure for a season.   The interests of Mexico, therefore, could in nothing be better consulted than in a peace with her neighbors which would result in the establishment of a permanent boundary.   Upon the ratification of the treaty the Executive was prepared to treat with her on the most liberal basis.   Hence the boundaries of Texas were left undefined by the treaty.   The Executive proposed to settle these upon terms that all the world should have pronounced just and reasonable.   No negotiation upon that point could have been undertaken between the United States and Mexico in advance of the ratification of the treaty.   We should have had no right, no power, no authority, to have conducted such a negotiation, and to have undertaken it would have been an assumption equally revolting to the pride of Mexico and Texas and subjecting us to the charge of arrogance, while to have proposed in advance of annexation to satisfy Mexico for any contingent interest she might have in Texas would have been to have treated Texas not as an independent power, but as a mere dependency of Mexico. This assumption could not have been acted on by the Executive without setting at defiance your own solemn declaration that that Republic was an independent State. Mexico had, it is true, threatened war against the United States in the event the treaty of annexation was ratified. The Executive could not permit itself to be influenced by this threat. It represented in this the spirit of our people, who are ready to sacrifice much for peace, but nothing to intimidation. A war under any circumstances is greatly to be deplored, and the United States is the last nation to desire it; but if, as the condition of peace, it be required of us to forego the unquestionable right of treating with an independent power of our own continent upon matters highly interesting to both, and that upon a naked and unsustained pretension of claim by a third power to control the free will of the power with whom we treat, devoted as we may be to peace and anxious to cultivate friendly relations with the whole world, the Executive does not hesitate to say that the people of the United States would be ready to brave all consequences sooner than submit to such condition. But no apprehension of war was entertained by the Executive, and I must express frankly the opinion that had the treaty been ratified by the Senate it would have been followed by a prompt settlement, to the entire satisfaction of Mexico, of every matter in difference between the two countries. Seeing, then, that new preparations for hostile invasion of Texas were about to be adopted by Mexico, and that these were brought about because Texas had adopted the suggestions of the Executive upon the subject of annexation, it could not passively have folded its arms and permitted a war, threatened to be accompanied by every act that could mark a barbarous age, to be waged against her because she had done so.

Other considerations of a controlling character influenced the course of the Executive. The treaty which had thus been negotiated had failed to receive the ratification of the Senate. One of the chief objections which was urged against it was found to consist in the fact that the question of annexation had not been submitted to the ordeal of public opinion in the United States. However untenable such an objection was esteemed to be, in view of the unquestionable power of the Executive to negotiate the treaty and the great and lasting interests involved in the question, I felt it to be my duty to submit the whole subject to Congress as the best expounders of popular sentiment. No definitive action having been taken on the subject by Congress, the question referred itself directly to the decision of the States and people. The great popular election which has just terminated afforded the best opportunity of ascertaining the will of the States and the people upon it. Pending that issue it became the imperative duty of the Executive to inform Mexico that the question of annexation was still before the American people, and that until their decision was pronounced any serious invasion of Texas would be regarded as an attempt to forestall their judgment and could not be looked upon with indifference. I am most happy to inform you that no such invasion has taken place; and I trust that whatever your action may be upon it Mexico will see the importance of deciding the matter by a resort to peaceful expedients in preference to those of arms. The decision of the people and the States on this great and interesting subject has been decisively manifested. The question of annexation has been presented nakedly to their consideration. By the treaty itself all collateral and incidental issues which were calculated to divide and distract the public councils were carefully avoided. These were left to the wisdom of the future to determine. It presented, I repeat, the isolated question of annexation, and in that form it has been submitted to the ordeal of public sentiment. A controlling majority of the people and a large majority of the States have declared in favor of immediate annexation. Instructions have thus come up to both branches of Congress from their respective constituents in terms the most emphatic. It is the will of both the people and the States that Texas shall be annexed to the Union promptly and immediately. It may be hoped that in carrying into execution the public will thus declared all collateral issues may be avoided. Future Legislatures can best decide as to the number of States which should be formed out of the territory when the time has arrived for deciding that question. So with all others. By the treaty the United States assumed the payment of the debts of Texas to an amount not exceeding $10,000,000, to be paid, with the exception of a sum falling short of $400,000, exclusively out of the proceeds of the sales of her public lands. We could not with honor take the lands without assuming the full payment of all incumbrances upon them.

Nothing has occurred since your last session to induce a doubt that the dispositions of Texas remain unaltered. No intimation of an altered determination on the part of her Government and people has been furnished to the Executive. She still desires to throw herself under the protection of our laws and to partake of the blessings of our federative system, while every American interest would seem to require it. The extension of our coastwise and foreign trade to an amount almost incalculable, the enlargement of the market for our manufactures, a constantly growing market for our agricultural productions, safety to our frontiers, and additional strength and stability to the Union—these are the results which would rapidly develop themselves upon the consummation of the measure of annexation. In such event I will not doubt but that Mexico would find her true interest to consist in meeting the advances of this Government in a spirit of amity. Nor do I apprehend any serious complaint from any other quarter; no sufficient ground exists for such complaint. We should interfere in no respect with the rights of any other nation. There can not be gathered from the act any design on our part to do so with their possessions on this continent. We have interposed no impediments in the way of such acquisitions of territory, large and extensive as many of them are, as the leading powers of Europe have made from time to time in every part of the world. We seek no conquest made by war. No intrigue will have been resorted to or acts of diplomacy essayed to accomplish the annexation of Texas. Free and independent herself, she asks to be received into our Union. It is a question for our own decision whether she shall be received or not.

The two Governments having already agreed through their respective organs on the terms of annexation, I would recommend their adoption by Congress in the form of a joint resolution or act to be perfected and made binding on the two countries when adopted in like manner by the Government of Texas.

In order that the subject may be fully presented in all its bearings, the correspondence which has taken place in reference to it since the adjournment of Congress between the United States, Texas, and Mexico is herewith transmitted.

The amendments proposed by the Senate to the convention concluded between the United States and Mexico on the 20th of November, 1843, have been transmitted through our minister for the concurrence of the Mexican Government, but, although urged thereto, no action has yet been had on the subject, nor has any answer been given which would authorize a favorable conclusion in the future.

The decree of September, 1843, in relation to the retail trade, the order for the expulsion of foreigners, and that of a more recent date in regard to passports—all which are considered as in violation of the treaty of amity and commerce between the two countries—have led to a correspondence of considerable length between the minister for foreign relations and our representatives at Mexico, but without any satisfactory result. They remain still unadjusted, and many and serious inconveniences have already resulted to our citizens in consequence of them.

Questions growing out of the act of disarming a body of Texan troops under the command of Major Snively by an officer in the service of the United States, acting under the orders of our Government, and the forcible entry into the custom-house at Bryarlys Landing, on Red River, by certain citizens of the United States, and taking away therefrom the goods seized by the collector of the customs as forfeited under the laws of Texas, have been adjusted so far as the powers of the Executive extend. The correspondence between the two Governments in reference to both subjects will be found amongst the accompanying documents. It contains a full statement of all the facts and circumstances, with the views taken on both sides and the principles on which the questions have been adjusted. It remains for Congress to make the necessary appropriation to carry the arrangement into effect, which I respectfully recommend.

The greatly improved condition of the Treasury affords a subject for general congratulation. The paralysis which had fallen on trade and commerce, and which subjected the Government to the necessity of resorting to loans and the issue of Treasury notes to a large amount, has passed away, and after the payment of upward of $7,000,000 on account of the interest, and in redemption of more than $5,000,000 of the public debt which falls due on the 1st of January next, and setting apart upward of $2,000,000 for the payment of outstanding Treasury notes and meeting an installment of the debts of the corporate cities of the District of Columbia, an estimated surplus of upward of $7,000,000 over and above the existing appropriations will remain in the Treasury at the close of the fiscal year. Should the Treasury notes continue outstanding as heretofore, that surplus will be considerably augmented. Although all interest has ceased upon them and the Government has invited their return to the Treasury, yet they remain outstanding, affording great facilities to commerce, and establishing the fact that under a well-regulated system of finance the Government has resources within itself which render it independent in time of need, not only of private loans, but also of bank facilities.

The only remaining subject of regret is that the remaining stocks of the Government do not fall due at an earlier day, since their redemption would be entirely within its control. As it is, it may be well worthy the consideration of Congress whether the law establishing the sinking fund (under the operation of which the debts of the Revolution and last war with Great Britain were to a great extent extinguished) should not, with proper modifications, so as to prevent an accumulation of surpluses, and limited in amount to a specific sum, be reenacted. Such provision, which would authorize the Government to go into the market for a purchase of its own stock on fair terms, would serve to maintain its credit at the highest point and prevent to a great extent those fluctuations in the price of its securities which might under other circumstances affect its credit. No apprehension of this sort is at this moment entertained, since the stocks of the Government, which but two years ago were offered for sale to capitalists at home and abroad at a depreciation, and could find no purchasers, are now greatly above par in the hands of the holders; but a wise and prudent forecast admonishes us to place beyond the reach of contingency the public credit.

It must also be a matter of unmingled gratification that under the existing financial system (resting upon the act of 1789 and the resolution of 1816) the currency of the country has attained a state of perfect soundness; and the rates of exchange between different parts of the Union, which in 1841 denoted by their enormous amount the great depreciation and, in fact, worthlessness of the currency in most of the States, are now reduced to little more than the mere expense of transporting specie from place to place and the risk incident to the operation. In a new country like that of the United States, where so many inducements are held out for speculation, the depositories of the surplus revenue, consisting of banks of any description, when it reaches any considerable amount, require the closest vigilance on the part of the Government. All banking institutions, under whatever denomination they may pass, are governed by an almost exclusive regard to the interest of the stockholders. That interest consists in the augmentation of profits in the form of dividends, and a large surplus revenue intrusted to their custody is but too apt to lead to excessive loans and to extravagantly large issues of paper. As a necessary consequence prices are nominally increased and the speculative mania very soon seizes upon the public mind. A fictitious state of prosperity for a season exists, and, in the language of the day, money becomes plenty. Contracts are entered into by individuals resting on this unsubstantial state of things, but the delusion speedily passes away and the country is overrun with an indebtedness so weighty as to overwhelm many and to visit every department of industry with great and ruinous embarrassment. The greatest vigilance becomes necessary on the part of Government to guard against this state of things. The depositories must be given distinctly to understand that the favors of the Government will be altogether withdrawn, or substantially diminished, if its revenues shall be regarded as additions to their banking capital or as the foundation of an enlarged circulation.

The Government, through its revenue, has at all times an important part to perform in connection with the currency, and it greatly depends upon its vigilance and care whether the country be involved in embarrassments similar to those which it has had recently to encounter, or, aided by the action of the Treasury, shall be preserved in a sound and healthy condition.

The dangers to be guarded against are greatly augmented by too large a surplus of revenue. When that surplus greatly exceeds in amount what shall be required by a wise and prudent forecast to meet unforeseen contingencies, the Legislature itself may come to be seized with a disposition to indulge in extravagant appropriations to objects many of which may, and most probably would, be found to conflict with the Constitution. A fancied expediency is elevated above constitutional authority, and a reckless and wasteful extravagance but too certainly follows.

The important power of taxation, which when exercised in its most restricted form is a burthen on labor and production, is resorted to under various pretexts for purposes having no affinity to the motives which dictated its grant, and the extravagance of Government stimulates individual extravagance until the spirit of a wild and ill-regulated speculation involves one and all in its unfortunate results. In view of such fatal consequences, it may be laid down as an axiom founded in moral and political truth that no greater taxes should be imposed than are necessary for an economical administration of the Government, and that whatever exists beyond should be reduced or modified.   This doctrine does in no way conflict with the exercise of a sound discrimination in the selection of the articles to be taxed, which a due regard to the public weal would at all times suggest to the legislative mind.   It leaves the range of selection undefined; and such selection should always be made with an eye to the great interests of the country.   Composed as is the Union of separate and independent States, a patriotic Legislature will not fail in consulting the interests of the parts to adopt such course as will be best calculated to advance the harmony of the whole, and thus insure that permanency in the policy of the Government without which all efforts to advance the public prosperity are vain and fruitless.

This great and vitally important task rests with Congress, and the Executive can do no more than recommend the general principles which should govern in its execution.

I refer you to the report of the Secretary of War for an exhibition of the condition of the Army, and recommend to you as well worthy your best consideration many of the suggestions it contains.   The Secretary in no degree exaggerates the great importance of pressing forward without delay in the work of erecting and finishing the fortifications to which he particularly alludes.   Much has been done toward placing our cities and roadsteads in a state of security against the hazards of hostile attack within the last four years; but considering the new elements which have been of late years employed in the propelling of ships and the formidable implements of destruction which have been brought into service, we can not be too active or vigilant in preparing and perfecting the means of defense.   I refer you also to his report for a full statement of the condition of the Indian tribes within our jurisdiction.   The Executive has abated no effort in carrying into effect the well-established policy of the Government which contemplates a removal of all the tribes residing within the limits of the several States beyond those limits, and it is now enabled to congratulate the country at the prospect of an early consummation of this object.   Many of the tribes have already made great progress in the arts of civilized life, and through the operation of the schools established among them, aided by the efforts of the pious men of various religious denominations who devote themselves to the task of their improvement, we may fondly hope that the remains of the formidable tribes which were once masters of this country will in their transition from the savage state to a condition of refinement and cultivation add another bright trophy to adorn the labors of a well-directed philanthropy.

The accompanying report of the Secretary of the Navy will explain to you the situation of that branch of the service.   The present organization of the Department imparts to its operations great efficiency, but I concur fully in the propriety of a division of the Bureau of Construction, Equipment, Increase, and Repairs into two bureaus.   The subjects as now arranged are incongruous, and require to a certain extent information and qualifications altogether dissimilar.

The operations of the squadron on the coast of Africa have been conducted with all due attention to the object which led to its origination, and I am happy to say that the officers and crews have enjoyed the best possible health under the system adopted by the officer in command. It is believed that the United States is the only nation which has by its laws subjected to the punishment of death as pirates those who may be engaged in the slave trade. A similar enactment on the part of other nations would not fail to be attended by beneficial results.

In consequence of the difficulties which have existed in the way of securing titles for the necessary grounds, operations have not yet been commenced toward the establishment of the navy-yard at Memphis. So soon as the title is perfected no further delay will be permitted to intervene. It is well worthy of your consideration whether Congress should not direct the establishment of a ropewalk in connection with the contemplated navy-yard, as a measure not only of economy, but as highly useful and necessary. The only establishment of the sort now connected with the service is located at Boston, and the advantages of a similar establishment convenient to the hemp-growing region must be apparent to all.

The report of the Secretary presents other matters to your consideration of an important character in connection with the service.

In referring you to the accompanying report of the Postmaster-General it affords me continued cause of gratification to be able to advert to the fact that the affairs of the Department for the last four years have been so conducted as from its unaided resources to meet its large expenditures. On my coming into office a debt of nearly $500,000 existed against the Department, which Congress discharged by an appropriation from the Treasury. The Department on the 4th of March next will be found, under the management of its present efficient head, free of debt or embarrassment, which could only have been done by the observance and practice of the greatest vigilance and economy. The laws have contemplated throughout that the Department should be self-sustained, but it may become necessary, with the wisest regard to the public interests, to introduce amendments and alterations in the system.

There is a strong desire manifested in many quarters so to alter the tariff of letter postage as to reduce the amount of tax at present imposed. Should such a measure be carried into effect to the full extent desired, it can not well be doubted but that for the first years of its operation a diminished revenue would be collected, the supply of which would necessarily constitute a charge upon the Treasury. Whether such a result would be desirable it will be for Congress in its wisdom to determine. It may in general be asserted as true that radical alterations in any system should rather be brought about gradually than by sudden changes, and by pursuing this prudent policy in the reduction of letter postage the Department might still sustain itself through the revenue which would accrue by the increase of letters. The state and condition of the public Treasury has heretofore been such as to have precluded the recommendation of any material change. The difficulties upon this head have, however, ceased, and a larger discretion is now left to the Government.

I can not too strongly urge the policy of authorizing the establishment of a line of steamships regularly to ply between this country and foreign ports and upon our own waters for the transportation of the mail. The example of the British Government is well worthy of imitation in this respect. The belief is strongly entertained that the emoluments arising from the transportation of mail matter to foreign countries would operate of itself as an inducement to cause individual enterprise to undertake that branch of the task, and the remuneration of the Government would consist in the addition readily made to our steam navy in case of emergency by the ships so employed. Should this suggestion meet your approval, the propriety of placing such ships under the command of experienced officers of the Navy will not escape your observation. The application of steam to the purposes of naval warfare cogently recommends an extensive steam marine as important in estimating the defenses of the country. Fortunately this may be obtained by us to a great extent without incurring any large amount of expenditure. Steam vessels to be engaged in the transportation of the mails on our principal water courses, lakes, and ports of our coast could also be so constructed as to be efficient as war vessels when needed, and would of themselves constitute a formidable force in order to repel attacks from abroad. We can not be blind to the fact that other nations have already added large numbers of steamships to their naval armaments and that this new and powerful agent is destined to revolutionize the condition of the world. It becomes the United States, therefore, looking to their security, to adopt a similar policy, and the plan suggested will enable them to do so at a small comparative cost.

I take the greatest pleasure in bearing testimony to the zeal and untiring industry which has characterized the conduct of the members of the Executive Cabinet. Each in his appropriate sphere has rendered me the most efficient aid in carrying on the Government, and it will not, I trust, appear out of place for me to bear this public testimony. The cardinal objects which should ever be held in view by those intrusted with the administration of public affairs are rigidly, and without favor or affection, so to interpret the national will expressed in the laws as that injustice should be done to none, justice to all. This has been the rule upon which they have acted, and thus it is believed that few cases, if any, exist wherein our fellow-citizens, who from time to time have been drawn to the seat of Government for the settlement of their transactions with the Government, have gone away dissatisfied. Where the testimony has been perfected and was esteemed satisfactory their claims have been promptly audited, and this in the absence of all favoritism or partiality. The Government which is not just to its own people can neither claim their affection nor the respect of the world. At the same time, the closest attention has been paid to those matters which relate more immediately to the great concerns of the country. Order and efficiency in each branch of the public service have prevailed, accompanied by a system of the most rigid responsibility on the part of the receiving and disbursing agents. The fact, in illustration of the truth of this remark, deserves to be noticed that the revenues of the Government, amounting in the last four years to upward of $120,000,000, have been collected and disbursed through the numerous governmental agents without the loss by default of any amount worthy of serious commentary.

The appropriations made by Congress for the improvement of the rivers of the West and of the harbors on the Lakes are in a course of judicious expenditure under suitable agents, and are destined, it is to be hoped, to realize all the benefits designed to be accomplished by Congress. I can not, however, sufficiently impress upon Congress the great importance of withholding appropriations from improvements which are not ascertained by previous examination and survey to be necessary for the shelter and protection of trade from the dangers of storms and tempests. Without this precaution the expenditures are but too apt to inure to the benefit of individuals, without reference to the only consideration which can render them constitutional—the public interests and the general good.

I can not too earnestly urge upon you the interests of this District, over which by the Constitution Congress has exclusive jurisdiction. It would be deeply to be regretted should there be at any time ground to complain of neglect on the part of a community which, detached as it is from the parental care of the States of Virginia and Maryland, can only expect aid from Congress as its local legislature. Amongst the subjects which claim your attention is the prompt organization of an asylum for the insane who may be found from time to time sojourning within the District. Such course is also demanded by considerations which apply to branches of the public service. For the necessities in this behalf I invite your particular attention to the report of the Secretary of the Navy.

I have thus, gentlemen of the two Houses of Congress, presented you a true and faithful picture of the condition of public affairs, both foreign and domestic. The wants of the public service are made known to you, and matters of no ordinary importance are urged upon your consideration. Shall I not be permitted to congratulate you on the happy auspices under which you have assembled and at the important change in the condition of things which has occurred in the last three years? During that period questions with foreign powers of vital importance to the peace of our country have been settled and adjusted. A desolating and wasting war with savage tribes has been brought to a close. The

internal tranquillity of the country, threatened by agitating questions, has
been preserved. The credit of the Government, which had experienced
a temporary embarrassment, has been thoroughly restored. Its coffers,
which for a season were empty, have been replenished. A currency
nearly uniform in its value has taken the place of one depreciated and
almost worthless. Commerce and manufactures, which had suffered
in common with every other interest, have once more revived, and the
whole country exhibits an aspect of prosperity and happiness. Trade
and barter, no longer governed by a wild and speculative mania, rest
upon a solid and substantial footing, and the rapid growth of our cities
in every direction bespeaks most strongly the favorable circumstances
by which we are surrounded. My happiness in the retirement which
shortly awaits me is the ardent hope which I experience that this state
of prosperity is neither deceptive nor destined to be short lived, and that
measures which have not yet received its sanction, but which I can not
but regard as closely connected with the honor, the glory, and still more
enlarged prosperity of the country, are destined at an early day to receive
the approval of Congress. Under these circumstances and with these
anticipations I shall most gladly leave to others more able than myself
the noble and pleasing task of sustaining the public prosperity. I shall
carry with me into retirement the gratifying reflection that as my sole
object throughout has been to advance the public good I may not entirely
have failed in accomplishing it; and this gratification is heightened in
no small degree by the fact that when under a deep and abiding sense
of duty I have found myself constrained to resort to the qualified veto it
has neither been followed by disapproval on the part of the people nor
weakened in any degree their attachment to that great conservative
feature of our Government.   JOHN TYLER.

SPECIAL MESSAGES.

WASHINGTON, *December 10, 1844.*
To the Senate of the United States:

I have great pleasure in submitting to the Senate, for its ratification
and approval, a treaty which has been concluded between Mr. Cushing,
the United States commissioner, and the Chinese Empire..

                                                   JOHN TYLER.

WASHINGTON, *December 10, 1844.*
To the Senate of the United States:

I submit copies of two private and confidential letters addressed by
Mr. Fay, acting in his place during the absence of Mr. Wheaton from

Berlin, from which it appears that should the Senate see cause to ratify the treaty with the States composing the Zollverein without reference to the fact that the time limited for the exchange of its ratification had expired the Germanic States would regard the time fixed for the exchange of ratifications as immaterial and would give by their action upon it vitality and force to the treaty. I submit it to your mature consideration whether, in view of the important benefits arising from the treaty to the trade and commerce of the United States and to their agriculture, it would not comport with sound policy to adopt that course.

The Executive, not regarding the action of the Senate upon the treaty as expressive of its decisive opinion, deemed it proper to reopen the negotiations so far as to obtain an extension of time for the interchange of ratifications. The negotiation failed, however, in this particular, out of no disinclination to abide by the terms of the treaty on the part of the Zollverein, but from a belief that it would not fully comport with its dignity to do so.

JOHN TYLER.

WASHINGTON, *December 10, 1844.*

To the Senate and House of Representatives:

I communicate to you an extract of a dispatch from Mr. Hall to the Secretary of State, which has been received by me since my message of the 3d instant, containing the pleasing intelligence that the indemnity assumed to be paid by the Republic of Venezuela in the case of the brig *Morris* has been satisfactorily arranged.

JOHN TYLER.

WASHINGTON, *December 18, 1844.*

To the Senate and House of Representatives:

I transmit herewith copies of dispatches received from our minister at Mexico since the commencement of your present session, which claim from their importance, and I doubt not will receive, your calm and deliberate consideration. The extraordinary and highly offensive language which the Mexican Government has thought proper to employ in reply to the remonstrance of the Executive, through Mr. Shannon, against the renewal of the war with Texas while the question of annexation was pending before Congress and the people, and also the proposed manner of conducting that war, will not fail to arrest your attention. Such remonstrance, urged in no unfriendly spirit to Mexico, was called for by considerations of an imperative character, having relation as well to the peace of this country and honor of this Government as to the cause of humanity and civilization. Texas had entered into the treaty of annexation upon the invitation of the Executive, and when for that act she was threatened with a renewal of the war on the part of Mexico she naturally looked to this Government to interpose its efforts to ward off the threatened blow.   But one course was left the Executive, acting within the limits of its constitutional competency, and that was to protest in respectful, but at the same time strong and decided, terms against it.   The war thus threatened to be renewed was promulgated by edicts and decrees, which ordered on the part of the Mexican military the desolation of whole tracts of country and the destruction without discrimination of all ages, sexes, and conditions of existence.   Over the manner of conducting war Mexico possesses no exclusive control.   She has no right to violate at pleasure the principles which an enlightened civilization has laid down for the conduct of nations at war, and thereby retrograde to a period of barbarism, which happily for the world has long since passed away.   All nations are interested in enforcing an observance of those principles, and the United States, the oldest of the American Republics and the nearest of the civilized powers to the theater on which these enormities were proposed to be enacted, could not quietly content themselves to witness such a state of things.   They had through the Executive on another occasion, and, as was believed, with the approbation of the whole country, remonstrated against outrages similar but even less inhuman than those which by her new edicts and decrees she has threatened to perpetrate, and of which the late inhuman massacre at Tabasco was but the precursor.

The bloody and inhuman murder of Fannin and his companions, equaled only in savage barbarity by the usages of the untutored Indian tribes, proved how little confidence could be placed on the most solemn stipulations of her generals, while the fate of others who became her captives in war—many of whom, no longer able to sustain the fatigues and privations of long journeys, were shot down by the wayside, while their companions who survived were subjected to sufferings even more painful than death—had left an indelible stain on the page of civilization.   The Executive, with the evidence of an intention on the part of Mexico to renew scenes so revolting to humanity, could do no less than renew remonstrances formerly urged.   For fulfilling duties so imperative Mexico has thought proper, through her accredited organs, because she has had represented to her the inhumanity of such proceedings, to indulge in language unknown to the courtesy of diplomatic intercourse and offensive in the highest degree to this Government and people.   Nor has she offended in this only.   She has not only violated existing conventions between the two countries by arbitrary and unjust decrees against our trade and intercourse, but withholds installments of debt due to our citizens which she solemnly pledged herself to pay under circumstances which are fully explained by the accompanying letter from Mr. Green, our secretary of legation.   And when our minister has invited the attention of her Government to wrongs committed by her local authorities, not only on the property but on the persons of our fellow-citizens engaged in prosecuting fair and honest pursuits, she has added insult to injury by not even deigning for months together to return an answer to his representations. Still further to manifest her unfriendly feelings toward the United States, she has issued decrees expelling from some of her Provinces American citizens engaged in the peaceful pursuits of life, and now denies to those of our citizens prosecuting the whale fishery on the northwest coast of the Pacific the privilege, which has through all time heretofore been accorded to them, of exchanging goods of a small amount in value at her ports in California for supplies indispensable to their health and comfort.

Nor will it escape the observation of Congress that in conducting a correspondence with a minister of the United States, who can not and does not know any distinction between the geographical sections of the Union, charges wholly unfounded are made against particular States, and an appeal to others for aid and protection against supposed wrongs. In this same connection, sectional prejudices are attempted to be excited and the hazardous and unpardonable effort is made to foment divisions amongst the States of the Union and thereby imbitter their peace. Mexico has still to learn that however freely we may indulge in discussion among ourselves, the American people will tolerate no interference in their domestic affairs by any foreign government, and in all that concerns the constitutional guaranties and the national honor the people of the United States have but one mind and one heart.

The subject of annexation addresses itself, most fortunately, to every portion of the Union. The Executive would have been unmindful of its highest obligations if it could have adopted a course of policy dictated by sectional interests and local feelings. On the contrary, it was because the question was neither local nor sectional, but made its appeal to the interests of the whole Union, and of every State in the Union, that the negotiation, and finally the treaty of annexation, was entered into; and it has afforded me no ordinary pleasure to perceive that so far as demonstrations have been made upon it by the people they have proceeded from all portions of the Union. Mexico may seek to excite divisions amongst us by uttering unjust denunciations against particular States, but when she comes to know that the invitations addressed to our fellow-citizens by Spain, and afterwards by herself, to settle Texas were accepted by emigrants from all the States, and when, in addition to this, she refreshes her recollection with the fact that the first effort which was made to acquire Texas was during the Administration of a distinguished citizen from an Eastern State, which was afterwards renewed under the auspices of a President from the Southwest, she will awake to a knowledge of the futility of her present purpose of sowing dissensions among us or producing distraction in our councils by attacks either on particular States or on persons who are now in the retirement of private life.

Considering the appeal which she now makes to eminent citizens by name, can she hope to escape censure for having ascribed to them, as well as to others, a design, as she pretends now for the first time revealed, of having originated negotiations to despoil her by duplicity and falsehood of a portion of her territory? The opinion then, as now, prevailed with the Executive that the annexation of Texas to the Union was a matter of vast importance. In order to acquire that territory before it had assumed a position among the independent powers of the earth, propositions were made to Mexico for a cession of it to the United States. Mexico saw in these proceedings at the time no cause of complaint. She is now, when simply reminded of them, awakened to the knowledge of the fact, which she, through her secretary of state, promulgates to the whole world as true, that those negotiations were founded in deception and falsehood and superinduced by unjust and iniquitous motives. While Texas was a dependency of Mexico the United States opened negotiations with the latter power for the cession of her then acknowledged territory, and now that Texas is independent of Mexico and has maintained a separate existence for nine years, during which time she has been received into the family of nations and is represented by accredited ambassadors at many of the principal Courts of Europe, and when it has become obvious to the whole world that she is forever lost to Mexico, the United States is charged with deception and falsehood in all relating to the past, and condemnatory accusations are made against States which have had no special agency in the matter, because the Executive of the whole Union has negotiated with free and independent Texas upon a matter vitally important to the interests of both countries; and after nine years of unavailing war Mexico now announces her intention, through her secretary of foreign affairs, never to consent to the independence of Texas or to abandon the effort to reconquer that Republic. She thus announces a perpetual claim, which at the end of a century will furnish her as plausible a ground for discontent against any nation which at the end of that time may enter into a treaty with Texas as she possesses at this moment against the United States. The lapse of time can add nothing to her title to independence.

A course of conduct such as has been described on the part of Mexico, in violation of all friendly feeling and of the courtesy which should characterize the intercourse between the nations of the earth, might well justify the United States in a resort to any measures to vindicate their national honor; but, actuated by a sincere desire to preserve the general peace, and in view of the present condition of Mexico, the Executive, resting upon its integrity, and not fearing but that the judgment of the world will duly appreciate its motives, abstains from recommending to Congress a resort to measures of redress and contents itself with reurging upon that body prompt and immediate action on the subject of annexation. By adopting that measure the United States will be in the exercise of an undoubted right; and if Mexico, not regarding their forbearance, shall aggravate the injustice of her conduct by a declaration of war against them, upon her head will rest all the responsibility.

JOHN TYLER.

WASHINGTON, *December 23, 1844.*

To the Senate of the United States:

The messenger who lately bore to Berlin the ratified copy of the convention for the mutual abolition of the *droit d'aubaine* and taxes on emigration between the United States of America and the Grand Duchy of Hesse, has just returned to Washington, bearing with him the exchange copy of said convention. It appears that the exchange of ratifications did not take place until the 16th day of October, twenty days after the period fixed by the convention itself for that purpose. This informality, which it would seem was occasioned by the absence from Berlin of the plenipotentiary from Hesse and by the time necessarily required for the preparation of the document, has been waived by the representative of that Government.

This subject is now submitted for the consideration of the Senate.

JOHN TYLER.

WASHINGTON, *December 23, 1844.*

To the Senate of the United States:

I herewith transmit a letter from the Secretary of State, accompanied by copies of the correspondence* asked for by your resolution of the 12th instant.

JOHN TYLER.

WASHINGTON, *January 2, 1845.*

To the Senate of the United States:

I transmit herewith a letter from the Secretary of State, accompanied by a copy of a letter† from Mr. Raymond, secretary of legation and chargé d'affaires *ad interim* of the Republic of Texas, in answer to the Senate's resolution of the 16th December last.

JOHN TYLER.

WASHINGTON, *January 2, 1845.*

To the Senate of the United States:

In answer to your resolution of the 19th December last, I herewith transmit a letter‡ from the Secretary of State and the accompanying documents.

JOHN TYLER.

WASHINGTON, *January 9, 1845.*

To the House of Representatives:

I herewith transmit to the House of Representatives, in reply to their resolution of the 14th of June last, a report from the Secretary of State, with accompanying papers.§

JOHN TYLER.

---

* Extracts from the instructions of the Department of State to the United States minister to France relative to the proposed annexation of Texas, etc.

† Relating to the public debt and public lands of the Republic of Texas.

‡ Transmitting copies of treaties between the Republic of Texas and Great Britain and France.

§ Copy of the instructions to George W. Erving upon his appointment as minister to Spain in 1814 and during his mission to that Court.

WASHINGTON, *January 9, 1845.*

To the Senate of the United States:

I transmit herewith additional documents having relation to the treaty with China, which may enable the Senate more satisfactorily to act upon it.

JOHN TYLER.

WASHINGTON, *January 22, 1845.*

To the Senate and House of Representatives of the United States:

I communicate herewith an abstract of the treaty between the United States of America and the Chinese Empire concluded at Wang-Hiya on the 3d of July last, and ratified by the Senate on the 16th instant, and which, having also been ratified by the Emperor of China, now awaits only the exchange of the ratifications in China, from which it will be seen that the special mission authorized by Congress for this purpose has fully succeeded in the accomplishment so far of the great objects for which it was appointed, and in placing our relations with China on a new footing eminently favorable to the commerce and other interests of the United States.

In view of the magnitude and importance of our national concerns, actual and prospective, in China, I submit to the consideration of Congress the expediency of providing for the preservation and cultivation of the subsisting relations of amity between the United States and the Chinese Government, either by means of a permanent minister or commissioner with diplomatic functions, as in the case of certain of the Mohammedan States. It appears by one of the extracts annexed that the establishment of the British Government in China consists both of a plenipotentiary and also of paid consuls for all the five ports, one of whom has the title and exercises the functions of consul-general; and France has also a salaried consul-general, and the interests of the United States seem in like manner to call for some representative in China of a higher class than an ordinary commercial consulate.

I also submit to the consideration of Congress the expediency of making some special provision by law for the security of the independent and honorable position which the treaty of Wang-Hiya confers on citizens of the United States residing or doing business in China. By the twenty-first and twenty-fifth articles of the treaty (copies of which are subjoined *in extenso*) citizens of the United States in China are wholly exempted, as well in criminal as in civil matters, from the local jurisdiction of the Chinese Government and made amenable to the laws and subject to the jurisdiction of the appropriate authorities of the United States alone. Some action on the part of Congress seems desirable in order to give full effect to these important concessions of the Chinese Government.

JOHN TYLER.

WASHINGTON, *January 29, 1845.*
To the Senate and House of Representatives of the United States:

In compliance with the request of the governor of the State of Illinois, I transmit herewith a copy of certain resolutions* adopted by the general assembly of that State.

JOHN TYLER.

WASHINGTON, *February 3, 1845.*
To the Senate of the United States:

In answer to the resolution of the Senate of the 2d ultimo, calling for information in reference to the indemnities stipulated to be paid pursuant to the convention between the United States and the Mexican Republic of the 30th of January, 1843, I transmit herewith reports from the Secretaries of State and of the Treasury and the documents which accompanied them.

JOHN TYLER.

WASHINGTON, *February 3, 1845.*
To the House of Representatives:

In answer to the resolution of the House of Representatives of the 23d ultimo, requesting information upon the subject of embezzlement of public money, I transmit herewith a report from the Secretary of State.

JOHN TYLER.

WASHINGTON, *February 3, 1845.*
To the House of Representatives:

In answer to the resolution of the House of Representatives of the 16th ultimo, calling for information upon the subject of the boundaries of the Republic of Texas and for copies of treaties between that Republic and other powers, I transmit herewith a report from the Secretary of State and the documents which accompanied it.

JOHN TYLER.

WASHINGTON, *February 4, 1845.*
To the Senate of the United States:

In compliance with the resolution of the Senate of the 5th December, I herewith transmit copies of the proceedings in the case of the inquiry into the official conduct of Silas Reed, principal surveyor of Missouri and Illinois, together with all the complaints against him and all the evidence taken in relation thereto. I did not consider the irregularities into which the surveyor-general had fallen as of sufficient magnitude to induce his dismissal from office at the time that the papers reached me, having become convinced, upon inquiry of the Commissioner of the General Land Office, of the ability, efficiency, and fidelity of the surveyor-general in all things

---

*Asking the publication and distribution of the decisions of the Supreme Court of the United States.

appertaining to his office; but since the passage of the resolution by the Senate I regarded the matter as so augmented in importance as to induce me to refer the subject to the Commissioner of the General Land Office for a minute and thorough examination. A copy of the report which he has made, and also the defense of Dr. Reed, accompanies the papers. It has seemed to me that the facts set forth by the report exhibit certain irregularities which are properly reprehensible, but from which neither the surveyor-general, in a pecuniary point of view, derived profit nor the Government sustained loss, and which the reproof contained in the Commissioner's report will in all future cases restrain; while the high testimony borne by the Commissioner to the generally excellent deportment in office of the surveyor-general has seemed to me to mark the case more as one meriting disapproval and correction in future than the severe punishment of dismissal.

JOHN TYLER.

WASHINGTON, *February 5, 1845.*

To the House of Representatives of the United States:

I herewith transmit to the House of Representatives, in answer to its resolution of the 31st ultimo, a report from the Secretary of State, together with copies of documents* therein referred to.

JOHN TYLER.

WASHINGTON, *February 5, 1845.*

To the Senate of the United States:

In compliance with the resolution of the Senate of the 10th of December last, requesting further correspondence touching the relations between the United States and the Mexican Republic, I transmit herewith a report from the Secretary of State and the documents which accompanied it.

JOHN TYLER.

WASHINGTON, *February 7, 1845.*

To the Senate of the United States:

I transmit herewith the report † requested by the resolution of the Senate of the 2d of January last.

JOHN TYLER.

WASHINGTON, *February 7, 1845.*

To the Senate of the United States:

In answer to the resolution of the Senate of the 4th instant, requesting information relative to the employment of Mr. Duff Green in the service of this Government, I transmit herewith a report from the Secretary of State.

JOHN TYLER.

*Correspondence relative to the surrender by Great Britain of fugitive criminals from Florida under the treaty of Washington.
† Of Lieutenant H. Wager Halleck, of the Engineer Corps, on the means of national defense.

WASHINGTON, *February 12, 1845.*

To the House of Representatives of the United States:

I transmit herewith a copy of the correspondence relating to the claims of citizens of the United States upon the Mexican Republic, requested by the resolution of the House of Representatives of the 10th of January, 1844.

JOHN TYLER.

WASHINGTON, *February 12, 1845.*

To the Senate of the United States:

I transmit herewith a copy of the correspondence relative to claims of citizens of the United States on the Mexican Republic, requested by the resolution of the Senate of the 26th December, 1843.

JOHN TYLER.

WASHINGTON CITY, *February 13, 1845.*

To the Senate of the United States:

I transmit herewith, for the advice and approbation of the Senate, a treaty with the Creek and Seminole tribes of Indians, concluded on the 4th day of January last.

JOHN TYLER.

WASHINGTON, *February 14, 1845.*

To the Senate of the United States:

I herewith transmit certain documents connected with the case of Silas Reed,* and which were inadvertently omitted in the packet of papers which accompanied my message to the Senate on this subject.

JOHN TYLER.

WASHINGTON, *February 17, 1845.*

To the House of Representatives:

In compliance with the resolution of the House of Representatives of the 30th of December last, requesting information with reference to indemnities for claims of citizens of the United States upon the Mexican Government, I transmit herewith a report from the Secretary of State and the documents which accompanied it.

JOHN TYLER.

WASHINGTON, *February 19, 1845.*

To the Senate of the United States:

In answer to the resolution of the Senate of the 11th December, 1844, requesting the President ''to lay before the Senate, if in his judgment

* Principal surveyor of Missouri and Illinois, official conduct of.

that may be done without prejudice to the public interests, a copy of any instructions which may have been given by the Executive to the American minister in England on the subject of the title to and occupation of the Territory of Oregon since the 4th day of March, 1841; also a copy of any correspondence which may have passed between this Government and that of Great Britain, or between either of the two Governments and the minister of the other, in relation to that subject since that time," I have to say that in my opinion, as the negotiation is still pending, the information sought for can not be communicated without prejudice to the public service.

I deem it, however, proper to add that considerable progress has been made in the discussion, which has been carried on in a very amicable spirit between the two Governments, and that there is reason to hope that it may be terminated and the negotiation brought to a close within a short period.

I have delayed answering the resolution under the expectation expressed in my annual message that the negotiation would have been terminated before the close of the present session of Congress, and that the information called for by the resolution of the Senate might be communicated.

JOHN TYLER.

WASHINGTON, February 20, 1845.

To the Senate of the United States:

I herewith communicate to the Senate a report* from the Secretary of State, in reply to the inquiries contained in their resolution of the 17th instant.

JOHN TYLER.

WASHINGTON, February 20, 1845.

To the Senate and House of Representatives of the United States:

I transmit herewith, for the information of Congress, copies of certain dispatches recently received from Mr. Wise, our envoy extraordinary and minister plenipotentiary at the Court of Brazil, upon the subject of the slave trade, developing the means used and the devices resorted to in order to evade existing enactments upon that subject.

Anxiously desirous as are the United States to suppress a traffic so revolting to humanity, in the efforts to accomplish which they have been the pioneers of civilized states, it can not but be a subject of the most profound regret that any portion of our citizens should be found acting in cooperation with the subjects of other powers in opposition to the policy of their own Government, thereby subjecting to suspicion and to the hazard of disgrace the flag of their own country. It is true that this

---

* Relating to redress from the British Government for the illegal capture of the fishing schooner *Argus* and other American vessels engaged in the fisheries, under a pretended infraction of the convention of October 20, 1818.

traffic is carried on altogether in foreign parts and that our own coasts are free from its pollution; but the crime remains the same wherever perpetrated, and there are many circumstances to warrant the belief that some of our citizens are deeply involved in its guilt. The mode and manner of carrying on this trade are clearly and fearlessly set forth in the accompanying documents, and it would seem that a regular system has been adopted for the purpose of thwarting the policy and evading the penalties of our laws. American vessels, with the knowledge, as there are good reasons to believe, of the owners and masters, are *chartered*, or rather purchased, by notorious slave dealers in Brazil, aided by English brokers and capitalists, with this intent. The vessel is only nominally chartered at so much per month, while in truth it is actually sold, to be delivered on the coast of Africa; the charter party binding the owners in the meantime to take on board *as passengers* a new crew in Brazil, who, when delivered on the coast, are to navigate her back to the ports of Brazil with her cargo of slaves. Under this agreement the vessel clears from the United States for some port in Great Britain, where a cargo of merchandise known as "coast goods," and designed especially for the African trade, is purchased, shipped, and consigned, together with the vessel, either directly to the slave dealer himself or to his agents or accomplices in Brazil. On her arrival a new crew is put on board *as passengers* and the vessel and cargo consigned to an equally guilty factor or agent on the coast of Africa, where the unlawful purpose originally designed is finally consummated. The merchandise is exchanged for slaves, the vessel is delivered up, her name obliterated, her papers destroyed, her American crew discharged, to be provided for by the charterers, and the new or *passenger* crew put in command to carry back its miserable freight to the first contrivers of the voyage, or their *employees* in Brazil.

During the whole progress of this tortuous enterprise it is possible that neither the American crew originally enlisted nor the *passenger* crew put on board in the Brazilian ports are aware of the nature of the voyage, and yet it is on these principally, ignorant if not innocent, that the penalties of the law are inflicted, while the guilty contrivers—the charterers, brokers, owners, and masters; in short, all who are most deeply concerned in the crime and its rewards—for the most part escape unpunished.

It will be seen from the examinations which have recently taken place at Rio that the subjects of Her Britannic Majesty as well as our own citizens are deeply implicated in this inhuman traffic. British factors and agents, while they supply Africa with British fabrics in exchange for slaves, are chiefly instrumental in the abuse of the American flag; and the suggestions contained in the letter of Mr. Wise (whose judicious and zealous efforts in the matter can not be too highly commended), addressed to Mr. Hamilton, the British envoy, as to the best mode of suppressing the evil, deserve your most deliberate consideration, as they will receive, I doubt not, that of the British Government.

It is also worthy of consideration whether any other measures than those now existing are necessary to give greater efficacy to the just and humane policy of our laws, which already provide for the restoration to Africa of slaves captured at sea by American cruisers. From time to time provision has been made by this Government for their comfortable support and maintenance during a limited period after their restoration, and it is much to be regretted that this liberal policy has not been adopted by Great Britain. As it is, it seems to me that the policy it has adopted is calculated rather to perpetuate than to suppress the trade by enlisting very large interests in its favor. Merchants and capitalists furnish the means of carrying it on; manufactures, for which the negroes are exchanged, are the products of her workshops; the slaves, when captured, instead of being returned back to their homes are transferred to her colonial possessions in the West Indies and made the means of swelling the amount of their products by a system of apprenticeship for a term of years; and the officers and crews who capture the vessels receive on the whole number of slaves so many pounds sterling *per capita* by way of bounty.

It must be obvious that while these large interests are enlisted in favor of its continuance it will be difficult, if not impossible, to suppress the nefarious traffic, and that its results would be in effect but a continuance of the slave trade in another and more cruel form; for it can be but a matter of little difference to the African whether he is torn from his country and transported to the West Indies as a slave in the regular course of the trade, or captured by a cruiser, transferred to the same place, and made to perform the same labor under the name of an apprentice, which is at present the practical operation of the policy adopted.

It is to be hoped that Her Britannic Majesty's Government will, upon a review of all the circumstances stated in these dispatches, adopt more efficient measures for the suppression of the trade, which she has so long attempted to put down, with, as yet, so little success, and more consonant with the original policy of restoring the captured African to his home.

JOHN TYLER.

WASHINGTON, *February 21, 1845.*

To the Senate of the United States:

I transmit to the Senate, for its consideration with a view to ratification, a treaty of peace, friendship, navigation, and commerce between the United States and the Republic of New Granada, signed at Bogota on the 20th of December last. A copy of the papers on file in the Department of State relating to the treaty is also herewith communicated, for the information of the Senate.

JOHN TYLER.

WASHINGTON, *February 21, 1845.*

To the Senate of the United States:

I herewith transmit to the Senate, in answer to their resolution of the 14th instant, a report of the Secretary of State, with the accompanying papers.* JOHN TYLER.

WASHINGTON, *February 21, 1845.*

To the House of Representatives of the United States:

In compliance with your resolution of the 23d January last, asking information "if any, and what, officers of the United States have been guilty of embezzlement of public money since the 19th August, 1841, and, further, whether such officers have been criminally prosecuted for such embezzlement, and, if not, that the reasons why they have not been so prosecuted be communicated," I herewith transmit letters from the Secretaries of the Treasury, War, and Navy Departments and the Postmaster-General, and from various heads of bureaus, from which it will be seen that no case of embezzlement by any person holding office under the Government is known to have occurred since the 19th August, 1841, unless exceptions are to be found in the cases of the postmaster at Tompkinsville, Ky., who was instantly removed from office, and all papers necessary for his prosecution were transmitted to the United States district attorney, and John Flanagan, superintendent of lead mines of the Upper Mississippi, who was also removed, and whose place of residence, as will be seen by the letter of the head of the Ordnance Bureau, has been, and still is, unknown. JOHN TYLER.

WASHINGTON, *February 24, 1845.*

To the Senate of the United States:

I herewith communicate to the Senate, for its consideration, a convention concluded by the minister of the United States at Berlin with the Kingdom of Bavaria, dated on the 21st day of January, 1845, for the mutual abolition of the *droit d'aubaine* and taxes on emigration between that Government and the United States, and also a copy of a dispatch from the minister explanatory of the sixth article of the same.

JOHN TYLER.

WASHINGTON, *February 26, 1845.*

To the Senate of the United States:

I transmit herewith a communication from the Secretary of the Treasury, inclosing reports from the Commissioner of the General Land Office, dated the 25th instant, and accompanying papers, in compliance with your resolution of the 17th instant, asking for information relative to reservations of mineral lands in the State of Illinois south of the base line and west of the third principal meridian. JOHN TYLER.

---

*Instructions to Hon. Caleb Cushing, commissioner to China and envoy extraordinary and minister plenipotentiary to the Court of China, etc.

WASHINGTON, *February 26, 1845.*

To the Senate of the United States:

I herewith communicate a dispatch recently received, and an extract from one of a prior date, from our minister at Mexico, which I deem it important to lay confidentially before the Senate.

JOHN TYLER.

WASHINGTON, *February 26, 1845.*

To the Senate of the United States:

In compliance with the resolution of the Senate of the 3d instant, I herewith transmit the information* called for.

JOHN TYLER.

WASHINGTON, *February 26, 1845.*

To the Senate of the United States:

I herewith transmit to the Senate, for its approval, an additional article to the treaty of extradition between the United States and France of the 9th of November, 1843. It will be found to contain the amendments suggested by the resolution of the Senate of the 15th of June last.

JOHN TYLER.

WASHINGTON, *February 28, 1845.*

To the Senate of the United States:

I transmit herewith to the Senate, in answer to its resolution of the 17th instant, a report† from the Secretary of State, together with the copies of papers therein referred to.

JOHN TYLER.

VETO MESSAGE.

WASHINGTON, *February 20, 1845.*

To the Senate of the United States:

I herewith return the bill entitled "An act relating to revenue cutters and steamers," with the following objections to its becoming a law:

The Executive has found it necessary and esteemed it important to the public interests to direct the building of two revenue boats, to be propelled by wind or steam, as occasion may require—the one for the coast of Georgia and the other for Mobile Bay, to be used as dispatch

---

* Operations of the United States squadron on the west coast of Africa, the growth, condition, and influence of the American colonies there, and the nature, extent, and progress of the commerce of the United States with the same.

† Relating to redress from the British Government for the illegal capture of the fishing schooner *Argus* and other American vessels engaged in the fisheries, under a pretended infraction of the convention of October 20, 1818.

vessels if necessary. The models have been furnished by the Navy Department and side wheels have been ordered, as being best tested and least liable to failure. The one boat is directed to be built at Richmond, Va., the other at Pittsburg, Pa., and contracts have been regularly entered into for their construction. The contractors have made and are making all necessary arrangements in procuring materials and sites for building, etc., and have doubtless been at considerable expense in the necessary preparations for completing their engagements. It was no part of the intention of the Senate in originating the bill, I am well convinced, to violate the sanctity of contracts regularly entered into by the Government. The language of the act, nevertheless, is of a character to produce in all probability that effect. Its language is "that no revenue cutter or revenue steamer shall hereafter be built (*excepting such as are now in the course of building or equipment*) nor purchased unless an appropriation be first made by law therefor." The *building* of the two cutters under contract can not be said properly to have commenced, although preparations have been made for building; but even if the construction be ambiguous, it is better that all ambiguity should be removed and thus the hazard of violating the pledged faith of the country be removed along with it.

I am free to confess that, existing contracts being guarded and protected, the law to operate *in futuro* would be regarded as both proper and wise.

With these objections, I return the bill to the House in which it originated for its final constitutional action.

JOHN TYLER.

PROCLAMATION.

[From Senate Journal, Twenty-eighth Congress, second session, p. 271.]

WASHINGTON, *January 8, 1845.*

To the Senators of the United States, respectively.

SIR: Objects interesting to the United States requiring that the Senate should be in session on Tuesday, the 4th of March next, to receive and act upon such communications as may be made to it on the part of the Executive, your attendance in the Senate Chamber, in this city, on that day at 10 o'clock in the forenoon is accordingly requested.

JOHN TYLER.

James K. Polk

March 4, 1845, to March 4, 1849

James K. Polk

JAMES KNOX POLK was born in Mecklenburg County, N. C., November 2, 1795. He was a son of Samuel Polk, a farmer, whose father, Ezekiel, and his brother, Colonel Thomas Polk, one of the signers of the Mecklenburg Declaration of Independence, were sons of Robert Polk (or Pollock), who was born in Ireland and emigrated to America. His mother was Jane, daughter of James Knox, a resident of Iredell County, N. C., and a captain in the War of the Revolution. His father removed to Tennessee in the autumn of 1806, and settled in the valley of Duck River, a tributary of the Tennessee, in a section that was erected the following year into the county of Maury; he died in 1827. James was brought up on the farm; was inclined to study, and was fond of reading. He was sent to school, and had succeeded in mastering the English branches when ill health compelled his removal. Was then placed with a merchant, but, having a strong dislike to commercial pursuits, soon returned home, and in July, 1813, was given in charge of a private tutor. In 1815 entered the sophomore class at the University of North Carolina. As a student he was correct, punctual, and industrious. At his graduation in 1818 he was officially acknowledged to be the best scholar in both the classics and mathematics, and delivered the Latin salutatory. In 1847 the university conferred upon him the degree of LL. D. In 1819 he entered the law office of Felix Grundy, then at the head of the Tennessee bar. While pursuing his legal studies he attracted the attention of Andrew Jackson, and an intimacy was thus begun between the two men. In 1820 Mr. Polk was admitted to the bar, and established himself at Columbia, the county seat of Maury County. He attained immediate success, his career at the bar only ending with his election to the governorship of Tennessee in 1839. Brought up as a Jeffersonian and early taking an interest in politics, he was frequently heard in public as an exponent of the views of his party. His style of oratory was so popular that his services soon came to be in great demand, and he was not long in earning the title of the "Napoleon of the Stump." His first public employment was that of chief clerk to the Tennessee house of representatives. In 1823 was elected a member of that body. In January, 1824, he married Sarah, daughter of Joel Childress, a merchant of Rutherford County, Tenn. In August, 1825, he was elected to Congress from the Duck River district, and reelected at every succeeding election till 1839, when he withdrew from the contest to become a candidate for governor. With one or two exceptions, he was the youngest member of the Nineteenth Congress. He was prominently connected with every leading question, and upon all he struck what proved to be the keynote for the action of his party. His maiden speech was in defense of the proposed amendment to the Constitution giving the choice of the President and Vice-President directly to the people. It at once placed him in the front rank of Congressional debaters. He opposed the appropriation for the Panama mission, asked for by President Adams, contending that such action would tend to involve the United States in a war with Spain and establish an unfortunate precedent. In December, 1827, he was placed on the Committee on Foreign Affairs, and afterwards was also appointed chairman of the select committee to which was referred that portion of President Adams's message calling attention to the probable accumulation of a surplus in the Treasury after the anticipated extinguishment of the national debt. As the head of the latter committee he made a report denying the constitutional power of Congress to collect from the people for distribution a surplus beyond the wants of the Government, and maintaining that the revenue should be reduced to the requirements of the public service. During the whole period of President Jackson's Administration he was one of its leading supporters, and at times its chief reliance. Early in 1833, as a member of the Ways and Means Committee, he made a minority report unfavorable to the Bank of the United States. During the entire contest between the bank and President Jackson, caused by the removal of the deposits in October, 1833, Mr. Polk, as chairman of the Ways and Means Committee, supported the Executive. He was elected Speaker of the House of Representatives in December, 1835, and held that office till 1839. It was his fortune to preside over the House at a period when party feelings were excited to an unusual degree, and notwithstanding the fact that during the first session more appeals were taken from his decisions than were ever known before, he was uniformly sustained by the House, and frequently by leading members of the Whig party. He gave to the Administration of Martin Van Buren the same unhesitating support he had accorded to that of President Jackson. On leaving Congress he became the candidate of the Democrats of Tennessee for governor, and was elected by over 2,500 majority. He was an unsuccessful candidate for governor again in 1841 and 1843. In 1839 he was nominated by the legislatures of Tennessee and other States for Vice-President of the United States, but Richard M. Johnson, of Kentucky, was the choice of the great body of the Democratic party, and was accordingly nominated. On May 27, 1844, Mr. Polk was nominated for President of the

United States by the national Democratic convention at Baltimore, and on November 12 was elected, receiving about 40,000 majority on the popular vote, and 170 electoral votes to 105 that were cast for Henry Clay. He was inaugurated March 4, 1845. Among the important events of his Administration were the establishment of the United States Naval Academy; the consummation of the annexation of Texas; the admission of Texas, Iowa, and Wisconsin as States; the war with Mexico, resulting in a treaty of peace, by which the United States acquired New Mexico and Upper California; the treaty with Great Britain settling the Oregon boundary; the establishment of the "warehouse system;" the reenactment of the independent-treasury system; the passage of the act establishing the Smithsonian Institution; the treaty with New Granada, the thirty-fifth article of which secured for citizens of the United States the right of way across the Isthmus of Panama; and the creation of the Department of the Interior. He declined to become a candidate for reelection, and at the conclusion of his term retired to his home in Nashville. He died June 15, 1849, and was buried at Polk Place, in Nashville. September 19, 1893, the remains were removed by the State to Capitol Square.

INAUGURAL ADDRESS.

FELLOW-CITIZENS: Without solicitation on my part, I have been chosen by the free and voluntary suffrages of my countrymen to the most honorable and most responsible office on earth. I am deeply impressed with gratitude for the confidence reposed in me. Honored with this distinguished consideration at an earlier period of life than any of my predecessors, I can not disguise the diffidence with which I am about to enter on the discharge of my official duties.

If the more aged and experienced men who have filled the office of President of the United States even in the infancy of the Republic distrusted their ability to discharge the duties of that exalted station, what ought not to be the apprehensions of one so much younger and less endowed now that our domain extends from ocean to ocean, that our people have so greatly increased in numbers, and at a time when so great diversity of opinion prevails in regard to the principles and policy which should characterize the administration of our Government? Well may the boldest fear and the wisest tremble when incurring responsibilities on which may depend our country's peace and prosperity, and in some degree the hopes and happiness of the whole human family.

In assuming responsibilities so vast I fervently invoke the aid of that Almighty Ruler of the Universe in whose hands are the destinies of nations and of men to guard this Heaven-favored land against the mischiefs which without His guidance might arise from an unwise public policy. With a firm reliance upon the wisdom of Omnipotence to sustain and direct me in the path of duty which I am appointed to pursue, I stand in the presence of this assembled multitude of my countrymen to take upon myself the solemn obligation "to the best of my ability to preserve, protect, and defend the Constitution of the United States."

A concise enumeration of the principles which will guide me in the administrative policy of the Government is not only in accordance with the examples set me by all my predecessors, but is eminently befitting the occasion.

The Constitution itself, plainly written as it is, the safeguard of our federative compact, the offspring of concession and compromise, binding together in the bonds of peace and union this great and increasing family of free and independent States, will be the chart by which I shall be directed.

It will be my first care to administer the Government in the true spirit of that instrument, and to assume no powers not expressly granted or clearly implied in its terms. The Government of the United States is one of delegated and limited powers, and it is by a strict adherence to the clearly granted powers and by abstaining from the exercise of doubtful or unauthorized implied powers that we have the only sure guaranty against the recurrence of those unfortunate collisions between the Federal and State authorities which have occasionally so much disturbed the harmony of our system and even threatened the perpetuity of our glorious Union.

"To the States, respectively, or to the people" have been reserved "the powers not delegated to the United States by the Constitution nor prohibited by it to the States." Each State is a complete sovereignty within the sphere of its reserved powers. The Government of the Union, acting within the sphere of its delegated authority, is also a complete sovereignty. While the General Government should abstain from the exercise of authority not clearly delegated to it, the States should be equally careful that in the maintenance of their rights they do not overstep the limits of powers reserved to them. One of the most distinguished of my predecessors attached deserved importance to "the support of the State governments in all their rights, as the most competent administration for our domestic concerns and the surest bulwark against antirepublican tendencies," and to the "preservation of the General Government in its whole constitutional vigor, as the sheet anchor of our peace at home and safety abroad."

To the Government of the United States has been intrusted the exclusive management of our foreign affairs. Beyond that it wields a few general enumerated powers. It does not force reform on the States. It leaves individuals, over whom it casts its protecting influence, entirely free to improve their own condition by the legitimate exercise of all their mental and physical powers. It is a common protector of each and all the States; of every man who lives upon our soil, whether of native or foreign birth; of every religious sect, in their worship of the Almighty according to the dictates of their own conscience; of every shade of opinion, and the most free inquiry; of every art, trade, and occupation consistent with the laws of the States. And we rejoice in the general happiness, prosperity, and advancement of our country, which have been the offspring of freedom, and not of power.

This most admirable and wisest system of well-regulated self-government among men ever devised by human minds has been tested by its successful operation for more than half a century, and if preserved from the usurpations of the Federal Government on the one hand and the exercise by the States of powers not reserved to them on the other, will, I fervently hope and believe, endure for ages to come and dispense the blessings of civil and religious liberty to distant generations. To effect objects so dear to every patriot I shall devote myself with anxious solicitude. It will be my desire to guard against that most fruitful source of danger to the harmonious action of our system which consists in substituting the mere discretion and caprice of the Executive or of majorities in the legislative department of the Government for powers which have been withheld from the Federal Government by the Constitution. By the theory of our Government majorities rule, but this right is not an arbitrary or unlimited one. It is a right to be exercised in subordination to the Constitution and in conformity to it. One great object of the Constitution was to restrain majorities from oppressing minorities or encroaching upon their just rights. Minorities have a right to appeal to the Constitution as a shield against such oppression.

That the blessings of liberty which our Constitution secures may be enjoyed alike by minorities and majorities, the Executive has been wisely invested with a qualified veto upon the acts of the Legislature. It is a negative power, and is conservative in its character. It arrests for the time hasty, inconsiderate, or unconstitutional legislation, invites reconsideration, and transfers questions at issue between the legislative and executive departments to the tribunal of the people. Like all other powers, it is subject to be abused. When judiciously and properly exercised, the Constitution itself may be saved from infraction and the rights of all preserved and protected.

The inestimable value of our Federal Union is felt and acknowledged by all. By this system of united and confederated States our people are permitted collectively and individually to seek their own happiness in their own way, and the consequences have been most auspicious. Since the Union was formed the number of the States has increased from thirteen to twenty-eight; two of these have taken their position as members of the Confederacy within the last week. Our population has increased from three to twenty millions. New communities and States are seeking protection under its ægis, and multitudes from the Old World are flocking to our shores to participate in its blessings. Beneath its benign sway peace and prosperity prevail. Freed from the burdens and miseries of war, our trade and intercourse have extended throughout the world. Mind, no longer tasked in devising means to accomplish or resist schemes of ambition, usurpation, or conquest, is devoting itself to man's true interests in developing his faculties and powers and the capacity of nature to minister to his enjoyments. Genius is free to announce its inventions and discoveries, and the hand is free to accomplish whatever the head conceives not incompatible with the rights of a fellow-being. All distinctions of birth or of rank have been abolished. All citizens, whether native or adopted, are placed upon terms of precise equality. All are entitled to equal rights and equal protection. No union exists between church and state, and perfect freedom of opinion is guaranteed to all sects and creeds.

These are some of the blessings secured to our happy land by our Federal Union. To perpetuate them it is our sacred duty to preserve it. Who shall assign limits to the achievements of free minds and free hands under the protection of this glorious Union? No treason to mankind since the organization of society would be equal in atrocity to that of him who would lift his hand to destroy it. He would overthrow the noblest structure of human wisdom, which protects himself and his fellow-man. He would stop the progress of free government and involve his country either in anarchy or despotism. He would extinguish the fire of liberty, which warms and animates the hearts of happy millions and invites all the nations of the earth to imitate our example. If he say that error and wrong are committed in the administration of the Government, let him remember that nothing human can be perfect, and that under no other system of government revealed by Heaven or devised by man has reason been allowed so free and broad a scope to combat error. Has the sword of despots proved to be a safer or surer instrument of reform in government than enlightened reason? Does he expect to find among the ruins of this Union a happier abode for our swarming millions than they now have under it? Every lover of his country must shudder at the thought of the possibility of its dissolution, and will be ready to adopt the patriotic sentiment, ''Our Federal Union—it must be preserved.'' To preserve it the compromises which alone enabled our fathers to form a common constitution for the government and protection of so many States and distinct communities, of such diversified habits, interests, and domestic institutions, must be sacredly and religiously observed. Any attempt to disturb or destroy these compromises, being terms of the compact of union, can lead to none other than the most ruinous and disastrous consequences.

It is a source of deep regret that in some sections of our country misguided persons have occasionally indulged in schemes and agitations whose object is the destruction of domestic institutions existing in other sections—institutions which existed at the adoption of the Constitution and were recognized and protected by it. All must see that if it were possible for them to be successful in attaining their object the dissolution of the Union and the consequent destruction of our happy form of government must speedily follow.

I am happy to believe that at every period of our existence as a nation there has existed, and continues to exist, among the great mass of our people a devotion to the Union of the States which will shield and protect it against the moral treason of any who would seriously contemplate its destruction. To secure a continuance of that devotion the compromises of the Constitution must not only be preserved, but sectional jealousies and heartburnings must be discountenanced, and all should remember that they are members of the same political family, having a common destiny. To increase the attachment of our people to the Union, our laws should be just. Any policy which shall tend to favor monopolies or the peculiar interests of sections or classes must operate to the prejudice of the interests of their fellow-citizens, and should be avoided. If the compromises of the Constitution be preserved, if sectional jealousies and heartburnings be discountenanced, if our laws be just and the Government be practically administered strictly within the limits of power prescribed to it, we may discard all apprehensions for the safety of the Union.

With these views of the nature, character, and objects of the Government and the value of the Union, I shall steadily oppose the creation of those institutions and systems which in their nature tend to pervert it from its legitimate purposes and make it the instrument of sections, classes, and individuals. We need no national banks or other extraneous institutions planted around the Government to control or strengthen it in opposition to the will of its authors. Experience has taught us how unnecessary they are as auxiliaries of the public authorities—how impotent for good and how powerful for mischief.

Ours was intended to be a plain and frugal government, and I shall regard it to be my duty to recommend to Congress and, as far as the Executive is concerned, to enforce by all the means within my power the strictest economy in the expenditure of the public money which may be compatible with the public interests.

A national debt has become almost an institution of European monarchies. It is viewed in some of them as an essential prop to existing governments. Melancholy is the condition of that people whose government can be sustained only by a system which periodically transfers large amounts from the labor of the many to the coffers of the few. Such a system is incompatible with the ends for which our republican Government was instituted. Under a wise policy the debts contracted in our Revolution and during the War of 1812 have been happily extinguished. By a judicious application of the revenues not required for other necessary purposes, it is not doubted that the debt which has grown out of the circumstances of the last few years may be speedily paid off.

I congratulate my fellow-citizens on the entire restoration of the credit of the General Government of the Union and that of many of the States. Happy would it be for the indebted States if they were freed from their liabilities, many of which were incautiously contracted. Although the Government of the Union is neither in a legal nor a moral sense bound for the debts of the States, and it would be a violation of our compact of union to assume them, yet we can not but feel a deep interest in seeing all the States meet their public liabilities and pay off their just debts at the earliest practicable period. That they will do so as soon as it can be done without imposing too heavy burdens on their citizens there is no reason to doubt. The sound moral and honorable feeling of the people of the indebted States can not be questioned, and we are happy to perceive a settled disposition on their part, as their ability returns after a season of unexampled pecuniary embarrassment, to pay off all just demands and to acquiesce in any reasonable measures to accomplish that object.

One of the difficulties which we have had to encounter in the practical administration of the Government consists in the adjustment of our revenue laws and the levy of the taxes necessary for the support of Government. In the general proposition that no more money shall be collected than the necessities of an economical administration shall require all parties seem to acquiesce. Nor does there seem to be any material difference of opinion as to the absence of right in the Government to tax one section of country, or one class of citizens, or one occupation, for the mere profit of another. "Justice and sound policy forbid the Federal Government to foster one branch of industry to the detriment of another, or to cherish the interests of one portion to the injury of another portion of our common country." I have heretofore declared to my fellow-citizens that "in my judgment it is the duty of the Government to extend, as far as it may be practicable to do so, by its revenue laws and all other means within its power, fair and just protection to all the great interests of the whole Union, embracing agriculture, manufactures, the mechanic arts, commerce, and navigation." I have also declared my opinion to be "in favor of a tariff for revenue," and that "in adjusting the details of such a tariff I have sanctioned such moderate discriminating duties as would produce the amount of revenue needed and at the same time afford reasonable incidental protection to our home industry," and that I was "opposed to a tariff for protection merely, and not for revenue."

The power "to lay and collect taxes, duties, imposts, and excises" was an indispensable one to be conferred on the Federal Government, which without it would possess no means of providing for its own support. In executing this power by levying a tariff of duties for the support of Government, the raising of *revenue* should be the *object* and *protection* the *incident*. To reverse this principle and make *protection* the *object* and *revenue* the *incident* would be to inflict manifest injustice upon all other than the protected interests. In levying duties for revenue it is doubtless proper to make such discriminations within the *revenue principle* as will afford incidental protection to our home interests. Within the revenue limit there is a discretion to discriminate; beyond that limit the rightful exercise of the power is not conceded. The incidental protection afforded to our home interests by discriminations within the revenue range it is believed will be ample. In making discriminations all our home interests should as far as practicable be equally protected. The largest portion of our people are agriculturists. Others are employed in manufactures, commerce, navigation, and the mechanic arts. They are all engaged in their respective pursuits, and their joint labors constitute the national or home industry. To tax one branch of this home industry for the benefit of another would be unjust. No one of these interests can rightfully claim an advantage over the others, or to be enriched by impoverishing the others. All are equally entitled to the fostering care and protection of the Government. In exercising a sound discretion in levying discriminating duties within the limit prescribed, care should be taken that it be done in a manner not to benefit the wealthy few at the expense of the toiling millions by taxing *lowest* the luxuries of life, or articles of superior quality and high price, which can only be consumed by the wealthy, and *highest* the necessaries of life, or articles of coarse quality and low price, which the poor and great mass of our people must consume. The burdens of government should as far as practicable be distributed justly and equally among all classes of our population. These general views, long entertained on this subject, I have deemed it proper to reiterate. It is a subject upon which conflicting interests of sections and occupations are supposed to exist, and a spirit of mutual concession and compromise in adjusting its details should be cherished by every part of our widespread country as the only means of preserving harmony and a cheerful acquiescence of all in the operation of our revenue laws. Our patriotic citizens in every part of the Union will readily submit to the payment of such taxes as shall be needed for the support of their Government, whether in peace or in war, if they are so levied as to distribute the burdens as equally as possible among them.

The Republic of Texas has made known her desire to come into our Union, to form a part of our Confederacy and enjoy with us the blessings of liberty secured and guaranteed by our Constitution. Texas was once a part of our country—was unwisely ceded away to a foreign power—is now independent, and possesses an undoubted right to dispose of a part or the whole of her territory and to merge her sovereignty as a separate and independent state in ours. I congratulate my country that by an act of the late Congress of the United States the assent of this Government has been given to the reunion, and it only remains for the two countries to agree upon the terms to consummate an object so important to both.

I regard the question of annexation as belonging exclusively to the United States and Texas. They are independent powers competent to contract, and foreign nations have no right to interfere with them or to take exceptions to their reunion. Foreign powers do not seem to appreciate the true character of our Government. Our Union is a confederation of independent States, whose policy is peace with each other and all the world. To enlarge its limits is to extend the dominions of peace over additional territories and increasing millions. The world has nothing to fear from military ambition in our Government. While the Chief Magistrate and the popular branch of Congress are elected for short terms by the suffrages of those millions who must in their own persons bear all the burdens and miseries of war, our Government can not be otherwise than pacific. Foreign powers should therefore look on the annexation of Texas to the United States not as the conquest of a nation seeking to extend her dominions by arms and violence, but as the peaceful acquisition of a territory once her own, by adding another member to our confederation, with the consent of that member, thereby diminishing the chances of war and opening to them new and ever-increasing markets for their products.

To Texas the reunion is important, because the strong protecting arm of our Government would be extended over her, and the vast resources of her fertile soil and genial climate would be speedily developed, while the safety of New Orleans and of our whole southwestern frontier against hostile aggression, as well as the interests of the whole Union, would be promoted by it.

In the earlier stages of our national existence the opinion prevailed with some that our system of confederated States could not operate successfully over an extended territory, and serious objections have at different times been made to the enlargement of our boundaries. These objections were earnestly urged when we acquired Louisiana. Experience has shown that they were not well founded. The title of numerous Indian tribes to vast tracts of country has been extinguished; new States have been admitted into the Union; new Territories have been created and our jurisdiction and laws extended over them. As our population has expanded, the Union has been cemented and strengthened. As our boundaries have been enlarged and our agricultural population has been spread over a large surface, our federative system has acquired additional strength and security. It may well be doubted whether it would not be in greater danger of overthrow if our present population were confined to the comparatively narrow limits of the original thirteen States than it is now that they are sparsely settled over a more expanded territory. It is confidently believed that our system may be safely extended to the utmost bounds of our territorial limits, and that as it shall be extended the bonds of our Union, so far from being weakened, will become stronger.

None can fail to see the danger to our safety and future peace if Texas remains an independent state or becomes an ally or dependency of some foreign nation more powerful than herself. Is there one among our citizens who would not prefer perpetual peace with Texas to occasional wars, which so often occur between bordering independent nations? Is there one who would not prefer free intercourse with her to high duties on all our products and manufactures which enter her ports or cross her frontiers? Is there one who would not prefer an unrestricted communication with her citizens to the frontier obstructions which must occur if she remains out of the Union? Whatever is good or evil in the local institutions of Texas will remain her own whether annexed to the United States or not. None of the present States will be responsible for them any more than they are for the local institutions of each other. They have confederated together for certain specified objects. Upon the same principle that they would refuse to form a perpetual union with Texas because of her local institutions our forefathers would have been prevented from forming our present Union. Perceiving no valid objection to the measure and many reasons for its adoption vitally affecting the peace, the safety, and the prosperity of both countries, I shall on the broad principle which formed the basis and produced the adoption of our Constitution, and not in any narrow spirit of sectional policy, endeavor by all constitutional, honorable, and appropriate means to consummate the expressed will of the people and Government of the United States by the reannexation of Texas to our Union at the earliest practicable period.

Nor will it become in a less degree my duty to assert and maintain by all constitutional means the right of the United States to that portion of our territory which lies beyond the Rocky Mountains. Our title to the country of the Oregon is "clear and unquestionable," and already are our people preparing to perfect that title by occupying it with their wives and children. But eighty years ago our population was confined on the west by the ridge of the Alleghanies. Within that period—within the lifetime, I might say, of some of my hearers—our people, increasing to many millions, have filled the eastern valley of the Mississippi, adventurously ascended the Missouri to its headsprings, and are already engaged in establishing the blessings of self-government in valleys of which the rivers flow to the Pacific. The world beholds the peaceful triumphs of the industry of our emigrants. To us belongs the duty of protecting them adequately wherever they may be upon our soil. The jurisdiction of our laws and the benefits of our republican institutions should be extended over them in the distant regions which they have selected for their homes. The increasing facilities of intercourse will easily bring the States, of which the formation in that part of our territory can not be long delayed, within the sphere of our federative Union. In the meantime every obligation imposed by treaty or conventional stipulations should be sacredly respected.

In the management of our foreign relations it will be my aim to observe a careful respect for the rights of other nations, while our own will be the subject of constant watchfulness. Equal and exact justice should characterize all our intercourse with foreign countries. All alliances having a tendency to jeopard the welfare and honor of our country or sacrifice any one of the national interests will be studiously avoided, and yet no opportunity will be lost to cultivate a favorable understanding with foreign governments by which our navigation and commerce may be extended and the ample products of our fertile soil, as well as the manufactures of our skillful artisans, find a ready market and remunerating prices in foreign countries.

In taking "care that the laws be faithfully executed," a strict performance of duty will be exacted from all public officers. From those officers, especially, who are charged with the collection and disbursement of the public revenue will prompt and rigid accountability be required. Any culpable failure or delay on their part to account for the moneys intrusted to them at the times and in the manner required by law will in every instance terminate the official connection of such defaulting officer with the Government.

Although in our country the Chief Magistrate must almost of necessity be chosen by a party and stand pledged to its principles and measures, yet in his official action he should not be the President of a part only, but of the whole people of the United States. While he executes the laws with an impartial hand, shrinks from no proper responsibility, and faithfully carries out in the executive department of the Government the principles and policy of those who have chosen him, he should not be unmindful that our fellow-citizens who have differed with him in opinion are entitled to the full and free exercise of their opinions and judgments, and that the rights of all are entitled to respect and regard.

Confidently relying upon the aid and assistance of the coordinate departments of the Government in conducting our public affairs, I enter upon the discharge of the high duties which have been assigned me by the people, again humbly supplicating that Divine Being who has watched over and protected our beloved country from its infancy to the present hour to continue His gracious benedictions upon us, that we may continue to be a prosperous and happy people.

MARCH 4, 1845.

SPECIAL MESSAGE.

WASHINGTON, *March 15, 1845.*

To the Senate of the United States:

I have received and maturely considered the two resolutions adopted by the Senate in executive session on the 12th instant, the first requesting the President to communicate information to the Senate (in confidence) of any steps which have been taken, if any were taken, by the late President in execution of the resolution of Congress entitled "A joint resolution for the annexation of Texas to the United States," and if any such steps have been taken, then to inform the Senate whether anything has been done by him to counteract, suspend, or reverse the action of the late President in the premises; and the second requesting the President "to inform the Senate what communications have been made by the Mexican minister in consequence of the proceedings of Congress and the Executive in relation to Texas."

With the highest respect for the Senate and a sincere desire to furnish all the information requested by the first resolution, I yet entertain strong apprehensions lest such a communication might delay and ultimately endanger the success of the great measure which Congress so earnestly sought to accomplish by the passage of the "joint resolution for the annexation of Texas to the United States." The initiatory proceedings which have been adopted by the Executive to give effect to this resolution can not, therefore, in my judgment, at this time and under existing circumstances, be communicated without injury to the public interest.

In conformity with the second resolution, I herewith transmit to the Senate the copy of a note, dated on the 6th instant, addressed by General Almonte, envoy extraordinary and minister plenipotentiary of the Mexican Republic, to the Hon. John C. Calhoun, late Secretary of State, which is the only communication that has been made by the Mexican minister to the Department of State since the passage of the joint resolution of Congress for the annexation of Texas; and I also transmit a copy of the answer of the Secretary of State to this note of the Mexican minister.

JAMES K. POLK.

EXECUTIVE ORDERS.

WASHINGTON CITY, *June 16, 1845*.

Andrew Jackson is no more. He departed this life on Sunday, the 8th instant, full of days and full of honors. His country deplores his loss, and will ever cherish his memory. Whilst a nation mourns it is proper that business should be suspended, at least for one day, in the Executive Departments, as a tribute of respect to the illustrious dead.

I accordingly direct that the Departments of State, the Treasury, War, the Navy, the Post-Office, the office of the Attorney-General, and the Executive Mansion be instantly put into mourning, and that they be closed during the whole day to-morrow.

JAMES K. POLK.

GENERAL ORDERS, No. 27.

WAR DEPARTMENT,
ADJUTANT-GENERAL'S OFFICE,
Washington, June 16, 1845.

The following general order of the President, received through the War Department, announces to the Army the death of the illustrious ex-President, General Andrew Jackson:

GENERAL ORDER.

WASHINGTON, *June 16, 1845.*

The President of the United States with heartfelt sorrow announces to the Army, the Navy, and the Marine Corps the death of Andrew Jackson. On the evening of Sunday, the 8th day of June, about 6 o'clock, he resigned his spirit to his Heavenly Father. The nation, while it learns with grief the death of its most illustrious citizen, fiuds solace in contemplating his venerable character and services. The Valley of the Mississippi beheld in him the bravest and wisest and most fortunate of its defenders; the country raised him to the highest trusts in military and in civil life with a confidence that never abated and an affection that followed him in undiminished vigor to retirement, watched over his latest hours, and pays its tribute at his grave. Wherever his lot was cast he appeared among those around him first in natural endowments and resources, not less than first in authority and station. The power of his mind impressed itself on the policy of his country, and still lives, and will live forever in the memory of its people. Child of a forest region and a settler of the wilderness, his was a genius which, as it came to the guidance of affairs, instinctively attached itself to general principles, and inspired by the truth which his own heart revealed to him in singleness and simplicity, he found always a response in the breast of his countrymen. Crowned with glory in war, in his whole career as a statesman he showed himself the friend and lover of peace. With an American heart, whose throbs were all for republican freedom and his native land, he yet longed to promote the widest intercourse and most intimate commerce between the many nations of mankind. He was the servant of humanity. Of a vehement will, he was patient in council, deliberating long, hearing all things, yet in the moment of action deciding with rapidity. Of a noble nature and incapable of disguise, his thoughts lay open to all around him and won their confidence by his ingenuous frankness. His judgment was of that solidity that he ever tempered vigor with prudence. The flushings of anger could never cloud his faculties, but rather kindled and lighted them up, quickening their energy without disturbing their balance. In war his eye at a glance discerned his plans with unerring sagacity; in peace he proposed measures with an instinctive wisdom of which the inspirations were prophecy. In discipline stern, in a just resolution inflexible, he was full of the gentlest affections, ever ready to solace the distressed and to relieve the needy, faithful to his friends, fervid for his country. Indifferent to other rewards, he aspired throughout life to an honorable fame, and so loved his fellow-men that he longed to dwell in their affectionate remembrance. Heaven gave him length of days and he filled them with deeds of greatness. He was always happy—happy in his youth, which shared the achievement of our national independence; happy in his after years, which beheld the Valley of the West cover itself with the glory of free and ever-increasing States; happy in his age, which saw the people multiply from two to twenty millions and freedom and union make their pathway from the Atlantic to the Pacific; thrice happy in death, for while he believed the liberties of his country imperishable and was cheered by visions of its constant advancement, he departed from this life in a full hope of a blessed immortality through the merits and atonement of the Redeemer.

Officers of the Army, the Navy, and the Marine Corps will wear crape on the left arm and on their swords and the colors of the several regiments will be put in mourning for the period of six months. At the naval stations and the public vessels in commission the flags will be worn at half-mast for one week, and on the day after this order is received twenty-one minute guns will be fired, beginning at 12 o'clock.

At each military station the day after the reception of this order the national flag will be displayed at half-staff from sunrise to sunset, thirteen guns will be fired at daybreak, half-hour guns during the day, and at the close of the day a general salute. The troops will be paraded at 10 o'clock and this order read to them, on which the labors of the day will cease.

Let the virtues of the illustrious dead retain their influence, and when energy and courage are called to trial emulate his example.

GEORGE BANCROFT,
Acting Secretary of War, and Secretary of the Navy.

By order:

R. JONES, *Adjutant-General.*

FIRST ANNUAL MESSAGE.

WASHINGTON, *December 2, 1845.*

Fellow-Citizens of the Senate and House of Representatives:

It is to me a source of unaffected satisfaction to meet the representatives of the States and the people in Congress assembled, as it will be to receive the aid of their combined wisdom in the administration of public affairs. In performing for the first time the duty imposed on me by the

Constitution of giving to you information of the state of the Union and recommending to your consideration such measures as in my judgment are necessary and expedient, I am happy that I can congratulate you on the continued prosperity of our country. Under the blessings of Divine Providence and the benign influence of our free institutions, it stands before the world a spectacle of national happiness.

With our unexampled advancement in all the elements of national greatness, the affection of the people is confirmed for the Union of the States and for the doctrines of popular liberty which lie at the foundation of our Government.

It becomes us in humility to make our devout acknowledgments to the Supreme Ruler of the Universe for the inestimable civil and religious blessings with which we are favored.

In calling the attention of Congress to our relations with foreign powers, I am gratified to be able to state that though with some of them there have existed since your last session serious causes of irritation and misunderstanding, yet no actual hostilities have taken place. Adopting the maxim in the conduct of our foreign affairs ''to ask nothing that is not right and submit to nothing that is wrong,'' it has been my anxious desire to preserve peace with all nations, but at the same time to be prepared to resist aggression and maintain all our just rights.

In pursuance of the joint resolution of Congress ''for annexing Texas to the United States,'' my predecessor, on the 3d day of March, 1845, elected to submit the first and second sections of that resolution to the Republic of Texas as an overture on the part of the United States for her admission as a State into our Union. This election I approved, and accordingly the chargé d'affaires of the United States in Texas, under instructions of the 10th of March, 1845, presented these sections of the resolution for the acceptance of that Republic. The executive government, the Congress, and the people of Texas in convention have successively complied with all the terms and conditions of the joint resolution. A constitution for the government of the State of Texas, formed by a convention of deputies, is herewith laid before Congress. It is well known, also, that the people of Texas at the polls have accepted the terms of annexation and ratified the constitution. I communicate to Congress the correspondence between the Secretary of State and our chargé d'affaires in Texas, and also the correspondence of the latter with the authorities of Texas, together with the official documents transmitted by him to his own Government. The terms of annexation which were offered by the United States having been accepted by Texas, the public faith of both parties is solemnly pledged to the compact of their union. Nothing remains to consummate the event but the passage of an act by Congress to admit the State of Texas into the Union upon an equal footing with the original States. Strong reasons exist why this should be done at an early period of the session. It will be observed

that by the constitution of Texas the existing government is only continued temporarily till Congress can act, and that the third Monday of the present month is the day appointed for holding the first general election. On that day a governor, a lieutenant-governor, and both branches of the legislature will be chosen by the people. The President of Texas is required, immediately after the receipt of official information that the new State has been admitted into our Union by Congress, to convene the legislature, and upon its meeting the existing government will be superseded and the State government organized. Questions deeply interesting to Texas, in common with the other States, the extension of our revenue laws and judicial system over her people and territory, as well as measures of a local character, will claim the early attention of Congress, and therefore upon every principle of republican government she ought to be represented in that body without unnecessary delay. I can not too earnestly recommend prompt action on this important subject. As soon as the act to admit Texas as a State shall be passed the union of the two Republics will be consummated by their own voluntary consent.

This accession to our territory has been a bloodless achievement. No arm of force has been raised to produce the result. The sword has had no part in the victory. We have not sought to extend our territorial possessions by conquest, or our republican institutions over a reluctant people. It was the deliberate homage of each people to the great principle of our federative union. If we consider the extent of territory involved in the annexation, its prospective influence on America, the means by which it has been accomplished, springing purely from the choice of the people themselves to share the blessings of our union, the history of the world may be challenged to furnish a parallel. The jurisdiction of the United States, which at the formation of the Federal Constitution was bounded by the St. Marys on the Atlantic, has passed the capes of Florida and been peacefully extended to the Del Norte. In contemplating the grandeur of this event it is not to be forgotten that the result was achieved in despite of the diplomatic interference of European monarchies. Even France, the country which had been our ancient ally, the country which has a common interest with us in maintaining the freedom of the seas, the country which, by the cession of Louisiana, first opened to us access to the Gulf of Mexico, the country with which we have been every year drawing more and more closely the bonds of successful commerce, most unexpectedly, and to our unfeigned regret, took part in an effort to prevent annexation and to impose on Texas, as a condition of the recognition of her independence by Mexico, that she would never join herself to the United States. We may rejoice that the tranquil and pervading influence of the American principle of self-government was sufficient to defeat the purposes of British and French interference, and that the almost unanimous voice of the people of Texas has given to that interference a peaceful and effective rebuke. From this example European

Constitution of giving to you information of the state of the Union and recommending to your consideration such measures as in my judgment are necessary and expedient, I am happy that I can congratulate you on the continued prosperity of our country. Under the blessings of Divine Providence and the benign influence of our free institutions, it stands before the world a spectacle of national happiness.

With our unexampled advancement in all the elements of national greatness, the affection of the people is confirmed for the Union of the States and for the doctrines of popular liberty which lie at the foundation of our Government.

It becomes us in humility to make our devout acknowledgments to the Supreme Ruler of the Universe for the inestimable civil and religious blessings with which we are favored.

In calling the attention of Congress to our relations with foreign powers, I am gratified to be able to state that though with some of them there have existed since your last session serious causes of irritation and misunderstanding, yet no actual hostilities have taken place. Adopting the maxim in the conduct of our foreign affairs "to ask nothing that is not right and submit to nothing that is wrong," it has been my anxious desire to preserve peace with all nations, but at the same time to be prepared to resist aggression and maintain all our just rights.

In pursuance of the joint resolution of Congress "for annexing Texas to the United States," my predecessor, on the 3d day of March, 1845, elected to submit the first and second sections of that resolution to the Republic of Texas as an overture on the part of the United States for her admission as a State into our Union. This election I approved, and accordingly the chargé d'affaires of the United States in Texas, under instructions of the 10th of March, 1845, presented these sections of the resolution for the acceptance of that Republic. The executive government, the Congress, and the people of Texas in convention have successively complied with all the terms and conditions of the joint resolution. A constitution for the government of the State of Texas, formed by a convention of deputies, is herewith laid before Congress. It is well known, also, that the people of Texas at the polls have accepted the terms of annexation and ratified the constitution. I communicate to Congress the correspondence between the Secretary of State and our chargé d'affaires in Texas, and also the correspondence of the latter with the authorities of Texas, together with the official documents transmitted by him to his own Government. The terms of annexation which were offered by the United States having been accepted by Texas, the public faith of both parties is solemnly pledged to the compact of their union. Nothing remains to consummate the event but the passage of an act by Congress to admit the State of Texas into the Union upon an equal footing with the original States. Strong reasons exist why this should be done at an early period of the session. It will be observed

that by the constitution of Texas the existing government is only continued temporarily till Congress can act, and that the third Monday of the present month is the day appointed for holding the first general election. On that day a governor, a lieutenant-governor, and both branches of the legislature will be chosen by the people. The President of Texas is required, immediately after the receipt of official information that the new State has been admitted into our Union by Congress, to convene the legislature, and upon its meeting the existing government will be superseded and the State government organized. Questions deeply interesting to Texas, in common with the other States, the extension of our revenue laws and judicial system over her people and territory, as well as measures of a local character, will claim the early attention of Congress, and therefore upon every principle of republican government she ought to be represented in that body without unnecessary delay. I can not too earnestly recommend prompt action on this important subject. As soon as the act to admit Texas as a State shall be passed the union of the two Republics will be consummated by their own voluntary consent.

This accession to our territory has been a bloodless achievement. No arm of force has been raised to produce the result. The sword has had no part in the victory. We have not sought to extend our territorial possessions by conquest, or our republican institutions over a reluctant people. It was the deliberate homage of each people to the great principle of our federative union. If we consider the extent of territory involved in the annexation, its prospective influence on America, the means by which it has been accomplished, springing purely from the choice of the people themselves to share the blessings of our union, the history of the world may be challenged to furnish a parallel. The jurisdiction of the United States, which at the formation of the Federal Constitution was bounded by the St. Marys on the Atlantic, has passed the capes of Florida and been peacefully extended to the Del Norte. In contemplating the grandeur of this event it is not to be forgotten that the result was achieved in despite of the diplomatic interference of European monarchies. Even France, the country which had been our ancient ally, the country which has a common interest with us in maintaining the freedom of the seas, the country which, by the cession of Louisiana, first opened to us access to the Gulf of Mexico, the country with which we have been every year drawing more and more closely the bonds of successful commerce, most unexpectedly, and to our unfeigned regret, took part in an effort to prevent annexation and to impose on Texas, as a condition of the recognition of her independence by Mexico, that she would never join herself to the United States. We may rejoice that the tranquil and pervading influence of the American principle of self-government was sufficient to defeat the purposes of British and French interference, and that the almost unanimous voice of the people of Texas has given to that interference a peaceful and effective rebuke. From this example European

Constitution of giving to you information of the state of the Union and recommending to your consideration such measures as in my judgment are necessary and expedient, I am happy that I can congratulate you on the continued prosperity of our country.   Under the blessings of Divine Providence and the benign influence of our free institutions, it stands before the world a spectacle of national happiness.

With our unexampled advancement in all the elements of national greatness, the affection of the people is confirmed for the Union of the States and for the doctrines of popular liberty which lie at the foundation of our Government.

It becomes us in humility to make our devout acknowledgments to the Supreme Ruler of the Universe for the inestimable civil and religious blessings with which we are favored.

In calling the attention of Congress to our relations with foreign powers, I am gratified to be able to state that though with some of them there have existed since your last session serious causes of irritation and misunderstanding, yet no actual hostilities have taken place.   Adopting the maxim in the conduct of our foreign affairs "to ask nothing that is not right and submit to nothing that is wrong," it has been my anxious desire to preserve peace with all nations, but at the same time to be prepared to resist aggression and maintain all our just rights.

In pursuance of the joint resolution of Congress "for annexing Texas to the United States," my predecessor, on the 3d day of March, 1845, elected to submit the first and second sections of that resolution to the Republic of Texas as an overture on the part of the United States for her admission as a State into our Union.   This election I approved, and accordingly the chargé d'affaires of the United States in Texas, under instructions of the 10th of March, 1845, presented these sections of the resolution for the acceptance of that Republic.   The executive government, the Congress, and the people of Texas in convention have successively complied with all the terms and conditions of the joint resolution. A constitution for the government of the State of Texas, formed by a convention of deputies, is herewith laid before Congress.   It is well known, also, that the people of Texas at the polls have accepted the terms of annexation and ratified the constitution.   I communicate to Congress the correspondence between the Secretary of State and our chargé d'affaires in Texas, and also the correspondence of the latter with the authorities of Texas, together with the official documents transmitted by him to his own Government.   The terms of annexation which were offered by the United States having been accepted by Texas, the public faith of both parties is solemnly pledged to the compact of their union.   Nothing remains to consummate the event but the passage of an act by Congress to admit the State of Texas into the Union upon an equal footing with the original States.   Strong reasons exist why this should be done at an early period of the session.   It will be observed

that by the constitution of Texas the existing government is only continued temporarily till Congress can act, and that the third Monday of the present month is the day appointed for holding the first general election. On that day a governor, a lieutenant-governor, and both branches of the legislature will be chosen by the people. The President of Texas is required, immediately after the receipt of official information that the new State has been admitted into our Union by Congress, to convene the legislature, and upon its meeting the existing government will be superseded and the State government organized. Questions deeply interesting to Texas, in common with the other States, the extension of our revenue laws and judicial system over her people and territory, as well as measures of a local character, will claim the early attention of Congress, and therefore upon every principle of republican government she ought to be represented in that body without unnecessary delay. I can not too earnestly recommend prompt action on this important subject. As soon as the act to admit Texas as a State shall be passed the union of the two Republics will be consummated by their own voluntary consent.

This accession to our territory has been a bloodless achievement. No arm of force has been raised to produce the result. The sword has had no part in the victory. We have not sought to extend our territorial possessions by conquest, or our republican institutions over a reluctant people. It was the deliberate homage of each people to the great principle of our federative union. If we consider the extent of territory involved in the annexation, its prospective influence on America, the means by which it has been accomplished, springing purely from the choice of the people themselves to share the blessings of our union, the history of the world may be challenged to furnish a parallel. The jurisdiction of the United States, which at the formation of the Federal Constitution was bounded by the St. Marys on the Atlantic, has passed the capes of Florida and been peacefully extended to the Del Norte. In contemplating the grandeur of this event it is not to be forgotten that the result was achieved in despite of the diplomatic interference of European monarchies. Even France, the country which had been our ancient ally, the country which has a common interest with us in maintaining the freedom of the seas, the country which, by the cession of Louisiana, first opened to us access to the Gulf of Mexico, the country with which we have been every year drawing more and more closely the bonds of successful commerce, most unexpectedly, and to our unfeigned regret, took part in an effort to prevent annexation and to impose on Texas, as a condition of the recognition of her independence by Mexico, that she would never join herself to the United States. We may rejoice that the tranquil and pervading influence of the American principle of self-government was sufficient to defeat the purposes of British and French interference, and that the almost unanimous voice of the people of Texas has given to that interference a peaceful and effective rebuke. From this example European

practicable period, which it is expected will be in time to enable me to communicate the result to Congress during the present session. Until that result is known I forbear to recommend to Congress such ulterior measures of redress for the wrongs and injuries we have so long borne as it would have been proper to make had no such negotiation been instituted.

Congress appropriated at the last session the sum of $275,000 for the payment of the April and July installments of the Mexican indemnities for the year 1844:

Provided it shall be ascertained to the satisfaction of the American Government that said installments have been paid by the Mexican Government to the agent appointed by the United States to receive the same in such manner as to discharge all claim on the Mexican Government, and said agent to be delinquent in remitting the money to the United States.

The unsettled state of our relations with Mexico has involved this subject in much mystery. The first information in an authentic form from the agent of the United States, appointed under the Administration of my predecessor, was received at the State Department on the 9th of November last. This is contained in a letter, dated the 17th of October, addressed by him to one of our citizens then in Mexico with a view of having it communicated to that Department. From this it appears that the agent on the 20th of September, 1844, gave a receipt to the treasury of Mexico for the amount of the April and July installments of the indemnity. In the same communication, however, he asserts that he had not received a single dollar in cash, but that he holds such securities as warranted him at the time in giving the receipt, and entertains no doubt but that he will eventually obtain the money. As these installments appear never to have been actually paid by the Government of Mexico to the agent, and as that Government has not, therefore, been released so as to discharge the claim, I do not feel myself warranted in directing payment to be made to the claimants out of the Treasury without further legislation. Their case is undoubtedly one of much hardship, and it remains for Congress to decide whether any, and what, relief ought to be granted to them. Our minister to Mexico has been instructed to ascertain the facts of the case from the Mexican Government in an authentic and official form and report the result with as little delay as possible.

My attention was early directed to the negotiation which on the 4th of March last I found pending at Washington between the United States and Great Britain on the subject of the Oregon Territory. Three several attempts had been previously made to settle the questions in dispute between the two countries by negotiation upon the principle of compromise, but each had proved unsuccessful. These negotiations took place at London in the years 1818, 1824, and 1826—the two first under the Administration of Mr. Monroe and the last under that of Mr. Adams.

The negotiation of 1818, having failed to accomplish its object, resulted in the convention of the 20th of October of that year.

By the third article of that convention it was—

Agreed that any country that may be claimed by either party on the northwest coast of America westward of the Stony Mountains shall, together with its harbors, bays, and creeks, and the navigation of all rivers within the same, be free and open for the term of ten years from the date f the signature of the , resent convention to the vessels, citizens, and subjects of the two powers; it being well understood that this agreement is not to be construed to the prejudice of any claim which either of the two high contracting parties may have to any part of the said country, nor shall it be taken to affect the claims of any other power or state to any part of the said country, the only object of the high contracting parties in that respect being to prevent disputes and differences amongst themselves.

The negotiation of 1824 was productive of no result, and the convention of 1818 was left unchanged.

The negotiation of 1826, having also failed to effect an adjustment by compromise, resulted in the convention of August 6, 1827, by which it was agreed to continue in force for an indefinite period the provisions of the third article of the convention of the 20th of October, 1818; and it was further provided that—

It shall be competent, however, to either of the contracting parties, in case either should think fit, at any time after the 20th of October, 1828, on giving due notice of twelve months to the other contracting party, to annul and abrogate this convention; and it shall in such case be accordingly entirely annulled and abrogated after the expiration of the said term of notice.

In these attempts to adjust the controversy the parallel of the forty-ninth degree of north latitude had been offered by the United States to Great Britain, and in those of 1818 and 1826, with a further concession of the free navigation of the Columbia River south of that latitude. The parallel of the forty-ninth degree from the Rocky Mountains to its intersection with the northeasternmost branch of the Columbia, and thence down the channel of that river to the sea, had been offered by Great Britain, with an addition of a small detached territory north of the Columbia. Each of these propositions had been rejected by the parties respectively. In October, 1843, the envoy extraordinary and minister plenipotentiary of the United States in London was authorized to make a similar offer to those made in 1818 and 1826. Thus stood the question when the negotiation was shortly afterwards transferred to Washington, and on the 23d of August, 1844, was formally opened under the direction of my immediate predecessor. Like all the previous negotiations, it was based upon principles of "compromise," and the avowed purpose of the parties was "to treat of the respective claims of the two countries to the Oregon Territory with the view to establish a permanent boundary between them westward of the Rocky Mountains to the Pacific Ocean."

Accordingly, on the 26th of August, 1844, the British plenipotentiary offered to divide the Oregon Territory by the forty-ninth parallel of north latitude from the Rocky Mountains to the point of its intersection with the northeasternmost branch of the Columbia River, and thence down that river to the sea, leaving the free navigation of the river to be enjoyed in common by both parties, the country south of this line to belong to the United States and that north of it to Great Britain.   At the same time he proposed in addition to yield to the United States a detached territory north of the Columbia extending along the Pacific and the Straits of Fuca from Bulfinchs Harbor, inclusive, to Hoods Canal, and to make free to the United States any port or ports south of latitude 49° which they might desire, either on the mainland or on Quadra and Vancouvers Island.   With the exception of the free ports, this was the same offer which had been made by the British and rejected by the American Government in the negotiation of 1826.   This proposition was properly rejected by the American plenipotentiary on the day it was submitted.   This was the only proposition of compromise offered by the British plenipotentiary.   The proposition on the part of Great Britain having been rejected, the British plenipotentiary requested that a proposal should be made by the United States for ''an equitable adjustment of the question.''   When I came into office I found this to be the state of the negotiation.   Though entertaining the settled conviction that the British pretensions of title could not be maintained to any portion of the Oregon Territory upon any principle of public law recognized by nations, yet in deference to what had been done by my predecessors, and especially in consideration that propositions of compromise had been thrice made by two preceding Administrations to adjust the question on the parallel of 49°, and in two of them yielding to Great Britain the free navigation of the Columbia, and that the pending negotiation had been commenced on the basis of compromise, I deemed it to be my duty not abruptly to break it off.   In consideration, too, that under the conventions of 1818 and 1827 the citizens and subjects of the two powers held a joint occupancy of the country, I was induced to make another effort to settle this long-pending controversy in the spirit of moderation which had given birth to the renewed discussion.   A proposition was accordingly made, which was rejected by the British plenipotentiary, who, without submitting any other proposition, suffered the negotiation on his part to drop, expressing his trust that the United States would offer what he saw fit to call ''some further proposal for the settlement of the Oregon question more consistent with fairness and equity and with the reasonable expectations of the British Government.''   The proposition thus offered and rejected repeated the offer of the parallel of 49° of north latitude, which had been made by two preceding Administrations, but without proposing to surrender to Great Britain, as they had done, the free navigation of the Columbia River.   The right of any foreign power to the free navigation of any of our rivers through the heart of our country was one which I was unwilling to concede.   It also embraced a provision to make free to Great Britain any port or ports on the cap of Quadra and Vancouvers Island south of this parallel. Had this been a new question, coming under discussion for the first time, this proposition would not have been made. The extraordinary and wholly inadmissible demands of the British Government and the rejection of the proposition made in deference alone to what had been done by my predecessors and the implied obligation which their acts seemed to impose afford satisfactory evidence that no compromise which the United States ought to accept can be effected. With this conviction the proposition of compromise which had been made and rejected was by my direction subsequently withdrawn and our title to the whole Oregon Territory asserted, and, as is believed, maintained by irrefragable facts and arguments.

The civilized world will see in these proceedings a spirit of liberal concession on the part of the United States, and this Government will be relieved from all responsibility which may follow the failure to settle the controversy.

All attempts at compromise having failed, it becomes the duty of Congress to consider what measures it may be proper to adopt for the security and protection of our citizens now inhabiting or who may hereafter inhabit Oregon, and for the maintenance of our just title to that Territory. In adopting measures for this purpose care should be taken that nothing be done to violate the stipulations of the convention of 1827, which is still in force. The faith of treaties, in their letter and spirit, has ever been, and, I trust, will ever be, scrupulously observed by the United States. Under that convention a year's notice is required to be given by either party to the other before the joint occupancy shall terminate and before either can rightfully assert or exercise exclusive jurisdiction over any portion of the territory. This notice it would, in my judgment, be proper to give, and I recommend that provision be made by law for giving it accordingly, and terminating in this manner the convention of the 6th of August, 1827.

It will become proper for Congress to determine what legislation they can in the meantime adopt without violating this convention. Beyond all question the protection of our laws and our jurisdiction, civil and criminal, ought to be immediately extended over our citizens in Oregon. They have had just cause to complain of our long neglect in this particular, and have in consequence been compelled for their own security and protection to establish a provisional government for themselves. Strong in their allegiance and ardent in their attachment to the United States, they have been thus cast upon their own resources. They are anxious that our laws should be extended over them, and I recommend that this be done by Congress with as little delay as possible in the full extent to which the British Parliament have proceeded in regard to British subjects in that Territory by their act of July 2, 1821, "for regulating the fur trade and establishing a criminal and civil jurisdiction within certain parts of

North America." By this act Great Britain extended her laws and jurisdiction, civil and criminal, over her subjects engaged in the fur trade in
that Territory. By it the courts of the Province of Upper Canada were
empowered to take cognizance of causes civil and criminal. Justices of
the peace and other judicial officers were authorized to be appointed in
Oregon with power to execute all process issuing from the courts of that
Province, and to "sit and hold courts of record for the trial of criminal
offenses and misdemeanors" not made the subject of capital punishment,
and also of civil cases where the cause of action shall not "exceed in value
the amount or sum of £200."

Subsequent to the date of this act of Parliament a grant was made
from the "British Crown" to the Hudsons Bay Company of the exclusive trade with the Indian tribes in the Oregon Territory, subject to a
reservation that it shall not operate to the exclusion "of the subjects of
any foreign states who, under or by force of any convention for the time
being between us and such foreign states, respectively, may be entitled
to and shall be engaged in the said trade." It is much to be regretted
that while under this act British subjects have enjoyed the protection
of British laws and British judicial tribunals throughout the whole of
Oregon, American citizens in the same Territory have enjoyed no such
protection from their Government. At the same time, the result illustrates the character of our people and their institutions. In spite of this
neglect they have multiplied, and their number is rapidly increasing in
that Territory. They have made no appeal to arms, but have peacefully
fortified themselves in their new homes by the adoption of republican
institutions for themselves, furnishing another example of the truth that
self-government is inherent in the American breast and must prevail.
It is due to them that they should be embraced and protected by our
laws. It is deemed important that our laws regulating trade and intercourse with the Indian tribes east of the Rocky Mountains should be
extended to such tribes as dwell beyond them. The increasing emigration to Oregon and the care and protection which is due from the Government to its citizens in that distant region make it our duty, as it is
our interest, to cultivate amicable relations with the Indian tribes of that
Territory. For this purpose I recommend that provision be made for
establishing an Indian agency and such subagencies as may be deemed
necessary beyond the Rocky Mountains.

For the protection of emigrants whilst on their way to Oregon against
the attacks of the Indian tribes occupying the country through which
they pass, I recommend that a suitable number of stockades and block-
house forts be erected along the usual route between our frontier settlements on the Missouri and the Rocky Mountains, and that an adequate
force of mounted riflemen be raised to guard and protect them on their
journey. The immediate adoption of these recommendations by Congress will not violate the provisions of the existing treaty. It will be

doing nothing more for American citizens than British laws have long since done for British subjects in the same territory.

It requires several months to perform the voyage by sea from the Atlantic States to Oregon, and although we have a large number of whale ships in the Pacific, but few of them afford an opportunity of interchanging intelligence without great delay between our settlements in that distant region and the United States. An overland mail is believed to be entirely practicable, and the importance of establishing such a mail at least once a month is submitted to the favorable consideration of Congress.

It is submitted to the wisdom of Congress to determine whether at their present session, and until after the expiration of the year's notice, any other measures may be adopted consistently with the convention of 1827 for the security of our rights and the government and protection of our citizens in Oregon. That it will ultimately be wise and proper to make liberal grants of land to the patriotic pioneers who amidst privations and dangers lead the way through savage tribes inhabiting the vast wilderness intervening between our frontier settlements and Oregon, and who cultivate and are ever ready to defend the soil, I am fully satisfied. To doubt whether they will obtain such grants as soon as the convention between the United States and Great Britain shall have ceased to exist would be to doubt the justice of Congress; but, pending the year's notice, it is worthy of consideration whether a stipulation to this effect may be made consistently with the spirit of that convention.

The recommendations which I have made as to the best manner of securing our rights in Oregon are submitted to Congress with great deference. Should they in their wisdom devise any other mode better calculated to accomplish the same object, it shall meet with my hearty concurrence.

At the end of the year's notice, should Congress think it proper to make provision for giving that notice, we shall have reached a period when the national rights in Oregon must either be abandoned or firmly maintained. That they can not be abandoned without a sacrifice of both national honor and interest is too clear to admit of doubt.

Oregon is a part of the North American continent, to which, it is confidently affirmed, the title of the United States is the best now in existence. For the grounds on which that title rests I refer you to the correspondence of the late and present Secretary of State with the British plenipotentiary during the negotiation. The British proposition of compromise, which would make the Columbia the line south of 49°, with a trifling addition of detached territory to the United States north of that river, and would leave on the British side two-thirds of the whole Oregon Territory, including the free navigation of the Columbia and all the valuable harbors on the Pacific, can never for a moment be entertained by the United States without an abandonment of their just and clear territorial rights, their own self-respect, and the national honor.   For the information of Congress, I communicate herewith the correspondence which took place between the two Governments during the late negotiation.

The rapid extension of our settlements over our territories heretofore unoccupied, the addition of new States to our Confederacy, the expansion of free principles, and our rising greatness as a nation are attracting the attention of the powers of Europe, and lately the doctrine has been broached in some of them of a "balance of power" on this continent to check our advancement.   The United States, sincerely desirous of preserving relations of good understanding with all nations, can not in silence permit any European interference on the North American continent, and should any such interference be attempted will be ready to resist it at any and all hazards.

It is well known to the American people and to all nations that this Government has never interfered with the relations subsisting between other governments.   We have never made ourselves parties to their wars or their alliances; we have not sought their territories by conquest; we have not mingled with parties in their domestic struggles; and believing our own form of government to be the best, we have never attempted to propagate it by intrigues, by diplomacy, or by force.   We may claim on this continent a like exemption from European interference.   The nations of America are equally sovereign and independent with those of Europe.   They possess the same rights, independent of all foreign interposition, to make war, to conclude peace, and to regulate their internal affairs.   The people of the United States can not, therefore, view with indifference attempts of European powers to interfere with the independent action of the nations on this continent.   The American system of government is entirely different from that of Europe.   Jealousy among the different sovereigns of Europe, lest any one of them might become too powerful for the rest, has caused them anxiously to desire the establishment of what they term the "balance of power."   It can not be permitted to have any application on the North American continent, and especially to the United States.   We must ever maintain the principle that the people of this continent alone have the right to decide their own destiny.   Should any portion of them, constituting an independent state, propose to unite themselves with our Confederacy, this will be a question for them and us to determine without any foreign interposition. We can never consent that European powers shall interfere to prevent such a union because it might disturb the "balance of power" which they may desire to maintain upon this continent.   Near a quarter of a century ago the principle was distinctly announced to the world, in the annual message of one of my predecessors, that—

The American continents, by the free and independent condition which they have assumed and maintain, are henceforth not to be considered as subjects for future colonization by any European powers.

This principle will apply with greatly increased force should any European power attempt to establish any new colony in North America. In the existing circumstances of the world the present is deemed a proper occasion to reiterate and reaffirm the principle avowed by Mr. Monroe and to state my cordial concurrence in its wisdom and sound policy. The reassertion of this principle, especially in reference to North America, is at this day but the promulgation of a policy which no European power should cherish the disposition to resist. Existing rights of every European nation should be respected, but it is due alike to our safety and our interests that the efficient protection of our laws should be extended over our whole territorial limits, and that it should be distinctly announced to the world as our settled policy that no future European colony or dominion shall with our consent be planted or established on any part of the North American continent.

A question has recently arisen under the tenth article of the subsisting treaty between the United States and Prussia. By this article the consuls of the two countries have the right to sit as judges and arbitrators "in such differences as may arise between the captains and crews of the vessels belonging to the nation whose interests are committed to their charge without the interference of the local authorities, unless the conduct of the crews or of the captain should disturb the order or tranquillity of the country, or the said consuls should require their assistance to cause their decisions to be carried into effect or supported."

The Prussian consul at New Bedford in June, 1844, applied to Mr. Justice Story to carry into effect a decision made by him between the captain and crew of the Prussian ship *Borussia*, but the request was refused on the ground that without previous legislation by Congress the judiciary did not possess the power to give effect to this article of the treaty. The Prussian Government, through their minister here, have complained of this violation of the treaty, and have asked the Government of the United States to adopt the necessary measures to prevent similar violations hereafter. Good faith to Prussia, as well as to other nations with whom we have similar treaty stipulations, requires that these should be faithfully observed. I have deemed it proper, therefore, to lay the subject before Congress and to recommend such legislation as may be necessary to give effect to these treaty obligations.

By virtue of an arrangement made between the Spanish Government and that of the United States in December, 1831, American vessels, since the 29th of April, 1832, have been admitted to entry in the ports of Spain, including those of the Balearic and Canary islands, on payment of the same tonnage duty of 5 cents per ton, as though they had been Spanish vessels; and this whether our vessels arrive in Spain directly from the United States or indirectly from any other country. When Congress, by the act of 13th July, 1832, gave effect to this arrangement between the two Governments, they confined the reduction of tonnage duty merely to Spanish vessels "coming from a port in Spain," leaving the former discriminating duty to remain against such vessels coming from a port in any other country. It is manifestly unjust that whilst American vessels arriving in the ports of Spain from other countries pay no more duty than Spanish vessels, Spanish vessels arriving in the ports of the United States from other countries should be subjected to heavy discriminating tonnage duties. This is neither equality nor reciprocity, and is in violation of the arrangement concluded in December, 1831, between the two countries. The Spanish Government have made repeated and earnest remonstrances against this inequality, and the favorable attention of Congress has been several times invoked to the subject by my predecessors. I recommend, as an act of justice to Spain, that this inequality be removed by Congress and that the discriminating duties which have been levied under the act of the 13th of July, 1832, on Spanish vessels coming to the United States from any other foreign country be refunded. This recommendation does not embrace Spanish vessels arriving in the United States from Cuba and Porto Rico, which will still remain subject to the provisions of the act of June 30, 1834, concerning tonnage duty on such vessels. By the act of the 14th of July, 1832, coffee was exempted from duty altogether. This exemption was universal, without reference to the country where it was produced or the national character of the vessel in which it was imported. By the tariff act of the 30th of August, 1842, this exemption from duty was restricted to coffee imported in American vessels from the place of its production, whilst coffee imported under all other circumstances was subjected to a duty of 20 per cent *ad valorem*. Under this act and our existing treaty with the King of the Netherlands Java coffee imported from the European ports of that Kingdom into the United States, whether in Dutch or American vessels, now pays this rate of duty. The Government of the Netherlands complains that such a discriminating duty should have been imposed on coffee the production of one of its colonies, and which is chiefly brought from Java to the ports of that Kingdom and exported from thence to foreign countries. Our trade with the Netherlands is highly beneficial to both countries and our relations with them have ever been of the most friendly character. Under all the circumstances of the case, I recommend that this discrimination should be abolished and that the coffee of Java imported from the Netherlands be placed upon the same footing with that imported directly from Brazil and other countries where it is produced.

Under the eighth section of the tariff act of the 30th of August, 1842, a duty of 15 cents per gallon was imposed on port wine in casks, while on the red wines of several other countries, when imported in casks, a duty of only 6 cents per gallon was imposed. This discrimination, so far as regarded the port wine of Portugal, was deemed a violation of our treaty with that power, which provides that—

No higher or other duties shall be imposed on the importation into the United States of America of any article the growth, produce, or manufacture of the Kingdom and possessions of Portugal than such as are or shall be payable on the like article being the growth, produce, or manufacture of any other foreign country.

Accordingly, to give effect to the treaty as well as to the intention of Congress, expressed in a proviso to the tariff act itself, that nothing therein contained should be so construed as to interfere with subsisting treaties with foreign nations, a Treasury circular was issued on the 16th of July, 1844, which, among other things, declared the duty on the port wine of Portugal, in casks, under the existing laws and treaty to be 6 cents per gallon, and directed that the excess of duties which had been collected on such wine should be refunded. By virtue of another clause in the same section of the act it is provided that all imitations of port or any other wines "shall be subject to the duty provided for the genuine article." Imitations of port wine, the production of France, are imported to some extent into the United States, and the Government of that country now claims that under a correct construction of the act these imitations ought not to pay a higher duty than that imposed upon the original port wine of Portugal. It appears to me to be unequal and unjust that French imitations of port wine should be subjected to a duty of 15 cents, while the more valuable article from Portugal should pay a duty of 6 cents only per gallon. I therefore recommend to Congress such legislation as may be necessary to correct the inequality.

The late President, in his annual message of December last, recommended an appropriation to satisfy the claims of the Texan Government against the United States, which had been previously adjusted so far as the powers of the Executive extend. These claims arose out of the act of disarming a body of Texan troops under the command of Major Snively by an officer in the service of the United States, acting under the orders of our Government, and the forcible entry into the custom-house at Bryarlys Landing, on Red River, by certain citizens of the United States and taking away therefrom the goods seized by the collector of the customs as forfeited under the laws of Texas. This was a liquidated debt ascertained to be due to Texas when an independent state. Her acceptance of the terms of annexation proposed by the United States does not discharge or invalidate the claim. I recommend that provision be made for its payment.

The commissioner appointed to China during the special session of the Senate in March last shortly afterwards set out on his mission in the United States ship *Columbus*. On arriving at Rio de Janeiro on his passage the state of his health had become so critical that by the advice of his medical attendants he returned to the United States early in the month of October last. Commodore Biddle, commanding the East India Squadron, proceeded on his voyage in the *Columbus*, and was charged by the commissioner with the duty of exchanging with the proper authorities the ratifications of the treaty lately concluded with the Emperor of China. Since the return of the commissioner to the United States his health has been much improved, and he entertains the confident belief that he will soon be able to proceed on his mission.

Unfortunately, differences continue to exist among some of the nations of South America which, following our example, have established their independence, while in others internal dissensions prevail. It is natural that our sympathies should be warmly enlisted for their welfare; that we should desire that all controversies between them should be amicably adjusted and their Governments administered in a manner to protect the rights and promote the prosperity of their people. It is contrary, however, to our settled policy to interfere in their controversies, whether external or internal.

I have thus adverted to all the subjects connected with our foreign relations to which I deem it necessary to call your attention. Our policy is not only peace with all, but good will toward all the powers of the earth. While we are just to all, we require that all shall be just to us. Excepting the differences with Mexico and Great Britain, our relations with all civilized nations are of the most satisfactory character. It is hoped that in this enlightened age these differences may be amicably adjusted.

The Secretary of the Treasury in his annual report to Congress will communicate a full statement of the condition of our finances. The imports for the fiscal year ending on the 30th of June last were of the value of $117,254,564, of which the amount exported was $15,346,830, leaving a balance of $101,907,734 for domestic consumption. The exports for the same year were of the value of $114,646,606, of which the amount of domestic articles was $99,299,776. The receipts into the Treasury during the same year were $29,769,133.56, of which there were derived from customs $27,528,112.70, from sales of public lands $2,077,022.30, and from incidental and miscellaneous sources $163,998.56. The expenditures for the same period were $29,968,206.98, of which $8,588,157.62 were applied to the payment of the public debt. The balance in the Treasury on the 1st of July last was $7,658,306.22. The amount of the public debt remaining unpaid on the 1st of October last was $17,075,445.52. Further payments of the public debt would have been made, in anticipation of the period of its reimbursement under the authority conferred upon the Secretary of the Treasury by the acts of July 21, 1841, and of April 15, 1842, and March 3, 1843, had not the unsettled state of our relations with Mexico menaced hostile collision with that power. In view of such a contingency it was deemed prudent to retain in the Treasury an amount unusually large for ordinary purposes.

A few years ago our whole national debt growing out of the Revolution and the War of 1812 with Great Britain was extinguished, and we presented to the world the rare and noble spectacle of a great and growing people who had fully discharged every obligation. Since that time the existing debt has been contracted, and, small as it is in comparison with the similar burdens of most other nations, it should be extinguished at the earliest practicable period. Should the state of the country permit, and especially if our foreign relations interpose no obstacle, it is contemplated to apply all the moneys in the Treasury as they accrue, beyond what is required for the appropriations by Congress, to its liquidation. I cherish the hope of soon being able to congratulate the country on its recovering once more the lofty position which it so recently occupied. Our country, which exhibits to the world the benefits of self-government, in developing all the sources of national prosperity owes to mankind the permanent example of a nation free from the blighting influence of a public debt.

The attention of Congress is invited to the importance of making suitable modifications and reductions of the rates of duty imposed by our present tariff laws. The object of imposing duties on imports should be to raise revenue to pay the necessary expenses of Government. Congress may undoubtedly, in the exercise of a sound discretion, discriminate in arranging the rates of duty on different articles, but the discriminations should be within the revenue standard and be made with the view to raise money for the support of Government.

It becomes important to understand distinctly what is meant by a revenue standard the maximum of which should not be exceeded in the rates of duty imposed. It is conceded, and experience proves, that duties may be laid so high as to diminish or prohibit altogether the importation of any given article, and thereby lessen or destroy the revenue which at lower rates would be derived from its importation. Such duties exceed the revenue rates and are not imposed to raise money for the support of Government. If Congress levy a duty for revenue of 1 per cent on a given article, it will produce a given amount of money to the Treasury and will incidentally and necessarily afford protection or advantage to the amount of 1 per cent to the home manufacturer of a similar or like article over the importer. If the duty be raised to 10 per cent, it will produce a greater amount of money and afford greater protection. If it be still raised to 20, 25, or 30 per cent, and if as it is raised the revenue derived from it is found to be increased, the protection or advantage will also be increased; but if it be raised to 31 per cent, and it is found that the revenue produced at that rate is less than at 30 per cent, it ceases to be a revenue duty. The precise point in the ascending scale of duties at which it is ascertained from experience that the revenue is greatest is the maximum rate of duty which can be laid for the *bona fide* purpose of collecting money for the support of Government. To raise the duties higher than that point, and thereby diminish the amount collected, is to levy them for protection merely, and not for revenue. As long, then, as Congress may gradually increase the rate of duty on a given article, and the revenue is increased by such increase of duty, they are within the revenue standard. When they go beyond that point, and as they increase the duties, the revenue is diminished or destroyed; the act ceases to have for its object the raising of money to support Government, but is for protection merely. It does not follow that Congress should levy the highest duty on all articles of import which they will bear within the revenue standard, for such rates would probably produce a much larger amount than the economical administration of the Government would require. Nor does it follow that the duties on all articles should be at the same or a horizontal rate. Some articles will bear a much ·higher revenue duty than others. Below the maximum of the revenue standard Congress may and ought to discriminate in the rates imposed, taking care so to adjust them on different articles as to produce in the aggregate the amount which, when added to the proceeds of the sales of public lands, may be needed to pay the economical expenses of the Government.

In levying a tariff of duties Congress exercise the taxing power, and for purposes of revenue may select the objects of taxation. They may exempt certain articles altogether and permit their importation free of duty. On others they may impose low duties. In these classes should be embraced such articles of necessity as are in general use, and especially such as are consumed by the laborer and poor as well as by the wealthy citizen. Care should be taken that all the great interests of the country, including manufactures, agriculture, commerce, navigation, and the mechanic arts, should, as far as may be practicable, derive equal advantages from the incidental protection which a just system of revenue duties may afford. Taxation, direct or indirect, is a burden, and it should be so imposed as to operate as equally as may be on all classes in the proportion of their ability to bear it. To make the taxing power an actual benefit to one class necessarily increases the burden of the others beyond their proportion, and would be manifestly unjust. The terms "protection to domestic industry" are of popular import, but they should apply under a just system to all the various branches of industry in our country. The farmer or planter who toils yearly in his fields is engaged in "domestic industry," and is as much entitled to have his labor "protected" as the manufacturer, the man of commerce, the navigator, or the mechanic, who are engaged also in "domestic industry" in their different pursuits. The joint labors of all these classes constitute the aggregate of the "domestic industry" of the nation, and they are equally entitled to the nation's "protection." No one of them can justly claim to be the exclusive recipient of "protection," which can only be afforded by increasing burdens on the "domestic industry" of the others.

If these views be correct, it remains to inquire how far the tariff act of 1842 is consistent with them. That many of the provisions of that act are in violation of the cardinal principles here laid down all must concede. The rates of duty imposed by it on some articles are prohibitory and on others so high as greatly to diminish importations and to produce a less amount of revenue than would be derived from lower rates. They operate as "protection merely" to one branch of "domestic industry" by taxing other branches.

By the introduction of minimums, or assumed and false values, and by the imposition of specific duties the injustice and inequality of the act of 1842 in its practical operations on different classes and pursuits are seen and felt. Many of the oppressive duties imposed by it under the operation of these principles range from 1 per cent to more than 200 per cent. They are prohibitory on some articles and partially so on others, and bear most heavily on articles of common necessity and but lightly on articles of luxury. It is so framed that much the greatest burden which it imposes is thrown on labor and the poorer classes, who are least able to bear it, while it protects capital and exempts the rich from paying their just proportion of the taxation required for the support of Government. While it protects the capital of the wealthy manufacturer and increases his profits, it does not benefit the operatives or laborers in his employment, whose wages have not been increased by it. Articles of prime necessity or of coarse quality and low price, used by the masses of the people, are in many instances subjected by it to heavy taxes, while articles of finer quality and higher price, or of luxury, which can be used only by the opulent, are lightly taxed. It imposes heavy and unjust burdens on the farmer, the planter, the commercial man, and those of all other pursuits except the capitalist who has made his investments in manufactures. All the great interests of the country are not as nearly as may be practicable equally protected by it.

The Government in theory knows no distinction of persons or classes, and should not bestow upon some favors and privileges which all others may not enjoy. It was the purpose of its illustrious founders to base the institutions which they reared upon the great and unchanging principles of justice and equity, conscious that if administered in the spirit in which they were conceived they would be felt only by the benefits which they diffused, and would secure for themselves a defense in the hearts of the people more powerful than standing armies and all the means and appliances invented to sustain governments founded in injustice and oppression.

The well-known fact that the tariff act of 1842 was passed by a majority of one vote in the Senate and two in the House of Representatives, and that some of those who felt themselves constrained, under the peculiar circumstances existing at the time, to vote in its favor, proclaimed its defects and expressed their determination to aid in its modification on the first opportunity, affords strong and conclusive evidence that it was not intended to be permanent, and of the expediency and necessity of its thorough revision.

In recommending to Congress a reduction of the present rates of duty and a revision and modification of the act of 1842, I am far from entertaining opinions unfriendly to the manufacturers. On the contrary, I desire to see them prosperous as far as they can be so without imposing unequal burdens on other interests. The advantage under any system of indirect taxation, even within the revenue standard, must be in favor of the manufacturing interest, and of this no other interest will complain.

I recommend to Congress the abolition of the minimum principle, or assumed, arbitrary, and false values, and of specific duties, and the substitution in their place of *ad valorem* duties as the fairest and most equitable indirect tax which can be imposed. By the *ad valorem* principle all articles are taxed according to their cost or value, and those which are of inferior quality or of small cost bear only the just proportion of the tax with those which are of superior quality or greater cost. The articles consumed by all are taxed at the same rate. A system of *ad valorem* revenue duties, with proper discriminations and proper guards against frauds in collecting them, it is not doubted will afford ample incidental advantages to the manufacturers and enable them to derive as great profits as can be derived from any other regular business. It is believed that such a system strictly within the revenue standard will place the manufacturing interests on a stable footing and inure to their permanent advantage, while it will as nearly as may be practicable extend to all the great interests of the country the incidental protection which can be afforded by our revenue laws. Such a system, when once firmly established, would be permanent, and not be subject to the constant complaints, agitations, and changes which must ever occur when duties are not laid for revenue, but for the "protection merely" of a favored interest.

In the deliberations of Congress on this subject it is hoped that a spirit of mutual concession and compromise between conflicting interests may prevail, and that the result of their labors may be crowned with the happiest consequences.

By the Constitution of the United States it is provided that "no money shall be drawn from the Treasury but in consequence of appropriations made by law." A public treasury was undoubtedly contemplated and intended to be created, in which the public money should be kept from the period of collection until needed for public uses. In the collection and disbursement of the public money no agencies have ever been employed by law except such as were appointed by the Government, directly responsible to it and under its control. The safe-keeping of the public money should be confided to a public treasury created by law and under like responsibility and control. It is not to be imagined that the framers of the Constitution could have intended that a treasury should be created as a place of deposit and safe-keeping of the public money which was irresponsible to the Government. The first Congress under the Constitution, by the act of the 2d of September, 1789, "to establish the Treasury Department," provided for the appointment of a Treasurer, and made it his duty "to receive and keep the moneys of the United States" and "at all times to submit to the Secretary of the Treasury and the Comptroller, or either of them, the inspection of the moneys in his hands."

That banks, national or State, could not have been intended to be used as a substitute for the Treasury spoken of in the Constitution as keepers of the public money is manifest from the fact that at that time there was no national bank, and but three or four State banks, of limited capital, existed in the country. Their employment as depositories was at first resorted to to a limited extent, but with no avowed intention of continuing them permanently in place of the Treasury of the Constitution. When they were afterwards from time to time employed, it was from motives of supposed convenience. Our experience has shown that when banking corporations have been the keepers of the public money, and been thereby made in effect the Treasury, the Government can have no guaranty that it can command the use of its own money for public purposes. The late Bank of the United States proved to be faithless. The State banks which were afterwards employed were faithless. But a few years ago, with millions of public money in their keeping, the Government was brought almost to bankruptcy and the public credit seriously impaired because of their inability or indisposition to pay on demand to the public creditors in the only currency recognized by the Constitution. Their failure occurred in a period of peace, and great inconvenience and loss were suffered by the public from it. Had the country been involved in a foreign war, that inconvenience and loss would have been much greater, and might have resulted in extreme public calamity. The public money should not be mingled with the private funds of banks or individuals or be used for private purposes. When it is placed in banks for safe-keeping, it is in effect loaned to them without interest, and is loaned by them upon interest to the borrowers from them. The public money is converted into banking capital, and is used and loaned out for the private profit of bank stockholders, and when called for, as was the case in 1837, it may be in the pockets of the borrowers from the banks instead of being in the public Treasury contemplated by the Constitution. The framers of the Constitution could never have intended that the money paid into the Treasury should be thus converted to private use and placed beyond the control of the Government.

Banks which hold the public money are often tempted by a desire of gain to extend their loans, increase their circulation, and thus stimulate, if not produce, a spirit of speculation and extravagance which sooner or later must result in ruin to thousands. If the public money be not permitted to be thus used, but be kept in the Treasury and paid out to the public creditors in gold and silver, the temptation afforded by its deposit with banks to an undue expansion of their business would be checked, while the amount of the constitutional currency left in circulation would be enlarged by its employment in the public collections and disbursements, and the banks themselves would in consequence be found in a safer and sounder condition. At present State banks are employed as depositories, but without adequate regulation of law whereby the public money can be secured against the casualties and excesses, revulsions, suspensions, and defalcations to which from overissues, overtrading, an inordinate desire for gain, or other causes they are constantly exposed. The Secretary of the Treasury has in all cases when it was practicable taken collateral security for the amount which they hold, by the pledge of stocks of the United States or such of the States as were in good credit. Some of the deposit banks have given this description of security and others have declined to do so.

Entertaining the opinion that "the separation of the moneys of the Government from banking institutions is indispensable for the safety of the funds of the Government and the rights of the people," I recommend to Congress that provision be made by law for such separation, and that a constitutional treasury be created for the safe-keeping of the public money. The constitutional treasury recommended is designed as a secure depository for the public money, without any power to make loans or discounts or to issue any paper whatever as a currency or circulation. I can not doubt that such a treasury as was contemplated by the Constitution should be independent of all banking corporations. The money of the people should be kept in the Treasury of the people created by law, and be in the custody of agents of the people chosen by themselves according to the forms of the Constitution—agents who are directly responsible to the Government, who are under adequate bonds and oaths, and who are subject to severe punishments for any embezzlement, private use, or misapplication of the public funds, and for any failure in other respects to perform their duties. To say that the people or their Government are incompetent or not to be trusted with the custody of their own money in their own Treasury, provided by themselves, but must rely on the presidents, cashiers, and stockholders of banking corporations, not appointed by them nor responsible to them, would be to concede that they are incompetent for self-government

In recommending the establishment of a constitutional treasury in which the public money shall be kept, I desire that adequate provision be made by law for its safety and that all Executive discretion or control over it shall be removed, except such as may be necessary in directing its disbursement in pursuance of appropriations made by law.

Under our present land system, limiting the minimum price at which the public lands can be entered to $1.25 per acre, large quantities of lands of inferior quality remain unsold because they will not command that price. From the records of the General Land Office it appears that of the public lands remaining unsold in the several States and Territories in which they are situated, 39,105,577 acres have been in the market subject to entry more than twenty years, 49,638,644 acres for more than fifteen years, 73,074,600 acres for more than ten years, and 106,176,961 acres for more than five years. Much the largest portion of these lands will continue to be unsalable at the minimum price at which they are permitted to be sold so long as large territories of lands from which the more valuable portions have not been selected are annually brought into market by the Government. With the view to the sale and settlement of these inferior lands, I recommend that the price be graduated and reduced below the present minimum rate, confining the sales at the reduced prices to settlers and cultivators, in limited quantities. If graduated and reduced in price for a limited term to $1 per acre, and after the expiration of that period for a second and third term to lower rates, a large portion of these lands would be purchased, and many worthy citizens who are unable to pay higher rates could purchase homes for themselves and their families. By adopting the policy of graduation and reduction of price these inferior lands will be sold for their real value, while the States in which they lie will be freed from the inconvenience, if not injustice, to which they are subjected in consequence of the United States continuing to own large quantities of the public lands within their borders not liable to taxation for the support of their local governments.

I recommend the continuance of the policy of granting preemptions in its most liberal extent to all those who have settled or may hereafter settle on the public lands, whether surveyed or unsurveyed, to which the Indian title may have been extinguished at the time of settlement. It has been found by experience that in consequence of combinations of purchasers and other causes a very small quantity of the public lands, when sold at public auction, commands a higher price than the minimum rates established by law. The settlers on the public lands are, however, but rarely able to secure their homes and improvements at the public sales at that rate, because these combinations, by means of the capital they command and their superior ability to purchase, render it impossible for the settler to compete with them in the market. By putting down all competition these combinations of capitalists and speculators are usually enabled to purchase the lands, including the improvements of the settlers, at the minimum price of the Government, and either turn them out of their homes or extort from them, according to their ability to pay, double or quadruple the amount paid for them to the Government. It is to the enterprise and perseverance of the hardy pioneers of the West, who penetrate the wilderness with their families, suffer the dangers, the privations, and hardships attending the settlement of a new country, and prepare the way for the body of emigrants who in the course of a few years usually follow them, that we are in a great degree indebted for the rapid extension and aggrandizement of our country.

Experience has proved that no portion of our population are more patriotic than the hardy and brave men of the frontier, or more ready to obey the call of their country and to defend her rights and her honor whenever and by whatever enemy assailed. They should be protected from the grasping speculator and secured, at the minimum price of the public lands, in the humble homes which they have improved by their labor.

With this end in view, all vexatious or unnecessary restrictions imposed upon them by the existing preemption laws should be repealed or modified. It is the true policy of the Government to afford facilities to its citizens to become the owners of small portions of our vast public domain at low and moderate rates.

The present system of managing the mineral lands of the United States is believed to be radically defective. More than 1,000,000 acres of the public lands, supposed to contain lead and other minerals, have been reserved from sale, and numerous leases upon them have been granted to individuals upon a stipulated rent. The system of granting leases has proved to be not only unprofitable to the Government, but unsatisfactory to the citizens who have gone upon the lands, and must, if continued, lay the foundation of much future difficulty between the Government and the lessees. According to the official records, the amount of rents received by the Government for the years 1841, 1842, 1843, and 1844 was $6,354.74, while the expenses of the system during the same period, including salaries of superintendents, agents, clerks, and incidental expenses, were $26,111.11, the income being less than one-fourth of the expenses. To this pecuniary loss may be added the injury sustained by the public in consequence of the destruction of timber and the careless and wasteful manner of working the mines. The system has given rise to much litigation between the United States and individual citizens, producing irritation and excitement in the mineral region, and involving the Government in heavy additional expenditures. It is believed that similar losses and embarrassments will continue to occur while the present system of leasing these lands remains unchanged. These lands are now under the superintendence and care of the War Department, with the ordinary duties of which they have no proper or natural connection. I recommend the repeal of the present system, and that these lands be placed under the superintendence and management of the General Land Office, as other public lands, and be brought into market and sold upon such terms as Congress in their wisdom may prescribe, reserving to the Government an equitable percentage of the gross amount of mineral product, and that the preemption principle be extended to resident miners and settlers upon them at the minimum price which may be established by Congress.

I refer you to the accompanying report of the Secretary of War for information respecting the present situation of the Army and its operations during the past year, the state of our defenses, the condition of the public works, and our relations with the various Indian tribes within our limits or upon our borders. I invite your attention to the suggestions contained in that report in relation to these prominent objects of national interest. When orders were given during the past summer for concentrating a military force on the western frontier of Texas, our troops were widely dispersed and in small detachments, occupying posts remote from each other. The prompt and expeditious manner in which an army embracing more than half our peace establishment was drawn together on an emergency so sudden reflects great credit on the officers who were intrusted with the execution of these orders, as well as upon the discipline of the Army itself. To be in strength to protect and defend the people and territory of Texas in the event Mexico should commence hostilities or invade her territories with a large army, which she threatened, I authorized the general assigned to the command of the army of occupation to make requisitions for additional forces from several of the States nearest the Texan territory, and which could most expeditiously furnish them, if in his opinion a larger force than that under his command and the auxiliary aid which under like circumstances he was authorized to receive from Texas should be required. The contingency upon which the exercise of this authority depended has not occurred. The circumstances under which two companies of State artillery from the city of New Orleans were sent into Texas and mustered into the service of the United States are fully stated in the report of the Secretary of War. I recommend to Congress that provision be made for the payment of these troops, as well as a small number of Texan volunteers whom the commanding general thought it necessary to receive or muster into our service.

During the last summer the First Regiment of Dragoons made extensive excursions through the Indian country on our borders, a part of them advancing nearly to the possessions of the Hudsons Bay Company in the north, and a part as far as the South Pass of the Rocky Mountains and the head waters of the tributary streams of the Colorado of the West. The exhibition of this military force among the Indian tribes in those distant regions and the councils held with them by the commanders of the expeditions, it is believed, will have a salutary influence in restraining them from hostilities among themselves and maintaining friendly relations between them and the United States. An interesting account of one of these excursions accompanies the report of the Secretary of War. Under the directions of the War Department Brevet Captain Frémont, of the Corps of Topographical Engineers, has been employed since 1842 in exploring the country west of the Mississippi and beyond the Rocky Mountains. Two expeditions have already been brought to a close, and the reports of that scientific and enterprising officer have furnished much interesting and valuable information. He is now engaged in a third expedition, but it is not expected that this arduous service will be completed in season to enable me to communicate the result to Congress at the present session.

Our relations with the Indian tribes are of a favorable character. The policy of removing them to a country designed for their permanent residence west of the Mississippi, and without the limits of the organized States and Territories, is better appreciated by them than it was a few years ago, while education is now attended to and the habits of civilized life are gaining ground among them.

Serious difficulties of long standing continue to distract the several parties into which the Cherokees are unhappily divided. The efforts of the Government to adjust the difficulties between them have heretofore proved unsuccessful, and there remains no probability that this desirable object can be accomplished without the aid of further legislation by Congress. I will at an early period of your session present the subject for your consideration, accompanied with an exposition of the complaints and claims of the several parties into which the nation is divided, with a view to the adoption of such measures by Congress as may enable the Executive to do justice to them, respectively, and to put an end, if possible, to the dissensions which have long prevailed and still prevail among them.

I refer you to the report of the Secretary of the Navy for the present condition of that branch of the national defense and for grave suggestions having for their object the increase of its efficiency and a greater economy in its management. During the past year the officers and men have performed their duty in a satisfactory manner. The orders which have been given have been executed with promptness and fidelity. A larger force than has often formed one squadron under our flag was readily concentrated in the Gulf of Mexico, and apparently without unusual effort. It is especially to be observed that notwithstanding the union of so considerable a force, no act was committed that even the jealousy of an irritated power could construe as an act of aggression, and that the commander of the squadron and his officers, in strict conformity with their instructions, holding themselves ever ready for the most active duty, have achieved the still purer glory of contributing to the preservation of peace. It is believed that at all our foreign stations the honor of our flag has been maintained and that generally our ships of war have been distinguished for their good discipline and order. I am happy to add that the display of maritime force which was required by the events of the summer has been made wholly within the usual appropriations for the service of the year, so that no additional appropriations are required.

The commerce of the United States, and with it the navigating interests, have steadily and rapidly increased since the organization of our Government, until, it is believed, we are now second to but one power in the world, and at no distant day we shall probably be inferior to none. Exposed as they must be, it has been a wise policy to afford to these important interests protection with our ships of war distributed in the great highways of trade throughout the world. For more than thirty years appropriations have been made and annually expended for the gradual increase of our naval forces. In peace our Navy performs the important duty of protecting our commerce, and in the event of war will be, as it has been, a most efficient means of defense.

The successful use of steam navigation on the ocean has been followed by the introduction of war steamers in great and increasing numbers into the navies of the principal maritime powers of the world. A due regard to our own safety and to an efficient protection to our large and increasing commerce demands a corresponding increase on our part. No country has greater facilities for the construction of vessels of this description than ours, or can promise itself greater advantages from their employment. They are admirably adapted to the protection of our commerce, to the rapid transmission of intelligence, and to the coast defense. In pursuance of the wise policy of a gradual increase of our Navy, large supplies of live-oak timber and other materials for shipbuilding have been collected and are now under shelter and in a state of good preservation, while iron steamers can be built with great facility in various parts of the Union. The use of iron as a material, especially in the construction of steamers which can enter with safety many of the harbors along our coast now inaccessible to vessels of greater draft, and the practicability of constructing them in the interior, strongly recommend that liberal appropriations should be made for this important object. Whatever may have been our policy in the earlier stages of the Government, when the nation was in its infancy, our shipping interests and commerce comparatively small, our resources limited, our population sparse and scarcely extending beyond the limits of the original thirteen States, that policy must be essentially different now that we have grown from three to more than twenty millions of people, that our commerce, carried in our own ships, is found in every sea, and that our territorial boundaries and settlements have been so greatly expanded. Neither our commerce nor our long line of coast on the ocean and on the Lakes can be successfully defended against foreign aggression by means of fortifications alone. These are essential at important commercial and military points, but our chief reliance for this object must be on a well-organized, efficient navy. The benefits resulting from such a navy are not confined to the Atlantic States. The productions of the interior which seek a market abroad are directly dependent on the safety and freedom of our commerce. The occupation of the Balize below New Orleans by a hostile force would embarrass, if not stagnate, the whole export trade of the Mississippi and affect the value of the agricultural products of the entire valley of that mighty river and its tributaries.

It has never been our policy to maintain large standing armies in time of peace. They are contrary to the genius of our free institutions, would impose heavy burdens on the people and be dangerous to public liberty. Our reliance for protection and defense on the land must be mainly on our citizen soldiers, who will be ever ready, as they ever have been ready in times past, to rush with alacrity, at the call of their country, to her defense. This description of force, however, can not defend our coast, harbors, and inland seas, nor protect our commerce on the ocean or the Lakes. These must be protected by our Navy.

Considering an increased naval force, and especially of steam vessels, corresponding with our growth and importance as a nation, and proportioned to the increased and increasing naval power of other nations, of vast importance as regards our safety, and the great and growing interests to be protected by it, I recommend the subject to the favorable consideration of Congress.

The report of the Postmaster-General herewith communicated contains a detailed statement of the operations of his Department during the past year. It will be seen that the income from postages will fall short of the expenditures for the year between $1,000,000 and $2,000,000. This deficiency has been caused by the reduction of the rates of postage, which was made by the act of the 3d of March last. No principle has been more generally acquiesced in by the people than that this Department should sustain itself by limiting its expenditures to its income. Congress has never sought to make it a source of revenue for general purposes except for a short period during the last war with Great Britain, nor should it ever become a charge on the general Treasury. If Congress shall adhere to this principle, as I think they ought, it will be necessary either to curtail the present mail service so as to reduce the expenditures, or so to modify the act of the 3d of March last as to improve its revenues. The extension of the mail service and the additional facilities which will be demanded by the rapid extension and increase of population on our western frontier will not admit of such curtailment as will materially reduce the present expenditures. In the adjustment of the tariff of postages the interests of the people demand that the lowest rates be adopted which will produce the necessary revenue to meet the expenditures of the Department. I invite the attention of Congress to the suggestions of the Postmaster-General on this subject, under the belief that such a modification of the late law may be made as will yield sufficient revenue without further calls on the Treasury, and with very little change in the present rates of postage. Proper measures have been taken in pursuance of the act of the 3d of March last for the establishment of lines of mail steamers between this and foreign countries. The importance of this service commends itself strongly to favorable consideration.

With the growth of our country the public business which devolves on the heads of the several Executive Departments has greatly increased. In some respects the distribution of duties among them seems to be incongruous, and many of these might be transferred from one to another with advantage to the public interests. A more auspicious time for the consideration of this subject by Congress, with a view to system in the organization of the several Departments and a more appropriate division of the public business, will not probably occur.

The most important duties of the State Department relate to our foreign affairs. By the great enlargement of the family of nations, the increase of our commerce, and the corresponding extension of our consular system the business of this Department has been greatly increased.

In its present organization many duties of a domestic nature and consisting of details are devolved on the Secretary of State, which do not appropriately belong to the foreign department of the Government and may properly be transferred to some other Department. One of these grows out of the present state of the law concerning the Patent Office, which a few years since was a subordinate clerkship, but has become a distinct bureau of great importance. With an excellent internal organization, it is still connected with the State Department. In the transaction of its business questions of much importance to inventors and to the community frequently arise, which by existing laws are referred for decision to a board of which the Secretary of State is a member. These questions are legal, and the connection which now exists between the State Department and the Patent Office may with great propriety and advantage be transferred to the Attorney-General.

In his last annual message to Congress Mr. Madison invited attention to a proper provision for the Attorney-General as "an important improvement in the executive establishment." This recommendation was repeated by some of his successors. The official duties of the Attorney-General have been much increased within a few years, and his office has become one of great importance. His duties may be still further increased with advantage to the public interests. As an executive officer his residence and constant attention at the seat of Government are required. Legal questions involving important principles and large amounts of public money are constantly referred to him by the President and Executive Departments for his examination and decision. The public business under his official management before the judiciary has been so augmented by the extension of our territory and the acts of Congress authorizing suits against the United States for large bodies of valuable public lands as greatly to increase his labors and responsibilities. I therefore recommend that the Attorney-General be placed on the same footing with the heads of the other Executive Departments, with such subordinate officers provided by law for his Department as may be required to discharge the additional duties which have been or may be devolved upon him.

Congress possess the power of exclusive legislation over the District of Columbia, and I commend the interests of its inhabitants to your favorable consideration. The people of this District have no legislative body of their own, and must confide their local as well as their general interests to representatives in whose election they have no voice and over whose official conduct they have no control. Each member of the National Legislature should consider himself as their immediate representative, and should be the more ready to give attention to their interests and wants because he is not responsible to them. I recommend that a liberal and generous spirit may characterize your measures in relation to them. I shall be ever disposed to show a proper regard for their wishes and, within constitutional limits, shall at all times cheerfully cooperate with you for the advancement of their welfare.

I trust it may not be deemed inappropriate to the occasion for me to dwell for a moment on the memory of the most eminent citizen of our country who during the summer that is gone by has descended to the tomb. The enjoyment of contemplating, at the advanced age of near fourscore years, the happy condition of his country cheered the last hours of Andrew Jackson, who departed this life in the tranquil hope of a blessed immortality. His death was happy, as his life had been eminently useful. He had an unfaltering confidence in the virtue and capacity of the people and in the permanence of that free Government which he had largely contributed to establish and defend. His great deeds had secured to him the affections of his fellow-citizens, and it was his happiness to witness the growth and glory of his country, which he loved so well. He departed amidst the benedictions of millions of free-men. The nation paid its tribute to his memory at his tomb. Coming generations will learn from his example the love of country and the rights of man. In his language on a similar occasion to the present, "I now commend you, fellow-citizens, to the guidance of Almighty God, with a full reliance on His merciful providence for the maintenance of our free institutions, and with an earnest supplication that whatever errors it may be my lot to commit in discharging the arduous duties which have devolved on me will find a remedy in the harmony and wisdom of your counsels."

JAMES K. POLK.

SPECIAL MESSAGES.

WASHINGTON, *December 9, 1845.*

To the Senate and House of Representatives:

I communicate herewith a letter received from the President of the existing Government of the State of Texas, transmitting duplicate copies of the constitution formed by the deputies of the people of Texas in convention assembled, accompanied by official information that the said constitution had been ratified, confirmed, and adopted by the people of Texas themselves, in accordance with the joint resolution for annexing Texas to the United States, and in order that Texas might be admitted as one of the States of that Union.

JAMES K. POLK.

WASHINGTON, *December 10, 1845.*

To the Senate of the United States:

I transmit herewith a report of the Secretary of War, in answer to a resolution of the Senate of the 4th instant, calling for information "with respect to the practicability and utility of a fort or forts on Ship Island, on the coast of Mississippi, with a view to the protection of said coast."

JAMES K. POLK.

WASHINGTON, *December 15, 1845.*
To the Senate of the United States:

I herewith communicate to the Senate, for its consideration, a convention signed on the 14th May of the present year by the minister of the United States at Berlin with the minister of Saxony at the same Court, for the mutual abolition of the *droit d'aubaine, droit de détraction,* and taxes on emigration between the United States and Saxony; and I communicate with the convention an explanatory dispatch of the minister of the United States, dated on the 14th May, 1845, and numbered 267.

JAMES K. POLK.

WASHINGTON, *December 16, 1845.*
To the Senate of the United States:

I herewith communicate to the Senate, for its consideration, a convention concluded and signed at Berlin on the 29th day of January, 1845, between the United States and Prussia, together with certain other German States, for the mutual extradition of fugitives from justice in certain cases; and I communicate with the convention the correspondence necessary to explain it.

In submitting this convention to the Senate I deem it proper to call their attention to the third article, by which it is stipulated that "none of the contracting parties shall be bound to deliver up its own citizens or subjects under the stipulations of this convention."

No such reservation is to be found in our treaties of extradition with Great Britain and France, the only two nations with whom we have concluded such treaties. These provide for the surrender of all persons who are fugitives from justice, without regard to the country to which they may belong. Under this article, if German subjects of any of the parties to the convention should commit crimes within the United States and fly back to their native country from justice, they would not be surrendered. This is clear in regard to all such Germans as shall not have been naturalized under our laws. But even after naturalization difficult and embarrassing questions might arise between the parties. These German powers, holding the doctrine of perpetual allegiance, might refuse to surrender German naturalized citizens, whilst we must ever maintain the principle that the rights and duties of such citizens are the same as if they had been born in the United States.

I would also observe that the fourth article of the treaty submitted contains a provision not to be found in our conventions with Great Britain and France.

JAMES K. POLK.

WASHINGTON, *December 16, 1845.*

To the Senate of the United States:

I herewith transmit a report from the Secretary of State, containing the information called for by the resolution of the Senate of the 8th of January last, in relation to the claim of the owners of the brig *General Armstrong* against the Government of Portugal.*

JAMES K. POLK.

WASHINGTON, *December 19, 1845.*

To the House of Representatives:

I communicate to the House of Representatives, in reply to their resolution of the 25th of February last, a report from the Secretary of State, together with the correspondence of George W. Slacum, late consul of the United States at Rio de Janeiro, with the Department of State, relating to the African slave trade.

JAMES K. POLK.

WASHINGTON, *December 22, 1845.*

To the Congress of the United States:

I transmit to Congress a communication from the Secretary of State, with a statement of the expenditures from the appropriation made by the act entitled "An act providing the means of future intercourse between the United States and the Government of China," approved the 3d of March, 1843.

JAMES K. POLK.

WASHINGTON, *January 3, 1846.*

To the Senate of the United States:

I transmit to the Senate a report of the Secretary of the Navy, communicating the information called for by their resolution of the 18th of December, 1845, in relation to the "number of agents now employed for the preservation of timber, their salaries, the authority of law under which they are paid, and the allowances of every description made within the last twenty years in the settlement of the accounts of said agents."

JAMES K. POLK.

WASHINGTON, *January 6, 1846.*

To the Senate of the United States:

I communicate to the Senate the information called for by their resolution of December 31, 1845, "requesting the President to cause to be communicated to the Senate copies of the correspondence between the

---

*For failing to protect the American armed brig *General Armstrong*, while lying in the port of Fnyal, Azores, from attack by British armed ships on September 26, 1814.

Attorney-General and the Solicitor of the Treasury and the judicial officers of Florida in relation to the authority of the Territorial judges as Federal judges since the 3d of March, 1845.''

JAMES K. POLK.

WASHINGTON, January 12, 1846.

To the Senate of the United States:

I nominate the persons named in the accompanying list * of promotions and appointments in the Army of the United States to the several grades annexed to their names, as proposed by the Secretary of War.

JAMES K. POLK.

WAR DEPARTMENT, January 8, 1846.

The PRESIDENT OF THE UNITED STATES.

SIR: I have the honor respectfully to propose for your approbation the annexed list * of officers for promotion and persons for appointment in the Army of the United States.

I am, sir, with great respect, your obedient servant,   W. L. MARCY.

ADJUTANT-GENERAL'S OFFICE,
Washington, January 8, 1846.

Hon. W. L. MARCY,
   Secretary of War.

SIR: I respectfully submit the accompanying list * of promotions and appointments to fill the vacancies in the Army which are known to have happened since the date of the last list, December 12, 1845. The promotions are all regular except that of Captain Martin Scott, Fifth Infantry, whose name, agreeably to the decision of the President and your instructions, is submitted to fill the vacancy of major in the First Regiment of Infantry (*vice* Dearborn, promoted), over the two senior captains of infantry, Captain John B. Clark, of the Third Regiment, and Brevet Major Thomas Noel, of the Sixth. The reasons for this departure from the ordinary course (as in other like cases of disability) are set forth in the Adjutant-General's report of the 27th ultimo and the General in Chief's indorsement thereon, of which copies are herewith respectfully annexed, marked A.

I am, sir, with great respect, your obedient servant,

R. JONES, *Adjutant-General.*

A.

ADJUTANT-GENERAL'S OFFICE,
Washington, December 27, 1845.

Major-General WINFIELD SCOTT,
   Commanding the Army.

SIR: The death of Lieutenant-Colonel Hoffman, Seventh Infantry, on the 26th ultimo, having caused a vacancy in the grade of major, to which, under the rule, Captain J. B. Clark, Third Infantry, would be entitled to succeed, I deem it proper to submit the following statement, extracted from the official returns of his regiment, touching his physical capacity for the performance of military duty.

In May, 1836, Captain Clark went on the recruiting service, where he remained till October 4, 1838, when he was granted a three months' leave. He joined his company at Fort Towson in May, 1839, and continued with it from that time till

* Omitted.

March, 1841, accompanying it meanwhile (October, 1840) to Florida. He obtained a three months' leave on surgeon's certificate of ill health March 23, 1841, but did not rejoin till February 16, 1842. In the interim he was placed on duty for a short time as a member of a general court-martial, which happened to be convened at St. Louis, where he was then staying. He remained with his company from February to November, 1842, when he again received a leave for the benefit of his health, and did not return to duty till April 26, 1843 (after his regiment had been ordered to Florida), when he rejoined it at Jefferson Barracks. He continued with it (with the exception of one short leave) from April, 1843, till June, 1845, but the returns show him to have been frequently on the sick report during that period. On the 2d of June, 1845, his company being then encamped near Fort Jessup in expectation of orders for Texas, he again procured a leave on account of his health, and has not since been able to rejoin, reporting monthly that his health unfitted him for the performance of duty. The signature of his last report (not written by himself), of November 30 (herewith*), would seem to indicate great physical derangement or decrepitude, approaching, perhaps, to paralysis.

From the foregoing it appears that during the last seven years (since October, 1838) Captain Clark has been off duty two years and four months, the greater part of the time on account of sickness, and that even when present with his company his health is so much impaired that very often he is unable to perform the ordinary garrison duties.

Under these circumstances it is respectfully submitted, for the consideration of the proper authority, whether the senior captain of infantry should not be passed over and (as Brevet Major Noel,† the next in rank, is utterly disqualified) Captain Martin Scott, of the Fifth Infantry, promoted to the vacant majority.

It is proper to state that Captain Clark has always been regarded as a perfect gentleman, and as such, as far as I know, is equal to any officer in the Army.

I am, sir, most respectfully, your obedient servant,

R. JONES, *Adjutant-General.*

[Remarks indorsed on the foregoing report by the General in Chief.]

DECEMBER 30, 1845.

This report presents grave points for consideration. It is highly improbable that the Captain will ever be fit for the active duties of his profession. The question, therefore, seems to be whether he shall be a pensioner on full pay as captain or as major, for he has long been, not in name, but in fact, a pensioner on full pay. We have no half pay in the Army to relieve marching regiments of crippled and superannuated officers. We have many such—Colonel Maury, of the Third Infantry (superannuated), and Majors Cobb and McClintock, Fifth Infantry and Third Artillery (crippled). Many others are fast becoming superannuated. The three named are on indefinite leaves of absence, and so are Majors Searle and Noel, permanent cripples from wounds. General Cass's resolution of yesterday refers simply to age. A half pay or retired list with half pay would be much better. There are some twenty officers who ought at once to be placed on such list and their places filled by promotion.

Upon the whole, I think it best that Captain M. Scott should be promoted, *vice* Dearborn, *vice* Lieutenant-Colonel Hoffman.

Respectfully submitted to the Secretary of War.

WINFIELD SCOTT.

*Omitted.

†In 1839 Brevet Major Noel, Sixth Infantry, was severely wounded (serving in the Florida War at the time) by the accidental discharge of his own pistol. He left his company February 16, 1839, and has ever since been absent from his regiment, the state of his wound and great suffering rendering him utterly incapable of performing any kind of duty whatever; nor is there any reason to hope he will ever be able to resume his duties.　　　R. JONES, *Adjutant-General.*

JANUARY 8, 1846.

It appearing from the within statements of the Commanding General and the Adjutant-General that the two officers proposed to be passed over are physically unable to perform the duties of major, and their inability is not temporary, I recommend that Captain Martin Scott be promoted to the vacant majority 3d January, 1846.

W. L. MARCY.

WASHINGTON, *January 13, 1846.*

To the Senate of the United States:

I transmit to the Senate a report of the Secretary of War, with accompanying papers, showing the measures which have been adopted in relation to the transfer of certain stocks between the Chickasaw and Choctaw Indians under the treaty between those tribes of the 24th March, 1837. The claim presented by the Choctaw General Council, if deemed to be founded in equity, can not be adjusted without the previous advice and consent of the Senate.

JAMES K. POLK.

WASHINGTON, *January 20, 1846.*

To the Senate of the United States:

On the 15th of January, 1846, I withdrew the nomination of James H. Tate, of Mississippi, as consul at Buenos Ayres. The withdrawal was made upon the receipt on that day of a letter addressed to me by the Senators from the State of Mississippi advising it. I transmit their letter herewith to the Senate. At that time I had not been furnished with a copy of the Executive Journal of the Senate, and had no knowledge of the pendency of the resolution before that body in executive session in relation to this nomination. Having since been furnished by the Secretary of the Senate with a copy of the Executive Journal containing the resolution referred to, I deem it proper and due to the Senate to reinstate the nomination in the condition in which it was before it was withdrawn. And with that view I nominate James H. Tate, of Mississippi, to be consul at Buenos Ayres.

JAMES K. POLK.

WASHINGTON, *January 28, 1846.*

To the Senate of the United States:

I herewith communicate to the Senate, for its consideration with regard to its ratification, a treaty of commerce and navigation between the United States and the Kingdom of the Two Sicilies, concluded and signed on the 1st day of December last at Naples by the chargé d'affaires of the United States with the plenipotentiaries of His Majesty the King of the Kingdom of the Two Sicilies.

And I communicate at the same time portions of the correspondence (so far as it has been received) in explanation of the treaty.

JAMES K. POLK.

WASHINGTON, *February 3, 1846.*

To the Senate of the United States:

I herewith communicate to the Senate, for its consideration in reference to its ratification, a treaty of commerce and navigation between the United States and Belgium, concluded and signed on the 10th November last at Brussels by the chargé d'affaires of the United States with the minister of foreign affairs of His Majesty the King of the Belgians.

And I communicate at the same time the correspondence and other papers in explanation of the treaty.

JAMES K. POLK.

WASHINGTON, *February 5, 1846.*

To the Senate of the United States:

In pursuance with the request of the Senate in their resolution of the 4th instant, I "return" herewith, "for their further action, the resolution advising and consenting to the appointment of Isaac H. Wright as navy agent at Boston." It will be observed that the resolution of the Senate herewith returned contains the advice and consent of that body to the appointment of several other persons to other offices not embraced in their resolution of the 4th instant, and it being impossible to comply with the request of the Senate without communicating to them the whole resolution, I respectfully request that so far as it relates to the other cases than that of Mr. Wright it may be returned to me.

JAMES K. POLK.

WASHINGTON, *February 7, 1846.*

To the Senate of the United States:

In compliance with the request of the Senate in their resolution of the 29th January last, I herewith communicate a report from the Secretary of State, with the accompanying correspondence, which has taken place between the Secretary of State and the minister of the United States at London and between the Government of the United States and that of England on the "subject of Oregon" since my communication of the 2d of December last was made to Congress.

JAMES K. POLK.

WASHINGTON, *February 7, 1846.*

To the House of Representatives of the United States:

In compliance with the request of the House of Representatives in their resolution of the 3d instant, I herewith communicate a report from the Secretary of State, with the accompanying "correspondence, which has taken place" between the Secretary of State and the minister of the United States at London and "between the Government of Great Britain and this Government in relation to the country west of the Rocky Mountains since the last annual message of the President" to Congress.

JAMES K. POLK.

WASHINGTON, *February 9, 1846.*
To the House of Representatives of the United States:

I communicate herewith, in answer to the resolution of the House of Representatives of the 19th of December last, the report of the Secretary of State inclosing "copies of correspondence between this Government and Great Britain within the last two years in relation to the Washington treaty, and particularly in relation to the free navigation of the river St. John, and in relation to the disputed-territory fund named in said treaty;" and also the accompanying copies of documents filed in the Department of State, which embrace the correspondence and information called for by the said resolution.

JAMES K. POLK.

WASHINGTON, *February 9, 1846.*
To the Senate of the United States:

In compliance with the request of the Senate in their resolution of the 5th instant, I herewith return "the resolution of the Senate advising and consenting to the appointment of F. G. Mayson to be a second lieutenant in the Marine Corps." As the same resolution which contains the advice and consent of the Senate to the appointment of Mr. Mayson contains also the advice and consent of that body to the appointment of several other persons to other offices, to whom commissions have been since issued, I respectfully request that the resolution, so far as it relates to the persons other than Mr. Mayson, may be returned to me.

JAMES K. POLK.

WASHINGTON, *February 12, 1846.*
To the Senate of the United States:

I transmit herewith, for the consideration and advice of the Senate with regard to its ratification, a treaty concluded on the 14th day of January last by Thomas H. Harvey and Richard W. Cummins, commissioners on the part of the United States, and the chiefs and headmen of the Kansas tribe of Indians, together with a report of the Commissioner of Indian Affairs and other papers explanatory of the same.

JAMES K. POLK.

WASHINGTON, *February 16, 1846.*
To the Senate and House of Representatives:

I herewith transmit a communication from the Attorney-General relating to a contract entered into by him with Messrs. Little & Brown for certain copies of their proposed edition of the laws and treaties of the United States, in pursuance of the joint resolution of the 3d March, 1845.

JAMES K. POLK.

WASHINGTON, *February 16, 1846.*
To the Senate of the United States:

I herewith transmit a report from the Secretary of the Navy, communicating the correspondence called for by the resolution of the Senate of the 25th of February, 1845, between the commander of the East India Squadrons and foreign powers or United States agents abroad during the years 1842 and 1843, relating to the trade and other interests of this Government.

JAMES K. POLK.

WASHINGTON, *February 18, 1846.*
To the House of Representatives of the United States:

In compliance with the request of the House of Representatives in their resolution of the 12th instant, asking for information relative to the Mexican indemnity, I communicate herewith a report from the Secretary of State, with the paper accompanying it.

JAMES K. POLK.

[A similar message was sent to the Senate in compliance with a request of that body.]

WASHINGTON, *March 23, 1846.*
To the Senate and House of Representatives of the United States:

I transmit, for your consideration, a correspondence between the minister of Her Britannic Majesty in Washington and the Secretary of State, containing an arrangement for the adjustment and payment of the claims of the respective Governments upon each other arising from the collection of certain import duties in violation of the second article of the commercial convention of 3d of July, 1815, between the two countries, and I respectfully submit to Congress the propriety of making provision to carry this arrangement into effect.

The second article of this convention provides that "no higher or other duties shall be imposed on the importation into the United States of any articles the growth, produce, or manufacture of His Britannic Majesty's territories in Europe, and no higher or other duties shall be imposed on the importation into the territories of His Britannic Majesty in Europe of any articles the growth, produce, or manufacture of the United States, than are or shall be payable on the like articles being the growth, produce, or manufacture of any other foreign country."

Previous to the act of Parliament of the 13th of August, 1836, the duty on foreign rough rice imported into Great Britain was 2s. 6d. sterling per bushel. By this act the duty was reduced to 1 penny per quarter (of 8 bushels) on the rough rice "imported from the west coast of Africa."

Upon the earnest and repeated remonstrances of our ministers at London in opposition to this discrimination against American and in favor of African rice, as a violation of the subsisting convention, Parliament, by the act of 9th July, 1842, again equalized the duty on all foreign rough rice by fixing it at 7s. per quarter. In the intervening period, however, of nearly six years large importations had been made into Great Britain of American rough rice, which was subjected to a duty of 2s. 6d. per bushel; but the importers, knowing their rights under the convention, claimed that it should be admitted at the rate of 1 penny per quarter, the duty imposed on African rice. This claim was resisted by the British Government, and the excess of duty was paid, at the first under protest, and afterwards, in consequence of an arrangement with the board of customs, by the deposit of exchequer bills.

It seems to have been a clear violation both of the letter and spirit of the convention to admit rough rice "the growth" of Africa at 1 penny per quarter, whilst the very same article "the growth" of the United States was charged with a duty of 2s. 6d. per bushel.

The claim of Great Britain, under the same article of the convention, is founded on the tariff act of 30th August, 1842. Its twenty-fifth section provides "that nothing in this act contained shall apply to goods shipped in a vessel bound to any port of the United States, actually having left her last port of lading eastward of the Cape of Good Hope or beyond Cape Horn prior to the 1st day of September, 1842; and all legal provisions and regulations existing immediately before the 30th day of June, 1842, shall be applied to importations which may be made in vessels which have left such last port of lading eastward of the Cape of Good Hope or beyond Cape Horn prior to said 1st day of September, 1842."

The British Government contends that it was a violation of the second article of the convention for this act to require that "articles the growth, produce, or manufacture" of Great Britain, when imported into the United States in vessels which had left their last port of lading in Great Britain prior to the 1st day of September, 1842, should pay any "higher or other duties" than were imposed on "like articles" "the growth, produce, or manufacture" of countries beyond the Cape of Good Hope and Cape Horn.

Upon a careful consideration of the subject I arrived at the conclusion that this claim on the part of the British Government was well founded. I deem it unnecessary to state my reasons at length for adopting this opinion, the whole subject being fully explained in the letter of the Secretary of the Treasury and the accompanying papers.

The amount necessary to satisfy the British claim can not at present be ascertained with any degree of accuracy, no individual having yet presented his case to the Government of the United States. It is not apprehended that the amount will be large. After such examination of the subject as it has been in his power to make, the Secretary of the Treasury believes that it will not exceed $100,000.

On the other hand, the claims of the importers of rough rice into Great Britain have been already ascertained, as the duties were paid either under protest or in exchequer bills. Their amount is stated by Mr. Everett, our late minister at London, in a dispatch dated June 1, 1843, to be £88,886 16s. 10d. sterling, of which £60,006 4d. belong to citizens of the United States.

As it may be long before the amount of the British claim can be ascertained, and it would be unreasonable to postpone payment to the American claimants until this can be adjusted, it has been proposed to the British Government immediately to refund the excess of duties collected by it on American rough rice. I should entertain a confident hope that this proposal would be accepted should the arrangement concluded be sanctioned by an act of Congress making provision for the return of the duties in question. The claimants might then be paid as they present their demands, properly authenticated, to the Secretary of the Treasury.

JAMES K. POLK.

WASHINGTON, *March 24, 1846.*

To the Senate of the United States:

In answer to the inquiry of the Senate contained in their resolution of the 17th instant, whether in my "judgment any circumstances connected with or growing out of the foreign relations of this country require at this time an increase of our naval or military force," and, if so, "what those circumstances are," I have to express the opinion that a wise precaution demands such increase.

In my annual message of the 2d of December last I recommended to the favorable consideration of Congress an increase of our naval force, especially of our steam navy, and the raising of an adequate military force to guard and protect such of our citizens as might think proper to emigrate to Oregon. Since that period I have seen no cause to recall or modify these recommendations. On the contrary, reasons exist which, in my judgment, render it proper not only that they should be promptly carried into effect, but that additional provision should be made for the public defense.

The consideration of such additional provision was brought before appropriate committees of the two Houses of Congress, in answer to calls made by them, in reports prepared, with my sanction, by the Secretary of War and the Secretary of the Navy on the 29th of December and the 8th of January last—a mode of communication with Congress not unusual, and under existing circumstances believed to be most eligible. Subsequent events have confirmed me in the opinion that these recommendations were proper as precautionary measures.

It was a wise maxim of the Father of his Country that "to be prepared for war is one of the most efficient means of preserving peace," and that, "avoiding occasions of expense by cultivating peace," we should "remember also that timely disbursements to prepare for danger frequently prevent much greater disbursements to repel it.'' The general obligation to perform this duty is greatly strengthened by facts known to the whole world. A controversy respecting the Oregon Territory now exists between the United States and Great Britain, and while, as far as we know, the relations of the latter with all European nations are of the most pacific character, she is making unusual and extraordinary armaments and warlike preparations, naval and military, both at home and in her North American possessions.

It can not be disguised that, however sincere may be the desire of peace, in the event of a rupture these armaments and preparations would be used against our country. Whatever may have been the original purpose of these preparations, the fact is undoubted that they are now proceeding, in part at least, with a view to the contingent possibility of a war with the United States. The general policy of making additional warlike preparations was distinctly announced in the speech from the throne as late as January last, and has since been reiterated by the ministers of the Crown in both houses of Parliament. Under this aspect of our relations with Great Britain, I can not doubt the propriety of increasing our means of defense both by land and sea. This can give Great Britain no cause of offense nor increase the danger of a rupture. If, on the contrary, we should fold our arms in security and at last be suddenly involved in hostilities for the maintenance of our just rights without any adequate preparation, our responsibility to the country would be of the gravest character. Should collision between the two countries be avoided, as I sincerely trust it may be, the additional charge upon the Treasury in making the necessary preparations will not be lost, while in the event of such a collision they would be indispensable for the maintenance of our national rights and national honor.

I have seen no reason to change or modify the recommendations of my annual message in regard to the Oregon question. The notice to abrogate the treaty of the 6th of August, 1827, is authorized by the treaty itself and can not be regarded as a warlike measure, and I can not withhold my strong conviction that it should be promptly given. The other recommendations are in conformity with the existing treaty, and would afford to American citizens in Oregon no more than the same measure of protection which has long since been extended to British subjects in that Territory.

The state of our relations with Mexico is still in an unsettled condition. Since the meeting of Congress another revolution has taken place in that country, by which the Government has passed into the hands of new rulers. This event has procrastinated, and may possibly defeat, the settlement of the differences between the United States and that country. The minister of the United States to Mexico at the date of the last advices had not been received by the existing authorities. Demonstrations of a character hostile to the United States continue to be made in

Mexico, which has rendered it proper, in my judgment, to keep nearly two-thirds of our Army on our southwestern frontier. In doing this many of the regular military posts have been reduced to a small force inadequate to their defense should an emergency arise.

In view of these "circumstances," it is my "judgment" that "an increase of our naval and military force is at this time required" to place the country in a suitable state of defense. At the same time, it is my settled purpose to pursue such a course of policy as may be best calculated to preserve both with Great Britain and Mexico an honorable peace, which nothing will so effectually promote as unanimity in our councils and a firm maintenance of all our just rights.

JAMES K. POLK.

WASHINGTON, *April 1, 1846.*

To the House of Representatives of the United States:

I transmit herewith a letter received from the governor of the State of Ohio in answer to a communication addressed to him in compliance with a resolution of the House of Representatives of January 30, 1846, "requesting the President of the United States to apply to the governor of the State of Ohio for information in regard to the present condition of the Columbus and Sandusky turnpike road; whether the said road is kept in such a state of repair as will enable the Federal Government to realize in case of need the advantages contemplated by the act of Congress approved March 3, 1827."

JAMES K. POLK.

WASHINGTON, *April 1, 1846.*

To the Senate of the United States:

In compliance with the request of a delegation of the Tonawanda band of the Seneca Indians now in this city, I herewith transmit, for your consideration, a memorial addressed to the President and the Senate in relation to the treaty of January 15, 1838, with the "Six Nations of New York Indians," and that of May 20, 1842, with the "Seneca Nation of Indians."

JAMES K. POLK.

WASHINGTON, *April 3, 1846.*

To the Senate of the United States:

I transmit herewith a report from the Acting Secretary of State, with accompanying papers, in answer to the resolution of the Senate of the 23d ultimo, requesting the President to communicate to that body, "if not incompatible with public interests, any correspondence which took place between the Government of the United States and that of Great Britain on the subject of the northeastern boundary between the 20th of June, 1840, and the 4th of March, 1841."

JAMES K. POLK.

WASHINGTON, *April 13, 1846.*

To the Senate of the United States:

In answer to the resolution of the Senate of the 11th instant, calling for "copies of any correspondence that may have taken place between the authorities of the United States and those of Great Britain since the last documents transmitted to Congress in relation to the subject of the Oregon Territory, or so much thereof as may be communicated without detriment to the public interest," I have to state that no correspondence in relation to the Oregon Territory has taken place between the authorities of the United States and those of Great Britain since the date of the last documents on the subject transmitted by me to Congress.

JAMES K. POLK.

WASHINGTON, *April 13, 1846.*

To the Senate and House of Representatives:

In my annual message of the 2d of December last it was stated that serious difficulties of long standing continued to distract the several parties into which the Cherokee tribe of Indians is unhappily divided; that all the efforts of the Government to adjust these difficulties had proved to be unsuccessful, and would probably remain so without the aid of further legislation by Congress. Subsequent events have confirmed this opinion.

I communicate herewith, for the information of Congress, a report of the Secretary of War, transmitting a report of the Commissioner of Indian Affairs, with accompanying documents, together with memorials which have been received from the several bands or parties of the Cherokees themselves. It will be perceived that internal feuds still exist which call for the prompt intervention of the Government of the United States.

Since the meeting of Congress several unprovoked murders have been committed by the stronger upon the weaker party of the tribe, which will probably remain unpunished by the Indian authorities; and there is reason to apprehend that similar outrages will continue to be perpetrated unless restrained by the authorities of the United States.

Many of the weaker party have been compelled to seek refuge beyond the limits of the Indian country and within the State of Arkansas, and are destitute of the means for their daily subsistence. The military forces of the United States stationed on the western frontier have been active in their exertions to suppress these outrages and to execute the treaty of 1835, by which it is stipulated that "the United States agree to protect the Cherokee Nation from domestic strife and foreign enemies, and against intestine wars between the several tribes."

These exertions of the Army have proved to a great extent unavailing, for the reasons stated in the accompanying documents, including communications from the officer commanding at Fort Gibson.

I submit, for the consideration of Congress, the propriety of making such amendments of the laws regulating intercourse with the Indian tribes as will subject to trial and punishment in the courts of the United States all Indians guilty of murder and such other felonies as may be designated, when committed on other Indians within the jurisdiction of the United States.

Such a modification of the existing laws is suggested because if offenders against the laws of humanity in the Indian country are left to be punished by Indian laws they will generally, if not always, be permitted to escape with impunity. This has been the case in repeated instances among the Cherokees. For years unprovoked murders have been committed, and yet no effort has been made to bring the offenders to punishment. Should this state of things continue, it is not difficult to foresee that the weaker party will be finally destroyed. As the guardian of the Indian tribes, the Government of the United States is bound by every consideration of duty and humanity to interpose to prevent such a disaster.

From the examination which I have made into the actual state of things in the Cherokee Nation I am satisfied that there is no probability that the different bands or parties into which it is divided can ever again live together in peace and harmony, and that the well-being of the whole requires that they should be separated and live under separate governments as distinct tribes.

That portion who emigrated to the west of the Mississippi prior to the year 1819, commonly called the "Old Settlers," and that portion who made the treaty of 1835, known as the "treaty party," it is believed would willingly unite, and could live together in harmony. The number of these, as nearly as can be estimated, is about one-third of the tribe. The whole number of all the bands or parties does not probably exceed 20,000. The country which they occupy embraces 7,000,000 acres of land, with the privilege of an outlet to the western limits of the United States. This country is susceptible of division, and is large enough for all.

I submit to Congress the propriety of either dividing the country which they at present occupy or of providing by law a new home for the one or the other of the bands or parties now in hostile array against each other, as the most effectual, if not the only, means of preserving the weaker party from massacre and total extermination. Should Congress favor the division of the country as suggested, and the separation of the Cherokees into two distinct tribes, justice will require that the annuities and funds belonging to the whole, now held in trust for them by the United States, should be equitably distributed among the parties, according to their respective claims and numbers.

There is still a small number of the Cherokee tribe remaining within the State of North Carolina, who, according to the stipulations of the treaty of 1835, should have emigrated with their brethren to the west of the Mississippi. It is desirable that they should be removed, and in the event of a division of the country in the West, or of a new home being provided for a portion of the tribe, that they be permitted to join either party, as they may prefer, and be incorporated with them.

I submit the whole subject to Congress, that such legislative measures may be adopted as will be just to all the parties or bands of the tribe. Such measures, I am satisfied, are the only means of arresting the horrid and inhuman massacres which have marked the history of the Cherokees for the last few years, and especially for the last few months.

The Cherokees have been regarded as among the most enlightened of the Indian tribes, but experience has proved that they have not yet advanced to such a state of civilization as to dispense with the guardian care and control of the Government of the United States.

JAMES K. POLK.

WASHINGTON, *April 14, 1846.*

To the Senate and House of Representatives:

In compliance with the act of the 3d of March, 1845, I communicate herewith to Congress a report of the Secretaries of War and the Navy on the subject of a fireproof building for the War and Navy Departments, together with documents explaining the plans to which it refers and containing an estimate of the cost of erecting the buildings proposed.

Congress having made no appropriation for the employment of an architect to prepare and submit the necessary plans, none was appointed. Several skillful architects were invited to submit plans and estimates, and from those that were voluntarily furnished a selection has been made of such as would furnish the requisite building for the accommodation of the War and Navy Departments at the least expense.

All the plans and estimates which have been received are herewith communicated, for the information of Congress.

JAMES K. POLK.

WASHINGTON, *April 20, 1846.*

To the House of Representatives:

I have considered the resolution of the House of Representatives of the 9th instant, by which I am requested "to cause to be furnished to that House an account of all payments made on President's certificates from the fund appropriated by law, through the agency of the State Department, for the contingent expenses of foreign intercourse from the 4th of March, 1841, until the retirement of Daniel Webster from the Department of State, with copies of all entries, receipts, letters, vouchers, memorandums, or other evidence of such payments, to whom paid, for what, and particularly all concerning the northeastern-boundary dispute with Great Britain."

With an anxious desire to furnish to the House any information requested by that body which may be in the Executive Departments, I
have felt bound by a sense of public duty to inquire how far I could with
propriety, or consistently with the existing laws, respond to their call.

The usual annual appropriation "for the contingent expenses of intercourse between the United States and foreign nations" has been
disbursed since the date of the act of May 1, 1810, in pursuance of its
provisions. By the third section of that act it is provided—

> That when any sum or sums of money shall be drawn from the Treasury under
> any law making appropriation for the contingent expenses of intercourse between
> the United States and foreign nations the President shall be, and he is hereby,
> authorized to cause the same to be duly settled annually with the accounting offi-
> cers of the Treasury in the manner following; that is to say, by causing the same to
> be accounted for specially in all instances wherein the expenditure thereof may in
> his judgment be made public, and by making a certificate of the amount of such
> expenditures as he may think it advisable not to specify; and every such certificate
> shall be deemed a sufficient voucher for the sum or sums therein expressed to have
> been expended.

Two distinct classes of expenditure are authorized by this law—the
one of a public and the other of a private and confidential character.
The President in office at the time of the expenditure is made by the
law the sole judge whether it shall be public or private. Such sums
are to be "accounted for specially in all instances wherein the expenditure thereof may in his judgment be made public." All expenditures
"accounted for specially" are settled at the Treasury upon vouchers,
and not on "President's certificates," and, like all other public accounts,
are subject to be called for by Congress, and are open to public examination. Had information as respects this class of expenditures been
called for by the resolution of the House, it would have been promptly
communicated.

Congress, foreseeing that it might become necessary and proper to
apply portions of this fund for objects the original accounts and vouchers
for which could not be "made public" without injury to the public interests, authorized the President, instead of such accounts and vouchers, to
make a certificate of the amount "of such expenditures as he may think
it advisable not to specify," and have provided that "every such certificate shall be deemed a sufficient voucher for the sum or sums therein
expressed to have been expended."

The law making these provisions is in full force. It is binding upon
all the departments of the Government, and especially upon the Executive, whose duty it is "to take care that the laws be faithfully executed."
In the exercise of the discretion lodged by it in the Executive several
of my predecessors have made "certificates" of the amount "of such
expenditures as they have thought it advisable not to specify," and upon
these certificates as the only vouchers settlements have been made at
the Treasury.

It appears that within the period specified in the resolution of the

House certificates were given by my immediate predecessor, upon which settlements have been made at the Treasury, amounting to $5,460. He has solemnly determined that the objects and items of these expenditures should not be made public, and has given his certificates to that effect, which are placed upon the records of the country. Under the direct authority of an existing law, he has exercised the power of placing these expenditures under the seal of confidence, and the whole matter was terminated before I came into office. An important question arises, whether a subsequent President, either voluntarily or at the request of one branch of Congress, can without a violation of the spirit of the law revise the acts of his predecessor and expose to public view that which he had determined should not be "made public." If not a matter of strict duty, it would certainly be a safe general rule that this should not be done. Indeed, it may well happen, and probably would happen, that the President for the time being would not be in possession of the information upon which his predecessor acted, and could not, therefore, have the means of judging whether he had exercised his discretion wisely or not. The law requires no other voucher but the President's certificate, and there is nothing in its provisions which requires any "entries, receipts, letters, vouchers, memorandums, or other evidence of such payments" to be preserved in the executive department. The President who makes the "certificate" may, if he chooses, keep all the information and evidence upon which he acts in his own possession. If, for the information of his successors, he shall leave the evidence on which he acts and the items of the expenditures which make up the sum for which he has given his "certificate" on the confidential files of one of the Executive Departments, they do not in any proper sense become thereby public records. They are never seen or examined by the accounting officers of the Treasury when they settle an account on the "President's certificate." The First Congress of the United States on the 1st of July, 1790, passed an act "providing the means of intercourse between the United States and foreign nations," by which a similar provision to that which now exists was made for the settlement of such expenditures as in the judgment of the President ought not to be made public. This act was limited in its duration. It was continued for a limited term in 1793, and between that time and the date of the act of May 1, 1810, which is now in force, the same provision was revived and continued. Expenditures were made and settled under Presidential certificates in pursuance of these laws.

If the President may answer the present call, he must answer similar calls for every such expenditure of a confidential character, made under every Administration, in war and in peace, from the organization of the Government to the present period. To break the seal of confidence imposed by the law, and heretofore uniformly preserved, would be subversive of the very purpose for which the law was enacted, and might be productive of the most disastrous consequences. The expenditures of this confidential character, it is believed, were never before sought to be made public, and I should greatly apprehend the consequences of establishing a precedent which would render such disclosures hereafter inevitable.

I am fully aware of the strong and correct public feeling which exists throughout the country against secrecy of any kind in the administration of the Government, and especially in reference to public expenditures; yet our foreign negotiations are wisely and properly confined to the knowledge of the Executive during their pendency. Our laws require the accounts of every particular expenditure to be rendered and publicly settled at the Treasury Department. The single exception which exists is not that the amounts embraced under President's certificates shall be withheld from the public, but merely that the items of which these are composed shall not be divulged. To this extent, and no further, is secrecy observed.

The laudable vigilance of the people in regard to all the expenditures of the Government, as well as a sense of duty on the part of the President and a desire to retain the good opinion of his fellow-citizens, will prevent any sum expended from being accounted for by the President's certificate unless in cases of urgent necessity. Such certificates have therefore been resorted to but seldom throughout our past history.

For my own part, I have not caused any account whatever to be settled on a Presidential certificate. I have had no occasion rendering it necessary in my judgment to make such a certificate, and it would be an extreme case which would ever induce me to exercise this authority; yet if such a case should arise it would be my duty to assume the responsibility devolved on me by the law.

During my Administration all expenditures for contingent expenses of foreign intercourse in which the accounts have been closed have been settled upon regular vouchers, as all other public accounts are settled at the Treasury.

It may be alleged that the power of impeachment belongs to the House of Representatives, and that, with a view to the exercise of this power, that House has the right to investigate the conduct of all public officers under the Government. This is cheerfully admitted. In such a case the safety of the Republic would be the supreme law, and the power of the House in the pursuit of this object would penetrate into the most secret recesses of the Executive Departments. It could command the attendance of any and every agent of the Government, and compel them to produce all papers, public or private, official or unofficial, and to testify on oath to all facts within their knowledge. But even in a case of that kind they would adopt all wise precautions to prevent the exposure of all such matters the publication of which might injuriously affect the public interest, except so far as this might be necessary to accomplish the great ends of public justice. If the House of Representatives, as the grand inquest of the nation, should at any time have reason to believe that there has been malversation in office by an improper use or application of the public money by a public officer, and should think proper to institute an inquiry into the matter, all the archives and papers of the Executive Departments, public or private, would be subject to the inspection and control of a committee of their body and every facility in the power of the Executive be afforded to enable them to prosecute the investigation.

The experience of every nation on earth has demonstrated that emergencies may arise in which it becomes absolutely necessary for the public safety or the public good to make expenditures the very object of which would be defeated by publicity. Some governments have very large amounts at their disposal, and have made vastly greater expenditures than the small amounts which have from time to time been accounted for on President's certificates. In no nation is the application of such sums ever made public. In time of war or impending danger the situation of the country may make it necessary to employ individuals for the purpose of obtaining information or rendering other important services who could never be prevailed upon to act if they entertained the least apprehension that their names or their agency would in any contingency be divulged. So it may often become necessary to incur an expenditure for an object highly useful to the country; for example, the conclusion of a treaty with a barbarian power whose customs require on such occasions the use of presents. But this object might be altogether defeated by the intrigues of other powers if our purposes were to be made known by the exhibition of the original papers and vouchers to the accounting officers of the Treasury. It would be easy to specify other cases which may occur in the history of a great nation, in its intercourse with other nations, wherein it might become absolutely necessary to incur expenditures for objects which could never be accomplished if it were suspected in advance that the items of expenditure and the agencies employed would be made public.

Actuated undoubtedly by considerations of this kind, Congress provided such a fund, coeval with the organization of the Government, and subsequently enacted the law of 1810 as the permanent law of the land. While this law exists in full force I feel bound by a high sense of public policy and duty to observe its provisions and the uniform practice of my predecessors under it.

With great respect for the House of Representatives and an anxious desire to conform to their wishes, I am constrained to come to this conclusion.

If Congress disapprove the policy of the law, they may repeal its provisions.

In reply to that portion of the resolution of the House which calls for "copies of whatever communications were made from the Secretary of State during the last session of the Twenty-seventh Congress, particularly February, 1843, to Mr. Cushing and Mr. Adams, members of the Committee of this House on Foreign Affairs, of the wish of the President of the United States to institute a special mission to Great Britain," I have to state that no such communications or copies of them are found in the Department of State.

"Copies of all letters on the books of the Department of State to any officer of the United States or any person in New York concerning Alexander McLeod," which are also called for by the resolution, are herewith communicated.   JAMES K. POLK.

WASHINGTON, *April 20, 1846.*

To the Senate of the United States:

I herewith transmit to the Senate, in answer to their resolution of the 8th instant, a report from the Secretary of State, with accompanying papers, containing the information and correspondence referred to in that resolution, relative to the search of American vessels by British cruisers subsequent to the date of the treaty of Washington.

JAMES K. POLK.

WASHINGTON, *April 27, 1846.*

To the Senate of the United States:

I transmit herewith the information called for by a resolution of the Senate of the 3d December last, relating to "claims arising under the fourteenth article of the treaty of Dancing Rabbit Creek" with the Choctaw tribe of Indians, concluded in September, 1830.

JAMES K. POLK.

WASHINGTON, *April 27, 1846.*

To the House of Representatives:

I transmit herewith a report of the Secretary of War and accompanying papers, containing the information called for by the resolution of the House of Representatives of December 19, 1845, relating to certain claims of the Chickasaw tribe of Indians.   JAMES K. POLK.

WASHINGTON, *April 27, 1846.·*

To the House of Representatives:

I transmit herewith a report and accompanying papers from the Secretary of War, in reply to the resolution of the House of Representatives of the 31st of December last, in relation to claims arising under the

Choctaw treaty of 1830 which have been presented to and allowed or rejected by commissioners appointed in pursuance of the acts of 3d of March, 1837, and 23d of August, 1842.   JAMES K. POLK.

To the House of Representatives: WASHINGTON, *May 6, 1846.*

I transmit herewith reports from the Secretary of War and the Secretary of the Treasury, with additional papers, relative to the claims of certain Chickasaw Indians, which, with those heretofore communicated to Congress, contain all the information called for by the resolution of the House of Representatives of the 19th of December last.

JAMES K. POLK.

To the House of Representatives: WASHINGTON, *May 6, 1846.*

I transmit herewith a report from the Secretary of State, with accompanying papers, in answer to a resolution of the House of Representatives of the 8th ultimo, requesting the President to communicate to that body, "if not incompatible with the public interest, copies of the correspondence of George William Gordon, late consul of the United States at Rio de Janeiro, with the Department of State, relating to the slave trade in vessels and by citizens of the United States between the coast of Africa and Brazil."

JAMES K. POLK.

To the House of Representatives: WASHINGTON, *May 6, 1846.*

I transmit herewith a report of the Secretary of War, in answer to the resolution of the House of Representatives of the 4th instant, calling for information "whether any soldier or soldiers of the Army of the United States have been shot for desertion, or in the act of deserting, and, if so, by whose order and under what authority."

JAMES K. POLK.

WASHINGTON, *May 11, 1846.*

To the Senate and House of Representatives:

The existing state of the relations between the United States and Mexico renders it proper that I should bring the subject to the consideration of Congress. In my message at the commencement of your present session the state of these relations, the causes which led to the suspension of diplomatic intercourse between the two countries in March, 1845, and the long-continued and unredressed wrongs and injuries committed by the Mexican Government on citizens of the United States in their persons and property were briefly set forth.

As the facts and opinions which were then laid before you were carefully considered, I can not better express my present convictions of the condition of affairs up to that time than by referring you to that communication.

The strong desire to establish peace with Mexico on liberal and honorable terms, and the readiness of this Government to regulate and adjust our boundary and other causes of difference with that power on such fair and equitable principles as would lead to permanent relations of the most friendly nature, induced me in September last to seek the reopening of diplomatic relations between the two countries. Every measure adopted on our part had for its object the furtherance of these desired results. In communicating to Congress a succinct statement of the injuries which we had suffered from Mexico, and which have been accumulating during a period of more than twenty years, every expression that could tend to inflame the people of Mexico or defeat or delay a pacific result was carefully avoided. An envoy of the United States repaired to Mexico with full powers to adjust every existing difference. But though present on the Mexican soil by agreement between the two Governments, invested with full powers, and bearing evidence of the most friendly dispositions, his mission has been unavailing. The Mexican Government not only refused to receive him or listen to his propositions, but after a long-continued series of menaces have at last invaded our territory and shed the blood of our fellow-citizens on our own soil.

It now becomes my duty to state more in detail the origin, progress, and failure of that mission. In pursuance of the instructions given in September last, an inquiry was made on the 13th of October, 1845, in the most friendly terms, through our consul in Mexico, of the minister for foreign affairs, whether the Mexican Government "would receive an envoy from the United States intrusted with full powers to adjust all the questions in dispute between the two Governments," with the assurance that "should the answer be in the affirmative such an envoy would be immediately dispatched to Mexico." The Mexican minister on the 15th of October gave an affirmative answer to this inquiry, requesting at the same time that our naval force at Vera Cruz might be withdrawn, lest its continued presence might assume the appearance of menace and coercion pending the negotiations. This force was immediately withdrawn. On the 10th of November, 1845, Mr. John Slidell, of Louisiana, was commissioned by me as envoy extraordinary and minister plenipotentiary of the United States to Mexico, and was intrusted with full powers to adjust both the questions of the Texas boundary and of indemnification to our citizens. The redress of the wrongs of our citizens naturally and inseparably blended itself with the question of boundary. The settlement of the one question in any correct view of the subject involves that of the other. I could not for a moment entertain the idea that the claims of our much-injured and long-suffering citizens, many of which had existed for more than twenty years, should be postponed or separated from the settlement of the boundary question.

Mr. Slidell arrived at Vera Cruz on the 30th of November, and was courteously received by the authorities of that city. But the Government of General Herrera was then tottering to its fall. The revolutionary party had seized upon the Texas question to effect or hasten its overthrow. Its determination to restore friendly relations with the United States, and to receive our minister to negotiate for the settlement of this question, was violently assailed, and was made the great theme of denunciation against it. The Government of General Herrera, there is good reason to believe, was sincerely desirous to receive our minister; but it yielded to the storm raised by its enemies, and on the 21st of December refused to accredit Mr. Slidell upon the most frivolous pretexts. These are so fully and ably exposed in the note of Mr. Slidell of the 24th of December last to the Mexican minister of foreign relations, herewith transmitted, that I deem it unnecessary to enter into further detail on this portion of the subject.

Five days after the date of Mr. Slidell's note General Herrera yielded the Government to General Paredes without a struggle, and on the 30th of December resigned the Presidency. This revolution was accomplished solely by the army, the people having taken little part in the contest; and thus the supreme power in Mexico passed into the hands of a military leader.

Determined to leave no effort untried to effect an amicable adjustment with Mexico, I directed Mr. Slidell to present his credentials to the Government of General Paredes and ask to be officially received by him. There would have been less ground for taking this step had General Paredes come into power by a regular constitutional succession. In that event his administration would have been considered but a mere constitutional continuance of the Government of General Herrera, and the refusal of the latter to receive our minister would have been deemed conclusive unless an intimation had been given by General Paredes of his desire to reverse the decision of his predecessor. But the Government of General Paredes owes its existence to a military revolution, by which the subsisting constitutional authorities had been subverted. The form of government was entirely changed, as well as all the high functionaries by whom it was administered.

Under these circumstances, Mr. Slidell, in obedience to my direction, addressed a note to the Mexican minister of foreign relations, under date of the 1st of March last, asking to be received by that Government in the diplomatic character to which he had been appointed. This minister in his reply, under date of the 12th of March, reiterated the arguments of his predecessor, and in terms that may be considered as giving just grounds of offense to the Government and people of the United States denied the application of Mr. Slidell. Nothing therefore remained for our envoy but to demand his passports and return to his own country.

Thus the Government of Mexico, though solemnly pledged by official acts in October last to receive and accredit an American envoy, violated their plighted faith and refused the offer of a peaceful adjustment of our difficulties. Not only was the offer rejected, but the indignity of its rejection was enhanced by the manifest breach of faith in refusing to admit the envoy who came because they had bound themselves to receive him. Nor can it be said that the offer was fruitless from the want of opportunity of discussing it; our envoy was present on their own soil. Nor can it be ascribed to a want of sufficient powers; our envoy had full powers to adjust every question of difference. Nor was there room for complaint that our propositions for settlement were unreasonable; permission was not even given our envoy to make any proposition whatever. Nor can it be objected that we, on our part, would not listen to any reasonable terms of their suggestion; the Mexican Government refused all negotiation, and have made no proposition of any kind.

In my message at the commencement of the present session I informed you that upon the earnest appeal both of the Congress and convention of Texas I had ordered an efficient military force to take a position "between the Nueces and the Del Norte." This had become necessary to meet a threatened invasion of Texas by the Mexican forces, for which extensive military preparations had been made. The invasion was threatened solely because Texas had determined, in accordance with a solemn resolution of the Congress of the United States, to annex herself to our Union, and under these circumstances it was plainly our duty to extend our protection over her citizens and soil.

This force was concentrated at Corpus Christi, and remained there until after I had received such information from Mexico as rendered it probable, if not certain, that the Mexican Government would refuse to receive our envoy.

Meantime Texas, by the final action of our Congress, had become an integral part of our Union. The Congress of Texas, by its act of December 19, 1836, had declared the Rio del Norte to be the boundary of that Republic. Its jurisdiction had been extended and exercised beyond the Nueces. The country between that river and the Del Norte had been represented in the Congress and in the convention of Texas, had thus taken part in the act of annexation itself, and is now included within one of our Congressional districts. Our own Congress had, moreover, with great unanimity, by the act approved December 31, 1845, recognized the country beyond the Nueces as a part of our territory by including it within our own revenue system, and a revenue officer to reside within that district has been appointed by and with the advice and consent of the Senate. It became, therefore, of urgent necessity to provide for the defense of that portion of our country. Accordingly, on the 13th of January last instructions were issued to the general in command of these troops to occupy the left bank of the Del Norte. This river, which is the southwestern boundary of the State of Texas, is an exposed frontier.

From this quarter invasion was threatened; upon it and in its immediate vicinity, in the judgment of high military experience, are the proper stations for the protecting forces of the Government. In addition to this important consideration, several others occurred to induce this movement. Among these are the facilities afforded by the ports at Brazos Santiago and the mouth of the Del Norte for the reception of supplies by sea, the stronger and more healthful military positions, the convenience for obtaining a ready and a more abundant supply of provisions, water, fuel, and forage, and the advantages which are afforded by the Del Norte in forwarding supplies to such posts as may be established in the interior and upon the Indian frontier.

The movement of the troops to the Del Norte was made by the commanding general under positive instructions to abstain from all aggressive acts toward Mexico or Mexican citizens and to regard the relations between that Republic and the United States as peaceful unless she should declare war or commit acts of hostility indicative of a state of war. He was specially directed to protect private property and respect personal rights.

The Army moved from Corpus Christi on the 11th of March, and on the 28th of that month arrived on the left bank of the Del Norte opposite to Matamoras, where it encamped on a commanding position, which has since been strengthened by the erection of fieldworks. A depot has also been established at Point Isabel, near the Brazos Santiago, 30 miles in rear of the encampment. The selection of his position was necessarily confided to the judgment of the general in command.

The Mexican forces at Matamoras assumed a belligerent attitude, and on the 12th of April General Ampudia, then in command, notified General Taylor to break up his camp within twenty-four hours and to retire beyond the Nueces River, and in the event of his failure to comply with these demands announced that arms, and arms alone, must decide the question. But no open act of hostility was committed until the 24th of April. On that day General Arista, who had succeeded to the command of the Mexican forces, communicated to General Taylor that "he considered hostilities commenced and should prosecute them." A party of dragoons of 63 men and officers were on the same day dispatched from the American camp up the Rio del Norte, on its left bank, to ascertain whether the Mexican troops had crossed or were preparing to cross the river, "became engaged with a large body of these troops, and after a short affair, in which some 16 were killed and wounded, appear to have been surrounded and compelled to surrender."

The grievous wrongs perpetrated by Mexico upon our citizens throughout a long period of years remain unredressed, and solemn treaties pledging her public faith for this redress have been disregarded. A government either unable or unwilling to enforce the execution of such treaties fails to perform one of its plainest duties.

Our commerce with Mexico has been almost annihilated. It was formerly highly beneficial to both nations, but our merchants have been deterred from prosecuting it by the system of outrage and extortion which the Mexican authorities have pursued against them, whilst their appeals through their own Government for indemnity have been made in vain. Our forbearance has gone to such an extreme as to be mistaken in its character. Had we acted with vigor in repelling the insults and redressing the injuries inflicted by Mexico at the commencement, we should doubtless have escaped all the difficulties in which we are now involved.

Instead of this, however, we have been exerting our best efforts to propitiate her good will. Upon the pretext that Texas, a nation as independent as herself, thought proper to unite its destinies with our own, she has affected to believe that we have severed her rightful territory, and in official proclamations and manifestoes has repeatedly threatened to make war upon us for the purpose of reconquering Texas. In the meantime we have tried every effort at reconciliation. The cup of forbearance had been exhausted even before the recent information from the frontier of the Del Norte. But now, after reiterated menaces, Mexico has passed the boundary of the United States, has invaded our territory and shed American blood upon the American soil. She has proclaimed that hostilities have commenced, and that the two nations are now at war.

As war exists, and, notwithstanding all our efforts to avoid it, exists by the act of Mexico herself, we are called upon by every consideration of duty and patriotism to vindicate with decision the honor, the rights, and the interests of our country.

Anticipating the possibility of a crisis like that which has arrived, instructions were given in August last, "as a precautionary measure" against invasion or threatened invasion, authorizing General Taylor, if the emergency required, to accept volunteers, not from Texas only, but from the States of Louisiana, Alabama, Mississippi, Tennessee, and Kentucky, and corresponding letters were addressed to the respective governors of those States. These instructions were repeated, and in January last, soon after the incorporation of "Texas into our Union of States," General Taylor was further "authorized by the President to make a requisition upon the executive of that State for such of its militia force as may be needed to repel invasion or to secure the country against apprehended invasion." On the 2d day of March he was again reminded, "in the event of the approach of any considerable Mexican force, promptly and efficiently to use the authority with which he was clothed to call to him such auxiliary force as he might need." War actually existing and our territory having been invaded, General Taylor, pursuant to authority vested in him by my direction, has called on the governor of Texas for four regiments of State troops, two to be mounted and two to serve on foot, and on the governor of Louisiana for four regiments of infantry to be sent to him as soon as practicable.

In further vindication of our rights and defense of our territory, I invoke the prompt action of Congress to recognize the existence of the war, and to place at the disposition of the Executive the means of prosecuting the war with vigor, and thus hastening the restoration of peace. To this end I recommend that authority should be given to call into the public service a large body of volunteers to serve for not less than six or twelve months unless sooner discharged. A volunteer force is beyond question more efficient than any other description of citizen soldiers, and it is not to be doubted that a number far beyond that required would readily rush to the field upon the call of their country. I further recommend that a liberal provision be made for sustaining our entire military force and furnishing it with supplies and munitions of war.

The most energetic and prompt measures and the immediate appearance in arms of a large and overpowering force are recommended to Congress as the most certain and efficient means of bringing the existing collision with Mexico to a speedy and successful termination.

In making these recommendations I deem it proper to declare that it is my anxious desire not only to terminate hostilities speedily, but to bring all matters in dispute between this Government and Mexico to an early and amicable adjustment; and in this view I shall be prepared to renew negotiations whenever Mexico shall be ready to receive propositions or to make propositions of her own.

I transmit herewith a copy of the correspondence between our envoy to Mexico and the Mexican minister for foreign affairs, and so much of the correspondence between that envoy and the Secretary of State and between the Secretary of War and the general in command on the Del Norte as is necessary to a full understanding of the subject.

JAMES K. POLK.

WASHINGTON, *May 12, 1846.*

To the Senate and House of Representatives:

I herewith transmit to Congress a copy of a communication* from the officer commanding the Army in Texas, with the papers which accompanied it. They were received by the Southern mail of yesterday, some hours after my message of that date had been transmitted, and are of a prior date to one of the communications from the same officer which accompanied that message.

JAMES K. POLK.

WASHINGTON, *May 19, 1846.*

To the Senate of the United States:

I transmit herewith a report from the Secretary of War, in answer to a resolution of the Senate of the 4th of December last, which contains

---

* Relating to the operations of the Army near Matamoras, Mexico.

the information called for "with respect to the practicability and utility of a fort or forts on Ship Island, on the coast of Mississippi, with a view to the protection of said coast."

JAMES K. POLK.

WASHINGTON, *May 26, 1846.*

To the Senate of the United States:

A convention was concluded at Lima on 17th March, 1841, between the United States and the Republic of Peru, for the adjustment of claims of our citizens upon that Republic. It was stipulated by the seventh article of this convention that "it shall be ratified by the contracting parties, and the ratifications shall be exchanged within two years from its date, or sooner if possible, after having been approved by the President and Senate of the United States and by the Congress of Peru."

This convention was transmitted by the President to the Senate for their consideration during the extra session of 1841, but it did not receive their approbation until the 5th January, 1843. This delay rendered it impracticable that the convention should reach Lima before the 17th March, 1843, the last day when the ratifications could be exchanged under the terms of its seventh article. The Senate therefore extended the time for this purpose until the 20th December, 1843.

In the meantime, previous to the 17th March, 1843, General Menendez, the constitutional President of Peru, had ratified the convention, declaring, however, in the act of ratification itself (which is without date), that "the present convention and ratification are to be submitted within the time stipulated in the seventh article for the final approbation of the National Congress." This was, however, rendered impossible from the fact that no Peruvian Congress assembled from the date of the convention until the year 1845.

When the convention arrived at Lima General Menendez had been deposed by a revolution, and General Vivanco had placed himself at the head of the Government. On the 16th July, 1843, the convention was ratified by him in absolute terms without the reference to Congress which the constitution of Peru requires, because, as the ratification states, "under existing circumstances the Government exercises the legislative powers demanded by the necessities of the State." The ratifications were accordingly exchanged at Lima on the 22d July, 1843, and the convention itself was proclaimed at Washington by the President on the 21st day of February, 1844.

In the meantime General Vivanco was deposed, and on the 12th October, 1843, the Government then in existence published a decree declaring all his administrative acts to be null and void, and notwithstanding the earnest and able remonstrances of Mr. Pickett, our chargé d'affaires at Lima, the Peruvian Government have still persisted in declaring that the ratification of the convention by Vivanco was invalid.

After the meeting of the Peruvian Congress in 1845 the convention was submitted to that body, by which it was approved on the 21st of

October last, "with the condition, however, that the first installment of $30,000 on account of the principal of the debt thereby recognized, and to which the second article relates, should begin from the 1st day of January, 1846, and the interest on this annual sum, according to article 3, should be calculated and paid from the 1st day of January, 1842, following in all other respects besides this modification the terms of the convention."

I am not in possession of the act of the Congress of Peru containing this provision, but the information is communicated through a note under date of the 15th of November, 1845, from the minister of foreign affairs of Peru to the chargé d'affaires of the United States at Lima. A copy of this note has been transmitted to the Department of State both by our chargé d'affaires at Lima and by the Peruvian minister of foreign affairs, and a copy of the same is herewith transmitted.

Under these circumstances I submit to the Senate, for their consideration, the amendment to the convention thus proposed by the Congress of Peru, with a view to its ratification. It would have been more satisfactory to have submitted the act itself of the Peruvian Congress, but, on account of the great distance, if I should wait until its arrival another year might be consumed, whilst the American claimants have already been too long delayed in receiving the money justly due to them. Several of the largest of these claimants would, I am informed, be satisfied with the modification of the convention adopted by the Peruvian Congress.

A difficulty may arise in regard to the form of any proceeding which the Senate might think proper to adopt, from the fact that the original convention approved by them was sent to Peru and was exchanged for the other original, ratified by General Vivanco, which is now in the Department of State. In order to obviate this difficulty as far as may be in my power, I transmit a copy of the convention, under the seal of the United States, on which the Senate might found any action they may deem advisable.

I would suggest that should the Senate advise the adoption of the amendment proposed by the Peruvian Congress the time for exchanging the ratifications of the amended convention ought to be extended for a considerable period, so as to provide against all accidents in its transmission to Lima.

JAMES K. POLK.

To the House of Representatives: WASHINGTON, *May 27, 1846.*

In compliance with the request contained in the resolution of the House of Representatives of this date, I transmit copies of all the official dispatches which have been received from General Taylor, commanding the army of occupation on the Rio Grande, relating to the battles* of the 8th and 9th instant.

JAMES K. POLK.

* Palo Alto and Resaca de la Palma.

WASHINGTON, *May 28, 1846.*

To the Senate and House of Representatives:

I transmit a copy of a note, under date the 26th instant, from the envoy extraordinary and minister plenipotentiary of Her Britannic Majesty to the Secretary of State, communicating a dispatch, under date of the 4th instant, received by him from Her Majesty's principal secretary of state for foreign affairs.

From these it will be seen that the claims of the two Governments upon each other for a return of duties which had been levied in violation of the commercial convention of 1815 have been finally and satisfactorily adjusted. In making this communication I deem it proper to express my satisfaction at the prompt manner in which the British Government has acceded to the suggestion of the Secretary of State for the speedy termination of this affair.

JAMES K. POLK.

WASHINGTON, *June 1, 1846.*

To the Senate of the United States:

I propose, for the reason stated in the accompanying communication of the Secretary of War, that the confirmation of Brevet Second Lieutenant L. B. Wood by the Senate on the 5th of February, as a second lieutenant in the Fifth Regiment of Infantry, be canceled; and I nominate the officers named in the same communication for regular promotion in the Army.

JAMES K. POLK.

WAR DEPARTMENT, *May 15, 1846.*

The PRESIDENT OF THE UNITED STATES.

SIR: On the 12th of December last a list of promotions and appointments of officers of the Army was submitted to the Senate for confirmation, in which list Brevet Second Lieutenant L. B. Wood, of the Eighth Infantry, was nominated to the grade of second lieutenant in the Fifth Regiment of Infantry, *vice* Second Lieutenant Deas, promoted. He was entitled to this vacancy by *seniority*, but in a letter dated November 30, 1845, and received at the Adjutant-General's Office December 30, 1845 (eighteen days *after* the list referred to above had been sent to the Senate), he says: "I respectfully beg leave to be permitted to decline promotion in any other regiment, and to fill the first vacancy which may happen in the Eighth." This request was acceded to, and accordingly, on the first subsequent list submitted to the Senate, dated January 8, 1846, Brevet Second Lieutenant Charles S. Hamilton, of the Second Infantry (the next below Lieutenant Wood), was nominated to fill the vacancy in the *Fifth* Regiment and Lieutenant Wood to a vacancy which has occurred meanwhile (December 31) in the *Eighth.*

The foregoing circumstances were explained in a note to the nomination list of January 8, but it is probable the explanation escaped observation in the Senate, as on the 5th of February Lieutenant Wood was confirmed in the Fifth Infantry, agreeably to the first nomination, while no action appears to have been taken on his nomination or that of Lieutenant Hamilton on the subsequent list of January 8, 1846.

As no commissions have yet been issued to these officers, and as Lieutenant Wood has renewed his application to be continued in the Eighth Infantry, I respectfully suggest that the Senate be requested to cancel their confirmation, on the 5th of February, of his promotion as a second lieutenant in the Fifth Regiment of Infantry; and I have the honor to propose the renomination of the lieutenants whose names are annexed for regular promotion, to wit:

Fifth Regiment of Infantry.

Brevet Second Lieutenant Charles S. Hamilton, of the Second Regiment of Infantry, to be second lieutenant, November 17, 1846, *vice* Deas, promoted.

Eighth Regiment of Infantry.

Brevet Second Lieutenant Lafayette B. Wood to be second lieutenant, December 31, 1846, *vice* Maclay, promoted.

I am, sir, with great respect, your obedient servant,

W. L. MARCY.

WASHINGTON, *June 5, 1846.*

To the Senate of the United States:

In answer to the resolution of the Senate of the 22d ultimo, calling for information upon the subject of the treaties which were concluded between the late Republic of Texas and England and France, respectively, I transmit a report from the Secretary of State and the documents by which it was accompanied.

JAMES K. POLK.

WASHINGTON, *June 6, 1846.*

To the Senate of the United States:

In answer to the resolutions of the Senate of the 10th, 11th, and 22d of April last, I communicate herewith a report from the Secretary of State, accompanied with the correspondence between the Government of the United States and that of Great Britain in the years 1840, 1841, 1842, and 1843 respecting the right or practice of visiting or searching merchant vessels in time of peace, and also the protest addressed by the minister of the United States at Paris in the year 1842 against the concurrence of France in the quintuple treaty, together with all correspondence relating thereto.

JAMES K. POLK.

WASHINGTON, *June 6, 1846.*

To the Senate of the United States:

I herewith communicate to the Senate, for its consideration, a convention signed on the 2d day of May, 1846, by the minister of the United States at Berlin with the plenipotentiary of Hesse-Cassel, for the mutual abolition of the *droit d'aubaine* and duties on emigration between that German State and the United States; and I communicate with the convention an explanatory dispatch of the minister of the United States dated on the same day of the present year and numbered 284.

JAMES K. POLK.

WASHINGTON, *June 8, 1846.*

To the Senate of the United States:

I communicate herewith a report from the Secretary of War, transmitting the correspondence called for by the resolution of the Senate of the 5th instant with General Edmund P. Gaines and General Winfield Scott, of the Army of the United States.

The report of the Secretary of War and the accompanying correspondence with General Gaines contain all the information in my possession in relation to calls for "volunteers or militia into the service of the United States" "by any officer of the Army" without legal "authority therefor," and of the "measures which have been adopted" "in relation to such officer or troops so called into service."

In addition to the information contained in the report of the Secretary of War and the accompanying correspondence with "Major-General Scott, of the United States Army, upon the subject of his taking the command of the army of occupation on the frontier of Texas," I state that on the same day on which I approved and signed the act of the 13th of May, 1846, entitled "An act providing for the prosecution of the existing war between the United States and the Republic of Mexico," I communicated to General Scott, through the Secretary of War, and also in a personal interview with that officer, my desire that he should take command of the Army on the Rio Grande and of the volunteer forces which I informed him it was my intention forthwith to call out to march to that frontier to be employed in the prosecution of the war against Mexico. The tender of the command to General Scott was voluntary on my part, and was made without any request or intimation on the subject from him. It was made in consideration of his rank as Commander in Chief of the Army. My communications with General Scott assigning him the command were verbal, first through the Secretary of War and afterwards in person. No written order was deemed to be necessary. General Scott assented to assume the command, and on the following day I had another interview with him and the Secretary of War, in relation to the number and apportionment among the several States of the volunteer forces to be called out for immediate service, the forces which were to be organized and held in readiness subject to a future call should it become necessary, and other military preparations and movements to be made with a view to the vigorous prosecution of the war. It was distinctly settled, and was well understood by General Scott, that he was to command the Army in the war against Mexico, and so continued to be settled and understood without any other intention on my part until the Secretary of War submitted to me the letter of General Scott addressed to him under date of the 21st of May, 1846, a copy of which is herewith communicated. The character of that letter made it proper, in my judgment, to change my determination in regard to the command of the Army, and the Secretary of War, by my direction, in his letter of the 25th of May, 1846, a copy of which is also herewith communicated, for the reasons therein assigned, informed General Scott that he was relieved from the command of the Army destined to prosecute the war against Mexico, and that he would remain in the discharge of his duties at Washington. The command of the Army on the frontier of Mexico has since been assigned to General Taylor, with his brevet rank of major-general recently conferred upon him.

JAMES K. POLK.

WASHINGTON, *June 10, 1846.*

To the Senate of the United States:

I lay before the Senate a proposal, in the form of a convention, presented to the Secretary of State on the 6th instant by the envoy extraordinary and minister plenipotentiary of Her Britannic Majesty, for the adjustment of the Oregon question, together with a protocol of this proceeding. I submit this proposal to the consideration of the Senate, and request their advice as to the action which in their judgment it may be proper to take in reference to it.

In the early periods of the Government the opinion and advice of the Senate were often taken in advance upon important questions of our foreign policy. General Washington repeatedly consulted the Senate and asked their previous advice upon pending negotiations with foreign powers, and the Senate in every instance responded to his call by giving their advice, to which he always conformed his action. This practice, though rarely resorted to in later times, was, in my judgment, eminently wise, and may on occasions of great importance be properly revived. The Senate are a branch of the treaty-making power, and by consulting them in advance of his own action upon important measures of foreign policy which may ultimately come before them for their consideration the President secures harmony of action between that body and himself. The Senate are, moreover, a branch of the war-making power, and it may be eminently proper for the Executive to take the opinion and advice of that body in advance upon any great question which may involve in its decision the issue of peace or war. On the present occasion the magnitude of the subject would induce me under any circumstances to desire the previous advice of the Senate, and that desire is increased by the recent debates and proceedings in Congress, which render it, in my judgment, not only respectful to the Senate, but necessary and proper, if not indispensable to insure harmonious action between that body and the Executive. In conferring on the Executive the authority to give the notice for the abrogation of the convention of 1827 the Senate acted publicly so large a part that a decision on the proposal now made by the British Government, without a definite knowledge of the views of that body in reference to it, might render the question still more complicated and difficult of adjustment. For these reasons I invite the consideration of the Senate to the proposal of the British Government for the settlement of the Oregon question, and ask their advice on the subject.

My opinions and my action on the Oregon question were fully made known to Congress in my annual message of the 2d of December last, and the opinions therein expressed remain unchanged.

Should the Senate, by the constitutional majority required for the ratification of treaties, advise the acceptance of this proposition, or advise it with such modifications as they may upon full deliberation deem proper, I shall conform my action to their advice. Should the Senate, however, decline by such constitutional majority to give such advice or to express an opinion on the subject, I shall consider it my duty to reject the offer.

I also communicate herewith an extract from a dispatch of the Secretary of State to the minister of the United States at London under date of the 28th of April last, directing him, in accordance with the joint resolution of Congress "concerning the Oregon Territory," to deliver the notice to the British Government for the abrogation of the convention of the 6th of August, 1827, and also a copy of the notice transmitted to him for that purpose, together with extracts from a dispatch of that minister to the Secretary of State bearing date on the 18th day of May last.

JAMES K. POLK.

WASHINGTON, *June 11, 1846.*
To the Senate of the United States:

I transmit herewith a communication from the Secretary of War, which is accompanied by documents relating to General Gaines's calls for volunteers, received since the answer was made to the resolution of the Senate of the 5th instant on that subject, and which I deem it proper to submit for the further information of the Senate.

JAMES K. POLK.

WASHINGTON, *June 12, 1846.*
To the Senate and House of Representatives:

I transmit herewith, for the information of Congress, official reports received at the War Department from the officer commanding the Army on the Mexican frontier, giving a detailed report of the operations of the Army in that quarter, and particularly of the recent engagements* between the American and Mexican forces.

JAMES K. POLK.

WASHINGTON, *June 15, 1846.*
To the Senate of the United States:

I transmit herewith a communication from the Secretary of War, accompanied by a report of an expedition led by Lieutenant Abert on the

* Palo Alto and Resaca de la Palma.

Upper Arkansas and through the country of the Camanche Indians in the fall of the year 1845, as requested by the resolution of the Senate of the 9th instant.

JAMES K. POLK.

WASHINGTON, *June 16, 1846.*

To the Senate of the United States:

In answer to the resolution of the Senate of the 3d instant, I communicate herewith estimates prepared by the War and Navy Departments of the probable expenses of conducting the existing war with Mexico during the remainder of the present and the whole of the next fiscal year. I communicate also a report of the Secretary of the Treasury, based upon these estimates, containing recommendations of measures for raising the additional means required. It is probable that the actual expenses incurred during the period specified may fall considerably below the estimates submitted, which are for a larger number of troops than have yet been called to the field. As a precautionary measure, however, against any possible deficiency, the estimates have been made at the largest amount which any state of the service may require.

It will be perceived from the report of the Secretary of the Treasury that a considerable portion of the additional amount required may be raised by a modification of the rates of duty imposed by the existing tariff laws. The high duties at present levied on many articles totally exclude them from importation, whilst the quantity and amount of others which are imported are greatly diminished. By reducing these duties to a revenue standard, it is not doubted that a large amount of the articles on which they are imposed would be imported, and a corresponding amount of revenue be received at the Treasury from this source. By imposing revenue duties on many articles now permitted to be imported free of duty, and by regulating the rates within the revenue standard upon others, a large additional revenue will be collected. Independently of the high considerations which induced me in my annual message to recommend a modification and reduction of the rates of duty imposed by the act of 1842 as being not only proper in reference to a state of peace, but just to all the great interests of the country, the necessity of such modification and reduction as a war measure must now be manifest. The country requires additional revenue for the prosecution of the war. It may be obtained to a great extent by reducing the prohibitory and highly protective duties imposed by the existing laws to revenue rates, by imposing revenue duties on the free list, and by modifying the rates of duty on other articles.

The modifications recommended by the Secretary of the Treasury in his annual report in December last were adapted to a state of peace, and the additional duties now suggested by him are with a view strictly to raise revenue as a war measure. At the conclusion of the war these duties may and should be abolished and reduced to lower rates.

It is not apprehended that the existing war with Mexico will materially affect our trade and commerce with the rest of the world. On the contrary, the reductions proposed would increase that trade and augment the revenue derived from it.

When the country is in a state of war no contingency should be permitted to occur in which there would be a deficiency in the Treasury for the vigorous prosecution of the war, and to guard against such an event it is recommended that contingent authority be given to issue Treasury notes or to contract a loan for a limited amount, reimbursable at an early day. Should no occasion arise to exercise the power, still it may be important that the authority should exist should there be a necessity for it.

It is not deemed necessary to resort to direct taxes or excises, the measures recommended being deemed preferable as a means of increasing the revenue. It is hoped that the war with Mexico, if vigorously prosecuted, as is contemplated, may be of short duration. I shall be at all times ready to conclude an honorable peace whenever the Mexican Government shall manifest a like disposition. The existing war has been rendered necessary by the acts of Mexico, and whenever that power shall be ready to do us justice we shall be prepared to sheath the sword and tender to her the olive branch of peace.

JAMES K. POLK.

WASHINGTON, *June 16, 1846.*

To the Senate of the United States:

In accordance with the resolution of the Senate of the 12th instant, that "the President of the United States be, and he is hereby, advised to accept the proposal of the British Government accompanying his message to the Senate dated 10th June, 1846, for a convention to settle boundaries, etc., between the United States and Great Britain west of the Rocky or Stony Mountains," a convention was concluded and signed on the 15th instant by the Secretary of State, on the part of the United States, and the envoy extraordinary and minister plenipotentiary of Her Britannic Majesty, on the part of Great Britain.

This convention I now lay before the Senate, for their consideration with a view to its ratification.

JAMES K. POLK.

WASHINGTON, *June 17, 1846.*

To the House of Representatives of the United States:

I communicate herewith a report from the Secretary of the Navy, accompanied with the correspondence called for by the resolution of the House of Representatives of the 4th of May last, between Commander G. J. Pendergrast and the Governments on the Rio de la Plata, and the foreign naval commanders and the United States minister at Buénos

Ayres and the Navy Department, whilst or since said Pendergrast was in command of the United States ship *Boston* in the Rio de la Plata, touching said service.

JAMES K. POLK.

WASHINGTON, *June 23, 1846.*

To the Senate of the United States:

I herewith communicate to the Senate, for its consideration, a convention concluded by the minister of the United States at Berlin with the Duchy of Nassau, dated on the 27th May, 1846, for the mutual abolition of the *droit d'aubaine* and taxes on emigration between that State of the Germanic Confederation and the United States of America, and also a dispatch from the minister explanatory of the convention.

JAMES K. POLK.

WASHINGTON, *June 24, 1846.*

To the Senate:

I transmit herewith a communication from the Secretary of War, accompanied by a report from the Commissioner of Indian Affairs, in reply to the resolution of the Senate of the 9th instant, requiring information on the subject of the removal of the Chippewa Indians from the mineral lands on Lake Superior.

JAMES K. POLK.

WASHINGTON, *July 2, 1846.*

To the House of Representatives:

I transmit herewith a report from the Secretary of State, together with copies of the correspondence in the year 1841 between the President of the United States and the governor of New York relative to the appearance of Joshua A. Spencer, esq., district attorney of the United States for the western district of New York in the courts of the State of New York as counsel for Alexander McLeod, called for by the resolution of the House of Representatives of the 10th of April, 1846.

JAMES K. POLK.

WASHINGTON, *July 7, 1846.*

To the Senate of the United States:

I herewith communicate to the Senate, for its consideration, a treaty of commerce and navigation between the United States and the Kingdom of Hanover, concluded and signed at Hanover on the 10th ultimo by the respective plenipotentiaries.

And I communicate at the same time extracts of a dispatch from the agent of the United States explanatory of the treaty.

JAMES K. POLK.

WASHINGTON, *July 9, 1846.*

To the Senate of the United States:

I transmit herewith, for the consideration and advice of the Senate with regard to its ratification, a treaty concluded on the 5th and 17th days of June last by T. P. Andrews, Thomas A. Harvey, and Gideon C. Matlock, commissioners on the part of the United States, and the various bands of the Pottawatomies, Chippewa, and Ottawa Indians, together with a report of the Commissioner of Indian Affairs and other papers explanatory of the same.

JAMES K. POLK.

WASHINGTON, *July 9, 1846.*

To the Senate of the United States:

I communicate herewith a report from the Secretary of the Treasury, transmitting a report from the Commissioner of Public Lands in reply to the resolution of the Senate of the 22d of June, 1846, calling for information of the "progress which has been made in the surveys of the mineral region upon Lake Superior, and within what time such surveys may probably be prepared for the sales of the lands in that country." In answer to that portion of the resolution which calls for the "views" of the Executive "respecting the proper mode of disposing of said lands, keeping in view the interest of the United States and the equitable claims of individuals who, under the authority of the War Department, have made improvements thereon or acquired rights of possession," I recommend that these lands be brought into market and sold at such price and under such regulations as Congress may prescribe, and that the right of preemption be secured to such persons as have, under the authority of the War Department, made improvements or acquired rights of possession thereon. Should Congress deem it proper to authorize the sale of these lands, it will be necessary to attach them to suitable land districts, and that they be placed under the management and control of the General Land Office, as other public lands.

JAMES K. POLK.

WASHINGTON, *July 11, 1846.*

To the Senate of the United States.

I communicate herewith a report from the Secretary of War, together with copies of the reports of the board of engineers heretofore employed in an examination of the coast of Texas with a view to its defense and improvement, called for by the resolution of the 29th June, 1846.

JAMES K. POLK.

WASHINGTON, *July 15, 1846.*

To the Senate of the United States:

I transmit herewith, for the consideration of the Senate, a treaty concluded on the 15th day of May last with the Comanche and other tribes or bands of Indians of Texas and the Southwestern prairies. I also inclose a communication from the Secretary of War and a report from the Commissioner of Indian Affairs, with accompanying documents, which contain full explanations of the considerations which led to the negotiation of the treaty and the general objects sought to be accomplished by it.

JAMES K. POLK.

WASHINGTON, *July 21, 1846.*

To the Senate of the United States:

I herewith transmit, in compliance with the request of the Senate in their resolution of the 17th of June, 1846, a report of the Secretary of State, together with a copy of all "the dispatches and instructions" "relative to the Oregon treaty" "forwarded to our minister, Mr. McLane," "not heretofore communicated to the Senate," including a statement of the propositions for the adjustment of the Oregon question previously made and rejected by the respective Governments. This statement was furnished to Mr. McLane before his departure from the country, and is dated on the 12th July, 1845, the day on which the note was addressed by the Secretary of State to Mr. Pakenham offering to settle the controversy by the forty-ninth parallel of latitude, which was rejected by that minister on the 29th July following.

The Senate will perceive that extracts from but two of Mr. McLane's "dispatches and communications to this Government" are transmitted, and these only because they were necessary to explain the answers given to them by the Secretary of State.

These dispatches are both numerous and voluminous, and, from their confidential character, their publication, it is believed, would be highly prejudicial to the public interests.

Public considerations alone have induced me to withhold the dispatches of Mr. McLane addressed to the Secretary of State. I concur with the Secretary of State in the views presented in his report herewith transmitted, against the publication of these dispatches.

Mr. McLane has performed his whole duty to his country, and I am not only willing, but anxious, that every Senator who may desire it shall have an opportunity of perusing these dispatches at the Department of State. The Secretary of State has been instructed to afford every facility for this purpose.

JAMES K. POLK.

WASHINGTON, *July 21, 1846.*

To the Senate of the United States:

I communicate herewith a report from the Secretary of State, in answer to the resolution of the Senate of the 18th of June, 1846, calling for certain information in relation to the Oregon Territory.

JAMES K. POLK.

WASHINGTON, *August 4, 1846.*

To the Senate of the United States:

I herewith communicate to the Senate the copy of a letter, under date of the 27th ultimo, from the Secretary of State of the United States to the minister of foreign relations of the Mexican Republic, again proposing to open negotiations and conclude a treaty of peace which shall adjust all the questions in dispute between the two Republics. Considering the relative power of the two countries, the glorious events which have already signalized our arms, and the distracted condition of Mexico, I did not conceive that any point of national honor could exist which ought to prevent me from making this overture. Equally anxious to terminate by a peace honorable for both parties as I was originally to avoid the existing war, I have deemed it my duty again to extend the olive branch to Mexico. Should the Government of that Republic accept the offer in the same friendly spirit by which it was dictated, negotiations will speedily commence for the conclusion of a treaty.

The chief difficulty to be anticipated in the negotiation is the adjustment of the boundary between the parties by a line which shall at once be satisfactory to both, and such as neither will hereafter be inclined to disturb. This is the best mode of securing perpetual peace and good neighborhood between the two Republics. Should the Mexican Government, in order to accomplish these objects, be willing to cede any portion of their territory to the United States, we ought to pay them a fair equivalent—a just and honorable peace, and not conquest, being our purpose in the prosecution of the war.

Under these circumstances, and considering the exhausted and distracted condition of the Mexican Republic, it might become necessary in order to restore peace that I should have it in my power to advance a portion of the consideration money for any cession of territory which may be made. The Mexican Government might not be willing to wait for the payment of the whole until the treaty could be ratified by the Senate and an appropriation to carry it into effect be made by Congress, and the necessity for such a delay might defeat the object altogether. I would therefore suggest whether it might not be wise for Congress to appropriate a sum such as they might consider adequate for this purpose, to be paid, if necessary, immediately upon the ratification of the treaty by Mexico. This disbursement would of course be accounted for at the Treasury, not as secret-service money, but like other expenditures.

Two precedents for such a proceeding exist in our past history, during the Administration of Mr. Jefferson, to which I would call your attention. On the 26th February, 1803, Congress passed an act appropriating $2,000,000 "for the purpose of defraying any extraordinary expenses which may be incurred in the intercourse between the United States and foreign nations," "to be applied under the direction of the President of the United States, who shall cause an account of the expenditure thereof to be laid before Congress as soon as may be;'' and on the 13th February, 1806, an appropriation was made of the same amount and in the same terms. The object in the first case was to enable the President to obtain the cession of Louisiana, and in the second that of the Florida. In neither case was the money actually drawn from the Treasury, and I should hope that the result might be similar in this respect on the present occasion, though the appropriation is deemed expedient as a precautionary measure.

I refer the whole subject to the Senate in executive session. If they should concur in opinion with me, then I recommend the passage of a law appropriating such a sum as Congress may deem adequate, to be used by the Executive, if necessary, for the purpose which I have indicated.

In the two cases to which I have referred the special purpose of the appropriation did not appear on the face of the law, as this might have defeated the object; neither, for the same reason, in my opinion, ought it now to be stated.

I also communicate to the Senate the copy of a letter from the Secretary of State to Commodore Conner of the 29th ultimo, which was transmitted to him on the day it bears date.

JAMES K. POLK.

WASHINGTON, *August 5, 1846.*
To the Senate and House of Representatives of the United States:

I communicate herewith a copy of a convention for the settlement and adjustment of the Oregon question, which was concluded in this city on the 15th day of June last between the United States and Her Britannic Majesty. This convention has since been duly ratified by the respective parties, and the ratifications were exchanged at London on the 17th day of July, 1846.

It now becomes important that provision should be made by law at the earliest practicable period for the organization of a Territorial government in Oregon.

It is also deemed proper that our laws regulating trade and intercourse with the Indian tribes east of the Rocky Mountains should be extended to such tribes within our territory as dwell beyond them, and that a suitable number of Indian agents should be appointed for the purpose of carrying these laws into execution.

It is likewise important that mail facilities, so indispensable for the diffusion of information and for binding together the different portions of our extended Confederacy, should be afforded to our citizens west of the Rocky Mountains.

There is another subject to which I desire to call your special attention. It is of great importance to our country generally, and especially to our navigating and whaling interests, that the Pacific Coast, and, indeed, the whole of our territory west of the Rocky Mountains, should speedily be filled up by a hardy and patriotic population.   Emigrants to that territory have many difficulties to encounter and privations to endure in their long and perilous journey, and by the time they reach their place of destination their pecuniary means are generally much reduced, if not altogether exhausted.   Under these circumstances it is deemed but an act of justice that these emigrants, whilst most effectually advancing the interests and policy of the Government, should be aided by liberal grants of land.   I would therefore recommend that such grants be made to actual settlers upon the terms and under the restrictions and limitations which Congress may think advisable.

JAMES K. POLK.

WASHINGTON, *August 7, 1846.*

To the Senate of the United States:

I communicate herewith a report from the Secretary of the Navy, with the accompanying documents, in answer to the resolution of the Senate of August 6, 1846, calling for the report of the board of naval officers, recently in session in this city, including the orders under which it was convened and the evidence which may have been laid before it.

JAMES K. POLK.

WASHINGTON, *August 7, 1846.*

To the Senate of the United States:

I transmit herewith, for the consideration and constitutional action of the Senate, articles of a treaty which has been concluded by the commissioners appointed for the purpose with the different parties into which the Cherokee tribe of Indians has been divided, through their delegates now in Washington.   The same commissioners had previously been appointed to investigate the subject of the difficulties which have for years existed among the Cherokees, and which have kept them in a state of constant excitement and almost entirely interrupted all progress on their part in civilization and improvement in agriculture and the mechanic arts, and have led to many unfortunate acts of domestic strife, against which the Government is bound by the treaty of 1835 to protect them.   Their unfortunate internal dissensions had attracted the notice and excited the sympathies of the whole country, and it became evident that if something was not done to heal them they would terminate in a sanguinary war, in which other tribes of Indians might become involved and the lives and property of our own citizens on the frontier endangered. I recommended in my message to Congress on the 13th of April last such measures as I then thought it expedient should be adopted to restore peace and good order among the Cherokees, one of which was a division of the country which they occupy and separation of the tribe.   This recommendation was made under the belief that the different factions could not be reconciled and live together in harmony—a belief based in a great degree upon the representations of the delegates of the two divisions of the tribe. Since then, however, there appears to have been a change of opinion on this subject on the part of these divisions of the tribe, and on representations being made to me that by the appointment of commissioners to hear and investigate the causes of grievance of the parties against each other and to examine into their claims against the Government it would probably be found that an arrangement could be made which would once more harmonize the tribe and adjust in a satisfactory manner their claims upon and relations with the United States, I did not hesitate to appoint three persons for the purpose. The commissioners entered into an able and laborious investigation, and on their making known to me the probability of their being able to conclude a new treaty with the delegates of all the divisions of the tribe, who were fully empowered to make any new arrangement which would heal all dissensions among the Cherokees and restore them to their ancient condition of peace and good brotherhood, I authorized and appointed them to enter into negotiations with these delegates for the accomplishment of that object. The treaty now transmitted is the result of their labors, and it is hoped that it will meet the approbation of Congress, and, if carried out in good faith by all parties to it, it is believed it will effect the great and desirable ends had in view.

Accompanying the treaty is the report of the commissioners, and also a communication to them from John Ross and others, who represent what is termed the government party of the Cherokees, and which is transmitted at their request for the consideration of the Senate.

JAMES K. POLK.

WASHINGTON, *August 8, 1846.*
To the Senate and House of Representatives of the United States:

I invite your attention to the propriety of making an appropriation to provide for any expenditure which it may be necessary to make in advance for the purpose of settling all our difficulties with the Mexican Republic. It is my sincere desire to terminate, as it was originally to avoid, the existing war with Mexico by a peace just and honorable to both parties. It is probable that the chief obstacle to be surmounted in accomplishing this desirable object will be the adjustment of a boundary between the two Republics which shall prove satisfactory and convenient to both, and such as neither will hereafter be inclined to disturb. In the adjustment of this boundary we ought to pay a fair equivalent for any concessions which may be made by Mexico.

Under these circumstances, and considering the other complicated questions to be settled by negotiation with the Mexican Republic, I deem it important that a sum of money should be placed under the control of the Executive to be advanced, if need be, to the Government of that Republic immediately after their ratification of a treaty. It might be inconvenient for the Mexican Government to wait for the whole sum the payment of which may be stipulated by this treaty until it could be ratified by our Senate and an appropriation to carry it into effect made by Congress. Indeed, the necessity for this delay might defeat the object altogether. The disbursement of this money would of course be accounted for, not as secret-service money, but like other expenditures.

Two precedents for such a proceeding exist in our past history, during the Administration of Mr. Jefferson, to which I would call your attention: On the 26th February, 1803, an act was passed appropriating $2,000,000 "for the purpose of defraying any extraordinary expenses which may be incurred in the intercourse between the United States and foreign nations," "to be applied under the direction of the President of the United States, who shall cause an account of the expenditure thereof to be laid before Congress as soon as may be;" and on the 13th of February, 1806, an appropriation was made of the same amount and in the same terms. In neither case was the money actually drawn from the Treasury, and I should hope that the result in this respect might be similar on the present occasion, although the appropriation may prove to be indispensable in accomplishing the object. I would therefore recommend the passage of a law appropriating $2,000,000 to be placed at the disposal of the Executive for the purpose which I have indicated.

In order to prevent all misapprehension, it is my duty to state that, anxious as I am to terminate the existing war with the least possible delay, it will continue to be prosecuted with the utmost vigor until a treaty of peace shall be signed by the parties and ratified by the Mexican Republic.

JAMES K. POLK.

VETO MESSAGES.

WASHINGTON, *August 3, 1846.*

To the House of Representatives:

I have considered the bill entitled "An act making appropriations for the improvement of certain harbors and rivers" with the care which its importance demands, and now return the same to the House of Representatives, in which it originated, with my objections to its becoming a law. The bill proposes to appropriate $1,378,450 to be applied to more than forty distinct and separate objects of improvement. On examining its provisions and the variety of objects of improvement which it embraces, many of them of a local character, it is difficult to conceive, if it shall be sanctioned and become a law, what practical constitutional restraint can hereafter be imposed upon the most extended system of internal improvements by the Federal Government in all parts of the Union. The Constitution has not, in my judgment, conferred upon the Federal Government the power to construct works of internal improvement within the States, or to appropriate money from the Treasury for that purpose. That this bill assumes for the Federal Government the right to exercise this power can not, I think, be doubted. The approved course of the Government and the deliberately expressed judgment of the people have denied the existence of such a power under the Constitution. Several of my predecessors have denied its existence in the most solemn forms.

The general proposition that the Federal Government does not possess this power is so well settled and has for a considerable period been so generally acquiesced in that it is not deemed necessary to reiterate the arguments by which it is sustained. Nor do I deem it necessary, after the full and elaborate discussions which have taken place before the country on this subject, to do more than to state the general considerations which have satisfied me of the unconstitutionality and inexpediency of the exercise of such a power.

It is not questioned that the Federal Government is one of limited powers. Its powers are such, and such only, as are expressly granted in the Constitution or are properly incident to the expressly granted powers and necessary to their execution. In determining whether a given power has been granted a sound rule of construction has been laid down by Mr. Madison. That rule is that—

Whenever a question arises concerning a particular power, the first question is whether the power be expressed in the Constitution. If it be, the question is decided. If it be not expressed, the next inquiry must be whether it is properly an incident to an expressed power and necessary to its execution. If it be, it may be exercised by Congress. If it be not, Congress can not exercise it.

It is not pretended that there is any express grant in the Constitution conferring on Congress the power in question. Is it, then, an incidental power necessary and proper for the execution of any of the granted powers? All the granted powers, it is confidently affirmed, may be effectually executed without the aid of such an incident. "A power, to be incidental, must not be exercised for ends which make it a principal or substantive power, independent of the principal power to which it is an incident." It is not enough that it may be regarded by Congress as *convenient* or that its exercise would advance the public weal. It must be *necessary and proper* to the execution of the principal expressed power to which it is an incident, and without which such principal power can not be carried into effect. The whole frame of the Federal Constitution proves that the Government which it creates was intended to be one of limited and specified powers. A construction of the Constitution so broad as that by which the power in question is defended tends imperceptibly to a consolidation of power in a Government intended by its framers to be thus limited in its authority. ''The obvious tendency and inevitable result of a consolidation of the States into one sovereignty would be to transform the republican system of the United States into a monarchy.'' To guard against the assumption of all powers which encroach upon the reserved sovereignty of the States, and which consequently tend to consolidation, is the duty of all the true friends of our political system. That the power in question is not properly an incident to any of the granted powers I am fully satisfied; but if there were doubts on this subject, experience has demonstrated the wisdom of the rule that all the functionaries of the Federal Government should abstain from the exercise of all questionable or doubtful powers. If an enlargement of the powers of the Federal Government should be deemed proper, it is safer and wiser to appeal to the States and the people in the mode prescribed by the Constitution for the grant desired than to assume its exercise without an amendment of the Constitution. If Congress does not possess the general power to construct works of internal improvement within the States, or to appropriate money from the Treasury for that purpose, what is there to exempt some, at least, of the objects of appropriation included in this bill from the operation of the general rule? This bill assumes the existence of the power, and in some of its provisions asserts the principle that Congress may exercise it as fully as though the appropriations which it proposes were applicable to the construction of roads and canals. If there be a distinction in principle, it is not perceived, and should be clearly defined. Some of the objects of appropriation contained in this bill are local in their character, and lie within the limits of a single State; and though in the language of the bill they are called *harbors*, they are not connected with foreign commerce, nor are they places of refuge or shelter for our Navy or commercial marine on the ocean or lake shores. To call the mouth of a creek or a shallow inlet on our coast a harbor can not confer the authority to expend the public money in its improvement. Congress have exercised the power coeval with the Constitution of establishing light-houses, beacons, buoys, and piers on our ocean and lake shores for the purpose of rendering navigation safe and easy and of affording protection and shelter for our Navy and other shipping. These are safeguards placed in existing channels of navigation. After the long acquiescence of the Government through all preceding Administrations, I am not disposed to question or disturb the authority to make appropriations for such purposes.

When we advance a step beyond this point, and, in addition to the establishment and support, by appropriations from the Treasury, of light-houses, beacons, buoys, piers, and other improvements within the bays, inlets, and harbors on our ocean and lake coasts immediately connected with our foreign commerce, attempt to make improvements in the interior at points unconnected with foreign commerce, and where they are not needed for the protection and security of our Navy and commercial marine, the difficulty arises in drawing a line beyond which appropriations may not be made by the Federal Government.

One of my predecessors, who saw the evil consequences of the system proposed to be revived by this bill, attempted to define this line by declaring that "expenditures of this character" should be "confined *below* the ports of entry or delivery established by law." Acting on this restriction, he withheld his sanction from a bill which had passed Congress "to improve the navigation of the Wabash River." He was at the same time "sensible that this restriction was not as satisfactory as could be desired, and that much embarrassment may be caused to the executive department in its execution, by appropriations for remote and not well-understood objects." This restriction, it was soon found, was subject to be evaded and rendered comparatively useless in checking the system of improvements which it was designed to arrest, in consequence of the facility with which ports of entry and delivery may be established by law upon the upper waters, and in some instances almost at the head springs of some of the most unimportant of our rivers, and at points on our coast possessing no commercial importance and not used as places of refuge and safety by our Navy and other shipping. Many of the ports of entry and delivery now authorized by law, so far as foreign commerce is concerned, exist only in the statute books. No entry of foreign goods is ever made and no duties are ever collected at them. No exports of American products bound for foreign countries ever clear from them. To assume that their existence in the statute book as ports of entry or delivery warrants expenditures on the waters leading to them, which would be otherwise unauthorized, would be to assert the proposition that the lawmaking power may ingraft new provisions on the Constitution. If the restriction is a sound one, it can only apply to the bays, inlets, and rivers connected with or leading to such ports as actually have foreign commerce—ports at which foreign importations arrive in bulk, paying the duties charged by law, and from which exports are made to foreign countries. It will be found by applying the restriction thus understood to the bill under consideration that it contains appropriations for more than twenty objects of internal improvement, called in the bill *harbors*, at places which have never been declared by law either ports of entry or delivery, and at which, as appears from the records of the Treasury, there has never been an arrival of foreign merchandise, and from which there has never been a vessel cleared for a foreign country. It will be found that many of these works are new, and at places for the improvement of which appropriations are now for the first time proposed. It will be found also that the bill contains appropriations for rivers upon which there not only exists no foreign commerce, but upon which there has not been established even a paper port of entry, and for the mouths of creeks, denominated harbors, which if improved can benefit only the particular neighborhood in which they are situated. It will be found, too, to contain appropriations the expenditure of which will only have the effect of improving one place at the expense of the local natural advantages of another in its vicinity.   Should this bill become a law, the same *principle* which authorizes the appropriations which it proposes to make would also authorize similar appropriations for the improvement of all the other bays, inlets, and creeks, which may with equal propriety be called harbors, and of all the rivers, important or unimportant, in every part of the Union.   To sanction the bill with such provisions would be to concede the *principle* that the Federal Government possesses the power to expend the public money in a general system of internal improvements, limited in its extent only by the ever-varying discretion of successive Congresses and successive Executives.   It would be to efface and remove the limitations and restrictions of power which the Constitution has wisely provided to limit the authority and action of the Federal Government to a few well-defined and specified objects. Besides these objections, the practical evils which must flow from the exercise on the part of the Federal Government of the powers asserted in this bill impress my mind with a grave sense of my duty to avert them from the country as far as my constitutional action may enable me to do so.

It not only leads to a consolidation of power in the Federal Government at the expense of the rightful authority of the States, but its inevitable tendency is to embrace objects for the expenditure of the public money which are local in their character, benefiting but few at the expense of the common Treasury of the whole.   It will engender sectional feelings and prejudices calculated to disturb the harmony of the Union.   It will destroy the harmony which should prevail in our legislative councils.

It will produce combinations of local and sectional interests, strong enough when united to carry propositions for appropriations of public money which could not of themselves, and standing alone, succeed, and can not fail to lead to wasteful and extravagant expenditures.

It must produce a disreputable scramble for the public money, by the conflict which is inseparable from such a system between local and individual interests and the general interest of the whole.   It is unjust to those States which have with their own means constructed their own internal improvements to make from the common Treasury appropriations for similar improvements in other States.

In its operation it will be oppressive and unjust toward those States whose representatives and people either deny or doubt the existence of the power or think its exercise inexpedient, and who, while they equally contribute to the Treasury, can not consistently with their opinions engage in a general competition for a share of the public money.   Thus a large portion of the Union, in numbers and in geographical extent, contributing its equal proportion of taxes to the support of the Government, would under the operation of such a system be compelled to see the national treasure—the common stock of all—unequally disbursed, and often improvidently wasted for the advantage of small sections, instead of being applied to the great national purposes in which all have a common interest, and for which alone the power to collect the revenue was given. Should the system of internal improvements proposed prevail, all these evils will multiply and increase with the increase of the number of the States and the extension of the geographical limits of the settled portions of our country. With the increase of our numbers and the extension of our settlements the local objects demanding appropriations of the public money for their improvement will be proportionately increased. In each case the expenditure of the public money would confer benefits, direct or indirect, only on a section, while these sections would become daily less in comparison with the whole.

The wisdom of the framers of the Constitution in withholding power over such objects from the Federal Government and leaving them to the local governments of the States becomes more and more manifest with every year's experience of the operations of our system.

In a country of limited extent, with but few such objects of expenditure (if the form of government permitted it), a common treasury might be used for their improvement with much less inequality and injustice than in one of the vast extent which ours now presents in population and territory. The treasure of the world would hardly be equal to the improvement of every bay, inlet, creek, and river in our country which might be supposed to promote the agricultural, manufacturing, or commercial interests of a neighborhood.

The Federal Constitution was wisely adapted in its provisions to any expansion of our limits and population, and with the advance of the confederacy of the States in the career of national greatness it becomes the more apparent that the harmony of the Union and the equal justice to which all its parts are entitled require that the Federal Government should confine its action within the limits prescribed by the Constitution to its power and authority. Some of the provisions of this bill are not subject to the objections stated, and did they stand alone I should not feel it to be my duty to withhold my approval.

If no constitutional objections existed to the bill, there are others of a serious nature which deserve some consideration. It appropriates between $1,000,000 and $2,000,000 for objects which are of no pressing necessity, and this is proposed at a time when the country is engaged in a foreign war, and when Congress at its present session has authorized a loan or the issue of Treasury notes to defray the expenses of the war, to be resorted to if the "exigencies of the Government shall require it." It would seem to be the dictate of wisdom under such circumstances to husband our means, and not to waste them on comparatively unimportant objects, so that we may reduce the loan or issue of Treasury notes which may become necessary to the smallest practicable sum. It would seem to be wise, too, to abstain from such expenditures with a view to avoid the accumulation of a large public debt, the existence of which would be opposed to the interests of our people as well as to the genius of our free institutions.

Should this bill become a law, the principle which it establishes will inevitably lead to large and annually increasing appropriations and drains upon the Treasury, for it is not to be doubted that numerous other localities not embraced in its provisions, but quite as much entitled to the favor of the Government as those which are embraced, will demand, through their representatives in Congress, to be placed on an equal footing with them. With such an increase of expenditure must necessarily follow either an increased public debt or increased burdens upon the people by taxation to supply the Treasury with the means of meeting the accumulated demands upon it.

With profound respect for the opinions of Congress, and ever anxious, as far as I can consistently with my responsibility to our common constituents, to cooperate with them in the discharge of our respective duties, it is with unfeigned regret that I find myself constrained, for the reasons which I have assigned, to withhold my approval from this bill.

JAMES K. POLK.

WASHINGTON, *August 8, 1846.*

To the Senate of the United States:

I return to the Senate, in which it originated, the bill entitled "An act to provide for the ascertainment and satisfaction of claims of American citizens for spoliations committed by the French prior to the 31st day of July, 1801," which was presented to me on the 6th instant, with my objections to its becoming a law.

In attempting to give to the bill the careful examination it requires, difficulties presented themselves in the outset from the remoteness of the period to which the claims belong, the complicated nature of the transactions in which they originated, and the protracted negotiations to which they led between France and the United States.

The short time intervening between the passage of the bill by Congress and the approaching close of their session, as well as the pressure of other official duties, have not permitted me to extend my examination of the subject into its minute details; but in the consideration which I have been able to give to it I find objections of a grave character to its provisions.

For the satisfaction of the claims provided for by the bill it is proposed to appropriate $5,000,000. I can perceive no legal or equitable ground upon which this large appropriation can rest. A portion of the claims have been more than half a century before the Government in its executive or legislative departments, and all of them had their origin in events which occurred prior to the year 1800. Since 1802 they have been from time to time before Congress. No greater necessity or propriety exists for providing for these claims at this time than has existed for near half a century, during all which period this questionable measure has never until now received the favorable consideration of Congress. It is scarcely probable, if the claim had been regarded as obligatory upon the Government or constituting an equitable demand upon the Treasury, that those who were contemporaneous with the events which gave rise to it should not long since have done justice to the claimants. The Treasury has often been in a condition to enable the Government to do so without inconvenience if these claims had been considered just. Mr. Jefferson, who was fully cognizant of the early dissensions between the Governments of the United States and France, out of which the claims arose, in his annual message in 1808 adverted to the large surplus then in the Treasury and its "probable accumulation," and inquired whether it should "lie unproductive in the public vaults;" and yet these claims, though then before Congress, were not recognized or paid. Since that time the public debt of the Revolution and of the War of 1812 has been extinguished, and at several periods since the Treasury has been in possession of large surpluses over the demands upon it. In 1836 the surplus amounted to many millions of dollars, and, for want of proper objects to which to apply it, it was directed by Congress to be deposited with the States.

During this extended course of time, embracing periods eminently favorable for satisfying all just demands upon the Government, the claims embraced in this bill met with no favor in Congress beyond reports of committees in one or the other branch. These circumstances alone are calculated to raise strong doubts in respect to these claims, more especially as all the information necessary to a correct judgment concerning them has been long before the public. These doubts are strengthened in my mind by the examination I have been enabled to give to the transactions in which they originated.

The bill assumes that the United States have become liable in these ancient transactions to make reparation to the claimants for injuries committed by France. Nothing was obtained for the claimants by negotiation; and the bill assumes that the Government has become responsible to them for the aggressions of France. I have not been able to satisfy myself of the correctness of this assumption, or that the Government has become in any way responsible for these claims. The limited time allotted me before your adjournment precludes the possibility of reiterating the facts and arguments by which in preceding Congresses these claims have been successfully resisted.

The present is a period peculiarly unfavorable for the satisfaction of claims of so large an amount and, to say the least of them, of so doubtful a character. There is no surplus in the Treasury. A public debt of several millions of dollars has been created within the last few years.

We are engaged in a foreign war, uncertain in its duration and involving heavy expenditures, to prosecute which Congress has at its present session authorized a further loan; so that in effect the Government, should this bill become a law, borrows money and increases the public debt to pay these claims.

It is true that by the provisions of the bill payment is directed to be made in land scrip instead of money, but the effect upon the Treasury will be the same. The public lands constitute one of the sources of public revenue, and if these claims be paid in land scrip it will from the date of its issue to a great extent cut off from the Treasury the annual income from the sales of the public lands, because payments for lands sold by the Government may be expected to be made in scrip until it is all redeemed. If these claims be just, they ought to be paid in money, and not in anything less valuable. The bill provides that they shall be paid in land scrip, whereby they are made in effect to be a mortgage upon the public lands in the new States; a mortgage, too, held in great part, if not wholly, by nonresidents of the States in which the lands lie, who may secure these lands to the amount of several millions of acres, and then demand for them exorbitant prices from the citizens of the States who may desire to purchase them for settlement, or they may keep them out of the market, and thus retard the prosperity and growth of the States in which they are situated. Why this unusual mode of satisfying demands on the Treasury has been resorted to does not appear. It is not consistent with a sound public policy. If it be done in this case, it may be done in all others. It would form a precedent for the satisfaction of all other stale and questionable claims in the same manner, and would undoubtedly be resorted to by all claimants who after successive trials shall fail to have their claims recognized and paid in money by Congress.

This bill proposes to appropriate $5,000,000, to be paid in land scrip, and provides that "no claim or memorial shall be received by the commissioners" authorized by the act "unless accompanied by a release or discharge of the United States from all other and further compensation" than the claimant "may be entitled to receive under the provisions of this act." These claims are estimated to amount to a much larger sum than $5,000,000, and yet the claimant is required to release to the Government all other compensation, and to accept his share of a fund which is known to be inadequate. If the claims be well founded, it would be unjust to the claimants to repudiate any portion of them, and the payment of the remaining sum could not be hereafter resisted. This bill proposes to pay these claims not in the currency known to the Constitution, and not to their full amount.

Passed, as this bill has been, near the close of the session, and when many measures of importance necessarily claim the attention of Congress, and possibly without that full and deliberate consideration which the large sum it appropriates and the existing condition of the Treasury and of the country demand, I deem it to be my duty to withhold my approval, that it may hereafter undergo the revision of Congress. I have come to this conclusion with regret. In interposing my objections to its becoming a law I am fully sensible that it should be an extreme case which would make it the duty of the Executive to withhold his approval of any bill passed by Congress upon the ground of its inexpediency alone. Such a case I consider this to be.

JAMES K. POLK.

PROCLAMATIONS.

[From Statutes at Large (Little & Brown), Vol. IX, p. 999.]

By the President of the United States of America.

A PROCLAMATION.

Whereas by an act of the Congress of the United States of the 3d of March, 1845, entitled "An act allowing drawback upon foreign merchandise exported in the original packages to Chihuahua and Santa Fe, in Mexico, and to the British North American Provinces adjoining the United States," certain privileges are extended in reference to drawback to ports therein specially enumerated in the seventh section of said act, which also provides "that such other ports situated on the frontiers of the United States adjoining the British North American Provinces as may hereafter be found expedient may have extended to them the like privileges on the recommendation of the Secretary of the Treasury and proclamation duly made by the President of the United States specially designating the ports to which the aforesaid privileges are to be extended;" and

Whereas the Secretary of the Treasury has duly recommended to me the extension of the privileges of the law aforesaid to the port of Lewiston, in the collection district of Niagara, in the State of New York:

Now, therefore, I, James K. Polk, President of the United States of America, do hereby declare and proclaim that the port of Lewiston, in the collection district of Niagara, in the State of New York, is and shall be entitled to all the privileges extended to the other ports enumerated in the seventh section of the act aforesaid from and after the date of this proclamation.

In witness whereof I have hereunto set my hand and caused the seal of the United States to be affixed.

[SEAL.] Done at the city of Washington, this 17th day of January, A. D. 1846, and of the Independence of the United States of America the seventieth.

JAMES K. POLK.

By the President:

JAMES BUCHANAN,
Secretary of State.

By the President of the United States of America.

A PROCLAMATION.

Whereas the Congress of the United States, by virtue of the constitutional authority vested in them, have declared by their act bearing date this day that "by the act of the Republic of Mexico a state of war exists between that Government and the United States:"

Now, therefore, I, James K. Polk, President of the United States of America, do hereby proclaim the same to all whom it may concern; and I do specially enjoin on all persons holding offices, civil or military, under the authority of the United States that they be vigilant and zealous in discharging the duties respectively incident thereto; and I do, moreover, exhort all the good people of the United States, as they love their country, as they feel the wrongs which have forced on them the last resort of injured nations, and as they consult the best means, under the blessing of Divine Providence, of abridging its calamities, that they exert themselves in preserving order, in promoting concord, in maintaining the authority and the efficacy of the laws, and in supporting and invigorating all the measures which may be adopted by the constituted authorities for obtaining a speedy, a just, and an honorable peace.

In testimony whereof I have hereunto set my hand and caused the seal of the United States to be affixed to these presents.

[SEAL.]   Done at the city of Washington, the 13th day of May, A. D. 1846, and of the Independence of the United States the seventieth.

JAMES K. POLK.

By the President:
    JAMES BUCHANAN,
       Secretary of State.

By the President of the United States of America.

A PROCLAMATION.

Whereas by the act of Congress approved July 9, 1846, entitled "An act to retrocede the county of Alexandria, in the District of Columbia, to the State of Virginia," it is enacted that, with the assent of the people of the county and town of Alexandria, to be ascertained in the manner therein prescribed, all that portion of the District of Columbia ceded to the United States by the State of Virginia and all the rights and jurisdiction therewith ceded over the same shall be ceded and forever relinquished to the State of Virginia in full and absolute right and jurisdiction, as well of soil as of persons residing or to reside thereon; and

Whereas it is further provided that the said act "shall not be in force until after the assent of the people of the county and town of Alexandria shall be given to it in the mode therein provided," and, if a majority of the votes should be in favor of accepting the provisions of the said act, it shall be the duty of the President to make proclamation of the fact; and

Whereas on the 17th day of August, 1846, after the close of the late session of the Congress of the United States, I duly appointed five citizens of the county or town of Alexandria, being freeholders within the same, as commissioners, who, being duly sworn to perform the duties imposed on them as prescribed in the said act, did proceed within ten days after they were notified to fix upon the 1st and 2d days of September, 1846, as the time, the court-house of the county of Alexandria as the place, and *viva voce* as the manner of voting, and gave due notice of the same; and at the time and at the place, in conformity with the said notice, the said commissioners presiding and deciding all questions arising in relation to the right of voting under the said act, the votes of the citizens qualified to vote were taken *viva voce* and recorded in poll books duly kept, and on the 3d day of September instant, after the said polls were closed, the said commissioners did make out and on the next day did transmit to me a statement of the polls so held, upon oath and under their seals; and of the votes so cast and polled there were in favor of accepting the provisions of the said act 763 votes, and against accepting the same 222, showing a majority of 541 votes for the acceptance of the same:

Now, therefore, be it known that I, James K. Polk, President of the United States of America, in fulfillment of the duty imposed upon me by the said act of Congress, do hereby make proclamation of the "result" of said "poll" as above stated, and do call upon all and singular the persons whom it doth or may concern to take notice that the act aforesaid "is in full force and effect."

In witness whereof I have hereunto set my hand and caused the seal of the United States to be affixed.

[SEAL.]   Done at the city of Washington, this 7th day of September, A. D. 1846, and of the Independence of the United States the seventy-first.

JAMES K. POLK.

By the President:

N. P. TRIST,
Acting Secretary of State.

SECOND ANNUAL MESSAGE.

WASHINGTON, *December 8, 1846.*

Fellow-Citizens of the Senate and of the House of Representatives:

In resuming your labors in the service of the people it is a subject of congratulation that there has been no period in our past history when all the elements of national prosperity have been so fully developed. Since your last session no afflicting dispensation has visited our country. General good health has prevailed, abundance has crowned the toil of the husbandman, and labor in all its branches is receiving an ample reward, while education, science, and the arts are rapidly enlarging the means of social happiness. The progress of our country in her career of greatness, not only in the vast extension of our territorial limits and the rapid increase of our population, but in resources and wealth and in the happy condition of our people, is without an example in the history of nations.

As the wisdom, strength, and beneficence of our free institutions are unfolded, every day adds fresh motives to contentment and fresh incentives to patriotism.

Our devout and sincere acknowledgments are due to the gracious Giver of All Good for the numberless blessings which our beloved country enjoys.

It is a source of high satisfaction to know that the relations of the United States with all other nations, with a single exception, are of the most amicable character. Sincerely attached to the policy of peace early adopted and steadily pursued by this Government, I have anxiously desired to cultivate and cherish friendship and commerce with every foreign power. The spirit and habits of the American people are favorable to the maintenance of such international harmony. In adhering to this wise policy, a preliminary and paramount duty obviously consists in the protection of our national interests from encroachment or sacrifice and our national honor from reproach. These must be maintained at any hazard. They admit of no compromise or neglect, and must be scrupulously and constantly guarded. In their vigilant vindication collision and conflict with foreign powers may sometimes become unavoidable. Such has been our scrupulous adherence to the dictates of justice in all our foreign intercourse that, though steadily and rapidly advancing in prosperity and power, we have given no just cause of complaint to any nation and have enjoyed the blessings of peace for more than thirty years. From a policy so sacred to humanity and so salutary in its effects upon our political system we should never be induced voluntarily to depart.

The existing war with Mexico was neither desired nor provoked by the United States. On the contrary, all honorable means were resorted to to avert it. After years of endurance of aggravated and unredressed wrongs on our part, Mexico, in violation of solemn treaty stipulations and of every principle of justice recognized by civilized nations, commenced hostilities, and thus by her own act forced the war upon us. Long before the advance of our Army to the left bank of the Rio Grande we had ample cause of war against Mexico, and had the United States resorted to this extremity we might have appealed to the whole civilized world for the justice of our cause. I deem it to be my duty to present to you on the present occasion a condensed review of the injuries we had sustained, of the causes which led to the war, and of its progress since its commencement. This is rendered the more necessary because of the misapprehensions which have to some extent prevailed as to its origin and true character. The war has been represented as unjust and unnecessary and as one of aggression on our part upon a weak and injured enemy. Such erroneous views, though entertained by but few, have been widely and extensively circulated, not only at home, but have been spread throughout Mexico and the whole world. A more effectual means could not have been devised to encourage the enemy and protract the war than to advocate and adhere to their cause, and thus give them "aid and comfort." It is a source of national pride and exultation that the great body of our people have thrown no such obstacles in the way of the Government in prosecuting the war successfully, but have shown themselves to be eminently patriotic and ready to vindicate their country's honor and interests at any sacrifice. The alacrity and promptness with which our volunteer forces rushed to the field on their country's call prove not only their patriotism, but their deep conviction that our cause is just.

The wrongs which we have suffered from Mexico almost ever since she became an independent power and the patient endurance with which we have borne them are without a parallel in the history of modern civilized nations. There is reason to believe that if these wrongs had been resented and resisted in the first instance the present war might have been avoided. One outrage, however, permitted to pass with impunity almost necessarily encouraged the perpetration of another, until at last Mexico seemed to attribute to weakness and indecision on our part a forbearance which was the offspring of magnanimity and of a sincere desire to preserve friendly relations with a sister republic.

Scarcely had Mexico achieved her independence, which the United States were the first among the nations to acknowledge, when she commenced the system of insult and spoliation which she has ever since pursued. Our citizens engaged in lawful commerce were imprisoned, their vessels seized, and our flag insulted in her ports. If money was wanted, the lawless seizure and confiscation of our merchant vessels and their cargoes was a ready resource, and if to accomplish their purposes it became necessary to imprison the owners, captains, and crews, it was done. Rulers superseded rulers in Mexico in rapid succession, but still there was no change in this system of depredation. The Government of the United States made repeated reclamations on behalf of its citizens, but these were answered by the perpetration of new outrages. Promises of redress made by Mexico in the most solemn forms were postponed or evaded. The files and records of the Department of State contain conclusive proofs of numerous lawless acts perpetrated upon the property and persons of our citizens by Mexico, and of wanton insults to our national flag. The interposition of our Government to obtain redress was again and again invoked under circumstances which no nation ought to disregard. It was hoped that these outrages would cease and that

Mexico would be restrained by the laws which regulate the conduct of civilized nations in their intercourse with each other after the treaty of amity, commerce, and navigation of the 5th of April, 1831, was concluded between the two Republics; but this hope soon proved to be vain. The course of seizure and confiscation of the property of our citizens, the violation of their persons, and the insults to our flag pursued by Mexico previous to that time were scarcely suspended for even a brief period, although the treaty so clearly defines the rights and duties of the respective parties that it is impossible to misunderstand or mistake them. In less than seven years after the conclusion of that treaty our grievances had become so intolerable that in the opinion of President Jackson they should no longer be endured. In his message to Congress in February, 1837, he presented them to the consideration of that body, and declared that—

The length of time since some of the injuries have been committed, the repeated and unavailing applications for redress, the wanton character of some of the outrages upon the property and persons of our citizens, upon the officers and flag of the United States, independent of recent insults to this Government and people by the late extraordinary Mexican minister, would justify in the eyes of all nations immediate war.

In a spirit of kindness and forbearance, however, he recommended reprisals as a milder mode of redress. He declared that war should not be used as a remedy "by just and generous nations, confiding in their strength for injuries committed, if it can be honorably avoided," and added:

It has occurred to me that, considering the present embarrassed condition of that country, we should act with both wisdom and moderation by giving to Mexico one more opportunity to atone for the past before we take redress into our own hands. To avoid all misconception on the part of Mexico, as well as to protect our own national character from reproach, this opportunity should be given with the avowed design and full preparation to take immediate satisfaction if it should not be obtained on a repetition of the demand for it. To this end I recommend that an act be passed authorizing reprisals, and the use of the naval force of the United States by the Executive against Mexico to enforce them, in the event of a refusal by the Mexican Government to come to an amicable adjustment of the matters in controversy between us upon another demand thereof made from on board one of our vessels of war on the coast of Mexico.

Committees of both Houses of Congress, to which this message of the President was referred, fully sustained his views of the character of the wrongs which we had suffered from Mexico, and recommended that another demand for redress should be made before authorizing war or reprisals. The Committee on Foreign Relations of the Senate, in their report, say:

After such a demand, should prompt justice be refused by the Mexican Government, we may appeal to all nations, not only for the equity and moderation with which we shall have acted toward a sister republic, but for the necessity which will then compel us to seek redress for our wrongs, either by actual war or by reprisals. The subject will then be presented before Congress, at the commencement of the next session, in a clear and distinct form, and the committee can not doubt but that such measures will be immediately adopted as may be necessary to vindicate the honor of the country and insure ample reparation to our injured fellow-citizens.

The Committee on Foreign Affairs of the House of Representatives made a similar recommendation. In their report they say that—

They fully concur with the President that ample cause exists for taking redress into our own hands, and believe that we should be justified in the opinion of other nations for taking such a step. But they are willing to try the experiment of another demand, made in the most solemn form, upon the justice of the Mexican Government before any further proceedings are adopted.

No difference of opinion upon the subject is believed to have existed in Congress at that time; the executive and legislative departments concurred; and yet such has been our forbearance and desire to preserve peace with Mexico that the wrongs of which we then complained, and which gave rise to these solemn proceedings, not only remain unredressed to this day, but additional causes of complaint of an aggravated character have ever since been accumulating. Shortly after these proceedings a special messenger was dispatched to Mexico to make a final demand for redress, and on the 20th of July, 1837, the demand was made. The reply of the Mexican Government bears date on the 29th of the same month, and contains assurances of the "anxious wish" of the Mexican Government "not to delay the moment of that final and equitable adjustment which is to terminate the existing difficulties between the two Governments;" that "nothing should be left undone which may contribute to the most speedy and equitable determination of the subjects which have so seriously engaged the attention of the American Government;" that the "Mexican Government would adopt as the only guides for its conduct the plainest principles of public right, the sacred obligations imposed by international law, and the religious faith of treaties," and that "whatever reason and justice may dictate respecting each case will be done." The assurance was further given that the decision of the Mexican Government upon each cause of complaint for which redress had been demanded should be communicated to the Government of the United States by the Mexican minister at Washington.

These solemn assurances in answer to our demand for redress were disregarded. By making them, however, Mexico obtained further delay. President Van Buren, in his annual message to Congress of the 5th of December, 1837, states that "although the larger number" of our demands for redress, "and many of them aggravated cases of personal wrongs, have been now for years before the Mexican Government, and some of the causes of national complaint, and those of the most offensive character, admitted of immediate, simple, and satisfactory replies, it is only within a few days past that any specific communication in answer to our last demand, made five months ago, has been received from the Mexican minister;" and that "for not one of our public complaints has satisfaction been given or offered, that but one of the cases of personal wrong has been favorably considered, and that but four cases of both descriptions out of all those formally presented and earnestly pressed have as yet been decided upon by the Mexican Government.'' President Van Buren, believing that it would be vain to make any further attempt to obtain redress by the ordinary means within the power of the Executive, communicated this opinion to Congress in the message referred to, in which he said:

On a careful and deliberate examination of their contents [of the correspondence with the Mexican Government], and considering the spirit manifested by the Mexican Government, it has become my painful duty to return the subject as it now stands to Congress, to whom it belongs to decide upon the time, the mode, and the measure of redress.

Had the United States at that time adopted compulsory measures and taken redress into their own hands, all our difficulties with Mexico would probably have been long since adjusted and the existing war have been averted. Magnanimity and moderation on our part only had the effect to complicate these difficulties and render an amicable settlement of them the more embarrassing. That such measures of redress under similar provocations committed by any of the powerful nations of Europe would have been promptly resorted to by the United States can not be doubted. The national honor and the preservation of the national character throughout the world, as well as our own self-respect and the protection due to our own citizens, would have rendered such a resort indispensable. The history of no civilized nation in modern times has presented within so brief a period so many wanton attacks upon the honor of its flag and upon the property and persons of its citizens as had at that time been borne by the United States from the Mexican authorities and people. But Mexico was a sister republic on the North American continent, occupying a territory contiguous to our own, and was in a feeble and distracted condition, and these considerations, it is presumed, induced Congress to forbear still longer.

Instead of taking redress into our own hands, a new negotiation was entered upon with fair promises on the part of Mexico, but with the real purpose, as the event has proved, of indefinitely postponing the reparation which we demanded, and which was so justly due. This negotiation, after more than a year's delay, resulted in the convention of the 11th of April, 1839, ''for the adjustment of claims of citizens of the United States of America upon the Government of the Mexican Republic.'' The joint board of commissioners created by this convention to examine and decide upon these claims was not organized until the month of August, 1840, and under the terms of the convention they were to terminate their duties within eighteen months from that time. Four of the eighteen months were consumed in preliminary discussions on frivolous and dilatory points raised by the Mexican commissioners, and it was not until the month of December, 1840, that they commenced the examination of the claims of our citizens upon Mexico. Fourteen months only remained to examine and decide upon these numerous and complicated cases. In the month of February, 1842, the term of the commission expired, leaving many claims undisposed of for want of time. The claims which were allowed by the board and by the umpire authorized by the convention to decide in case of disagreement between the Mexican and American commissioners amounted to $2,026,139.68. There were pending before the umpire when the commission expired additional claims, which had been examined and awarded by the American commissioners and had not been allowed by the Mexican commissioners, amounting to $928,627.88, upon which he did not decide, alleging that his authority had ceased with the termination of the joint commission. Besides these claims, there were others of American citizens amounting to $3,336,837.05, which had been submitted to the board, and upon which they had not time to decide before their final adjournment.

The sum of $2,026,139.68, which had been awarded to the claimants, was a liquidated and ascertained debt due by Mexico, about which there could be no dispute, and which she was bound to pay according to the terms of the convention. Soon after the final awards for this amount had been made the Mexican Government asked for a postponement of the time of making payment, alleging that it would be inconvenient to make the payment at the time stipulated. In the spirit of forbearing kindness toward a sister republic, which Mexico has so long abused, the United States promptly complied with her request. A second convention was accordingly concluded between the two Governments on the 30th of January, 1843, which upon its face declares that "this new arrangement is entered into for the accommodation of Mexico." By the terms of this convention all the interest due on the awards which had been made in favor of the claimants under the convention of the 11th of April, 1839, was to be paid to them on the 30th of April, 1843, and "the principal of the said awards and the interest accruing thereon" was stipulated to "be paid in five years, in equal installments every three months." Notwithstanding this new convention was entered into at the request of Mexico and for the purpose of relieving her from embarrassment, the claimants have only received the interest due on the 30th of April, 1843, and three of the twenty installments. Although the payment of the sum thus liquidated and confessedly due by Mexico to our citizens as indemnity for acknowledged acts of outrage and wrong was secured by treaty, the obligations of which are ever held sacred by all just nations, yet Mexico has violated this solemn engagement by failing and refusing to make the payment. The two installments due in April and July, 1844, under the peculiar circumstances connected with them, have been assumed by the United States and discharged to the claimants, but they are still due by Mexico. But this is not all of which we have just cause of complaint. To provide a remedy for the claimants whose cases were not decided by the joint commission under the convention of April 11, 1839, it was expressly stipulated by the sixth article of the convention of the 30th of January, 1843, that—

> A new convention shall be entered into for the settlement of all claims of the Government and citizens of the United States against the Republic of Mexico which were not finally decided by the late commission which met in the city of Washington, and of all claims of the Government and citizens of Mexico against the United States.

In conformity with this stipulation, a third convention was concluded and signed at the city of Mexico on the 20th of November, 1843, by the plenipotentiaries of the two Governments, by which provision was made for ascertaining and paying these claims. In January, 1844, this convention was ratified by the Senate of the United States with two amendments, which were manifestly reasonable in their character. Upon a reference of the amendments proposed to the Government of Mexico, the same evasions, difficulties, and delays were interposed which have so long marked the policy of that Government toward the United States. It has not even yet decided whether it would or would not accede to them, although the subject has been repeatedly pressed upon its consideration. Mexico has thus violated a second time the faith of treaties by failing or refusing to carry into effect the sixth article of the convention of January, 1843.

Such is the history of the wrongs which we have suffered and patiently endured from Mexico through a long series of years. So far from affording reasonable satisfaction for the injuries and insults we had borne, a great aggravation of them consists in the fact that while the United States, anxious to preserve a good understanding with Mexico, have been constantly but vainly employed in seeking redress for past wrongs, new outrages were constantly occurring, which have continued to increase our causes of complaint and to swell the amount of our demands. While the citizens of the United States were conducting a lawful commerce with Mexico under the guaranty of a treaty of "amity, commerce, and navigation," many of them have suffered all the injuries which would have resulted from open war. This treaty, instead of affording protection to our citizens, has been the means of inviting them into the ports of Mexico that they might be, as they have been in numerous instances, plundered of their property and deprived of their personal liberty if they dared insist on their rights. Had the unlawful seizures of American property and the violation of the personal liberty of our citizens, to say nothing of the insults to our flag, which have occurred in the ports of Mexico taken place on the high seas, they would themselves long since have constituted a state of actual war between the two countries. In so long suffering Mexico to violate her most solemn treaty obligations, plunder our citizens of their property, and imprison their persons without affording them any redress we have failed to perform one of the first and highest duties which every government owes to its citizens, and the consequence has been that many of them have been reduced from a state of affluence to bankruptcy. The proud name of American citizen, which ought to protect all who bear it from insult and injury throughout the world, has afforded no such protection to our citizens in Mexico. We had ample cause of war against Mexico long before the breaking out of · hostilities; but even then we forbore to take redress into our own hands until Mexico herself became the aggressor by invading our soil in hostile array and shedding the blood of our citizens.

Such are the grave causes of complaint on the part of the United States against Mexico—causes which existed long before the annexation of Texas to the American Union; and yet, animated by the love of peace and a magnanimous moderation, we did not adopt those measures of redress which under such circumstances are the justified resort of injured nations.

The annexation of Texas to the United States constituted no just cause of offense to Mexico. The pretext that it did so is wholly inconsistent and irreconcilable with well-authenticated facts connected with the revolution by which Texas became independent of Mexico. That this may be the more manifest, it may be proper to advert to the causes and to the history of the principal events of that revolution.

Texas constituted a portion of the ancient Province of Louisiana, ceded to the United States by France in the year 1803. In the year 1819 the United States, by the Florida treaty, ceded to Spain all that part of Louisiana within the present limits of Texas, and Mexico, by the revolution which separated her from Spain and rendered her an independent nation, succeeded to the rights of the mother country over this territory. In the year 1824 Mexico established a federal constitution, under which the Mexican Republic was composed of a number of sovereign States confederated together in a federal union similar to our own. Each of these States had its own executive, legislature, and judiciary, and for all except federal purposes was as independent of the General Government and that of the other States as is Pennsylvania or Virginia under our Constitution. Texas and Coahuila united and formed one of these Mexican States. The State constitution which they adopted, and which was approved by the Mexican Confederacy, asserted that they were "free and independent of the other Mexican United States and of every other power and dominion whatsoever," and proclaimed the great principle of human liberty that "the sovereignty of the state resides originally and essentially in the general mass of the individuals who compose it." To the Government under this constitution, as well as to that under the federal constitution, the people of Texas owed allegiance.

Emigrants from foreign countries, including the United States, were invited by the colonization laws of the State and of the Federal Government to settle in Texas. Advantageous terms were offered to induce them to leave their own country and become Mexican citizens. This invitation was accepted by many of our citizens in the full faith that in their new home they would be governed by laws enacted by representatives elected by themselves, and that their lives, liberty, and property would be protected by constitutional guaranties similar to those which existed in the Republic they had left. Under a Government thus organized they continued until the year 1835, when a military revolution broke out in the City of Mexico which entirely subverted the federal and State constitutions and placed a military dictator at the head of the Government. By a sweeping decree of a Congress subservient to the will of the Dictator the several State constitutions were abolished and the States themselves converted into mere departments of the central Government. The people of Texas were unwilling to submit to this usurpation. Resistance to such tyranny became a high duty. Texas was fully absolved from all allegiance to the central Government of Mexico from the moment that Government had abolished her State constitution and in its place substituted an arbitrary and despotic central government. Such were the principal causes of the Texan revolution. The people of Texas at once determined upon resistance and flew to arms. In the midst of these important and exciting events, however, they did not omit to place their liberties upon a secure and permanent foundation. They elected members to a convention, who in the month of March, 1836, issued a formal declaration that their "political connection with the Mexican nation has forever ended, and that the people of Texas do now constitute a *free, sovereign, and independent Republic*, and are fully invested with all the rights and attributes which properly belong to independent nations." They also adopted for their government a liberal republican constitution. About the same time Santa Anna, then the Dictator of Mexico, invaded Texas with a numerous army for the purpose of subduing her people and enforcing obedience to his arbitrary and despotic Government. On the 21st of April, 1836, he was met by the Texan citizen soldiers, and on that day was achieved by them the memorable victory of San Jacinto, by which they conquered their independence. Considering the numbers engaged on the respective sides, history does not record a more brilliant achievement. Santa Anna himself was among the captives.

In the month of May, 1836, Santa Anna acknowledged by a treaty with the Texan authorities in the most solemn form "the full, entire, and perfect independence of the Republic of Texas." It is true he was then a prisoner of war, but it is equally true that he had failed to reconquer Texas, and had met with signal defeat; that his authority had not been revoked, and that by virtue of this treaty he obtained his personal release. By it hostilities were suspended, and the army which had invaded Texas under his command returned in pursuance of this arrangement unmolested to Mexico.

From the day that the battle of San Jacinto was fought until the present hour Mexico has never possessed the power to reconquer Texas. In the language of the Secretary of State of the United States in a dispatch to our minister in Mexico under date of the 8th of July, 1842—

Mexico may have chosen to consider, and may still choose to consider, Texas as having been at all times since 1835, and as still continuing, a rebellious province; but the world has been obliged to take a very different view of the matter. From the time of the battle of San Jacinto, in April, 1836, to the present moment, Texas has exhibited the same external signs of national independence as Mexico herself, and with quite as much stability of government. Practically free and independent, acknowledged as a political sovereignty by the principal powers of the world, no hostile foot finding rest within her territory for six or seven years, and Mexico herself refraining for all that period from any further attempt to reestablish her own authority over that territory, it can not but be surprising to find Mr. De Bocanegra [the secretary of foreign affairs of Mexico] complaining that for that whole period citizens of the United States or its Government have been favoring the rebels of Texas and supplying them with vessels, ammunition, and money, as if the war for the reduction of the Province of Texas had been constantly prosecuted by Mexico, and her success prevented by these influences from abroad.

In the same dispatch the Secretary of State affirms that—

Since 1837 the United States have regarded Texas as an independent sovereignty as much as Mexico, and that trade and commerce with citizens of a government at war with Mexico can not on that account be regarded as an intercourse by which assistance and succor are given to Mexican rebels. The whole current of Mr. De Bocanegra's remarks runs in the same direction, as if the independence of Texas had not been acknowledged. It has been acknowledged; it was acknowledged in 1837 against the remonstrance and protest of Mexico, and most of the acts of any importance of which Mr. De Bocanegra complains flow necessarily from that recognition. He speaks of Texas as still being "an integral part of the territory of the Mexican Republic," but he can not but understand that the United States do not so regard it. The real complaint of Mexico, therefore, is in substance neither more nor less than a complaint against the recognition of Texan independence. It may be thought rather late to repeat that complaint, and not quite just to confine it to the United States to the exemption of England, France, and Belgium, unless the United States, having been the first to acknowledge the independence of Mexico herself, are to be blamed for setting an example for the recognition of that of Texas.

And he added that—

The Constitution, public treaties, and the laws oblige the President to regard Texas as an independent state, and its territory as no part of the territory of Mexico.

Texas had been an independent state, with an organized government, defying the power of Mexico to overthrow or reconquer her, for more than ten years before Mexico commenced the present war against the United States. Texas had given such evidence to the world of her ability to maintain her separate existence as an independent nation that she had been formally recognized as such not only by the United States, but by several of the principal powers of Europe. These powers had entered into treaties of amity, commerce, and navigation with her. They had received and accredited her ministers and other diplomatic agents at their respective courts, and they had commissioned ministers and diplomatic agents on their part to the Government of Texas. If Mexico,

notwithstanding all this and her utter inability to subdue or reconquer Texas, still stubbornly refused to recognize her as an independent
nation, she was none the less so on that account. Mexico herself had
been recognized as an independent nation by the United States and by
other powers many years before Spain, of which before her revolution
she had been a colony, would agree to recognize her as such; and yet
Mexico was at that time in the estimation of the civilized world, and in
fact, none the less an independent power because Spain still claimed her
as a colony. If Spain had continued until the present period to assert
that Mexico was one of her colonies in rebellion against her, this would
not have made her so or changed the fact of her independent existence.
Texas at the period of her annexation to the United States bore the
same relation to Mexico that Mexico had borne to Spain for many years
before Spain acknowledged her independence, with this important difference, that before the annexation of Texas to the United States was
consummated Mexico herself, by a formal act of her Government, had
acknowledged the independence of Texas as a nation. It is true that
in the act of recognition she prescribed a condition which she had no
power or authority to impose—that Texas should not annex herself to
any other power—but this could not detract in any degree from the recognition which Mexico then made of her actual independence. Upon this
plain statement of facts, it is absurd for Mexico to allege as a pretext
for commencing hostilities against the United States that Texas is still
a part of her territory.

But there are those who, conceding all this to be true, assume the
ground that the true western boundary of Texas is the Nueces instead
of the Rio Grande, and that therefore in marching our Army to the east
bank of the latter river we passed the Texan line and invaded the territory of Mexico. A simple statement of facts known to exist will conclusively refute such an assumption. Texas, as ceded to the United States
by France in 1803, has been always claimed as extending west to the Rio
Grande or Rio Bravo. This fact is established by the authority of our
most eminent statesmen at a period when the question was as well, if not
better, understood than it is at present. During Mr. Jefferson's Administration Messrs. Monroe and Pinckney, who had been sent on a special
mission to Madrid, charged among other things with the adjustment of
boundary between the two countries, in a note addressed to the Spanish minister of foreign affairs under date of the 28th of January, 1805,
assert that the boundaries of Louisiana, as ceded to the United States by
France, "are the river Perdido on the east and the river Bravo on the
west," and they add that "the facts and principles which justify this
conclusion are so satisfactory to our Government as to convince it that
the United States have not a better right to the island of New Orleans
under the cession referred to than they have to the whole district of
territory which is above described." Down to the conclusion of the

Florida treaty, in February, 1819, by which this territory was ceded to Spain, the United States asserted and maintained their territorial rights to this extent. In the month of June, 1818, during Mr. Monroe's Administration, information having been received that a number of foreign adventurers had landed at Galveston with the avowed purpose of forming a settlement in that vicinity, a special messenger was dispatched by the Government of the United States with instructions from the Secretary of State to warn them to desist, should they be found there, "or any other place north of the Rio Bravo, and within the territory claimed by the United States." He was instructed, should they be found in the country north of that river, to make known to them "the surprise with which the President has seen possession thus taken, without authority from the United States, of a place within their territorial limits, and upon which no lawful settlement can be made without their sanction." He was instructed to call upon them to "avow under what national authority they profess to act," and to give them due warning "that the place is within the United States, who will suffer no permanent settlement to be made there under any authority other than their own." As late as the 8th of July, 1842, the Secretary of State of the United States, in a note addressed to our minister in Mexico, maintains that by the Florida treaty of 1819 the territory as far west as the Rio Grande was confirmed to Spain. In that note he states that—

By the treaty of the 22d of February, 1819, between the United States and Spain, the Sabine was adopted as the line of boundary between the two powers. Up to that period no considerable colonization had been effected in Texas; but the territory between the Sabine and the Rio Grande being confirmed to Spain by the treaty, applications were made to that power for grants of land, and such grants or permissions of settlement were in fact made by the Spanish authorities in favor of citizens of the United States proposing to emigrate to *Texas* in numerous families before the declaration of independence by Mexico.

The Texas which was ceded to Spain by the Florida treaty of 1819 embraced all the country now claimed by the State of Texas between the Nueces and the Rio Grande. The Republic of Texas always claimed this river as her western boundary, and in her treaty made with Santa Anna in May, 1836, he recognized it as such. By the constitution which Texas adopted in March, 1836, senatorial and representative districts were organized extending west of the Nueces. The Congress of Texas on the 19th of December, 1836, passed "An act to define the boundaries of the Republic of Texas," in which they declared the Rio Grande from its mouth to its source to be their boundary, and by the said act they extended their "civil and political jurisdiction" over the country up to that boundary. During a period of more than nine years which intervened between the adoption of her constitution and her annexation as one of the States of our Union Texas asserted and exercised many acts of sovereignty and jurisdiction over the territory and inhabitants west of the Nueces. She organized and defined the limits of counties extending to the Rio Grande; she established courts of justice and extended her judicial system over the territory; she established a custom-house and collected duties, and also post-offices and post-roads, in it; she established a land office and issued numerous grants for land within its limits; a senator and a representative residing in it were elected to the Congress of the Republic and served as such before the act of annexation took place. In both the Congress and convention of Texas which gave their assent to the terms of annexation to the United States proposed by our Congress were representatives residing west of the Nueces, who took part in the act of annexation itself. This was the Texas which by the act of our Congress of the 29th of December, 1845, was admitted as one of the States of our Union. That the Congress of the United States understood the State of Texas which they admitted into the Union to extend beyond the Nueces is apparent from the fact that on the 31st of December, 1845. only two days after the act of admission, they passed a law ''to establish a collection district in the State of Texas,'' by which they created a port of delivery at Corpus Christi, situated west of the Nueces, and being the same point at which the Texas custom-house under the laws of that Republic had been located, and directed that a surveyor to collect the revenue should be appointed for that port by the President, by and with the advice and consent of the Senate. A surveyor was accordingly nominated, and confirmed by the Senate, and has been ever since in the performance of his duties. All these acts of the Republic of Texas and of our Congress preceded the orders for the advance of our Army to the east bank of the Rio Grande. Subsequently Congress passed an act ''establishing certain post routes'' extending west of the Nueces. The country west of that river now constitutes a part of one of the Congressional districts of Texas and is represented in the House of Representatives. The Senators from that State were chosen by a legislature in which the country west of that river was represented. In view of all these facts it is difficult to conceive upon what ground it can be maintained that in occupying the country west of the Nueces with our Army, with a view solely to its security and defense, we invaded the territory of Mexico. But it would have been still more difficult to justify the Executive, whose duty it is to see that the laws be faithfully executed, if in the face of all these proceedings, both of the Congress of Texas and of the United States, he had assumed the responsibility of yielding up the territory west of the Nueces to Mexico or of refusing to protect and defend this territory and its inhabitants, including Corpus Christi as well as the remainder of Texas, against the threatened Mexican invasion.

But Mexico herself has never placed the war which she has waged upon the ground that our Army occupied the intermediate territory between the Nueces and the Rio Grande. Her refuted pretension that Texas was not in fact an independent state, but a rebellious province, was obstinately persevered in, and her avowed purpose in commencing a war with the United States was to reconquer Texas and to restore Mexican authority over the whole territory—not to the Nueces only, but to the Sabine. In view of the proclaimed menaces of Mexico to this effect, I deemed it my duty, as a measure of precaution and defense, to order our Army to occupy a position on our frontier as a military post, from which our troops could best resist and repel any attempted invasion which Mexico might make. Our Army had occupied a position at Corpus Christi, west of the Nueces, as early as August, 1845, without complaint from any quarter. Had the Nueces been regarded as the true western boundary of Texas, that boundary had been passed by our Army many months before it advanced to the eastern bank of the Rio Grande. In my annual message of December last I informed Congress that upon the invitation of both the Congress and convention of Texas I had deemed it proper to order a strong squadron to the coasts of Mexico and to concentrate an efficient military force on the western frontier of Texas to protect and defend the inhabitants against the menaced invasion of Mexico. In that message I informed Congress that the moment the terms of annexation offered by the United States were accepted by Texas the latter became so far a part of our own country as to make it our duty to afford such protection and defense, and that for that purpose our squadron had been ordered to the Gulf and our Army to take a "position between the Nueces and the Del Norte" or Rio Grande and to "repel any invasion of the Texan territory which might be attempted by the Mexican forces."

It was deemed proper to issue this order, because soon after the President of Texas, in April, 1845, had issued his proclamation convening the Congress of that Republic for the purpose of submitting to that body the terms of annexation proposed by the United States the Government of Mexico made serious threats of invading the Texan territory. These threats became more imposing as it became more apparent in the progress of the question that the people of Texas would decide in favor of accepting the terms of annexation, and finally they had assumed such a formidable character as induced both the Congress and convention of Texas to request that a military force should be sent by the United States into her territory for the purpose of protecting and defending her against the threatened invasion. It would have been a violation of good faith toward the people of Texas to have refused to afford the aid which they desired against a threatened invasion to which they had been exposed by their free determination to annex themselves to our Union in compliance with the overture made to them by the joint resolution of our Congress. Accordingly, a portion of the Army was ordered to advance into Texas. Corpus Christi was the position selected by General Taylor. He encamped at that place in August, 1845, and the Army remained in that position until the 11th of March, 1846, when it moved westward, and on the 28th of that month reached the east bank of the Rio Grande opposite to Matamoras. This movement was made in pursuance of orders from the War Department, issued on the 13th of January, 1846. Before these orders were issued the dispatch of our minister in Mexico transmitting the decision of the council of government of Mexico advising that he should not be received, and also the dispatch of our consul residing in the City of Mexico, the former bearing date on the 17th and the latter on the 18th of December, 1845, copies of both of which accompanied my message to Congress of the 11th of May last, were received at the Department of State. These communications rendered it highly probable, if not absolutely certain, that our minister would not be received by the Government of General Herrera. It was also well known that but little hope could be entertained of a different result from General Paredes in case the revolutionary movement which he was prosecuting should prove successful, as was highly probable. The partisans of Paredes, as our minister in the dispatch referred to states, breathed the fiercest hostility against the United States, denounced the proposed negotiation as treason, and openly called upon the troops and the people to put down the Government of Herrera by force. The reconquest of Texas and war with the United States were openly threatened. These were the circumstances existing when it was deemed proper to order the Army under the command of General Taylor to advance to the western frontier of Texas and occupy a position on or near the Rio Grande.

The apprehensions of a contemplated Mexican invasion have been since fully justified by the event. The determination of Mexico to rush into hostilities with the United States was afterwards manifested from the whole tenor of the note of the Mexican minister of foreign affairs to our minister bearing date on the 12th of March, 1846. Paredes had then revolutionized the Government, and his minister, after referring to the resolution for the annexation of Texas which had been adopted by our Congress in March, 1845, proceeds to declare that—

A fact such as this, or, to speak with greater exactness, so notable an act of usurpation, created an imperious necessity that Mexico, for her own honor, should repel it with proper firmness and dignity. The supreme Government had beforehand declared that it would look upon such an act as a *casus belli*, and as a consequence of this declaration negotiation was by its very nature at an end, and war was the only recourse of the Mexican Government.

It appears also that on the 4th of April following General Paredes, through his minister of war, issued orders to the Mexican general in command on the Texan frontier to "attack" our Army "by every means which war permits." To this General Paredes had been pledged to the army and people of Mexico during the military revolution which had brought him into power. On the 18th of April, 1846, General Paredes addressed a letter to the commander on that frontier in which he stated to him: "At the present date I suppose you, at the head of that valiant army, either fighting already or preparing for the operations of a campaign;'' and, "Supposing you already on the theater of operations and with all the forces assembled, it is indispensable that hostilities be commenced, yourself taking the initiative against the enemy.''

The movement of our Army to the Rio Grande was made by the commanding general under positive orders to abstain from all aggressive acts toward Mexico or Mexican citizens, and to regard the relations between the two countries as peaceful unless Mexico should declare war or commit acts of hostility indicative of a state of war, and these orders he faithfully executed. Whilst occupying his position on the east bank of the Rio Grande, within the limits of Texas, then recently admitted as one of the States of our Union, the commanding general of the Mexican forces, who, in pursuance of the orders of his Government, had collected a large army on the opposite shore of the Rio Grande, crossed the river, invaded our territory, and commenced hostilities by attacking our forces. Thus, after all the injuries which we had received and borne from Mexico, and after she had insultingly rejected a minister sent to her on a mission of peace, and whom she had solemnly agreed to receive, she consummated her long course of outrage against our country by commencing an offensive war and shedding the blood of our citizens on our own soil.

The United States never attempted to acquire Texas by conquest. On the contrary, at an early period after the people of Texas had achieved their independence they sought to be annexed to the United States. At a general election in September, 1836, they decided with great unanimity in favor of "annexation," and in November following the Congress of the Republic authorized the appointment of a minister to bear their request to this Government. This Government, however, having remained neutral between Texas and Mexico during the war between them, and considering it due to the honor of our country and our fair fame among the nations of the earth that we should not at this early period consent to annexation, nor until it should be manifest to the whole world that the reconquest of Texas by Mexico was impossible, refused to accede to the overtures made by Texas. On the 12th of April, 1844, after more than seven years had elapsed since Texas had established her independence, a treaty was concluded for the annexation of that Republic to the United States, which was rejected by the Senate. Finally, on the 1st of March, 1845, Congress passed a joint resolution for annexing her to the United States upon certain preliminary conditions to which her assent was required. The solemnities which characterized the deliberations and conduct of the Government and people of Texas on the deeply interesting questions presented by these resolutions are known to the world. The Congress, the Executive, and the people of Texas, in a convention elected for that purpose, accepted with great unanimity the proposed terms of annexation, and thus consummated on her part the great act of restoring to our Federal Union a vast territory which had been ceded to Spain by the Florida treaty more than a quarter of a century before.

After the joint resolution for the annexation of Texas to the United States had been passed by our Congress the Mexican minister at Washington addressed a note to the Secretary of State, bearing date on the 6th of March, 1845, protesting against it as "an act of aggression the most unjust which can be found recorded in the annals of modern history, namely, that of despoiling a friendly nation like Mexico of a considerable portion of her territory," and protesting against the resolution of annexation as being an act "whereby the Province of Texas, an integral portion of the Mexican territory, is agreed and admitted into the American Union;" and he announced that as a consequence his mission to the United States had terminated, and demanded his passports, which were granted. It was upon the absurd pretext, made by Mexico (herself indebted for her independence to a successful revolution), that the Republic of Texas still continued to be, notwithstanding all that had passed, a Province of Mexico that this step was taken by the Mexican minister.

Every honorable effort has been used by me to avoid the war which followed, but all have proved vain. All our attempts to preserve peace have been met by insult and resistance on the part of Mexico. My efforts to this end commenced in the note of the Secretary of State of the 10th of March, 1845, in answer to that of the Mexican minister. Whilst declining to reopen a discussion which had already been exhausted, and proving again what was known to the whole world, that Texas had long since achieved her independence, the Secretary of State expressed the regret of this Government that Mexico should have taken offense at the resolution of annexation passed by Congress, and gave assurance that our "most strenuous efforts shall be devoted to the amicable adjustment of every cause of complaint between the two Governments and to the cultivation of the kindest and most friendly relations between the sister Republics." That I have acted in the spirit of this assurance will appear from the events which have since occurred. Notwithstanding Mexico had abruptly terminated all diplomatic intercourse with the United States, and ought, therefore, to have been the first to ask for its resumption, yet, waiving all ceremony, I embraced the earliest favorable opportunity "to ascertain from the Mexican Government whether they would receive an envoy from the United States intrusted with full power to adjust all the questions in dispute between the two Governments." In September, 1845, I believed the propitious moment for such an overture had arrived. Texas, by the enthusiastic and almost unanimous will of her people, had pronounced in favor of annexation. Mexico herself had agreed to acknowledge the independence of Texas, subject to a condition, it is true, which she had no right to impose and no power to enforce. The last lingering hope of Mexico, if she still could have retained any, that Texas would ever again become one of her Provinces, must have been abandoned.

The consul of the United States at the City of Mexico was therefore instructed by the Secretary of State on the 15th of September, 1845, to make the inquiry of the Mexican Government. The inquiry was made, and on the 15th of October, 1845, the minister of foreign affairs of the Mexican Government, in a note addressed to our consul, gave a favorable response, requesting at the same time that our naval force might be withdrawn from Vera Cruz while negotiations should be pending. Upon the receipt of this note our naval force was promptly withdrawn from Vera Cruz. A minister was immediately appointed, and departed to Mexico. Everything bore a promising aspect for a speedy and peaceful adjustment of all our difficulties. At the date of my annual message to Congress in December last no doubt was entertained but that he would be received by the Mexican Government, and the hope was cherished that all cause of misunderstanding between the two countries would be speedily removed. In the confident hope that such would be the result of his mission, I informed Congress that I forbore at that time to ''recommend such ulterior measures of redress for the wrongs and injuries we had so long borne as it would have been proper to make had no such negotiation been instituted.'' To my surprise and regret the Mexican Government, though solemnly pledged to do so, upon the arrival of our minister in Mexico refused to receive and accredit him. When he reached Vera Cruz, on the 30th of November, 1845, he found that the aspect of affairs had undergone an unhappy change. The Government of General Herrera, who was at that time President of the Republic, was tottering to its fall. General Paredes, a military leader, had manifested his determination to overthrow the Government of Herrera by a military revolution, and one of the principal means which he employed to effect his purpose and render the Government of Herrera odious to the army and people of Mexico was by loudly condemning its determination to receive a minister of peace from the United States, alleging that it was the intention of Herrera, by a treaty with the United States, to dismember the territory of Mexico by ceding away the department of Texas. The Government of Herrera is believed to have been well disposed to a pacific adjustment of existing difficulties, but probably alarmed for its own security, and in order to ward off the danger of the revolution led by Paredes, violated its solemn agreement and refused to receive or accredit our minister; and this although informed that he had been invested with full power to adjust all questions in dispute between the two Governments. Among the frivolous pretexts for this refusal, the principal one was that our minister had not gone upon a special mission confined to the question of Texas alone, leaving all the outrages upon our flag and our citizens unredressed. The Mexican Government well knew that both our national honor and the protection due to our citizens imperatively required that the two questions of boundary and indemnity should be treated of together, as naturally and inseparably blended, and they ought to have seen that this course was best calculated to enable the United States to extend to them the most liberal justice. On the 30th of December, 1845, General Herrera resigned the Presidency and yielded up the Government to General Paredes without a struggle. Thus a revolution was accomplished solely by the army commanded by Paredes, and the supreme power in Mexico passed into the hands of a military usurper who was known to be bitterly hostile to the United States.

Although the prospect of a pacific adjustment with the new Government was unpromising from the known hostility of its head to the United States, yet, determined that nothing should be left undone on our part to restore friendly relations between the two countries, our minister was instructed to present his credentials to the new Government and ask to be accredited by it in the diplomatic character in which he had been commissioned. These instructions he executed by his note of the 1st of March, 1846, addressed to the Mexican minister of foreign affairs, but his request was insultingly refused by that minister in his answer of the 12th of the same month. No alternative remained for our minister but to demand his passports and return to the United States.

Thus was the extraordinary spectacle presented to the civilized world of a Government, in violation of its own express agreement, having twice rejected a minister of peace invested with full powers to adjust all the existing differences between the two countries in a manner just and honorable to both. I am not aware that modern history presents a parallel case in which in time of peace one nation has refused even to hear propositions from another for terminating existing difficulties between them. Scarcely a hope of adjusting our difficulties, even at a remote day, or of preserving peace with Mexico, could be cherished while Paredes remained at the head of the Government. He had acquired the supreme power by a military revolution and upon the most solemn pledges to wage war against the United States and to reconquer Texas, which he claimed as a revolted province of Mexico. He had denounced as guilty of treason all those Mexicans who considered Texas as no longer constituting a part of the territory of Mexico and who were friendly to the cause of peace. The duration of the war which he waged against the United States was indefinite, because the end which he proposed of the reconquest of Texas was hopeless. Besides, there was good reason to believe from all his conduct that it was his intention to convert the Republic of Mexico into a monarchy and to call a foreign European prince to the throne. Preparatory to this end, he had during his short rule destroyed the liberty of the press, tolerating that portion of it only which openly advocated the establishment of a monarchy. The better to secure the success of his ultimate designs, he had by an arbitrary decree convoked a Congress, not to be elected by the free voice of the people, but to be chosen in a manner to make them subservient to his will and to give him absolute control over their deliberations.

Under all these circumstances it was believed that any revolution in Mexico founded upon opposition to the ambitious projects of Paredes would tend to promote the cause of peace as well as prevent any attempted European interference in the affairs of the North American continent, both objects of deep interest to the United States. Any such foreign interference, if attempted, must have been resisted by the United States. My views upon that subject were fully communicated to Congress in my last annual message. In any event, it was certain that no change whatever in the Government of Mexico which would deprive Paredes of power could be for the worse so far as the United States were concerned, while it was highly probable that any change must be for the better. This was the state of affairs existing when Congress, on the 13th of May last, recognized the existence of the war which had been commenced by the Government of Paredes; and it became an object of much importance, with a view to a speedy settlement of our difficulties and the restoration of an honorable peace, that Paredes should not retain power in Mexico.

Before that time there were symptoms of a revolution in Mexico, favored, as it was understood to be, by the more liberal party, and especially by those who were opposed to foreign interference and to the monarchical form of government. Santa Anna was then in exile in Havana, having been expelled from power and banished from his country by a revolution which occurred in December, 1844; but it was known that he had still a considerable party in his favor in Mexico. It was also equally well known that no vigilance which could be exerted by our squadron would in all probability have prevented him from effecting a landing somewhere on the extensive Gulf coast of Mexico if he desired to return to his country. He had openly professed an entire change of policy, had expressed his regret that he had subverted the federal constitution of 1824, and avowed that he was now in favor of its restoration. He had publicly declared his hostility, in strongest terms, to the establishment of a monarchy and to European interference in the affairs of his country. Information to this effect had been received, from sources believed to be reliable, at the date of the recognition of the existence of the war by Congress, and was afterwards fully confirmed by the receipt of the dispatch of our consul in the City of Mexico, with the accompanying documents, which are herewith transmitted. Besides, it was reasonable to suppose that he must see the ruinous consequences to Mexico of a war with the United States, and that it would be his interest to favor peace.

It was under these circumstances and upon these considerations that it was deemed expedient not to obstruct his return to Mexico should he attempt to do so. Our object was the restoration of peace, and, with that view, no reason was perceived why we should take part with Paredes and aid him by means of our blockade in preventing the return of his rival to Mexico. On the contrary, it was believed that the intestine divisions which ordinary sagacity could not but anticipate as the fruit of Santa Anna's return to Mexico, and his contest with Paredes, might strongly tend to produce a disposition with both parties to restore and preserve peace with the United States. Paredes was a soldier by profession and a monarchist in principle. He had but recently before been successful in a military revolution, by which he had obtained power. He was the sworn enemy of the United States, with which he had involved his country in the existing war. Santa Anna had been expelled from power by the army, was known to be in open hostility to Paredes, and publicly pledged against foreign intervention and the restoration of monarchy in Mexico. In view of these facts and circumstances it was that when orders were issued to the commander of our naval forces in the Gulf, on the 13th day of May last, the same day on which the existence of the war was recognized by Congress, to place the coasts of Mexico under blockade, he was directed not to obstruct the passage of Santa Anna to Mexico should he attempt to return.

A revolution took place in Mexico in the early part of August following, by which the power of Paredes was overthrown, and he has since been banished from the country, and is now in exile. Shortly afterwards Santa Anna returned. It remains to be seen whether his return may not yet prove to be favorable to a pacific adjustment of the existing difficulties, it being manifestly his interest not to persevere in the prosecution of a war commenced by Paredes to accomplish a purpose so absurd as the reconquest of Texas to the Sabine. Had Paredes remained in power, it is morally certain that any pacific adjustment would have been hopeless.

Upon the commencement of hostilities by Mexico against the United States the indignant spirit of the nation was at once aroused. Congress promptly responded to the expectations of the country, and by the act of the 13th of May last recognized the fact that war existed, by the act of Mexico, between the United States and that Republic, and granted the means necessary for its vigorous prosecution. Being involved in a war thus commenced by Mexico, and for the justice of which on our part we may confidently appeal to the whole world, I resolved to prosecute it with the utmost vigor. Accordingly the ports of Mexico on the Gulf and on the Pacific have been placed under blockade and her territory invaded at several important points. The reports from the Departments of War and of the Navy will inform you more in detail of the measures adopted in the emergency in which our country was placed and of the gratifying results which have been accomplished.

The various columns of the Army have performed their duty under great disadvantages with the most distinguished skill and courage. The victories of Palo Alto and Resaca de la Palma and of Monterey, won against greatly superior numbers and against most decided advantages in other respects on the part of the enemy, were brilliant in their execution, and entitle our brave officers and soldiers to the grateful thanks of their country. The nation deplores the loss of the brave officers and men who have gallantly fallen while vindicating and defending their country's rights and honor.

It is a subject of pride and satisfaction that our volunteer citizen soldiers, who so promptly responded to their country's call, with an experience of the discipline of a camp of only a few weeks, have borne their part in the hard-fought battle of Monterey with a constancy and courage equal to that of veteran troops and worthy of the highest admiration. The privations of long marches through the enemy's country and through a wilderness have been borne without a murmur. By rapid movements the Province of New Mexico, with Santa Fe, its capital, has been captured without bloodshed. The Navy has cooperated with the Army and rendered important services; if not so brilliant, it is because the enemy had no force to meet them on their own element and because of the defenses which nature has interposed in the difficulties of the navigation on the Mexican coast. Our squadron in the Pacific, with the cooperation of a gallant officer of the Army and a small force hastily collected in that distant country, has acquired bloodless possession of the Californias, and the American flag has been raised at every important point in that Province.

I congratulate you on the success which has thus attended our military and naval operations. In less than seven months after Mexico commenced hostilities, at a time selected by herself, we have taken possession of many of her principal ports, driven back and pursued her invading army, and acquired military possession of the Mexican Provinces of New Mexico, New Leon, Coahuila, Tamaulipas, and the Californias, a territory larger in extent than that embraced in the original thirteen States of the Union, inhabited by a considerable population, and much of it more than 1,000 miles from the points at which we had to collect our forces and commence our movements. By the blockade the import and export trade of the enemy has been cut off. Well may the American people be proud of the energy and gallantry of our regular and volunteer officers and soldiers. The events of these few months afford a gratifying proof that our country can under any emergency confidently rely for the maintenance of her honor and the defense of her rights on an effective force, ready at all times voluntarily to relinquish the comforts of home for the perils and privations of the camp. And though such a force may be for the time expensive, it is in the end economical, as the ability to command it removes the necessity of employing a large standing army in time of peace, and proves that our people love their institutions and are ever ready to defend and protect them.

While the war was in a course of vigorous and successful prosecution, being still anxious to arrest its evils, and considering that after the brilliant victories of our arms on the 8th and 9th of May last the national honor could not be compromitted by it, another overture was made to Mexico, by my direction, on the 27th of July last to terminate hostilities by a peace just and honorable to both countries. On the 31st of August following the Mexican Government declined to accept this friendly overture, but referred it to the decision of a Mexican Congress to be assembled in the early part of the present month. I communicate to you herewith a copy of the letter of the Secretary of State proposing to reopen negotiations, of the answer of the Mexican Government, and of the reply thereto of the Secretary of State.

The war will continue to be prosecuted with vigor as the best means of securing peace. It is hoped that the decision of the Mexican Congress, to which our last overture has been referred, may result in a speedy and honorable peace. With our experience, however, of the unreasonable course of the Mexican authorities, it is the part of wisdom not to relax in the energy of our military operations until the result is made known. In this view it is deemed important to hold military possession of all the Provinces which have been taken until a definitive treaty of peace shall have been concluded and ratified by the two countries.

The war has not been waged with a view to conquest, but, having been commenced by Mexico, it has been carried into the enemy's country and will be vigorously prosecuted there with a view to obtain an honorable peace, and thereby secure ample indemnity for the expenses of the war, as well as to our much-injured citizens, who hold large pecuniary demands against Mexico.

By the laws of nations a conquered country is subject to be governed by the conqueror during his military possession and until there is either a treaty of peace or he shall voluntarily withdraw from it. The old civil government being necessarily superseded, it is the right and duty of the conqueror to secure his conquest and to provide for the maintenance of civil order and the rights of the inhabitants. This right has been exercised and this duty performed by our military and naval commanders by the establishment of temporary governments in some of the conquered Provinces of Mexico, assimilating them as far as practicable to the free institutions of our own country. In the Provinces of New Mexico and of the Californias little, if any, further resistance is apprehended from the inhabitants to the temporary governments which have thus, from the necessity of the case and according to the laws of war, been established. It may be proper to provide for the security of these important conquests by making an adequate appropriation for the purpose of erecting fortifications and defraying the expenses necessarily incident to the maintenance of our possession and authority over them.

Near the close of your last session, for reasons communicated to Congress, I deemed it important as a measure for securing a speedy peace with Mexico, that a sum of money should be appropriated and placed in the power of the Executive, similar to that which had been made upon two former occasions during the Administration of President Jefferson.

On the 26th of February, 1803, an appropriation of $2,000,000 was made and placed at the disposal of the President. Its object is well known. It was at that time in contemplation to acquire Louisiana from France, and it was intended to be applied as a part of the consideration which might be paid for that territory. On the 13th of February, 1806, the same sum was in like manner appropriated, with a view to the purchase of the Floridas from Spain. These appropriations were made to facilitate negotiations and as a means to enable the President to accomplish the important objects in view. Though it did not become necessary for the President to use these appropriations, yet a state of things might have arisen in which it would have been highly important for him to do so, and the wisdom of making them can not be doubted. It is believed that the measure recommended at your last session met with the approbation of decided majorities in both Houses of Congress. Indeed, in different forms, a bill making an appropriation of $2,000,000 passed each House, and it is much to be regretted that it did not become a law. The reasons which induced me to recommend the measure at that time still exist, and I again submit the subject for your consideration and suggest the importance of early action upon it. Should the appropriation be made and be not needed, it will remain in the Treasury; should it be deemed proper to apply it in whole or in part, it will be accounted for as other public expenditures.

Immediately after Congress had recognized the existence of the war with Mexico my attention was directed to the danger that privateers might be fitted out in the ports of Cuba and Porto Rico to prey upon the commerce of the United States, and I invited the special attention of the Spanish Government to the fourteenth article of our treaty with that power of the 27th of October, 1795, under which the citizens and subjects of either nation who shall take commissions or letters of marque to act as privateers against the other "shall be punished as pirates."

It affords me pleasure to inform you that I have received assurances from the Spanish Government that this article of the treaty shall be faithfully observed on its part. Orders for this purpose were immediately transmitted from that Government to the authorities of Cuba and Porto Rico to exert their utmost vigilance in preventing any attempts to fit out privateers in those islands against the United States. From the good faith of Spain I am fully satisfied that this treaty will be executed in its spirit as well as its letter, whilst the United States will on their part faithfully perform all the obligations which it imposes on them.

Information has been recently received at the Department of State that the Mexican Government has sent to Havana blank commissions to privateers and blank certificates of naturalization signed by General Salas, the present head of the Mexican Government. There is also reason to apprehend that similar documents have been transmitted to other parts of the world. Copies of these papers, in translation, are herewith transmitted.

As the preliminaries required by the practice of civilized nations for commissioning privateers and regulating their conduct appear not to have been observed, and as these commissions are in blank, to be filled up with the names of citizens and subjects of all nations who may be willing to purchase them, the whole proceeding can only be construed as an invitation to all the freebooters upon earth who are willing to pay for the privilege to cruise against American commerce. It will be for our courts of justice to decide whether under such circumstances these Mexican letters of marque and reprisal shall protect those who accept them, and commit robberies upon the high seas under their authority, from the pains and penalties of piracy.

If the certificates of naturalization thus granted be intended by Mexico to shield Spanish subjects from the guilt and punishment of pirates under our treaty with Spain, they will certainly prove unavailing. Such a subterfuge would be but a weak device to defeat the provisions of a solemn treaty.

I recommend that Congress should immediately provide by law for the trial and punishment as pirates of Spanish subjects who, escaping the vigilance of their Government, shall be found guilty of privateering against the United States. I do not apprehend serious danger from these privateers. Our Navy will be constantly on the alert to protect our commerce. Besides, in case prizes should be made of American vessels, the utmost vigilance will be exerted by our blockading squadron to prevent the captors from taking them into Mexican ports, and it is not apprehended that any nation will violate its neutrality by suffering such prizes to be condemned and sold within its jurisdiction.

I recommend that Congress should immediately provide by law for granting letters of marque and reprisal against vessels under the Mexican flag. It is true that there are but few, if any, commercial vessels of Mexico upon the high seas, and it is therefore not probable that many American privateers would be fitted out in case a law should pass authorizing this mode of warfare. It is, notwithstanding, certain that such privateers may render good service to the commercial interests of the country by recapturing our merchant ships should any be taken by armed vessels under the Mexican flag, as well as by capturing these vessels themselves. Every means within our power should be rendered available for the protection of our commerce.

The annual report of the Secretary of the Treasury will exhibit a detailed statement of the condition of the finances. The imports for the fiscal year ending on the 30th of June last were of the value of $121,691,797, of which the amount exported was $11,346,623, leaving the amount retained in the country for domestic consumption $110,345,-174. The value of the exports for the same period was $113,488,516, of which $102,141,893 consisted of domestic productions and $11,346,623 of foreign articles.

The receipts into the Treasury for the same year were $29,499,247.06, of which there was derived from customs $26,712,667.87, from the sales of public lands $2,694,452.48, and from incidental and miscellaneous sources $92,126.71. The expenditures for the same period were $28,-031,114.20, and the balance in the Treasury on the 1st day of July last was $9,126,439.08.

The amount of the public debt, including Treasury notes, on the 1st of the present month was $24,256,494.60, of which the sum of $17,788,-799.62 was outstanding on the 4th of March, 1845, leaving the amount incurred since that time $6,467,694.98.

In order to prosecute the war with Mexico with vigor and energy, as the best means of bringing it to a speedy and honorable termination, a further loan will be necessary to meet the expenditures for the present and the next fiscal year. If the war should be continued until the 30th of June, 1848, being the end of the next fiscal year, it is estimated that an additional loan of $23,000,000 will be required. This estimate is made upon the assumption that it will be necessary to retain constantly in the Treasury $4,000,000 to guard against contingencies. If such surplus were not required to be retained, then a loan of $19,000,000 would be sufficient. If, however, Congress should at the present session impose a revenue duty on the principal articles now embraced in the free list, it is estimated that an additional annual revenue of about two millions and a half, amounting, it is estimated, on the 30th of June, 1848, to $4,000,000, would be derived from that source, and the loan required would be reduced by that amount. It is estimated also that should Congress graduate and reduce the price of such of the public lands as have been long in the market the additional revenue derived from that source would be annually, for several years to come, between half a million and a million dollars; and the loan required may be reduced by that amount also. Should these measures be adopted, the loan required would not probably exceed $18,000,000 or $19,000,000, leaving in the Treasury a constant surplus of $4,000,000. The loan proposed, it is estimated, will be sufficient to cover the necessary expenditures both for the war and for all other purposes up to the 30th of June, 1848, and an amount of this loan not exceeding one-half may be required during the present fiscal year, and the greater part of the remainder during the first half of the fiscal year succeeding.

In order that timely notice may be given and proper measures taken to effect the loan, or such portion of it as may be required, it is important that the authority of Congress to make it be given at an early period of your present session. It is suggested that the loan should be contracted for a period of twenty years, with authority to purchase the stock and pay it off at an earlier period at its market value out of any surplus which may at any time be in the Treasury applicable to that purpose. After the establishment of peace with Mexico, it is supposed that a considerable surplus will exist, and that the debt may be extinguished in a much shorter period than that for which it may be contracted. The period of twenty years, as that for which the proposed loan may be contracted, in preference to a shorter period, is suggested, because all experience, both at home and abroad, has shown that loans are effected upon much better terms upon long time than when they are reimbursable at short dates.

Necessary as this measure is to sustain the honor and the interests of the country engaged in a foreign war, it is not doubted but that Congress will promptly authorize it.

The balance in the Treasury on the 1st July last exceeded $9,000,000, notwithstanding considerable expenditures had been made for the war during the months of May and June preceding. But for the war the whole public debt could and would have been extinguished within a short period; and it was a part of my settled policy to do so, and thus relieve the people from its burden and place the Government in a position which would enable it to reduce the public expenditures to that economical standard which is most consistent with the general welfare and the pure and wholesome progress of our institutions.

Among our just causes of complaint against Mexico arising out of her refusal to treat for peace, as well before as since the war so unjustly commenced on her part, are the extraordinary expenditures in which we have been involved. Justice to our own people will make it proper that Mexico should be held responsible for these expenditures.

Economy in the public expenditures is at all times a high duty which all public functionaries of the Government owe to the people. This duty becomes the more imperative in a period of war, when large and extraordinary expenditures become unavoidable. During the existence of the war with Mexico all our resources should be husbanded, and no appropriations made except such as are absolutely necessary for its vigorous prosecution and the due administration of the Government. Objects of appropriation which in peace may be deemed useful or proper, but which are not indispensable for the public service, may when the country is engaged in a foreign war be well postponed to a future period. By the observance of this policy at your present session large amounts may be saved to the Treasury and be applied to objects of pressing and urgent necessity, and thus the creation of a corresponding amount of public debt may be avoided.

It is not meant to recommend that the ordinary and necessary appropriations for the support of Government should be withheld; but it is well known that at every session of Congress appropriations are proposed for numerous objects which may or may not be made without materially affecting the public interests, and these it is recommended should not be granted.

The act passed at your last session "reducing the duties on imports" not having gone into operation until the 1st of the present month, there has not been time for its practical effect upon the revenue and the business of the country to be developed. It is not doubted, however, that the just policy which it adopts will add largely to our foreign trade and promote the general prosperity. Although it can not be certainly foreseen what amount of revenue it will yield, it is estimated that it will exceed that produced by the act of 1842, which it superseded. The leading principles established by it are to levy the taxes with a view to raise revenue and to impose them upon the articles imported according to their actual value.

The act of 1842, by the excessive rates of duty which it imposed on many articles, either totally excluded them from importation or greatly reduced the amount imported, and thus diminished instead of producing revenue. By it the taxes were imposed not for the legitimate purpose of raising revenue, but to afford advantages to favored classes at the expense of a large majority of their fellow-citizens. Those employed in agriculture, mechanical pursuits, commerce, and navigation were compelled to contribute from their substance to swell the profits and overgrown wealth of the comparatively few who had invested their capital in manufactures. The taxes were not levied in proportion to the value of the articles upon which they were imposed, but, widely departing from this just rule, the lighter taxes were in many cases levied upon articles of luxury and high price and the heavier taxes on those of necessity and low price, consumed by the great mass of the people. It was a system the inevitable effect of which was to relieve favored classes and the wealthy few from contributing their just proportion for the support of Government, and to lay the burden on the labor of the many engaged in other pursuits than manufactures.

A system so unequal and unjust has been superseded by the existing law, which imposes duties not for the benefit or injury of classes or pursuits, but distributes and, as far as practicable, equalizes the public burdens among all classes and occupations. The favored classes who under the unequal and unjust system which has been repealed have heretofore realized large profits, and many of them amassed large fortunes at the expense of the many who have been made tributary to them, will have no reason to complain if they shall be required to bear their just proportion of the taxes necessary for the support of Government. So far from it, it will be perceived by an examination of the existing law that discriminations in the rates of duty imposed within the revenue principle have been retained in their favor. The incidental aid against foreign competition which they still enjoy gives them an advantage which no other pursuits possess, but of this none others will complain, because the duties levied are necessary for revenue. These revenue duties, including freights and charges, which the importer must pay before he can come in competition with the home manufacturer in our markets, amount on nearly all our leading branches of manufacture to more than one-third of the value of the imported article, and in some cases to almost one-half its value. With such advantages it is not doubted that our domestic manufacturers will continue to prosper, realizing in well-conducted establishments even greater profits than can be derived from any other regular business. Indeed, so far from requiring the protection of even incidental revenue duties, our manufacturers in several leading branches are extending their business, giving evidence of great ingenuity and skill and of their ability to compete, with increased prospect of success, for the open market of the world. Domestic manufactures to the value of several millions of dollars, which can not find a market at home, are annually exported to foreign countries. With such rates of duty as those established by the existing law the system will probably be permanent, and capitalists who are made or shall hereafter make their investments in manufactures will know upon what to rely. The country will be satisfied with these rates, because the advantages which the manufacturers still enjoy result necessarily from the collection of revenue for the support of Government. High protective duties, from their unjust operation upon the masses of the people, can not fail to give rise to extensive dissatisfaction and complaint and to constant efforts to change or repeal them, rendering all investments in manufactures uncertain and precarious. Lower and more permanent rates of duty, at the same time that they will yield to the manufacturer fair and remunerating profits, will secure him against the danger of frequent changes in the system, which can not fail to ruinously affect his interests.

Simultaneously with the relaxation of the restrictive policy by the United States, Great Britain, from whose example we derived the system, has relaxed hers. She has modified her corn laws and reduced many other duties to moderate revenue rates. After ages of experience the statesmen of that country have been constrained by a stern necessity and by a public opinion having its deep foundation in the sufferings and wants of impoverished millions to abandon a system the effect of which was to build up immense fortunes in the hands of the few and to reduce the laboring millions to pauperism and misery. Nearly in the same ratio that labor was depressed capital was increased and concentrated by the British protective policy.

The evils of the system in Great Britain were at length rendered intolerable, and it has been abandoned, but not without a severe struggle on the part of the protected and favored classes to retain the unjust advantages which they have so long enjoyed. It was to be expected that a similar struggle would be made by the same classes in the United States whenever an attempt was made to modify or abolish the same unjust system here. The protective policy had been in operation in the United States for a much shorter period, and its pernicious effects were not, therefore, so clearly perceived and felt. Enough, however, was known of these effects to induce its repeal.

It would be strange if in the face of the example of *Great Britain,* our principal foreign customer, and of the evils of a system rendered manifest in that country by long and painful experience, and in the face of the immense advantages which under a more liberal commercial policy we are already deriving, and must continue to derive, by supplying her starving population with food, the United States should restore a policy which she has been compelled to abandon, and thus diminish her ability to purchase from us the food and other articles which she so much needs and we so much desire to sell. By the simultaneous abandonment of the protective policy by Great Britain and the United States new and important markets have already been opened for our agricultural and other products, commerce and navigation have received a new impulse, labor and trade have been released from the artificial trammels which have so long fettered them, and to a great extent reciprocity in the exchange of commodities has been introduced at the same time by both countries, and greatly for the benefit of both. Great Britain has been forced by the pressure of circumstances at home to abandon a policy which has been upheld for ages, and to open her markets for our immense surplus of breadstuffs, and it is confidently believed that other powers of Europe will ultimately see the wisdom, if they be not compelled by the pauperism and sufferings of their crowded population, to pursue a similar policy.

Our farmers are more deeply interested in maintaining the just and liberal policy of the existing law than any other class of our citizens. They constitute a large majority of our population, and it is well known that when they prosper all other pursuits prosper also. They have heretofore not only received none of the bounties or favors of Government, but by the unequal operations of the protective policy have been made by the burdens of taxation which it imposed to contribute to the bounties which have enriched others.

When a foreign as well as a home market is opened to them, they must receive, as they are now receiving, increased prices for their products. They will find a readier sale, and at better prices, for their wheat, flour, rice, Indian corn, beef, pork, lard, butter, cheese, and other articles which they produce. The home market alone is inadequate to enable them to dispose of the immense surplus of food and other articles which they are capable of producing, even at the most reduced prices, for the manifest reason that they can not be consumed in the country. The United States can from their immense surplus supply not only the home demand, but the deficiencies of food required by the whole world.

That the reduced production of some of the chief articles of food in Great Britain and other parts of Europe may have contributed to increase the demand for our breadstuffs and provisions is not doubted, but that the great and efficient cause of this increased demand and of increased prices consists in the removal of artificial restrictions heretofore imposed is deemed to be equally certain. That our exports of food, already increased and increasing beyond former example under the more liberal policy which has been adopted, will be still vastly enlarged unless they be checked or prevented by a restoration of the protective policy can not be doubted. That our commercial and navigating interests will be enlarged in a corresponding ratio with the increase of our trade is equally certain, while our manufacturing interests will still be the favored interests of the country and receive the incidental protection afforded them by revenue duties; and more than this they can not justly demand.

In my annual message of December last a tariff of revenue duties based upon the principles of the existing law was recommended, and I have seen no reason to change the opinions then expressed. In view of the probable beneficial effects of that law, I recommend that the policy established by it be maintained. It has but just commenced to operate, and to abandon or modify it without giving it a fair trial would be inexpedient and unwise. Should defects in any of its details be ascertained by actual experience to exist, these may be hereafter corrected; but until such defects shall become manifest the act should be fairly tested.

It is submitted for your consideration whether it may not be proper, as a war measure, to impose revenue duties on some of the articles now embraced in the free list. Should it be deemed proper to impose such duties with a view to raise revenue to meet the expenses of the war with Mexico or to avoid to that extent the creation of a public debt, they may be repealed when the emergency which gave rise to them shall cease to exist, and constitute no part of the permanent policy of the country.

The act of the 6th of August last, "to provide for the better organization of the Treasury and for the collection, safe-keeping, transfer, and disbursement of the public revenue," has been carried into execution as rapidly as the delay necessarily arising out of the appointment of new officers, taking and approving their bonds, and preparing and securing proper places for the safe-keeping of the public money would permit. It is not proposed to depart in any respect from the principles or policy on which this great measure is founded. There are, however, defects in the details of the measure, developed by its practical operation, which are fully set forth in the report of the Secretary of the Treasury, to which the attention of Congress is invited. These defects would impair to some extent the successful operation of the law at all times, but are especially embarrassing when the country is engaged in a war, when the expenditures are greatly increased, when loans are to be effected and the disbursements are to be made at points many hundred miles distant, in some cases, from any depository, and a large portion of them in a foreign country. The modifications suggested in the report of the Secretary of the Treasury are recommended to your favorable consideration.

In connection with this subject I invite your attention to the importance of establishing a branch of the Mint of the United States at New York. Two-thirds of the revenue derived from customs being collected at that point, the demand for specie to pay the duties will be large, and a branch mint where foreign coin and bullion could be immediately converted into American coin would greatly facilitate the transaction of the public business, enlarge the circulation of gold and silver, and be at the same time a safe depository of the public money.

The importance of graduating and reducing the price of such of the public lands as have been long offered in the market at the minimum rate authorized by existing laws, and remain unsold, induces me again to recommend the subject to your favorable consideration. Many millions of acres of these lands have been offered in the market for more than thirty years and larger quantities for more than ten or twenty years, and, being of an inferior quality, they must remain unsalable for an indefinite period unless the price at which they may be purchased shall be reduced. To place a price upon them above their real value is not only to prevent their sale, and thereby deprive the Treasury of any income from that source, but is unjust to the States in which they lie, because it retards their growth and increase of population, and because they have no power to levy a tax upon them as upon other lands within their limits, held by other proprietors than the United States, for the support of their local governments.

The beneficial effects of the graduation principle have been realized by some of the States owning the lands within their limits in which it has been adopted. They have been demonstrated also by the United States acting as the trustee of the Chickasaw tribe of Indians in the sale of their lands lying within the States of Mississippi and Alabama. The Chickasaw lands, which would not command in the market the minimum price established by the laws of the United States for the sale of their lands, were, in pursuance of the treaty of 1834 with that tribe, subsequently offered for sale at graduated and reduced rates for limited periods. The result was that large quantities of these lands were purchased which would otherwise have remained unsold. The lands were disposed of at their real value, and many persons of limited means were enabled to purchase small tracts, upon which they have settled with their families. That similar results would be produced by the adoption of the graduation policy by the United States in all the States in which they are the owners of large bodies of lands which have been long in the market can not be doubted. It can not be a sound policy to withhold large quantities of the public lands from the use and occupation of our citizens by fixing upon them prices which experience has shown they will not command. On the contrary, it is a wise policy to afford facilities to our citizens to become the owners at low and moderate rates of freeholds of their own instead of being the tenants and dependents of others. If it be apprehended that these lands if reduced in price would be secured in large quantities by speculators or capitalists, the sales may be restricted in limited quantities to actual settlers or persons purchasing for purposes of cultivation.

In my last annual message I submitted for the consideration of Congress the present system of managing the mineral lands of the United States, and recommended that they should be brought into market and sold upon such terms and under such restrictions as Congress might prescribe. By the act of the 11th of July last "the reserved lead mines and contiguous lands in the States of Illinois and Arkansas and Territories of Wisconsin and Iowa" were authorized to be sold. The act is confined in its operation to "lead mines and contiguous lands." A large portion of the public lands, containing copper and other ores, is represented to be very valuable, and I recommend that provision be made authorizing the sale of these lands upon such terms and conditions as from their supposed value may in the judgment of Congress be deemed advisable, having due regard to the interests of such of our citizens as may be located upon them.

It will be important during your present session to establish a Territorial government and to extend the jurisdiction and laws of the United States over the Territory of Oregon. Our laws regulating trade and intercourse with the Indian tribes east of the Rocky Mountains should be extended to the Pacific Ocean; and for the purpose of executing them and preserving friendly relations with the Indian tribes within our limits, an additional number of Indian agencies will be required, and should be authorized by law. The establishment of custom-houses and of post-offices and post-roads and provision for the transportation of the mail on such routes as the public convenience will suggest require legislative authority. It will be proper also to establish a surveyor-general's office in that Territory and to make the necessary provision for surveying the public lands and bringing them into market. As our citizens who now reside in that distant region have been subjected to many hardships, privations, and sacrifices in their emigration, and by their improvements have enhanced the value of the public lands in the neighborhood of their settlements, it is recommended that liberal grants be made to them of such portions of these lands as they may occupy, and that similar grants or rights of preemption be made to all who may emigrate thither within a limited period, prescribed by law.

The report of the Secretary of War contains detailed information relative to the several branches of the public service connected with that Department. The operations of the Army have been of a satisfactory and highly gratifying character. I recommend to your early and favorable consideration the measures proposed by the Secretary of War for speedily filling up the rank and file of the Regular Army, for its greater efficiency in the field, and for raising an additional force to serve during the war with Mexico.

Embarrassment is likel. to arise for want of legal provision authorizing compensation to be made to the agents employed in the several States and Territories to pay the Revolutionary and other pensioners the amounts allowed them by law. Your attention is invited to the recommendations of the Secretary of War on this subject. These agents incur heavy responsibilities and perform important duties, and no reason exists why they should not be placed on the same footing as to compensation with other disbursing officers.

Our relations with the various Indian tribes continue to be of a pacific character. The unhappy dissensions which have existed among the Cherokees for many years past have been healed. Since my last annual message important treaties have been negotiated with some of the tribes, by which the Indian title to large tracts of valuable land within the limits of the States and Territories has been extinguished and arrangements made for removing them to the country west of the Mississippi. Between 3,000 and 4,000 of different tribes have been removed to the country provided for them by treaty stipulations, and arrangements have been made for others to follow.

In our intercourse with the several tribes particular attention has been given to the important subject of education. The number of schools established among them has been increased, and additional means provided not only for teaching them the rudiments of education, but of instructing them in agriculture and the mechanic arts.

I refer you to the report of the Secretary of the Navy for a satisfactory view of the operations of the Department under his charge during the past year. It is gratifying to perceive that while the war with Mexico has rendered it necessary to employ an unusual number of our armed vessels on her coasts, the protection due to our commerce in other quarters of the world has not proved insufficient. No means will be spared to give efficiency to the naval service in the prosecution of the war; and I am happy to know that the officers and men anxiously desire to devote themselves to the service of their country in any enterprise, however difficult of execution.

I recommend to your favorable consideration the proposition to add to each of our foreign squadrons an efficient sea steamer, and, as especially demanding attention, the establishment at Pensacola of the necessary means of repairing and refitting the vessels of the Navy employed in the Gulf of Mexico.

There are other suggestions in the report which deserve and I doubt not will receive your consideration.

The progress and condition of the mail service for the past year are fully presented in the report of the Postmaster-General. The revenue for the year ending on the 30th of June last amounted to $3,487,199, which is $802,642.45 less than that of the preceding year. The payments for that Department during the same time amounted to $4,084,297.22. Of this sum $597,097.80 have been drawn from the Treasury. The disbursements for the year were $236,434.77 less than those of the preceding year. While the disbursements have been thus diminished, the mail facilities have been enlarged by new mail routes of 5,739 miles, an increase of transportation of 1,764,145 miles, and the establishment of 418 new post-offices. Contractors, postmasters, and others engaged in this branch of the service have performed their duties with energy and faithfulness deserving commendation. For many interesting details connected with the operations of this establishment you are referred to the report of the Postmaster-General, and his suggestions for improving its revenues are recommended to your favorable consideration. I repeat the opinion expressed in my last annual message that the business of this Department should be so regulated that the revenues derived from it should be made to equal the expenditures, and it is believed that this may be done by proper modifications of the present laws, as suggested in the report of the Postmaster-General, without changing the present rates of postage.

With full reliance upon the wisdom and patriotism of your deliberations, it will be my duty, as it will be my anxious desire, to cooperate with you in every constitutional effort to promote the welfare and maintain the honor of our common country.   JAMES K. POLK.

SPECIAL MESSAGES.

WASHINGTON, *December 14, 1846.*

To the Senate of the United States:

I transmit to the Senate, for their consideration and advice with regard to its ratification, a convention for the mutual surrender of criminals between the United States and the Swiss Confederation, signed by their respective plenipotentiaries on the 15th of September last at Paris.

I transmit also a copy of a dispatch from the plenipotentiary of the United States, with the accompanying documents.

JAMES K. POLK.

WASHINGTON, *December 22, 1846.*

To the House of Representatives of the United States:

In compliance with the request contained in the resolution of the House of Representatives of the 15th instant, I communicate herewith reports from the Secretary of War and the Secretary of the Navy, with the documents which accompany them.

These documents contain all the "orders or instructions" to any military, naval, or other officer of the Government "in relation to the establishment or organization of civil government in any portion of the territory of Mexico which has or might be taken possession of by the Army or Navy of the United States."

These orders and instructions were given to regulate the exercise of the rights of a belligerent engaged in actual war over such portions of the territory of our enemy as by military conquest might be "taken possession of" and be occupied by our armed forces—rights necessarily resulting from a state of war and clearly recognized by the laws of nations. This was all the authority which could be delegated to our military and naval commanders, and its exercise was indispensable to the secure occupation and possession of territory of the enemy which might be conquered. The regulations authorized were temporary, and dependent on the rights acquired by conquest. They were authorized as belligerent rights, and were to be carried into effect by military or naval officers. They were but the amelioration of martial law, which modern civilization requires, and were due as well to the security of the conquest as to the inhabitants of the conquered territory.

The documents communicated also contain the reports of several highly meritorious officers of our Army and Navy who have conquered and taken possession of portions of the enemy's territory.

Among the documents accompanying the report of the Secretary of War will be found a "form of government" "established and organized" by the military commander who conquered and occupied with his forces the Territory of New Mexico. This document was received at the War Department in the latter part of the last month, and, as will be perceived by the report of the Secretary of War, was not, for the reasons stated by that officer, brought to my notice until after my annual message of the 8th instant was communicated to Congress.

It is declared on its face to be a "temporary government of the said Territory," but there are portions of it which purport to "establish and organize" a permanent Territorial government of the United States over the Territory and to impart to its inhabitants political rights which under the Constitution of the United States can be enjoyed permanently only by citizens of the United States. These have not been "approved and recognized" by me. Such organized regulations as have been established in any of the conquered territories for the security of our conquest, for the preservation of order, for the protection of the rights of the inhabitants, and for depriving the enemy of the advantages of these territories while the military possession of them by the forces of the United States continues will be recognized and approved.

It will be apparent from the reports of the officers who have been required by the success which has crowned their arms to exercise the powers of temporary government over the conquered territories that if any excess of power has been exercised the departure has been the offspring of a patriotic desire to give to the inhabitants the privileges and immunities so cherished by the people of our own country, and which they believed calculated to improve their condition and promote their prosperity. Any such excess has resulted in no practical injury, but can and will be early corrected in a manner to alienate as little as possible the good feelings of the inhabitants of the conquered territory.

JAMES K. POLK.

WASHINGTON, *December 29, 1846.*

To the Senate and House of Representatives of the United States:

In order to prosecute the war against Mexico with vigor and success, it is necessary that authority should be promptly given by Congress to increase the Regular Army and to remedy existing defects in its organization. With this view your favorable attention is invited to the annual report of the Secretary of War, which accompanied my message of the 8th instant, in which he recommends that ten additional regiments of regular troops shall be raised, to serve during the war.

Of the additional regiments of volunteers which have been called for from several of the States, some have been promptly raised; but this has not been the case in regard to all. The existing law, requiring that they should be organized by the independent action of the State governments, has in some instances occasioned considerable delay, and it is yet uncertain when the troops required can be ready for service in the field.

It is our settled policy to maintain in time of peace as small a Regular Army as the exigencies of the public service will permit. In a state of war, notwithstanding the great advantage with which our volunteer citizen soldiers can be brought into the field, this small Regular Army must be increased in its numbers in order to render the whole force more efficient.

Additional officers as well as men then become indispensable. Under the circumstances of our service a peculiar propriety exists for increasing the officers, especially in the higher grades. The number of such officers who from age and other causes are rendered incapable of active service in the field has seriously impaired the efficiency of the Army.

From the report of the Secretary of War it appears that about two-thirds of the whole number of regimental field officers are either permanently disabled or are necessarily detached from their commands on other duties. The long enjoyment of peace has prevented us from experiencing much embarrassment from this cause, but now, in a state of war, conducted in a foreign country, it has produced serious injury to the public service.

An efficient organization of the Army, composed of regulars and volunteers, whilst prosecuting the war in Mexico, it is believed would require the appointment of a general officer to take the command of all our military forces in the field. Upon the conclusion of the war the services of such an officer would no longer be necessary, and should be dispensed with upon the reduction of the Army to a peace establishment.

I recommend that provision be made by law for the appointment of such a general officer to serve during the war.

It is respectfully recommended that early action should be had by Congress upon the suggestions submitted for their consideration, as necessary to insure active and efficient service in prosecuting the war, before the present favorable season for military operations in the enemy's country shall have passed away.

JAMES K. POLK.

WASHINGTON, *January 4, 1847.*

To the Senate of the United States:

I communicate herewith a report of the Postmaster-General, which contains the information called for by the resolution of the Senate of the 16th instant, in relation to the means which have been taken for the transmission of letters and papers to and from the officers and soldiers now in the service of the United States in Mexico. In answer to the inquiry whether any legislation is necessary to secure the speedy transmission and delivery of such letters and papers, I refer you to the suggestions of the Postmaster-General, which are recommended to your favorable consideration.

JAMES K. POLK.

WASHINGTON, *January 11, 1847.*

To the Senate of the United States:

In answer to the resolution of the Senate of the 22d ultimo, calling for information relative to the negotiation of the treaty of commerce with the Republic of New Granada signed on the 20th of December, 1844, I transmit a report from the Secretary of State and the documents by which it was accompanied.

JAMES K. POLK.

WASHINGTON, *January 19, 1847.*

To the House of Representatives of the United States:

I transmit herewith a report of the Secretary of War, with the accompanying report from the Adjutant-General of the Army, made in compliance with the resolution of the House of Representatives of the 5th instant, requesting the President to communicate to the House "the whole number of volunteers which have been mustered into the service of the United States since the 1st day of May last, designating the number mustered for three months, six months, and twelve months; the number of those who have been discharged before they served two months, number discharged after two months' service, and the number of volunteer officers who have resigned, and the dates of their resignations."

JAMES K. POLK.

WASHINGTON, *January 20, 1847.*

To the House of Representatives of the United States:

I communicate herewith a letter received from the president of the convention of delegates of the people of Wisconsin, transmitting a certified copy of the constitution adopted by the delegates of the people of Wisconsin in convention assembled, also a copy of the act of the legislature of the Territory of Wisconsin providing for the calling of said convention, and also a copy of the last census, showing the number of inhabitants in said Territory, requesting the President to "lay the same before the Congress of the United States with the request that Congress act upon the same at its present session."

JAMES K. POLK.

WASHINGTON, *January 25, 1847.*

To the House of Representatives of the United States:

I communicate herewith a report of the Secretary of the Treasury, accompanied by a statement of the Register of the Treasury prepared in compliance with a resolution of the House of Representatives of the 7th instant, requesting the President "to furnish the House with a statement showing the whole amount allowed and paid at the Treasury during the year ending 30th June, 1846, for postages of the Executive Departments of the Government and for the several officers and persons authorized by the act approved 3d March, 1846, to send or receive matter through the mails free, including the amount allowed or allowable, if charged in the postages of any officers or agents, military, naval, or civil, employed in or by any of said Departments." It will be perceived that said statement is as full and accurate as can be made during the present session of Congress.

JAMES K. POLK.

WASHINGTON, *January 29, 1847.*

To the House of Representatives of the United States:

I communicate herewith a report of the Secretary of War, together with reports of the Adjutant-General and Paymaster-General of the Army, in answer to a resolution of the House of Representatives of the 20th instant, requesting the President to communicate to the House "whether any, and, if any, which, of the Representatives named in the list annexed have held any office or offices under the United States since the commencement of the Twenty-ninth Congress, designating the office or offices held by each, and whether the same are now so held, and including in said information the names of all who are now serving in the Army of the United States as officers and receiving pay as such, and when and by whom they were commissioned."

JAMES K. POLK.

WASHINGTON, *February 3, 1847.*

To the Senate of the United States:

I communicate herewith reports of the Secretary of War and the Secretary of the Treasury, with accompanying documents, in answer to a resolution of the Senate "requesting the President to inform the Senate whether any funds of the Government, and, if any, what amount, have been remitted from the Atlantic States to New Orleans or to the disbursing officers of the American Army in Mexico since the 1st of September last, and, if any remitted, in what funds remitted, whether in gold or silver coin, Treasury notes, bank notes, or bank checks, and, if in whole or in part remitted in gold and silver, what has been the expense to the Government of each of said remittances.''

JAMES K. POLK.

WASHINGTON, *February 10, 1847.*

To the Senate of the United States:

I transmit to the Senate, for their advice with regard to its ratification, ''a general treaty of peace, amity, navigation, and commerce between the United States of America and the Republic of New Granada,'' concluded at Bogota on the 12th December last by Benjamin A. Bidlack, chargé d'affaires of the United States, on their part, and by Manuel Maria Mallarino, secretary of state and foreign relations, on the part of that Republic.

It will be perceived by the thirty-fifth article of this treaty that New Granada proposes to guarantee to the Government and citizens of the United States the right of passage across the Isthmus of Panama over the natural roads and over any canal or railroad which may be constructed to unite the two seas, on condition that the United States shall make a similar guaranty to New Granada of the neutrality of this portion of her territory and her sovereignty over the same.

The reasons which caused the insertion of this important stipulation in the treaty will be fully made known to the Senate by the accompanying documents. From these it will appear that our chargé d'affaires acted in this particular upon his own responsibility and without instructions. Under such circumstances it became my duty to decide whether I would submit the treaty to the Senate, and after mature consideration I have determined to adopt this course.

The importance of this concession to the commercial and political interests of the United States can not easily be overrated. The route by the Isthmus of Panama is the shortest between the two oceans, and from the information herewith communicated it would seem to be the most practicable for a railroad or canal.

The vast advantages to our commerce which would result from such a communication, not only with the west coast of America, but with Asia and the islands of the Pacific, are too obvious to require any detail. Such a passage would relieve us from a long and dangerous navigation of more than 9,000 miles around Cape Horn and render our communication with our possessions on the northwest coast of America comparatively easy and speedy.

The communication across the Isthmus has attracted the attention of the Government of the United States ever since the independence of the South American Republics.   On the 3d of March, 1835, a resolution passed the Senate in the following words:

Resolved, That the President of the United States be respectfully requested to consider the expediency of opening negotiations with the governments of other nations, and particularly with the Governments of Central America and New Granada, for the purpose of effectually protecting, by suitable treaty stipulations with them, such individuals or companies as may undertake to open a communication between the Atlantic and Pacific oceans by the construction of a ship canal across the isthmus which connects North and South America, and of securing forever by such stipulations the free and equal right of navigating such canal to all nations on the payment of such reasonable tolls as may be established to compensate the capitalists who may engage in such undertaking and complete the work.

No person can be more deeply sensible than myself of the danger of entangling alliances with any foreign nation.   That we should avoid such alliances has become a maxim of our policy consecrated by the most venerated names which adorn our history and sanctioned by the unanimous voice of the American people.   Our own experience has taught us the wisdom of this maxim in the only instance, that of the guaranty to France of her American possessions, in which we have ever entered into such an alliance.   If, therefore, the very peculiar circumstances of the present case do not greatly impair, if not altogether destroy, the force of this objection, then we ought not to enter into the stipulation, whatever may be its advantages.   The general considerations which have induced me to transmit the treaty to the Senate for their advice may be summed up in the following particulars:

1. The treaty does not propose to guarantee a territory to a foreign nation in which the United States will have no common interest with that nation.   On the contrary, we are more deeply and directly interested in the subject of this guaranty than New Granada herself or any other country.

2. The guaranty does not extend to the territories of New Granada generally, but is confined to the single Province of the Isthmus of Panama, where we shall acquire by the treaty a common and coextensive right of passage with herself.

3. It will constitute no alliance for any political object, but for a purely commercial purpose, in which all the navigating nations of the world have a common interest.

4. In entering into the mutual guaranties proposed by the thirty-fifth article of the treaty neither the Government of New Granada nor that of the United States has any narrow or exclusive views.   The ultimate object, as presented by the Senate of the United States in their resolution to which I have already referred, is to secure to all nations the free and equal right of passage over the Isthmus.   If the United States, as the chief of the American nations, should first become a party to this guaranty, it can not be doubted—indeed, it is confidently expected by the Government of New Granada—that similar guaranties will be given to that Republic

by Great Britain and France. Should the proposition thus tendered be rejected we may deprive the United States of the just influence which its acceptance might secure to them and confer the glory and benefits of being the first among the nations in concluding such an arrangement upon the Government either of Great Britain or France. That either of these Governments would embrace the offer can not be doubted, because there does not appear to be any other effectual means of securing to all nations the advantages of this important passage but the guaranty of great commercial powers that the Isthmus shall be neutral territory. The interests of the world at stake are so important that the security of this passage between the two oceans can not be suffered to depend upon the wars and revolutions which may arise among different nations.

Besides, such a guaranty is almost indispensable to the construction of a railroad or canal across the territory. Neither sovereign states nor individuals would expend their capital in the construction of these expensive works without some such security for their investments.

The guaranty of the sovereignty of New Granada over the Isthmus is a natural consequence of the guaranty of its neutrality, and there does not seem to be any other practicable mode of securing the neutrality of this territory. New Granada would not consent to yield up this Province in order that it might become a neutral state, and if she should it is not sufficiently populous or wealthy to establish and maintain an independent sovereignty. But a civil government must exist there in order to protect the works which shall be constructed. New Granada is a power which will not excite the jealousy of any nation. If Great Britain, France, or the United States held the sovereignty over the Isthmus, other nations might apprehend that in case of war the Government would close up the passage against the enemy, but no such fears can ever be entertained in regard to New Granada.

This treaty removes the heavy discriminating duties against us in the ports of New Granada, which have nearly destroyed our commerce and navigation with that Republic, and which we have been in vain endeavoring to abolish for the last twenty years.

It may be proper also to call the attention of the Senate to the twenty-fifth article of the treaty, which prohibits privateering in case of war between the two Republics, and also to the additional article, which nationalizes all vessels of the parties which "shall be provided by the respective Governments with a patent issued according to its laws," and in this particular goes further than any of our former treaties.

JAMES K. POLK.

WASHINGTON, *February 13, 1847.*

To the Senate and House of Representatives of the United States:

Congress, by the act of the 13th of May last, declared that "by the act of the Republic of Mexico a state of war exists between that Government and the United States," and "for the purpose of enabling the

Government of the United States to prosecute said war to a speedy and successful termination" authority was vested in the President to employ the "naval and military forces of the United States."

It has been my unalterable purpose since the commencement of hostilities by Mexico and the declaration of the existence of war by Congress to prosecute the war in which the country was unavoidably involved with the utmost energy, with a view to its "speedy and successful termination" by an honorable peace. ·

Accordingly all the operations of our naval and military forces have been directed with this view. While the sword has been held in one hand and our military movements pressed forward into the enemy's country and its coasts invested by our Navy, the tender of an honorable peace has been constantly presented to Mexico in the other.

Hitherto the overtures of peace which have been made by this Government have not been accepted by Mexico. With a view to avoid a protracted war, which hesitancy and delay on our part would be so well calculated to produce, I informed you in my annual message of the 8th December last that the war would "continue to be prosecuted with vigor, as the best means of securing peace," and recommended to your early and favorable consideration the measures proposed by the Secretary of War in his report accompanying that message.

In my message of the 4th January last these and other measures deemed to be essential to the "speedy and successful termination" of the war and the attainment of a just and honorable peace were recommended to your early and favorable consideration.   :

The worst state of things which could exist in a war with such a power as Mexico would be a course of indecision and inactivity on our part. Being charged by the Constitution and the laws with the conduct of the war, I have availed myself of all the means at my command to prosecute it with energy and vigor.

The act "to raise for a limited time an additional military force, and for other purposes," and which authorizes the raising of ten additional regiments to the Regular Army, to serve during the war and to be disbanded at its termination, which was presented to me on the 11th instant and approved on that day, will constitute an important part of our military force. These regiments will be raised and moved to the seat of war with the least practicable delay.

It will be perceived that this act makes no provision for the organization into brigades and divisions of the increased force which it authorizes, nor for the appointment of general officers to command it. It will be proper that authority be given by law to make such organization, and to appoint, by and with the advice and consent of the Senate, such number of major-generals and brigadier-generals as the efficiency of the service may demand. The number of officers of these grades now in service are not more than are required for their respective commands; but further legislative action during your present session will, in my judgment, be required, and to which it is my duty respectfully to invite your attention.

Should the war, contrary to my earnest desire, be protracted to the close of the term of service of the volunteers now in Mexico, who engaged for twelve months, an additional volunteer force will probably become necessary to supply their place. Many of the volunteers now serving in Mexico, it is not doubted, will cheerfully engage at the conclusion of their present term to serve during the war. They would constitute a more efficient force than could be speedily obtained by accepting the services of any new corps who might offer their services. They would have the advantage of the experience and discipline of a year's service, and will have become accustomed to the climate and be in less danger than new levies of suffering from the diseases of the country. I recommend, therefore, that authority be given to accept the services of such of the volunteers now in Mexico as the state of the public service may require, and who may at the termination of their present term voluntarily engage to serve during the war with Mexico, and that provision be made for commissioning the officers. Should this measure receive the favorable consideration of Congress, it is recommended that a bounty be granted to them upon their voluntarily extending their term of service. This would not only be due to these gallant men, but it would be economy to the Government, because if discharged at the end of the twelve months the Government would be bound to incur a heavy expense in bringing them back to their homes and in sending to the seat of war new corps of fresh troops to supply their place.

By the act of the 13th of May last the President was authorized to accept the services of volunteers "in companies, battalions, squadrons, and regiments," but no provision was made for filling up vacancies which might occur by death or discharges from the service on account of sickness or other casualties. In consequence of this omission many of the corps now in service have been much reduced in numbers. Nor was any provision made for filling vacancies of regimental or company officers who might die or resign. Information has been received at the War Department of the resignation of more than 100 of these officers. They were appointed by the State authorities, and no information has been received except in a few instances that their places have been filled; and the efficiency of the service has been impaired from this cause. To remedy these defects, I recommend that authority be given to accept the services of individual volunteers to fill up the places of such as may die or become unfit for the service and be discharged, and that provision be also made for filling the places of regimental and company officers who may die or resign. By such provisions the volunteer corps may be constantly kept full or may approximate the maximum number authorized and called into service in the first instance.

While it is deemed to be our true policy to prosecute the war in the manner indicated, and thus make the enemy feel its pressure and its evils, I shall be at all times ready, with the authority conferred on me by the Constitution and with all the means which may be placed at my command by Congress, to conclude a just and honorable peace.

Of equal importance with an energetic and vigorous prosecution of the war are the means required to defray its expenses and to uphold and maintain the public credit.

In my annual message of the 8th December last I submitted for the consideration of Congress the propriety of imposing, as a war measure, revenue duties on some of the articles now embraced in the free list. The principal articles now exempt from duty from which any considerable revenue could be derived are tea and coffee. A moderate revenue duty on these articles it is estimated would produce annually an amount exceeding $2,500,000. Though in a period of peace, when ample means could be derived from duties on other articles for the support of the Government, it may have been deemed proper not to resort to a duty on these articles, yet when the country is engaged in a foreign war and all our resources are demanded to meet the unavoidable increased expenditure in maintaining our armies in the field no sound reason is perceived why we should not avail ourselves of the revenues which may be derived from this source. The objections which have heretofore existed to the imposition of these duties were applicable to a state of peace, when they were not needed. We are now, however, engaged in a foreign war. We need money to prosecute it and to maintain the public honor and credit. It can not be doubted that the patriotic people of the United States would cheerfully and without complaint submit to the payment of this additional duty or any other that may be necessary to maintain the honor of the country, provide for the unavoidable expenses of the Government, and to uphold the public credit. It is recommended that any duties which may be imposed on these articles be limited in their duration to the period of the war.

An additional annual revenue, it is estimated, of between half a million and a million of dollars would be derived from the graduation and reduction of the price of such of the public lands as have been long offered in the market at the minimum price established by the existing laws and have remained unsold. And in addition to other reasons commending the measure to favorable consideration, it is recommended as a financial measure. The duty suggested on tea and coffee and the graduation and reduction of the price of the public lands would secure an additional annual revenue to the Treasury of not less than $3,000,000, and would thereby prevent the necessity of incurring a public debt annually to that amount, the interest on which must be paid semiannually, and ultimately the debt itself by a tax on the people.

It is a sound policy and one which has long been approved by the Government and people of the United States never to resort to loans unless in cases of great public emergency, and then only for the smallest amount which the public necessities will permit.

The increased revenues which the measures now recommended would produce would, moreover, enable the Government to negotiate a loan for any additional sum which may be found to be needed with more facility and at cheaper rates than can be done without them.

Under the injunction of the Constitution which makes it my duty "from time to time to give to Congress information of the state of the Union and to recommend to their consideration such measures" as shall be judged "necessary and expedient," I respectfully and earnestly invite the action of Congress on the measures herein presented for their consideration. The public good, as well as a sense of my responsibility to our common constituents, in my judgment imperiously demands that I should present them for your enlightened consideration and invoke favorable action upon them before the close of your present session.

JAMES K. POLK.

WASHINGTON, February 13, 1847.

To the Senate of the United States:

I nominate the officers named in the accompanying communication for regular promotion in the Army of the United States, as proposed by the Secretary of War.

JAMES K. POLK.

WAR DEPARTMENT,
Washington, February 13, 1847.

The PRESIDENT OF THE UNITED STATES.

SIR: I have the honor respectfully to propose for your approbation the following-named captains* for promotion to the rank of major in the existing regiments of the Army, in conformity with the third section of the act approved February 11, 1847, which authorizes one additional major to each of the regiments of dragoons, artillery, infantry, and riflemen.

The promotions are all regular with one exception, that of Captain Washington Seawell, of the Seventh Infantry, instead of Captain Edgar Hawkins, of the same regiment, who stands at the head of the list of his grade in the infantry arm. Captain Hawkins, who distinguished himself in the defense of Fort Brown, is passed over on the ground of mental alienation, it being officially reported that he is "insane," on which account he was recently sent from the Army in Mexico. He is now in New York, and is reported to be "unable to perform any duty." An officer just returned from the Army in Mexico, and who had recently served with Captain Hawkins, informed the Adjutant-General that he was quite deranged, but that he had hopes of his recovery, as the malady was probably caused by sickness. Should these hopes be realized at some future day, Captain Hawkins will then of course be promoted without loss of rank; meanwhile I respectfully recommend that he be passed over, as the declared object of these additional majors (as set forth in the Adjutant-General's report to this Department of the 30th of July last) was to insure the presence of an adequate number of *efficient* field officers for duty with the marching regiments, which object would be neutralized in part should Captain Hawkins now receive the appointment.

I am, sir, with great respect, your obedient servant, W. L. MARCY.

* List omitted.

WASHINGTON, *February 20, 1847.*

To the Senate of the United States:

I communicate herewith a report of the Secretary of State, with the accompanying documents, in answer to a resolution of the Senate of the 2d instant, requesting the President to communicate such information in possession of the Executive Departments in relation to the importation of foreign criminals and paupers as he may deem consistent with the public interests to communicate.　　　JAMES K. POLK.

WASHINGTON, *February 26, 1847.*

To the Senate of the United States:

I nominate the persons named in the accompanying list* of promotions and appointments in the Army of the United States to the several grades annexed to their names, as proposed by the Secretary of War.

　　　JAMES K. POLK.

WAR DEPARTMENT, *February 26, 1847.*

The PRESIDENT OF THE UNITED STATES.

SIR: I have the honor respectfully to propose for your approbation the annexed list* of officers for regular promotion and persons for appointment in the Army of the United States.

It having been decided to be just and proper to restore Grafton D. Hanson, late a lieutenant in the Eighth Infantry, to his former regiment and rank, whose resignation was accepted in June, 1845, contrary to his wish, he having in due time recalled the same, it will be seen that he is reappointed accordingly. I deem it proper to state that the vacancy of first lieutenant in the Eighth Infantry, now proposed to be filled by Mr. Hanson's restoration and reappointment, has been occasioned by the appointment of the senior captain of the regiment to be major under the recent act authorizing an additional major to each regiment, being an original vacancy, and therefore the less reason for any objection in respect to the general principles and usages of the service, which guarantee regular promotions to fill vacancies which occur by accident, etc.

I am, sir, with great respect, your obedient servant,　　　W. L. MARCY.

WASHINGTON, *February 26, 1847.*

To the Senate of the United States:

I nominate the officers named in the accompanying list* for brevet promotion in the Army of the United States, for gallant conduct in the actions at Monterey.

　　　JAMES K. POLK.

WAR DEPARTMENT, *February 19, 1847.*

The PRESIDENT.

SIR: I present to you the following list* of officers engaged in the actions at Monterey, whose distinguished conduct therein entitles them, in my judgment, to the promotion by brevet. This list has been prepared after a particular and careful examination of all the documents in this Department in relation to the military operations at that place.

*Omitted.

Lieutenant-Colonel Garland and Brevet Lieutenant-Colonel Childs (then a captain of the line) also behaved in the actions of Monterey in a manner deserving of particular notice, but as their names are now before the Senate for colonelcies by brevet, I have not presented them for further promotion. I am not aware that any officer below the lineal rank of colonel has ever been made a brigadier-general by brevet.

I have the honor to be, very respectfully, your obedient servant,

W. L. MARCY.

WASHINGTON, *February 27, 1847.*

To the House of Representatives of the United States:

I communicate herewith a report of the Secretary of War, with the accompanying documents, in answer to the resolution of the House of Representatives of the 1st instant, requesting the President "to communicate to the House of Representatives all the correspondence with General Taylor since the commencement of hostilities with Mexico which has not yet been published, and the publication of which may not be deemed detrimental to the public service; also the correspondence of the Quartermaster-General in relation to transportation for General Taylor's Army; also the reports of Brigadier-Generals Hamer and Quitman of the operations of their respective brigades on the 21st of September last."

As some of these documents relate to military operations of our forces which may not have been fully executed, I might have deemed it proper to withhold parts of them under the apprehension that their publication at this time would be detrimental to the public service; but I am satisfied that these operations are now so far advanced and that the enemy has already received so much information from other sources in relation to the intended movements of our Army as to render this precaution unnecessary.

JAMES K. POLK.

WASHINGTON, *March 2, 1847.*

To the Senate of the United States:

I communicate herewith a report of the Secretary of War, with the accompanying documents, in answer to the resolution of the Senate of the 27th ultimo, requesting to be informed "why the name of Captain Theophilus H. Holmes was not sent in for brevet promotion amongst the other officers who distinguished themselves at the military operations at Monterey."

The report of the Secretary of War discloses the reasons for the omission of the name of Captain Holmes in the list of brevet promotions in my message of the —— ultimo. Upon the additional testimony in Captain Holmes's case which has been received at the War Department, and to which the Secretary of War refers in his report, I deem it proper to nominate him for brevet promotion.

I therefore nominate Captain Theophilus H. Holmes, of the Seventh Regiment of Infantry, to be major by brevet from the 23d September, 1846, in the Army of the United States.

JAMES K. POLK.

WAR DEPARTMENT, *March 1, 1847.*

The PRESIDENT OF THE UNITED STATES.

SIR: With a special reference to the resolution of the Senate of the 27th ultimo, requesting to be informed "why the name of Captain Theophilus H. Holmes was not sent in for brevet promotion amongst the other officers who distinguished themselves at the military operations at Monterey," I have again examined the official reports of those operations. I do not find that Captain Holmes is mentioned in General Taylor's report, nor in that of any other officer except the report of Brigadier-General Worth. The following extract from the latter contains all that is said having relation to the conduct of Captain Holmes:

"My thanks are also especially due to Lieutenant-Colonel Stanford, Eighth, commanding First Brigade; Major Munroe, chief of artillery, general staff; Brevet Major Brown and Captain J. R. Vinton, artillery battalion; Captain J. B. Scott, artillery battalion, light troops; Major Scott (commanding) and Captain Merrill, Fifth; Captain Miles (commanding), Holmes, and Ross, Seventh Infantry, and Captain Screven, commanding Eighth Infantry; to Lieutenant-Colonel Walker, captain of rifles; Major Chevalier and Captain McCulloch, of the Texan, and Captain Blanchard, of the Louisiana, Volunteers; to Lieutenant Mackall, commanding battery; Roland, Martin, Hays, Irons, Clark, and Curd, horse artillery; Lieutenant Longstreet, commanding light company, Eighth; Lieutenant Ayers, artillery battalion, who was among the first in the assault upon the place and who secured the colors. Each of the officers named either headed special detachments, columns of attack, storming parties, or detached guns, and all were conspicuous for conduct and courage."

It will be perceived that in this list there are twenty-one officers (besides the medical staff and officers of volunteers) who are highly commended by General Worth for gallant conduct. That they were justly entitled to the praise bestowed on them is not doubted; but if I had recommended all of them to be brevetted, together with all those in the reports of other generals also in like manner highly commended, the number of officers in my list submitted for your consideration would have been probably trebled. Indeed, the whole Army behaved most gallantly on that occasion. It was deemed proper to discriminate and select from among the well deserving those who had peculiar claims to dis'inction. In making this selection I exercised my best judgment, regarding the official reports as the authentic source of information. Six or seven only of the officers named in the foregoing extract from General Worth's report were placed on the list. A close examination of the reports will, I think, disclose the ground for the discrimination, and I hope justify the distinction which I felt it my duty to make. Without disparagement to Captain Holmes, whose conduct was highly creditable, it appears to me that a rule of selection which would have brought him upon the list for promotion by brevet would also have placed on the same list nearly everyone named with him in General Worth's report, and many on the reports of other generals not presented in my report to you of the 19th ultimo. There is not time before the adjournment of the Senate to make the thorough examination which a due regard to the relative claims of the gallant officers engaged in the actions of Monterey would require if the list of brevet promotions is to be enlarged to this extent. Such enlargement would not accord with my own views on the subject of bestowing brevet rewards.

There are on file other papers relative to Captain Holmes. They were not written with reference to his brevet promotion, but for an appointment in the new regiments. Copies of those are herewith transmitted. The letter of the Hon. W. P.

Mangum inclosing the statement from Generals Twiggs and Smith is dated the 26th, and my report the 19th ultimo, and was not, consequently, received at this Department until some days after the list for brevets was made out and presented to you.

From the facts and recommendations of the official reports of the actions at Monterey I should not feel warranted in presenting Captain Holmes for brevet promotion without at the same time including on the same list many others not recommended in my report of the 19th ultimo; but as his conduct fell under the immediate observation of General Smith (General Twiggs commanded in a different part of the town), it may be proper to regard their statement, received since my former report was prepared and handed to you, as additional evidence of his gallantry and of claims to your particular notice. I therefore recommend him to be promoted major by brevet.

I have the honor to be, very respectfully, your obedient servant,

W. L. MARCY,
Secretary of War.

PROCLAMATIONS.

[From Statutes at Large (Little & Brown), Vol. IX, p. 1001.]

BY THE PRESIDENT OF THE UNITED STATES OF AMERICA.

A PROCLAMATION.

Whereas by an act of the Congress of the United States approved the 3d day of March, 1845, entitled "An act regulating commercial intercourse within the islands of Miquelon and St. Pierre," it is provided that all French vessels coming directly from those islands, either in ballast or laden with articles the growth or manufacture of either of said islands, and which are permitted to be exported therefrom in American vessels, may be admitted into the ports of the United States on payment of no higher duties of tonnage or on their cargoes aforesaid than are imposed on American vessels and on like cargoes imported in American vessels, provided that this act shall not take effect until the President of the United States shall have received satisfactory information that similar privileges have been allowed to American vessels and their cargoes at said islands by the Government of France and shall have made proclamation accordingly; and

Whereas satisfactory information has been received by me that similar privileges have been allowed to American vessels and their cargoes at said islands by the Government of France:

Now, therefore, I, James K. Polk, President of the United States of America, do hereby declare and proclaim that all French vessels coming directly from the islands of Miquelon and St. Pierre, either in ballast or laden with articles the growth or manufacture of either of said islands, and which are permitted to be exported therefrom in American vessels, shall from this date be admitted into the ports of the United States on payment of no higher duties on tonnage or on their cargoes aforesaid than are imposed on American vessels and on like cargoes imported in American vessels.

Given under my hand, at the city of Washington, the 20th day of April, A. D. 1847, and of the Independence of the United States the seventy-first.

JAMES K. POLK.

By the President:

JAMES BUCHANAN,
    Secretary of State.

BY THE PRESIDENT OF THE UNITED STATES OF AMERICA.

A PROCLAMATION.

Whereas by an act of the Congress of the United States of the 24th of May, 1828, entitled "An act in addition to an act entitled 'An act concerning discriminating duties of tonnage and impost' and to equalize the duties on Prussian vessels and their cargoes," it is provided that upon satisfactory evidence being given to the President of the United States by the government of any foreign nation that no discriminating duties of tonnage or impost are imposed or levied in the ports of the said nation upon vessels wholly belonging to citizens of the United States, or upon the produce, manufactures, or merchandise imported in the same from the United States or from any foreign country, the President is thereby authorized to issue his proclamation declaring that the foreign discriminating duties of tonnage and impost within the United States are and shall be suspended and discontinued so far as respects the vessels of the said foreign nation and the produce, manufactures, or merchandise imported into the United States in the same from the said foreign nation or from any other foreign country, the said suspension to take effect from the time of such notification being given to the President of the United States and to continue so long as the reciprocal exemption of vessels belonging to citizens of the United States and their cargoes as aforesaid shall be continued, and no longer; and

Whereas satisfactory evidence has lately been received by me from His Majesty the Emperor of Brazil, through an official communication of Mr. Felippe José Pereira Leal, his chargé d'affaires in the United States, under date of the 25th of October, 1847, that no other or higher duties of tonnage and impost are imposed or levied in the ports of Brazil upon vessels wholly belonging to citizens of the United States and upon the produce, manufactures, or merchandise imported in the same from the United States and from any foreign country whatever than are levied on Brazilian ships and their cargoes in the same ports under like circumstances:

Now, therefore, I, James K. Polk, President of the United States of America, do hereby declare and proclaim that so much of the several acts imposing discriminating duties of tonnage and impost within the United States are and shall be suspended and discontinued so far as respects the vessels of Brazil and the produce, manufactures, and merchandise imported into the United States in the same from Brazil and from any other foreign country whatever, the said suspension to take effect from the day above mentioned and to continue thenceforward so long as the reciprocal exemption of the vessels of the United States and the produce, manufactures, and merchandise imported into Brazil in the same as aforesaid shall be continued on the part of the Government of Brazil.

Given under my hand, at the city of Washington, this 4th day of November, A. D. 1847, and the seventy-second of the Independence of the United States.

JAMES K. POLK.

By the President:

JAMES BUCHANAN,
Secretary of State.

EXECUTIVE ORDERS.

WASHINGTON, *March 23, 1847.*

The SECRETARY OF THE TREASURY.

SIR: The Government of Mexico having repeatedly rejected the friendly overtures of the United States to open negotiations with a view to the restoration of peace, sound policy and a just regard to the interests of our own country require that the enemy should be made, as far as practicable, to bear the expenses of a war of which they are the authors, and which they obstinately persist in protracting.

It is the right of the conqueror to levy contribution upon the enemy in their seaports, towns, or provinces which may be in his military possession by conquest and to apply the same to defray the expenses of the war. The conqueror possesses the right also to establish a temporary military government over such seaports, towns, or provinces and to prescribe the conditions and restrictions upon which commerce with such places may be permitted. He may, in his discretion, exclude all trade, or admit it with limitation or restriction, or impose terms the observance of which will be the condition of carrying it on. One of these conditions may be the payment of a prescribed rate of duties on tonnage and imports.

In the exercise of these unquestioned rights of war, I have, on full consideration, determined to order that all the ports or places in Mexico which now are or hereafter may be in the actual possession of our land and naval forces by conquest shall be opened while our military occupation may continue to the commerce of all neutral nations, as well as our own, in articles not contraband of war, upon the payment of prescribed rates of duties, which will be made known and enforced by our military and naval commanders.

While the adoption of this policy will be to impose a burden on the enemy, and at the same time to deprive them of the revenue to be derived from trade at such ports or places, as well as to secure it to ourselves, whereby the expenses of the war may be diminished, a just regard to the general interests of commerce and the obvious advantages of uniformity in the exercise of these belligerent rights require that well-considered regulations and restrictions should be prepared for the guidance of those who may be charged with carrying it into effect.

You are therefore instructed to examine the existing Mexican tariff of duties and report to me a schedule of articles of trade to be admitted at such ports or places as may be at any time in our military possession, with such rates of duty on them and also on tonnage as will be likely to produce the greatest amount of revenue. You will also communicate the considerations which may recommend the scale of duties which you may propose, and will submit such regulations as you may deem advisable in order to enforce their collection.

As the levy of the contribution proposed is a military right, derived from the laws of nations, the collection and disbursement of the duties will be made, under the orders of the Secretary of War and the Secretary of the Navy, by the military and naval commanders at the ports or places in Mexico which may be in possession of our arms. The report requested is therefore necessary in order to enable me to give the proper directions to the War and Navy Departments.

JAMES K. POLK.

TREASURY DEPARTMENT, *March 30, 1847.*
The PRESIDENT.

SIR: Your instructions of the 23d instant have been received by this Department, and in conformity thereto I present you herewith, for your consideration, a scale of duties proposed to be collected as a military contribution during the war in the ports of Mexico in possession of our Army or Navy by conquest, with regulations for the ascertainment and collection of such duties, together with the reasons which appear to me to recommend their adoption.

It is clear that we must either adopt our own tariff or that of Mexico, or establish a new system of duties. Our own tariff could not be adopted, because the Mexican exports and imports are so different from our own that different rates of duties are indispensable in order to collect the largest revenue. Thus upon many articles produced in great abundance here duties must be imposed at the lowest rate in order to collect any revenue, whereas many of the same articles are not produced in Mexico, or to a very inconsiderable extent, and would therefore bear there a much higher duty for revenue. A great change is also rendered necessary by the proposed exaction of duties on all imports to any Mexican port in our possession from any other Mexican port occupied by us in the same manner. This measure would largely increase the revenue which we might collect. It is recommended, however, for reasons of obvious safety, that this Mexican coastwise trade should be confined to our own vessels, as well as the interior trade above any port of entry in our possession, but that in all other respects the ports of Mexico held by us should be freely opened at the rate of duties herein recommended to the vessels and commerce of all the world. The *ad valorem* system of duties adopted by us, although by far the most just and equitable, yet requires an appraisement to ascertain the actual value of every article. This demands great mercantile skill, knowledge, and experience, and therefore, for the want of skillful appraisers (a class of officers wholly unknown in Mexico), could not at once be put into successful operation there. If also, as proposed, these duties are to be ascertained and collected as a military contribution through the officers of our Army and Navy, those brave men would more easily perform almost any other duty than that of estimating the value of every description of goods, wares, and merchandise.

The system of specific duties already prevails in Mexico, and may be put by us into immediate operation; and if, as conceded, specific duties should be more burdensome upon the people of Mexico, the more onerous the operation of these duties upon them the sooner it is likely that they will force their military rulers to agree to a peace. It is certain that a mild and forbearing system of warfare, collecting no duties in their ports in our possession on the Gulf and levying no contributions, whilst our armies purchase supplies from them at high prices, by rendering the war a benefit to the people of Mexico rather than an injury has not hastened the conclusion of a peace. It may be, however, that specific duties, onerous as they are, and heavy contributions, accompanied by a vigorous prosecution of the war, may more speedily insure that peace which we have failed to obtain from magnanimous forbearance, from brilliant victories, or from proffered negotiation. The duties, however, whilst they may be specific, and therefore more onerous than *ad valorem* duties, should not be so high as to defeat revenue.

It is impossible to adopt as a basis the tariff of Mexico, because the duties are extravagantly high, defeating importation, commerce, and revenue and producing innumerable frauds and smuggling. There are also sixty articles the importation of which into Mexico is strictly prohibited by their tariff, embracing most of the necessaries of life and far the greater portion of our products and fabrics.

Among the sixty prohibited articles are sugar, rice, cotton, boots and half-boots, coffee, nails of all kinds, leather of most kinds, flour, cotton yarn and thread, soap of all kinds, common earthenware, lard, molasses, timber of all kinds, saddles of all kinds, coarse woolen cloth, cloths for cloaks, ready-made clothing of all kinds, salt, tobacco of all kinds, cotton goods or textures, chiefly such as are made by ourselves; pork, fresh or salted, smoked or corned; woolen or cotton blankets or counterpanes, shoes and slippers, wheat and grain of all kinds. Such is a list of but part of the articles whose importation is prohibited by the Mexican tariff. These prohibitions should not be permitted to continue, because they exclude most of our products and fabrics and prevent the collection of revenue. We turn from the prohibitions to the actual duties imposed by Mexico. The duties are specific throughout, and almost universally by weight, irrespective of value; are generally protective or exorbitant, and without any discrimination for revenue. The duties proposed to be substituted are moderate when compared with those imposed by Mexico, being generally reduced to a standard more than one-half below the Mexican duties. The duties are also based upon a discrimination throughout for revenue, and, keeping in view the customs and habits of the people of Mexico, so different from our own, are fixed in each case at that rate which it is believed will produce in the Mexican ports the largest amount of revenue.

In order to realize from this system the largest amount of revenue, it would be necessary that our Army and Navy should seize every important port or place upon the Gulf of Mexico or California, or on the Pacific, and open the way through the interior for the free transit of exports and imports, and especially that the interior passage through the Mexican isthmus should be secured from ocean to ocean, for the benefit of our commerce and that of all the world. This measure, whilst it would greatly increase our revenue from these duties and facilitate communication between our forces upon the eastern and western coasts of Mexico, would probably lead at the conclusion of a peace to results of incalculable importance to our own commerce and to that of all the world.

In the meantime the Mexican Government monopoly in tobacco, from which a considerable revenue is realized by Mexico, together with the culture there which yields that revenue, should be abolished, so as to diminish the resources of that Government and augment our own by collecting the duty upon all the imported tobacco. The Mexican interior transit duties should also be abolished, and also their internal Government duty on coin and bullion. The prohibition of exports and the duties upon exports should be annulled, and especially the heavy export duty on coin and bullion, so as to cheapen and facilitate the purchase of imports and permit the precious metals, untaxed, to flow out freely from Mexico into general circulation. Quicksilver and machinery for working the mines of precious metals in Mexico, for the same reasons, should also be admitted duty free, which, with the measures above indicated, would largely increase the production and circulation of the precious metals, improve our own commerce and industry and that of all neutral powers.

In thus opening the ports of Mexico to the commerce of the world you will present to all nations with whom we are at peace the best evidence of your desire to maintain with them our friendly relations, to render the war to them productive of as little injury as possible, and even to advance their interests, so far as it safely can be done, by affording to them in common with ourselves the advantages of a liberal commerce with Mexico. To extend this commerce, you will have unsealed the ports of Mexico, repealed their interior transit duties, which obstruct the passage of merchandise to and from the coast; you will have annulled the Government duty on coin and bullion and abolished the heavy export duties on the precious metals, so as to permit them to flow out freely for the benefit of mankind; you will have expunged the long list of their prohibited articles and reduced more than one-half their duties on imports, whilst the freest scope would be left for the mining of the precious metals. These are great advantages which would be secured to friendly nations, especially when compared with the exclusion of their commerce by rigorous blockades. It is true, the duties collected from these imports would be for the benefit of our own Government, but it is equally true that the expenses of the war, which Mexico insists upon prosecuting, are borne exclusively by ourselves, and not by foreign nations. It can not be doubted but that all neutral nations will see in the adoption of such a course by you a manifestation of your good will toward them and a strong desire to advance those just and humane principles which make it the duty of belligerents, as we have always contended, to render the war in which they are engaged as little injurious as practicable to neutral powers.

These duties would not be imposed upon any imports into our own country, but only upon imports into Mexico, and the tax would fall upon the people of Mexico in the enhancement to them of the prices of these imports. Nearly all our own products are excluded by the Mexican tariff even in time of peace; they are excluded also during the war so far as we continue the system of blockading any of the ports of Mexico; and they are also excluded even from the ports not blockaded in possession of Mexico; whereas the new system would soon open to our commerce all the ports of Mexico as they shall fall into our military possession. Neither our own nor foreign merchants are required to send any goods to Mexico, and if they do so voluntarily it will be because they can make a profit upon the importation there, and therefore they will have no right to complain of the duties levied in the ports of Mexico upon the consumers of those goods—the people of Mexico. The whole money collected would inure to the benefit of our own Government and people, to sustain the war and to prevent to that extent new loans and increased taxation. Indeed, in view of the fact that the Government is thrown upon the ordinary revenues for peace, with no other additional resources but loans to carry on the war, the income to be derived from the new system, which it is believed will be large if these suggestions are adopted, would be highly important to sustain the credit of the Government, to prevent the embarrassment of the Treasury, and to save the country from such ruinous sacrifices as occurred during the last war, including the inevitable legacy to posterity of a large public debt and onerous taxation. The new system would not only arrest the expensive transfer and ruinous drain of specie to Mexico, but would cause it, in duties and in return for our exports, to reflow into our country to an amount, perhaps, soon exceeding the $9,000,000 which it had reached in 1835 even under the restrictive laws of Mexico, thus relieving our own people from a grievous tax and imposing it where it should fall, upon our enemies, the people of Mexico, as a contribution levied upon them to conquer a peace as well as to defray the expenses of the war; whereas by admitting our exports freely, without duty, into the Mexican ports which we may occupy from time to time, and affording those goods, including the necessaries of life, at less than one-half the prices which they had heretofore paid for them, the war might in time become a benefit instead of a burden to the people of Mexico; and they would therefore be unwilling to terminate the contest. It is hoped also that Mexico, after a peace, will never renew her present prohibitory and protective system, so nearly resembling that of ancient China or Japan, but that, liberalized, enlightened, and regenerated by the contact and intercourse with our people and those of other civilized nations, she will continue the far more moderate system of duties resembling that prescribed by these regulations.

In the meantime it is not just that Mexico, by her obstinate persistence in this contest, should compel us to overthrow our own financial policy and arrest this great nation in her high and prosperous career. To reimpose high duties would be alike injurious to ourselves and to all neutral powers, and, unless demanded by a stern necessity, ungenerous to those enlightened nations which have adopted cotemporaneously with us a more liberal commercial policy. The system you now propose of imposing the burden as far as practicable upon our enemies, the people of Mexico, and not upon ourselves or upon friendly nations, appears to be most just in itself, and is further recommended as the only policy which is likely to hasten the conclusion of a just and honorable peace.

A tonnage duty on all vessels, whether our own or of neutral powers, of $1 per ton, which is greatly less than that imposed by Mexico, is recommended in lieu of all port duties and charges. Appended to these regulations are tables of the rates at which foreign money is fixed by law, as also a separate table of currencies by usage, in which a certificate of value is required to be attached to the invoice. There is also annexed a table of foreign weights and measures reduced to the standard of the United States, together with blank forms to facilitate the transaction of business.

It is recommended that the duties herein suggested shall be collected exclusively in gold or silver coin. These duties can only be collected as a military contribution through the agency of our brave officers of the Army and Navy, who will no doubt cheerfully and faithfully collect and keep these moneys and account for them, not to the Treasury, but to the Secretaries of War or of the Navy, respectively.

It is recommended that these duties be performed by the commandant of the port, whether naval or military, aided by the paymaster or purser or other officer, the accounts of each being countersigned by the other, as a check upon mistakes or error, in the same manner as is now the case with the collector and naval officer of our several principal ports, which has introduced so much order and accuracy in our system. It is suggested that as in some cases the attention of the commandant of the port might be necessary for the performance of other duties that he be permitted to substitute some other officer, making known the fact to the Secretaries of War or of the Navy, and subject to their direction.

I have the honor to be, with great respect, your obedient servant,

R. J. WALKER,
Secretary of the Treasury.

WASHINGTON, *March 31, 1847.*

SIR:* Being charged by the Constitution with the prosecution of the existing war with Mexico, I deem it proper, in the exercise of an undoubted belligerent right, to order that military contributions be levied upon the enemy in such of their ports or other places as now are or may be hereafter in the possession of our land and naval forces by conquest, and that the same be collected and applied toward defraying the expenses of the war. As one means of effecting this object, the blockade at such conquered ports will be raised, and they will be opened to our own commerce and that of all neutral nations in articles not contraband of war during our military occupation of them, and duties on tonnage and imports will be levied and collected through the agency of our military and naval officers in command at such ports, acting under orders from the War and Navy Departments.

I transmit to you herewith, for your information and guidance, a copy of a communication addressed by me to the Secretary of the Treasury on the 23d instant, instructing him to examine the existing Mexican tariff and to report to me, for my consideration, a scale of duties which he would recommend to be levied on tonnage and imports in such conquered ports, together with such regulations as he would propose as necessary and proper in order to carry this policy into effect; and also a copy of the report of the Secretary of the Treasury made on the 30th instant in answer to my communication to him. The scale of duties and the regulations for their collection as military contributions exacted from the enemy, recommended by the Secretary of the Treasury in this report, have been approved by me.

*Addressed to the Secretaries of War and of the Navy.

You will, after consulting with the Secretary of the Navy, so as t
secure concert of action between the War and Navy Departments, issu
the necessary orders to carry the measure proposed into immediate effect.

JAMES K. POLK.

TREASURY DEPARTMENT, *June 10, 1847.*

The PRESIDENT.

SIR: In compliance with your directions, I have examined the questions presented by the Secretary of War in regard to the military contri
butions proposed to be levied in Mexico under the tariff and regulation
sanctioned by you on the 31st of March last, and respectfully recommen
the following modifications, namely:

First. On all manufactures of cotton, or of cotton mixed with an
other material except wool, worsted, and silk, in the piece or in an
other form, a duty, as a military contribution, of 30 per cent *ad valorem*

Second. When goods on which the duties are levied by weight are im
ported into said ports in the package, the duties shall be collected on th
net weight only; and in all cases an allowance shall be made for all defi
ciencies, leakage, breakage, or damage proved to have actually occurr
during the voyage of importation, and made known before the goods ar
warehoused.

Third. The period named in the eighth of said regulations durin,
which the goods may remain in warehouse before the payment of dutie
is extended from thirty to ninety days, and within said period of ninet
days any portion of the said goods on which the duties, as a military
contribution, have been paid may be taken, after such payment, from
the warehouse and entered free of any further duty at any other port
or ports of Mexico in our military possession, the facts of the case, with
a particular description of said goods and a statement that the dutie
thereon have been paid, being certified by the proper officer of the port
or ports of reshipment.

Fourth. It is intended to provide by the treaty of peace that all goods
imported during the war into any of the Mexican ports in our military
possession shall be exempt from any new import duty or confiscation by
Mexico in the same manner as if said goods had been imported and paid
the import duties prescribed by the Government of Mexico.

Most respectfully, your obedient servant,

R. J. WALKER,
Secretary of the Treasury.

JUNE 11, 1847.

The modifications as above recommended by the Secretary of the
Treasury are approved by me, and the Secretary of War and the Secretary of the Navy will give the proper orders to carry them into effect.

JAMES K. POLK.

TREASURY DEPARTMENT, *November 5, 1847.*
The PRESIDENT.

SIR: The military contributions in the form of duties upon imports into Mexican ports have been levied by the Departments of War and of the Navy during the last six months under your order of the 31st of March last, and in view of the experience of the practical operation of the system I respectfully recommend the following modifications in some of its details, which will largely augment the revenue:

That the duty on silk, flax, hemp or grass, cotton, wool, worsted or any manufactures of the same, or of either or mixtures thereof; coffee, teas, sugar, molasses, tobacco and all manufactures thereof, including cigars and cigarritos; glass, china, and stoneware, iron and steel and all manufactures of either not prohibited, be 30 per cent *ad valorem;* on copper and all manufactures thereof, tallow, tallow candles, soap, fish, beef, pork, hams, bacon, tongues, butter, lard, cheese, rice, Indian corn and meal, potatoes, wheat, rye, oats, and all other grain, rye meal and oat meal, flour, whale and sperm oil, clocks, boots and shoes, pumps, bootees and slippers, bonnets, hats, caps, beer, ale, porter, cider, timber, boards, planks, scantling, shingles, laths, pitch, tar, rosin, turpentine, spirits of turpentine, vinegar, apples, ship bread, hides, leather and manufactures thereof, and paper of all kinds, 20 per cent *ad valorem;* and these reduced rates shall also apply to all goods on which the duties are not paid remaining not exceeding ninety days in deposit in the Mexican ports, introduced under previous regulations enforcing military contributions.

Yours, most respectfully,

R. J. WALKER,
Secretary of the Treasury.

NOVEMBER 6, 1847.

The modifications as above recommended by the Secretary of the Treasury are approved by me, and the Secretary of War and the Secretary of the Navy will give the proper orders to carry them into effect.

JAMES K. POLK.

TREASURY DEPARTMENT, *November 16, 1847.*
The PRESIDENT.

SIR: With a view to augment the military contributions now collected by the Departments of War and of the Navy under your order of the 31st of March last, I recommend that the export duty exacted before the war by the Government of Mexico be now collected at the port of exportation by the same officers of the Army or Navy of the United States in the Mexican ports in our possession who are authorized to collect the import duties, abolishing, however, the prohibition of export established in certain cases by the Mexican Government, as also all interior transit duties; dispensing also with the necessity of any certificate of having paid any duty to the Mexican Government.

The export duty would then be as follows:

	Per cent.
Gold, coined or wrought..	3
Silver, coined	6
Silver, wrought, with or without certificate of having paid any duty to the Mexican Government..	7
Silver, refined or pure, wrought in ingots, with or without certificate of having paid the Mexican Government duty..	7
Gold, unwrought or in a state of ore or dust..	3
Silver, unwrought or in a state of ore..	7

Where gold or silver in any form is taken from any interior Mexican city in our military possession, the export duty must be paid there to the officer of the United States commanding, and his certificate of such prepayment must be produced at the Mexican port of exportation; otherwise a double duty will be collected upon the arrival of such gold or silver at the Mexican port of exportation. Whenever it is practicable, all internal taxes of every description, whether upon persons or property, exacted by the Government of Mexico, or by any department, town, or city thereof, should be collected by our military officers in possession and appropriated as a military contribution toward defraying the expenses of the war, excluding however, all duties on the transit of goods from one department to another, which duties, being prejudicial to revenue and restrictive of the exchange of imports for exports, were abolished by your order of the 31st of March last.

Yours, most respectfully,

R. J. WALKER,
Secretary of the Treasury.

NOVEMBER 16, 1847.

The modifications and military contributions as above recommended by the Secretary of the Treasury are approved by me, and the Secretary of War and the Secretary of the Navy will give the proper orders to carry them into effect.

JAMES K. POLK.

THIRD ANNUAL MESSAGE.

WASHINGTON, *December 7, 1847.*

Fellow-Citizens of the Senate and of the House of Representatives:

The annual meeting of Congress is always an interesting event. The representatives of the States and of the people come fresh from their constituents to take counsel together for the common good.

After an existence of near three-fourths of a century as a free and independent Republic, the problem no longer remains to be solved whether man is capable of self-government. The success of our admirable system is a conclusive refutation of the theories of those in other countries who

maintain that a "favored few" are born to rule and that the mass of mankind must be governed by force. Subject to no arbitrary or hereditary authority, the people are the only sovereigns recognized by our Constitution.

Numerous emigrants, of every lineage and language, attracted by the civil and religious freedom we enjoy and by our happy condition, annually crowd to our shores, and transfer their heart, not less than their allegiance, to the country whose dominion belongs alone to the people.

No country has been so much favored, or should acknowledge with deeper reverence the manifestations of the divine protection. An all-wise Creator directed and guarded us in our infant struggle for freedom and has constantly watched over our surprising progress until we have become one of the great nations of the earth.

It is in a country thus favored, and under a Government in which the executive and legislative branches hold their authority for limited periods alike from the people, and where all are responsible to their respective constituencies, that it is again my duty to communicate with Congress upon the state of the Union and the present condition of public affairs.

During the past year the most gratifying proofs are presented that our country has been blessed with a widespread and universal prosperity. There has been no period since the Government was founded when all the industrial pursuits of our people have been more successful or when labor in all branches of business has received a fairer or better reward. From our abundance we have been enabled to perform the pleasing duty of furnishing food for the starving millions of less favored countries.

In the enjoyment of the bounties of Providence at home such as have rarely fallen to the lot of any people, it is cause of congratulation that our intercourse with all the powers of the earth except Mexico continues to be of an amicable character.

It has ever been our cherished policy to cultivate peace and good will with all nations, and this policy has been steadily pursued by me.

No change has taken place in our relations with Mexico since the adjournment of the last Congress. The war in which the United States were forced to engage with the Government of that country still continues.

I deem it unnecessary, after the full exposition of them contained in my message of the 11th of May, 1846, and in my annual message at the commencement of the session of Congress in December last, to reiterate the serious causes of complaint which we had against Mexico before she commenced hostilities.

It is sufficient on the present occasion to say that the wanton violation of the rights of person and property of our citizens committed by Mexico, her repeated acts of bad faith through a long series of years, and her disregard of solemn treaties stipulating for indemnity to our injured

citizens not only constituted ample cause of war on our part, but were of such an aggravated character as would have justified us before the whole world in resorting to this extreme remedy. With an anxious desire to avoid a rupture between the two countries, we forbore for years to assert our clear rights by force, and continued to seek redress for the wrongs we had suffered by amicable negotiation in the hope that Mexico might yield to pacific counsels and the demands of justice. In this hope we were disappointed. Our minister of peace sent to Mexico was insultingly rejected. The Mexican Government refused even to hear the terms of adjustment which he was authorized to propose, and finally, under wholly unjustifiable pretexts, involved the two countries in war by invading the territory of the State of Texas, striking the first blow, and shedding the blood of our citizens on our own soil.

Though the United States were the aggrieved nation, Mexico commenced the war, and we were compelled in self-defense to repel the invader and to vindicate the national honor and interests by prosecuting it with vigor until we could obtain a just and honorable peace.

On learning that hostilities had been commenced by Mexico I promptly communicated that fact, accompanied with a succinct statement of our other causes of complaint against Mexico, to Congress, and that body, by the act of the 13th of May, 1846, declared that "by the act of the Republic of Mexico a state of war exists between that Government and the United States." This act declaring "the war to exist by the act of the Republic of Mexico," and making provision for its prosecution "to a speedy and successful termination," was passed with great unanimity by Congress, there being but two negative votes in the Senate and but fourteen in the House of Representatives.

The existence of the war having thus been declared by Congress, it became my duty under the Constitution and the laws to conduct and prosecute it. This duty has been performed, and though at every stage of its progress I have manifested a willingness to terminate it by a just peace, Mexico has refused to accede to any terms which could be accepted by the United States consistently with the national honor and interest.

The rapid and brilliant successes of our arms and the vast extent of the enemy's territory which had been overrun and conquered before the close of the last session of Congress were fully known to that body. Since that time the war has been prosecuted with increased energy, and, I am gratified to state, with a success which commands universal admiration. History presents no parallel of so many glorious victories achieved by any nation within so short a period. Our Army, regulars and volunteers, have covered themselves with imperishable honors. Whenever and wherever our forces have encountered the enemy, though he was in vastly superior numbers and often intrenched in fortified positions of his own selection and of great strength, he has been defeated. Too much praise can not be bestowed upon our officers and men, regulars and

volunteers, for their gallantry, discipline, indomitable courage, and perseverance, all seeking the post of danger and vying with each other in
deeds of noble daring.

While every patriot's heart must exult and a just national pride ani-
mate every bosom in beholding the high proofs of courage, consummate
military skill, steady discipline, and humanity to the vanquished enemy
exhibited by our gallant Army, the nation is called to mourn over the
loss of many brave officers and soldiers, who have fallen in defense of
their country's honor and interests. The brave dead met their melancholy fate in a foreign land, nobly discharging their duty, and with their
country's flag waving triumphantly in the face of the foe. Their patriotic deeds are justly appreciated, and will long be remembered by their
grateful countrymen. The parental care of the Government they loved
and served should be extended to their surviving families.

Shortly after the adjournment of the last session of Congress the gratifying intelligence was received of the signal victory of Buena Vista, and
of the fall of the city of Vera Cruz, and with it the strong castle of San
Juan de Ulloa, by which it was defended. Believing that after these
and other successes so honorable to our arms and so disastrous to Mexico the period was propitious to afford her another opportunity, if she
thought proper to embrace it, to enter into negotiations for peace, a
commissioner was appointed to proceed to the headquarters of our Army
with full powers to enter upon negotiations and to conclude a just and
honorable treaty of peace. He was not directed to make any new overtures of peace, but was the bearer of a dispatch from the Secretary of
State of the United States to the minister of foreign affairs of Mexico,
in reply to one received from the latter of the 22d of February, 1847,
in which the Mexican Government was informed of his appointment
and of his presence at the headquarters of our Army, and that he was
invested with full powers to conclude a definitive treaty of peace whenever the Mexican Government might signify a desire to do so. While I
was unwilling to subject the United States to another indignant refusal,
I was yet resolved that the evils of the war should not be protracted a
day longer than might be rendered absolutely necessary by the Mexican
Government.

Care was taken to give no instructions to the commissioner which could
in any way interfere with our military operations or relax our energies in
the prosecution of the war. He possessed no authority in any manner to
control these operations. He was authorized to exhibit his instructions
to the general in command of the Army, and in the event of a treaty
being concluded and ratified on the part of Mexico he was directed to
give him notice of that fact. On the happening of such contingency, and
on receiving notice thereof, the general in command was instructed by
the Secretary of War to suspend further active military operations until
further orders. These instructions were given with a view to intermit

hostilities until the treaty thus ratified by Mexico could be transmitted to Washington and receive the action of the Government of the United States. The commissioner was also directed on reaching the Army to deliver to the general in command the dispatch which he bore from the Secretary of State to the minister of foreign affairs of Mexico, and on receiving it the general was instructed by the Secretary of War to cause it to be transmitted to the commander of the Mexican forces, with a request that it might be communicated to his Government.

The commissioner did not reach the headquarters of the Army until after another brilliant victory had crowned our arms at Cerro Gordo.

The dispatch which he bore from the Secretary of War to the general in command of the Army was received by that officer, then at Jalapa, on the 7th of May, 1847, together with the dispatch from the Secretary of State to the minister of foreign affairs of Mexico, having been transmitted to him from Vera Cruz. The commissioner arrived at the headquarters of the Army a few days afterwards. His presence with the Army and his diplomatic character were made known to the Mexican Government from Puebla on the 12th of June, 1847, by the transmission of the dispatch from the Secretary of State to the minister of foreign affairs of Mexico.

Many weeks elapsed after its receipt, and no overtures were made nor was any desire expressed by the Mexican Government to enter into negotiations for peace.

Our Army pursued its march upon the capital, and as it approached it was met by formidable resistance. Our forces first encountered the enemy, and achieved signal victories in the severely contested battles of Contreras and Churubusco. It was not until after these actions had resulted in decisive victories and the capital of the enemy was within our power that the Mexican Government manifested any disposition to enter into negotiations for peace, and even then, as events have proved, there is too much reason to believe they were insincere, and that in agreeing to go through the forms of negotiation the object was to gain time to strengthen the defenses of their capital and to prepare for fresh resistance.

The general in command of the Army deemed it expedient to suspend hostilities temporarily by entering into an armistice with a view to the opening of negotiations. Commissioners were appointed on the part of Mexico to meet the commissioner on the part of the United States. The result of the conferences which took place between these functionaries of the two Governments was a failure to conclude a treaty of peace.

The commissioner of the United States took with him the project of a treaty already prepared, by the terms of which the indemnity required by the United States was a cession of territory.

It is well known that the only indemnity which it is in the power of Mexico to make in satisfaction of the just and long-deferred claims of our citizens against her and the only means by which she can reimburse the United States for the expenses of the war is a cession to the United States of a portion of her territory. Mexico has no money to pay, and no other means of making the required indemnity. If we refuse this, we can obtain nothing else. To reject indemnity by refusing to accept a cession of territory would be to abandon all our just demands, and to wage the war, bearing all its expenses, without a purpose or definite object.

A state of war abrogates treaties previously existing between the belligerents and a treaty of peace puts an end to all claims for indemnity for tortious acts committed under the authority of one government against the citizens or subjects of another unless they are provided for in its stipulations. A treaty of peace which would terminate the existing war without providing for indemnity would enable Mexico, the acknowledged debtor and herself the aggressor in the war, to relieve herself from her just liabilities. By such a treaty our citizens who hold just demands against her would have no remedy either against Mexico or their own Government. Our duty to these citizens must forever prevent such a peace, and no treaty which does not provide ample means of discharging these demands can receive my sanction.

A treaty of peace should settle all existing differences between the two countries. If an adequate cession of territory should be made by such a treaty, the United States should release Mexico from all her liabilities and assume their payment to our own citizens. If instead of this the United States were to consent to a treaty by which Mexico should again engage to pay the heavy amount of indebtedness which a just indemnity to our Government and our citizens would impose on her, it is notorious that she does not possess the means to meet such an undertaking. From such a treaty no result could be anticipated but the same irritating disappointments which have heretofore attended the violations of similar treaty stipulations on the part of Mexico. Such a treaty would be but a temporary cessation of hostilities, without the restoration of the friendship and good understanding which should characterize the future intercourse between the two countries.

That Congress contemplated the acquisition of territorial indemnity when that body made provision for the prosecution of the war is obvious. Congress could not have meant when, in May, 1846, they appropriated $10,000,000 and authorized the President to employ the militia and naval and military forces of the United States and to accept the services of 50,000 volunteers to enable him to prosecute the war, and when, at their last session, and after our Army had invaded Mexico, they made additional appropriations and authorized the raising of additional troops for the same purpose, that no indemnity was to be obtained from Mexico at the conclusion of the war; and yet it was certain that if no Mexican territory was acquired no indemnity could be obtained. It is further manifest that Congress contemplated territorial indemnity from the fact that at their last session an act was passed, upon the Executive recommendation, appropriating $3,000,000 with that express object. This appropriation was made ''to enable the President to conclude a treaty of peace, limits, and boundaries with the Republic of Mexico, to be used by him in the event that said treaty, when signed by the authorized agents of the two Governments and duly ratified by Mexico, shall call for the expenditure of the same or any part thereof.'' The object of asking this appropriation was distinctly stated in the several messages on the subject which I communicated to Congress. Similar appropriations made in 1803 and 1806, which were referred to, were intended to be applied in part consideration for the cession of Louisiana and the Floridas. In like manner it was anticipated that in settling the terms of a treaty of ''limits and boundaries'' with Mexico a cession of territory estimated to be of greater value than the amount of our demands against her might be obtained, and that the prompt payment of this sum in part consideration for the territory ceded, on the conclusion of a treaty and its ratification on her part, might be an inducement with her to make such a cession of territory as would be satisfactory to the United States; and although the failure to conclude such a treaty has rendered it unnecessary to use any part of the $3,000,000 appropriated by that act, and the entire sum remains in the Treasury, it is still applicable to that object should the contingency occur making such application proper.

The doctrine of no territory is the doctrine of no indemnity, and if sanctioned would be a public acknowledgment that our country was wrong and that the war declared by Congress with extraordinary unanimity was unjust and should be abandoned—an admission unfounded in fact and degrading to the national character.

The terms of the treaty proposed by the United States were not only just to Mexico, but, considering the character and amount of our claims, the unjustifiable and unprovoked commencement of hostilities by her, the expenses of the war to which we have been subjected, and the success which had attended our arms, were deemed to be of a most liberal character.

The commissioner of the United States was authorized to agree to the establishment of the Rio Grande as the boundary from its entrance into the Gulf to its intersection with the southern boundary of New Mexico, in north latitude about 32°, and to obtain a cession to the United States of the Provinces of New Mexico and the Californias and the privilege of the right of way across the Isthmus of Tehuantepec. The boundary of the Rio Grande and the cession to the United States of New Mexico and Upper California constituted an ultimatum which our commissioner was under no circumstances to yield.

That it might be manifest, not only to Mexico, but to all other nations, that the United States were not disposed to take advantage of a feeble power by insisting upon wresting from her all the other Provinces, including many of her principal towns and cities, which we had conquered and held in our military occupation, but were willing to conclude a treaty in

a spirit of liberality, our commissioner was authorized to stipulate for the restoration to Mexico of all our other conquests.

As the territory to be acquired by the boundary proposed might be estimated to be of greater value than a fair equivalent for our just demands, our commissioner was authorized to stipulate for the payment of such additional pecuniary consideration as was deemed reasonable.

The terms of a treaty proposed by the Mexican commissioners were wholly inadmissible. They negotiated as if Mexico were the victorious, and not the vanquished, party. They must have known that their ultimatum could never be accepted. It required the United States to dismember Texas by surrendering to Mexico that part of the territory of that State lying between the Nueces and the Rio Grande, included within her limits by her laws when she was an independent republic, and when she was annexed to the United States and admitted by Congress as one of the States of our Union. It contained no provision for the payment by Mexico of the just claims of our citizens. It required indemnity to Mexican citizens for injuries they may have sustained by our troops in the prosecution of the war. It demanded the right for Mexico to levy and collect the Mexican tariff of duties on goods imported into her ports while in our military occupation during the war, and the owners of which had paid to officers of the United States the military contributions which had been levied upon them; and it offered to cede to the United States, for a pecuniary consideration, that part of Upper California lying north of latitude 37°. Such were the unreasonable terms proposed by the Mexican commissioners.

The cession to the United States by Mexico of the Provinces of New Mexico and the Californias, as proposed by the commissioner of the United States, it was believed would be more in accordance with the convenience and interests of both nations than any other cession of territory which it was probable Mexico could be induced to make.

It is manifest to all who have observed the actual condition of the Mexican Government for some years past and at present that if these Provinces should be retained by her she could not long continue to hold and govern them. Mexico is too feeble a power to govern these Provinces, lying as they do at a distance of more than 1,000 miles from her capital, and if attempted to be retained by her they would constitute but for a short time even nominally a part of her dominions. This would be especially the case with Upper California.

The sagacity of powerful European nations has long since directed their attention to the commercial importance of that Province, and there can be little doubt that the moment the United States shall relinquish their present occupation of it and their claim to it as indemnity an effort would be made by some foreign power to possess it, either by conquest or by purchase. If no foreign government should acquire it in either of these modes, an independent revolutionary government would probably

that at their last session an act was passed, upon the Executive recommendation, appropriating $3,000,000 with that express object. This appropriation was made "to enable the President to conclude a treaty of peace, limits, and boundaries with the Republic of Mexico, to be used by him in the event that said treaty, when signed by the authorized agents of the two Governments and duly ratified by Mexico, shall call for the expenditure of the same or any part thereof." The object of asking this appropriation was distinctly stated in the several messages on the subject which I communicated to Congress. Similar appropriations made in 1803 and 1806, which were referred to, were intended to be applied in part consideration for the cession of Louisiana and the Floridas. In like manner it was anticipated that in settling the terms of a treaty of "limits and boundaries" with Mexico a cession of territory estimated to be of greater value than the amount of our demands against her might be obtained, and that the prompt payment of this sum in part consideration for the territory ceded, on the conclusion of a treaty and its ratification on her part, might be an inducement with her to make such a cession of territory as would be satisfactory to the United States; and although the failure to conclude such a treaty has rendered it unnecessary to use any part of the $3,000,000 appropriated by that act, and the entire sum remains in the Treasury, it is still applicable to that object should the contingency occur making such application proper.

The doctrine of no territory is the doctrine of no indemnity, and if sanctioned would be a public acknowledgment that our country was wrong and that the war declared by Congress with extraordinary unanimity was unjust and should be abandoned—an admission unfounded in fact and degrading to the national character.

The terms of the treaty proposed by the United States were not only just to Mexico, but, considering the character and amount of our claims, the unjustifiable and unprovoked commencement of hostilities by her, the expenses of the war to which we have been subjected, and the success which had attended our arms, were deemed to be of a most liberal character.

The commissioner of the United States was authorized to agree to the establishment of the Rio Grande as the boundary from its entrance into the Gulf to its intersection with the southern boundary of New Mexico, in north latitude about 32°, and to obtain a cession to the United States of the Provinces of New Mexico and the Californias and the privilege of the right of way across the Isthmus of Tehuantepec. The boundary of the Rio Grande and the cession to the United States of New Mexico and Upper California constituted an ultimatum which our commissioner was under no circumstances to yield.

That it might be manifest, not only to Mexico, but to all other nations, that the United States were not disposed to take advantage of a feeble power by insisting upon wresting from her all the other Provinces, including many of her principal towns and cities, which we had conquered and held in our military occupation, but were willing to conclude a treaty in

a spirit of liberality, our commissioner was authorized to stipulate for the restoration to Mexico of all our other conquests.

As the territory to be acquired by the boundary proposed might be estimated to be of greater value than a fair equivalent for our just demands, our commissioner was authorized to stipulate for the payment of such additional pecuniary consideration as was deemed reasonable.

The terms of a treaty proposed by the Mexican commissioners were wholly inadmissible. They negotiated as if Mexico were the victorious, and not the vanquished, party. They must have known that their ultimatum could never be accepted. It required the United States to dismember Texas by surrendering to Mexico that part of the territory of that State lying between the Nueces and the Rio Grande, included within her limits by her laws when she was an independent republic, and when she was annexed to the United States and admitted by Congress as one of the States of our Union. It contained no provision for the payment by Mexico of the just claims of our citizens. It required indemnity to Mexican citizens for injuries they may have sustained by our troops in the prosecution of the war. It demanded the right for Mexico to levy and collect the Mexican tariff of duties on goods imported into her ports while in our military occupation during the war, and the owners of which had paid to officers of the United States the military contributions which had been levied upon them; and it offered to cede to the United States, for a pecuniary consideration, that part of Upper California lying north of latitude 37°. Such were the unreasonable terms proposed by the Mexican commissioners.

The cession to the United States by Mexico of the Provinces of New Mexico and the Californias, as proposed by the commissioner of the United States, it was believed would be more in accordance with the convenience and interests of both nations than any other cession of territory which it was probable Mexico could be induced to make.

It is manifest to all who have observed the actual condition of the Mexican Government for some years past and at present that if these Provinces should be retained by her she could not long continue to hold and govern them. Mexico is too feeble a power to govern these Provinces, lying as they do at a distance of more than 1,000 miles from her capital, and if attempted to be retained by her they would constitute but for a short time even nominally a part of her dominions. This would be especially the case with Upper California.

The sagacity of powerful European nations has long since directed their attention to the commercial importance of that Province, and there can be little doubt that the moment the United States shall relinquish their present occupation of it and their claim to it as indemnity an effort would be made by some foreign power to possess it, either by conquest or by purchase. If no foreign government should acquire it in either of these modes, an independent revolutionary government would probably

that at their last session an act was passed, upon the Executive recommendation, appropriating $3,000,000 with that express object. This appropriation was made ''to enable the President to conclude a treaty of peace, limits, and boundaries with the Republic of Mexico, to be used by him in the event that said treaty, when signed by the authorized agents of the two Governments and duly ratified by Mexico, shall call for the expenditure of the same or any part thereof.'' The object of asking this appropriation was distinctly stated in the several messages on the subject which I communicated to Congress. Similar appropriations made in 1803 and 1806, which were referred to, were intended to be applied in part consideration for the cession of Louisiana and the Floridas. In like manner it was anticipated that in settling the terms of a treaty of ''limits and boundaries'' with Mexico a cession of territory estimated to be of greater value than the amount of our demands against her might be obtained, and that the prompt payment of this sum in part consideration for the territory ceded, on the conclusion of a treaty and its ratification on her part, might be an inducement with her to make such a cession of territory as would be satisfactory to the United States; and although the failure to conclude such a treaty has rendered it unnecessary to use any part of the $3,000,000 appropriated by that act, and the entire sum remains in the Treasury, it is still applicable to that object should the contingency occur making such application proper.

The doctrine of no territory is the doctrine of no indemnity, and if sanctioned would be a public acknowledgment that our country was wrong and that the war declared by Congress with extraordinary unanimity was unjust and should be abandoned—an admission unfounded in fact and degrading to the national character.

The terms of the treaty proposed by the United States were not only just to Mexico, but, considering the character and amount of our claims, the unjustifiable and unprovoked commencement of hostilities by her, the expenses of the war to which we have been subjected, and the success which had attended our arms, were deemed to be of a most liberal character.

The commissioner of the United States was authorized to agree to the establishment of the Rio Grande as the boundary from its entrance into the Gulf to its intersection with the southern boundary of New Mexico, in north latitude about 32°, and to obtain a cession to the United States of the Provinces of New Mexico and the Californias and the privilege of the right of way across the Isthmus of Tehuantepec. The boundary of the Rio Grande and the cession to the United States of New Mexico and Upper California constituted an ultimatum which our commissioner was under no circumstances to yield.

That it might be manifest, not only to Mexico, but to all other nations, that the United States were not disposed to take advantage of a feeble power by insisting upon wresting from her all the other Provinces, including many of her principal towns and cities, which we had conquered and held in our military occupation, but were willing to conclude a treaty in

a spirit of liberality, our commissioner was authorized to stipulate for the restoration to Mexico of all our other conquests.

As the territory to be acquired by the boundary proposed might be estimated to be of greater value than a fair equivalent for our just demands, our commissioner was authorized to stipulate for the payment of such additional pecuniary consideration as was deemed reasonable.

The terms of a treaty proposed by the Mexican commissioners were wholly inadmissible. They negotiated as if Mexico were the victorious, and not the vanquished, party. They must have known that their ultimatum could never be accepted. It required the United States to dismember Texas by surrendering to Mexico that part of the territory of that State lying between the Nueces and the Rio Grande, included within her limits by her laws when she was an independent republic, and when she was annexed to the United States and admitted by Congress as one of the States of our Union. It contained no provision for the payment by Mexico of the just claims of our citizens. It required indemnity to Mexican citizens for injuries they may have sustained by our troops in the prosecution of the war. It demanded the right for Mexico to levy and collect the Mexican tariff of duties on goods imported into her ports while in our military occupation during the war, and the owners of which had paid to officers of the United States the military contributions which had been levied upon them; and it offered to cede to the United States, for a pecuniary consideration, that part of Upper California lying north of latitude 37°. Such were the unreasonable terms proposed by the Mexican commissioners.

The cession to the United States by Mexico of the Provinces of New Mexico and the Californias, as proposed by the commissioner of the United States, it was believed would be more in accordance with the convenience and interests of both nations than any other cession of territory which it was probable Mexico could be induced to make.

It is manifest to all who have observed the actual condition of the Mexican Government for some years past and at present that if these Provinces should be retained by her she could not long continue to hold and govern them. Mexico is too feeble a power to govern these Provinces, lying as they do at a distance of more than 1,000 miles from her capital, and if attempted to be retained by her they would constitute but for a short time even nominally a part of her dominions. This would be especially the case with Upper California.

The sagacity of powerful European nations has long since directed their attention to the commercial importance of that Province, and there can be little doubt that the moment the United States shall relinquish their present occupation of it and their claim to it as indemnity an effort would be made by some foreign power to possess it, either by conquest or by purchase. If no foreign government should acquire it in either of these modes, an independent revolutionary government would probably

be established by the inhabitants and such foreigners as may remain in or remove to the country as soon as it shall be known that the United States have abandoned it. Such a government would be too feeble long to maintain its separate independent existence, and would finally become annexed to or be a dependent colony of some more powerful state.

Should any foreign government attempt to possess it as a colony, or otherwise to incorporate it with itself, the principle avowed by President Monroe in 1824, and reaffirmed in my first annual message, that no foreign power shall with our consent be permitted to plant or establish any new.colony or dominion on any part of the North American continent must be maintained. In maintaining this principle and in resisting its invasion by any foreign power we might be involved in other wars more expensive and more difficult than that in which we are now engaged.

The Provinces of New Mexico and the Californias are contiguous to the territories of the United States, and if brought under the government of our laws their resources—mineral, agricultural, manufacturing, and commercial—would soon be developed.

Upper California is bounded on the north by our Oregon possessions, and if held by the United States would soon be settled by a hardy, enterprising, and intelligent portion of our population. The Bay of San Francisco and other harbors along the Californian coast would afford shelter for our Navy, for our numerous whale ships, and other merchant vessels employed in the Pacific Ocean, and would in a short period become the marts of an extensive and profitable commerce with China and other countries of the East.

These advantages, in which the whole commercial world would participate, would at once be secured to the United States by the cession of this territory; while it is certain that as long as it remains a part of the Mexican dominions they can be enjoyed neither by Mexico herself nor by any other nation.

New Mexico is a frontier Province, and has never been of any considerable value to Mexico. From its locality it is naturally connected with our Western settlements. The territorial limits of the State of Texas, too, as defined by her laws before her admission into our Union, embrace all that portion of New Mexico lying east of the Rio Grande, while Mexico still claims to hold this territory as a part of her dominions. The adjustment of this question of boundary is important.

There is another consideration which induced the belief that the Mexican Government might even desire to place this Province under the protection of the Government of the United States. Numerous bands of fierce and warlike savages wander over it and upon its borders. Mexico has been and must continue to be too feeble to restrain them from committing depredations, robberies, and murders, not only upon the inhabitants of New Mexico itself, but upon those of the other northern States of Mexico. It would be a blessing to all these northern States to have their citizens protected against them by the power of the United States. At this moment many Mexicans, principally females and children, are in captivity among them. If New Mexico were held and governed by the United States, we could effectually prevent these tribes from committing such outrages, and compel them to release these captives and restore them to their families and friends.

In proposing to acquire New Mexico and the Californias, it was known that but an inconsiderable portion of the Mexican people would be transferred with them, the country embraced within these Provinces being chiefly an uninhabited region.

These were the leading considerations which induced me to authorize the terms of peace which were proposed to Mexico. They were rejected, and, negotiations being at an end, hostilities were renewed. An assault was made by our gallant Army upon the strongly fortified places near the gates of the City of Mexico and upon the city itself, and after several days of severe conflict the Mexican forces, vastly superior in number to our own, were driven from the city, and it was occupied by our troops.

Immediately after information was received of the unfavorable result of the negotiations, believing that his continued presence with the Army could be productive of no good, I determined to recall our commissioner. A dispatch to this effect was transmitted to him on the 6th of October last. The Mexican Government will be informed of his recall, and that in the existing state of things I shall not deem it proper to make any further overtures of peace, but shall be at all times ready to receive and consider any proposals which may be made by Mexico.

Since the liberal proposition of the United States was authorized to be made, in April last, large expenditures have been incurred and the precious blood of many of our patriotic fellow-citizens has been shed in the prosecution of the war. This consideration and the obstinate perseverance of Mexico in protracting the war must influence the terms of peace which it may be deemed proper hereafter to accept.

Our arms having been everywhere victorious, having subjected to our military occupation a large portion of the enemy's country, including his capital, and negotiations for peace having failed, the important questions arise, in what manner the war ought to be prosecuted and what should be our future policy. I can not doubt that we should secure and render available the conquests which we have already made, and that with this view we should hold and occupy by our naval and military forces all the ports, towns, cities, and Provinces now in our occupation or which may hereafter fall into our possession; that we should press forward our military operations and levy such military contributions on the enemy as may, as far as practicable, defray the future expenses of the war.

Had the Government of Mexico acceded to the equitable and liberal

The export duty would then be as follows:

	Per cent.
Gold, coined or wrought	3
Silver, coined	6
Silver, wrought, with or without certificate of having paid any duty to the Mexican Government	7
Silver, refined or pure, wrought in ingots, with or without certificate of having paid the Mexican Government duty	7
Gold, unwrought or in a state of ore or dust	3
Silver, unwrought or in a state of ore	7

Where gold or silver in any form is taken from any interior Mexican city in our military possession, the export duty must be paid there to the officer of the United States commanding, and his certificate of such prepayment must be produced at the Mexican port of exportation; otherwise a double duty will be collected upon the arrival of such gold or silver at the Mexican port of exportation. Whenever it is practicable, all internal taxes of every description, whether upon persons or property, exacted by the Government of Mexico, or by any department, town, or city thereof, should be collected by our military officers in possession and appropriated as a military contribution toward defraying the expenses of the war, excluding however, all duties on the transit of goods from one department to another, which duties, being prejudicial to revenue and restrictive of the exchange of imports for exports, were abolished by your order of the 31st of March last.

Yours, most respectfully,

R. J. WALKER,
Secretary of the Treasury.

NOVEMBER 16, 1847.

The modifications and military contributions as above recommended by the Secretary of the Treasury are approved by me, and the Secretary of War and the Secretary of the Navy will give the proper orders to carry them into effect.

JAMES K. POLK.

THIRD ANNUAL MESSAGE.

WASHINGTON, *December 7, 1847.*

Fellow-Citizens of the Senate and of the House of Representatives:

The annual meeting of Congress is always an interesting event. The representatives of the States and of the people come fresh from their constituents to take counsel together for the common good.

After an existence of near three-fourths of a century as a free and independent Republic, the problem no longer remains to be solved whether man is capable of self-government. The success of our admirable system is a conclusive refutation of the theories of those in other countries who maintain that a "favored few" are born to rule and that the mass of mankind must be governed by force. Subject to no arbitrary or hereditary authority, the people are the only sovereigns recognized by our Constitution.

Numerous emigrants, of every lineage and language, attracted by the civil and religious freedom we enjoy and by our happy condition, annually crowd to our shores, and transfer their heart, not less than their allegiance, to the country whose dominion belongs alone to the people.

No country has been so much favored, or should acknowledge with deeper reverence the manifestations of the divine protection. An all-wise Creator directed and guarded us in our infant struggle for freedom and has constantly watched over our surprising progress until we have become one of the great nations of the earth.

It is in a country thus favored, and under a Government in which the executive and legislative branches hold their authority for limited periods alike from the people, and where all are responsible to their respective constituencies, that it is again my duty to communicate with Congress upon the state of the Union and the present condition of public affairs.

During the past year the most gratifying proofs are presented that our country has been blessed with a widespread and universal prosperity. There has been no period since the Government was founded when all the industrial pursuits of our people have been more successful or when labor in all branches of business has received a fairer or better reward. From our abundance we have been enabled to perform the pleasing duty of furnishing food for the starving millions of less favored countries.

In the enjoyment of the bounties of Providence at home such as have rarely fallen to the lot of any people, it is cause of congratulation that our intercourse with all the powers of the earth except Mexico continues to be of an amicable character.

It has ever been our cherished policy to cultivate peace and good will with all nations, and this policy has been steadily pursued by me.

No change has taken place in our relations with Mexico since the adjournment of the last Congress. The war in which the United States were forced to engage with the Government of that country still continues.

I deem it unnecessary, after the full exposition of them contained in my message of the 11th of May, 1846, and in my annual message at the commencement of the session of Congress in December last, to reiterate the serious causes of complaint which we had against Mexico before she commenced hostilities.

It is sufficient on the present occasion to say that the wanton violation of the rights of person and property of our citizens committed by Mexico, her repeated acts of bad faith through a long series of years, and her disregard of solemn treaties stipulating for indemnity to our injured prevented it would not be such as to render impracticable the levy of forced contributions for its support, and on the 1st of September and again on the 6th of October, 1847, the order was repeated in dispatches addressed by the Secretary of War to General Scott, and his attention was again called to the importance of making the enemy bear the burdens of the war by requiring them to furnish the means of supporting our Army, and he was directed to adopt this policy unless by doing so there was danger of depriving the Army of the necessary supplies. Copies of these dispatches were forwarded to General Taylor for his government.

On the 31st of March last I caused an order to be issued to our military and naval commanders to levy and collect a military contribution upon all vessels and merchandise which might enter any of the ports of Mexico in our military occupation, and to apply such contributions toward defraying the expenses of the war. By virtue of the right of conquest and the laws of war, the conqueror, consulting his own safety or convenience, may either exclude foreign commerce altogether from all such ports or permit it upon such terms and conditions as he may prescribe. Before the principal ports of Mexico were blockaded by our Navy the revenue derived from import duties under the laws of Mexico was paid into the Mexican treasury. After these ports had fallen into our military possession the blockade was raised and commerce with them permitted upon prescribed terms and conditions. They were opened to the trade of all nations upon the payment of duties more moderate in their amount than those which had been previously levied by Mexico, and the revenue, which was formerly paid into the Mexican treasury, was directed to be collected by our military and naval officers and applied to the use of our Army and Navy. Care was taken that the officers, soldiers, and sailors of our Army and Navy should be exempted from the operations of the order, and, as the merchandise imported upon which the order operated must be consumed by Mexican citizens, the contributions exacted were in effect the seizure of the public revenues of Mexico and the application of them to our own use. In directing this measure the object was to compel the enemy to contribute as far as practicable toward the expenses of the war.

For the amount of contributions which have been levied in this form I refer you to the accompanying reports of the Secretary of War and of the Secretary of the Navy, by which it appears that a sum exceeding half a million of dollars has been collected. This amount would undoubtedly have been much larger but for the difficulty of keeping open communications between the coast and the interior, so as to enable the owners of the merchandise imported to transport and vend it to the inhabitants of the country. It is confidently expected that this difficulty will to a great extent be soon removed by our increased forces which have been sent to the field.

Measures have recently been adopted by which the internal as well as the external revenues of .Mexico in all places in our military occupation will be seized and appropriated to the use of our Army and Navy.

The policy of levying upon the enemy contributions in every form consistently with the laws of nations, which it may be practicable for our military commanders to adopt, should, in my judgment, be rigidly enforced, and orders to this effect have accordingly been given. By such a policy, at the same time that our own Treasury will be relieved from a heavy drain, the Mexican people will be made to feel the burdens of the war, and, consulting their own interests, may be induced the more readily to require their rulers to accede to a just peace.

After the adjournment of the last session of Congress events transpired in the prosecution of the war which in my judgment required a greater number of troops in the field than had been anticipated. The strength of the Army was accordingly increased by "accepting" the services of all the volunteer forces authorized by the act of the 13th of May, 1846, without putting a construction on that act the correctness of which was seriously questioned. The volunteer forces now in the field, with those which had been "accepted" to "serve for twelve months" and were discharged at the end of their term of service, exhaust the 50,000 men authorized by that act. Had it been clear that a proper construction of the act warranted it, the services of an additional number would have been called for and accepted; but doubts existing upon this point, the power was not exercised. It is deemed important that Congress should at an early period of their session confer the authority to raise an additional regular force to serve during the war with Mexico and to be discharged upon the conclusion and ratification of a treaty of peace. I invite the attention of Congress to the views presented by the Secretary of War in his report upon this subject.

I recommend also that authority be given by law to call for and accept the services of an additional number of volunteers, to be exercised at such time and to such extent as the emergencies of the service may require.

In prosecuting the war with Mexico, whilst the utmost care has been taken to avoid every just cause of complaint on the part of neutral nations, and none has been given, liberal privileges have been granted to their commerce in the ports of the enemy in our military occupation.

The difficulty with the Brazilian Government, which at one time threatened to interrupt the friendly relations between the two countries, will, I trust, be speedily adjusted. I have received information that an envoy extraordinary and minister plenipotentiary to the United States will shortly be appointed by His Imperial Majesty, and it is hoped that he will come instructed and prepared to adjust all remaining differences between the two Governments in a manner acceptable and honorable to both. In the meantime, I have every reason to believe that nothing will occur to interrupt our amicable relations with Brazil.

It has been my constant effort to maintain and cultivate the most intimate relations of friendship with all the independent powers of South
America, and this policy has been attended with the happiest results.
It is true that the settlement and payment of many just claims of American citizens against these nations have been long delayed.   The peculiar
position in which they have been placed and the desire on the part of
my predecessors as well as myself to grant them the utmost indulgence
have hitherto prevented these claims from being urged in a manner
demanded by strict justice.   The time has arrived when they ought to
be finally adjusted and liquidated, and efforts are now making for that
purpose.

It is proper to inform you that the Government of Peru has in good
faith paid the first two installments of the indemnity of $30,000 each,
and the greater portion of the interest due thereon, in execution of the
convention between that Government and the United States the ratifications of which were exchanged at Lima on the 31st of October, 1846.
The Attorney-General of the United States early in August last completed the adjudication of the claims under this convention, and made
his report thereon in pursuance of the act of the 8th of August, 1846.
The sums to which the claimants are respectively entitled will be paid
on demand at the Treasury.

I invite the early attention of Congress to the present condition of
our citizens in China.   Under our treaty with that power American
citizens are withdrawn from the jurisdiction, whether civil or criminal,
of the Chinese Government and placed under that of our public functionaries in that country.   By these alone can our citizens be tried and
punished for the commission of any crime; by these alone can questions
be decided between them involving the rights of persons and property,
and by these alone can contracts be enforced into which they may have
entered with the citizens or subjects of foreign powers.   The merchant
vessels of the United States lying in the waters of the five ports of
China open to foreign commerce are under the exclusive jurisdiction of
officers of their own Government.   Until Congress shall establish competent tribunals to try and punish crimes and to exercise jurisdiction in
civil cases in China, American citizens there are subject to no law whatever.   Crimes may be committed with impunity and debts may be contracted without any means to enforce their payment.   Inconveniences
have already resulted from the omission of Congress to legislate upon the
subject, and still greater are apprehended.   The British authorities in
China have already complained that this Government has not provided
for the punishment of crimes or the enforcement of contracts against
American citizens in that country, whilst their Government has established tribunals by which an American citizen can recover debts due
from British subjects.

Accustomed, as the Chinese are, to summary justice, they could not be made to comprehend why criminals who are citizens of the United States should escape with impunity, in violation of treaty obligations, whilst the punishment of a Chinese who had committed any crime against an American citizen would be rigorously exacted. Indeed, the consequences might be fatal to American citizens in China should a flagrant crime be committed by any one of them upon a Chinese, and should trial and punishment not follow according to the requisitions of the treaty. This might disturb, if not destroy, our friendly relations with that Empire, and cause an interruption of our valuable commerce.

Our treaties with the Sublime Porte, Tripoli, Tunis, Morocco, and Muscat also require the legislation of Congress to carry them into execution, though the necessity for immediate action may not be so urgent as in regard to China.

The Secretary of State has submitted an estimate to defray the expense of opening diplomatic relations with the Papal States. The interesting political events now in progress in these States, as well as a just regard to our commercial interests, have, in my opinion, rendered such a measure highly expedient.

Estimates have also been submitted for the outfits and salaries of chargés d'affaires to the Republics of Bolivia, Guatemala, and Ecuador. The manifest importance of cultivating the most friendly relations with all the independent States upon this continent has induced me to recommend appropriations necessary for the maintenance of these missions.

I recommend to Congress that an appropriation be made to be paid to the Spanish Government for the purpose of distribution among the claimants in the *Amistad* case.. I entertain the conviction that this is due to Spain under the treaty of the 20th of October, 1795, and, moreover, that from the earnest manner in which the claim continues to be urged so long as it shall remain unsettled it will be a source of irritation and discord between the two countries, which may prove highly prejudicial to the interests of the United States. Good policy, no less than a faithful compliance with our treaty obligations, requires that the inconsiderable appropriation demanded should be made.

A detailed statement of the condition of the finances will be presented in the annual report of the Secretary of the Treasury. The imports for the last fiscal year, ending on the 30th of June, 1847, were of the value of $146,545,638, of which the amount exported was $8,011,158, leaving $138,534,480 in the country for domestic use. The value of the exports for the same period was $158,648,622, of which $150,637,464 consisted of domestic productions and $8,011,158 of foreign articles.

The receipts into the Treasury for the same period amounted to $26,-346,790.37, of which there was derived from customs $23,747,864.66, from sales of public lands $2,498,335.20, and from incidental and miscellaneous sources $100,570.51. The last fiscal year, during which this amount was received, embraced five months under the operation of the tariff act of 1842 and seven months during which the tariff act of 1846 was in force. During the five months under the act of 1842 the amount received from customs was $7,842,306.90, and during the seven months under the act of 1846 the amount received was $15,905,557.76.

The net revenue from customs during the year ending on the 1st of December, 1846, being the last year under the operation of the tariff act of 1842, was $22,971,403.10, and the net revenue from customs during the year ending on the 1st of December, 1847, being the first year under the operations of the tariff act of 1846, was about $31,500,000, being an increase of revenue for the first year under the tariff of 1846 of more than $8,500,000 over that of the last year under the tariff of 1842.

The expenditures during the fiscal year ending on the 30th of June last were $59,451,177.65, of which $3,522,082.37 was on account of payment of principal and interest of the public debt, including Treasury notes redeemed and not funded. The expenditures exclusive of payment of public debt were $55,929,095.28.

It is estimated that the receipts into the Treasury for the fiscal year ending on the 30th of June, 1848, including the balance in the Treasury on the 1st of July last, will amount to $42,886,545.80, of which $31,000,000, it is estimated, will be derived from customs, $3,500,000 from the sale of the public lands, $400,000 from incidental sources, including sales made by the Solicitor of the Treasury, and $6,285,294.55 from loans already authorized by law, which, together with the balance in the Treasury on the 1st of July last, make the sum estimated.

The expenditures for the same period, if peace with Mexico shall not be concluded and the Army shall be increased as is proposed, will amount, including the necessary payments on account of principal and interest of the public debt and Treasury notes, to $58,615,660.07.

On the 1st of the present month the amount of the public debt actually incurred, including Treasury notes, was $45,659,659.40. The public debt due on the 4th of March, 1845, including Treasury notes, was $17,788,799.62, and consequently the addition made to the public debt since that time is $27,870,859.78.

Of the loan of twenty-three millions authorized by the act of the 28th of January, 1847, the sum of five millions was paid out to the public creditors or exchanged at par for specie; the remaining eighteen millions was offered for specie to the highest bidder not below par, by an advertisement issued by the Secretary of the Treasury and published from the 9th of February until the 10th of April, 1847, when it was awarded to the several highest bidders at premiums varying from one-eighth of 1 per cent to 2 per cent above par. The premium has been paid into the Treasury and the sums awarded deposited in specie in the Treasury as fast as it was required by the wants of the Government.

To meet the expenditures for the remainder of the present and for the next fiscal year, ending on the 30th of June, 1849, a further loan in aid of the ordinary revenues of the Government will be necessary. Retaining a sufficient surplus in the Treasury, the loan required for the remainder of the present fiscal year will be about $18,500,000. If the duty on tea and coffee be imposed and the graduation of the price of the public lands shall be made at an early period of your session, as recommended, the loan for the present fiscal year may be reduced to $17,000,000. The loan may be further reduced by whatever amount of expenditures can be saved by military contributions collected in Mexico. The most vigorous measures for the augmentation of these contributions have been directed and a very considerable sum is expected from that source. Its amount can not, however, be calculated with any certainty. It is recommended that the loan to be made be authorized upon the same terms and for the same time as that which was authorized under the provisions of the act of the 28th of January, 1847.

Should the war with Mexico be continued until the 30th of June, 1849, it is estimated that a further loan of $20,500,000 will be required for the fiscal year ending on that day, in case no duty be imposed on tea and coffee, and the public lands be not reduced and graduated in price, and no military contributions shall be collected in Mexico. If the duty on tea and coffee be imposed and the lands be reduced and graduated in price as proposed, the loan may be reduced to $17,000,000, and will be subject to be still further reduced by the amount of the military contributions which may be collected in Mexico. It is not proposed, however, at present to ask Congress for authority to negotiate this loan for the next fiscal year, as it is hoped that the loan asked for the remainder of the present fiscal year, aided by military contributions which may be collected in Mexico, may be sufficient. If, contrary to my expectation, there should be a necessity for it, the fact will be communicated to Congress in time for their action during the present session. In no event will a sum exceeding $6,000,000 of this amount be needed before the meeting of the session of Congress in December, 1848.

The act of the 30th of July, 1846, "reducing the duties on imports," has been in force since the 1st of December last, and I am gratified to state that all the beneficial effects which were anticipated from its operation have been fully realized. The public revenue derived from customs during the year ending on the 1st of December, 1847, exceeds by more than $8,000,000 the amount received in the preceding year under the operation of the act of 1842, which was superseded and repealed by it. Its effects are visible in the great and almost unexampled prosperity which prevails in every branch of business.

While the repeal of the prohibitory and restrictive duties of the act of 1842 and the substitution in their place of reasonable revenue rates levied on articles imported according to their actual value has increased the revenue and augmented our foreign trade, all the great interests of the country have been advanced and promoted.

The great and important interests of agriculture, which had been not only too much neglected, but actually taxed under the protective policy for the benefit of other interests, have been relieved of the burdens which that policy imposed on them; and our farmers and planters, under a more just and liberal commercial policy, are finding new and profitable markets abroad for their augmented products. Our commerce is rapidly increasing, and is extending more widely the circle of international exchanges. Great as has been the increase of our imports during the past year, our exports of domestic products sold in foreign markets have been still greater.

Our navigating interest is eminently prosperous. The number of vessels built in the United States has been greater than during any preceding period of equal length. Large profits have been derived by those who have constructed as well as by those who have navigated them. Should the ratio of increase in the number of our merchant vessels be progressive, and be as great for the future as during the past year, the time is not distant when our tonnage and commercial marine will be larger than that of any other nation in the world.

Whilst the interests of agriculture, of commerce, and of navigation have been enlarged and invigorated, it is highly gratifying to observe that our manufactures are also in a prosperous condition. None of the ruinous effects upon this interest which were apprehended by some as the result of the operation of the revenue system established by the act of 1846 have been experienced. On the contrary, the number of manufactories and the amount of capital invested in them is steadily and rapidly increasing, affording gratifying proofs that American enterprise and skill employed in this branch of domestic industry, with no other advantages than those fairly and incidentally accruing from a just system of revenue duties, are abundantly able to meet successfully all competition from abroad and still derive fair and remunerating profits. While capital invested in manufactures is yielding adequate and fair profits under the new system, the wages of labor, whether employed in manufactures, agriculture, commerce, or navigation, have been augmented. The toiling millions whose daily labor furnishes the supply of food and raiment and all the necessaries and comforts of life are receiving higher wages and more steady and permanent employment than in any other country or at any previous period of our own history.

So successful have been all branches of our industry that a foreign war, which generally diminishes the resources of a nation, has in no essential degree retarded our onward progress or checked our general prosperity.

With such gratifying evidences of prosperity and of the successful operation of the revenue act of 1846, every consideration of public policy recommends that it shall remain unchanged. It is hoped that the system of impost duties which it established may be regarded as the permanent policy of the country, and that the great interests affected by it may not again be subject to be injuriously disturbed, as they have heretofore been, by frequent and sometimes sudden changes.

For the purpose of increasing the revenue, and without changing or modifying the rates imposed by the act of 1846 on the dutiable articles embraced by its provisions, I again recommend to your favorable consideration the expediency of levying a revenue duty on tea and coffee. The policy which exempted these articles from duty during peace, and when the revenue to be derived from them was not needed, ceases to exist when the country is engaged in war and requires the use of all of its available resources. It is a tax which would be so generally diffused among the people that it would be felt oppressively by none and be complained of by none. It is believed that there are not in the list of imported articles any which are more properly the subject of war duties than tea and coffee.

It is estimated that $3,000,000 would be derived annually by a moderate duty imposed on these articles.

Should Congress avail itself of this additional source of revenue, not only would the amount of the public loan rendered necessary by the war with Mexico be diminished to that extent, but the public credit and the public confidence in the ability and determination of the Government to meet all its engagements promptly would be more firmly established, and the reduced amount of the loan which it may be necessary to negotiate could probably be obtained at cheaper rates.

Congress is therefore called upon to determine whether it is wiser to impose the war duties recommended or by omitting to do so increase the public debt annually $3,000,000 so long as loans shall be required to prosecute the war, and afterwards provide in some other form to pay the semiannual interest upon it, and ultimately to extinguish the principal. If in addition to these duties Congress should graduate and reduce the price of such of the public lands as experience has proved will not command the price placed upon them by the Government, an additional annual income to the Treasury of between half a million and a million of dollars, it is estimated, would be derived from this source. Should both measures receive the sanction of Congress, the annual amount of public debt necessary to be contracted during the continuance of the war would be reduced near $4,000,000. The duties recommended to be levied on tea and coffee it is proposed shall be limited in their duration to the end of the war, and until the public debt rendered necessary to be contracted by it shall be discharged. The amount of the public debt to be contracted should be limited to the lowest practicable sum, and should be extinguished as early after the conclusion of the war as the means of the Treasury will permit.

With this view, it is recommended that as soon as the war shall be over all the surplus in the Treasury not needed for other indispensable objects shall constitute a sinking fund and be applied to the purchase of the funded debt, and that authority be conferred by laws for that purpose.

The act of the 6th of August, 1846, "to establish a warehousing system," has been in operation more than a year, and has proved to be an important auxiliary to the tariff act of 1846 in augmenting the revenue and extending the commerce of the country. Whilst it has tended to enlarge commerce, it has been beneficial to our manufactures by diminishing forced sales at auction of foreign goods at low prices to raise the duties to be advanced on them, and by checking fluctuations in the market. The system, although sanctioned by the experience of other countries, was entirely new in the United States, and is susceptible of improvement in some of its provisions. The Secretary of the Treasury, upon whom was devolved large discretionary powers in carrying this measure into effect, has collected and is now collating the practical results of the system in other countries where it has long been established, and will report at an early period of your session such further regulations suggested by the investigation as may render it still more effective and beneficial.

By the act to "provide for the better organization of the Treasury and for the collection, safe-keeping, and disbursement of the public revenue" all banks were discontinued as fiscal agents of the Government, and the paper currency issued by them was no longer permitted to be received in payment of public dues. The constitutional treasury created by this act went into operation on the 1st of January last. Under the system established by it the public moneys have been collected, safely kept, and disbursed by the direct agency of officers of the Government in gold and silver, and transfers of large amounts have been made from points of collection to points of disbursement without loss to the Treasury or injury or inconvenience to the trade of the country.

While the fiscal operations of the Government have been conducted with regularity and ease under this system, it has had a salutary effect in checking and preventing an undue inflation of the paper currency issued by the banks which exist under State charters. Requiring, as it does, all dues to the Government to be paid in gold and silver, its effect is to restrain excessive issues of bank paper by the banks disproportioned to the specie in their vaults, for the reason that they are at all times liable to be called on by the holders of their notes for their redemption in order to obtain specie for the payment of duties and other public dues. The banks, therefore, must keep their business within prudent limits, and be always in a condition to meet such calls, or run the hazard of being compelled to suspend specie payments and be thereby discredited. The amount of specie imported into the United States during the last fiscal year was $24,121,289, of which there was retained in the country $22,276,170. Had the former financial system prevailed and the public moneys been placed on deposit in the banks, nearly the whole of this amount would have gone into their vaults, not to be thrown into circulation by them, but to be withheld from the hands of the people as a currency and made the basis of new and enormous issues of bank paper. A large proportion of the specie imported has been paid into the Treasury for public dues, and after having been to a great extent recoined at the

Mint has been paid out to the public creditors and gone into circulation as a currency among the people. The amount of gold and silver coin now in circulation in the country is larger than at any former period.

The financial system established by the constitutional treasury has been thus far eminently successful in its operations, and I recommend an adherence to all its essential provisions, and especially to that vital provision which wholly separates the Government from all connection with banks and excludes bank paper from all revenue receipts.

In some of its details, not involving its general principles, the system is defective and will require modification. These defects and such amendments as are deemed important were set forth in the last annual report of the Secretary of the Treasury. These amendments are again recommended to the early and favorable consideration of Congress.

During the past year the coinage at the Mint and its branches has exceeded $20,000,000. This has consisted chiefly in converting the coins of foreign countries into American coin.

The largest amount of foreign coin imported has been received at New York, and if a branch mint were established at that city all the foreign coin received at that port could at once be converted into our own coin without the expense, risk, and delay of transporting it to the Mint for that purpose, and the amount recoined would be much larger.

Experience has proved that foreign coin, and especially foreign gold coin, will not circulate extensively as a currency among the people. The important measure of extending our specie circulation, both of gold and silver, and of diffusing it among the people can only be effected by converting such foreign coin into American coin. I repeat the recommendation contained in my last annual message for the establishment of a branch of the Mint of the United States at the city of New York.

All the public lands which had been surveyed and were ready for market have been proclaimed for sale during the past year. The quantity offered and to be offered for sale under proclamations issued since the 1st of January last amounts to 9,138,531 acres. The prosperity of the Western States and Territories in which these lands lie will be advanced by their speedy sale. By withholding them from market their growth and increase of population would be retarded, while thousands of our enterprising and meritorious frontier population would be deprived of the opportunity of securing freeholds for themselves and their families. But in addition to the general considerations which rendered the early sale of these lands proper, it was a leading object at this time to derive as large a sum as possible from this source, and thus diminish by that amount the public loan rendered necessary by the existence of a foreign war.

It is estimated that not less than 10,000,000 acres of the public lands will be surveyed and be in a condition to be proclaimed for sale during the year 1848.

In my last annual message I presented the reasons which in my judgment rendered it proper to graduate and reduce the price of such of the public lands as have remained unsold for long periods after they had been offered for sale at public auction.

Many millions of acres of public lands lying within the limits of several of the Western States have been offered in the market and been subject to sale at private entry for more than twenty years and large quantities for more than thirty years at the lowest price prescribed by the existing laws, and it has been found that they will not command that price. They must remain unsold and uncultivated for an indefinite period unless the price demanded for them by the Government shall be reduced. No satisfactory reason is perceived why they should be longer held at rates above their real value. At the present period an additional reason exists for adopting the measure recommended. When the country is engaged in a foreign war, and we must necessarily resort to loans, it would seem to be the dictate of wisdom that we should avail ourselves of all our resources and thus limit the amount of the public indebtedness to the lowest possible sum.

I recommend that the existing laws on the subject of preemption rights be amended and modified so as to operate prospectively and to embrace all who may settle upon the public lands and make improvements upon them, before they are surveyed as well as afterwards, in all cases where such settlements may be made after the Indian title shall have been extinguished.

If the right of preemption be thus extended, it will embrace a large and meritorious class of our citizens. It will increase the number of small freeholders upon our borders, who will be enabled thereby to educate their children and otherwise improve their condition, while they will be found at all times, as they have ever proved themselves to be in the hour of danger to their country, among our hardiest and best volunteer soldiers, ever ready to attend to their services in cases of emergencies and among the last to leave the field as long as an enemy remains to be encountered. Such a policy will also impress these patriotic pioneer emigrants with deeper feelings of gratitude for the parental care of their Government, when they find their dearest interests secured to them by the permanent laws of the land and that they are no longer in danger of losing their homes and hard-earned improvements by being brought into competition with a more wealthy class of purchasers at the land sales.

The attention of Congress was invited at their last and the preceding session to the importance of establishing a Territorial government over our possessions in Oregon, and it is to be regretted that there was no legislation on the subject. Our citizens who inhabit that distant region of country are still left without the protection of our laws, or any regularly organized government. Before the question of limits and boundaries of the Territory of Oregon was definitely settled, from the necessity of their condition the inhabitants had established a temporary government of their own. Besides the want of legal authority for continuing such a government, it is wholly inadequate to protect them in their rights of person and property, or to secure to them the enjoyment of the privileges of other citizens, to which they are entitled under the Constitution of the United States. They should have the right of suffrage, be represented in a Territorial legislature and by a Delegate in Congress, and possess all the rights and privileges which citizens of other portions of the territories of the United States have heretofore enjoyed or may now enjoy.

Our judicial system, revenue laws, laws regulating trade and intercourse with the Indian tribes, and the protection of our laws generally should be extended over them.

In addition to the inhabitants in that Territory who had previously emigrated to it, large numbers of our citizens have followed them during the present year, and it is not doubted that during the next and subsequent years their numbers will be greatly increased.

Congress at its last session established post routes leading to Oregon, and between different points within that Territory, and authorized the establishment of post-offices at "Astoria and such other places on the coasts of the Pacific within the territory of the United States as the public interests may require." Post-offices have accordingly been established, deputy postmasters appointed, and provision made for the transportation of the mails.

The preservation of peace with the Indian tribes residing west of the Rocky Mountains will render it proper that authority should be given by law for the appointment of an adequate number of Indian agents to reside among them.

I recommend that a surveyor-general's office be established in that Territory, and that the public lands be surveyed and brought into market at an early period.

I recommend also that grants, upon liberal terms, of limited quantities of the public lands be made to all citizens of the United States who have emigrated, or may hereafter within a prescribed period emigrate, to Oregon and settle upon them. These hardy and adventurous citizens, who have encountered the dangers and privations of a long and toilsome journey, and have at length found an abiding place for themselves and their families upon the utmost verge of our western limits, should be secured in the homes which they have improved by their labor.

I refer you to the accompanying report of the Secretary of War for a detailed account of the operations of the various branches of the public service connected with the Department under his charge. The duties devolving on this Department have been unusually onerous and responsible during the past year, and have been discharged with ability and success.

Pacific relations continue to exist with the various Indian tribes, and most of them manifest a strong friendship for the United States. Some depredations were committed during the past year upon our trains transporting supplies for the Army, on the road between the western border of Missouri and Santa Fe. These depredations, which are supposed to have been committed by bands from the region of New Mexico, have been arrested by the presence of a military force ordered out for that purpose. Some outrages have been perpetrated by a portion of the northwestern bands upon the weaker and comparatively defenseless neighboring tribes. Prompt measures were taken to prevent such occurrences in future.

Between 1,000 and 2,000 Indians, belonging to several tribes, have been removed during the year from the east of the Mississippi to the country allotted to them west of that river as their permanent home, and arrangements have been made for others to follow.

Since the treaty of 1846 with the Cherokees the feuds among them appear to have subsided, and they have become more united and contented than they have been for many years past. The commissioners appointed in pursuance of the act of June 27, 1846, to settle claims arising under the treaty of 1835–36 with that tribe have executed their duties, and after a patient investigation and a full and fair examination of all the cases brought before them closed their labors in the month of July last. This is the fourth board of commissioners which has been organized under this treaty. Ample opportunity has been afforded to all those interested to bring forward their claims. No doubt is entertained that impartial justice has been done by the late board, and that all valid claims embraced by the treaty have been considered and allowed. This result and the final settlement to be made with this tribe under the treaty of 1846, which will be completed and laid before you during your session, will adjust all questions of controversy between them and the United States and produce a state of relations with them simple, well defined, and satisfactory.

Under the discretionary authority conferred by the act of the 3d of March last the annuities due to the various tribes have been paid during the present year to the heads of families instead of to their chiefs or such persons as they might designate, as required by the law previously existing. This mode of payment has given general satisfaction to the great body of the Indians. Justice has been done to them, and they are grateful to the Government for it. A few chiefs and interested persons may object to this mode of payment, but it is believed to be the only mode of preventing fraud and imposition from being practiced upon the great body of common Indians, constituting a majority of all the tribes.

It is gratifying to perceive that a number of the tribes have recently manifested an increased interest in the establishment of schools among them, and are making rapid advances in agriculture, some of them producing a sufficient quantity of food for their support and in some cases a surplus to dispose of to their neighbors. The comforts by which those who have received even a very limited education and have engaged in agriculture are surrounded tend gradually to draw off their less civilized brethren from the precarious means of subsistence by the chase to habits of labor and civilization.

The accompanying report of the Secretary of the Navy presents a satisfactory and gratifying account of the condition and operations of the naval service during the past year. Our commerce has been pursued with increased activity and with safety and success in every quarter of the globe under the protection of our flag, which the Navy has caused to be respected in the most distant seas.

In the Gulf of Mexico and in the Pacific the officers and men of our squadrons have displayed distinguished gallantry and performed valuable services. In the early stages of the war with Mexico her ports on both coasts were blockaded, and more recently many of them have been captured and held by the Navy. When acting in cooperation with the land forces, the naval officers and men have performed gallant and distinguished services on land as well as on water, and deserve the high commendation of the country.

While other maritime powers are adding to their navies large numbers of war steamers, it was a wise policy on our part to make similar additions to our Navy. The four war steamers authorized by the act of the 3d of March, 1847, are in course of construction.

In addition to the four war steamers authorized by this act, the Secretary of the Navy has, in pursuance of its provisions, entered into contracts for the construction of five steamers to be employed in the transportation of the United States mail "from New York to New Orleans, touching at Charleston, Savannah, and Havana, and from Havana to Chagres;" for three steamers to be employed in like manner from Panama to Oregon, "so as to connect with the mail from Havana to Chagres across the Isthmus;" and for five steamers to be employed in like manner from New York to Liverpool. These steamers will be the property of the contractors, but are to be built "under the superintendence and direction of a naval constructor in the employ of the Navy Department, and to be so constructed as to render them convertible at the least possible expense into war steamers of the first class." A prescribed number of naval officers, as well as a post-office agent, are to be on board of them, and authority is reserved to the Navy Department at all times to "exercise control over said steamships" and "to have the right to take them for the exclusive use and service of the United States upon making proper compensation to the contractors therefor."

Whilst these steamships will be employed in transporting the mails of the United States coastwise and to foreign countries upon an annual compensation to be paid to the owners, they will be always ready, upon an emergency requiring it, to be converted into war steamers; and the right reserved to take them for public use will add greatly to the efficiency and strength of this description of our naval force.   To the steamers thus authorized under contracts made by the Secretary of the Navy should be added five other steamers authorized under contracts made in pursuance of laws by the Postmaster-General, making an addition, in the whole, of eighteen war steamers subject to be taken for public use.   As further contracts for the transportation of the mail to foreign countries may be authorized by Congress, this number may be enlarged indefinitely.

The enlightened policy by which a rapid communication with the various distant parts of the globe is established, by means of American-built sea steamers, would find an ample reward in the increase of our commerce and in making our country and its resources more favorably known abroad; but the national advantage is still greater—of having our naval officers made familiar with steam navigation and of having the privilege of taking the ships already equipped for immediate service at a moment's notice, and will be cheaply purchased by the compensation to be paid for the transportation of the mail in them over and above the postages received.

A just national pride, no less than our commercial interests, would seem to favor the policy of augmenting the number of this description of vessels.   They can be built in our country cheaper and in greater numbers than in any other in the world.

I refer you to the accompanying report of the Postmaster-General for a detailed and satisfactory account of the condition and operations of that Department during the past year.   It is gratifying to find that within so short a period after the reduction in the rates of postage, and notwithstanding the great increase of mail service, the revenue received for the year will be sufficient to defray all the expenses, and that no further aid will be required from the Treasury for that purpose.

The first of the American mail steamers authorized by the act of the 3d of March, 1845, was completed and entered upon the service on the 1st of June last, and is now on her third voyage to Bremen and other intermediate ports.   The other vessels authorized under the provisions of that act are in course of construction, and will be put upon the line as soon as completed.   Contracts have also been made for the transportation of the mail in a steamer from Charleston to Havana.

A reciprocal and satisfactory postal arrangement has been made by the Postmaster-General with the authorities of Bremen, and no difficulty is apprehended in making similar arrangements with all other powers with which we may have communications by mail steamers, except with Great Britain.

On the arrival of the first of the American steamers bound to Bremen at Southampton, in the month of June last, the British post-office directed the collection of discriminating postages on all letters and other mailable matter which she took out to Great Britain or which went into the British post-office on their way to France and other parts of Europe. The effect of the order of the British post-office is to subject all letters and other matter transported by American steamers to double postage, one postage having been previously paid on them to the United States, while letters transported in British steamers are subject to pay but a single postage. This measure was adopted with the avowed object of protecting the British line of mail steamers now running between Boston and Liverpool, and if permitted to continue must speedily put an end to the transportation of all letters and other matter by American steamers and give to British steamers a monopoly of the business. A just and fair reciprocity is all that we desire, and on this we must insist. By our laws no such discrimination is made against British steamers bringing letters into our ports, but all letters arriving in the United States are subject to the same rate of postage, whether brought in British or American vessels. I refer you to the report of the Postmaster-General for a full statement of the facts of the case and of the steps taken by him to correct this inequality. He has exerted all the power conferred upon him by the existing laws.

The minister of the United States at London has brought the subject to the attention of the British Government, and is now engaged in negotiations for the purpose of adjusting reciprocal postal arrangements which shall be equally just to both countries. Should he fail in concluding such arrangements, and should Great Britain insist on enforcing the unequal and unjust measure she has adopted, it will become necessary to confer additional powers on the Postmaster-General in order to enable him to meet the emergency and to put our own steamers on an equal footing with British steamers engaged in transporting the mails between the two countries, and I recommend that such powers be conferred.

In view of the existing state of our country, I trust it may not be inappropriate, in closing this communication, to call to mind the words of wisdom and admonition of the first and most illustrious of my predecessors in his Farewell Address to his countrymen.

That greatest and best of men, who served his country so long and loved it so much, foresaw with "serious concern" the danger to our Union of "characterizing parties by *geographical* discriminations—*Northern* and *Southern*, *Atlantic* and *Western*—whence designing men may endeavor to excite a belief that there is a real difference of local interests and views," and warned his countrymen against it.

, So deep and solemn was his conviction of the importance of the Union and of preserving harmony between its different parts, that he declared to his countrymen in that address:

It is of infinite moment that you should properly estimate the immense value of your national union to your collective and individual happiness; that you should cherish a cordial, habitual, and immovable attachment to it; accustoming yourselves to think and speak of it as of the palladium of your political safety and prosperity; watching for its preservation with jealous anxiety; discountenancing whatever may suggest even a suspicion that it can in any event be abandoned, and indignantly frowning upon the first dawning of every attempt to alienate any portion of our country from the rest or to enfeeble the sacred ties which now link together the various parts.

After the lapse of half a century these admonitions of Washington fall upon us with all the force of truth. It *is* difficult to estimate the "immense value" of our glorious Union of confederated States, to which we are so much indebted for our growth in population and wealth and for all that constitutes us a great and a happy nation. How unimportant are all our differences of opinion upon minor questions of public policy compared with its preservation, and how scrupulously should we avoid all agitating topics which may tend to distract and divide us into contending parties, separated by geographical lines, whereby it may be weakened or endangered.

Invoking the blessing of the Almighty Ruler of the Universe upon your deliberations, it will be my highest duty, no less than my sincere pleasure, to cooperate with you in all measures which may tend to promote the honor and enduring welfare of our common country.

JAMES K. POLK.

SPECIAL MESSAGES.

WASHINGTON, *December 20, 1847.*

To the Senate of the United States:

I herewith communicate to the Senate, for their consideration and advice with regard to its ratification, a convention between the United States and the Swiss Confederation, signed in this city by their respective plenipotentiaries on the 18th day of May last, for the mutual abolition of the *droit d'aubaine* and of taxes on emigration.

JAMES K. POLK.

WASHINGTON, *December 21, 1847.*

To the Senate of the United States:

I submit herewith, for the consideration and constitutional action of the Senate, two treaties with the Chippewa Indians of Lake Superior and the Upper Mississippi, for a portion of the lands possessed by those Indians west of the Mississippi River. The treaties are accompanied by communications from the Secretary of War and Commissioner of Indian Affairs, which fully explain their nature and objects.

JAMES K. POLK.

WASHINGTON, *December 22, 1847.*

To the Senate and House of Representatives:

I communicate herewith a report of the Secretary of the Navy, containing a statement of the measures which have been taken in execution of the act of 3d March last, relating to the construction of floating dry docks at Pensacola, Philadelphia, and Kittery.

JAMES K. POLK.

WASHINGTON, *January 4, 1848.*

To the House of Representatives of the United States:

I communicate herewith a report of the Secretary of War, with accompanying documents, being in addition to a report made on the 27th of February, 1847, in answer to a resolution of the House of Representatives of the 1st of that month, requesting the President "to communicate to the House of Representatives all the correspondence with General Taylor since the commencement of hostilities with Mexico which has not yet been published, and the publication of which may not be deemed detrimental to the public service; also the correspondence of the Quartermaster-General in relation to transportation for General Taylor's Army; also the reports of Brigadier-Generals Hamer and Quitman of the operations of their respective brigades on the 21st of September last" (1846).

JAMES K. POLK.

WASHINGTON, *January 12, 1848.*

To the House of Representatives of the United States:

I have carefully considered the resolution of the House of Representatives of the 4th instant, requesting the President to communicate to that House "any instructions which may have been given to any of the officers of the Army or Navy of the United States, or other persons, in regard to the return of President General Lopez de Santa Anna, or any other Mexican, to the Republic of Mexico prior or subsequent to the order of the President or Secretary of War issued in January, 1846, for the march of the Army from the Nueces River, across the 'stupendous deserts' which intervene, to the Rio Grande; that the date of all such instructions, orders, and correspondence be set forth, together with the instructions and orders issued to Mr. Slidell at any time prior or subsequent to his departure for Mexico as minister plenipotentiary of the United States to that Republic;" and requesting the President also to "communicate all the orders and correspondence of the Government in relation to the return of General Paredes to Mexico."

I transmit herewith reports from the Secretary of State, the Secretary of War, and the Secretary of the Navy, with the documents accompanying the same, which contain all the information in the possession of the Executive which it is deemed compatible with the public interests to communicate.

For further information relating to the return of Santa Anna to Mexico I refer you to my annual message of December 8, 1846. The facts and considerations stated in that message induced the order of the Secretary of the Navy to the commander of our squadron in the Gulf of Mexico a copy of which is herewith communicated. This order was issued simultaneously with the order to blockade the coasts of Mexico, both bearing date the 13th of May, 1846, the day on which the existence of the war

with Mexico was recognized by Congress.   It was issued solely upon
the views of policy presented in that message, and without any understanding on the subject, direct or indirect, with Santa Anna or any other
person.

General Paredes evaded the vigilance of our combined forces by land
and sea, and made his way back to Mexico from the exile into which he
had been driven, landing at Vera Cruz after that city and the castle of
San Juan de Ulloa were in our military occupation, as will appear from
the accompanying reports and documents.

The resolution calls for the "instructions and orders issued to Mr.
Slidell at any time prior or subsequent to his departure for Mexico as
minister plenipotentiary of the United States to that Republic."   The
customary and usual reservation contained in calls of either House of
Congress upon the Executive for information relating to our intercourse
with foreign nations has been omitted in the resolution before me.   The
call of the House is unconditional.   It is that the information requested
be communicated, and thereby be made public, whether in the opinion
of the Executive (who is charged by the Constitution with the duty of
conducting negotiations with foreign powers) such information, when
disclosed, would be prejudicial to the public interest or not.   It has been
a subject of serious deliberation with me whether I could, consistently
with my constitutional duty and my sense of the public interests involved and to be affected by it, violate an important principle, always
heretofore held sacred by my predecessors, as I should do by a compliance with the request of the House.   President Washington, in a message to the House of Representatives of the 30th of March, 1796, declined
to comply with a request contained in a resolution of that body, to lay
before them "a copy of the instructions to the minister of the United
States who negotiated the treaty with the King of Great Britain, together
with the correspondence and other documents relative to that treaty,
excepting such of the said papers as any existing negotiation may render
improper to be disclosed."   In assigning his reasons for declining to comply with the call he declared that—

The nature of foreign negotiations requires caution, and their success must often
depend on secrecy; and even when brought to a conclusion a full disclosure of all
the measures, demands, or eventual concessions which may have been proposed or
contemplated would be extremely impolitic; for this might have a pernicious influence on future negotiations, or produce immediate inconveniences, perhaps danger
and mischief, in relation to other powers.   The necessity of such caution and secrecy
was one cogent reason for vesting the power of making treaties in the President,
with the advice and consent of the Senate, the principle on which that body was
formed confining it to a small number of members.   To admit, then, a right in the
House of Representatives to demand and to have as a matter of course all the papers respecting a negotiation with a foreign power would be to establish a dangerous
precedent.

In that case the instructions and documents called for related to a
treaty which had been concluded and ratified by the President and Senate, and the negotiations in relation to it had been terminated.   There

was an express reservation, too, "excepting" from the call all such papers as related to "any existing negotiations" which it might be improper to disclose. In that case President Washington deemed it to be a violation of an important principle, the establishment of a "dangerous precedent," and prejudicial to the public interests to comply with the call of the House. Without deeming it to be necessary on the present occasion to examine or decide upon the other reasons assigned by him for his refusal to communicate the information requested by the House, the one which is herein recited is in my judgment conclusive in the case under consideration.

Indeed, the objections to complying with the request of the House contained in the resolution before me are much stronger than those which existed in the case of the resolution in 1796. This resolution calls for the "instructions and orders" to the minister of the United States to Mexico which relate to negotiations which have not been terminated, and which may be resumed. The information called for respects negotiations which the United States offered to open with Mexico immediately preceding the commencement of the existing war. The instructions given to the minister of the United States relate to the differences between the two countries out of which the war grew and the terms of adjustment which we were prepared to offer to Mexico in our anxiety to prevent the war. These differences still remain unsettled, and to comply with the call of the House would be to make public through that channel, and to communicate to Mexico, now a public enemy engaged in war, information which could not fail to produce serious embarrassment in any future negotiation between the two countries. I have heretofore communicated to Congress all the correspondence of the minister of the United States to Mexico which in the existing state of our relations with that Republic can, in my judgment, be at this time communicated without serious injury to the public interest.

Entertaining this conviction, and with a sincere desire to furnish any information which may be in possession of the executive department, and which either House of Congress may at any time request, I regard it to be my constitutional right and my solemn duty under the circumstances of this case to decline a compliance with the request of the House contained in their resolution.

JAMES K. POLK.

WASHINGTON, *January 21, 1848.*
To the Senate of the United States:

I herewith communicate to the Senate, for its consideration, a declaration of the Government of the Grand Duchy of Mecklenburg-Schwerin, bearing date at the city of Schwerin on the 9th December, 1847, acceding substantially to the stipulations of our treaty of commerce and navigation with Hanover of the 10th June, 1846.

Under the twelfth article of this treaty—

The United States agree to extend all the advantages and privileges contained in the stipulations of the present treaty to one or more of the other States of the Germanic Confederation which may wish to accede to them, by means of an official exchange of declarations, provided that such State or States shall confer similar favors upon the said United States to those conferred by the Kingdom of Hanover, and observe and be subject to the same conditions, stipulations, and obligations.

This declaration of the Grand Duchy of Mecklenburg-Schwerin is submitted to the Senate, because in its eighth and eleventh articles it is not the same in terms with the corresponding articles of our treaty with Hanover. The variations, however, are deemed unimportant, while the admission of our " paddy," or rice in the husk, into Mecklenburg-Schwerin free of import duty is an important concession not contained in the Hanoverian treaty. Others might be mentioned, which will appear upon inspection. Still, as the stipulations in the two articles just mentioned in the declaration are not the same as those contained in the corresponding articles of our treaty with Hanover, I deem it proper to submit this declaration to the Senate for their consideration before issuing a proclamation to give it effect.

I also communicate a dispatch from the special agent on the part of the United States, which accompanied the declaration.

JAMES K. POLK.

WASHINGTON, *January 24, 1848.*

To the Senate of the United States:

In compliance with the request of the Senate in their resolution of the 13th instant, I herewith communicate a report from the Secretary of War, with the accompanying correspondence, containing the information called for, in relation to forced contributions in Mexico.

JAMES K. POLK.

WASHINGTON, *January 31, 1848.*

To the Senate of the United States:

I transmit herewith a report from the Secretary of War, containing the information called for in the resolution of the Senate of the 20th instant, in relation to General Orders, No. 376,* issued by General Scott at headquarters, Mexico, bearing date the 15th December last.

JAMES K. POLK.

WASHINGTON, *January 31, 1848.*

To the Senate of the United States:

I communicate herewith a report of the Secretary of War, with the accompanying documents, in answer to the resolution of the Senate of

* Relating to the levying of taxes and duties upon Mexican products, etc., for the support of the United States Army in Mexico.

the 24th instant, requesting to be furnished with "copies of the letters, reports, or other communications which are referred to in the letter of General Zachary Taylor dated at New Orleans, 20th July, 1845, and addressed to the Secretary of War, and which are so referred to as containing the views of General Taylor, previously communicated, in regard to the line proper to be occupied at that time by the troops of the United States; and any similar communication from any officer of the Army on the same subject."

JAMES K. POLK.

WASHINGTON, *February 2, 1848.*

To the Senate of the United States:

In answer to a resolution of the Senate of the 13th January, 1848, calling for information on the subject of the negotiation between the commissioner of the United States and the commissioners of Mexico during the suspension of hostilities after the battles of Contreras and Churubusco, I transmit a report from the Secretary of State and the documents which accompany it.

I deem it proper to add that the invitation from the commissioner of the United States to submit the proposition of boundary referred to in his dispatch (No. 15) of the 4th of September, 1847, herewith communicated, was unauthorized by me, and was promptly disapproved; and this disapproval was communicated to the commissioner of the United States with the least possible delay.

JAMES K. POLK.

WASHINGTON, *February 3, 1848.*

To the House of Representatives of the United States:

In compliance with the request of the House of Representatives contained in their resolution of the 31st of January, 1848, I communicate herewith a report of the Secretary of War, transmitting "a copy of General Taylor's answer* to the letter dated January 27, 1847," addressed to him by the Secretary of War.

JAMES K. POLK.

WASHINGTON, *February 8, 1848.*

To the House of Representatives of the United States:

In compliance with the resolution of the House of Representatives of the 31st January last, I communicate herewith the report of the Secretary of State, accompanied by "the documents and correspondence not already published relating to the final adjustment of the difficulties between Great Britain and the United States concerning rough rice and paddy."

JAMES K. POLK.

* Relating to the publication of a letter from General Taylor to General Gaines concerning the operations of the United S'ates forces in Mexico.

WASHINGTON, *February 10, 1848.*

To the Senate of the United States:

In answer to the resolution of the Senate of the 1st instant, requesting to be informed whether "any taxes, duties, or imposts" have been "laid and collected upon goods and merchandise belonging to citizens of the United States exported by such citizens from the United States to Mexico, and, if so, what is the rate of such duties, and what amount has been collected, and also by what authority of law the same have been laid and collected," I refer the Senate to my annual message of the 7th of December last, in which I informed Congress that orders had been given to our military and naval commanders in Mexico to adopt the policy, as far as practicable, of levying military contributions upon the enemy for the support of our Army.

As one of the modes adopted for levying such contributions, it was stated in that message that—

On the 31st of March last I caused an order to be issued to our military and naval commanders to levy and collect a military contribution upon all vessels and merchandise which might enter any of the ports of Mexico in our military occupation, and to apply such contributions toward defraying the expenses of the war. By virtue of the right of conquest and the laws of war, the conqueror, consulting his own safety or convenience, may either exclude foreign commerce altogether from all such ports or permit it upon such terms and conditions as he may prescribe. Before the principal ports of Mexico were blockaded by our Navy the revenue derived from import duties under the laws of Mexico was paid into the Mexican treasury. After these ports had fallen into our military possession the blockade was raised and commerce with them permitted upon prescribed terms and conditions. They were opened to the trade of all nations upon the payment of duties more moderate in their amount than those which had been previously levied by Mexico, and the revenue, which was formerly paid into the Mexican treasury, was directed to be collected by our military and naval officers and applied to the use of our Army and Navy. Care was taken that the officers, soldiers, and sailors of our Army and Navy should be exempted from the operations of the order, and, as the merchandise imported upon which the order operated must be consumed by Mexican citizens, the contributions exacted were in effect the seizure of the public revenues of Mexico and the application of them to our own use. In directing this measure the object was to compel the enemy to contribute as far as practicable toward the expenses of the war.

A copy of the order referred to, with the documents accompanying it, has been communicated to Congress.

The order operated upon the vessels and merchandise of all nations, whether belonging to citizens of the United States or to foreigners, arriving in any of the ports in Mexico in our military occupation. The contributions levied were a tax upon Mexican citizens, who were the consumers of the merchandise imported. But for the permit or license granted by the order all vessels and merchandise belonging to citizens of the United States were necessarily excluded from all commerce with Mexico from the commencement of the war. The coasts and ports of Mexico were ordered to be placed under blockade on the day Congress declared the war to exist, and by the laws of nations the blockade applied to the vessels of the United States as well as to the vessels of all other nations. Had no blockade been declared, or had any of our merchant vessels entered any of the ports of Mexico not blockaded, they would have been liable to be seized and condemned as lawful prize by the Mexican authorities. When the order was issued, it operated as a privilege to the vessels of the United States as well as to those of foreign countries to enter the ports held by our arms upon prescribed terms and conditions. It was altogether optional with citizens of the United States and foreigners to avail themselves of the privileges granted upon the terms prescribed.

Citizens of the United States and foreigners have availed themselves of these privileges.

No principle is better established than that a nation at war has the right of shifting the burden off itself and imposing it on the enemy by exacting military contributions. The mode of making such exactions must be left to the discretion of the conqueror, but it should be exercised in a manner conformable to the rules of civilized warfare.

The right to levy these contributions is essential to the successful prosecution of war in an enemy's country, and the practice of nations has been in accordance with this principle. It is as clearly necessary as the right to fight battles, and its exercise is often essential to the subsistence of the army.

Entertaining no doubt that the military right to exclude commerce altogether from the ports of the enemy in our military occupation included the minor right of admitting it under prescribed conditions, it became an important question at the date of the order whether there should be a discrimination between vessels and cargoes belonging to citizens of the United States and vessels and cargoes belonging to neutral nations.

Had the vessels and cargoes belonging to citizens of the United States been admitted without the payment of any duty, while a duty was levied on foreign vessels and cargoes, the object of the order would have been defeated. The whole commerce would have been conducted in American vessels, no contributions could have been collected, and the enemy would have been furnished with goods without the exaction from him of any contribution whatever, and would have been thus benefited by our military occupation, instead of being made to feel the evils of the war. In order to levy these contributions and to make them available for the support of the Army, it became, therefore, absolutely necessary that they should be collected upon imports into Mexican ports, whether in vessels belonging to citizens of the United States or to foreigners.

It was deemed proper to extend the privilege to vessels and their cargoes belonging to neutral nations. It has been my policy since the commencement of the war with Mexico to act justly and liberally toward all neutral nations, and to afford to them no just cause of complaint; and we have seen the good consequences of this policy by the general satisfaction which it has given.

In answer to the inquiry contained in the resolution as to the rates of duties imposed, I refer you to the documents which accompanied my annual message of the 7th of December last, which contain the information.

From the accompanying reports of the Secretary of War and the Secretary of the Navy it will be seen that the contributions have been collected on all vessels and cargoes, whether American or foreign; but the returns to the Departments do not show with exactness the amounts collected on American as distinguishable from foreign vessels and merchandise.

JAMES K. POLK.

WASHINGTON, *February 10, 1848.*

To the House of Representatives of the United States:

In answer to the resolution of the House of Representatives of the 7th instant, I transmit herewith a report from the Secretary of State.

No communication has been received from Mexico "containing propositions from the Mexican authorities or commissioners for a treaty of peace," except the "counter projet" presented by the Mexican commissioners to the commissioners of the United States on the 6th of September last, a copy of which, with the documents accompanying it, I communicated to the Senate of the United States on the 2d instant. A copy of my communication to the Senate embracing this "projet" is herewith communicated.

JAMES K. POLK.

WASHINGTON, *February 14, 1848.*

To the Senate of the United States:

I transmit, for the consideration of the Senate with a view to ratification, a treaty of peace, friendship, commerce, and navigation between the United States and the Republic of Peru, concluded and signed in this city on the 9th instant by the Secretary of State and the minister plenipotentiary of Peru, in behalf of their respective Governments. I also transmit a copy of the correspondence between them which led to the treaty.

JAMES K. POLK.

WASHINGTON, *February 15, 1848.*

To the Senate of the United States:

I communicate herewith a report of the Secretary of War, together with the accompanying report of the Adjutant-General, in answer to the resolution of the Senate of the 7th instant, calling for information in regard to the order or law by virtue of which certain words "in relation to the promotion of cadets have been inserted in the Army Register of the United States, page 45, in the year 1847."

JAMES K. POLK.

WASHINGTON, *February 22, 1848.*

To the Senate of the United States:

I lay before the Senate, for their consideration and advice as to its ratification, a treaty of peace, friendship, limits, and settlement, signed at the city of Guadalupe Hidalgo on the 2d day of February, 1848, by N. P. Trist on the part of the United States, and by plenipotentiaries appointed for that purpose on the part of the Mexican Government.

I deem it to be my duty to state that the recall of Mr. Trist as commissioner of the United States, of which Congress was informed in my annual message, was dictated by a belief that his continued presence with the Army could be productive of no good, but might do much harm by encouraging the delusive hopes and false impressions of the Mexicans, and that his recall would satisfy Mexico that the United States had no terms of peace more favorable to offer. Directions were given that any propositions for peace which Mexico might make should be received and transmitted by the commanding general of our forces to the United States.

It was not expected that Mr. Trist would remain in Mexico or continue in the exercise of the functions of the office of commissioner after he received his letter of recall. He has, however, done so, and the plenipotentiaries of the Government of Mexico, with a knowledge of the fact, have concluded with him this treaty. I have examined it with a full sense of the extraneous circumstances attending its conclusion and signature, which might be objected to, but conforming as it does substantially on the main questions of boundary and indemnity to the terms which our commissioner, when he left the United States in April last, was authorized to offer, and animated as I am by the spirit which has governed all my official conduct toward Mexico, I have felt it to be my duty to submit it to the Senate for their consideration with a view to its ratification.

To the tenth article of the treaty there are serious objections, and no instructions given to Mr. Trist contemplated or authorized its insertion. The public lands within the limits of Texas belong to that State, and this Government has no power to dispose of them or to change the conditions of grants already made. All valid titles to lands within the other territories ceded to the United States will remain unaffected by the change of sovereignty; and I therefore submit that this article should not be ratified as a part of the treaty.

There may be reason to apprehend that the ratification of the "additional and secret article" might unreasonably delay and embarrass the final action on the treaty by Mexico. I therefore submit whether that article should not be rejected by the Senate.

If the treaty shall be ratified as proposed to be amended, the cessions of territory made by it to the United States as indemnity, the provision for the satisfaction of the claims of our injured citizens, and the permanent establishment of the boundary of one of the States of the Union are objects gained of great national importance, while the magnanimous forbearance exhibited toward Mexico, it is hoped, may insure a lasting peace and good neighborhood between the two countries.

I communicate herewith a copy of the instructions given to Mr. Slidell in November, 1845, as envoy extraordinary and minister plenipotentiary to Mexico; a copy of the instructions given to Mr. Trist in April last, and such of the correspondence of the latter with the Department of State, not heretofore communicated to Congress, as will enable the Senate to understand the action which has been had with a view to the adjustment of our difficulties with Mexico.

JAMES K. POLK.

WASHINGTON, *February 28, 1848.*
To the Senate of the United States:

In answer to the resolution of the Senate of the 24th instant, requesting to be informed whether the active operations of the Army of the United States in Mexico have been, and now are, suspended, and, if so, by whose agency and in virtue of what authority such armistice has been effected, I have to state that I have received no information relating to the subject other than that communicated to the Senate with my executive message of the 22d instant.

JAMES K. POLK.

WASHINGTON, *February 29, 1848.*
To the Senate of the United States:

In compliance with the resolution of the Senate passed in "executive session" on yesterday, requesting the President "to communicate to the Senate, *in confidence*, the entire correspondence between Mr. Trist and the Mexican commissioners from the time of his arrival in Mexico until the time of the negotiation of the treaty submitted to the Senate; and also the entire correspondence between Mr. Trist and the Secretary of State in relation to his negotiations with the Mexican commissioners; also all the correspondence between General Scott and the Government and between General Scott and Mr. Trist since the arrival of Mr. Trist in Mexico which may be in the possession of the Government," I transmit herewith the correspondence called for. These documents are very voluminous, and presuming that the Senate desired them in reference to early action on the treaty with Mexico submitted to the consideration of that body by my message of the 22d instant, the originals of several of the letters of Mr. Trist are herewith communicated, in order to save the time which would necessarily be required to make copies of them. These original letters, it is requested, may be returned when the Senate shall have no further use for them.

The letters of Mr. Trist to the Secretary of State, and especially such of them as bear date subsequent to the receipt by him of his letter of recall as commissioner, it will be perceived, contain much matter that is impertinent, irrelevant, and highly exceptionable. Four of these letters, bearing date, respectively, the 29th December, 1847, January 12, January 22, and January 25, 1848, have been received since the treaty was submitted to the Senate. In the latter it is stated that the Mexican commissioners who signed the treaty derived "their full powers, bearing date on the 30th December, 1847, from the President *ad interim* of the Republic (General Anaya), constitutionally elected to that office in November by the Sovereign Constituent Congress" of Mexico. It is impossible that I can approve the conduct of Mr. Trist in disobeying the positive orders of his Government contained in the letter recalling him, or do otherwise than condemn much of the matter with which he has chosen to encumber his voluminous correspondence. Though all of his acts since his recall might have been disavowed by his Government, yet Mexico can take no such exception. The treaty which the Mexican commissioners have negotiated with him, with a full knowledge on their part that he had been recalled from his mission, *is* binding on Mexico.

Looking at the actual condition of Mexico, and believing that if the present treaty be rejected the war will probably be continued at great expense of life and treasure for an indefinite period, and considering that the terms, with the exceptions mentioned in my message of the 22d instant, conform substantially, so far as relates to the main question of boundary, to those authorized by me in April last, I considered it to be my solemn duty to the country, uninfluenced by the exceptionable conduct of Mr. Trist, to submit the treaty to the Senate with a recommendation that it be ratified, with the modifications suggested.

Nothing contained in the letters received from Mr. Trist since it was submitted to the Senate has changed my opinion on the subject.

The resolution also calls for "all the correspondence between General Scott and the Government since the arrival of Mr. Trist in Mexico." A portion of that correspondence, relating to Mr. Trist and his mission, accompanies this communication. The remainder of the "correspondence between General Scott and the Government" relates mainly, if not exclusively, to military operations. A part of it was communicated to Congress with my annual message, and the whole of it will be sent to the Senate if it shall be desired by that body. As coming within the purview of the resolution, I also communicate copies of the letters of the Secretary of War to Major-General Butler in reference to Mr. Trist's remaining at the headquarters of the Army in the assumed exercise of his powers of commissioner.

JAMES K. POLK.

WASHINGTON, *March 2, 1848.*

To the Senate of the United States:

In answer to a resolution of the Senate of the 3d of January, 1848, I communicate herewith a report from the Secretary of State, with the accompanying documents, containing the correspondence of Mr. Wise, late minister of the United States at the Court of Brazil, relating to the subject of the slave trade.

JAMES K. POLK.

WASHINGTON, *March 2, 1848.*

To the Senate of the United States:

I communicate herewith a report of the Secretary of War, with the accompanying documents, in answer to the resolution of the Senate of the 28th February, 1848, requesting the President to communicate "any information he may at any time have received of the desire of any considerable portion of the people of any of the States of Mexico to be incorporated within the limits of any territory to be acquired from the Republic of Mexico, and particularly that he communicate any late proposition which has been made to that effect through General Wool or any other military officer in Mexico."

JAMES K. POLK.

WASHINGTON, *March 7, 1848.*

To the Senate of the United States:

I lay before the Senate a letter of the 12th February, 1848, from N. P. Trist, together with the authenticated map of the United Mexican States and of the plan of the port of San Diego, referred to in the fifth article of the treaty "of peace, friendship, limits, and settlement between the United States of America and the Mexican Republic," which treaty was transmitted to the Senate with my message of the 22d ultimo.

JAMES K. POLK.

WASHINGTON, *March 8, 1848.*

To the Senate of the United States:

In answer to the resolution of the Senate of this date, requesting the President "to inform the Senate of the terms of the authority given to Mr. Trist to draw for the $3,000,000 authorized by the act of the 2d of March, 1847," I communicate herewith a report from the Secretary of State, with the accompanying documents, which contain the information called for.

JAMES K. POLK.

WASHINGTON, *March 8, 1848.*

To the Senate of the United States:

In answer to the resolution of the Senate of this date, requesting the President to communicate to that body, "confidentially, any additional dispatches which may have been received from Mr. Trist, and especially those which are promised by him in his letter to Mr. Buchanan of the 2d of February last, if the same have been received," I have to state that all the dispatches which have been received from Mr. Trist have been heretofore communicated to the Senate.

JAMES K. POLK.

WASHINGTON, *March 10, 1848.*

To the House of Representatives:

I transmit herewith reports from the Secretary of State and the Secretary of War, with the accompanying documents, in compliance with the resolution of the House of Representatives of the 7th February, 1848, requesting the President to communicate to that House "copies of all correspondence between the Secretary of War and Major-General Scott, and between the Secretary of War and Major-General Taylor, and between Major-General Scott and N. P. Trist, late commissioner of the United States to Mexico, and between the latter and Secretary of State, which has not heretofore been published, and the publication of which may not be incompatible with the public interest."

JAMES K. POLK.

To the House of Representatives:

I communicate herewith a copy of the constitution of State government formed by a convention of the people of the Territory of Wisconsin in pursuance of the act of Congress of August 6, 1846, entitled "An act to enable the people of Wisconsin Territory to form a constitution and State government, and for the admission of such State into the Union."

I communicate also the documents accompanying the constitution, which have been transmitted to me by the president of the convention.

MARCH 16, 1848.   JAMES K. POLK.

WASHINGTON, *March 18, 1848.*

To the Senate of the United States:

Sudden and severe indisposition has prevented, and may for an indefinite period continue to prevent, Ambrose H. Sevier, recently appointed commissioner to Mexico, from departing on his mission. The public interest requires that a diplomatic functionary should proceed without delay to Mexico, bearing with him the treaty between the United States and the Mexican Republic, lately ratified, with amendments, by and with the advice and consent of the Senate of the United States. It is deemed proper, with this view, to appoint an associate commissioner, with full powers to act separately or jointly with Mr. Sevier.

I therefore nominate Nathan Clifford, of the State of Maine, to be a commissioner, with the rank of envoy extraordinary and minister pleni-potentiary, of the United States to the Mexican Republic.

JAMES K. POLK.

WASHINGTON, *March 22, 1848.*

To the Senate of the United States:

I transmit herewith a report from the Secretary of State, with the ac-companying documents, in compliance with the resolution of the Senate of the 24th January, 1848, requesting the President to communicate to the Senate, if not inconsistent with the public interest, the correspond-ence of Mr. Wise, late minister of the United States at the Court of Bra-zil, with the Department of State of the United States.

JAMES K. POLK.

WASHINGTON, *March 24, 1848.*

To the Senate of the United States:

In answer to the resolution of the Senate of the 17th instant, request-ing the President to transmit to that body "a copy of a dispatch to the United States consul at Monterey, T. O. Larkin, esq., forwarded in November, 1845, by Captain Gillespie, of the Marine Corps, and which was by him destroyed before entering the port of Vera Cruz, if a com-munication of the same be not, in his opinion, incompatible with the public interests," I communicate herewith a report of the Secretary of State, with a copy of the dispatch referred to. The resolution of the Senate appears to have been passed in legislative session. Entertaining the opinion that the publication of this dispatch at this time will not be "compatible with the public interests," but unwilling to withhold from the Senate information deemed important by that body, I communicate a copy of it to the Senate in executive session.

JAMES K. POLK.

To the House of Representatives of the United States:

I transmit herewith a report from the Secretary of State, with the ac-companying documents, in compliance with the resolution of the House of Representatives of the 8th instant, calling for "any correspondence which may have recently taken place with the British Government rela-tive to the adoption of principles of reciprocity in the trade and shipping of the two countries."

JAMES K. POLK.

MARCH 24, 1848.

To the Senate of the United States:

I transmit herewith a report of the Secretary of State, with accom-panying documents, in compliance with the resolution of the Senate of the 17th instant, requesting the President to communicate to that body

"copies of the correspondence between the minister of the United States
at London and any authorities of the British Government in relation to a
postal arrangement between the two countries."

MARCH 27, 1848.   JAMES K. POLK.

WASHINGTON, *April 3, 1848.*

To the Senate and House of Representatives of the United States:

I communicate to Congress, for their information, a copy of a dispatch, with the accompanying documents, received at the Department
of State from the envoy extraordinary and minister plenipotentiary of
the United States at Paris, giving official information of the overthrow
of the French Monarchy, and the establishment in its stead of a "provisional government based on republican principles."

This great event occurred suddenly, and was accomplished almost
without bloodshed. The world has seldom witnessed a more interesting or sublime spectacle than the peaceful rising of the French people,
resolved to secure for themselves enlarged liberty, and to assert, in the
majesty of their strength, the great truth that in this enlightened age
man is capable of governing himself.

The prompt recognition of the new Government by the representative
of the United States at the French Court meets my full and unqualified
approbation, and he has been authorized in a suitable manner to make
known this fact to the constituted authorities of the French Republic.

Called upon to act upon a sudden emergency, which could not have
been anticipated by his instructions, he judged rightly of the feelings
and sentiments of his Government and of his countrymen, when, in
advance of the diplomatic representatives of other countries, he was the
first to recognize, so far as it was in his power, the free Government
established by the French people.

The policy of the United States has ever been that of nonintervention
in the domestic affairs of other countries, leaving to each to establish the
form of government of its own choice. While this wise policy will be
maintained toward France, now suddenly transformed from a monarchy
into a republic, all our sympathies are naturally enlisted on the side of
a great people who, imitating our example, have resolved to be free.
That such sympathy should exist on the part of the people of the United
States with the friends of free government in every part of the world,
and especially in France, is not remarkable. We can never forget that
France was our early friend in our eventful Revolution, and generously
aided us in shaking off a foreign yoke and becoming a free and independent people.

We have enjoyed the blessings of our system of well-regulated self-
government for near three-fourths of a century, and can properly appreciate its value. Our ardent and sincere congratulations are extended to

the patriotic people of France upon their noble and thus far successful efforts to found for their future government liberal institutions similar to our own.

It is not doubted that under the benign influence of free institutions the enlightened statesmen of republican France will find it to be for her true interests and permanent glory to cultivate with the United States the most liberal principles of international intercourse and commercial reciprocity, whereby the happiness and prosperity of both nations will be promoted.   JAMES K. POLK.

WASHINGTON, *April 7, 1848.*
To the Senate of the United States:

In answer to a resolution of the Senate of the 29th of March, 1848, I transmit herewith a report of the Secretary of War, with the accompanying documents, containing the information called for, relative to the services of Captain McClellan's company of Florida volunteers in the year 1840.   JAMES K. POLK.

WASHINGTON, *April 7, 1848.*
To the Senate of the United States:

I communicate herewith a report of the Secretary of War, transmitting a copy of the proceedings of the general court-martial in the case of Lieutenant-Colonel Frémont, called for by a resolution of the Senate of the 29th February, 1848.   JAMES K. POLK.

WASHINGTON, *April 10, 1848.*
To the Senate of the United States:

I communicate herewith a report of the Secretary of State, together with a copy of the correspondence between the Secretary of State and "the Brazilian chargé d'affaires at Washington," called for by the resolution of the Senate of the 28th of March, 1848.

JAMES K. POLK.

WASHINGTON, *April 13, 1848.*
To the Senate of the United States:

In answer to the resolution of the Senate of the 28th of March, 1848, I communicate herewith a report of the Secretary of War, transmitting a report of the head of the Ordnance Bureau, with the accompanying papers, relative to "the repeating firearms invented by Samuel Colt."

Such is the favorable opinion entertained of the value of this arm, particularly for a mounted corps, that the Secretary of War, as will be seen by his report, has contracted with Mr. Colt for 2,000 of his pistols.   He has offered to contract for an additional number at liberal prices, but the inventor is unwilling to furnish them at the prices offered.

The invention for the construction of these arms being patented, the United States can not manufacture them at the Government armories without a previous purchase of the right so to do. The right to use his patent by the United States the inventor is unwilling to dispose of at a price deemed reasonable.

JAMES K. POLK.

WASHINGTON, *April 25, 1848.*

To the House of Representatives of the United States:

I communicate herewith a report of the Secretary of War, with accompanying documents, submitted by him as embracing the papers and the correspondence* between the Secretary of War and Major-General Scott, called for by the resolution of the House of Representatives of the 17th instant.

JAMES K. POLK.

WASHINGTON, *April 29, 1848.*

To the Senate and House of Representatives of the United States:

I submit for the consideration of Congress several communications received at the Department of State from Mr. Justo Sierra, commissioner of Yucatan, and also a communication from the Governor of that State, representing the condition of extreme suffering to which their country has been reduced by an insurrection of the Indians within its limits, and asking the aid of the United States.

These communications present a case of human suffering and misery which can not fail to excite the sympathies of all civilized nations. From these and other sources of information it appears that the Indians of Yucatan are waging a war of extermination against the white race. In this civil war they spare neither age nor sex, but put to death, indiscriminately, all who fall within their power. The inhabitants, panic stricken and destitute of arms, are flying before their savage pursuers toward the coast, and their expulsion from their country or their extermination would seem to be inevitable unless they can obtain assistance from abroad.

In this condition they have, through their constituted authorities, implored the aid of this Government to save them from destruction, offering in case this should be granted to transfer the "dominion and sovereignty of the peninsula" to the United States. Similar appeals for aid and protection have been made to the Spanish and the English Governments.

Whilst it is not my purpose to recommend the adoption of any measure with a view to the acquisition of the "dominion and sovereignty"

---

* Relating to the conduct of the war in Mexico and the recall of General Scott from the command of the Army.

over Yucatan, yet, according to our established policy, we could not consent to a transfer of this "dominion and sovereignty" either to Spain, Great Britain, or any other European power. In the language of President Monroe in his message of December, 1823—

We should consider any attempt on their part to extend their system to any portion of this hemisphere as dangerous to our peace and safety.

In my annual message of December, 1845, I declared that—

Near a quarter of a century ago the principle was distinctly announced to the world, in the annual message of one of my predecessors, that "the American continents, by the free and independent condition which they have assumed and maintain, are henceforth not to be considered as subjects for future colonization by any European powers." This principle will apply with greatly increased force should any European power attempt to establish any new colony in North America. In the existing circumstances of the world, the present is deemed a proper occasion to reiterate and reaffirm the principle avowed by Mr. Monroe, and to state my cordial concurrence in its wisdom and sound policy. The reassertion of this principle, especially in reference to North America, is at this day but the promulgation of a policy which no European power should cherish the disposition to resist. Existing rights of every European nation should be respected, but it is due alike to our safety and our interests that the efficient protection of our laws should be extended over our whole territorial limits, and that it should be distinctly announced to the world as our settled policy that no future European colony or dominion shall with our consent be planted or established on any part of the North American continent.

Our own security requires that the established policy thus announced should guide our conduct, and this applies with great force to the peninsula of Yucatan. It is situate in the Gulf of Mexico, on the North American continent, and, from its vicinity to Cuba, to the capes of Florida, to New Orleans, and, indeed, to our whole southwestern coast, it would be dangerous to our peace and security if it should become a colony of any European nation.

We have now authentic information that if the aid asked from the United States be not granted such aid will probably be obtained from some European power, which may hereafter assert a claim to "dominion and sovereignty" over Yucatan.

Our existing relations with Yucatan are of a peculiar character, as will be perceived from the note of the Secretary of State to their commissioner dated on the 24th of December last, a copy of which is herewith transmitted. Yucatan has never declared her independence, and we treated her as a State of the Mexican Republic. For this reason we have never officially received her commissioner; but whilst this is the case, we have to a considerable extent recognized her as a neutral in our war with Mexico. Whilst still considering Yucatan as a portion of Mexico, if we had troops to spare for this purpose I would deem it proper, during the continuance of the war with Mexico, to occupy and hold military possession of her territory and to defend the white inhabitants against the incursions of the Indians, in the same way that we have employed our troops in other States of the Mexican Republic in our possession in repelling the attacks of savages upon the inhabitants who have maintained their neutrality in the war. But, unfortunately, we can not at the present time, without serious danger, withdraw our forces from other portions of the Mexican territory now in our occupation and send them to Yucatan. All that can be done under existing circumstances is to employ our naval forces in the Gulf not required at other points to afford them relief; but it is not to be expected that any adequate protection can thus be afforded, as the operations of such naval forces must of necessity be confined to the coast.

I have considered it proper to communicate the information contained in the accompanying correspondence, and I submit to the wisdom of Congress to adopt such measures as in their judgment may be expedient to prevent Yucatan from becoming a colony of any European power, which in no event could be permitted by the United States, and at the same time to rescue the white race from extermination or expulsion from their country.

JAMES K. POLK.

WASHINGTON, *May 5, 1848.*

To the Senate of the United States:

I communicate herewith a report from the Secretary of State, together with the correspondence "between the Secretary of State and Don Justo Sierra, the representative of Yucatan," called for by the resolution of the Senate of the 4th instant.

I communicate also additional documents relating to the same subject.

JAMES K. POLK.

WASHINGTON, *May 8, 1848.*

To the Senate of the United States:

I communicate herewith a report of the Secretary of War, together with the accompanying documents, in compliance with the resolution of the Senate of the 25th April, requesting the President to cause to be sent to the Senate a copy of the opinion of the Attorney-General, with copies of the accompanying papers, on the claim made by the Choctaw Indians for $5,000, with interest thereon from the date of the transfer, being the difference between the cost of the stock and the par value thereof transferred to them by the Chickasaws under the convention of the 17th of January, 1837.

JAMES K. POLK.

WASHINGTON, *May 9, 1848.*

To the Senate of the United States:

In answer to the resolution of the Senate of the 8th instant, requesting further information in relation to the condition of Yucatan, I transmit herewith a report of the Secretary of the Navy, with the accompanying copies of communications from officers of the Navy on the subject.

JAMES K. POLK.

WASHINGTON, *May 9, 1848.*

To the Senate of the United States:

I herewith communicate to the Senate, for their consideration with a view to its ratification, a convention for the extension of certain stipulations* contained in the treaty of commerce and navigation of August 27, 1829, between the United States and Austria, concluded and signed in this city on the 8th instant by the respective plenipotentiaries.

JAMES K. POLK.

WASHINGTON, *May 15, 1848.*

To the Senate of the United States:

I communicate herewith a report from the Secretary of the Navy, together with the accompanying documents, in compliance with the resolution of the Senate of the 13th instant, requesting information as to the measures taken for the protection of the white population of Yucatan by the naval forces of the United States.   JAMES K. POLK.

WASHINGTON, *May 19, 1848.*

To the Senate and House of Representatives of the United States:

I transmit for the information of Congress a communication from the Secretary of War and a report from the Commissioner of Indian Affairs, showing the result of the settlement required by the treaty of August, 1846, with the Cherokees, and the appropriations requisite to carry the provisions of that treaty into effect.   JAMES K. POLK.

WASHINGTON, *May 29, 1848.*

To the Senate and House of Representatives of the United States:

I lay before Congress the accompanying memorial and papers, which have been transmitted to me, by a special messenger employed for that purpose, by the governor and legislative assembly of Oregon Territory, who constitute the temporary government which the inhabitants of that distant region of our country have, from the necessity of their condition, organized for themselves. The memorialists are citizens of the United States. They express ardent attachment to their native land, and in their present perilous and distressed situation they earnestly invoke the aid and protection of their Government.

They represent that "the proud and powerful tribes of Indians" residing in their vicinity have recently raised "the war whoop and crimsoned their tomahawks in the blood of their citizens;" that they apprehend that "many of the powerful tribes inhabiting the upper valley of the

* Relating to disposal of property, etc.

Columbia have formed an alliance for the purpose of carrying on hostilities against their settlements;'' that the number of the white population is far inferior to that of the savages; that they are deficient in arms
and money, and fear that they do not possess strength to repel the ''attack
of so formidable a foe and protect their families and property from violence and rapine.'' They conclude their appeal to the Government of
the United States for relief by declaring:

> If it be at all the intention of our honored parent to spread her guardian wing over
> her sons and daughters in Oregon, she surely will not refuse to do it now, when they
> are struggling with all the ills of a weak and temporary government, and when perils
> are daily thickening around them and preparing to burst upon their heads. When
> the ensuing summer's sun shall have dispelled the snow from the mountains, we shall
> look with glowing hope and restless anxiety for the coming of your laws and your
> arms.

In my message of the 5th of August, 1846, communicating ''a copy of
the convention for the settlement and adjustment of the Oregon boundary,'' I recommended to Congress that ''provision should be made by
law, at the earliest practicable period, for the organization of a Territorial
government in Oregon.'' In my annual message of December, 1846,
and again in December, 1847, this recommendation was repeated.

The population of Oregon is believed to exceed 12,000 souls, and it is
known that it will be increased by a large number of emigrants during
the present season. The facts set forth in the accompanying memorial
and papers show that the dangers to which our fellow-citizens are exposed
are so imminent that I deem it to be my duty again to impress on Congress the strong claim which the inhabitants of that distant country have
to the benefit of our laws and to the protection of our Government.

I therefore again invite the attention of Congress to the subject, and
recommend that laws be promptly passed establishing a Territorial government and granting authority to raise an adequate volunteer force for
the defense and protection of its inhabitants. It is believed that a regiment of mounted men, with such additional force as may be raised in
Oregon, will be sufficient to afford the required protection. It is recommended that the forces raised for this purpose should engage to serve for
twelve months, unless sooner discharged. No doubt is entertained that,
with proper inducements in land bounties, such a force can be raised in
a short time. Upon the expiration of their service many of them will
doubtless desire to remain in the country and settle upon the land which
they may receive as bounty. It is deemed important that provision be
made for the appointment of a suitable number of Indian agents to reside
among the various tribes in Oregon, and that appropriations be made to
enable them to treat with these tribes with a view to restore and preserve
peace between them and the white inhabitants.

Should the laws recommended be promptly passed, the measures for
their execution may be completed during the present season, and before
the severity of winter will interpose obstacles in crossing the Rocky

Mountains. If not promptly passed, a delay of another year will be the consequence, and may prove destructive to the white settlements in Oregon.

                                                    JAMES K. POLK.

WASHINGTON, *May 31, 1848.*

To the Senate of the United States:

I transmit herewith reports from the Secretary of State and the Secretary of the Navy, with the accompanying correspondence, which contains the information called for by the Senate in their resolution of the 30th instant, relating to the existing condition of affairs in Yucatan.

                                                    JAMES K. POLK.

WASHINGTON, *June 12, 1848.*

To the Senate of the United States:

I communicate herewith a report of the Secretary of State, together with the accompanying documents, in compliance with the resolution of the Senate of the 31st ultimo, ''requesting the President to communicate the correspondence not heretofore communicated between the Secretary of State and the minister of the United States at Paris since the recent change in the Government of France.''

                                                    JAMES K. POLK.

WASHINGTON, *June 23, 1848.*

To the Senate of the United States:

I communicate herewith a report of the Secretary of War, with the accompanying documents, in answer to a resolution of the Senate of the 21st instant, requesting the President to communicate to the Senate, in executive session, as early as practicable, the papers heretofore in the possession of the Senate and returned to the War Department, together with a statement from the Adjutant-General of the Army as to the merits or demerits of the claim of James W. Schaumburg to be restored to rank in the Army.

                                                    JAMES K. POLK.

WASHINGTON, *July 5, 1848.*

To the Senate of the United States:

I submit herewith, for such action as the Senate shall deem proper, a report of the Secretary of War, suggesting a discrepancy between the resolutions of the Senate of the 15th and the 27th ultimo, advising and consenting to certain appointments and promotions in the Army of the United States.

                                                    JAMES K. POLK.

WAR DEPARTMENT,
Washington, July 1, 1848.

The PRESIDENT OF THE UNITED STATES.

SIR: I have the honor to submit herewith a report from the Adjutant-General of the Army, inviting attention to a difficulty arising from the terms of certain confirmations made by the resolutions of the Senate of the 15th and 27th ultimo, the former advising and consenting to the reappointment of Captain Edward Deas, Fourth Artillery, who had been dismissed the service, and the latter advising and consenting to the promotion of First Lieutenant Joseph Roberts to be captain, *vice* Deas, dismissed, and Second Lieutenant John A. Brown to be first lieutenant, *vice* Roberts, promoted.

Very respectfully, your obedient servant,

W. L. MARCY,
Secretary of War.

ADJUTANT-GENERAL'S OFFICE,
Washington, June 29, 1848.

Hon. W. L. MARCY,
Secretary of War.

SIR: In a list of confirmations of regular promotions just received from the Senate, dated the 27th instant, it is observed, under the heading "Fourth Regiment of Artillery," that First Lieutenant Joseph Roberts is confirmed as a captain, *vice* Deas, dismissed, and Second Lieutenant John A. Brown as first lieutenant, *vice* Roberts, promoted.

The President, having decided to reinstate Captain Deas, nominated him for restoration to the Senate the 12th instant, withdrawing, as the records show, at the same time the names of Lieutenants Roberts and Brown. This nomination of Captain Deas was confirmed the 15th of June, and he has been commissioned accordingly. I respectfully bring this matter to your notice under the impression that as the resolutions of June 15 and June 27 conflict with each other it may be the wish of the Senate to reconcile them by rescinding that portion of the latter which advises and consents to the promotions of Lieutenants Roberts and Brown.

Respectfully submitted.

R. JONES, *Adjutant-General.*

WASHINGTON, *July 6, 1848.*

To the Senate and House of Representatives of the United States:

I lay before Congress copies of a treaty of peace, friendship, limits, and settlement between the United States and the Mexican Republic, the ratifications of which were duly exchanged at the city of Queretaro, in Mexico, on the 30th day of May, 1848.

The war in which our country was reluctantly involved, in the necessary vindication of the national rights and honor, has been thus terminated, and I congratulate Congress and our common constituents upon the restoration of an honorable peace.

The extensive and valuable territories ceded by Mexico to the United States constitute indemnity for the past, and the brilliant achievements and signal successes of our arms will be a guaranty of security for the future, by convincing all nations that our rights must be respected. The results of the war with Mexico have given to the United States a national character abroad which our country never before enjoyed. Our power and our resources have become known and are respected throughout the world, and we shall probably be saved from the necessity of engaging in another foreign war for a long series of years. It is a subject of congratulation that we have passed through a war of more than two years' duration with the business of the country uninterrupted, with our resources unexhausted, and the public credit unimpaired.

I communicate for the information of Congress the accompanying documents and correspondence, relating to the negotiation and ratification of the treaty.

Before the treaty can be fully executed on the part of the United States legislation will be required.

It will be proper to make the necessary appropriations for the payment of the $12,000,000 stipulated by the twelfth article to be paid to Mexico in four equal annual installments. Three million dollars were appropriated by the act of March 3, 1847, and that sum was paid to the Mexican Government after the exchange of the ratifications of the treaty.

The fifth article of the treaty provides that—

In order to designate the boundary line with due precision upon authoritative maps, and to establish upon the ground landmarks which shall show the limits of both Republics as described in the present article, the two Governments shall each appoint a commissioner and a surveyor, who, before the expiration of one year from the date of the exchange of ratifications of this treaty, shall meet at the port of San Diego and proceed to run and mark the said boundary in its whole course to the mouth of the Rio Bravo del Norte.

It will be necessary that provision should be made by law for the appointment of a commissioner and surveyor on the part of the United States to act in conjunction with a commissioner and surveyor appointed by Mexico in executing the stipulations of this article.

It will be proper also to provide by law for the appointment of a "board of commissioners" to adjudicate and decide upon all claims of our citizens against the Mexican Government, which by the treaty have been assumed by the United States.

New Mexico and Upper California have been ceded by Mexico to the United States, and now constitute a part of our country. Embracing nearly ten degrees of latitude, lying adjacent to the Oregon Territory, and extending from the Pacific Ocean to the Rio Grande, a mean distance of nearly 1,000 miles, it would be difficult to estimate the value of these possessions to the United States. They constitute of themselves a country large enough for a great empire, and their acquisition is second only in importance to that of Louisiana in 1803. Rich in mineral and agricultural resources, with a climate of great salubrity, they embrace the most important ports on the whole Pacific coast of the continent of North America. The possession of the ports of San Diego and Monterey and the Bay of San Francisco will enable the United States to command the already valuable and rapidly increasing commerce of the Pacific. The number of our whale ships alone now employed in that sea exceeds 700, requiring more than 20,000 seamen to navigate them, while the capital invested in this particular branch of commerce is estimated at not less than $40,000,000. The excellent harbors of Upper California will under our flag afford security and repose to our commercial marine, and American mechanics will soon furnish ready means of shipbuilding and repair, which are now so much wanted in that distant sea.

By the acquisition of these possessions we are brought into immediate proximity with the west coast of America, from Cape Horn to the Russian possessions north of Oregon, with the islands of the Pacific Ocean, and by a direct voyage in steamers we will be in less than thirty days of Canton and other ports of China.

In this vast region, whose rich resources are soon to be developed by American energy and enterprise, great must be the augmentation of our commerce, and with it new and profitable demands for mechanic labor in all its branches and new and valuable markets for our manufactures and agricultural products.

While the war has been conducted with great humanity and forbearance and with complete success on our part, the peace has been concluded on terms the most liberal and magnanimous to Mexico. In her hands the territories now ceded had remained, and, it is believed, would have continued to remain, almost unoccupied, and of little value to her or to any other nation, whilst as a part of our Union they will be productive of vast benefits to the United States, to the commercial world, and the general interests of mankind.

The immediate establishment of Territorial governments and the extension of our laws over these valuable possessions are deemed to be not only important, but indispensable to preserve order and the due administration of justice within their limits, to afford protection to the inhabitants, and to facilitate the development of the vast resources and wealth which their acquisition has added to our country.

The war with Mexico having terminated, the power of the Executive to establish or to continue temporary civil governments over these territories, which existed under the laws of nations whilst they were regarded as conquered provinces in our military occupation, has ceased. By their cession to the United States Mexico has no longer any power over them, and until Congress shall act the inhabitants will be without any organized government. Should they be left in this condition, confusion and anarchy will be likely to prevail.

Foreign commerce to a considerable amount is now carried on in the ports of Upper California, which will require to be regulated by our laws. As soon as our system shall be extended over this commerce, a revenue of considerable amount will be at once collected, and it is not doubted that it will be annually increased. For these and other obvious reasons I deem it to be my duty earnestly to recommend the action of Congress on the subject at the present session.

In organizing governments over these territories, fraught with such vast advantages to every portion of our Union, I invoke that spirit of concession, conciliation, and compromise in your deliberations in which the Constitution was framed, in which it should be administered, and which is so indispensable to preserve and perpetuate the harmony and union of the States. We should never forget that this Union of confederated States was established and cemented by kindred blood and by the common toils, sufferings, dangers, and triumphs of all its parts, and has been the ever-augmenting source of our national greatness and of all our blessings.

There has, perhaps, been no period since the warning so impressively given to his countrymen by Washington to guard against geographical divisions and sectional parties which appeals with greater force than the present to the patriotic, sober-minded, and reflecting of all parties and of all sections of our country. Who can calculate the value of our glorious Union? It is a model and example of free government to all the world, and is the star of hope and haven of rest to the oppressed of every clime. By its preservation we have been rapidly advanced as a nation to a height of strength, power, and happiness without a parallel in the history of the world. As we extend its blessings over new regions, shall we be so unwise as to endanger its existence by geographical divisions and dissensions?

With a view to encourage the early settlement of these distant possessions, I recommend that liberal grants of the public lands be secured to all our citizens who have settled or may in a limited period settle within their limits.

In execution of the provisions of the treaty, orders have been issued to our military and naval forces to evacuate without delay the Mexican Provinces, cities, towns, and fortified places in our military occupation, and which are not embraced in the territories ceded to the United States. The Army is already on its way to the United States. That portion of it, as well regulars as volunteers, who engaged to serve during the war with Mexico will be discharged as soon as they can be transported or marched to convenient points in the vicinity of their homes. A part of the Regular Army will be employed in New Mexico and Upper California to afford protection to the inhabitants and to guard our interests in these territories.

The old Army, as it existed before the commencement of the war with Mexico, especially if authority be given to fill up the rank and file of the several corps to the maximum number authorized during the war, it is believed, will be a sufficient force to be retained in service during a period of peace. A few additional officers in the line and staff of the Army have been authorized, and these, it is believed, will be necessary in the peace establishment, and should be retained in the service.

The number of the general officers may be reduced, as vacancies occur by the casualties of the service, to what it was before the war.

While the people of other countries who live under forms of government less free than our own have been for ages oppressed by taxation to support large standing armies in periods of peace, our experience has shown that such establishments are unnecessary in a republic. Our standing army is to be found in the bosom of society. It is composed of free citizens, who are ever ready to take up arms in the service of their country when an emergency requires it. Our experience in the war just closed fully confirms the opinion that such an army may be raised upon a few weeks' notice, and that our citizen soldiers are equal to any troops in the world. No reason, therefore, is perceived why we should enlarge our land forces and thereby subject the Treasury to an annual increased charge. Sound policy requires that we should avoid the creation of a large standing army in a period of peace. No public exigency requires it. Such armies are not only expensive and unnecessary, but may become dangerous to liberty.

Besides making the necessary legislative provisions for the execution of the treaty and the establishment of Territorial governments in the ceded country, we have, upon the restoration of peace, other important duties to perform. Among these I regard none as more important than the adoption of proper measures for the speedy extinguishment of the national debt. It is against sound policy and the genius of our institutions that a public debt should be permitted to exist a day longer than the means of the Treasury will enable the Government to pay it off. We should adhere to the wise policy laid down by President Washington, of "avoiding likewise the accumulation of debt, not only by shunning occasions of expense, but by vigorous exertions in time of peace to discharge the debts which unavoidable wars have occasioned, not ungenerously throwing upon posterity the burthen which we ourselves ought to bear."

At the commencement of the present Administration the public debt amounted to $17,788,799.62. In consequence of the war with Mexico, it has been necessarily increased, and now amounts to $65,778,450.41, including the stock and Treasury notes which may yet be issued under the act of January 28, 1847, and the $16,000,000 loan recently negotiated under the act of March 31, 1848.

In addition to the amount of the debt, the treaty stipulates that $12,-000,000 shall be paid to Mexico, in four equal annual installments of $3,000,000 each, the first of which will fall due on the 30th day of May, 1849. The treaty also stipulates that the United States shall "assume and pay" to our own citizens "the claims already liquidated and decided against the Mexican Republic," and "all claims not heretofore decided against the Mexican Government," "to an amount not exceeding three and a quarter millions of dollars." The "liquidated" claims of citizens of the United States against Mexico, as decided by the joint board of commissioners under the convention between the United States and Mexico of the 11th of April, 1839, amounted to $2,026,139.68. This sum was payable in twenty equal annual installments. Three of them have been paid to the claimants by the Mexican Government and two by the

United States, leaving to be paid of the principal of the liquidated amount assumed by the United States the sum of $1,519,604.76, together with the interest thereon. These several amounts of "liquidated" and unliquidated claims assumed by the United States, it is believed, may be paid as they fall due out of the accruing revenue, without the issue of stock or the creation of any additional public debt.

I can not too strongly recommend to Congress the importance of husbanding all our national resources, of limiting the public expenditures to necessary objects, and of applying all the surplus at any time in the Treasury to the redemption of the debt. I recommend that authority be vested in the Executive by law to anticipate the period of reimbursement of such portion of the debt as may not be now redeemable, and to purchase it at par, or at the premium which it may command in the market, in all cases in which that authority has not already been granted. A premium has been obtained by the Government on much the larger portion of the loans, and if when the Government becomes a purchaser of its own stock it shall command a premium in the market, it will be sound policy to pay it rather than to pay the semiannual interest upon it. The interest upon the debt, if the outstanding Treasury notes shall be funded, from the end of the last fiscal year until it shall fall due and be redeemable will be very nearly equal to the principal, which must itself be ultimately paid.

Without changing or modifying the present tariff of duties, so great has been the increase of our commerce under its benign operation that the revenue derived from that source and from the sales of the public lands will, it is confidently believed, enable the Government to discharge annually several millions of the debt and at the same time possess the means of meeting necessary appropriations for all other proper objects. Unless Congress shall authorize largely increased expenditures for objects not of absolute necessity, the whole public debt existing before the Mexican war and that created during its continuance may be paid off without any increase of taxation on the people long before it falls due.

Upon the restoration of peace we should adopt the policy suited to a state of peace. In doing this the earliest practicable payment of the public debt should be a cardinal principle of action. Profiting by the experience of the past, we should avoid the errors into which the country was betrayed shortly after the close of the war with Great Britain in 1815. In a few years after that period a broad and latitudinous construction of the powers of the Federal Government unfortunately received but too much countenance. Though the country was burdened with a heavy public debt, large, and in some instances unnecessary and extravagant, expenditures were authorized by Congress. The consequence was that the payment of the debt was postponed for more than twenty years, and even then it was only accomplished by the stern will and unbending policy of President Jackson, who made its payment a leading measure of his Administration. He resisted the attempts which were made to divert the public money from that great object and apply it in wasteful and extravagant expenditures for other objects, some of them of more than doubtful constitutional authority and expediency.

If the Government of the United States shall observe a proper economy in its expenditures, and be confined in its action to the conduct of our foreign relations and to the few general objects of its care enumerated in the Constitution, leaving all municipal and local legislation to the States, our greatness as a nation, in moral and physical power and in wealth and resources, can not be calculated.

By pursuing this policy oppressive measures, operating unequally and unjustly upon sections and classes, will be avoided, and the people, having no cause of complaint, will pursue their own interests under the blessings of equal laws and the protection of a just and paternal Government. By abstaining from the exercise of all powers not clearly conferred, the current of our glorious Union, now numbering thirty States, will be strengthened as we grow in age and increase in population, and our future destiny will be without a parallel or example in the history of nations.

JAMES K. POLK.

WASHINGTON, *July 7, 1848.*

To the Senate of the United States:

For the reasons mentioned in the accompanying letter of the Secretary of War, I ask that the date in the promotion of Captain W. J. Hardee, Second Dragoons, to be major by brevet for gallant and meritorious conduct in the affair at Madellin, Mexico, be changed to the 25th of March, 1847, the day on which the action occurred.

JAMES K. POLK.

WAR DEPARTMENT,
Washington, July 7, 1848.

The PRESIDENT OF THE UNITED STATES.

SIR: Captain W. J. Hardee, Second Dragoons, has been promoted to be major by brevet for gallant and meritorious conduct in the affair at Madellin, Mexico, to date from the 26th of March, 1847. As this affair took place on the 25th of that month, I respectfully recommend that the Senate be asked to change the date of Captain Hardee's brevet rank so as to correspond with the date of the action, to wit, the 25th of March, 1847. Brevets which have been conferred upon other officers in the same affair take the latter date.

Very respectfully, your obedient servant,

W. L. MARCY,
Secretary of War.

WASHINGTON, *July 12, 1848.*

To the Senate of the United States:

In compliance with a resolution of the Senate, of the 21st June, 1848, I herewith communicate to the Senate a report of the Secretary of War, with the accompanying documents, containing the proceedings of a court of inquiry which convened at Saltillo, Mexico, January 12, 1848, and which was instituted for the purpose of obtaining full information relative to an alleged mutiny in the camp of Buena Vista, Mexico, on or about the 15th of August, 1847.   JAMES K. POLK.

WASHINGTON, *July 14, 1848.*

To the Senate of the United States:

In compliance with the resolution of the Senate of July 13, 1848, I transmit herewith a report of the Secretary of War and accompanying documents, containing all the proceedings of the two courts of inquiry in the case of Major-General Pillow, the one commenced and terminated in Mexico, the other commenced in Mexico and terminated in the United States.   JAMES K. POLK.

WASHINGTON, *July 24, 1848.*

To the House of Representatives of the United States:

In answer to the resolutions of the House of Representatives of the 10th instant, requesting information in relation to New Mexico and California, I communicate herewith reports from the Secretary of State, the Secretary of the Treasury, the Secretary of War, and the Secretary of the Navy, with the documents which accompany the same. These reports and documents contain information upon the several points of inquiry embraced by the resolutions. "The proper limits and boundaries of New Mexico and California" are delineated on the map referred to in the late treaty with Mexico, an authentic copy of which is herewith transmitted; and all the additional information upon that subject, and also the most reliable information in respect to the population of these respective Provinces, which is in the possession of the Executive will be found in the accompanying report of the Secretary of State.

The resolutions request information in regard to the existence of civil governments in New Mexico and California, their "form and character," by "whom instituted," by "what authority," and how they are "maintained and supported."

In my message of December 22, 1846, in answer to a resolution of the House of Representatives calling for information "in relation to the establishment or organization of civil government in any portion of the territory of Mexico which has or might be taken possession of by the Army or Navy of the United States," I communicated the orders which had been given to the officers of our Army and Navy, and stated the general authority upon which temporary military governments had been established over the conquered portion of Mexico then in our military occupation.

The temporary governments authorized were instituted by virtue of the rights of war. The power to declare war against a foreign country, and to prosecute it according to the general laws of war, as sanctioned by civilized nations, it will not be questioned, exists under our Constitution. When Congress has declared that war exists with a foreign nation, "the general laws of war apply to our situation," and it becomes the duty of the President, as the constitutional "Commander in Chief of the Army and Navy of the United States," to prosecute it.

In prosecuting a foreign war thus duly declared by Congress, we have the right, by "conquest and military occupation," to acquire possession of the territories of the enemy, and, during the war, to "exercise the fullest rights of sovereignty over it." The sovereignty of the enemy is in such case "suspended," and his laws can "no longer be rightfully enforced" over the conquered territory "or be obligatory upon the inhabitants who remain and submit to the conqueror. By the surrender the inhabitants pass under a temporary allegiance" to the conqueror, and are "bound by such laws, and such only, as" he may choose to recognize and impose. "From the nature of the case, no other laws could be obligatory upon them, for where there is no protection or allegiance or sovereignty there can be no claim to obedience." These are well-established principles of the laws of war, as recognized and practiced by civilized nations, and they have been sanctioned by the highest judicial tribunal of our own country.

The orders and instructions issued to the officers of our Army and Navy, applicable to such portions of the Mexican territory as had been or might be conquered by our arms, were in strict conformity to these principles. They were, indeed, ameliorations of the rigors of war upon which we might have insisted. They substituted for the harshness of military rule something of the mildness of civil government, and were not only the exercise of no excess of power, but were a relaxation in favor of the peaceable inhabitants of the conquered territory who had submitted to our authority, and were alike politic and humane.

It is from the same source of authority that we derive the unquestioned right, after the war has been declared by Congress, to blockade the ports and coasts of the enemy, to capture his towns, cities, and provinces, and to levy contributions upon him for the support of our Army. Of the same character with these is the right to subject to our temporary military government the conquered territories of our enemy. They are all belligerent rights, and their exercise is as essential to the successful prosecution of a foreign war as the right to fight battles.

New Mexico and Upper California were among the territories conquered and occupied by our forces, and such temporary governments were established over them. They were established by the officers of our Army and Navy in command, in pursuance of the orders and instructions accompanying my message to the House of Representatives of

December 22, 1846.   In their form and detail, as at first established, they exceeded in some respects, as was stated in that message, the authority which had been given, and instructions for the correction of the error were issued in dispatches from the War and Navy Departments of the 11th of January, 1847, copies of which are herewith transmitted.   They have been maintained and supported out of the military exactions and contributions levied upon the enemy, and no part of the expense has been paid out of the Treasury of the United States.

In the routine of duty some of the officers of the Army and Navy who first established temporary governments in California and New Mexico have been succeeded in command by other officers, upon whom light duties devolved; and the agents employed or designated by them to conduct the temporary governments have also, in some instances, been superseded by others.   Such appointments for temporary civil duty during our military occupation were made by the officers in command in the conquered territories, respectively.

On the conclusion and exchange of ratifications of a treaty of peace with Mexico, which was proclaimed on the 4th instant, these temporary governments necessarily ceased to exist.   In the instructions to establish a temporary government over New Mexico, no distinction was made between that and the other Provinces of Mexico which might be conquered and held in our military occupation.

The Province of New Mexico, according to its ancient boundaries, as claimed by Mexico, lies on both sides of the Rio Grande.   That part of it on the east of that river was in dispute when the war between the United States and Mexico commenced.   Texas, by a successful revolution in April, 1836, achieved, and subsequently maintained, her independence.   By an act of the Congress of Texas passed in December, 1836, her western boundary was declared to be the Rio Grande from its mouth to its source, and thence due north to the forty-second degree of north latitude.   Though the Republic of Texas, by many acts of sovereignty which she asserted and exercised, some of which were stated in my annual message of December, 1846, had established her clear title to the country west of the Nueces, and bordering upon that part of the Rio Grande which lies below the Province of New Mexico, she had never conquered or reduced to actual possession and brought under her Government and laws that part of New Mexico lying east of the Rio Grande, which she claimed to be within her limits.   On the breaking out of the war we found Mexico in possession of this disputed territory.   As our Army approached Sante Fe (the capital of New Mexico) it was found to be held by a governor under Mexican authority, with an armed force collected to resist our advance.   The inhabitants were Mexicans, acknowledging allegiance to Mexico.   The boundary in dispute was the line between the two countries engaged in actual war, and the settlement of it of necessity depended on a treaty of peace.   Finding the Mexican authorities and people in possession, our forces conquered them, and extended military rule over them and the territory which they actually occupied, in lieu of the sovereignty which was displaced. It was not possible to disturb or change the practical boundary line in the midst of the war, when no negotiation for its adjustment could be opened, and when Texas was not present, by her constituted authorities, to establish and maintain government over a hostile Mexican population who acknowledged no allegiance to her. There was, therefore, no alternative left but to establish and maintain military rule during the war over the conquered people in the disputed territory who had submitted to our arms, or to forbear the exercise of our belligerent rights and leave them in a state of anarchy and without control.

Whether the country in dispute rightfully belonged to Mexico or to Texas, it was our right in the first case, and our duty as well as our right in the latter, to conquer and hold it. Whilst this territory was in our possession as conquerors, with a population hostile to the United States, which more than once broke out in open insurrection, it was our unquestionable duty to continue our military occupation of it until the conclusion of the war, and to establish over it a military government, necessary for our own security as well as for the protection of the conquered people.

By the joint resolution of Congress of March 1, 1845, "for annexing Texas to the United States," the "adjustment of all questions of boundary which may arise with other governments" was reserved to this Government. When the conquest of New Mexico was consummated by our arms, the question of boundary remained still unadjusted. Until the exchange of the ratifications of the late treaty, New Mexico never became an undisputed portion of the United States, and it would therefore have been premature to deliver over to Texas that portion of it on the east side of the Rio Grande, to which she asserted a claim. However just the right of Texas may have been to it, that right had never been reduced into her possession, and it was contested by Mexico.

By the cession of the whole of New Mexico, on both sides of the Rio Grande, to the United States, the question of disputed boundary, so far as Mexico is concerned, has been settled, leaving the question as to the true limits of Texas in New Mexico to be adjusted between that State and the United States.

Under the circumstances existing during the pendency of the war, and while the whole of New Mexico, as claimed by our enemy, was in our military occupation, I was not unmindful of the rights of Texas to that portion of it which she claimed to be within her limits. In answer to a letter from the governor of Texas dated on the 4th of January, 1847, the Secretary of State, by my direction, informed him in a letter of the 12th of February, 1847, that in the President's annual message of December, 1846—

You have already perceived that New Mexico is at present in the temporary occupation of the troops of the United States, and the government over it is military in its character. It is merely such a government as must exist under the laws of nations and of war to preserve order and protect the rights of the inhabitants, and will cease on the conclusion of a treaty of peace with Mexico. Nothing, therefore, can be more certain than that this temporary government, resulting from necessity, can never injuriously affect the right which the President believes to be justly asserted by Texas to the whole territory on this side of the Rio Grande whenever the Mexican claim to it shall have been extinguished by treaty. But this is a subject which more properly belongs to the legislative than the executive branch of the Government.

The result of the whole is that Texas had asserted a right to that part of New Mexico east of the Rio Grande, which is believed, under the acts of Congress for the annexation and admission of Texas into the Union as a State, and under the constitution and laws of Texas, to be well founded; but this right had never been reduced to her actual possession and occupancy. The General Government, possessing exclusively the war-making power, had the right to take military possession of this disputed territory, and until the title to it was perfected by a treaty of peace it was their duty to hold it and to establish a temporary military government over it for the preservation of the conquest itself, the safety of our Army, and the security of the conquered inhabitants.

The resolutions further request information whether any persons have been tried and condemned for ''treason against the United States in that part of New Mexico lying east of the Rio Grande since the same has been in the occupancy of our Army,'' and, if so, before ''what tribunal'' and ''by what authority of law such tribunal was established.'' It appears that after the territory in question was ''in the occupancy of our Army'' some of the conquered Mexican inhabitants, who had at first submitted to our authority, broke out in open insurrection, murdering our soldiers and citizens and committing other atrocious crimes. Some of the principal offenders who were apprehended were tried and condemned by a tribunal invested with civil and criminal jurisdiction, which had been established in the conquered country by the military officer in command. That the offenders deserved the punishment inflicted upon them there is no reason to doubt, and the error in the proceedings against them consisted in designating and describing their crimes as ''treason against the United States.'' This error was pointed out, and its recurrence thereby prevented, by the Secretary of War in a dispatch to the officer in command in New Mexico dated on the 26th of June, 1847, a copy of which, together with copies of all communications relating to the subject which have been received at the War Department, is herewith transmitted.

The resolutions call for information in relation to the quantity of the public lands acquired within the ceded territory, and ''how much of the same is within the boundaries of Texas as defined by the act of the Congress of the Republic of Texas of the 19th day of December, 1836.'' No means of making an accurate estimate on the subject is in the possession of the executive department. The information which is possessed will be found in the accompanying report of the Secretary of the Treasury.

The country ceded to the United States lying west of the Rio Grande, and to which Texas has no title, is estimated by the commissioner of the General Land Office to contain 526,078 square miles, or 336,689,920 acres.

The period since the exchange of ratifications of the treaty has been too short to enable the Government to have access to or to procure abstracts or copies of the land titles issued by Spain or by the Republic of Mexico. Steps will be taken to procure this information at the earliest practicable period. It is estimated, as appears from the accompanying report of the Secretary of the Treasury, that much the larger portion of the land within the territories ceded remains vacant and unappropriated, and will be subject to be disposed of by the United States. Indeed, a very inconsiderable portion of the land embraced in the cession, it is believed, has been disposed of or granted either by Spain or Mexico.

What amount of money the United States may be able to realize from the sales of these vacant lands must be uncertain, but it is confidently believed that with prudent management, after making liberal grants to emigrants and settlers, it will exceed the cost of the war and all the expenses to which we have been subjected in acquiring it.

The resolutions also call for "the evidence, or any part thereof, that the 'extensive and valuable territories ceded by Mexico to the United States constitute indemnity for the past.'"

The immense value of the ceded country does not consist alone in the amount of money for which the public lands may be sold. If not a dollar could be realized from the sale of these lands, the cession of the jurisdiction over the country and the fact that it has become a part of our Union and can not be made subject to any European power constitute ample "indemnity for the past" in the immense value and advantages which its acquisition must give to the commercial, navigating, manufacturing, and agricultural interests of our country.

The value of the public lands embraced within the limits of the ceded territory, great as that value may be, is far less important to the people of the United States than the sovereignty over the country. Most of our States contain no public lands owned by the United States, and yet the sovereignty and jurisdiction over them is of incalculable importance to the nation. In the State of New York the United States is the owner of no public lands, and yet two-thirds of our whole revenue is collected at the great port of that State, and within her limits is found about one-seventh of our entire population. Although none of the future cities on our coast of California may ever rival the city of New York in wealth, population, and business, yet that important cities will grow up on the magnificent harbors of that coast, with a rapidly increasing commerce and population, and yielding a large revenue, would seem to be certain. By the possession of the safe and capacious harbors on the Californian coast we shall have great advantages in securing the rich commerce of the East, and shall thus obtain for our products new and increased markets and greatly enlarge our coasting and foreign trade, as well as augment our tonnage and revenue.

These great advantages, far more than the simple value of the public lands in the ceded territory, "constitute our indemnity for the past."

JAMES K. POLK.

WASHINGTON, *July 28, 1848.*

To the Senate of the United States:

I have received from the Senate the "convention for the mutual delivery of criminals, fugitives from justice, in certain cases, concluded on the 29th of January, 1845, between the United States on the one part and Prussia and other States of the German Confederation on the other part," with a copy of their resolution of the 21st of June last, advising and consenting to its ratification, with an amendment extending the period for the exchange of ratifications until the 28th of September, 1848.

I have taken this subject into serious and deliberate consideration, and regret that I can not ratify this convention, in conformity with the advice of the Senate, without violating my convictions of duty. Having arrived at this conclusion, I deem it proper and respectful, considering the peculiar circumstances of the present case and the intimate relations which the Constitution has established between the President and Senate, to make known to you the reasons which influence me to come to this determination.

On the 16th of December, 1845, I communicated this convention to the Senate for its consideration, at the same time stating my objections to the third article. I deemed this to be a more proper and respectful course toward the Senate, as well as toward Prussia and the other parties to it, than if I had withheld it and disapproved it altogether. Had the Senate concurred with me in opinion and rejected the third article, then the convention thus amended would have conformed to our treaties of extradition with Great Britain and France.

But the Senate did not act upon it within the period limited for the exchange of ratifications. From this I concluded that they had concurred with me in opinion in regard to the third article, and had for this and other reasons deemed it proper to take no proceedings upon the convention. After this date, therefore, I considered the affair as terminated.

Upon the presumption that this was the fact, new negotiations upon the subject were commenced, and several conferences were held between the Secretary of State and the Prussian minister. These resulted in a protocol signed at the Department of State on the 27th of April, 1847, in which the Secretary proposed either that the two Governments might agree to extend the time for the exchange of ratifications, and thus revive the convention, provided the Prussian Government would previously intimate its consent to the omission of the third article, or he "expressed his willingness immediately to conclude with Mr. Gerolt a new convention, if he possessed the requisite powers from his Government, embracing all the provisions contained in that of the 29th January, 1845, with the exception of the third article. To this Mr. Gerolt observed that he had no powers to conclude such a convention, but would submit the propositions of Mr. Buchanan to the Prussian Government for further instructions.''

Mr. Gerolt has never yet communicated in writing to the Department of State the answer of his Government to these propositions, but the Secretary of State, a few months after the date of the protocol, learned from him in conversation that they insisted upon the third article of the convention as a *sine qua non*. Thus the second negotiation had finally terminated by a disagreement between the parties, when, more than a year afterwards, on the 21st June, 1848, the Senate took the original convention into consideration and ratified it, retaining the third article.

After the second negotiation with the Prussian Government, in which the objections to the third article were stated, as they had been previously in my message of the 16th December, 1845, a strong additional difficulty was interposed to the ratification of the convention; but I might overcome this difficulty if my objections to the third article had not grown stronger by further reflection. For a statement of them in detail I refer you to the accompanying memorandum, prepared by the Secretary of State by my direction.

I can not believe that the sovereign States of this Union, whose administration of justice would be almost exclusively affected by such a convention, will ever be satisfied with a treaty of extradition under which if a German subject should commit murder or any other high crime in New York or New Orleans, and could succeed in escaping to his own country, he would thereby be protected from trial and punishment under the jurisdiction of our State laws which he had violated. It is true, as has been stated, that the German States, acting upon a principle springing from the doctrine of perpetual allegiance, still assert the jurisdiction of trying and punishing their subjects for crimes committed in the United States or any other portion of the world. It must, however, be manifest that individuals throughout our extended country would rarely, if ever, follow criminals to Germany with the necessary testimony for the purpose of prosecuting them to conviction before German courts for crimes committed in the United States.

On the other hand, the Constitution and laws of the United States, as well as of the several States, would render it impossible that crimes committed by our citizens in Germany could be tried and punished in any portion of this Union.

But if no other reason existed for withholding my ratification from this treaty, the great change which has recently occurred in the organization of the Government of the German States would be sufficient. By the last advices we learn that the German Parliament, at Frankfort, have already established a federal provisional Executive for all the States of Germany, and have elected the Archduke John of Austria to be "Administrator of the Empire." One of the attributes of this Executive is "to represent the Confederation in its relations with foreign nations and to appoint diplomatic agents, ministers, and consuls." Indeed, our minister at Berlin has already suggested the propriety of his transfer to Frankfort. In case this convention with nineteen of the thirty-nine German States should be ratified, this could amount to nothing more than a proposition on the part of the Senate and President to these nineteen States who were originally parties to the convention to negotiate anew on the subject of extradition. In the meantime a central German Government has been provisionally established, which extinguishes the right of these separate parties to enter into negotiations with foreign Governments on subjects of several interest to the whole.

Admitting such a treaty as that which has been ratified by the Senate to be desirable, the obvious course would now be to negotiate with the General Government of Germany. A treaty concluded with it would embrace all the thirty-nine States of Germany, and its authority, being coextensive with the Empire, fugitives from justice found in any of these States would be surrendered up on the requisition of our minister at Frankfort. This would be more convenient and effectual than to address such separate requisitions to each of the nineteen German States with which the convention was concluded.

I communicate herewith, for the information of the Senate, copies of a dispatch from our minister at Berlin and a communication from our consul at Darmstadt.

JAMES K. POLK.

WASHINGTON, *July 29, 1848.*

To the House of Representatives of the United States:

In answer to the resolution of the House of Representatives of the 17th instant, requesting the President "to communicate, if not inconsistent with the public interests, copies of all instructions given to the Hon. Ambrose H. Sevier and Nathan Clifford, commissioners appointed to conduct negotiations for the ratification of the treaty lately concluded between the United States and the Republic of Mexico," I have to state that in my opinion it would be "inconsistent with the public interests" to give publicity to these instructions at the present time.

I avail myself of this occasion to observe that, as a general rule applicable to all our important negotiations with foreign powers, it could not fail to be prejudicial to the public interest to publish the instructions to our ministers until some time had elapsed after the conclusion of such negotiations.

In the present case the object of the mission of our commissioners to

Mexico has been accomplished. The treaty, as amended by the Senate of the United States, has been ratified. The ratifications have been exchanged and the treaty has been proclaimed as the supreme law of the land. No contingency occurred which made it either necessary or proper for our commissioners to enter upon any negotiations with the Mexican Government further than to urge upon that Government the ratification of the treaty in its amended form.

JAMES K. POLK.

WASHINGTON, *July 31, 1848.*

To the Senate of the United States:

I communicate herewith a report from the Secretary of State, containing the information called for by the resolution of the Senate of the 24th of April, 1848, in relation "to the claim of the owners of the ship *Miles*, of Warren, in the State of Rhode Island, upon the Government of Portugal for the payment of a cargo of oil taken by the officers and applied to the uses of that Government."

JAMES K. POLK.

WASHINGTON, *July 31, 1848.*

To the Senate of the United States:

In compliance with the resolution of the Senate of the 28th instant, requesting the President to communicate to that body, "in confidence, if not inconsistent with the public interest, what steps, if any, have been taken by the Executive to extinguish the rights of the Hudsons Bay and Puget Sound Land Company within the Territory of Oregon, and such communications, if any, which may have been received from the British Government in relation to this subject," I communicate herewith a report from the Secretary of State, with the accompanying documents.

JAMES K. POLK.

WASHINGTON, *August 1, 1848.*

To the House of Representatives of the United States:

I communicate herewith a report from the Secretary of War, containing the information called for by the resolution of the House of Representatives of the 17th July, 1848, in relation to the number of Indians in Oregon, California, and New Mexico, the number of military posts, the number of troops which will be required in each, and "the whole military force which should constitute the peace establishment."

I have seen no reason to change the opinion expressed in my message to Congress of the 6th July, 1848, transmitting the treaty of peace with Mexico, that "the old Army, as it existed before the commencement of the war with Mexico, especially if authority be given to fill up the rank and file of the several corps to the maximum number authorized during the war, will be a sufficient force to be retained in service during a period of peace.''

The old Army consists of fifteen regiments. By the act of the 13th of May, 1846, the President was authorized, by ''voluntary enlistments, to increase the number of privates in each or any of the companies of the existing regiments of dragoons, artillery, and infantry to any number not exceeding 100,'' and to ''reduce the same to 64 when the exigencies requiring the present increase shall cease.'' Should this act remain in force, the maximum number of the rank and file of the Army authorized by it would be over 16,000 men, exclusive of officers. Should the authority conferred by this act be continued, it would depend on the exigencies of the service whether the number of the rank and file should be increased, and, if so, to what amount beyond the minimum number of 64 privates to a company.

Allowing 64 privates to a company, the Army would be over 10,000 men, exclusive of commissioned and noncommissioned officers, a number which, it is believed, will be sufficient; but, as a precautionary measure, it is deemed expedient that the Executive should possess the power of increasing the strength of the respective corps should the exigencies of the service be such as to require it. Should these exigencies not call for such increase, the discretionary power given by the act to the President will not be exercised.

It will be seen from the report of the Secretary of War that a portion of the forces will be employed in Oregon, New Mexico, and Upper California; a portion for the protection of the Texas frontier adjoining the Mexican possessions, and bordering on the territory occupied by the Indian tribes within her limits. After detailing the force necessary for these objects, it is believed a sufficient number of troops will remain to afford security and protection to our Indian frontiers in the West and Northwest and to occupy with sufficient garrisons the posts on our northern and Atlantic borders.

I have no reason at present to believe that any increase of the number of regiments or corps will be required during a period of peace.

JAMES K. POLK.

WASHINGTON, *August 3, 1848.*

To the Senate of the United States:

I communicate herewith a report from the Secretary of War, together with the accompanying documents, in compliance with the resolution of the Senate of the 24th July, 1848, requesting the President ''to transmit to the Senate the proceedings of the two courts of inquiry in the case of Major-General Pillow, the one commenced and terminated in Mexico, and the other commenced in Mexico and terminated in the United States.''

JAMES K. POLK.

To the Senate of the United States:

I nominate Andrew J. Donelson, of Tennessee, to be envoy extraordinary and minister plenipotentiary of the United States to the Federal Government of Germany.

In submitting this nomination I transmit, for the information of the Senate, an official dispatch received from the consul of the United States at Darmstadt, dated July 10, 1848. I deem it proper also to state that no such diplomatic agent as that referred to by the consul has been appointed by me. Mr. Deverre, the person alluded to, is unknown to me and has no authority to represent this Government in any capacity whatever.

JAMES K. POLK.

WASHINGTON, *August 5, 1848*.
To the House of Representatives of the United States:

I communicate herewith a report from the Secretary of War, together with the accompanying documents, in compliance with a resolution of the House of Representatives of the 17th of July, 1848, requesting the President to communicate to the House of Representatives "a copy of the proceedings of the court of inquiry in Mexico touching the matter which led to the dismissal from the public service of Lieutenants Joseph S. Pendée and George E. B. Singletary, of the North Carolina regiment of volunteers, and all the correspondence between the War Department and Generals Taylor and Wool in relation to the same."

JAMES K. POLK.

WASHINGTON, *August 8, 1848*.
To the Senate of the United States:

In reply to the resolution of the Senate of the 7th instant, requesting the President to inform that body "whether he has any information that any citizen or citizens of the United States is or are now preparing or intending to prepare within the United States an expedition to revolutionize by force any part of the Republic of Mexico, or to assist in so doing, and, if he has, what is the extent of such preparation, and whether he has or is about to take any steps to arrest the same," I have to state that the Executive is not in possession of any information of the character called for by the resolution.

The late treaty of peace with Mexico has been and will be faithfully observed on our part.

JAMES K. POLK.

WASHINGTON, *August 8, 1848*.
To the Senate and House of Representatives of the United States:

It affords me satisfaction to communicate herewith, for the information of Congress, copies of a decree adopted by the National Assembly of France in response to the resolution of the Congress of the United States passed on the 13th of April last, "tendering the congratulations of the American to the French people upon the success of their recent efforts to consolidate the principles of liberty in a republican form of government."

JAMES K. POLK.

WASHINGTON, *August 10, 1848.*

To the Senate of the United States:

I communicate herewith a report of the Secretary of the Navy, together with the accompanying documents, in answer to a resolution of the Senate of the 18th July, 1848, requesting the President to communicate to that body "any information which may be in the possession of the Executive relating to the seizure or capture of the American ship *Admittance* on the coast of California by a vessel of war of the United States, and whether any, and what, proceedings have occurred in regard to said vessel or her cargo, and to furnish the Senate with copies of all documents, papers, and communications in the possession of the Executive relating to the same."

JAMES K. POLK.

WASHINGTON, *August 11, 1848.*

To the House of Representatives of the United States:

I communicate herewith reports from the Secretary of the Treasury and the Secretary of War, together with the accompanying documents, in answer to a resolution of the House of Representatives of the 17th of July, 1848, requesting the President to inform that body what amount of public moneys had been respectively paid to Lewis Cass and Zachary Taylor from the time of their first entrance into the public service up to this time, distinguishing between regular and extra compensation; that he also state what amount of extra compensation has been claimed by either; the items composing the same; when filed; when and by whom allowed; if disallowed, when and by whom; the reasons for such disallowance; and whether or not any items so disallowed were subsequently presented for payment, and, if allowed, when and by whom.

JAMES K. POLK.

WASHINGTON, *August 14, 1848.*

To the House of Representatives of the United States:

When the President has given his official sanction to a bill which has passed Congress, usage requires that he shall notify the House in which it originated of that fact. The mode of giving this notification has been by an oral message delivered by his private secretary.

Having this day approved and signed an act entitled "An act to establish the Territorial government of Oregon," I deem it proper, under the existing circumstances, to communicate the fact in a more solemn form. The deeply interesting and protracted discussions which have taken place in both Houses of Congress and the absorbing interest which the subject has excited throughout the country justify, in my judgment, this departure from the form of notice observed in other cases. In this communication with a coordinate branch of the Government, made proper by the considerations referred to, I shall frankly and without reserve express the reasons which have constrained me not to withhold my signature from the bill to establish a government over Oregon, even though the two territories of New Mexico and California are to be left for the present without governments. None doubt that it is proper to establish a government in Oregon. Indeed, it has been too long delayed. I have made repeated recommendations to Congress to this effect. The petitions of the people of that distant region have been presented to the Government, and ought not to be disregarded. To give to them a regularly organized government and the protection of our laws, which, as citizens of the United States, they claim, is a high duty on our part, and one which we are bound to perform, unless there be controlling reasons to prevent it.

In the progress of all governments questions of such transcendent importance occasionally arise as to cast in the shade all those of a mere party character. But one such question can now be agitated in this country, and this may endanger our glorious Union, the source of our greatness and all our political blessings. This question is slavery. With the slaveholding States this does not embrace merely the rights of property, however valuable, but it ascends far higher, and involves the domestic peace and security of every family.

The fathers of the Constitution, the wise and patriotic men who laid the foundation of our institutions, foreseeing the danger from this quarter, acted in a spirit of compromise and mutual concession on this dangerous and delicate subject, and their wisdom ought to be the guide of their successors. Whilst they left to the States exclusively the question of domestic slavery within their respective limits, they provided that slaves who might escape into other States not recognizing the institution of slavery shall be "delivered up on the claim of the party to whom such service or labor may be due."

Upon this foundation the matter rested until the Missouri question arose.

In December, 1819, application was made to Congress by the people of the Missouri Territory for admission into the Union as a State. The discussion upon the subject in Congress involved the question of slavery, and was prosecuted with such violence as to produce excitements alarming to every patriot in the Union. But the good genius of conciliation, which presided at the birth of our institutions, finally prevailed, and the Missouri compromise was adopted. The eighth section of the act of Congress of the 6th of March, 1820, "to authorize the people of the

Missouri Territory to form a constitution and State government,'' etc.,
provides:

That in all that territory ceded by France to the United States under the name of
Louisiana which lies north of 36° 30′ north latitude, not included within the limits
of the State contemplated by this act, slavery and involuntary servitude, otherwise
than in the punishment of crimes, whereof the parties shall have been duly convicted,
shall be, and is hereby, forever prohibited: *Provided always*, That any person escaping into the same from whom labor or service is lawfully claimed in any State or
Territory of the United States, such fugitive may be lawfully reclaimed and conveyed
to the person claiming his or her labor or service as aforesaid.

This compromise had the effect of calming the troubled waves and
restoring peace and good will throughout the States of the Union.

The Missouri question had excited intense agitation of the public mind,
and threatened to divide the country into geographical parties, alienating the feelings of attachment which each portion of our Union should
bear to every other. The compromise allayed the excitement, tranquil-
ized the popular mind, and restored confidence and fraternal feelings. Its
authors were hailed as public benefactors.

I do not doubt that a similar adjustment of the questions which now
agitate the public mind would produce the same happy results. If the
legislation of Congress on the subject of the other Territories shall not be
adopted in a spirit of conciliation and compromise, it is impossible that
the country can be satisfied or that the most disastrous consequences
shall fail to ensue.

When Texas was admitted into the Union, the same spirit of compromise which guided our predecessors in the admission of Missouri a quarter
of a century before prevailed without any serious opposition. The joint
resolution for annexing Texas to the United States, approved March 1,
1845, provides that—

Such States as may be formed out of that portion of said territory lying south of
36° 30′ north latitude, commonly known as the Missouri compromise line, shall be
admitted into the Union with or without slavery, as the people of each State asking
admission may desire; and in such State or States as shall be formed out of said territory north of the Missouri compromise line slavery or involuntary servitude (except
for crime) shall be prohibited.

The Territory of Oregon lies far north of 36° 30′, the Missouri and
Texas compromise line. Its southern boundary is the parallel of 42°,
leaving the intermediate distance to be 330 geographical miles. And it
is because the provisions of this bill are not inconsistent with the laws
of the Missouri compromise, if extended from the Rio Grande to the
Pacific Ocean, that I have not felt at liberty to withhold my sanction.
Had it embraced territories south of that compromise, the question presented for my consideration would have been of a far different character,
and my action upon it must have corresponded with my convictions.

Ought we now to disturb the Missouri and Texas compromises? Ought
we at this late day, in attempting to annul what has been so long estab-

lished and acquiesced in, to excite sectional divisions and jealousies, to alienate the people of different portions of the Union from each other, and to endanger the existence of the Union itself?

From the adoption of the Federal Constitution, during a period of sixty years, our progress as a nation has been without example in the annals of history. Under the protection of a bountiful Providence, we have advanced with giant strides in the career of wealth and prosperity. We have enjoyed the blessings of freedom to a greater extent than any other people, ancient or modern, under a Government which has preserved order and secured to every citizen life, liberty, and property. We have now become an example for imitation to the whole world. The friends of freedom in every clime point with admiration to our institutions. Shall we, then, at the moment when the people of Europe are devoting all their energies in the attempt to assimilate their institutions to our own, peril all our blessings by despising the lessons of experience and refusing to tread in the footsteps which our fathers have trodden? And for what cause would we endanger our glorious Union? The Missouri compromise contains a prohibition of slavery throughout all that vast region extending twelve and a half degrees along the Pacific, from the parallel of 36° 30' to that of 49°, and east from that ocean to and beyond the summit of the Rocky Mountains. Why, then, should our institutions be endangered because it is proposed to submit to the people of the remainder of our newly acquired territory lying south of 36° 30', embracing less than four degrees of latitude, the question whether, in the language of the Texas compromise, they "shall be admitted [as a State] into the Union with or without slavery." Is this a question to be pushed to such extremities by excited partisans on the one side or the other, in regard to our newly acquired distant possessions on the Pacific, as to endanger the Union of thirty glorious States, which constitute our Confederacy? I have an abiding confidence that the sober reflection and sound patriotism of the people of all the States will bring them to the conclusion that the dictate of wisdom is to follow the example of those who have gone before us, and settle this dangerous question on the Missouri compromise, or some other equitable compromise which would respect the rights of all and prove satisfactory to the different portions of the Union.

Holding as a sacred trust the Executive authority for the whole Union, and bound to guard the rights of all, I should be constrained by a sense of duty to withhold my official sanction from any measure which would conflict with these important objects.

I can not more appropriately close this message than by quoting from the Farewell Address of the Father of his Country. His warning voice can never be heard in vain by the American people. If the spirit of prophecy had distinctly presented to his view more than a half century ago the present distracted condition of his country, the language which he then employed could not have been more appropriate than it is to the present occasion. He declared:

The unity of government which constitutes you one people is also now dear to you. It is justly so, for it is a main pillar in the edifice of your real independence, the support of your tranquillity at home, your peace abroad, of your safety, of your prosperity, of that very liberty which you so highly prize. But as it is easy to foresee that from different causes and from different quarters much pains will be taken, many artifices employed, to weaken in your minds the conviction of this truth, as this is the point in your political fortress against which the batteries of internal and external enemies will be most constantly and actively (though often covertly and insidiously) directed, it is of infinite moment that you should properly estimate the immense value of your national union to your collective and individual happiness; that you should cherish a cordial, habitual, and immovable attachment to it; accustoming yourselves to think and speak of it as of the palladium of your political safety and prosperity; watching for its preservation with jealous anxiety; discountenancing whatever may suggest even a suspicion that it can in any event be abandoned, and indignantly frowning upon the first dawning of every attempt to alienate any portion of our country from the rest or to enfeeble the sacred ties which now link together the various parts.

For this you have every inducement of sympathy and interest. Citizens by birth or choice of a common country, that country has a right to concentrate your affections. The name of American, which belongs to you in your national capacity, must always exalt the just pride of patriotism more than any appellation derived from local discriminations. With slight shades of difference, you have the same religion, manners, habits, and political principles. You have in a common cause fought and triumphed together. The independence and liberty you possess are the work of joint councils and joint efforts, of common dangers, sufferings, and successes.

* * * * * * *

With such powerful and obvious motives to union affecting all parts of our country, while experience shall not have demonstrated its impracticability, there will always be reason to distrust the patriotism of those who in any quarter may endeavor to weaken its bands.

In contemplating the causes which may disturb our union it occurs as matter of serious concern that any ground should have been furnished for characterizing parties by *geographical* discriminations—*Northern* and *Southern*, *Atlantic* and *Western*—whence designing men may endeavor to excite a belief that there is a real difference of local interests and views. One of the expedients of party to acquire influence within particular districts is to misrepresent the opinions and aims of other districts. You can not shield yourselves too much against the jealousies and heartburnings which spring from these misrepresentations; they tend to render alien to each other those who ought to be bound together by fraternal affection.

JAMES K. POLK.

VETO MESSAGE.*

WASHINGTON, *December 15, 1847.*

To the House of Representatives:

On the last day of the last session of Congress a bill entitled "An act to provide for continuing certain works in the Territory of Wisconsin, and for other purposes," which had passed both Houses, was presented to me for my approval. I entertained insuperable objections to its becom-

* Pocket veto.

ing a law, but the short period of the session which remained afforded me no sufficient opportunity to prepare my objections and communicate them with the bill to the House of Representatives, in which it originated. For this reason the bill was retained, and I deem it proper now to state my objections to it.

Although from the title of the bill it would seem that its main object was to make provision for continuing certain works already commenced in the Territory of Wisconsin, it appears on examination of its provisions that it contains only a single appropriation of $6,000 to be applied within that Territory, while it appropriates more than half a million of dollars for the improvement of numerous harbors and rivers lying within the limits and jurisdiction of several of the States of the Union.

At the preceding session of Congress it became my duty to return with my objections to the House in which it originated a bill making similar appropriations and involving like principles, and the views then expressed remain unchanged.

The circumstances under which this heavy expenditure of public money was proposed were of imposing weight in determining upon its expediency. Congress had recognized the existence of war with Mexico, and to prosecute it to "a speedy and successful termination" had made appropriations exceeding our ordinary revenues. To meet the emergency and provide for the expenses of the Government, a loan of $23,000,000 was authorized at the same session, which has since been negotiated. The practical effect of this bill, had it become a law, would have been to add the whole amount appropriated by it to the national debt. It would, in fact, have made necessary an additional loan to that amount as effectually as if in terms it had required the Secretary of the Treasury to borrow the money therein appropriated. The main question in that aspect is whether it is wise, while all the means and credit of the Government are needed to bring the existing war to an honorable close, to impair the one and endanger the other by borrowing money to be expended in a system of internal improvements capable of an expansion sufficient to swallow up the revenues not only of our own country, but of the civilized world? It is to be apprehended that by entering upon such a career at this moment confidence at home and abroad in the wisdom and prudence of the Government would be so far impaired as to make it difficult, without an immediate resort to heavy taxation, to maintain the public credit and to preserve the honor of the nation and the glory of our arms in prosecuting the existing war to a successful conclusion. Had this bill become a law, it is easy to foresee that largely increased demands upon the Treasury would have been made at each succeeding session of Congress for the improvements of numerous other harbors, bays, inlets, and rivers of equal importance with those embraced by its provisions. Many millions would probably have been added to the necessary amount of the war debt, the annual interest on which must also have been borrowed, and finally a permanent national debt been fastened on the country and entailed on posterity.

The policy of embarking the Federal Government in a general system of internal improvements had its origin but little more than twenty years ago. In a very few years the applications to Congress for appropriations in furtherance of such objects exceeded $200,000,000. In this alarming crisis President Jackson refused to approve and sign the Maysville road bill, the Wabash River bill, and other bills of similar character. His interposition put a check upon the new policy of throwing the cost of local improvements upon the National Treasury, preserved the revenues of the nation for their legitimate objects, by which he was enabled to extinguish the then existing public debt and to present to an admiring world the unprecedented spectacle in modern times of a nation free from debt and advancing to greatness with unequaled strides under a Government which was content to act within its appropriate sphere in protecting the States and individuals in their own chosen career of improvement and of enterprise. Although the bill under consideration proposes no appropriation for a road or canal, it is not easy to perceive the difference in principle or mischievous tendency between appropriations for making roads and digging canals and appropriations to deepen rivers and improve harbors. All are alike within the limits and jurisdiction of the States, and rivers and harbors alone open an abyss of expenditure sufficient to swallow up the wealth of the nation and load it with a debt which may fetter its energies and tax its industry for ages to come.

The experience of several of the States, as well as that of the United States, during the period that Congress exercised the power of appropriating the public money for internal improvements is full of eloquent warnings. It seems impossible, in the nature of the subject, as connected with local representation, that the several objects presented for improvement shall be weighed according to their respective merits and appropriations confined to those whose importance would justify a tax on the whole community to effect their accomplishment.

In some of the States systems of internal improvements have been projected, consisting of roads and canals, many of which, taken separately, were not of sufficient public importance to justify a tax on the entire population of the State to effect their construction, and yet by a combination of local interests, operating on a majority of the legislature, the whole have been authorized and the States plunged into heavy debts. To an extent so ruinous has this system of legislation been carried in some portions of the Union that the people have found it necessary to their own safety and prosperity to forbid their legislatures, by constitutional restrictions, to contract public debts for such purposes without their immediate consent.

If the abuse of power has been so fatal in the States, where the systems of taxation are direct and the representatives responsible at short periods to small masses of constituents, how much greater danger of abuse is to be apprehended in the General Government, whose revenues are raised by indirect taxation and whose functionaries are responsible to the people in larger masses and for longer terms.

Regarding only objects of improvement of the nature of those embraced in this bill, how inexhaustible we shall find them. Let the imagination run along our coast from the river St. Croix to the Rio Grande and trace every river emptying into the Atlantic and Gulf of Mexico to its source; let it coast along our lakes and ascend all their tributaries; let it pass to Oregon and explore all its bays, inlets, and streams; and then let it raise the curtain of the future and contemplate the extent of this Republic and the objects of improvement it will embrace as it advances to its high destiny, and the mind will be startled at the immensity and danger of the power which the principle of this bill involves.

Already our Confederacy consists of twenty-nine States. Other States may at no distant period be expected to be formed on the west of our present settlements. We own an extensive country in Oregon, stretching many hundreds of miles from east to west and seven degrees of latitude from south to north. By the admission of Texas into the Union we have recently added many hundreds of miles to our seacoast. In all this vast country, bordering on the Atlantic and Pacific, there are many thousands of bays, inlets, and rivers equally entitled to appropriations for their improvement with the objects embraced in this bill.

We have seen in our States that the interests of individuals or neighborhoods, combining against the general interest, have involved their governments in debts and bankruptcy; and when the system prevailed in the General Government, and was checked by President Jackson, it had begun to be considered the highest merit in a member of Congress to be able to procure appropriations of public money to be expended within his district or State, whatever might be the object. We should be blind to the experience of the past if we did not see abundant evidences that if this system of expenditure is to be indulged in combinations of individual and local interests will be found strong enough to control legislation, absorb the revenues of the country, and plunge the Government into a hopeless indebtedness.

What is denominated a harbor by this system does not necessarily mean a bay, inlet, or arm of the sea on the ocean or on our lake shores, on the margin of which may exist a commercial city or town engaged in foreign or domestic trade, but is made to embrace waters where there is not only no such city or town, but no commerce of any kind. By it a bay or sheet of shoal water is called a *harbor*, and appropriations demanded from Congress to deepen it with a view to draw commerce to it or to enable individuals to build up a town or city on its margin upon speculation and for their own private advantage.

What is denominated a river which may be improved in the system is equally undefined in its meaning. It may be the Mississippi or it may be the smallest and most obscure and unimportant stream bearing the name of river which is to be found in any State in the Union.

Such a system is subject, moreover, to be perverted to the accomplishment of the worst of political purposes. During the few years it was in full operation, and which immediately preceded the veto of President Jackson of the Maysville road bill, instances were numerous of public men seeking to gain popular favor by holding out to the people interested in particular localities the promise of large disbursements of public money. Numerous reconnoissances and surveys were made during that period for roads and canals through many parts of the Union, and the people in the vicinity of each were led to believe that their property would be enhanced in value and they themselves be enriched by the large expenditures which they were promised by the advocates of the system should be made from the Federal Treasury in their neighborhood. Whole sections of the country were thus sought to be influenced, and the system was fast becoming one not only of profuse and wasteful expenditure, but a potent political engine.

If the power to improve a harbor be admitted, it is not easy to perceive how the power to deepen every inlet on the ocean or the lakes and make harbors where there are none can be denied. If the power to clear out or deepen the channel of rivers near their mouths be admitted, it is not easy to perceive how the power to improve them to their fountain head and make them navigable to their sources can be denied. Where shall the exercise of the power, if it be assumed, stop? Has Congress the power when an inlet is deep enough to admit a schooner to deepen it still more, so that it will admit ships of heavy burden, and has it not the power when an inlet will admit a boat to make it deep enough to admit a schooner? May it improve rivers deep enough already to float ships and steamboats, and has it no power to improve those which are navigable only for flatboats and barges? May the General Government exercise power and jurisdiction over the soil of a State consisting of rocks and sand bars in the beds of its rivers, and may it not excavate a canal around its waterfalls or across its lands for precisely the same object?

Giving to the subject the most serious and candid consideration of which my mind is capable, I can not perceive any intermediate grounds. The power to improve harbors and rivers for purposes of navigation, by deepening or clearing out, by dams and sluices, by locking or canalling, must be admitted without any other limitation than the discretion of Congress, or it must be denied altogether. If it be admitted, how broad and how susceptible of enormous abuses is the power thus vested in the General Government! There is not an inlet of the ocean or the Lakes, not a river, creek, or streamlet within the States, which is not brought for this purpose within the power and jurisdiction of the General Government.

Speculation, disguised under the cloak of public good, will call on Congress to deepen shallow inlets, that it may build up new cities on their shores, or to make streams navigable which nature has closed by bars and rapids, that it may sell at a profit its lands upon their banks. To enrich neighborhoods by spending within them the moneys of the nation will be the aim and boast of those who prize their local interests above the good of the nation, and millions upon millions will be abstracted by tariffs and taxes from the earnings of the whole people to foster speculation and subserve the objects of private ambition.

Such a system could not be administered with any approach to equality among the several States and sections of the Union. There is no equality among them in the objects of expenditure, and if the funds were distributed according to the merits of those objects some would be enriched at the expense of their neighbors. But a greater practical evil would be found in the art and industry by which appropriations would be sought and obtained. The most artful and industrious would be the most successful. The true interests of the country would be lost sight of in an annual scramble for the contents of the Treasury, and the Member of Congress who could procure the largest appropriations to be expended in his district would claim the reward of victory from his enriched constituents. The necessary consequence would be sectional discontents and heartburnings, increased taxation, and a national debt never to be extinguished.

In view of these portentous consequences, I can not but think that this course of legislation should be arrested, even were there nothing to forbid it in the fundamental laws of our Union. This conclusion is fortified by the fact that the Constitution itself indicates a process by which harbors and rivers within the States may be improved—a process not susceptible of the abuses necessarily to flow from the assumption of the power to improve them by the General Government, just in its operation, and actually practiced upon, without complaint or interruption, during more than thirty years from the organization of the present Government.

The Constitution provides that "no State shall, without the consent of Congress, lay any duty of tonnage." With the "consent" of Congress, such duties may be levied, collected, and expended by the States. We are not left in the dark as to the objects of this reservation of power to the States. The subject was fully considered by the Convention that framed the Constitution. It appears in Mr. Madison's report of the proceedings of that body that one object of the reservation was that the States should not be restrained from laying duties of tonnage for the purpose of clearing harbors. Other objects were named in the debates, and among them the support of seamen. Mr. Madison, treating on this subject in the Federalist, declares that—

The restraint on the power of the States over imports and exports is enforced by all the arguments which prove the necessity of submitting the regulation of trade to the Federal councils. It is needless, therefore, to remark further on this head than that the manner in which the restraint is qualified seems well calculated at once to secure to the States a reasonable discretion in providing for the conveniency of their imports and exports, and to the United States a reasonable check against the abuse of this discretion.

The States may lay tonnage duties for clearing harbors, improving rivers, or for other purposes, but are restrained from abusing the power, because before such duties can take effect the "consent" of Congress must be obtained. Here is a safe provision for the improvement of harbors and rivers in the reserved powers of the States and in the aid they may derive from duties of tonnage levied with the consent of Congress. Its safeguards are, that both the State legislatures and Congress have to concur in the act of raising the funds; that they are in every instance to be levied upon the commerce of those ports which are to profit by the proposed improvement; that no question of conflicting power or jurisdiction is involved; that the expenditure, being in the hands of those who are to pay the money and be immediately benefited, will be more carefully managed and more productive of good than if the funds were drawn from the National Treasury and disbursed by the officers of the General Government; that such a system will carry with it no enlargement of Federal power and patronage, and leave the States to be the sole judges of their own wants and interests, with only a conservative negative in Congress upon any abuse of the power which the States may attempt.

Under this wise system the improvement of harbors and rivers was commenced, or rather continued, from the organization of the Government under the present Constitution. Many acts were passed by the several States levying duties of tonnage, and many were passed by Congress giving their consent to those acts. Such acts have been passed by Massachusetts, Rhode Island, Pennsylvania, Maryland, Virginia, North Carolina, South Carolina, and Georgia, and have been sanctioned by the consent of Congress. Without enumerating them all, it may be instructive to refer to some of them, as illustrative of the mode of improving harbors and rivers in the early periods of our Government, as to the constitutionality of which there can be no doubt.

In January, 1790, the State of Rhode Island passed a law levying a tonnage duty on vessels arriving in the port of Providence, "for the purpose of clearing and deepening the channel of Providence River and making the same more navigable."

On the 2d of February, 1798, the State of Massachusetts passed a law levying a tonnage duty on all vessels, whether employed in the foreign or coasting trade, which might enter into the Kennebunk River, for the improvement of the same by "rendering the passage in and out of said river less difficult and dangerous."

On the 1st of April, 1805, the State of Pennsylvania passed a law levying a tonnage duty on vessels, "to remove the obstructions to the navigation of the river Delaware below the city of Philadelphia."

On the 23d of January, 1804, the State of Virginia passed a law levying a tonnage duty on vessels, "for improving the navigation of James River."

On the 22d of February, 1826, the State of Virginia passed a law levying a tonnage duty on vessels, "for improving the navigation of James River from Warwick to Rocketts Landing."

On the 8th of December, 1824, the State of Virginia passed a law levying a tonnage duty on vessels, "for improving the navigation of Appomattox River from Pocahontas Bridge to Broadway."

In November, 1821, the State of North Carolina passed a law levying a tonnage duty on vessels, "for the purpose of opening an inlet at the lower end of Albemarle Sound, near a place called Nags Head, and improving the navigation of said sound, with its branches;" and in November, 1828, an amendatory law was passed.

On the 21st of December, 1804, the State of South Carolina passed a law levying a tonnage duty, for the purpose of "building a marine hospital in the vicinity of Charleston," and on the 17th of December, 1816, another law was passed by the legislature of that State for the "maintenance of a marine hospital."

On the 10th of February, 1787, the State of Georgia passed a law levying a tonnage duty on all vessels entering into the port of Savannah, for the purpose of "clearing" the Savannah River of "wrecks and other obstructions" to the navigation.

On the 12th of December, 1804, the State of Georgia passed a law levying a tonnage duty on vessels, "to be applied to the payment of the fees of the harbor master and health officer of the ports of Savannah and St. Marys."

In April, 1783, the State of Maryland passed a law laying a tonnage duty on vessels, for the improvement of the "basin" and "harbor" of Baltimore and the "river Patapsco."

On the 26th of December, 1791, the State of Maryland passed a law levying a tonnage duty on vessels, for the improvement of the "harbor and port of Baltimore."

On the 28th of December, 1793, the State of Maryland passed a law authorizing the appointment of a health officer for the port of Baltimore, and laying a tonnage duty on vessels to defray the expenses.

Congress has passed many acts giving its "consent" to these and other State laws, the first of which is dated in 1790 and the last in 1843. By the latter act the "consent" of Congress was given to the law of the legislature of the State of Maryland laying a tonnage duty on vessels for the improvement of the harbor of Baltimore, and continuing it in force until the 1st day of June, 1850. I transmit herewith copies of such of the acts of the legislatures of the States on the subject, and also the acts of Congress giving its "consent" thereto, as have been collated.

That the power was constitutionally and rightfully exercised in these cases does not admit of a doubt.

The injustice and inequality resulting from conceding the power to both Governments is illustrated by several of the acts enumerated. Take that for the improvement of the harbor of Baltimore. That improvement is paid for exclusively by a tax on the commerce of that city, but if an appropriation be made from the National Treasury for the improvement of the harbor of Boston it must be paid in part out of taxes levied on the commerce of Baltimore. The result is that the commerce of Baltimore pays the full cost of the harbor improvement designed for its own benefit, and in addition contributes to the cost of all other harbor and river improvements in the Union. The facts need but be stated to prove the inequality and injustice which can not but flow from the practice embodied in this bill. Either the subject should be left as it was during the first third of a century, or the practice of levying tonnage duties by the States should be abandoned altogether and all harbor and river improvements made under the authority of the United States, and by means of direct appropriations. In view not only of the constitutional difficulty, but as a question of policy, I am clearly of opinion that the whole subject should be left to the States, aided by such tonnage duties on vessels navigating their waters as their respective legislatures may think proper to propose and Congress see fit to sanction. This "consent" of Congress would never be refused in any case where the duty proposed to be levied by the State was reasonable and where the object of improvement was one of importance. The funds required for the improvement of harbors and rivers may be raised in this mode, as was done in the earlier periods of the Government, and thus avoid a resort to a strained construction of the Constitution not warranted by its letter. If direct appropriations be made of the money in the Federal Treasury for such purposes, the expenditures will be unequal and unjust. The money in the Federal Treasury is paid by a tax on the whole people of the United States, and if applied to the purposes of improving harbors and rivers it will be partially distributed and be expended for the advantage of particular States, sections, or localities at the expense of others.

By returning to the early and approved construction of the Constitution and to the practice under it this inequality and injustice will be avoided and at the same time all the really important improvements be made, and, as our experience has proved, be better made and at less cost than they would be by the agency of officers of the United States. The interests benefited by these improvements, too, would bear the cost of making them, upon the same principle that the expenses of the Post-Office establishment have always been defrayed by those who derive benefits from it. The power of appropriating money from the Treasury for such improvements was not claimed or exercised for more than thirty years after the organization of the Government in 1789, when a more latitudinous construction was indicated, though it was not broadly asserted and exercised until 1825. Small appropriations were first made in 1820 and 1821 for surveys. An act was passed on the 3d of March, 1823, authorizing the President to "cause an examination and survey to be made of the obstructions between the harbor of Gloucester and the harbor of Squam, in the State of Massachusetts," and of "the entrance of the harbor of the port of Presque Isle, in Pennsylvania," with a view to their removal, and a small appropriation was made to pay the necessary expenses. This appears to have been the commencement of harbor improvements by Congress, thirty-four years after the Government went into operation under the present Constitution. On the 30th of April, 1824, an act was passed making an appropriation of $30,000, and directing "surveys and estimates to be made of the routes of such roads and canals" as the President "may deem of national importance in a commercial or military point of view or necessary for the transportation of the mails." This act evidently looked to the adoption of a general system of internal improvements, to embrace roads and canals as well as harbors and rivers. On the 26th May, 1824, an act was passed making appropriations for "deepening the channel leading into the harbor of Presque Isle, in the State of Pennsylvania," and to "repair Plymouth Beach, in the State of Massachusetts, and thereby prevent the harbor at that place from being destroyed."

President Monroe yielded his approval to these measures, though he entertained, and had, in a message to the House of Representatives on the 4th of May, 1822, expressed, the opinion that the Constitution had not conferred upon Congress the power to "adopt and execute a system of internal improvements." He placed his approval upon the ground, not that Congress possessed the power to "adopt and execute" such a system by virtue of any or all of the enumerated grants of power in the Constitution, but upon the assumption that the power to make appropriations of the public money was limited and restrained only by the discretion of Congress. In coming to this conclusion he avowed that "in the more early stage of the Government" he had entertained a different opinion. He avowed that his first opinion had been that "as the National Government is a Government of limited powers, it has no right to expend money except in the performance of acts authorized by the other specific grants, according to a strict construction of their powers," and that the power to make appropriations gave to Congress no discretionary authority to apply the public money to any other purposes or objects except to "carry into effect the powers contained in the other grants." These sound views, which Mr. Monroe entertained "in the early stage of the Government," he gave up in 1822, and declared that—

The right of appropriation is nothing more than a right to apply the public money to this or that purpose. It has no incidental power, nor does it draw after it any consequences of that kind. All that Congress could do under it in the case of internal improvements would be to appropriate the money necessary to make them. For every act requiring legislative sanction or support the State authority must be relied on. The condemnation of the land, if the proprietors should refuse to sell it, the establishment of turnpikes and tolls, and the protection of the work when finished must be done by the State. To these purposes the powers of the General Government are believed to be utterly incompetent.

But it is impossible to conceive on what principle the power of appropriating public money when in the Treasury can be construed to extend to objects for which the Constitution does not authorize Congress to levy taxes or imposts to raise money. The power of appropriation is but the consequence of the power to raise money; and the true inquiry is whether Congress has the right to levy taxes for the object over which power is claimed.

During the four succeeding years embraced by the Administration of President Adams the power not only to appropriate money, but to apply it, under the direction and authority of the General Government, as well to the construction of roads as to the improvement of harbors and rivers, was fully asserted and exercised.

Among other acts assuming the power was one passed on the 20th of May, 1826, entitled "An act for improving certain harbors and the navigation of certain rivers and creeks, and for authorizing surveys to be made of certain bays, sounds, and rivers therein mentioned." By that act large appropriations were made, which were to be "applied, under the direction of the President of the United States," to numerous improvements in ten of the States. This act, passed thirty-seven years after the organization of the present Government, contained the first appropriation ever made for the improvement of a navigable river, unless it be small appropriations for examinations and surveys in 1820. During the residue of that Administration many other appropriations of a similar character were made, embracing roads, rivers, harbors, and canals, and objects claiming the aid of Congress multiplied without number.

This was the first breach effected in the barrier which the universal opinion of the framers of the Constitution had for more than thirty years thrown in the way of the assumption of this power by Congress. The general mind of Congress and the country did not appreciate the distinction taken by President Monroe between the right to appropriate money for an object and the right to apply and expend it without the embarrassment and delay of applications to the State governments. Probably no instance occurred in which such an application was made, and the flood gates being thus hoisted the principle laid down by him was disregarded, and applications for aid from the Treasury, virtually to make harbors as well as improve them, clear out rivers, cut canals, and construct roads, poured into Congress in torrents until arrested by the veto of President Jackson. His veto of the Maysville road bill was followed up by his refusal to sign the "Act making appropriations for building light-houses, light-boats, beacons, and monuments, placing buoys, improving harbors, and directing surveys;" "An act authorizing subscriptions for stock in the Louisville and Portland Canal Company;" "An act for the improvement of certain harbors and the navigation of certain rivers;" and, finally, "An act to improve the navigation of the Wabash River." In his objections to the act last named he says:

> The desire to embark the Federal Government in works of internal improvement prevailed in the highest degree during the first session of the first Congress that I had the honor to meet in my present situation. When the bill authorizing a subscription on the part of the United States for stock in the Maysville and Lexington Turnpike Company passed the two Houses, there had been reported by the Committees of Internal Improvements bills containing appropriations for such objects, inclusive of those for the Cumberland road and for harbors and light-houses, to the amount of $106,000,000. In this amount was included authority to the Secretary of the Treasury to subscribe for the stock of different companies to a great extent, and the residue was principally for the direct construction of roads by this Government. In addition to these projects, which had been presented to the two Houses under the sanction and recommendation of their respective Committees on Internal Improvements, there were then still pending before the committees and in memorials to Congress presented but not referred different projects for works of a similar character, the expense of which can not be estimated with certainty, but must have exceeded $100,000,000.

Thus, within the brief period of less than ten years after the commencement of internal improvements by the General Government the sum asked for from the Treasury for various projects amounted to more than $200,000,000. President Jackson's powerful and disinterested appeals to his country appear to have put down forever the assumption of power to make roads and cut canals, and to have checked the prevalent disposition to bring all rivers in any degree navigable within the control of the General Government. But an immense field for expending the public money and increasing the power and patronage of this Government was left open in the concession of even a limited power of Congress to improve harbors and rivers—a field which millions will not fertilize to the satisfaction of those local and speculating interests by which these projects are in general gotten up. There can not be a just and equal distribution of public burdens and benefits under such a system, nor can the States be relieved from the danger of fatal encroachment, nor the United States from the equal danger of consolidation, otherwise than by an arrest of the system and a return to the doctrines and practices which prevailed during the first thirty years of the Government.

How forcibly does the history of this subject illustrate the tendency of power to concentration in the hands of the General Government. The power to improve their own harbors and rivers was clearly reserved to the States, who were to be aided by tonnage duties levied and collected by themselves, with the consent of Congress. For thirty-four years improvements were carried on under that system, and so careful was Congress not to interfere, under any implied power, with the soil or jurisdiction of the States that they did not even assume the power to erect light-houses or build piers without first purchasing the ground, with the consent of the States, and obtaining jurisdiction over it. At length, after the lapse of thirty-three years, an act is passed providing for the examination of certain obstructions at the mouth of one or two harbors almost unknown. It is followed by acts making small appropriations for the removal of those obstructions. The obstacles interposed by President Monroe, after conceding the power to appropriate, were soon swept away. Congress virtually assumed jurisdiction of the soil and waters of the States, without their consent, for the purposes of internal improvement, and the eyes of eager millions were turned from the State governments to Congress as the fountain whose golden streams were to deepen their harbors and rivers, level their mountains, and fill their valleys with canals. To what consequences this assumption of power was rapidly leading is shown by the veto messages of President Jackson, and to what end it is again tending is witnessed by the provisions of this bill and bills of similar character.

In the proceedings and debates of the General Convention which formed the Constitution and of the State conventions which adopted it nothing is found to countenance the idea that the one intended to propose or the others to concede such a grant of power to the General Government as the building up and maintaining of a system of internal improvements within the States necessarily implies. Whatever the General Government may constitutionally create, it may lawfully protect. If it may make a road upon the soil of the States, it may protect it from destruction or injury by penal laws. So of canals, rivers, and harbors. If it may put a dam in a river, it may protect that dam from removal or injury, in direct opposition to the laws, authorities, and people of the State in which it is situated. If it may deepen a harbor, it may by its own laws protect its agents and contractors from being driven from their work even by the laws and authorities of the State. The power to make a road or canal or to dig up the bottom of a harbor or river implies a right in the soil of the State and a jurisdiction over it, for which it would be impossible to find any warrant.

The States were particularly jealous of conceding to the General Government any right of jurisdiction over their soil, and in the Constitution restricted the exclusive legislation of Congress to such places as might be "purchased with the consent of the States in which the same shall be, for the erection of forts, magazines, dockyards, and other needful buildings." That the United States should be prohibited from purchasing lands within the States without their consent, even for the most essential purposes of national defense, while left at liberty to purchase or seize them for roads, canals, and other improvements of immeasurably less importance, is not to be conceived.

A proposition was made in the Convention to provide for the appointment of a "Secretary of Domestic Affairs," and make it his duty, among other things, "to attend to the opening of roads and navigation and the facilitating communications through the United States." It was referred to a committee, and that appears to have been the last of it. On a subsequent occasion a proposition was made to confer on Congress the power to "provide for the cutting of canals when deemed necessary," which was rejected by the strong majority of eight States to three. Among the reasons given for the rejection of this proposition, it was urged that "the expense in such cases will fall on the United States and the benefits accrue to the places where the canals may be cut."

During the consideration of this proposition a motion was made to enlarge the proposed power for "cutting canals" into a power "to grant charters of incorporation when the interest of the United States might require and the legislative provisions of the individual States may be incompetent;" and the reason assigned by Mr. Madison for the proposed enlargement of the power was that it would "secure an easy communication between the States, which the free intercourse now to be opened seemed to call for. The political obstacles being removed, a removal of the natural ones, as far as possible, ought to follow."

The original proposition and all the amendments were rejected, after deliberate discussion, not on the ground, as so much of that discussion as has been preserved indicates, that no direct grant was necessary, but because it was deemed inexpedient to grant it at all. When it is considered that some of the members of the Convention, who afterwards participated in the organization and administration of the Government, advocated and practiced upon a very liberal construction of the Constitution, grasping at many high powers as implied in its various provisions, not one of them, it is believed, at that day claimed the power to make roads and canals, or improve rivers and harbors, or appropriate money for that purpose. Among our early statesmen of the strict-construction class the opinion was universal, when the subject was first broached, that Congress did not possess the power, although some of them thought it desirable.

President Jefferson, in his message to Congress in 1806, recommended an amendment of the Constitution, with a view to apply an anticipated surplus in the Treasury "to the great purposes of the public education, roads, rivers, canals, and such other objects of public improvement as it may be thought proper to add to the constitutional enumeration of Federal powers." And he adds:

I suppose an amendment to the Constitution, by consent of the States, necessary, because the objects now recommended are not among those enumerated in the Constitution, and to which it permits the public moneys to be applied.

In 1825 he repeated, in his published letters, the opinion that no such power has been conferred upon Congress.

President Madison, in a message to the House of Representatives of the 3d of March, 1817, assigning his objections to a bill entitled "An act to set apart and pledge certain funds for internal improvements," declares that—

"The power to regulate commerce among the several States" can not include a power to construct roads and canals and to *improve the navigation of water courses* in order to facilitate, promote, and secure such a commerce without a latitude of construction departing from the ordinary import of the terms, strengthened by the known inconveniences which doubtless led to the grant of this remedial power to Congress.

President Monroe, in a message to the House of Representatives of the 4th of May, 1822, containing his objections to a bill entitled "An act for the preservation and repair of the Cumberland road," declares:

Commerce between independent powers or communities is universally regulated by duties and imposts. It was so regulated by the States before the adoption of this Constitution, equally in respect to each other and to foreign powers. The goods and vessels employed in the trade are the only subjects of regulation. It can act on none other. A power, then, to impose such duties and imposts in regard to foreign nations and to prevent any on the trade between the States was the only power granted.

If we recur to the causes which produced the adoption of this Constitution, we shall find that injuries resulting from the regulation of trade by the States respectively and the advantages anticipated from the transfer of the power to Congress were among those which had the most weight. Instead of acting as a nation in regard to foreign powers, the States individually had commenced a system of restraint on each other whereby the interests of foreign powers were promoted at their expense. If one State imposed high duties on the goods or vessels of a foreign power to countervail the regulations of such power, the next adjoining States imposed lighter duties to invite those articles into their ports, that they might be transferred thence into the other States, securing the duties to themselves. This contracted policy in some of the States was soon counteracted by others. Restraints were immediately laid on such commerce by the suffering States; and thus had grown up a state of affairs disorderly and unnatural, the tendency of which was to destroy the Union itself and with it all hope of realizing those blessings which we had anticipated from the glorious Revolution which had been so recently achieved. From this deplorable dilemma, or, rather, certain ruin, we were happily rescued by the adoption of the Constitution.

Among the first and most important effects of this great Revolution was the complete abolition of this pernicious policy. The States were brought together by the Constitution, as to commerce, into one community, equally in regard to foreign nations and each other. The regulations that were adopted regarded us in both respects as one people. The duties and imposts that were laid on the vessels and merchandise of foreign nations were all uniform throughout the United States, and in the intercourse between the States themselves no duties of any kind were imposed other than between different ports and counties within the same State.

This view is supported by a series of measures, all of a marked character, preceding the adoption of the Constitution. As early as the year 1781 Congress recommended it to the States to vest in the United States a power to levy a duty of 5 per cent on all goods imported from foreign countries into the United States for the term of fifteen years. In 1783 this recommendation, with alterations as to the kind of duties and an extension of this term to twenty-five years, was repeated and more earnestly urged. In 1784 it was recommended to the States to authorize Congress to prohibit, under certain modifications, the importation of goods from foreign powers into the United States for fifteen years. In 1785 the consideration of the subject was resumed, and a proposition presented in a new form, with an address to the States explaining fully the principles on which a grant of the power to regulate trade was deemed indispensable. In 1786 a meeting took place at Annapolis of delegates from several of the States on this subject, and on their report a convention was formed at Philadelphia the ensuing year from all the States, to whose deliberations we are indebted for the present Constitution.

In none of these measures was the subject of internal improvement mentioned or even glanced at. Those of 1784, 1785, 1786, and 1787, leading step by step to the adoption of the Constitution, had in view only the obtaining of a power to enable Congress to regulate trade with foreign powers. It is manifest that the regulation of trade with the several States was altogether a secondary object, suggested by and adopted in connection with the other. If the power necessary to this system of improvement is included under either branch of this grant, I should suppose that it was the first rather than the second. The pretension to it, however, under that branch has never been set up. In support of the claim under the second no reason has been assigned which appears to have the least weight.

Such is a brief history of the origin, progress, and consequences of a system which for more than thirty years after the adoption of the Constitution was unknown. The greatest embarrassment upon the subject consists in the departure which has taken place from the early construction of the Constitution and the precedents which are found in the legislation of Congress in later years. President Jackson, in his veto of the Wabash River bill, declares that "to inherent embarrassments have been added others resulting from the course of our legislation concerning it." In his vetoes on the Maysville road bill, the Rockville road bill, the Wabash River bill, and other bills of like character he reversed the precedents which existed prior to that time on the subject of internal improvements. When our experience, observation, and reflection have convinced us that a legislative precedent is either unwise or unconstitutional, it should not be followed.

No express grant of this power is found in the Constitution. Its advocates have differed among themselves as to the source from which it is derived as an incident. In the progress of the discussions upon this subject the power to regulate commerce seems now to be chiefly relied upon, especially in reference to the improvement of harbors and rivers.

In relation to the regulation of commerce, the language of the grant in the Constitution is:

Congress shall have power to regulate commerce with foreign nations, and among the several States, and with the Indian tribes.

That to "regulate commerce" does not mean to make a road, or dig a canal, or clear out a river, or deepen a harbor would seem to be obvious to the common understanding. To "regulate" admits or affirms the preexistence of the thing to be regulated. In this case it presupposes the existence of commerce, and, of course, the means by which and the channels through which commerce is carried on. It confers no creative power; it only assumes control over that which may have been brought into existence through other agencies, such as State legislation and the industry and enterprise of individuals. If the definition of the word "regulate" is to include the provision of means to carry on commerce, then have Congress not only power to deepen harbors, clear out rivers, dig canals, and make roads, but also to build ships, railroad cars, and other vehicles, all of which are necessary to commerce. There is no

M P—VOL IV—40

middle ground.   If the power to regulate can be legitimately construed into a power to create or facilitate, then not only the bays and harbors, but the roads and canals and all the means of transporting merchandise among the several States, are put at the disposition of Congress.   This power to regulate commerce was construed and exercised immediately after the adoption of the Constitution, and has been exercised to the present day, by prescribing general rules by which commerce should be conducted.   With foreign nations it has been regulated by treaties defining the rights of citizens and subjects, as well as by acts of Congress imposing duties and restrictions embracing vessels, seamen, cargoes, and passengers.   It has been regulated among the States by acts of Congress relating to the coasting trade and the vessels employed therein, and for the better security of passengers in vessels propelled by steam, and by the removal of all restrictions upon internal trade.   It has been regulated with the Indian tribes by our intercourse laws, prescribing the manner in which it shall be carried on.   Thus each branch of this grant of power was exercised soon after the adoption of the Constitution, and has continued to be exercised to the present day.   If a more extended construction be adopted, it is impossible for the human mind to fix on a limit to the exercise of the power other than the will and discretion of Congress. It sweeps into the vortex of national power and jurisdiction not only harbors and inlets, rivers and little streams, but canals, turnpikes, and railroads—every species of improvement which can facilitate or create trade and intercourse "with foreign nations, and among the several States, and with the Indian tribes."

Should any great object of improvement exist in our widely extended country which can not be effected by means of tonnage duties levied by the States with the concurrence of Congress, it is safer and wiser to apply to the States in the mode prescribed by the Constitution for an amendment of that instrument whereby the powers of the General Government may be enlarged, with such limitations and restrictions as experience has shown to be proper, than to assume and exercise a power which has not been granted, or which may be regarded as doubtful in the opinion of a large portion of our constituents.   This course has been recommended successively by Presidents Jefferson, Madison, Monroe, and Jackson, and I fully concur with them in opinion.   If an enlargement of power should be deemed proper, it will unquestionably be granted by the States; if otherwise, it will be withheld; and in either case their decision should be final.   In the meantime I deem it proper to add that the investigation of this subject has impressed me more strongly than ever with the solemn conviction that the usefulness and permanency of this Government and the happiness of the millions over whom it spreads its protection will be best promoted by carefully abstaining from the exercise of all powers not clearly granted by the Constitution.

JAMES K. POLK.

PROCLAMATION.

BY THE PRESIDENT OF THE UNITED STATES OF AMERICA.

A PROCLAMATION.

Whereas a treaty of peace, friendship, limits, and settlement between the United States of America and the Mexican Republic was concluded and signed at the city of Guadalupe Hidalgo on the 2d day of February, 1848, which treaty, as amended by the Senate of the United States, and being in the English and Spanish languages, is word for word as follows:

[Here follows the treaty.]

And whereas the said treaty, as amended, has been duly ratified on both parts, and the respective ratifications of the same were exchanged at Queretaro on the 30th day of May last by Ambrose H. Sevier and Nathan Clifford, commissioners on the part of the Government of the United States, and by Señor Don Luis de la Rosa, minister of relations of the Mexican Republic, on the part of that Government:

Now, therefore, be it known that I, James K. Polk, President of the United States of America, have caused the said treaty to be made public, to the end that the same and every clause and article thereof may be observed and fulfilled with good faith by the United States and the citizens thereof.

In witness whereof I have hereunto set my hand and caused the seal of the United States to be affixed.

[SEAL.]   Done at the city of Washington, this 4th day of July, 1848, and of the Independence of the United States the seventy-third.

JAMES K. POLK.

By the President:
JAMES BUCHANAN, *Secretary of State.*

EXECUTIVE ORDER.

GENERAL ORDERS, No. 9.

WAR DEPARTMENT, ADJUTANT-GENERAL'S OFFICE,
Washington, February 24, 1848.

I. The following orders of the President of the United States and Secretary of War announce to the Army the death of the illustrious ex-President John Quincy Adams:

BY THE PRESIDENT OF THE UNITED STATES.

WASHINGTON, *February 24, 1848.*

It has pleased Divine Providence to call hence a great and patriotic citizen. John Quincy Adams is no more. At the advanced age of more than fourscore years, he was suddenly stricken from his seat in the House of Representatives by the hand of disease on the 21st, and expired in the Capitol a few minutes after 7 o'clock on the evening of the 23d of February, 1848.

He had for more than half a century filled the most important public stations, and among them that of President of the United States.   The two Houses of Congress, of one of which he was a venerable and most distinguished member, will doubtless prescribe appropriate ceremonies to be observed as a mark of respect for the memory of this eminent citizen.

The nation mourns his loss; and as a further testimony of respect for his memory I direct that all the executive offices at Washington be placed in mourning and that all business be suspended during this day and to-morrow.

JAMES K. POLK.

WAR DEPARTMENT, *February 24, 1848.*

The President of the United States with deep regret announces to the Army the death of John Quincy Adams, our eminent and venerated fellow-citizen.

While occupying his seat as a member of the House of Representatives, on the 21st instant he was suddenly prostrated by disease, and on the 23d expired, without having been removed from the Capitol.   He had filled many honorable and responsible stations in the service of his country, and among them that of President of the United States; and he closed his long and eventful life in the actual discharge of his duties as one of the Representatives of the people.

From sympathy with his relatives and the American people for his loss and from respect for his distinguished public services, the President orders that funeral honors shall be paid to his memory at each of the military stations.

The Adjutant-General will give the necessary instructions for carrying into effect the foregoing orders.

W. L. MARCY,
Secretary of War.

II. On the day succeeding the arrival of this general order at each military post the troops will be paraded at 10 o'clock a. m. and the order read to them, after which all labors for the day will cease.

The national flag will be displayed at half-staff.

At dawn of day thirteen guns will be fired, and afterwards, at intervals of thirty minutes between the rising and setting sun, a single gun, and at the close of the day a national salute of twenty-nine guns.

The officers of the Army will wear crape on the left arm and on their swords and the colors of the several regiments will be put in mourning for the period of six months.

By order:

R. JONES,
Adjutant-General.

FOURTH ANNUAL MESSAGE.

WASHINGTON, *December 5, 1848.*

Fellow-Citizens of the Senate and of the House of Representatives:

Under the benignant providence of Almighty God the representatives of the States and of the people are again brought together to deliberate for the public good. The gratitude of the nation to the Sovereign Arbiter of All Human Events should be commensurate with the boundless blessings which we enjoy.

Peace, plenty, and contentment reign throughout our borders, and our beloved country presents a sublime moral spectacle to the world.

The troubled and unsettled condition of some of the principal European powers has had a necessary tendency to check and embarrass trade and to depress prices throughout all commercial nations, but notwithstanding these causes, the United States, with their abundant products, have felt their effects less severely than any other country, and all our great interests are still prosperous and successful.

In reviewing the great events of the past year and contrasting the agitated and disturbed state of other countries with our own tranquil and happy condition, we may congratulate ourselves that we are the most favored people on the face of the earth. While the people of other countries are struggling to establish free institutions, under which man may govern himself, we are in the actual enjoyment of them—a rich inheritance from our fathers. While enlightened nations of Europe are convulsed and distracted by civil war or intestine strife, we settle all our political controversies by the peaceful exercise of the rights of freemen at the ballot box.

The great republican maxim, so deeply engraven on the hearts of our people, that the will of the majority, constitutionally expressed, shall prevail, is our sure safeguard against force and violence. It is a subject of just pride that our fame and character as a nation continue rapidly to advance in the estimation of the civilized world.

To our wise and free institutions it is to be attributed that while other nations have achieved glory at the price of the suffering, distress, and impoverishment of their people, we have won our honorable position in the midst of an uninterrupted prosperity and of an increasing individual comfort and happiness.

I am happy to inform you that our relations with all nations are friendly and pacific. Advantageous treaties of commerce have been concluded within the last four years with New Granada, Peru, the Two Sicilies, Belgium, Hanover, Oldenburg, and Mecklenburg-Schwerin. Pursuing our example, the restrictive system of Great Britain, our principal foreign customer, has been relaxed, a more liberal commercial policy has been adopted by other enlightened nations, and our trade has been greatly enlarged and extended. Our country stands higher in the respect of the world than at any former period. To continue to occupy this proud position, it is only necessary to preserve peace and faithfully adhere to the great and fundamental principle of our foreign policy of noninterference in the domestic concerns of other nations. We recognize in all nations the right which we enjoy ourselves, to change and reform their political institutions according to their own will and pleasure. Hence we do not look behind existing governments capable of maintaining their own authority. We recognize all such actual governments, not only from the dictates of true policy, but from a sacred regard for the independence of nations. While this is our settled policy, it does not follow that we can ever be indifferent spectators of the progress of liberal principles. The Government and people of the United States hailed with enthusiasm and delight the establishment of the French Republic, as we now hail the efforts in progress to unite the States of Germany in a confederation similar in many respects to our own Federal Union. If the great and enlightened German States, occupying, as they do, a central and commanding position in Europe, shall succeed in establishing such a confederated government, securing at the same time to the citizens of each State local governments adapted to the peculiar condition of each, with unrestricted trade and intercourse with each other, it will be an important era in the history of human events. Whilst it will consolidate and strengthen the power of Germany, it must essentially promote the cause of peace, commerce, civilization, and constitutional liberty throughout the world.

With all the Governments on this continent our relations, it is believed, are now on a more friendly and satisfactory footing than they have ever been at any former period.

Since the exchange of ratifications of the treaty of peace with Mexico our intercourse with the Government of that Republic has been of the most friendly character. The envoy extraordinary and minister plenipotentiary of the United States to Mexico has been received and accredited, and a diplomatic representative from Mexico of similar rank has been received and accredited by this Government The amicable relations between the two countries, which had been suspended, have been happily restored, and are destined, I trust, to be long preserved. The two Republics, both situated on this continent, and with coterminous territories, have every motive of sympathy and of interest to bind them together in perpetual amity.

This gratifying condition of our foreign relations renders it unnecessary for me to call your attention more specifically to them.

It has been my constant aim and desire to cultivate peace and commerce with all nations. Tranquillity at home and peaceful relations abroad constitute the true permanent policy of our country. War, the scourge of nations, sometimes becomes inevitable, but is always to be avoided when it can be done consistently with the rights and honor of a nation.

One of the most important results of the war into which we were recently forced with a neighboring nation is the demonstration it has afforded of the military strength of our country. Before the late war with Mexico European and other foreign powers entertained imperfect and erroneous views of our physical strength as a nation and of our ability to prosecute war, and especially a war waged out of our own country. They saw that our standing Army on the peace establishment did not exceed 10,000 men. Accustomed themselves to maintain in peace large standing armies for the protection of thrones against their own subjects, as well as against foreign enemies, they had not conceived that it was possible for a nation without such an army, well disciplined and of long service, to wage war successfully. They held in low repute our militia, and were far from regarding them as an effective force, unless it might be for temporary defensive operations when invaded on our own soil. The events of the late war with Mexico have not only undeceived them, but have removed erroneous impressions which prevailed to some extent even among a portion of our own countrymen. That war has demonstrated that upon the breaking out of hostilities not anticipated, and for which no previous preparation had been made, a volunteer army of citizen soldiers equal to veteran troops, and in numbers equal to any emergency, can in a short period be brought into the field. Unlike what would have occurred in any other country, we were under no necessity of resorting to drafts or conscriptions. On the contrary, such was the number of volunteers who patriotically tendered their services that the chief difficulty was in making selections and determining who should be disappointed and compelled to remain at home. Our citizen soldiers are unlike those drawn from the population of any other country. They are composed indiscriminately of all professions and pursuits—of farmers, lawyers, physicians, merchants, manufacturers, mechanics, and laborers—and this not only among the officers, but the private soldiers in the ranks. Our citizen soldiers are unlike those of any other country in other respects. They are armed, and have been accustomed from their youth up to handle and use firearms, and a large proportion of them, especially in the Western and more newly settled States, are expert marksmen. They are men who have a reputation to maintain at home by their good conduct in the field. They are intelligent, and there is an individuality of character which is found in the ranks of no other army. In battle each private man, as well as every officer, fights not only for his country, but for glory and distinction among his fellow-citizens when he shall return to civil life.

The war with Mexico has demonstrated not only the ability of the Government to organize a numerous army upon a sudden call, but also to provide it with all the munitions and necessary supplies with dispatch, convenience, and ease, and to direct its operations with efficiency.   The strength of our institutions has not only been displayed in the valor and skill of our troops engaged in active service in the field, but in the organization of those executive branches which were charged with the general direction and conduct of the war.   While too great praise can not be bestowed upon the officers and men who fought our battles, it would be unjust to withhold from those officers necessarily stationed at home, who were charged with the duty of furnishing the Army in proper time and at proper places with all the munitions of war and other supplies so necessary to make it efficient, the commendation to which they are entitled.   The credit due to this class of our officers is the greater when it is considered that no army in ancient or modern times was ever better appointed or provided than our Army in Mexico.   Operating in an enemy's country, removed 2,000 miles from the seat of the Federal Government, its different corps spread over a vast extent of territory, hundreds and even thousands of miles apart from each other, nothing short of the untiring vigilance and extraordinary energy of these officers could have enabled them to provide the Army at all points and in proper season with all that was required for the most efficient service.

It is but an act of justice to declare that the officers in charge of the several executive bureaus, all under the immediate eye and supervision of the Secretary of War, performed their respective duties with ability, energy, and efficiency.   They have reaped less of the glory of the war, not having been personally exposed to its perils in battle, than their companions in arms; but without their forecast, efficient aid, and cooperation those in the field would not have been provided with the ample means they possessed of achieving for themselves and their country the unfading honors which they have won for both.

When all these facts are considered, it may cease to be a matter of so much amazement abroad how it happened that our noble Army in Mexico, regulars and volunteers, were victorious upon every battlefield, however fearful the odds against them.

The war with Mexico has thus fully developed the capacity of republican governments to prosecute successfully a just and necessary foreign war with all the vigor usually attributed to more arbitrary forms of government.   It has been usual for writers on public law to impute to republics a want of that unity, concentration of purpose, and vigor of execution which are generally admitted to belong to the monarchical and aristocratic forms; and this feature of popular government has been supposed to display itself more particularly in the conduct of a war carried on in an enemy's territory.   The war with Great Britain in 1812 was to a great extent confined within our own limits, and shed but little light on this subject; but the war which we have just closed by an honorable peace evinces beyond all doubt that a popular representative government is equal to any emergency which is likely to arise in the affairs of a nation.

The war with Mexico has developed most strikingly and conspicuously another feature in our institutions. It is that without cost to the Government or danger to our liberties we have in the bosom of our society of freemen, available in a just and necessary war, virtually a standing army of 2,000,000 armed citizen soldiers, such as fought the battles of Mexico. But our military strength does not consist alone in our capacity for extended and successful operations on land. The Navy is an important arm of the national defense. If the services of the Navy were not so brilliant as those of the Army in the late war with Mexico, it was because they had no enemy to meet on their own element. While the Army had opportunity of performing more conspicuous service, the Navy largely participated in the conduct of the war. Both branches of the service performed their whole duty to the country. For the able and gallant services of the officers and men of the Navy, acting independently as well as in cooperation with our troops, in the conquest of the Californias, the capture of Vera Cruz, and the seizure and occupation of other important positions on the Gulf and Pacific coasts, the highest praise is due. Their vigilance, energy, and skill rendered the most effective service in excluding munitions of war and other supplies from the enemy, while they secured a safe entrance for abundant supplies for our own Army. Our extended commerce was nowhere interrupted, and for this immunity from the evils of war the country is indebted to the Navy.

High praise is due to the officers of the several executive bureaus, navy-yards, and stations connected with the service, all under the immediate direction of the Secretary of the Navy, for the industry, foresight, and energy with which everything was directed and furnished to give efficiency to that branch of the service. The same vigilance existed in directing the operations of the Navy as of the Army. There was concert of action and of purpose between the heads of the two arms of the service. By the orders which were from time to time issued, our vessels of war on the Pacific and the Gulf of Mexico were stationed in proper time and in proper positions to cooperate efficiently with the Army. By this means their combined power was brought to bear successfully on the enemy.

The great results which have been developed and brought to light by this war will be of immeasurable importance in the future progress of our country. They will tend powerfully to preserve us from foreign collisions, and to enable us to pursue uninterruptedly our cherished policy of "peace with all nations, entangling alliances with none."

Occupying, as we do, a more commanding position among nations than at any former period, our duties and our responsibilities to ourselves and to posterity are correspondingly increased. This will be the more obvious when we consider the vast additions which have been recently made to our territorial possessions and their great importance and value.

Within less than four years the annexation of Texas to the Union has been consummated; all conflicting title to the Oregon Territory south of the forty-ninth degree of north latitude, being all that was insisted on by any of my predecessors, has been adjusted, and New Mexico and Upper California have been acquired by treaty. The area of these several Territories, according to a report carefully prepared by the Commissioner of the General Land Office from the most authentic information in his possession, and which is herewith transmitted, contains 1,193,061 square miles, or 763,559,040 acres; while the area of the remaining twenty-nine States and the territory not yet organized into States east of the Rocky Mountains contains 2,059,513 square miles, or 1,318,126,058 acres. These estimates show that the territories recently acquired, and over which our exclusive jurisdiction and dominion have been extended, constitute a country more than half as large as all that which was held by the United States before their acquisition. If Oregon be excluded from the estimate, there will still remain within the limits of Texas, New Mexico, and California 851,598 square miles, or 545,012,720 acres, being an addition equal to more than one-third of all the territory owned by the United States before their acquisition, and, including Oregon, nearly as great an extent of territory as the whole of Europe, Russia only excepted. The Mississippi, so lately the frontier of our country, is now only its center. With the addition of the late acquisitions, the United States are now estimated to be nearly as large as the whole of Europe. It is estimated by the Superintendent of the Coast Survey in the accompanying report that the extent of the seacoast of Texas on the Gulf of Mexico is upward of 400 miles; of the coast of Upper California on the Pacific, of 970 miles, and of Oregon, including the Straits of Fuca, of 650 miles, making the whole extent of seacoast on the Pacific 1,620 miles and the whole extent on both the Pacific and the Gulf of Mexico 2,020 miles. The length of the coast on the Atlantic from the northern limits of the United States around the capes of Florida to the Sabine, on the eastern boundary of Texas, is estimated to be 3,100 miles; so that the addition of seacoast, including Oregon, is very nearly two-thirds as great as all we possessed before, and, excluding Oregon, is an addition of 1,370 miles, being nearly equal to one-half of the extent of coast which we possessed before these acquisitions. We have now three great maritime fronts— on the Atlantic, the Gulf of Mexico, and the Pacific—making in the whole an extent of seacoast exceeding 5,000 miles. This is the extent of the seacoast of the United States, not including bays, sounds, and small irregularities of the main shore and of the sea islands. If these be included, the length of the shore line of coast, as estimated by the Superintendent of the Coast Survey in his report, would be 33,063 miles.

It would be difficult to calculate the value of these immense additions to our territorial possessions. Texas, lying contiguous to the western boundary of Louisiana, embracing within its limits a part of the navigable tributary waters of the Mississippi and an extensive seacoast, could not long have remained in the hands of a foreign power without endangering the peace of our southwestern frontier. Her products in the vicinity of the tributaries of the Mississippi must have sought a market through these streams, running into and through our territory, and the danger of irritation and collision of interests between Texas as a foreign state and ourselves would have been imminent, while the embarrassments in the commercial intercourse between them must have been constant and unavoidable. Had Texas fallen into the hands or under the influence and control of a strong maritime or military foreign power, as she might have done, these dangers would have been still greater. They have been avoided by her voluntary and peaceful annexation to the United States. Texas, from her position, was a natural and almost indispensable part of our territories. Fortunately, she has been restored to our country, and now constitutes one of the States of our Confederacy, "upon an equal footing with the original States." The salubrity of climate, the fertility of soil, peculiarly adapted to the production of some of our most valuable staple commodities, and her commercial advantages must soon make her one of our most populous States.

New Mexico, though situated in the interior and without a seacoast, is known to contain much fertile land, to abound in rich mines of the precious metals, and to be capable of sustaining a large population. From its position it is the intermediate and connecting territory between our settlements and our possessions in Texas and those on the Pacific Coast.

Upper California, irrespective of the vast mineral wealth recently developed there, holds at this day, in point of value and importance, to the rest of the Union the same relation that Louisiana did when that fine territory was acquired from France forty-five years ago. Extending nearly ten degrees of latitude along the Pacific, and embracing the only safe and commodious harbors on that coast for many hundred miles, with a temperate climate and an extensive interior of fertile lands, it is scarcely possible to estimate its wealth until it shall be brought under the government of our laws and its resources fully developed. From its position it must command the rich commerce of China, of Asia, of the islands of the Pacific, of western Mexico, of Central America, the South American States, and of the Russian possessions bordering on that ocean. A great emporium will doubtless speedily arise on the Californian coast which may be destined to rival in importance New Orleans itself. The depot of the vast commerce which must exist on the Pacific will probably be at some point on the Bay of San Francisco, and will occupy the same relation to the whole western coast of that ocean as New Orleans does to the valley of the Mississippi and the Gulf of Mexico. To this depot our numerous whale ships will resort with their cargoes to trade, refit, and obtain supplies. This of itself will largely contribute to build up a city, which would soon become the center of a great and rapidly increasing commerce. Situated on a safe harbor, sufficiently capacious for all the navies as well as the marine of the world, and convenient to excellent timber for ship-building, owned by the United States, it must become our great Western naval depot.

It was known that mines of the precious metals existed to a considerable extent in California at the time of its acquisition. Recent discoveries render it probable that these mines are more extensive and valuable than was anticipated. The accounts of the abundance of gold in that territory are of such an extraordinary character as would scarcely command belief were they not corroborated by the authentic reports of officers in the public service who have visited the mineral district and derived the facts which they detail from personal observation. Reluctant to credit the reports in general circulation as to the quantity of gold, the officer commanding our forces in California visited the mineral district in July last for the purpose of obtaining accurate information on the subject. His report to the War Department of the result of his examination and the facts obtained on the spot is herewith laid before Congress. When he visited the country there were about 4,000 persons engaged in collecting gold. There is every reason to believe that the number of persons so employed has since been augmented. The explorations already made warrant the belief that the supply is very large and that gold is found at various places in an extensive district of country.

Information received from officers of the Navy and other sources, though not so full and minute, confirms the accounts of the commander of our military force in California. It appears also from these reports that mines of quicksilver are found in the vicinity of the gold region. One of them is now being worked, and is believed to be among the most productive in the world.

The effects produced by the discovery of these rich mineral deposits and the success which has attended the labors of those who have resorted to them have produced a surprising change in the state of affairs in California. Labor commands a most exorbitant price, and all other pursuits but that of searching for the precious metals are abandoned. Nearly the whole of the male population of the country have gone to the gold districts. Ships arriving on the coast are deserted by their crews and their voyages suspended for want of sailors. Our commanding officer there entertains apprehensions that soldiers can not be kept in the public service without a large increase of pay. Desertions in his command have become frequent, and he recommends that those who shall withstand the strong temptation and remain faithful should be rewarded.

This abundance of gold and the all-engrossing pursuit of it have already caused in California an unprecedented rise in the price of all the necessaries of life.

That we may the more speedily and fully avail ourselves of the undeveloped wealth of these mines, it is deemed of vast importance that a branch of the Mint of the United States be authorized to be established at your present session in California. Among other signal advantages which would result from such an establishment would be that of raising the gold to its par value in that territory. A branch mint of the United States at the great commercial depot on the west coast would convert into our own coin not only the gold derived from our own rich mines, but also the bullion and specie which our commerce may bring from the whole west coast of Central and South America. The west coast of America and the adjacent interior embrace the richest and best mines of Mexico, New Granada, Central America, Chili, and Peru. The bullion and specie drawn from these countries, and especially from those of western Mexico and Peru, to an amount in value of many millions of dollars, are now annually diverted and carried by the ships of Great Britain to her own ports, to be recoined or used to sustain her national bank, and thus contribute to increase her ability to command so much of the commerce of the world. If a branch mint be established at the great commercial point upon that coast, a vast amount of bullion and specie would flow thither to be recoined, and pass thence to New Orleans, New York, and other Atlantic cities. The amount of our constitutional currency at home would be greatly increased, while its circulation abroad would be promoted. It is well known to our merchants trading to China and the west coast of America that great inconvenience and loss are experienced from the fact that our coins are not current at their par value in those countries.

The powers of Europe, far removed from the west coast of America by the Atlantic Ocean, which intervenes, and by a tedious and dangerous navigation around the southern cape of the continent of America, can never successfully compete with the United States in the rich and extensive commerce which is opened to us at so much less cost by the acquisition of California.

The vast importance and commercial advantages of California have heretofore remained undeveloped by the Government of the country of which it constituted a part. Now that this fine province is a part of our country, all the States of the Union, some more immediately and directly than others, are deeply interested in the speedy development of its wealth and resources. No section of our country is more interested or will be more benefited than the commercial, navigating, and manufacturing interests of the Eastern States. Our planting and farming interests in every part of the Union will be greatly benefited by it. As our commerce and navigation are enlarged and extended, our exports of agricultural products and of manufactures will be increased, and in the new markets thus opened they can not fail to command remunerating and profitable prices.

The acquisition of California and New Mexico, the settlement of the Oregon boundary, and the annexation of Texas, extending to the Rio . Grande, are results which, combined, are of greater consequence and will add more to the strength and wealth of the nation than any which have preceded them since the adoption of the Constitution.

But to effect these great results not only California, but New Mexico, must be brought under the control of regularly organized governments. The existing condition of California and of that part of New Mexico lying west of the Rio Grande and without the limits of Texas imperiously demands that Congress should at its present session organize Territorial governments over them.

Upon the exchange of ratifications of the treaty of peace with Mexico, on the 30th of May last, the temporary governments which had been established over New Mexico and California by our military and naval commanders by virtue of the rights of war ceased to derive any obligatory force from that source of authority, and having been ceded to the United States, all government and control over them under the authority of Mexico had ceased to exist. Impressed with the necessity of establishing Territorial governments over them, I recommended the subject to the favorable consideration of Congress in my message communicating the ratified treaty of peace, on the 6th of July last, and invoked their action at that session. Congress adjourned without making any provision for their government. The inhabitants by the transfer of their country had become entitled to the benefit of our laws and Constitution, and yet were left without any regularly organized government. Since that time the very limited power possessed by the Executive has been exercised to preserve and protect them from the inevitable consequences of a state of anarchy. The only government which remained was that established by the military authority during the war. Regarding this to be a *de facto* government, and that by the presumed consent of the inhabitants it might be continued temporarily, they were advised to conform and submit to it for the short intervening period before Congress would again assemble and could legislate on the subject. The views entertained by the Executive on this point are contained in a communication of the Secretary of State dated the 7th of October last, which was forwarded for publication to California and New Mexico, a copy of which is herewith transmitted. The small military force of the Regular Army which was serving within the limits of the acquired territories at the close of the war was retained in them, and additional forces have been ordered there for the protection of the inhabitants and to preserve and secure the rights and interests of the United States.

No revenue has been or could be collected at the ports in California, because Congress failed to authorize the establishment of custom-houses or the appointment of officers for that purpose.

The Secretary of the Treasury, by a circular letter addressed to collectors of the customs on the 7th day of October last, a copy of which is herewith transmitted, exercised all the power with which he was invested by law.

In pursuance of the act of the 14th of August last, extending the benefit of our post-office laws to the people of California, the Postmaster-General has appointed two agents, who have proceeded, the one to California and the other to Oregon, with authority to make the necessary arrangements for carrying its provisions into effect.

The monthly line of mail steamers from Panama to Astoria has been required to "stop and deliver and take mails at San Diego, Monterey, and San Francisco." These mail steamers, connected by the Isthmus of Panama with the line of mail steamers on the Atlantic between New York and Chagres, will establish a regular mail communication with California.

It is our solemn duty to provide with the least practicable delay for New Mexico and California regularly organized Territorial governments. The causes of the failure to do this at the last session of Congress are well known and deeply to be regretted. With the opening prospects of increased prosperity and national greatness which the acquisition of these rich and extensive territorial possessions affords, how irrational it would be to forego or to reject these advantages by the agitation of a domestic question which is coeval with the existence of our Government itself, and to endanger by internal strifes, geographical divisions, and heated contests for political power, or for any other cause, the harmony of the glorious Union of our confederated States—that Union which binds us together as one people, and which for sixty years has been our shield and protection against every danger. In the eyes of the world and of posterity how trivial and insignificant will be all our internal divisions and struggles compared with the preservation of this Union of the States in all its vigor and with all its countless blessings! No patriot would foment and excite geographical and sectional divisions. No lover of his country would deliberately calculate the value of the Union. Future generations would look in amazement upon the folly of such a course. Other nations at the present day would look upon it with astonishment, and such of them as desire to maintain and perpetuate thrones and monarchical or aristocratical principles will view it with exultation and delight, because in it they will see the elements of faction, which they hope must ultimately overturn our system. Ours is the great example of a prosperous and free self-governed republic, commanding the admiration and the imitation of all the lovers of freedom throughout the world. How solemn, therefore, is the duty, how impressive the call upon us and upon all parts of our country, to cultivate a patriotic spirit of harmony, of good-fellowship, of compromise and mutual concession, in the administration of the incomparable system of government formed by our fathers in the midst of almost insuperable difficulties, and transmitted to us with the injunction that we should enjoy its blessings and hand it down unimpaired to those who may come after us.

In view of the high and responsible duties which we owe to ourselves and to mankind, I trust you may be able at your present session to approach the adjustment of the only domestic question which seriously threatens, or probably ever can threaten, to disturb the harmony and successful operations of our system.

The immensely valuable possessions of New Mexico and California are already inhabited by a considerable population. Attracted by their great fertility, their mineral wealth, their commercial advantages, and the salubrity of the climate, emigrants from the older States in great numbers are already preparing to seek new homes in these inviting regions. Shall the dissimilarity of the domestic institutions in the different States prevent us from providing for them suitable governments? These institutions existed at the adoption of the Constitution, but the obstacles which they interposed were overcome by that spirit of compromise which is now invoked. In a conflict of opinions or of interests, real or imaginary, between different sections of our country, neither can justly demand all which it might desire to obtain. Each, in the true spirit of our institutions, should concede something to the other.

Our gallant forces in the Mexican war, by whose patriotism and unparalleled deeds of arms we obtained these possessions as an indemnity for our just demands against Mexico, were composed of citizens who belonged to no one State or section of our Union. They were men from slaveholding and nonslaveholding States, from the North and the South, from the East and the West. They were all companions in arms and fellow-citizens of the same common country, engaged in the same common cause. When prosecuting that war they were brethren and friends, and shared alike with each other common toils, dangers, and sufferings. Now, when their work is ended, when peace is restored, and they return again to their homes, put off the habiliments of war, take their places in society, and resume their pursuits in civil life, surely a spirit of harmony and concession and of equal regard for the rights of all and of all sections of the Union ought to prevail in providing governments for the acquired territories—the fruits of their common service. The whole people of the United States, and of every State, contributed to defray the expenses of that war, and it would not be just for any one section to exclude another from all participation in the acquired territory. This would not be in consonance with the just system of government which the framers of the Constitution adopted.

The question is believed to be rather abstract than practical, whether slavery ever can or would exist in any portion of the acquired territory even if it were left to the option of the slaveholding States themselves. From the nature of the climate and productions in much the larger portion of it it is certain it could never exist, and in the remainder the probabilities are it would not. But however this may be, the question, involving, as it does, a principle of equality of rights of the separate and several States as equal copartners in the Confederacy, should not be disregarded.

In organizing governments over these territories no duty imposed on Congress by the Constitution requires that they should legislate on the subject of slavery, while their power to do so is not only seriously questioned, but denied by many of the soundest expounders of that instrument. Whether Congress shall legislate or not, the people of the acquired territories, when assembled in convention to form State constitutions, will possess the sole and exclusive power to determine for themselves whether slavery shall or shall not exist within their limits. If Congress shall abstain from interfering with the question, the people of these territories will be left free to adjust it as they may think proper when they apply for admission as States into the Union. No enactment of Congress could restrain the people of any of the sovereign States of the Union, old or new, North or South, slaveholding or nonslaveholding, from determining the character of their own domestic institutions as they may deem wise and proper. Any and all the States possess this right, and Congress can not deprive them of it. The people of Georgia might if they chose so alter their constitution as to abolish slavery within its limits, and the people of Vermont might so alter their constitution as to admit slavery within its limits. Both States would possess the right, though, as all know, it is not probable that either would exert it.

It is fortunate for the peace and harmony of the Union that this question is in its nature temporary and can only continue for the brief period which will intervene before California and New Mexico may be admitted as States into the Union. From the tide of population now flowing into them it is highly probable that this will soon occur.

Considering the several States and the citizens of the several States as equals and entitled to equal rights under the Constitution, if this were an original question it might well be insisted on that the principle of noninterference is the true doctrine and that Congress could not, in the absence of any express grant of power, interfere with their relative rights. Upon a great emergency, however, and under menacing dangers to the Union, the Missouri compromise line in respect to slavery was adopted. The same line was extended farther west in the acquisition of Texas. After an acquiescence of nearly thirty years in the principle of compromise recognized and established by these acts, and to avoid the danger to the Union which might follow if it were now disregarded, I have heretofore expressed the opinion that that line of compromise should be extended on the parallel of 36° 30' from the western boundary of Texas, where it now terminates, to the Pacific Ocean. This is the middle ground of compromise, upon which the different sections of the Union may meet, as they have heretofore met. If this be done, it is confidently believed a large majority of the people of every section of the country, however widely their abstract opinions on the subject of slavery may differ, would cheerfully and patriotically acquiesce in it, and peace and harmony would again fill our borders.

The restriction north of the line was only yielded to in the case of Missouri and Texas upon a principle of compromise, made necessary for the sake of preserving the harmony and possibly the existence of the Union.

It was upon these considerations that at the close of your last session I gave my sanction to the principle of the Missouri compromise line by approving and signing the bill to establish "the Territorial government of Oregon." From a sincere desire to preserve the harmony of the Union, and in deference for the acts of my predecessors, I felt constrained to yield my acquiescence to the extent to which they had gone in compromising this delicate and dangerous question. But if Congress shall now reverse the decision by which the Missouri compromise was effected, and shall propose to extend the restriction over the whole territory, south as well as north of the parallel of 36° 30', it will cease to be a compromise, and must be regarded as an original question.

If Congress, instead of observing the course of noninterference, leaving the adoption of their own domestic institutions to the people who may inhabit these territories, or if, instead of extending the Missouri compromise line to the Pacific, shall prefer to submit the legal and constitutional questions which may arise to the decision of the judicial tribunals, as was proposed in a bill which passed the Senate at your last session, an adjustment may be effected in this mode. If the whole subject be referred to the judiciary, all parts of the Union should cheerfully acquiesce in the final decision of the tribunal created by the Constitution for the settlement of all questions which may arise under the Constitution, treaties, and laws of the United States.

Congress is earnestly invoked, for the sake of the Union, its harmony, and our continued prosperity as a nation, to adjust at its present session this, the only dangerous question which lies in our path, if not in some one of the modes suggested, in some other which may be satisfactory.

In anticipation of the establishment of regular governments over the acquired territories, a joint commission of officers of the Army and Navy has been ordered to proceed to the coast of California and Oregon for the purpose of making reconnoissances and a report as to the proper sites for the erection of fortifications or other defensive works on land and of suitable situations for naval stations. The information which may be expected from a scientific and skillful examination of the whole face of the coast will be eminently useful to Congress when they come to consider the propriety of making appropriations for these great national objects. Proper defenses on land will be necessary for the security and protection of our possessions, and the establishment of navy-yards and a dock for the repair and construction of vessels will be important alike to our Navy and commercial marine. Without such establishments every vessel, whether of the Navy or of the merchant service, requiring repair must at great expense come round Cape Horn to one of our Atlantic yards for that purpose. With such establishments vessels, it is believed, may be built or repaired as cheaply in California as upon the Atlantic coast. They would give employment to many of our enterprising ship-builders and mechanics and greatly facilitate and enlarge our commerce in the Pacific.

As it is ascertained that mines of gold, silver, copper, and quicksilver exist in New Mexico and California, and that nearly all the lands where they are found belong to the United States, it is deemed important to the public interest that provision be made for a geological and mineral-ogical examination of these regions. Measures should be adopted to pre-serve the mineral lands, especially such as contain the precious metals, for the use of the United States, or, if brought into market, to sepa-rate them from the farming lands and dispose of them in such manner as to secure a large return of money to the Treasury and at the same time to lead to the development of their wealth by individual proprie-tors and purchasers. To do this it will be necessary to provide for an immediate survey and location of the lots. If Congress should deem it proper to dispose of the mineral lands, they should be sold in small quantities and at a fixed minimum price.

I recommend that surveyors-general's offices be authorized to be estab-lished in New Mexico and California and provision made for surveying and bringing the public lands into market at the earliest practicable period. In disposing of these lands, I recommend that the right of pre-emption be secured and liberal grants made to the early emigrants who have settled or may settle upon them.

It will be important to extend our revenue laws over these territories, and especially over California, at an early period. There is already a considerable commerce with California, and until ports of entry shall be established and collectors appointed no revenue can be received.

If these and other necessary and proper measures be adopted for the development of the wealth and resources of New Mexico and California and regular Territorial governments be established over them, such will probably be the rapid enlargement of our commerce and navigation and such the addition to the national wealth that the present generation may live to witness the controlling commercial and monetary power of the world transferred from London and other European emporiums to the city of New York.

The apprehensions which were entertained by some of our statesmen in the earlier periods of the Government that our system was incapable of operating with sufficient energy and success over largely extended territorial limits, and that if this were attempted it would fall to pieces by its own weakness, have been dissipated by our experience. By the division of power between the States and Federal Government the latter is found to operate with as much energy in the extremes as in the center. It is as efficient in the remotest of the thirty States which now compose the Union as it was in the thirteen States which formed our Constitu-tion. Indeed, it may well be doubted whether if our present population had been confined within the limits of the original thirteen States the tendencies to centralization and consolidation would not have been such as to have encroached upon the essential reserved rights of the States, and thus to have made the Federal Government a widely different one, practically, from what it is in theory and was intended to be by its framers. So far from entertaining apprehensions of the safety of our system by the extension of our territory, the belief is confidently entertained that each new State gives strength and an additional guaranty for the preservation of the Union itself.

In pursuance of the provisions of the thirteenth article of the treaty of peace, friendship, limits, and settlement with the Republic of Mexico, and of the act of July 29, 1848, claims of our citizens, which had been "already liquidated and decided, against the Mexican Republic" amounting, with the interest thereon, to $2,023,832.51 have been liquidated and paid. There remain to be paid of these claims $74,192.26.

Congress at its last session having made no provision for executing the fifteenth article of the treaty, by which the United States assume to make satisfaction for the "unliquidated claims" of our citizens against Mexico to "an amount not exceeding three and a quarter millions of dollars," the subject is again recommended to your favorable consideration.

The exchange of ratifications of the treaty with Mexico took place on the 30th of May, 1848. Within one year after that time the commissioner and surveyor which each Government stipulates to appoint are required to meet "at the port of San Diego and proceed to run and mark the said boundary in its whole course to the mouth of the Rio Bravo del Norte." It will be seen from this provision that the period within which a commissioner and surveyor of the respective Governments are to meet at San Diego will expire on the 30th of May, 1849. Congress at the close of its last session made an appropriation for "the expenses of running and marking the boundary line" between the two countries, but did not fix the amount of salary which should be paid to the commissioner and surveyor to be appointed on the part of the United States. It is desirable that the amount of compensation which they shall receive should be prescribed by law, and not left, as at present, to Executive discretion.

Measures were adopted at the earliest practicable period to organize the "Territorial government of Oregon," as authorized by the act of the 14th of August last. The governor and marshal of the Territory, accompanied by a small military escort, left the frontier of Missouri in September last, and took the southern route, by the way of Santa Fe and the river Gila, to California, with the intention of proceeding thence in one of our vessels of war to their destination. The governor was fully advised of the great importance of his early arrival in the country, and it is confidently believed he may reach Oregon in the latter part of the present month or early in the next. The other officers for the Territory have proceeded by sea.

In the month of May last I communicated information to Congress that an Indian war had broken out in Oregon, and recommended that authority be given to raise an adequate number of volunteers to proceed without delay to the assistance of our fellow-citizens in that Territory. The authority to raise such a force not having been granted by Congress, as soon as their services could be dispensed with in Mexico orders were issued to the regiment of mounted riflemen to proceed to Jefferson Barracks, in Missouri, and to prepare to march to Oregon as soon as the necessary provision could be made. Shortly before it was ready to march it was arrested by the provision of the act passed by Congress on the last day of the last session, which directed that all the noncommissioned officers, musicians, and privates of that regiment who had been in service in Mexico should, upon their application, be entitled to be discharged. The effect of this provision was to disband the rank and file of the regiment, and before their places could be filled by recruits the season had so far advanced that it was impracticable for it to proceed until the opening of the next spring.

In the month of October last the accompanying communication was received from the governor of the temporary government of Oregon, giving information of the continuance of the Indian disturbances and of the destitution and defenseless condition of the inhabitants. Orders were immediately transmitted to the commander of our squadron in the Pacific to dispatch to their assistance a part of the naval forces on that station, to furnish them with arms and ammunition, and to continue to give them such aid and protection as the Navy could afford until the Army could reach the country.

It is the policy of humanity, and one which has always been pursued by the United States, to cultivate the good will of the aboriginal tribes of this continent and to restrain them from making war and indulging in excesses by mild means rather than by force. That this could have been done with the tribes in Oregon had that Territory been brought under the government of our laws at an earlier period, and had other suitable measures been adopted by Congress, such as now exist in our intercourse with the other Indian tribes within our limits, can not be doubted. Indeed, the immediate and only cause of the existing hostility of the Indians of Oregon is represented to have been the long delay of the United States in making to them some trifling compensation, in such articles as they wanted, for the country now occupied by our emigrants, which the Indians claimed and over which they formerly roamed. This compensation had been promised to them by the temporary government established in Oregon, but its fulfillment had been postponed from time to time for nearly two years, whilst those who made it had been anxiously waiting for Congress to establish a Territorial government over the country. The Indians became at length distrustful of their good faith and sought redress by plunder and massacre, which finally led to the present difficulties. A few thousand dollars in suitable presents, as a compensation for the country which had been taken possession of by our citizens, would have satisfied the Indians and have prevented the war. A small amount properly distributed, it is confidently believed, would soon restore quiet. In this Indian war our fellow-citizens of Oregon have been compelled to take the field in their own defense, have performed valuable military services, and been subjected to expenses which have fallen heavily upon them. Justice demands that provision should be made by Congress to compensate them for their services and to refund to them the necessary expenses which they have incurred.

I repeat the recommendation heretofore made to Congress, that provision be made for the appointment of a suitable number of Indian agents to reside among the tribes of Oregon, and that a small sum be appropriated to enable these agents to cultivate friendly relations with them. If this be done, the presence of a small military force will be all that is necessary to keep them in check and preserve peace. I recommend that similar provisions be made as regards the tribes inhabiting northern Texas, New Mexico, California, and the extensive region lying between our settlements in Missouri and these possessions, as the most effective means of preserving peace upon our borders and within the recently acquired territories.

The Secretary of the Treasury will present in his annual report a highly satisfactory statement of the condition of the finances.

The imports for the fiscal year ending on the 30th of June last were of the value of $154,977,876, of which the amount exported was $21,128,010, leaving $133,849,866 in the country for domestic use. The value of the exports for the same period was $154,032,131, consisting of domestic productions amounting to $132,904,121 and $21,128,010 of foreign articles. The receipts into the Treasury for the same period, exclusive of loans, amounted to $35,436,750.59, of which there was derived from customs $31,757,070.96, from sales of public lands $3,328,642.56, and from miscellaneous and incidental sources $351,037.07.

It will be perceived that the revenue from customs for the last fiscal year exceeded by $757,070.96 the estimate of the Secretary of the Treasury in his last annual report, and that the aggregate receipts during the same period from customs, lands, and miscellaneous sources also exceeded the estimate by the sum of $536,750.59, indicating, however, a very near approach in the estimate to the actual result.

The expenditures during the fiscal year ending on the 30th of June last, including those for the war and exclusive of payments of principal and interest for the public debt, were $42,811,970.03.

It is estimated that the receipts into the Treasury for the fiscal year ending on the 30th of June, 1849, including the balance in the Treasury on the 1st of July last, will amount to the sum of $57,048,969.90, of which $32,000,000, it is estimated, will be derived from customs, $3,000,000 from the sales of the public lands, and $1,200,000 from miscellaneous and incidental sources, including the premium upon the loan, and the amount paid and to be paid into the Treasury on account of military contributions in Mexico, and the sales of arms and vessels and other public property rendered unnecessary for the use of the Government by the termination of the war, and $20,695,435.30 from loans already negotiated, including Treasury notes funded, which, together with the balance in the Treasury on the 1st of July last, make the sum estimated.

The expenditures for the same period, including the necessary payment on account of the principal and interest of the public debt, and the principal and interest of the first installment due to Mexico on the 30th of May next, and other expenditures growing out of the war to be paid during the present year, will amount, including the reimbursement of Treasury notes, to the sum of $54,195,275.06, leaving an estimated balance in the Treasury on the 1st of July, 1849, of $2,853,694.84.

The Secretary of the Treasury will present, as required by law, the estimate of the receipts and expenditures for the next fiscal year. The expenditures as estimated for that year are $33,213,152.73, including $3,799,102.18 for the interest on the public debt and $3,540,000 for the principal and interest due to Mexico on the 30th of May, 1850, leaving the sum of $25,874,050.35, which, it is believed, will be ample for the ordinary peace expenditures.

The operations of the tariff act of 1846 have been such during the past year as fully to meet the public expectation and to confirm the opinion heretofore expressed of the wisdom of the change in our revenue system which was effected by it. The receipts under it into the Treasury for the first fiscal year after its enactment exceeded by the sum of $5,044,403.09 the amount collected during the last fiscal year under the tariff act of 1842, ending the 30th of June, 1846. The total revenue realized from the commencement of its operation, on the 1st of December, 1846, until the close of the last quarter, on the 30th of September last, being twenty-two months, was $56,654,563.79, being a much larger sum than was ever before received from duties during any equal period under the tariff acts of 1824, 1828, 1832, and 1842. Whilst by the repeal of highly protective and prohibitory duties the revenue has been increased, the taxes on the people have been diminished. They have been relieved from the heavy amounts with which they were burthened under former laws in the form of increased prices or bounties paid to favored classes and pursuits.

The predictions which were made that the tariff act of 1846 would reduce the amount of revenue below that collected under the act of 1842, and would prostrate the business and destroy the prosperity of the country, have not been verified. With an increased and increasing revenue, the finances are in a highly flourishing condition. Agriculture, commerce, and navigation are prosperous; the prices of manufactured fabrics and of other products are much less injuriously affected than was to have been anticipated from the unprecedented revulsions which during the last and the present year have overwhelmed the industry and paralyzed the credit and commerce of so many great and enlightened nations of Europe.

Severe commercial revulsions abroad have always heretofore operated to depress and often to affect disastrously almost every branch of American industry. The temporary depression of a portion of our manufacturing interests is the effect of foreign causes, and is far less severe than has prevailed on all former similar occasions.

It is believed that, looking to the great aggregate of all our interests, the whole country was never more prosperous than at the present period, and never more rapidly advancing in wealth and population. Neither the foreign war in which we have been involved, nor the loans which have absorbed so large a portion of our capital, nor the commercial revulsion in Great Britain in 1847, nor the paralysis of credit and commerce throughout Europe in 1848, have affected injuriously to any considerable extent any of the great interests of the country or arrested our onward march to greatness, wealth, and power.

Had the disturbances in Europe not occurred, our commerce would undoubtedly have been still more extended, and would have added still more to the national wealth and public prosperity. But notwithstanding these disturbances, the operations of the revenue system established by the tariff act of 1846 have been so generally beneficial to the Government and the business of the country that no change in its provisions is demanded by a wise public policy, and none is recommended.

The operations of the constitutional treasury established by the act of the 6th of August, 1846, in the receipt, custody, and disbursement of the public money have continued to be successful. Under this system the public finances have been carried through a foreign war, involving the necessity of loans and extraordinary expenditures and requiring distant transfers and disbursements, without embarrassment, and no loss has occurred of any of the public money deposited under its provisions. Whilst it has proved to be safe and useful to the Government, its effects have been most beneficial upon the business of the country. It has tended powerfully to secure an exemption from that inflation and fluctuation of the paper currency so injurious to domestic industry and rendering so uncertain the rewards of labor, and, it is believed, has largely contributed to preserve the whole country from a serious commercial revulsion, such as often occurred under the bank deposit system. In the year 1847 there was a revulsion in the business of Great Britain of great extent and intensity, which was followed by failures in that Kingdom unprecedented in number and amount of losses. This is believed to be the first instance when such disastrous bankruptcies, occurring in a country with which we have such extensive commerce, produced little or no injurious effect upon our trade or currency. We remained but little affected in our money market, and our business and industry were still prosperous and progressive.

During the present year nearly the whole continent of Europe has been convulsed by civil war and revolutions, attended by numerous bankruptcies, by an unprecedented fall in their public securities, and an almost universal paralysis of commerce and industry; and yet, although our trade and the prices of our products must have been somewhat unfavorably affected by these causes, we have escaped a revulsion, our money market is comparatively easy, and public and private credit have advanced and improved.

It is confidently believed that we have been saved from their effect by the salutary operation of the constitutional treasury. It is certain that if the twenty-four millions of specie imported into the country during the fiscal year ending on the 30th of June, 1847, had gone into the banks, as to a great extent it must have done, it would in the absence of this system have been made the basis of augmented bank paper issues, probably to an amount not less than $60,000,000 or $70,000,000, producing, as an inevitable consequence of an inflated currency, extravagant prices for a time and wild speculation, which must have been followed, on the reflux to Europe the succeeding year of so much of that specie, by the prostration of the business of the country, the suspension of the banks, and most extensive bankruptcies. Occurring, as this would have done, at a period when the country was engaged in a foreign war, when considerable loans of specie were required for distant disbursements, and when the banks, the fiscal agents of the Government and the depositories of its money, were suspended, the public credit must have sunk, and many millions of dollars, as was the case during the War of 1812, must have been sacrificed in discounts upon loans and upon the depreciated paper currency which the Government would have been compelled to use.

Under the operations of the constitutional treasury not a dollar has been lost by the depreciation of the currency. The loans required to prosecute the war with Mexico were negotiated by the Secretary of the Treasury above par, realizing a large premium to the Government. The restraining effect of the system upon the tendencies to excessive paper issues by banks has saved the Government from heavy losses and thousands of our business men from bankruptcy and ruin. The wisdom of the system has been tested by the experience of the last two years, and it is the dictate of sound policy that it should remain undisturbed. The modifications in some of the details of this measure, involving none of its essential principles, heretofore recommended, are again presented for your favorable consideration.

In my message of the 6th of July last, transmitting to Congress the ratified treaty of peace with Mexico, I recommended the adoption of measures for the speedy payment of the public debt. In reiterating that recommendation I refer you to the considerations presented in that message in its support. The public debt, including that authorized to be negotiated in pursuance of existing laws, and including Treasury notes, amounted at that time to $65,778,450.41.

Funded stock of the United States amounting to about half a million of dollars has been purchased, as authorized by law, since that period, and the public debt has thus been reduced, the details of which will be presented in the annual report of the Secretary of the Treasury.

The estimates of expenditures for the next fiscal year, submitted by the Secretary of the Treasury, it is believed will be ample for all necessary purposes. If the appropriations made by Congress shall not exceed the amount estimated, the means in the Treasury will be sufficient to defray all the expenses of the Government, to pay off the next installment of $3,000,000 to Mexico, which will fall due on the 30th of May next, and still a considerable surplus will remain, which should be applied to the further purchase of the public stock and reduction of the debt. Should enlarged appropriations be made, the necessary consequence will be to postpone the payment of the debt. Though our debt, as compared with that of most other nations, is small, it is our true policy, and in harmony with the genius of our institutions, that we should present to the world the rare spectacle of a great Republic, possessing vast resources and wealth, wholly exempt from public indebtedness. This would add still more to our strength, and give to us a still more commanding position among the nations of the earth.

The public expenditures should be economical, and be confined to such necessary objects as are clearly within the powers of Congress. All such as are not absolutely demanded should be postponed, and the payment of the public debt at the earliest practicable period should be a cardinal principle of our public policy.

For the reason assigned in my last annual message, I repeat the recommendation that a branch of the Mint of the United States be established at the city of New York. The importance of this measure is greatly increased by the acquisition of the rich mines of the precious metals in New Mexico and California, and especially in the latter.

I repeat the recommendation heretofore made in favor of the graduation and reduction of the price of such of the public lands as have been long offered in the market and have remained unsold, and in favor of extending the rights of preemption to actual settlers on the unsurveyed as well as the surveyed lands.

The condition and operations of the Army and the state of other branches of the public service under the supervision of the War Department are satisfactorily presented in the accompanying report of the Secretary of War.

On the return of peace our forces were withdrawn from Mexico, and the volunteers and that portion of the Regular Army engaged for the war were disbanded. Orders have been issued for stationing the forces of our permanent establishment at various positions in our extended country where troops may be required. Owing to the remoteness of some of these positions, the detachments have not yet reached their destination. Notwithstanding the extension of the limits of our country and the forces required in the new territories, it is confidently believed that our present military establishment is sufficient for all exigencies so long as our peaceful relations remain undisturbed.

Of the amount of military contributions collected in Mexico, the sum of $769,650 was applied toward the payment of the first installment due under the treaty with Mexico. The further sum of $346,369.30 has been paid into the Treasury, and unexpended balances still remain in the hands of disbursing officers and those who were engaged in the collection of these moneys. After the proclamation of peace no further disbursements were made of any unexpended moneys arising from this source. The balances on hand were directed to be paid into the Treasury, and individual claims on the fund will remain unadjusted until Congress shall authorize their settlement and payment. These claims are not considerable in number or amount.

I recommend to your favorable consideration the suggestions of the Secretary of War and the Secretary of the Navy in regard to legislation on this subject.

Our Indian relations are presented in a most favorable view in the report from the War Department. The wisdom of our policy in regard to the tribes within our limits is clearly manifested by their improved and rapidly improving condition.

A most important treaty with the Menomonies has been recently negotiated by the Commissioner of Indian Affairs in person, by which all their land in the State of Wisconsin—being about 4,000,000 acres—has been ceded to the United States. This treaty will be submitted to the Senate for ratification at an early period of your present session.

Within the last four years eight important treaties have been negotiated with different Indian tribes, and at a cost of $1,842,000; Indian lands to the amount of more than 18,500,000 acres have been ceded to the United States, and provision has been made for settling in the country west of the Mississippi the tribes which occupied this large extent of the public domain. The title to all the Indian lands within the several States of our Union, with the exception of a few small reservations, is now extinguished, and a vast region opened for settlement and cultivation.

The accompanying report of the Secretary of the Navy gives a satisfactory exhibit of the operations and condition of that branch of the public service.

A number of small vessels, suitable for entering the mouths of rivers, were judiciously purchased during the war, and gave great efficiency to the squadron in the Gulf of Mexico. On the return of peace, when no longer valuable for naval purposes, and liable to constant deterioration, they were sold and the money placed in the Treasury.

The number of men in the naval service authorized by law during the war has been reduced by discharges below the maximum fixed for the peace establishment. Adequate squadrons are maintained in the several quarters of the globe where experience has shown their services may be most usefully employed, and the naval service was never in a condition of higher discipline or greater efficiency.

I invite attention to the recommendation of the Secretary of the Navy on the subject of the Marine Corps. The reduction of the Corps at the end of the war required that four officers of each of the three lower grades should be dropped from the rolls. A board of officers made the selection, and those designated were necessarily dismissed, but without any alleged fault. I concur in opinion with the Secretary that the service would be improved by reducing the number of landsmen and increasing the marines. Such a measure would justify an increase of the number of officers to the extent of the reduction by dismissal, and still the Corps would have fewer officers than a corresponding number of men in the Army.

The contracts for the transportation of the mail in steamships, convertible into war steamers, promise to realize all the benefits to our commerce and to the Navy which were anticipated. The first steamer thus secured to the Government was launched in January, 1847. There are now seven, and in another year there will probably be not less than seventeen afloat. While this great national advantage is secured, our social and commercial intercourse is increased and promoted with Germany, Great Britain, and other parts of Europe, with all the countries on the west coast of our continent, especially with Oregon and California, and between the northern and southern sections of the United States. Considerable revenue may be expected from postages, but the connected line from New York to Chagres, and thence across the Isthmus to Oregon, can not fail to exert a beneficial influence, not now to be estimated, on the interests of the manufactures, commerce, navigation, and currency of the United States. As an important part of the system, I recommend to your favorable consideration the establishment of the proposed line of steamers between New Orleans and Vera Cruz. It promises the most happy results in cementing friendship between the two Republics and extending reciprocal benefits to the trade and manufactures of both.

The report of the Postmaster-General will make known to you the operations of that Department for the past year.

It is gratifying to find the revenues of the Department, under the rates of postage now established by law, so rapidly increasing. The gross amount of postages during the last fiscal year amounted to $4,371,077, exceeding the annual average received for the nine years immediately preceding the passage of the act of the 3d of March, 1845, by the sum of $6,453, and exceeding the amount received for the year ending the 30th of June, 1847, by the sum of $425,184.

The expenditures for the year, excluding the sum of $94,672, allowed by Congress at its last session to individual claimants, and including the sum of $100,500, paid for the services of the line of steamers between Bremen and New York, amounted to $4,198,845, which is less than the annual average for the nine years previous to the act of 1845 by $300,748.

The mail routes on the 30th day of June last were 163,208 miles in extent, being an increase during the last year of 9,390 miles. The mails were transported over them during the same time 41,012,579 miles, making an increase of transportation for the year of 2,124,680 miles, whilst the expense was less than that of the previous year by $4,235.

The increase in the mail transportation within the last three years has been 5,378,310 miles, whilst the expenses were reduced $456,738, making an increase of service at the rate of 15 per cent and a reduction in the expenses of more than 15 per cent.

During the past year there have been employed, under contracts with the Post-Office Department, two ocean steamers in conveying the mails monthly between New York and Bremen, and one, since October last, performing semimonthly service between Charleston and Havana; and a contract has been made for the transportation of the Pacific mails across the Isthmus from Chagres to Panama.

Under the authority given to the Secretary of the Navy, three ocean steamers have been constructed and sent to the Pacific, and are expected to enter upon the mail service between Panama and Oregon and the intermediate ports on the 1st of January next; and a fourth has been engaged by him for the service between Havana and Chagres, so that a regular monthly mail line will be kept up after that time between the United States and our territories on the Pacific.

Notwithstanding this great increase in the mail service, should the revenue continue to increase the present year as it did in the last, there will be received near $450,000 more than the expenditures.

These considerations have satisfied the Postmaster-General that, with certain modifications of the act of 1845, the revenue may be still further increased and a reduction of postages made to a uniform rate of 5 cents, without an interference with the principle, which has been constantly and properly enforced, of making that Department sustain itself.

A well-digested cheap-postage system is the best means of diffusing intelligence among the people, and is of so much importance in a country so extensive as that of the United States that I recommend to your favorable consideration the suggestions of the Postmaster-General for its improvement.

Nothing can retard the onward progress of our country and prevent us from assuming and maintaining the first rank among nations but a disregard of the experience of the past and a recurrence to an unwise public policy. We have just closed a foreign war by an honorable peace—a war rendered necessary and unavoidable in vindication of the national rights and honor. The present condition of the country is similar in some respects to that which existed immediately after the close of the war with Great Britain in 1815, and the occasion is deemed to be a proper one to take a retrospect of the measures of public policy which followed that war. There was at that period of our history a departure from our earlier policy. The enlargement of the powers of the Federal Government by *construction*, which obtained, was not warranted by any just interpretation of the Constitution. A few years after the close of that war a series of measures was adopted which, united and combined, constituted what was termed by their authors and advocates the "American system."

The introduction of the new policy was for a time favored by the condition of the country, by the heavy debt which had been contracted during the war, by the depression of the public credit, by the deranged state of the finances and the currency, and by the commercial and pecuniary embarrassment which extensively prevailed. These were not the only causes which led to its establishment. The events of the war with Great Britain and the embarrassments which had attended its prosecution had left on the minds of many of our statesmen the impression that our Government was not strong enough, and that to wield its resources successfully in great emergencies, and especially in war, more power should be concentrated in its hands. This increased power they did not seek to obtain by the legitimate and prescribed mode—an amendment of the Constitution—but by *construction*. They saw Governments in the Old World based upon different orders of society, and so constituted as to throw the whole power of nations into the hands of a few, who taxed and controlled the many without responsibility or restraint. In that arrangement they conceived the strength of nations in war consisted. There was also something fascinating in the ease, luxury, and display of the higher orders, who drew their wealth from the toil of the laboring millions. The authors of the system drew their ideas of political economy from what they had witnessed in Europe, and particularly in Great Britain. They had viewed the enormous wealth concentrated in few hands and had seen the splendor of the overgrown establishments of an aristocracy which was upheld by the restrictive policy. They forgot to look down upon the poorer classes of the English population, upon whose daily and yearly labor the great establishments they so much admired were sustained and supported. They failed to perceive that the scantily fed and half-clad operatives were not only in abject poverty, but were bound in chains of oppressive servitude for the benefit of favored classes, who were the exclusive objects of the care of the Government.

It was not possible to reconstruct society in the United States upon the European plan. Here there was a written Constitution, by which orders and titles were not recognized or tolerated. A system of measures was therefore devised, calculated, if not intended, to withdraw power gradually and silently from the States and the mass of the people, and by *construction* to approximate our Government to the European models, substituting an aristocracy of wealth for that of orders and titles.

Without reflecting upon the dissimilarity of our institutions and of the condition of our people and those of Europe, they conceived the vain idea of building up in the United States a system similar to that which they admired abroad. Great Britain had a national bank of large capital, in whose hands was concentrated the controlling monetary and financial power of the nation—an institution wielding almost kingly power, and exerting vast influence upon all the operations of trade and upon the policy of the Government itself. Great Britain had an enormous public debt, and it had become a part of her public policy to regard this as a "public blessing." Great Britain had also a restrictive policy, which placed fetters and burdens on trade and trammeled the productive industry of the mass of the nation. By her combined system of policy the landlords and other property holders were protected and enriched by the enormous taxes which were levied upon the labor of the country for their advantage. Imitating this foreign policy, the first step in establishing the new system in the United States was the creation of a national bank. Not foreseeing the dangerous power and countless evils which such an institution might entail on the country, nor perceiving the connection which it was designed to form between the bank and the other branches of the miscalled "American system," but feeling the embarrassments of the Treasury and of the business of the country consequent upon the war, some of our statesmen who had held different and sounder views were induced to yield their scruples and, indeed, settled convictions of its unconstitutionality, and to give it their sanction as an expedient which they vainly hoped might produce relief. It was a most unfortunate error, as the subsequent history and final catastrophe of that dangerous and corrupt institution have abundantly proved. The bank, with its numerous branches ramified into the States, soon brought many of the active political and commercial men in different sections of the country into the relation of debtors to it and dependents upon it for pecuniary favors, thus diffusing throughout the mass of society a great number of individuals of power and influence to give tone to public opinion and to act in concert in cases of emergency. The corrupt power of such a political engine is no longer a matter of speculation, having been displayed in numerous instances, but most signally in the political struggles of 1832, 1833, and 1834 in opposition to the public will represented by a fearless and patriotic President.

But the bank was but one branch of the new system. A public debt of more than $120,000,000 existed, and it is not to be disguised that many of the authors of the new system did not regard its speedy payment as essential to the public prosperity, but looked upon its continuance as no national evil. Whilst the debt existed it furnished aliment to the national bank and rendered increased taxation necessary to the amount of the interest, exceeding $7,000,000 annually.

This operated in harmony with the next branch of the new system, which was a high protective tariff. This was to afford bounties to favored classes and particular pursuits at the expense of all others. A proposition to tax the whole people for the purpose of enriching a few was too monstrous to be openly made. The scheme was therefore veiled under the plausible but delusive pretext of a measure to protect "home industry," and many of our people were for a time led to believe that a tax which in the main fell upon labor was for the benefit of the laborer who paid it. This branch of the system involved a partnership between the Government and the favored classes, the former receiving the proceeds of the tax imposed on articles imported and the latter the increased price of similar articles produced at home, caused by such tax. It is obvious that the portion to be received by the favored classes would, as a general rule, be increased in proportion to the increase of the rates of tax imposed and diminished as those rates were reduced to the revenue standard required by the wants of the Government. The rates required to produce a sufficient revenue for the ordinary expenditures of Government for necessary purposes were not likely to give to the private partners in this scheme profits sufficient to satisfy their cupidity, and hence a variety of expedients and pretexts were resorted to for the purpose of enlarging the expenditures and thereby creating a necessity for keeping up a high protective tariff. The effect of this policy was to interpose artificial restrictions upon the natural course of the business and trade of the country, and to advance the interests of large capitalists and monopolists at the expense of the great mass of the people, who were taxed to increase their wealth.

Another branch of this system was a comprehensive scheme of internal improvements, capable of indefinite enlargement and sufficient to swallow up as many millions annually as could be exacted from the foreign commerce of the country. This was a convenient and necessary adjunct of the protective tariff: It was to be the great absorbent of any surplus which might at any time accumulate in the Treasury and of the taxes levied on the people, not for necessary revenue purposes, but for the avowed object of affording protection to the favored classes.

Auxiliary to the same end, if it was not an essential part of the system itself, was the scheme, which at a later period obtained, for distributing the proceeds of the sales of the public lands among the States. Other expedients were devised to take money out of the Treasury and prevent its coming in from any other source than the protective tariff. The authors and supporters of the system were the advocates of the largest expenditures, whether for necessary or useful purposes or not, because the larger the expenditures the greater was the pretext for high taxes in the form of protective duties.

These several measures were sustained by popular names and plausible arguments, by which thousands were deluded. The bank was represented to be an indispensable fiscal agent for the Government; was to equalize exchanges and to regulate and furnish a sound currency, always and everywhere of uniform value. The protective tariff was to give employment to "American labor" at advanced prices; was to protect "home industry" and furnish a steady market for the farmer. Internal improvements were to bring trade into every neighborhood and enhance the value of every man's property. The distribution of the land money was to enrich the States, finish their public works, plant schools throughout their borders, and relieve them from taxation. But the fact that for every dollar taken out of the Treasury for these objects a much larger sum was transferred from the pockets of the people to the favored classes was carefully concealed, as was also the tendency, if not the ultimate design, of the system to build up an aristocracy of wealth, to control the masses of society, and monopolize the political power of the country.

The several branches of this system were so intimately blended together that in their operation each sustained and strengthened the others. Their joint operation was to add new burthens of taxation and to encourage a largely increased and wasteful expenditure of public money. It was the interest of the bank that the revenue collected and the disbursements made by the Government should be large, because, being the depository of the public money, the larger the amount the greater would be the bank profits by its use. It was the interest of the favored classes, who were enriched by the protective tariff, to have the rates of that protection as high as possible, for the higher those rates the greater would be their advantage. It was the interest of the people of all those sections and localities who expected to be benefited by expenditures for internal improvements that the amount collected should be as large as possible, to the end that the sum disbursed might also be the larger. The States, being the beneficiaries in the distribution of the land money, had an interest in having the rates of tax imposed by the protective tariff large enough to yield a sufficient revenue from that source to meet the wants of the Government without disturbing or taking from them the land fund; so that each of the branches constituting the system had a common interest in swelling the public expenditures. They had a direct interest in maintaining the public debt unpaid and increasing its amount, because this would produce an annual increased drain upon the Treasury to the amount of the interest and render augmented taxes necessary. The operation and necessary effect of the whole system were to encourage large and extravagant expenditures, and thereby to increase the public patronage, and maintain a rich and splendid government at the expense of a taxed and impoverished people.

It is manifest that this scheme of enlarged taxation and expenditures, had it continued to prevail, must soon have converted the Government of the Union, intended by its framers to be a plain, cheap, and simple confederation of States, united together for common protection and charged with a few specific duties, relating chiefly to our foreign affairs, into a consolidated empire, depriving the States of their reserved rights and the people of their just power and control in the administration of their Government. In this manner the whole form and character of the Government would be changed, not by an amendment of the Constitution, but by resorting to an unwarrantable and unauthorized construction of that instrument.

The indirect mode of levying the taxes by a duty on imports prevents the mass of the people from readily perceiving the amount they pay, and has enabled the few who are thus enriched, and who seek to wield the political power of the country, to deceive and delude them. Were the taxes collected by a direct levy upon the people, as is the case in the States, this could not occur.

The whole system was resisted from its inception by many of our ablest statesmen, some of whom doubted its constitutionality and its expediency, while others believed it was in all its branches a flagrant and dangerous infraction of the Constitution.

That a national bank, a protective tariff—levied not to raise the revenue needed, but for protection merely—internal improvements, and the distribution of the proceeds of the sale of the public lands are measures without the warrant of the Constitution would, upon the maturest consideration, seem to be clear. It is remarkable that no one of these measures, involving such momentous consequences, is authorized by any express grant of power in the Constitution. No one of them is "incident to, as being necessary and proper for the execution of, the specific powers" granted by the Constitution. The authority under which it has been attempted to justify each of them is derived from inferences and constructions of the Constitution which its letter and its whole object and design do not warrant. Is it to be conceived that such immense powers would have been left by the framers of the Constitution to mere inferences and doubtful constructions? Had it been intended to confer them on the Federal Government, it is but reasonable to conclude that it would have been done by plain and unequivocal grants. This was not done; but the whole structure of which the "American system" consisted was reared on no other or better foundation than forced implications and inferences of power, which its authors assumed might be deduced by construction from the Constitution.

But it has been urged that the national bank, which constituted so essential a branch of this combined system of measures, was not a new measure, and that its constitutionality had been previously sanctioned, because a bank had been chartered in 1791 and had received the official signature of President Washington. A few facts will show the just weight to which this precedent should be entitled as bearing upon the question of constitutionality.

Great division of opinion upon the subject existed in Congress. It is well known that President Washington entertained serious doubts both as to the constitutionality and expediency of the measure, and while the bill was before him for his official approval or disapproval so great were these doubts that he required "the opinion in writing" of the members of his Cabinet to aid him in arriving at a decision. His Cabinet gave their opinions and were divided upon the subject, *General Hamilton* being in favor of and *Mr. Jefferson* and *Mr. Randolph* being opposed to the constitutionality and expediency of the bank. It is well known also that President Washington retained the bill from Monday, the 14th, when it was presented to him, until Friday, the 25th of February, being the last moment permitted him by the Constitution to deliberate, when he finally yielded to it his reluctant assent and gave it his signature. It is certain that as late as the 23d of February, being the ninth day after the bill was presented to him, he had arrived at no satisfactory conclusion, for on that day he addressed a note to General Hamilton in which he informs him that "this bill was presented to me by the joint committee of Congress at 12 o'clock on Monday, the 14th instant," and he requested his opinion "to what precise period, by legal interpretation of the Constitution, can the President retain it in his possession before it becomes a law by the lapse of ten days." If the proper construction was that the day on which the bill was presented to the President and the day on which his action was had upon it were both to be counted inclusive, then the time allowed him within which it would be competent for him to return it to the House in which it originated with his objections would expire on Thursday, the 24th of February. General Hamilton on the same day returned an answer, in which he states:

I give it as my opinion that you have ten days exclusive of that on which the bill was delivered to you and Sundays; hence, in the present case if it is returned on Friday it will be in time.

By this construction, which the President adopted, he gained another day for deliberation, and it was not until the 25th of February that he signed the bill, thus affording conclusive proof that he had at last obtained his own consent to sign it not without great and almost insuperable difficulty. Additional light has been recently shed upon the serious doubts which he had on the subject, amounting at one time to a conviction that it was his duty to withhold his approval from the bill. This is found among the manuscript papers of *Mr. Madison*, authorized to be purchased for the use of the Government by an act of the last session of Congress, and now for the first time accessible to the public. From these papers it appears that President Washington, while he yet held the bank bill in his hands, actually requested *Mr. Madison*, at that time a member of the House of Representatives, to prepare the draft of a veto message for him. *Mr. Madison*, at his request, did prepare the draft of such a message, and sent it to him on the 21st of February, 1791. A copy of this original draft, in Mr. Madison's own handwriting, was carefully preserved by him, and is among the papers lately purchased by Congress. It is preceded by a note, written on the same sheet, which is also in Mr. Madison's handwriting, and is as follows:

February 21, 1791.—Copy of a paper made out and sent to the President, *at his request*, to be ready in case his judgment should finally decide against the bill for incorporating a national bank, the bill being then before him.

Among the objections assigned in this paper to the bill, and which were submitted for the consideration of the President, are the following:

I object to the bill, because it is an essential principle of the Government that powers not delegated by the Constitution can not be rightfully exercised; because the power proposed by the bill to be exercised is not expressly delegated, and because I can not satisfy myself that it results from any express power by fair and safe rules of interpretation.

The weight of the precedent of the bank of 1791 and the sanction of the great name of Washington, which has been so often invoked in its support, are greatly weakened by the development of these facts.

The experiment of that bank satisfied the country that it ought not to be continued, and at the end of twenty years Congress refused to recharter it. It would have been fortunate for the country, and saved thousands from bankruptcy and ruin, had our public men of 1816 resisted the temporary pressure of the times upon our financial and pecuniary interests and refused to charter the second bank. Of this the country became abundantly satisfied, and at the close of its twenty years' duration, as in the case of the first bank, it also ceased to exist. Under the repeated blows of *President Jackson* it reeled and fell, and a subsequent attempt to charter a similar institution was arrested by the *veto* of President Tyler.

Mr. Madison, in yielding his signature to the charter of 1816, did so upon the ground of the respect due to precedents; and, as he subsequently declared—

The Bank of the United States, though on the original question held to be unconstitutional, received the Executive signature.

It is probable that neither the bank of 1791 nor that of 1816 would have been chartered but for the embarrassments of the Government in its finances, the derangement of the currency, and the pecuniary pressure which existed, the first the consequence of the War of the Revolution and the second the consequence of the War of 1812. Both were resorted to in the delusive hope that they would restore public credit and afford relief to the Government and to the business of the country.

Those of our public men who opposed the whole "American system" at its commencement and throughout its progress foresaw and predicted that it was fraught with incalculable mischiefs and must result in serious injury to the best interests of the country. For a series of years their wise counsels were unheeded, and the system was established. It was soon apparent that its practical operation was unequal and unjust upon different portions of the country and upon the people engaged in different pursuits. All were equally entitled to the favor and protection of the Government. It fostered and elevated the money power and enriched the favored few by taxing labor, and at the expense of the many. Its effect was to "make the rich richer and the poor poorer." Its tendency was to create distinctions in society based on wealth and to give to the favored classes undue control and sway in our Government. It was an organized money power, which resisted the popular will and sought to shape and control the public policy.

Under the pernicious workings of this combined system of measures the country witnessed alternate seasons of temporary apparent prosperity, of sudden and disastrous commercial revulsions, of unprecedented fluctuation of prices and depression of the great interests of agriculture, navigation, and commerce, of general pecuniary suffering, and of final bankruptcy of thousands. After a severe struggle of more than a quarter of a century, the system was overthrown.

The bank has been succeeded by a practical system of finance, conducted and controlled solely by the Government. The constitutional currency has been restored, the public credit maintained unimpaired even in a period of a foreign war, and the whole country has become satisfied that banks, national or State, are not necessary as fiscal agents of the Government. Revenue duties have taken the place of the protective tariff. The distribution of the money derived from the sale of the public lands has been abandoned and the corrupting system of internal improvements, it is hoped, has been effectually checked.

It is not doubted that if this whole train of measures, designed to take wealth from the many and bestow it upon the few, were to prevail the effect would be to change the entire character of the Government. One only danger remains. It is the seductions of that branch of the system which consists in internal improvements, holding out, as it does, inducements to the people of particular sections and localities to embark the Government in them without stopping to calculate the inevitable consequences. This branch of the system is so intimately combined and linked with the others that as surely as an effect is produced by an adequate cause, if it be resuscitated and revived and firmly established it requires no sagacity to foresee that it will necessarily and speedily draw after it the reestablishment of a national bank, the revival of a protective tariff, the distribution of the land money, and not only the postponement to the distant future of the payment of the present national debt, but its annual increase.

I entertain the solemn conviction that if the internal-improvement branch of the "American system" be not firmly resisted at this time the whole series of measures composing it will be speedily reestablished and the country be thrown back from its present high state of prosperity, which the existing policy has produced, and be destined again to witness all the evils, commercial revulsions, depression of prices, and pecuniary embarrassments through which we have passed during the last twenty-five years.

To guard against consequences so ruinous is an object of high national importance, involving, in my judgment, the continued prosperity of the country.

I have felt it to be an imperative obligation to withhold my constitutional sanction from two bills which had passed the two Houses of Congress, involving the principle of the internal-improvement branch of the "American system" and conflicting in their provisions with the views here expressed.

This power, conferred upon the President by the Constitution, I have on three occasions during my administration of the executive department of the Government deemed it my duty to exercise, and on this last occasion of making to Congress an annual communication "of the state of the Union" it is not deemed inappropriate to review the principles and considerations which have governed my action. I deem this the more necessary because, after the lapse of nearly sixty years since the adoption of the Constitution, the propriety of the exercise of this undoubted constitutional power by the President has for the first time been drawn seriously in question by a portion of my fellow-citizens.

The Constitution provides that—

Every bill which shall have passed the House of Representatives and the Senate shall, before it become a law, be presented to the President of the United States. If he approve he *shall* sign it, but if not he *shall* return it with his objections to that House in which it shall have originated, who shall enter the objections at large on their Journal and proceed to reconsider it.

The preservation of the Constitution from infraction is the President's highest duty. He is bound to discharge that duty at whatever hazard of incurring the displeasure of those who may differ with him in opinion. He is bound to discharge it as well by his obligations to the people who have clothed him with his exalted trust as by his oath of office, which he may not disregard. Nor are the obligations of the President in any degree lessened by the prevalence of views different from his own in one or both Houses of Congress. It is not alone hasty and inconsiderate legislation that he is required to check; but if at any time Congress shall, after apparently full deliberation, resolve on measures which he deems subversive of the Constitution or of the vital interests of the country, it is his solemn duty to stand in the breach and resist them. The President is bound to approve or disapprove every bill which passes Congress and is presented to him for his signature. The Constitution makes this his duty, and he can not escape it if he would. He has no election. In deciding upon any bill presented to him he must exercise his own best judgment. If he can not approve, the Constitution commands him to return the bill to the House in which it originated with his objections, and if he fail to do this within ten days (Sundays excepted) it shall become a law without his signature. Right or wrong, he may be overruled by a vote of two-thirds of each House, and in that event the bill becomes a law without his sanction. If his objections be not thus overruled, the subject is only postponed, and is referred to the States and the people for their consideration and decision. The President's power is negative merely, and not affirmative. He can enact no law. The only effect, therefore, of his withholding his approval of a bill passed by Congress is to suffer the existing laws to remain unchanged, and the delay occasioned is only that required to enable the States and the people to consider and act upon the subject in the election of public agents who will carry out their wishes and instructions. Any attempt to coerce the President to yield his sanction to measures which he can not approve would be a violation of the spirit of the Constitution, palpable and flagrant, and if successful would break down the independence of the executive department and make the President, elected by the people and clothed by the Constitution with power to defend their rights, the mere instrument of a majority of Congress. A surrender on his part of the powers with which the Constitution has invested his office would effect a practical alteration of that instrument without resorting to the prescribed process of amendment.

With the motives or considerations which may induce Congress to pass any bill the President can have nothing to do. He must presume them to be as pure as his own, and look only to the practical effect of their measures when compared with the Constitution or the public good.

But it has been urged by those who object to the exercise of this undoubted constitutional power that it assails the representative principle and the capacity of the people to govern themselves; that there is greater safety in a numerous representative body than in the single Executive created by the Constitution, and that the Executive veto is a "one-man power," despotic in its character. To expose the fallacy of this objection it is only necessary to consider the frame and true character of our system. Ours is not a consolidated empire, but a confederated union. The States before the adoption of the Constitution were coordinate, coequal, and separate independent sovereignties, and by its adoption they did not lose that character. They clothed the Federal Government with certain powers and reserved all others, including their own sovereignty, to themselves. They guarded their own rights as States and the rights of the people by the very limitations which they incorporated into the Federal Constitution, whereby the different departments of the General Government were checks upon each other. That the majority should govern is a general principle controverted by none, but they must govern according to the Constitution, and not according to an undefined and unrestrained discretion, whereby they may oppress the minority.

The people of the United States are not blind to the fact that they may be temporarily misled, and that their representatives, legislative and executive, may be mistaken or influenced in their action by improper motives. They have therefore interposed between themselves and the laws which may be passed by their public agents various representations, such as assemblies, senates, and governors in their several States, a House of Representatives, a Senate, and a President of the United States. The people can by their own direct agency make no law, nor can the House of Representatives, immediately elected by them, nor can the Senate, nor can both together without the concurrence of the President or a vote of two-thirds of both Houses.

Happily for themselves, the people in framing our admirable system of government were conscious of the infirmities of their representatives, and in delegating to them the power of legislation they have fenced them around with checks to guard against the effects of hasty action, of error, of combination, and of possible corruption. Error, selfishness, and faction have often sought to rend asunder this web of checks and subject the Government to the control of fanatic and sinister influences, but these efforts have only satisfied the people of the wisdom of the checks which they have imposed and of the necessity of preserving them unimpaired.

The true theory of our system is not to govern by the acts or decrees of any one set of representatives. The Constitution interposes checks upon all branches of the Government, in order to give time for error to be corrected and delusion to pass away; but if the people settle down into a firm conviction different from that of their representatives they give effect to their opinions by changing their public servants. The checks which the people imposed on their public servants in the adoption of the Constitution are the best evidence of their capacity for self-government. They know that the men whom they elect to public stations are of like infirmities and passions with themselves, and not to be trusted without being restricted by coordinate authorities and constitutional limitations. Who that has witnessed the legislation of Congress for the last thirty years will say that he knows of no instance in which measures not demanded by the public good have been carried? Who will deny that in the State governments, by combinations of individuals and sections, in derogation of the general interest, banks have been chartered, systems of internal improvements adopted, and debts entailed upon the people repressing their growth and impairing their energies for years to come?

After so much experience it can not be said that absolute unchecked power is safe in the hands of any one set of representatives, or that the capacity of the people for self-government, which is admitted in its broadest extent, is a conclusive argument to prove the prudence, wisdom, and integrity of their representatives.

The people, by the Constitution, have commanded the President, as much as they have commanded the legislative branch of the Government, to execute their will. They have said to him in the Constitution, which they require he shall take a solemn oath to support, that if Congress pass any bill which he can not approve ''he shall return it to the House in which it originated with his objections.'' In withholding from it his approval and signature he is executing the will of the people, constitutionally expressed, as much as the Congress that passed it. No bill is presumed to be in accordance with the popular will until it shall have passed through all the branches of the Government required by the Constitution to make it a law. A bill which passes the House of Representatives may be rejected by the Senate, and so a bill passed by the Senate may be rejected by the House. In each case the respective Houses exercise the veto power on the other.

Congress, and each House of Congress, hold under the Constitution a check upon the President, and he, by the power of the qualified veto, a check upon Congress. When the President recommends measures to Congress, he avows in the most solemn form his opinions, gives his voice in their favor, and pledges himself in advance to approve them if passed by Congress. If he acts without due consideration, or has been influenced by improper or corrupt motives, or if from any other cause Congress, or either House of Congress, shall differ with him in opinion, they exercise their *veto* upon his recommendations and reject them; and there is no appeal from their decision but to the people at the ballot box. These are proper checks upon the Executive, wisely interposed by the Constitution. None will be found to object to them or to wish them removed. It is equally important that the constitutional checks of the Executive upon the legislative branch should be preserved.

If it be said that the Representatives in the popular branch of Congress are chosen directly by the people, it is answered, the people elect the President. If both Houses represent the States and the people, so does the President. The President represents in the executive department the whole people of the United States, as each member of the legislative department represents portions of them.

The doctrine of restriction upon legislative and executive power, while a well-settled public opinion is enabled within a reasonable time to accomplish its ends, has made our country what it is, and has opened to us a career of glory and happiness to which all other nations have been strangers.

In the exercise of the power of the veto the President is responsible not only to an enlightened public opinion, but to the people of the whole Union, who elected him, as the representatives in the legislative branches who differ with him in opinion are responsible to the people of particular States or districts, who compose their respective constituencies. To deny to the President the exercise of this power would be to repeal that provision of the Constitution which confers it upon him. To charge that its exercise unduly controls the legislative will is to complain of the Constitution itself.

If the Presidential veto be objected to upon the ground that it checks and thwarts the popular will, upon the same principle the equality of representation of the States in the Senate should be stricken out of the Constitution. The vote of a Senator from Delaware has equal weight in deciding upon the most important measures with the vote of a Senator from New York, and yet the one represents a State containing, according to the existing apportionment of Representatives in the House of Representatives, but one thirty-fourth part of the population of the other. By the constitutional composition of the Senate a majority of that body from the smaller States represent less than one-fourth of the people of the Union. There are thirty States, and under the existing apportionment of Representatives there are 230 Members in the House of Representatives. Sixteen of the smaller States are represented in that House by but 50 Members, and yet the Senators from these States constitute a majority of the Senate. So that the President may recommend a measure to Congress, and it may receive the sanction and approval of more than three-fourths of the House of Representatives and of all the Senators from the large States, containing more than three-fourths of the whole population of the United States, and yet the measure may be defeated by the votes of the Senators from the smaller States. None, it is presumed, can be found ready to change the organization of the Senate on this account, or to strike that body practically out of existence by requiring that its action shall be conformed to the will of the more numerous branch.

Upon the same principle that the *veto* of the President should be practically abolished the power of the Vice-President to give the casting vote upon an equal division of the Senate should be abolished also. The Vice-President exercises the *veto* power as effectually by rejecting a bill by his casting vote as the President does by refusing to approve and sign it. This power has been exercised by the Vice-President in a few instances, the most important of which was the rejection of the bill to recharter the Bank of the United States in 1811. It may happen that a bill may be passed by a large majority of the House of Representatives, and may be supported by the Senators from the larger States, and the Vice-President may reject it by giving his vote with the Senators from the smaller States; and yet none, it is presumed, are prepared to deny to him the exercise of this power under the Constitution.

But it is, in point of fact, untrue that an act passed by Congress is conclusive evidence that it is an emanation of the popular will. A majority of the whole number elected to each House of Congress constitutes a quorum, and a majority of that quorum is competent to pass laws. It might happen that a quorum of the House of Representatives, consisting of a single member more than half of the whole number elected to that House, might pass a bill by a majority of a single vote, and in that case a fraction more than one-fourth of the people of the United States would be represented by those who voted for it. It might happen that the same bill might be passed by a majority of one of a quorum of the Senate, composed of Senators from the fifteen smaller States and a single Senator from a sixteenth State; and if the Senators voting for it happened to be from the eight of the smallest of these States, it would be passed by the votes of Senators from States having but fourteen Representatives in the House of Representatives, and containing less than one-sixteenth of the whole population of the United States. This extreme case is stated to illustrate the fact that the mere passage of a bill by Congress is no conclusive evidence that those who passed it represent the majority of the people of the United States or truly reflect their will. If such an extreme case is not likely to happen, cases that approximate it are of constant occurrence. It is believed that not a single law has been passed since the adoption of the Constitution upon which all the members elected to both Houses have been present and voted. Many of the most important acts which have passed Congress have been carried by a close vote in thin Houses. Many instances of this might be given. Indeed, our experience proves that many of the most important acts of Congress are postponed to the last days, and often the last hours, of a session, when they are disposed of in haste, and by Houses but little exceeding the number necessary to form a quorum.

Besides, in most of the States the members of the House of Representatives are chosen by pluralities, and not by majorities of all the voters in their respective districts, and it may happen that a majority of that House may be returned by a less aggregate vote of the people than that received by the minority.

If the principle insisted on be sound, then the Constitution should be so changed that no bill shall become a law unless it is voted for by members representing in each House a majority of the whole people of the United States. We must remodel our whole system, strike down and abolish not only the salutary checks lodged in the executive branch, but must strike out and abolish those lodged in the Senate also, and thus practically invest the whole power of the Government in a majority of a single assembly— a majority uncontrolled and absolute, and which may become despotic. To conform to this doctrine of the right of majorities to rule, independent of the checks and limitations of the Constitution, we must revolutionize our whole system; we must destroy the constitutional compact by which the several States agreed to form a Federal Union and rush into consolidation, which must end in monarchy or despotism. No one advocates such a proposition, and yet the doctrine maintained, if carried out, must lead to this result.

One great object of the Constitution in conferring upon the President a qualified negative upon the legislation of Congress was to protect minorities from injustice and oppression by majorities. The equality of their representation in the Senate and the veto power of the President are the constitutional guaranties which the smaller States have that their rights will be respected. Without these guaranties all their interests would be at the mercy of majorities in Congress representing the larger States. To the smaller and weaker States, therefore, the preservation of this power and its exercise upon proper occasions demanding it is of vital importance. They ratified the Constitution and entered into the Union, securing to themselves an equal representation with the larger States in the Senate; and they agreed to be bound by all laws passed by Congress upon the express condition, and none other, that they should be approved by the President or passed, his objections to the contrary notwithstanding, by a vote of two-thirds of both Houses. Upon this condition they have a right to insist as a part of the compact to which they gave their assent.

A bill might be passed by Congress against the will of the whole people of a particular State and against the votes of its Senators and all its Representatives. However prejudicial it might be to the interests of such State, it would be bound by it if the President shall approve it or it shall be passed by a vote of two-thirds of both Houses; but it has a right to demand that the President shall exercise his constitutional power and arrest it if his judgment is against it. If he surrender this power, or fail to exercise it in a case where he can not approve, it would make his formal approval a mere mockery, and would be itself a violation of the Constitution, and the dissenting State would become bound by a law which had not been passed according to the sanctions of the Constitution.

The objection to the exercise of the *veto* power is founded upon an idea respecting the popular will, which, if carried out, would annihilate State sovereignty and substitute for the present Federal Government a consolidation directed by a supposed numerical majority. A revolution of the Government would be silently effected and the States would be subjected to laws to which they had never given their constitutional consent.

The Supreme Court of the United States is invested with the power to declare, and has declared, acts of Congress passed with the concurrence of the Senate, the House of Representatives, and the approval of the President to be unconstitutional and void, and yet none, it is presumed, can be found who will be disposed to strip this highest judicial tribunal under the Constitution of this acknowledged power—a power necessary alike to its independence and the rights of individuals.

For the same reason that the Executive veto should, according to the doctrine maintained, be rendered nugatory, and be practically expunged from the Constitution, this power of the court should also be rendered nugatory and be expunged, because it restrains the legislative and Executive will, and because the exercise of such a power by the court may be regarded as being in conflict with the capacity of the people to govern themselves. Indeed, there is more reason for striking this power of the court from the Constitution than there is that of the qualified veto of the President, because the decision of the court is final, and can never be reversed even though both Houses of Congress and the President should be unanimous in opposition to it, whereas the veto of the President may be overruled by a vote of two-thirds of both Houses of Congress or by the people at the polls.

It is obvious that to preserve the system established by the Constitution each of the coordinate branches of the Government—the executive, legislative, and judicial—must be left in the exercise of its appropriate powers. If the executive or the judicial branch be deprived of powers conferred upon either as checks on the legislative, the preponderance of the latter will become disproportionate and absorbing and the others impotent for the accomplishment of the great objects for which they were established. Organized, as they are, by the Constitution, they work together harmoniously for the public good. If the Executive and the judiciary shall be deprived of the constitutional powers invested in them, and of their due proportions, the equilibrium of the system must be destroyed, and consolidation, with the most pernicious results, must ensue— a consolidation of unchecked, despotic power, exercised by majorities of the legislative branch.

The executive, legislative, and judicial each constitutes a separate coordinate department of the Government, and each is independent of the others. In the performance of their respective duties under the Constitution neither can in its legitimate action control the others. They each act upon their several responsibilities in their respective spheres. But if the doctrines now maintained be correct, the executive must become practically subordinate to the legislative, and the judiciary must become subordinate to both the legislative and the executive; and thus the whole power of the Government would be merged in a single department. Whenever, if ever, this shall occur, our glorious system of well-regulated self-government will crumble into ruins, to be succeeded, first by anarchy, and finally by monarchy or despotism. I am far from believing that this doctrine is the sentiment of the American people; and during the short period which remains in which it will be my duty to administer the executive department it will be my aim to maintain its independence and discharge its duties without infringing upon the powers or duties of either of the other departments of the Government.

The power of the Executive veto was exercised by the first and most illustrious of my predecessors and by four of his successors who preceded me in the administration of the Government, and it is believed in no instance prejudicially to the public interests. It has never been and there is but little danger that it ever can be abused. No President will ever desire unnecessarily to place his opinion in opposition to that of Congress. He must always exercise the power reluctantly, and only in cases where his convictions make it a matter of stern duty, which he can not escape. Indeed, there is more danger that the President, from the repugnance he must always feel to come in collision with Congress, may fail to exercise it in cases where the preservation of the Constitution from infraction, or the public good, may demand it than that he will ever exercise it unnecessarily or wantonly.

During the period I have administered the executive department of the Government great and important questions of public policy, foreign and domestic, have arisen, upon which it was my duty to act. It may, indeed, be truly said that my Administration has fallen upon eventful times. I have felt most sensibly the weight of the high responsibilities devolved upon me. With no other object than the public good, the enduring fame, and permanent prosperity of my country, I have pursued the convictions of my own best judgment. The impartial arbitrament of enlightened public opinion, present and future, will determine how far the public policy I have maintained and the measures I have from time to time recommended may have tended to advance or retard the public prosperity at home and to elevate or depress the estimate of our national character abroad.

Invoking the blessings of the Almighty upon your deliberations at your present important session, my ardent hope is that in a spirit of harmony and concord you may be guided to wise results, and such as may redound to the happiness, the honor, and the glory of our beloved country.

JAMES K. POLK.

SPECIAL MESSAGES.

WASHINGTON, *December 12, 1848.*

To the Senate of the United States:

I nominate Second Lieutenant Ulysses S. Grant (since promoted first lieutenant), of the Fourth Regiment of Infantry, to be first lieutenant by brevet for gallant and meritorious services in the battle of Chapultepec, September 13, 1847, as proposed in the accompanying communication from the Secretary of War.

JAMES K. POLK.

WAR DEPARTMENT, *December 11, 1848.*

The PRESIDENT OF THE UNITED STATES.

SIR: The brevet of captain conferred on Second Lieutenant Ulysses S. Grant (since promoted first lieutenant), of the Fourth Regiment of Infantry, and confirmed by the Senate on the 13th of July, 1848, "for gallant and meritorious conduct in the battle of Chapultepec, September 13, 1847," being the result of a misapprehension as to the grade held by that officer on the 13th of September, 1847 (he being then a second lieutenant), I have to propose that the brevet of captain be canceled and that the brevet of first lieutenant "for gallant and meritorious services in the battle of Chapultepec, September 13, 1847," be conferred in lieu thereof.

I am, sir, with great respect, your obedient servant,

W. L. MARCY.

WASHINGTON, *December 12, 1848.*

To the Senate of the United States:

I transmit herewith, for the consideration and advice of the Senate with regard to its ratification, a treaty concluded on the 6th of August, 1848, by L. E. Powell, on the part of the United States, and the chiefs and headmen of the confederated bands of the Pawnee Indians, together with a report of the Commissioner of Indian Affairs and other papers explanatory of the same.

JAMES K. POLK.

WASHINGTON, *December 12, 1848.*

To the Senate of the United States:

I transmit herewith, for the consideration and advice of the Senate with regard to its ratification, a treaty concluded on the 18th of October, 1848, by William Medill, Commissioner of Indian Affairs, on the part of the United States, and the chiefs and headmen of the Menomonee Indians, together with a report of the Commissioner of Indian Affairs and other papers explanatory of the same.

JAMES K. POLK.

WASHINGTON, *December 27, 1848.*

To the House of Representatives:

In compliance with the resolution of the House of the 11th instant, requesting the President to inform that body "whether he has received any information that American citizens have been imprisoned or arrested by British authorities in Ireland, and, if so, what have been the causes thereof and what steps have been taken for their release, and if not, in his opinion, inconsistent with public interest to furnish this House with copies of all correspondence in relation thereto," I communicate herewith a report of the Secretary of State, together with the accompanying correspondence upon the subject.

JAMES K. POLK.

WASHINGTON, *December 27, 1848.*

To the Senate of the United States:

I communicate herewith, in compliance with the request contained in the resolution of the Senate of the 19th instant, a report of the Secretary of the Treasury, with the accompanying statement, prepared by the Register of the Treasury, which exhibits the annual amount appropriated on account of the Coast Survey from the commencement of said Survey.

JAMES K. POLK.

WASHINGTON, *January 2, 1849.*

To the House of Representatives of the United States:

In answer to the resolution of the House of Representatives of the 18th of December, 1848, requesting information "under what law or provision of the Constitution, or by what other authority," the Secretary of the Treasury, with the "sanction and approval" of the President, established "a tariff of duties in the ports of the Mexican Republic during the war with Mexico," and "by what legal, constitutional, or other authority" the "revenue thus derived" was appropriated to "the support of the Army in Mexico," I refer the House to my annual message of the 7th of December, 1847, to my message to the Senate of the 10th of February, 1848, responding to a call of that body, a copy of which is herewith communicated, and to my message to the House of Representatives of the 24th of July, 1848, responding to a call of that House. The resolution assumes that the Secretary of the Treasury "established a tariff of duties in the ports of the Mexican Republic." The contributions collected in this mode were not established by the Secretary of the Treasury, but by a military order issued by the President through the War and Navy Departments. For his information the President directed the Secretary of the Treasury to prepare and report to him a scale of duties. That report was made, and the President's military order of the 31st of March, 1847, was based upon it. The documents communicated to Congress with my annual message of December, 1847, show the true character of that order.

The authority under which military contributions were exacted and collected from the enemy and applied to the support of our Army during the war with Mexico was stated in the several messages referred to. In the first of these messages I informed Congress that—

On the 31st of March last I caused an order to be issued to our military and naval commanders to levy and collect a military contribution upon all vessels and merchandise which might enter any of the ports of Mexico in our military occupation, and to apply such contributions toward defraying the expenses of the war. By virtue of the right of conquest and the laws of war, the conqueror, consulting his own safety or convenience, may either exclude foreign commerce altogether from all such ports or permit it upon such terms and conditions as he may prescribe. Before the principal ports of Mexico were blockaded by our Navy the revenue derived from import duties under the laws of Mexico was paid into the Mexican treasury. After these ports had fallen into our military possession the blockade was raised and commerce with them permitted upon prescribed terms and conditions. They were opened to the trade of all nations upon the payment of duties more moderate in their amount than those which had been previously levied by Mexico, and the revenue, which was formerly paid into the Mexican treasury, was directed to be collected by our military and naval officers and applied to the use of our Army and Navy. Care was taken that the officers, soldiers, and sailors of our Army and Navy should be exempted from the operations of the order, and, as the merchandise imported upon which the order operated must be consumed by Mexican citizens, the contributions exacted were in effect the seizure of the public revenues of Mexico and the application of them to our own use. In directing this measure the object was to compel the enemy to contribute as far as practicable toward the expenses of the war.

It was also stated in that message that—

Measures have recently been adopted by which the internal as well as the external revenues of Mexico in all places in our military occupation will be seized and appropriated to the use of our Army and Navy.

The policy of levying upon the enemy contributions in every form consistently with the laws of nations, which it may be practicable for our military commanders to adopt, should, in my judgment, be rigidly enforced, and orders to this effect have accordingly been given. By such a policy, at the same time that our own Treasury will be relieved from a heavy drain, the Mexican people will be made to feel the burdens of the war, and, consulting their own interests, may be induced the more readily to require their rulers to accede to a just peace.

In the same message I informed Congress that the amount of the "loan" which would be required for the further prosecution of the war might be "reduced by whatever amount of expenditures can be saved by military contributions collected in Mexico," and that " the most rigorous measures for the augmentation of these contributions have been directed, and a very considerable sum is expected from that source." The Secretary of the Treasury, in his annual report of that year, in making his estimate of the amount of loan which would probably be required, reduced the sum in consideration of the amount which would probably be derived from these contributions, and Congress authorized the loan upon this reduced estimate.

In the message of the 10th of February, 1848, to the Senate, it was stated that—

No principle is better established than that a nation at war has the right of shifting the burden off itself and imposing it on the enemy by exacting military contributions. The mode of making such exactions must be left to the discretion of the conqueror, but it should be exercised in a manner conformable to the rules of civilized warfare.

The right to levy these contributions is essential to the successful prosecution of war in an enemy's country, and the practice of nations has been in accordance with this principle. It is as clearly necessary as the right to fight battles, and its exercise is often essential to the subsistence of the army.

Entertaining no doubt that the military right to exclude commerce altogether from the ports of the enemy in our military occupation included the minor right of admitting it under prescribed conditions, it became an important question at the date of the order whether there should be a discrimination between vessels and cargoes belonging to citizens of the United States and vessels and cargoes belonging to neutral nations.

In the message to the House of Representatives of the 24th of July, 1848, it was stated that—

It is from the same source of authority that we derive the unquestioned right, after the war has been declared by Congress, to blockade the ports and coasts of the enemy, to capture his towns, cities, and provinces, and to levy contributions upon him for the support of our Army. Of the same character with these is the right to subject to our temporary military government the conquered territories of our enemy. They are all belligerent rights, and their exercise is as essential to the successful prosecution of a foreign war as the right to fight battles.

By the Constitution the power to "declare war" is vested in Congress, and by the same instrument it is provided that "the President shall be Commander in Chief of the Army and Navy of the United States" and that "he shall take care that the laws be faithfully executed."

When Congress have exerted their power by declaring war against a foreign nation, it is the duty of the President to prosecute it. The Constitution has prescribed no particular mode in which he shall perform this duty. The manner of conducting the war is not defined by the Constitution. The term *war* used in that instrument has a well-understood meaning among nations. That meaning is derived from the laws of nations, a code which is recognized by all civilized powers as being obligatory in a state of war. The power is derived from the Constitution and the manner of exercising it is regulated by the laws of nations. When Congress have declared war, they in effect make it the duty of the President in prosecuting it, by land and sea, to resort to all the modes and to exercise all the powers and rights which other nations at war possess. He is invested with the same power in this respect as if he were personally present commanding our fleets by sea or our armies by land. He may conduct the war by issuing orders for fighting battles, besieging and capturing cities, conquering and holding the provinces of the enemy, or by capturing his vessels and other property on the high seas. But these are not the only modes of prosecuting war which are recognized by the laws of nations and to which he is authorized to resort. The levy of contributions on the enemy is a right of war well established and universally acknowledged among nations, and one which every belligerent possessing the ability may properly exercise. The most approved writers on public law admit and vindicate this right as consonant with reason, justice, and humanity.

No principle is better established than that—

We have a right to deprive our enemy of his possessions, of everything which may augment his strength and enable him to make war. This everyone endeavors to accomplish in the manner most suitable to him. Whenever we have an opportunity we seize on the enemy's property and convert it to our own use, and thus, besides diminishing the enemy's power, we augment our own and obtain at least a partial indemnification or equivalent, either for what constitutes the subject of the war or for the expenses and losses incurred in its prosecution. In a word, we do ourselves justice.

"Instead of the custom of pillaging the open country and defenseless places," the levy of contributions has been "substituted."

Whoever carries on a just war has a right to make the enemy's country contribute to the support of his army and toward defraying all the charges of the war. Thus he obtains a part of what is due to him, and the enemy's subjects, by consenting to pay the sum demanded, have their property secured from pillage and the country is preserved.

These principles, it is believed, are uncontroverted by any civilized nation in modern times. The public law of nations, by which they are recognized, has been held by our highest judicial tribunal as a code which is applicable to our "situation" in a state of war and binding on the United States, while in admiralty and maritime cases it is often the governing rule. It is in a just war that a nation has the "right to make the enemy's country contribute to the support of his army." Not doubting that our late war with Mexico was just on the part of the United States, I did not hesitate when charged by the Constitution with its prosecution to exercise a power common to all other nations, and Congress was duly informed of the mode and extent to which that power had been and would be exercised at the commencement of their first session thereafter.

Upon the declaration of war against Mexico by Congress the United States were entitled to all the rights which any other nation at war would have possessed. These rights could only be demanded and enforced by the President, whose duty it was, as "Commander in Chief of the Army and Navy of the United States," to execute the law of Congress which declared the war. In the act declaring war Congress provided for raising men and money to enable the President "to prosecute it to a speedy and successful termination." Congress prescribed no mode of conducting it, but left the President to prosecute it according to the laws of nations as his guide. Indeed, it would have been impracticable for Congress to have provided for all the details of a campaign.

The mode of levying contributions must necessarily be left to the discretion of the conqueror, subject to be exercised, however, in conformity with the laws of nations. It may be exercised by requiring a given sum or a given amount of provisions to be furnished by the authorities of a captured city or province; it may be exercised by imposing an internal tax or a tax on the enemy's commerce, whereby he may be deprived of his revenues, and these may be appropriated to the use of the conqueror. The latter mode was adopted by the collection of duties in the ports of Mexico in our military occupation during the late war with that Republic.

So well established is the military right to do this under the laws of nations that our military and naval officers commanding our forces on the theater of war adopted the same mode of levying contributions from the enemy before the order of the President of the 31st of March, 1847, was issued. The general in command of the Army at Vera Cruz, upon his own view of his powers and duties, and without specific instructions to that effect, immediately after the capture of that city adopted this mode. By his order of the 28th of March, 1847, heretofore communicated to the House of Representatives, he directed a "temporary and moderate tariff of duties to be established." Such a tariff was established, and contributions were collected under it and applied to the uses of our Army.   At a still earlier period the same power was exercised by the naval officers in command of our squadron on the Pacific coast. * * * Not doubting the authority to resort to this mode, the order of the 31st of March, 1847, was issued, and was in effect but a modification of the previous orders of these officers, by making the rates of contribution uniform and directing their collection in all the ports of the enemy in our military occupation and under our temporary military government.

The right to levy contributions upon the enemy in the form of import and export duties in his ports was sanctioned by the treaty of peace with Mexico.   By that treaty both Governments recognized * * * and confirmed the exercise of that right.   By its provisions "the custom-houses at all the ports occupied by the forces of the United States" were, upon the exchange of ratifications, to be delivered up to the Mexican authorities, "together with all bonds and evidences of debt for duties on importations and exportations *not yet fallen due;*" and "all duties on imports and on exports collected at such custom-houses or elsewhere in Mexico by authority of the United States" before the ratification of the treaty by the Mexican Government were to be retained by the United States, and only the net amount of the duties collected after this period was to be "delivered to the Mexican Government."   By its provisions also all merchandise "imported previously to the restoration of the custom-houses to the Mexican authorities" or "exported from any Mexican port whilst in the occupation of the forces of the United States" was protected from confiscation and from the payment of any import or export duties to the Mexican Government, even although the importation of such merchandise " be prohibited by the Mexican tariff."   The treaty also provides that should the custom-houses be surrendered to the Mexican authorities in less than sixty days from the date of its signature, the rates of duty on merchandise imposed by the United States were in that event to survive the war until the end of this period; and in the meantime Mexican custom-house officers were bound to levy no other duties thereon "than the duties established by the tariff found in force at such custom-houses at the time of the restoration of the same."   The "tariff found in force at such custom-houses," which is recognized and sustained by this stipulation, was that established by the military order of the 31st of March, 1847, as a mode of levying and collecting military contributions from the enemy.

The right to blockade the ports and coasts of the enemy in war is no more provided for or prescribed by the Constitution than the right to levy and collect contributions from him in the form of duties or otherwise, and yet it has not been questioned that the President had the power after war had been declared by Congress to order our Navy to blockade the ports and coasts of Mexico.   The right in both cases exists under the laws of nations.   If the President can not order military contributions to be collected without an act of Congress, for the same reason he can not order a blockade; nor can he direct the enemy's vessels to be captured on the high seas; nor can he order our military and naval officers to invade the enemy's country, conquer, hold, and subject to our military government his cities and provinces; nor can he give to our military and naval commanders orders to perform many other acts essential to success in war.

If when the City of Mexico was captured the commander of our forces had found in the Mexican treasury public money which the enemy had provided to support his army, can it be doubted that he possessed the right to seize and appropriate it for the use of our own Army? If the money captured from the enemy could have been thus lawfully seized and appropriated, it would have been by virtue of the laws of war, recognized by all civilized nations; and by the same authority the sources of revenue and of supply of the enemy may be cut off from him, whereby he may be weakened and crippled in his means of continuing or waging the war. If the commanders of our forces, while acting under the orders of the President, in the heart of the enemy's country and surrounded by a hostile population, possess none of these essential and indispensable powers of war, but must halt the Army at every step of its progress and wait for an act of Congress to be passed to authorize them to do that which every other nation has the right to do by virtue of the laws of nations, then, indeed, is the Government of the United States in a condition of imbecility and weakness, which must in all future time render it impossible to prosecute a foreign war in an enemy's country successfully or to vindicate the national rights and the national honor by war.

The contributions levied were collected in the enemy's country, and were ordered to be "applied" in the enemy's country "toward defraying the expenses of the war," and the appropriations made by Congress for that purpose were thus relieved, and considerable balances remained undrawn from the Treasury. The amount of contributions remaining unexpended at the close of the war, as far as the accounts of collecting and disbursing officers have been settled, have been paid into the Treasury in pursuance of an order for that purpose, except the sum "applied toward the payment of the first installment due under the treaty with Mexico," as stated in my last annual message, for which an appropriation had been made by Congress. The accounts of some of these officers, as stated in the report of the Secretary of War accompanying that message, will require legislation before they can be finally settled.

In the late war with Mexico it is confidently believed that the levy of contributions and the seizure of the sources of public revenue upon which the enemy relied to enable him to continue the war essentially contributed to hasten peace. By those means the Government and people of Mexico were made to feel the pressure of the war and to realize that if it were protracted its burdens and inconveniences must be borne by themselves. Notwithstanding the great success of our arms, it may well be doubted whether an honorable peace would yet have been obtained but for the very contributions which were exacted.

JAMES K. POLK.

WASHINGTON, *January 4, 1849.*

To the Senate of the United States:

I transmit to the Senate, for their consideration and advice with regard to its ratification, a convention between the United States of America and the Government of Her Britannic Majesty, for the improvement of the communication by post between their respective territories, concluded and signed at London on the 15th December last, together with an explanatory dispatch from our minister at that Court.

JAMES K. POLK.

WASHINGTON, *January 29, 1849.*

To the Senate of the United States:

I communicate herewith a report of the Secretary of State, with the accompanying documents, in answer to a resolution of the Senate of the 21st December, 1848, requesting the President "to communicate to the Senate (if, in his opinion, not incompatible with the public service) a copy of the dispatches transmitted to the Secretary of State in August last by the resident minister at Rio de Janeiro in reference to the service and general conduct of Commodore G. W. Storer, commander in chief of the United States naval forces on the coast of Brazil."

JAMES K. POLK.

WASHINGTON, *January 29, 1849.*

To the House of Representatives of the United States:

I communicate herewith reports from the Secretary of War and the Secretary of the Navy, together with the accompanying documents, in answer to a resolution of the House of Representatives of December 20, 1848, requesting the President "to communicate to the House the amount of moneys and property received during the late war with the Republic of Mexico at the different ports of entry, or in any other way within her limits, and in what manner the same has been expended or appropriated."

JAMES K. POLK.

WASHINGTON, *February 1, 1849.*

To the Senate of the United States:

I communicate herewith reports from the Secretary of State, the Secretary of the Treasury, the Secretary of War, and the Secretary of the

Navy, together with the accompanying documents, in answer to a resolution of the Senate of the 15th January, 1849, "that the petition and papers of John B. Emerson be referred to the President of the United States, and that he be requested to cause a report thereon to be made to the Senate, wherein the public officer making such report shall state in what cases, if any, the United States have used or employed the invention of said Emerson contrary to law, and, further, whether any compensation therefor is justly due to said Emerson, and, if so, to what amount in each case."

JAMES K. POLK.

WASHINGTON, *February 5, 1849.*

To the Senate of the United States:

I transmit herewith, for the consideration and advice of the Senate with regard to its ratification, a treaty concluded on the 24th day of November, 1848, by Morgan L. Martin and Albert G. Ellis, commissioners on the part of the United States, and the sachem, councilors, and headmen of the Stockbridge tribe of Indians, together with a report of the Commissioner of Indian Affairs and other papers explanatory of the same.

JAMES K. POLK.

WASHINGTON, *February 8, 1849.*

To the House of Representatives of the United States:

In reply to the resolutions of the House of Representatives of the 5th instant, I communicate herewith a report from the Secretary of State, accompanied with all the documents and correspondence relating to the treaty of peace concluded between the United States and Mexico at Guadalupe Hidalgo on the 2d February, 1848, and to the amendments of the Senate thereto, as requested by the House in the said resolutions.

Amongst the documents transmitted will be found a copy of the instructions given to the commissioners of the United States who took to Mexico the treaty as amended by the Senate and ratified by the President of the United States. In my message to the House of Representatives of the 29th of July, 1848, I gave as my reason for declining to furnish these instructions in compliance with a resolution of the House that "in my opinion it would be inconsistent with the public interests to give publicity to them at the present time." Although it may still be doubted whether giving them publicity in our own country, and, as a necessary consequence, in Mexico, may not have a prejudicial influence on our public interests, yet, as they have been again called for by the House, and called for in connection with other documents, to the correct understanding of which they are indispensable, I have deemed it my duty to transmit them.

I still entertain the opinion expressed in the message referred to, that—

As a general rule applicable to all our important negotiations with foreign powers, it could not fail to be prejudicial to the public interests to publish the instructions to our ministers until some time had elapsed after the conclusion of such negotiations.

In these instructions of the 18th of March, 1848, it will be perceived that—

The task was assigned to the commissioners of the United States of consummating the treaty of peace, which was signed at Guadalupe Hidalgo on the 2d day of February last, between the United States and the Mexican Republic, and which on the 10th of March last was ratified by the Senate with amendments.

They were informed that—

This brief statement will indicate to you clearly the line of your duty. You are not sent to Mexico for the purpose of negotiating any new treaty, or of changing in any particular the ratified treaty which you will bear with you. None of the amendments adopted by the Senate can be rejected or modified except by the authority of that body. Your whole duty will, then, consist in using every honorable effort to obtain from the Mexican Government a ratification of the treaty in the form in which it has been ratified by the Senate, and this with the least practicable delay. * * * For this purpose it may, and most probably will, become necessary that you should explain to the Mexican minister for foreign affairs, or to the authorized agents of the Mexican Government, the reasons which have influenced the Senate in adopting these several amendments to the treaty. This duty you will perform as much as possible by personal conferences. Diplomatic notes are to be avoided unless in case of necessity. These might lead to endless discussions and indefinite delay. Besides, they could not have any practical result, as your mission is confined to procuring a ratification from the Mexican Government of the treaty as it came from the Senate, and does not extend to the slightest modification in any of its provisions.

The commissioners were sent to Mexico to procure the ratification of the treaty *as amended by the Senate*. Their instructions confined them to this point. It was proper that the amendments to the treaty adopted by the United States should be explained to the Mexican Government, and explanations were made by the Secretary of State in his letter of the 18th of March, 1848, to the Mexican minister for foreign affairs, under my direction. This dispatch was communicated to Congress with my message of the 6th of July last, communicating the treaty of peace, and published by their order. This dispatch was transmitted by our commissioners from the City of Mexico to the Mexican Government, then at Queretaro, on the 17th of April, 1848, and its receipt acknowledged on the 19th of the same month. During the whole time that the treaty, as amended, was before the Congress of Mexico these explanations of the Secretary of State, and these alone, were before them.

The President of Mexico, on these explanations, on the 8th day of May, 1848, submitted the amended treaty to the Mexican Congress, and on the 25th of May that Congress approved the treaty as amended, without modification or alteration. The final action of the Mexican Congress had taken place before the commissioners of the United States had been officially received by the Mexican authorities, or held any conference with them, or had any other communication on the subject of the treaty except to transmit the letter of the Secretary of State.

In their dispatch transmitted to Congress with my message of the 6th of July last, communicating the treaty of peace, dated "City of Queretaro, May 25, 1848, 9 o'clock p. m.," the commissioners say:

> We have the satisfaction to inform you that we reached this city this afternoon at about 5 o'clock, and that the treaty, as amended by the Senate of the United States, passed the Mexican Senate about the hour of our arrival by a vote of 33 to 5. It having previously passed the House of Deputies, nothing now remains but to exchange the ratifications of the treaty.

On the next day (the 26th of May) the commissioners were for the first time presented to the President of the Republic and their credentials placed in his hands. On this occasion the commissioners delivered an address to the President of Mexico, and he replied. In their dispatch of the 30th of May the commissioners say:

> We inclose a copy of our address to the President, and also a copy of his reply. Several conferences afterwards took place between Messrs. Rosa, Cuevas, Conto, and ourselves, which it is not thought necessary to recapitulate, as we inclose a copy of the protocol, which contains the substance of the conversations. We have now the satisfaction to announce that the exchange of ratifications was effected to-day.

This dispatch was communicated with my message of the 6th of July last, and published by order of Congress.

The treaty, as amended by the Senate of the United States, with the accompanying papers and the evidence that in that form it had been ratified by Mexico, was received at Washington on the 4th day of July, 1848, and immediately proclaimed as the supreme law of the land. On the 6th of July I communicated to Congress the ratified treaty, with such accompanying documents as were deemed material to a full understanding of the subject, to the end that Congress might adopt the legislation necessary and proper to carry the treaty into effect. Neither the address of the commissioners, nor the reply of the President of Mexico on the occasion of their presentation, nor the memorandum of conversations embraced in the paper called a protocol, nor the correspondence now sent, were communicated, because they were not regarded as in any way material; and in this I conformed to the practice of our Government. It rarely, if ever, happens that all the correspondence, and especially the instructions to our ministers, is communicated. Copies of these papers are now transmitted, as being within the resolutions of the House calling for all such "correspondence as appertains to said treaty."

When these papers were received at Washington, peace had been restored, the first installment of three millions paid to Mexico, the blockades were raised, the City of Mexico evacuated, and our troops on their return home. The war was at an end, and the treaty, as ratified by the United States, was binding on both parties, and already executed in a great degree. In this condition of things it was not competent for the

President alone, or for the President and Senate, or for the President, Senate, and House of Representatives combined, to abrogate the treaty, to annul the peace and restore a state of war, except by a solemn declaration of war.

Had the protocol varied the treaty as amended by the Senate of the United States, it would have had no binding effect.

It was obvious that the commissioners of the United States did not regard the protocol as in any degree a part of the treaty, nor as modifying or altering the treaty as amended by the Senate. They communicated it as the substance of conversations held after the Mexican Congress had ratified the treaty, and they knew that the approval of the Mexican Congress was as essential to the validity of a treaty in all its parts as the advice and consent of the Senate of the United States. They knew, too, that they had no authority to alter or modify the treaty in the form in which it had been ratified by the United States, but that, if failing to procure the ratification of the Mexican Government otherwise than with amendments, their duty, imposed by express instructions, was to ask of Mexico to send without delay a commissioner to Washington to exchange ratifications here if the amendments of the treaty proposed by Mexico, on being submitted, should be adopted by the Senate of the United States.

I was equally well satisfied that the Government of Mexico had agreed to the treaty as amended by the Senate of the United States, and did not regard the protocol as modifying, enlarging, or diminishing its terms or effect. The President of that Republic, in submitting the amended treaty to the Mexican Congress, in his message on the 8th day of May, 1848, said:

> If the treaty could have been submitted to your deliberation precisely as it came from the hands of the plenipotentiaries, my satisfaction at seeing the war at last brought to an end would not have been lessened as it this day is in consequence of the modifications introduced into it by the Senate of the United States, and which have received the sanction of the President. * * * At present it is sufficient for us to say to you that if in the opinion of the Government justice had not been evinced on the part of the Senate and Government of the United States in introducing such modifications, it is presumed, on the other hand, that they are not of such importance that they should set aside the treaty. I believe, on the contrary, that it ought to be ratified upon the same terms in which it has already received the sanction of the American Government. My opinion is also greatly strengthened by the fact that a new negotiation is neither expected nor considered possible. Much less could another be brought forward upon a basis more favorable for the Republic.

The deliberations of the Mexican Congress, with no explanation before that body from the United States except the letter of the Secretary of State, resulted in the ratification of the treaty, as recommended by the President of that Republic, in the form in which it had been amended and ratified by the United States. The conversations embodied in the paper called a protocol took place after the action of the Mexican Congress was complete, and there is no reason to suppose that the Government of Mexico ever submitted the protocol to the Congress, or ever treated or regarded it as in any sense a new negotiation, or as operating any modification or change of the amended treaty. If such had been its effect, it was a nullity until approved by the Mexican Congress; and such approval was never made or intimated to the United States. In the final consummation of the ratification of the treaty by the President of Mexico no reference is made to it. On the contrary, this ratification, which was delivered to the commissioners of the United States, and is now in the State Department, contains a full and explicit recognition of the amendments of the Senate just as they had been communicated to that Government by the Secretary of State and been afterwards approved by the Mexican Congress. It declares that—

Having seen and examined the said treaty and the modifications made by the Senate of the United States of America, and having given an account thereof to the General Congress, conformably to the requirement in the fourteenth paragraph of the one hundred and tenth article of the federal constitution of these United States, that body has thought proper to approve of the said treaty, with the modifications thereto, in all their parts; and in consequence thereof, exerting the power granted to me by the constitution, I accept, ratify, and confirm the said treaty with its modifications, and promise, in the name of the Mexican Republic, to fulfill and observe it, and to cause it to be fulfilled and observed.

Upon an examination of this protocol, when it was received with the ratified treaty, I did not regard it as material or as in any way attempting to modify or change the treaty as it had been amended by the Senate of the United States.

The first explanation which it contains is:

That the American Government, by suppressing the ninth article of the treaty of Guadalupe and substituting the third article of the treaty of Louisiana, did not intend to diminish in any way what was agreed upon by the aforesaid article (ninth) in favor of the inhabitants of the territories ceded by Mexico. Its understanding is that all of that agreement is contained in the third article of the treaty of Louisiana. In consequence, all the privileges and guaranties—civil, political, and religious—which would have been possessed by the inhabitants of the ceded territories if the ninth article of the treaty had been retained will be enjoyed by them without any difference under the article which has been substituted.

The ninth article of the original treaty stipulated for the incorporation of the Mexican inhabitants of the ceded territories and their admission into the Union "as soon as possible, according to the principles of the Federal Constitution, to the enjoyment of all the rights of citizens of the United States." It provided also that in the meantime they should be maintained in the enjoyment of their liberty, their property, and their civil rights now vested in them according to the Mexican laws. It secured to them similar political rights with the inhabitants of the other Territories of the United States, and at least equal to the inhabitants of Louisiana and Florida when they were in a Territorial condition. It then proceeded to guarantee that ecclesiastics and religious corporations should be protected in the discharge of the offices of their ministry and the enjoyment of their property of every kind, whether individual or corporate, and, finally, that there should be a free communication between the Catholics of the ceded territories and their ecclesiastical authorities, ''even although such authority should reside within the limits of the Mexican Republic as defined by this treaty.''

The ninth article of the treaty, as adopted by the Senate, is much more comprehensive in its terms and explicit in its meaning, and it clearly embraces in comparatively few words all the guaranties inserted in the original article. It is as follows:

Mexicans who, in the territories aforesaid, shall not preserve the character of citizens of the Mexican Republic, conformably with what is stipulated in the preceding article, shall be incorporated into the Union of the United States and be admitted at the proper time (to be judged of by the Congress of the United States) to the enjoyment of all the rights of citizens of the United States, according to the principles of the Constitution, and in the meantime shall be maintained and protected in the free enjoyment of their liberty and property and secured in the free exercise of their religion without restriction.

This article, which was substantially copied from the Louisiana treaty, provides equally with the original article for the admission of these inhabitants into the Union, and in the meantime, whilst they shall remain in a Territorial state, by one sweeping provision declares that they ''shall be maintained and protected in the free enjoyment of their liberty and property and secured in the free exercise of their religion without restriction.''

This guaranty embraces every kind of property, whether held by ecclesiastics or laymen, whether belonging to corporations or individuals. It secures to these inhabitants the free exercise of their religion without restriction, whether they choose to place themselves under the spiritual authority of pastors resident within the Mexican Republic or the ceded territories. It was, it is presumed, to place this construction beyond all question that the Senate superadded the words ''without restriction'' to the religious guaranty contained in the corresponding article of the Louisiana treaty. Congress itself does not possess the power under the Constitution to make any law prohibiting the free exercise of religion.

If the ninth article of the treaty, whether in its original or amended form, had been entirely omitted in the treaty, all the rights and privileges which either of them confers would have been secured to the inhabitants of the ceded territories by the Constitution and laws of the United States.

The protocol asserts that ''the American Government, by suppressing the tenth article of the treaty of Guadalupe, did not in any way intend to annul the grants of lands made by Mexico in the ceded territories;'' that ''these grants, notwithstanding the suppression of the article of the treaty, preserve the legal value which they may possess; and the grantees may cause their legitimate titles to be acknowledged before the American tribunals;'' and then proceeds to state that, ''conformably to the law of the United States, legitimate titles to every description of property, personal and real, existing in the ceded territories are those which were legitimate titles under the Mexican law in California and New Mexico up to the 13th of May, 1846, and in Texas up to the 2d of March, 1836.''

The former was the date of the declaration of war against Mexico and the latter that of the declaration of independence by Texas.

The objection to the tenth article of the original treaty was not that it protected legitimate titles, which our laws would have equally protected without it, but that it most unjustly attempted to resuscitate grants which had become a mere nullity by allowing the grantees the same period after the exchange of the ratifications of the treaty to which they had been originally entitled after the date of their grants for the purpose of performing the conditions on which they had been made. In submitting the treaty to the Senate I had recommended the rejection of this article. That portion of it in regard to lands in Texas did not receive a single vote in the Senate. This information was communicated by the letter of the Secretary of State to the minister for foreign affairs of Mexico, and was in possession of the Mexican Government during the whole period the treaty was before the Mexican Congress; and the article itself was reprobated in that letter in the strongest terms. Besides, our commissioners to Mexico had been instructed that—

Neither the President nor the Senate of the United States can ever consent to ratify any treaty containing the tenth article of the treaty of Guadalupe Hidalgo, in favor of grantees of land in Texas or elsewhere.

And again:

Should the Mexican Government persist in retaining this article, then all prospect of immediate peace is ended; and of this you may give them an absolute assurance.

On this point the language of the protocol is free from ambiguity, but if it were otherwise is there any individual American or Mexican who would place such a construction upon it as to convert it into a vain attempt to revive this article, which had been so often and so solemnly condemned? Surely no person could for one moment suppose that either the commissioners of the United States or the Mexican minister for foreign affairs ever entertained the purpose of thus setting at naught the deliberate decision of the President and Senate, which had been communicated to the Mexican Government with the assurance that their abandonment of this obnoxious article was essential to the restoration of peace.

But the meaning of the protocol is plain. It is simply that the nullification of this article was not intended to destroy valid, legitimate titles to land which existed and were in full force independently of the provisions and without the aid of this article. Notwithstanding it has been expunged from the treaty, these grants were to "preserve the legal value which they may possess." The refusal to revive grants which had become extinct was not to invalidate those which were in full force and vigor. That such was the clear understanding of the Senate of the United States, and this in perfect accordance with the protocol, is manifest from the fact that whilst they struck from the treaty this unjust article, they at the same time sanctioned and ratified the last paragraph of the eighth article of the treaty, which declares that—

In the said territories property of every kind now belonging to Mexicans not established there shall be inviolably respected. The present owners, the heirs of these, and all Mexicans who may hereafter acquire said property by contract shall enjoy with respect to it guaranties equally ample as if the same belonged to citizens of the United States.

Without any stipulation in the treaty to this effect, all such valid titles under the Mexican Government would have been protected under the Constitution and laws of the United States.

The third and last explanation contained in the protocol is that—

The Government of the United States, by suppressing the concluding paragraph of article 12 of the treaty, did not intend to deprive the Mexican Republic of the free and unrestrained faculty of ceding, conveying, or transferring at any time (as it may judge best) the sum of the $12,000,000 which the same Government of the United States is to deliver in the places designated by the amended article.

The concluding paragraph of the original twelfth article, thus suppressed by the Senate, is in the following language:

Certificates in proper form for the said installments, respectively, in such sums as shall be desired by the Mexican Government, and transferable by it, shall be delivered to the said Government by that of the United States.

From this bare statement of facts the meaning of the protocol is obvious. Although the Senate had declined to create a Government stock for the $12,000,000, and issue transferable certificates for the amount in such sums as the Mexican Government might desire, yet they could not have intended thereby to deprive that Government of the faculty which every creditor possesses of transferring for his own benefit the obligation of his debtor, whatever this may be worth, according to his will and pleasure.

It can not be doubted that the twelfth article of the treaty as it now stands contains a positive obligation, ''in consideration of the extension acquired by the boundaries of the United States,'' to pay to the Mexican Republic $12,000,000 in four equal annual installments of three millions each. This obligation may be assigned by the Mexican Government to any person whatever, but the assignee in such case would stand in no better condition than the Government. The amendment of the Senate prohibiting the issue of a Government transferable stock for the amount produces this effect and no more.

The protocol contains nothing from which it can be inferred that the assignee could rightfully demand the payment of the money in case the consideration should fail which is stated on the face of the obligation.

With this view of the whole protocol, and considering that the explanations which it contained were in accordance with the treaty, I did not deem it necessary to take any action upon the subject. Had it varied from the terms of the treaty as amended by the Senate, although it would even then have been a nullity in itself, yet duty might have required that I should make this fact known to the Mexican Government. This not being the case, I treated it in the same manner I would have done had these explanations been made verbally by the commissioners to the Mexican minister for foreign affairs and communicated in a dispatch to the State Department.

JAMES K. POLK.

WASHINGTON, *February 9, 1849.*

To the Senate of the United States:

In compliance with the resolution of the Senate of the 6th instant, requesting the President to cause to be laid before that body, in "executive or open session, in his discretion, any instructions given to Ambrose H. Sevier and Nathan Clifford, commissioned as ministers plenipotentiary on the part of the United States to the Government of Mexico, or to either of said ministers, prior to the ratification by the Government of Mexico of the treaty of peace between the United States and that Republic," and certain correspondence and other papers specified in the said resolution, I communicate herewith a report from the Secretary of State, together with copies of the documents called for.

Having on the 8th instant, in compliance with a resolution of the House of Representatives in its terms more comprehensive than that of the Senate, communicated these and all other papers appertaining to the same subject, with a message to that House, this communication is made to the Senate in "open" and not in "executive" session.

JAMES K. POLK.

WASHINGTON, *February 12, 1849.*

To the Senate of the United States:

I communicate herewith a report from the Secretary of the Treasury, with the accompanying documents, in answer to the resolution of the Senate of December 28, 1848, requesting "to be informed of the number of vessels annually employed in the Coast Survey, and the annual cost thereof, and out of what fund they were paid; also the number of persons annually employed in said Survey who were not of the Army and Navy of the United States; also the amount of money received by the United States for maps and charts made under such Survey and sold under the act of 1844."

JAMES K. POLK.

WASHINGTON, *February 14, 1849.*

To the Senate of the United States:

I transmit herewith a report from the Secretary of War, together with the accompanying papers, in compliance with a resolution of the

Senate of the 12th instant, requesting the President to communicate to that body the proceedings under the act of Congress of the last session to compensate R. M. Johnson for the erection of certain buildings for the use of the Choctaw academy; also the evidence of the cost of said buildings.

JAMES K.. POLK.

WASHINGTON, *February 23, 1849.*
To the Senate of the United States:

I communicate herewith a report of the Secretary of State, together with the accompanying documents, in compliance with a resolution of the Senate of the 23d ultimo, requesting the President "to transmit to the Senate, so far as is consistent with the public service, any correspondence between the Department of State and the Spanish authorities in the island of Cuba relating to the imprisonment in said island of William Henry Rush, a citizen of the United States."

JAMES K. POLK.

WASHINGTON, *February 27, 1849.*
To the Senate of the United States:

I communicate herewith a report from the Secretary of State, in compliance with a resolution of the Senate of the 3d ultimo, requesting the President to communicate to the Senate a list of all the treaties of commerce and navigation between the United States and foreign nations conferring upon the vessels of such nations the right of trading between the United States and the rest of the world in the productions of every country upon the same terms with American vessels, with the date of the proclamation of such treaties; also a list of the proclamations conferring similar rights upon the vessels of foreign nations issued by the President of the United States under the provisions of the first section of the act entitled "An act in addition to an act entitled 'An act concerning discriminating duties on tonnage and impost and to equalize the duties on Prussian vessels and their cargoes,'" approved May 24, 1828.

JAMES K. POLK.

WASHINGTON, *March 2, 1849.*
To the House of Representatives of the United States:

I communicate herewith a report of the Secretary of State, together with the accompanying papers, in compliance with the resolution of the House of Representatives of the 23d of December, 1848, requesting the President "to cause to be transmitted to the House, if compatible with the public interest, the correspondence of George W. Gordon, late, and Gorham Parks, the present, consul of the United States at Rio de Janeiro, with the Department of State on the subject of the African slave trade; also any unpublished correspondence on the same subject by the Hon. Henry A. Wise, our late minister to Brazil.''

JAMES K. POLK.

WASHINGTON, *March 2, 1849.*

To the House of Representatives of the United States:

I communicate herewith a report of the Secretary of State, together with the accompanying papers, in compliance with the resolution of the House of Representatives of the 20th ultimo, requesting the President to communicate to that House a list of all consuls, vice-consuls, and commercial agents now in the service of the United States, their residence, distinguishing such as are citizens of the United States from such as are not, and to inform the said House whether regular returns of their fees and perquisites and the tonnage and commerce of the United States within their respective consulates or agencies have been regularly made by each, and to communicate the amount of such fees and perquisites for certain years therein specified, together with the number of vessels and amount of tonnage which entered and cleared within each of the consulates and agencies for the same period; also the number of seamen of the United States who have been provided for and sent home from each of the said consulates for the time aforesaid.

JAMES K. POLK.

WASHINGTON, *March 2, 1849.*

To the Senate of the United States:

I herewith transmit a communication from the Secretary of the Treasury, accompanying a report from the Solicitor of the Treasury presenting a view of the operations of that office since its organization.

JAMES K. POLK.

PROCLAMATIONS.

[From Senate Journal, Thirtieth Congress, second session, p. 349.]

WASHINGTON, *January 2, 1849.*

To the Senators of the United States, respectively.

SIR: Objects interesting to the United States requiring that the Senate should be in session on Monday, the 5th of March next, to receive and act upon such communications as may be made to it on the part of the Executive, your attention in the Senate Chamber, in this city, on that day at 10 o'clock in the forenoon is accordingly requested.

JAMES K. POLK.

BY THE PRESIDENT OF THE UNITED STATES.

A PROCLAMATION.

Whereas by an act of the Congress of the United States of the 10th January, 1849, entitled "An act to extend certain privileges to the town of Whitehall, in the State of New York," the President of the United States, on the recommendation of the Secretary of the Treasury, is authorized to extend to the town of Whitehall the same privileges as are conferred on certain ports named in the seventh section of an act entitled "An act allowing drawback upon foreign merchandise exported in the original packages to Chihuahua and Santa Fe, in Mexico, and to the British North American Provinces adjoining the United States," passed 3d March, 1845, in the manner prescribed by the proviso contained in said section; and

Whereas the Secretary of the Treasury has duly recommended to me the extension of the privileges of the law aforesaid to the port of Whitehall, in the collection district of Champlain, in the State of New York:

Now, therefore, I, James K. Polk, President of the United States of America, do hereby declare and proclaim that the port of Whitehall, in the collection district of Champlain, in the State of New York, is and shall be entitled to all the privileges extended to the other ports enumerated in the seventh section of the act aforesaid from and after the date of this proclamation.

In witness whereof I have hereunto set my hand and caused the seal of the United States to be affixed.

[SEAL.]   Done at the city of Washington, this 2d day of March, A. D. 1849, and of the Independence of the United States of America the seventy-third.

JAMES K. POLK.

By the President:

JAMES BUCHANAN,
  Secretary of State.